International Financial Markets

This book provides an up-to-date series of advanced chapters on applied financial econometric techniques pertaining to the various fields of commodities finance, mathematics and stochastics, international macroeconomics, and financial econometrics.

International Financial Markets: Volume 1 provides a key repository on the current state of knowledge, the latest debates, and recent literature on international financial markets. Against the background of the "financialization of commodities" since the 2008 sub-prime crisis, Part 1 contains recent contributions on commodity and financial markets, pushing the frontiers of applied econometrics techniques. Part 2 is devoted to exchange rate and current account dynamics in an environment characterized by large global imbalances. Part 3 examines the latest research in the field of meta-analysis in economics and finance.

This book will be useful to students and researchers in applied econometrics: academics and students seeking convenient access to an unfamiliar area. It will also be of great interest established researchers seeking a single repository on the current state of knowledge, current debates, and relevant literature.

Julien Chevallier is Full Professor of Economics at the University Paris 8 (LED), France. He undertakes research and lectures on empirical finance, applied time-series econometrics, and commodity markets. He has published articles in leading refereed journals.

Stéphane Goutte is a Maître de Conférences-HDR of Financial Mathematics at University Paris 8, France and Senior Lecturer in Mathematics at University of Luxembourg. He is also a researcher at the Chair European Electricity Markets of Paris Dauphine PSL University.

David Guerreiro is an Assistant Professor of Economics at the University Paris 8 (LED), France. His fields of research are international macroeconomics, monetary economics, and meta-analysis, and he has published in numerous peer-reviewed journals.

Sophie Saglio is an Assistant Professor of Economics at the University Paris 8 (LED), France. Her research focuses on international economics and finance, and she has published in various peer-reviewed journals.

Bilel Sanhaji is an Assistant Professor of Economics at the University Paris 8 (LED), France. His main research focuses on nonlinear time series econometrics and modeling volatility. He has published theoretical and applied research papers in various peer-reviewed journals.

Routledge Advances in Applied Financial Econometrics
Julien Chevallier
University Paris 8, France

The Routledge Advances in Applied Financial Econometrics series brings together the latest research on econometric techniques and empirical cases in the fields of commodities finance, mathematics and stochastics, international macroeconomics and financial econometrics. It provides a single repository on the current state of knowledge, the latest debates and recent literature in the field.

International Financial Markets
Volume 1
Edited by Julien Chevallier, Stéphane Goutte, David Guerreiro, Sophie Saglio and Bilel Sanhaji

Financial Mathematics, Volatility and Covariance Modelling
Volume 2
Edited by Julien Chevallier, Stéphane Goutte, David Guerreiro, Sophie Saglio and Bilel Sanhaji

For more information about this series, please visit: www.routledge.com/Routledge-Advances-in-Applied-Financial-Econometrics/book-series/RAAFE

International Financial Markets

Volume 1

Edited by Julien Chevallier,
Stéphane Goutte, David Guerreiro,
Sophie Saglio and Bilel Sanhaji

Routledge
Taylor & Francis Group

LONDON AND NEW YORK

First published 2019
by Routledge
2 Park Square, Milton Park, Abingdon, Oxon OX14 4RN

and by Routledge
605 Third Avenue, New York, NY 10017

First issued in paperback 2021

Routledge is an imprint of the Taylor & Francis Group, an informa business

British Library Cataloguing-in-Publication Data
A catalogue record for this book is available from the British Library

Library of Congress Cataloging-in-Publication Data
Names: Chevallier, Julien, editor.
Title: International financial markets / edited by Julien Chevallier [and four others].
Description: Abingdon, Oxon ; New York, NY : Routledge, 2019. | Series: Routledge advances in applied financial econometrics ; volume 1 | Includes bibliographical references and index.
Identifiers: LCCN 2019008470 (print) | LCCN 2019011231 (ebook) | ISBN 9781315162775 (Ebook) | ISBN 9781138060920 (hardback : alk. paper)
Subjects: LCSH: International finance—Mathematical models. | International finance—Econometric models.
Classification: LCC HG3881 (ebook) | LCC HG3881 .I494 2019 (print) | DDC 332/.042—dc23
LC record available at https://lccn.loc.gov/2019008470

ISBN 13: 978-0-367-78556-7 (pbk)
ISBN 13: 978-1-138-06092-0 (hbk)

Typeset in Times New Roman
by Apex CoVantage, LLC

Contents

vi *Contents*

About the editors

Julien Chevallier is Full Professor of Economics at the University Paris 8 (LED). He undertakes research and lectures on empirical finance, applied time-series econometrics, and commodity markets. He has published articles in leading refereed journals, including the *Journal of Empirical Finance; International Review of Financial Analysis; Quantitative Finance; Journal of Forecasting; Journal of International Financial Markets, Institutions & Money*; and *Annals of Operations Research*.

Stéphane Goutte holds a Ph.D. in Mathematics. He is a Maître de Conférences-HDR of Financial Mathematics at University Paris 8 and Senior Lecturer in Mathematics at University of Luxembourg. He is also a researcher at the Chair European Electricity Markets of Paris Dauphine PSL University. He has several publications in peer-reviewed academic journals in the field of mathematical finance, theoretical probability, and energy economics.

David Guerreiro is Assistant Professor of Economics at the University Paris 8 (LED). His fields of research are international macroeconomics, monetary economics, and meta-analysis. He has published in peer-reviewed journals such as *World Development, Journal of Macroeconomics, Economic Modeling, Journal of Economic Integration*, and *Journal of International Trade and Economic Development*.

Sophie Saglio is Assistant Professor of Economics at the University Paris 8 (LED). Her research focuses on international economics and finance. She has published in peer-reviewed journals including *Review of International Economics* and *Oxford Bulletin of Economics and Statistics*.

Bilel Sanhaji is Assistant Professor of Economics at the University Paris 8 (LED). His main research focuses on nonlinear time series econometrics and modeling volatility. He has published theoretical and applied research papers in peer-reviewed journals such as *Annals of Economics and Statistics* and *Applied Economics*.

Contributors

Monica Billio
Department of Economics, Ca' Foscari University of Venice, Dorsoduro 3246, 30123 Venice (Italy), billio@unive.it (e-mail)

Jamal Bouoiyour
IRMAPE - ESC Pau Business School, France
CATT, University of Pau, France
Email: jamal.bouoiyour@univ-pau.fr

Marine Carrasco
Professor of Economics. Université de Montréal, CIRANO and CIREQ.
Email: marine.carrasco@umontreal.ca

Roberto Casarin
Department of Economics, Ca' Foscari University of Venice, Dorsoduro 3246, 30123 Venice (Italy), r.casarin@unive.it (e-mail)

Antoine Cazals
CERDI, CNRS-Universite Clermont Auvergne, Clermont Ferrand, France. CERDI (Centre d'Etudes et de Recherches sur le Developpement International), UMR 6587 CNRS-Universite Clermont Auvergne, 65 Boulevard Francois Mitterrand, 63009 Clermont-Ferrand, France. Email addresses: antoine.cazals@gmail.fr (Antoine Cazals)

Shyh-Wei Chen
Department of International Business, Tunghai University. No.1727, Sec.4, Taiwan Boulevard, Xitun District, Taichung 40704, Taiwan Tel: 886-4-23590121 ext 35310, Fax: 886-4-23592898. E-mail: shyhwei.chen@gmail.com, schen@thu.edu.tw.

Michele Costola
SAFE, House of Finance, Goethe University Frankfurt, Theodor-W.-Adorno-Platz 3, 60323 Frankfurt am Main (Germany), costola@safe.uni-frankfurt.de (e-mail)

Hristos Doucouliagos
Department of Economics and DeLMAR, Deakin University, Burwood, VIC 3125, Australia.

Lina Lassesen Ekern
Faculty of Economics
NTNU Trondheim, Norway

Lorenzo Frattarolo
Department of Economics, Ca' Foscari University of Venice, Dorsoduro
3246, 30123 Venice (Italy), lorenzo.frattarolo@unive.it (e-mail)

Elīna Gaillard-Ladinska
Fabernovel Innovate, 17 Rue du Faubourg du Temple, 75010 Paris, France.
E-mail: elina.gaillard@fabernovel.com

Matthew Greenwood-Nimmo
Department of Economics, University of Melbourne, 111 Barry Street,
Melbourne 3053, Australia. Tel.: +61 (0)383445354.
matthew.greenwood@unimelb.edu.au

Ichiro Iwasaki
Institute of Economic Research, Hitotsubashi (University, 2-1 Naka),
Kunitachi, Tokyo 186-8603, Japan. E-mail: iiwasaki@ier.hit-u.ac.jp

Jae H. Kim
Department of Economics and Finance, La Trobe Business School
La Trobe University, Bundoora
Victoria 3086, Australia
J.Kim@latrobe.edu.au

Rachidi Kotchoni
Associate Professor (Maître de Conférence) of Economics. Université
Paris Nanterre, CNRS-EconomiX. Email: rachidi.kotchoni@parisnanterre.fr

Christian Leschinski
Institute of Statistics, Faculty of Economics and Management, Leibniz
University Hannover, D-30167 Hannover, Germany

Pierre Mandon
CERDI, CNRS-Universite Clermont Auvergne, Clermont Ferrand, France.
CERDI (Centre d'Etudes et de Recherches sur le Developpement International),
UMR 6587 CNRS-Universite Clermont Auvergne, 65 Boulevard Francois Mitter-
rand, 63009 Clermont-Ferrand, France. Email addresses: pierr.mandon@gmail.
com (Pierre Mandon)

Ingrid Naustdal
Faculty of Economics
NTNU Trondheim, Norway

Viet Nguyen
Melbourne Institute of Applied Economic & Social Research, 111 Barry Street,
Melbourne 3053, Australia. vietn@unimelb.edu.au

Mariëlle Non
CPB Netherlands Bureau for Economic Policy Analysis, P.O. Box 80510, 2508GM The Hague, The Netherlands.
Email: m.c.non@cpb.nl

Florentina Paraschiv
Faculty of Economics
NTNU Trondheim, Norway

Malene Roland
Faculty of Economics
NTNU Trondheim, Norway

Refk Selmi
IRMAPE - ESC Pau Business School, France
CATT, University of Pau, France
Email: refk.selmi@univ-pau.fr

Yongcheol Shin
Department of Economic and Related Studies, University of York, Heslington, York, YO10 5DD, UK. yongcheol.shin@york.ac.uk

Philipp Sibbertsen
Institute of Statistics, Faculty of Economics and Management, Leibniz University Hannover, D-30167 Hannover, Germany

T.D. Stanley
School of Business and DeLMAR, Deakin
University, Burwood, VIC 3125, Australia.

Bas Straathof
Ministry of Finance, Financial and Economic Policy Directorate, P.O. Box 20201, 2500EE The Hague, The Netherlands.
E-mail: s.m.straathof@minfin.nl

Akira Uegaki
Department of Economics, Seinan Gakuin University, 6-2-92 Nishijin, Sawara-ku, Fukuoka 814-8511, Japan. E-mail: uegaki@seinan-gu.ac.jp

Michelle Voges
Institute of Statistics, Faculty of Economics and Management, Leibniz University Hannover, D-30167 Hannover, Germany

Sjur Westgaard
Faculty of Economics
NTNU Trondheim, Norway
sjur.westgaard@ntnu.no

Zixiong Xie
Department of International Economics and Trade, Institute of Resources, Environment, and Sustainable Development, College of Economics, Jinan University. E-mail: zixiong.xie@gmail.com, txiezixiong@jnu.edu.cn

Ting Yao
Business School, Hunan University, Changsha 410082, PR China. Center for Resource and Environmental Management, Hunan University, Changsha 410082, PR China

Yue-Jun Zhang
Business School, Hunan University, Changsha 410082, PR China. Center for Resource and Environmental Management, Hunan University, Changsha 410082, PR China

Introduction

Summary

The Routledge Advances in Applied Financial Econometrics series provides an up-to-date series of advanced chapters on applied financial econometric techniques pertaining the various fields of commodities finance, mathematics and stochastics, international macroeconomics, and financial econometrics. Applied econometrics being a booming academic discipline, with its well-established academic journals and associations, we hope that the contents of this series will be useful to students and researchers in applied econometrics; academics and students seeking convenient access to an unfamiliar area; as well as established researchers seeking a single repository on the current state of knowledge, current debates and relevant literature.

Structure of volume 1

Volume 1 is titled *"International Financial Markets"*. It contains 12 chapters organized in 3 sections.

Part 1 is devoted to commodities finance and market performance. Against the background of "financialization of commodities" since the 2008 sub-prime crisis, it contains recent contributions on commodity and financial markets pushing the frontiers of applied econometrics techniques.

Part 2 is devoted to exchange rate and current account dynamics in an economic and financial environment characterized by large global imbalances. This section presents recent research, which uses applied econometrics techniques in the field of international economics and finance.

Part 3 is devoted to meta-analyses in economics and finance. Initially coming from the medical field, this econometric methodology has been largely employed in economics during the last years to (1) scrutinize passed empirical literature, (2) assess publication bias, (3) test the robustness of the results, and (4) provide guidelines to improve the modeling.

A brief outline of the contribution of each chapter in the volume follows.

Chapter contributions

Part 1 tackles topics related to commodities finance and market performance.

Chapter 1, by Westgaard, Paraschiv, Ekern, Naustdal, and Roland, is interested in electricity price distribution forecasts that are crucial to energy risk management. The authors model and forecast Value-at-Risk (VaR) for the German EPEX spot price. They use variable selection with quantile regression, exponentially weighted quantile regression, exponentially weighted double kernel quantile regression, GARCH models with skewed-t error distributions, and various CAViaR models. The findings are (1) exponentially weighted quantile regression tends to perform best in terms of overall quantiles and hours, and (2) different variables are selected for the various quantiles and hours. They identify a nonlinear relationship between fundamentals and the electricity price, which differs between hours as the dynamics of the intra-daily prices are different. Quantile regression is able to capture these effects. As the input mix has changed in Germany over the last few years, exponentially weighted quantile regression which allows for time-varying parameters can also capture the effect of changing quantile sensitivities over time. Exponentially weighted quantile regression is also an easy model to implement compared with the other models investigated in this chapter.

Chapter 2, by Yao and Zhang, relies on Internet search data to effectively reflect the psychological behaviors of investors in the crude oil market. More precisely, the search data aggregated by Google is supposed to reflect investors' attention. The authors construct a direct, timely, and unambiguous proxy for investor attention in crude oil market by aggregating the Google search volume index (GSVI). They explore the effect and predictive power of the investor attention on crude oil price returns by using the autoregressive integrated moving average (ARMAX) models with exogenous variables and autoregressive integrated moving average with exogenous variable-generalized autoregressive conditional heteroskedastic (ARMAX-GARCH). Their findings indicate that there exists a negative effect of the Google index on crude oil returns. Besides, they identify that the incorporation of investor attention brings an improvement on the goodness-of-fit. Finally, the incorporation of investor attention fails to improve the forecasting performance in the crude oil market, specifically, the forecasting performance becomes worse after the incorporation of the investor attention according to almost all the loss functions.

***

Part 2 covers broad areas in international economics and finance.

Chapter 3, by Billio, Casarin, Costola, and Frattarolo, studies financial networks with the help of the graph theory. The strength of this approach is to be able to draw a financial network without transaction data between the institutions. First, this chapter introduces the notion of financial network and reviews some techniques used to extract financial networks from a panel of observations. The interdependence between financial institutions is measured by pairwise

Granger causality between returns. Second, the authors develop new measures of network connectivity: Von Neumann entropies and disagreement persistence index. These new measures are applied to a sequence of inferred pairwise-Granger networks and the authors use them to develop an early warning indicator for banking crises. Empirical analysis is made to European financial institutions. The database is composed by the daily closing price series for European financial institutions between December 1999 and January 2013. The authors analyze 437 European financial institutions according to the Industrial Classification Benchmark (ICB). The MSCI Europe index is used as the proxy for the market index. The authors show that entropy measures can be used fruitfully to generate early warning signals for banking crises.

Chapter 4, by Greenwood-Nimmo, Nguyen, and Shin, analyzes the transmission of information between currency spot markets using a classic dataset from the Reuters Dealing 2000–1 platform for the period May–August 1996. The authors refer to the microstructure literature which allows new avenues to model the informational linkages between markets; more precisely, they refer to the multi-currency portfolio shifts model developed by Evans and Lyons (2002) which explains how trading activity in one market can influence prices in other markets. Nevertheless, the model of Evans and Lyons has an important limitation: price-order flow interactions and cross-market linkages are addressed only in a static setting under the strong assumptions of continuous market equilibrium and unidirectional causality running from order flow to price. The authors exceed this limit by deriving a dynamic error correction representation of the Evans and Lyons multi-currency portfolio shifts model with the help of the global vector autoregressive (GVAR). They use the database used by Evans and Lyons which contains daily data on direct interdealer trading for 82 trading days over the four-month period from May 1 to August 31, 1996. The data is drawn from the Reuters D2000–1 platform and covers trades in the following eight currency spot markets against the US dollar: the German mark, the British pound, the Japanese yen, the Swiss franc, the French franc, the Belgian franc, the Italian lira, and the Dutch guilder. The GVAR model explicitly accounts for the dynamic interactions between exchange rate and order flows simultaneously and across all of the currency markets in the system. This model describes the complex network of interlinkages among the currency markets in the Evans and Lyons dataset in considerable detail for the first time.

In **Chapter 5**, Chen and Xie investigate the bubble-like behavior in the logarithm of the dividend yield of the G7 stock markets. This contribution is to take account of the possibility of a smooth break and non-linearity at the same time to explain the dynamics of the dividend yield. Indeed, nonlinearity and smooth break have often been studied separately in the empirical analysis. This paper fills this gap. By combining the LNV and ESTAR approaches, the authors test a possible mean reverting process (ESTAR model) after taking into account the structural changes in the deterministic components (by estimating the LNV equation). For the empirical application, the authors use monthly data on the dividend yield for the G7 stock markets, obtained from the Datastream. The sample periods were determined primarily based on the availability of the data. They show that the logarithms of the dividend yields of the G7 countries are mean-reverting processes after considering the properties of non-linearity and a smooth break. Their results are in line with the theoretical foundation presented in the first section of the paper.

Chapter 6, by Kotchoni and Carrasco, reviews the theory underlying the Continuum GMM procedure of Carrasco and Florens (2000), discusses the properties of the CGMM estimator and presents numerical algorithms for its implementation. The purpose of this chapter is to inform applied researchers of the usefulness of CGMM as this procedure is relevant for many econometrics models in economics and finance that can be specified in terms of their characteristic functions as their densities are unknown in closed form. As the standard GMM estimator (the GMM of Hansen), it is implemented in two steps, the first step leading to a consistent estimator and the second step delivering an efficient estimator. Furthermore, when a conditional moment restriction is converted into a continuum of moment condition, the CGMM permits to avoid the arbitrariness of the choice of the instruments and to efficiently exploit the information content of this restriction. An empirical application is proposed where a Variance Gamma model is fitted to the monthly increments of the USD/GBP exchange rates. The authors use the USD/GBP daily exchange rates from 1980–01–01 to 2017–05–01, which are publicly available on the website of the Federal Reserve Bank of St. Louis (the FRED database). They find that the posterior mean of the variance process is a poor predictor of the monthly realized variances inferred from daily data. They suggest that a model that specifies the variance of the exchange rate increment as IID should be avoided in empirical applications.

In **Chapter 7,** Voges, Leschinski, and Sibbertsen study the nature of intra-seasonality intraday trading volume and realized volatility in finance markets and propose a semiparametric test for stochastic seasonal long memory with a specific periodicity that is robust to the presence of short memory. The authors remove deterministic seasonality using the seasonally demeaned series and propose a modified version of the G-test developed by Leschinski and Sibbertsen (2014). This modified version assesses the presence of seasonal long memory without specifying the model. They construct a local version of the G-test using a predetermined set of Fourier frequencies to the left and the right of the frequency of interest. To analyze the finite performance of their G-test, the authors construct a Monte Carlo experiment (with 1,000 replications). The Monte Carlo simulation shows good finite-sample properties independent of short-run dynamics. The authors use intraday realized volatility and trading volume data of the DJIA index and its constituents. The authors study intraday realized volatility and trading volume data of the DJIA index and its constituents. They find for both the trading volume and the volatility that the majority of the constituents of the DJIA (almost two-thirds of them) exhibit seasonal long memory. However, they find that for the index, seasonality is deterministic.

Hence, the nature of intraday seasonality in the index and in its components is different and they should be modeled accordingly.

***

Part 3 develops meta-analysis, a growing strand of applied econometrics: it states its scope and value for research improvement and policy evaluation. Meta-analysis was imported from medicine into economics in 1989 by Stanley and Jarrell. It has since then been adapted to handle non-experimental data. It has spread considerably during these last years but remains under-recognized in economics. This part attempts to fill this gap and provides a panel of meta-analyses that covers different economic topics. We employ the most recent econometric advances in the field.

Our two first contributions focus on inflation. In **Chapter 8**, Iwasaki and Uegaki perform a comparative meta-analysis on the effect that central bank independence has on inflation; it compares transition economies against the rest of the world. The paper assesses the impact of independent monetary authorities on price dynamics in transition countries; it also compares transition countries with non-transition ones. Following the collapse of socialism, the transition toward a market-based economy implied a set of structural reforms and stabilizing macro-policies. Sound monetary policies, and particularly inflation levels, proved to be crucial. They did question the role of central banks in relation to political authorities. The authors apply standard meta-regression techniques on a data set relying on 28 studies, 337 estimates (125 for transition, 212 for non-transition countries): Funnel Asymmetry Tests (FAT), Precision Effect Tests (PET), and Precision Effect Estimate with Standard Error (PEESE). Robustness checks, employing different estimators, complete the analysis. The authors find that an increased central bank independence lowers inflation independently on the group of countries, thus confirming that independent monetary authorities perform better in controlling inflation. While studies dealing with non-transition countries do exhibit a publication selection bias, transition ones do not. The authors show that the heterogeneity of results in the primary literature is mainly due to the estimator choice of, the variable inflation type, to CBI measurement, and to the quality level of the study.

In **Chapter 9**, Bouoiyour and Selmi challenge inflation uncertainty, another important facet of the inflation problem. Inflation uncertainty has huge implications for policy-making and has been largely overlooked by economists since the 1980s. However, there still is an ongoing dispute concerning the nature and direction of the relationship between realized inflation and inflation uncertainty. The authors pay a special attention to the causal relationship between the two. To that purpose, they use a panel of 32 primary studies containing 812 estimates. They employ standard meta-regression techniques (FPP procedure)[1] to explain the contradictory findings in the primary literature. Their analysis benefits from newly developed meta-analytic tests (Meta-Granger Causality testing) that handle problems raised by VAR (Vectorial Auto-Regressive) models. They suggest that the heterogeneity of the results in primary literature is mainly due to an overfitting bias supplemented by the variety of model specifications, data sources, inflation uncertainty indicators, and idiosyncratic characteristics of countries. Concerning causality direction, results are mixed. While a genuine causal effect of inflation uncertainty on inflation is present, the inverse relation is not due to the problem of overfitting bias.

Chapter 10 applies meta-analysis to policy evaluation. At the end of the 1970s, there was a new interest for economic growth, especially regarding the role of public authorities in its promotion. The fear of a secular stagnation in recent time has eventually strengthened the reflection on this topic. Several measures have been implemented, one of them consisting in fostering research and development (R&D), as a driving force of innovation. Gaillard-Ladinska, Non, and Straathof establish the effectiveness of a particular policy, tax incentives, on private R&D expenditure. FPP procedures with different estimators and weights show the existence of strong publication bias: they employ a homogeneous set of 16 studies (86 estimates reported) working on the elasticity between use cost of R&D capital and private R&D expenditures. Once the publication bias is corrected, they find that a reduction of the user cost of capital of 10 percent raises R&D expenditure by 1.5 percent, suggesting that tax-reduction may help to increase the level of private R&D. However, this effect is relatively modest and may not be the major determinant of a country's innovativeness.

In **Chapter 11**, Cazals and Mandon deal with political business cycles (PBC). Despite a long research history, the magnitude of PBC or even their existence remains an open question, and thus an ideal case for meta-analysis. After having collected data from 46 studies (1,037 estimates), the authors run both usual techniques of meta-regression and Bayesian Model Averaging (BMA) to analyze heterogeneity. A deficiency of meta-models is that they may suffer, analogously to standard econometric models, from uncertainty and/or under-over-specification. The advantage of BMA is that it allows building a model that maximizes the explained variation of the dependent variable while limiting over-under-specification problems. Results show that if political cycles in revenue and fiscal balance are patently present, their magnitudes are rather negligible. Moreover, there also is publication bias. BMA does not radically change the results but it stresses the importance of sample characteristics such as geography, time, and the timespan of democratic institutions as well as methodological choices operated by the authors.

Chapter 12 is devoted to an assessment of financial markets efficiency, a keystone of finance with deep implications for market functioning, the role of regulators, and investor strategies. Despite extensive theoretical and empirical investigations, results are mixed. Kim, Doucouliagos, and Stanley check the validity of efficiency market hypothesis (EMH) for stock markets of 16 countries in Asia and Australasia. They draw on a strand of literature focusing on variance ratio tests, (29 studies, 1,560 estimates). They adopt a cross-country comparison and hence appraise stock market efficiency from a comparative perspective. In combination with the FPP procedure, the authors pay a special attention to the problem of the statistical power of primary estimates, introducing an emerging technique: the WAAP (Weighted Average of the Adequately Powered). Until recently, meta-analysis only handled the problem of significance, but it has been shown that lack of power (associated with publication bias) raises major concerns in reviewing quantitative literature. The authors put forward that EMH is rejected, with the inefficiency of stock markets being larger in less developed countries. However, they also identify efficiency to improve over time and that factors such as market capitalization and market linearization did positively impact efficiency. This suggests that efficiency should be thought of as a process rather than a steady state.

Note

1 FAT-PET-PEESE procedure.

Part 1

Commodities finance and market performance

1 Forecasting price distributions in the German electricity market

*Sjur Westgaard, Florentina Paraschiv,
Lina Lassesen Ekern, Ingrid Naustdal,
and Malene Roland*

1. Introduction

As electricity is a non-storable commodity, a stable power system requires a constant supply and demand balance. This makes electricity a unique commodity with complex price dynamics and relations to fundamentals. Prices are characterized by sudden (positive and negative) spikes, high volatility and volatility clustering, and seasonal patterns over the day, week, and year. Thus, forecasting in electricity markets is arguably more challenging than in traditional financial markets.

Electricity price forecasts are important inputs for decision making by energy companies. For day-to-day market operations, accurate forecasts of short-term prices are crucial. Price forecasts also assist producers, retailers, and speculators who seek to determine their optimal short-term strategies for production, consumption, hedging, and trading. Uncontrolled exposure to market price risk can have devastating consequences for market participants (see the discussion in Deng and Oren (2006)). This has led to an increased focus on risk management in power markets during the last few years.

The recent introduction of smart grids and renewable integration has created more uncertainty in future supply and demand conditions where both very low prices (often negative) and high prices might occur. Over the last 15 years, most research has been concerned with predicting the mean for electricity prices. As stakeholders require explicit control of the risk of both high and low extreme prices, point forecasts are inadequate in many cases (see Nowotarski and Weron (2017)). Academics and practitioners have come to understand that probabilistic electricity price forecasting is now more important for energy systems planning, risk management, and operations than ever before.

Value-at-Risk (VaR) is the market standard for risk measurement and is simply a given quantile that will be found directly from a price distribution forecast. Despite the importance of measuring risk management in power markets, Weron (2014) and Nowotarski and Weron (2017) find that distribution forecasting is "barely touched upon" in the electricity price forecasting literature. This statement is supported by Bunn et al. (2016), who argue that for electricity markets, VaR forecasting remains a highly "under-researched" area. Maciejowska et al. (2016) claim that the lack of such research is probably due to the embedded complexity of the research problem compared with point forecasting. The sparseness in the current literature, combined with the importance of density forecasting, is our motivation for investigating how state-of-the-art econometric models can be applied to forecast VaR. We have chosen to look at the German market for several reasons: (1) it is probably the most important electricity market in Europe; (2) data quality, transparency, and access are excellent; and (3) the input mix of production towards renewables has changed a lot over the years, challenging us to build models that capture this dynamics. We need to identify models that can capture the non-linear sensitivities of electricity prices to fundamentals because of the convex supply curve as well as time-varying sensitivities to fundamentals.

We argue for the use of quantile regression (QR) models when forecasting price distributions and estimating VaR. QR models estimate each quantile with a distinct regression. Moreover, they are simple, insensitive to outliers, avoid distributional assumptions, and help find non-linear sensitivities (e.g., that electricity price sensitivities to gas prices should be higher when electricity prices are higher since gas power plants are used in such a regime "at the end" of the supply or merit order curve). In addition, we also apply QR models with time-varying parameters taking into account that the input mix has changed over time.[1] These models are exponentially weighted QR (EWQR) and exponentially weighted double kernel QR (EWDKQR) as proposed by Taylor (2008b). We compare these alternatives with common benchmarks in the VaR prediction literature using GARCH and CAViaR types of models.

By using knowledge of market conditions, we form a set of fundamental factors (supply and demand variables) and perform a variable selection procedure for each trading period and quantile with the aim of (1) proper in-sample fit and (2) optimal out-of-sample fit for a given hour and a given quantile. Hence, in additional to the dimensions of the model choice, we stress the fact that variable selection should be carefully monitored as the various fundamentals influence hours and quantiles differently.

To sum up, the overall goal of our work is threefold. First, we want to identify appropriate fundamental variables for selected hours and quantiles of the price distribution. Second, we assess the gain of using more complex QR models compared to traditional QR models and given GARCH and CAViaR benchmarks. Third, to our knowledge, no such comprehensive VaR prediction study for the German electricity market has been performed.

The paper is structured as follows. In Section 2 we review relevant literature on fundamental electricity price modeling and VaR forecasting. Next, we describe the German power market and price formation process in Section 3. In Section 4 we present and analyze the data set. In Section 5, we give an explanation of the models and evaluation procedures for distributional forecasts. We present and discuss the empirical results in Section 6 and conclude in Section 7.

2. Literature review

We position ourselves between the following groups in the literature: (1) VaR forecasting of asset markets and more specifically energy commodities and (2) fundamental analyses of electricity price formation.

VaR forecasting is complicated by the fact that high-frequency asset prices (including electricity prices) exhibit challenging data features. Time-varying volatility, skewness, and kurtosis induce a lot of complexity to the modeling of VaR (see Hartz et al. (2006)). Kuester et al. (2006) provide a comprehensive review of VaR prediction strategies that can solve some of these issues.

In our context, available models for VaR forecasts can be classified into three main categories:

- *Fully parametric models assuming a given error distribution (e.g., a GARCH-skew-t model, EVT models).*
- *Non-parametric approaches such as historical simulation, where one computes empirical quantiles based on past data. Historical simulation can be filtered taking into account time-varying volatility.*
- *Semi-parametric approaches such as quantile regression that directly models specific quantiles with no assumption regarding the error distribution.*

Most of these models have been applied without using fundamentals when we look at the energy market literature. Gurrola-Perez and Murphy (2015) evaluate historical and filtered historical simulation models for energy markets. According to paper above these authors the latter approach should be used as it greatly improves the distributional forecast. At present, research on EVT for estimating VaR in energy markets is sparse. However, examples are found in Bystrom (2005), Chan and Gray (2006), and Paraschiv and Hadzi-Mishev (2016), who all report that their results are encouraging. Garcia et al. (2005) use two GARCH models to forecast spot prices for the Spanish and Californian markets: one with price as the only variable, and one including demand. They benchmark these against an ARIMA model. They find that GARCH with price only outperforms ARIMA when time-varying volatility and price spikes are present. Moreover, adding demand as an explanatory variable further improves the forecasting performance. When assuming t or skewed t distribution, GARCH models show promising results when forecasting VaR for commodities, including energy commodities (see Giot and Laurent (2003) and Fuss et al. (2010)). Conditional Autoregressive Value-at-Risk (CAViaR) models by Engle and Manganelli (2004) model quantiles directly as an autoregressive process. The estimation is based on a quantile regression approach. The performance of CAViaR models are promising for electricity markets (see Fuss et al. (2010) and Bunn et al. (2016)). Bunn et al. (2016) also find that classical quantile regression models give excellent VaR forecasts for UK electricity prices. Florentina and Hadzi-Mishev (2016) use a combination of GARCH and EVT to investigate the tails of the German electricity price change distribution. They find that the model delivers relatively precise quantile estimates; however, the quality of the estimates is sensitive to the threshold selected for the tail.

As mentioned, the other area of research is fundamental models for electricity markets. These models try to capture price dynamics by modeling the impact of exogenous (supply and demand) factors on the electricity prices. The main motivation for using such models is that characteristic electricity price patterns are the result of adaption to fundamentals. Prices are also functions of different drivers in a specific trading period. Prices have also different sensitivities to fundamentals depending on the level of electricity prices. In a comprehensive review of electricity forecasting literature, Weron (2014) finds that the majority of models include fundamentals. The fundamental type of models has been applied to the Nordic electricity market, where the effects of water reservoir levels, load, and gas and coal prices among other variables have been found important for the price formation. Examples of such studies are Lundby and Uppheim (2011), Huisman et al. (2015a, b), and Fleten et al. (2016). All these studies give empirical insights on the non-linear influence of the fundamentals on the electricity prices and well as time-varying sensitivity to these fundamentals. The methods applied are quantile regression, various non-linear models, and state space models. In the German market, there are several interesting studies. Paraschiv et al. (2014, 2016) emphasize the importance of using fundamentals and find variables for renewable power particularly influential. Their focus is the investigation of how the sensitivities to fundamentals change over time applying a state space model with Kalman filtering. Time-varying parameters are motivated because evolving factors, like technology, market structure, and participant conduct, affect the underlying price formation dynamically over time. Follow-up studies using quantile regression highlight that sensitivities change in relation to the level of electricity prices (Hagfors et al. (2016a)). The prediction of extreme price occurrences in the German day-ahead electricity market by using non-linear discrete choice models is found in Hagfors et al. (2016b). For the UK market there are several papers investigating the price formation with fundamentals using the state space model (Karakatsani and Bunn (2008)), regime switch models with non-linear transition functions of fundamentals (Bunn and Chen (2008)), and quantile regression (Bunn et al. (2016) and Hagfors et al. (2016)). One of the few papers focusing on predicting prices for the UK electricity market is Gonzales et al. (2012). They find improved accuracy by including fundamentals when forecasting UK spot prices. Moreover, they observe that the variable coefficients in their models evolve remarkably over time. Thus, they argue that dynamic specifications are necessary, and that forecasting models should be re-estimated day by day. They suggest constant monitoring of market conditions in order to select the appropriate model specification and fundamental drivers. The only paper we have found about predicting price *distributions* in the UK el-market is Bunn et al. (2016). They find improved forecasting accuracy by including fundamentals. Bunn et al. (2016) investigate the UK market using various forms of quantile regression and compare the out-of-sample forecast with various GARCH and CaViaR models. The general finding is that quantile regression models that include fundamentals perform just as well these advanced models at a much lower cost of implementation. Quantile regression models including fundamentals are also much easier to understand and enable risk management to perform scenario analyses and investigate how VaR is directly affected by changing values of risk factors. Market participants can use these in risk management and plan for a range of price scenarios given different input ranges for the fundamental variables. Maciejowska and Weron (2016) also find that the inclusion of fundamentals generally improves the forecasting performance of UK base load prices. However, they also emphasize that variable selection is crucial. For example, they observe that including gas prices increases forecasting performance, whereas variables related to system-wide demand and CO_2 prices decreases the performance of the predictions. We conclude that there is no general answer about which fundamentals are the best to include, as the optimal selection depends on both the forecasting horizon and trading period.

We want to extend the literature and understanding of electricity price distributional forecasting using dynamic quantile regression models. This is an area that lacks investigation. It is of specific interest in markets such as the German electricity market, where the input mix (and hence sensitivities to the drivers) clearly has changed over time. In particular we want to follow the models proposed by Taylor (2008a). He introduces exponentially weighted quantile regression (EWQR). The extension is motivated by the trade-off between including too few observations and getting large sampling errors, and including too many and getting a model that reacts slowly to changes in the true distribution. EWQR attempts to resolve this by placing exponentially decaying weights on the observations, which gives greater emphasis to newer observations. To the best of our knowledge, EWQR has received little attention in electricity price forecasting literature. It is challenging to estimate extreme quantiles due to the sparseness of observations in the tails. This is Taylor's (2008b) motivation for extending the EWQR model further, to exponentially weighted double kernel quantile regression (EWDKQR). The EWDKQR method is based on the paper by Jones and Yu (1998), who argue that double-kernel methods are useful for calculating quantiles. In empirical studies, Taylor finds that EWDKQR performs worse than EWQR in terms of the hit percentage. However, the dynamic properties of the quantiles are better explained by the EWDKQR model.

To sum up, we want to extend the analysis and understanding of electricity price formation with fundamentals using dynamic quantile regression models. In addition, we will investigate whether these models improve the forecast compared to static quantile regression, GARCH, and the CaViaR type of models. We also want to specifically find which combinations of drivers/fundamentals should be used in predicting VaR for specific hours and quantiles.

3. The German electricity market

In this section, we describe the German electricity market, the price drivers, and the price formation process. This will serve as guidance and motivation for choosing the fundamental variables.

The European Power Exchange (EPEX) is the main trading platform for electricity prices in Europe. It offers trading, clearing, and settlement in both the day-ahead and intraday markets. The day-ahead, hourly prices in Germany are traded on EPEX and are referred to as "Phelix". The day-ahead market is the primary market for power trading. Here, buyers and sellers make hourly contracts for the delivery of power the following day. This happens through a daily auction at 12 p.m., where the market clearing price is determined by matching supply and demand. The intraday market supplements the day-ahead market and helps secure the necessary demand-supply balance.

Seasonal fluctuations, substantial volatility clustering, large spikes and increasing occurrences of negative prices for certain hours characterize the German electricity market (see Reisch and Micklitz (2006), Paraschiv et al. (2014), and Hagfors et al. (2016b)).

Energy input mix

Table 1.1 shows the development of the energy mix in Germany from 2010 to 2016. It illustrates that power production in Germany mainly relies on fossil fuel power, particularly coal, with 40.3% of the total production in 2016. Moreover, there is a large share of intermittent renewable energy in the form of wind and solar power. The increase in renewable energy and reduction in nuclear power are the most notable developments during the period. The latter is due to the German government's decision to phase out nuclear energy by 2022. Regulatory changes are also the key driving force for the growth in renewables, as several subsidies and policy measures have been introduced during the recent period (see Federal Ministry for Economic Affairs and Energy (2017)).

Demand

Since electricity is a flow, it is produced and consumed continuously. The non-storable nature of electricity entails that a constant balance between supply and demand is necessary to ensure power system stability. Hence, hourly price variations are largely due to fluctuations in demand. Therefore, there are different dynamics in hourly prices. Demand is a function of temperature, seasonality and consumer patterns, which give rise to the periodic nature of electricity

Table 1.1 Electricity production in Germany by source (%). Data from AG Energibalanzen e.V. (2017) and Clean Energy Wire (2017).

Source	2010	2011	2012	2013	2014	2015	2016
Coal	41.6	42.9	44.1	45.2	43.8	42.1	40.3
Nuclear	22.2	17.6	15.8	15.3	15.5	14.2	13.1
Natural gas	14.1	14.1	12.2	10.6	9.7	9.6	12.4
Oil	1.4	1.2	1.2	1.1	0.9	1.0	0.9
Renewable energy:	16.5	20.1	22.6	23.7	25.8	29.0	29.0
Wind	6.0	8.0	8.1	8.1	9.1	12.3	11.9
Solar	1.9	3.2	4.2	4.9	5.7	6.0	5.9
Biomass	4.6	5.2	6.1	6.3	7.7	6.9	7.0
Hydro power	3.3	2.9	3.5	3.6	3.1	2.9	3.2
Waste to energy	0.7	0.8	0.8	0.8	1.0	0.9	0.9
Other	4.2	4.1	4.1	4.1	4.3	4.1	4.2

prices. As few options are available to consumers in response to price changes, demand is highly price inelastic in the short term. Positive price spikes are often caused by high (unexpected) demand. Producers with market power may also offer and create market prices substantially above marginal costs in times of scarcity and high demand. Including lagged price and volatility behavior might capture some of these effects (see Bunn et al. (2016) for discussion about how adaptive behavior can be specified in the model specifications).

Supply

The *merit order curve* plays a vital role in the electricity price formation process. This is the sorted marginal cost curve of electricity production, starting with the least expensive technologies to the left of the curve. Generally, the plants with the lowest marginal costs are the first to use to meet demand. Thus, we can use the merit order curve to determine the price setting technology, i.e., the production technology located at the intersection between supply and demand. The German merit order curve increases areas of flat and convex regions, hence inducing non-linearity in the elasticity between fundamentals and prices. During periods of low demand, base load power plants, such as nuclear and coal, usually serve as price setting technologies. These plants are inflexible, due to high ramp-up costs. Contrary, in times of high demand, prices are set by expensive peak load plants, like gas and oil power plants. These facilities have high flexibility and high marginal costs and give rise to the convex shape of the merit order curve. With the lowest marginal cost, renewable energy sources are at the bottom of the merit order curve. Increased supply of renewable energy shifts the curve to the right and thus lowers power prices. Coal is the largest source of electricity in Germany. Hence, coal is a generating technology in the mid-region of the supply function where demand tends to be most of the time. CO_2-producing companies are obliged to buy emission allowances. Since coal-fired power plants and to a lesser degree gas-fired power are CO_2 intensive, the price of CO_2 allowances influence the marginal cost of coal and gas power plants in a different way. During periods of high prices for emission allowances, a phenomenon called *fuel switch* may occur. This is a change in the merit order curve, where the marginal production costs of more efficient gas-fired power plants become less than those of CO_2-intense coal-fired power plants (see Erni (2012) and Paraschiv et al. (2014)).

Among the renewable energy sources in Table 1.1, wind and solar energy have attracted most attention in Germany over the past few years. In 2016, they contributed 18% of the total production in Germany. The supply of wind and solar energy is determined by meteorological conditions and features seasonal patterns. A notable observation from Paraschiv et al. (2014) is that wind infeed tends to be higher in the early morning and the afternoon hours. Due to intermittency, renewable energy sources pose significant challenges for modern energy markets (see EPEX Spot (2017)). Hours with increased supply of renewable energy cause difficulties for inflexible facilities that should run continuously. This is because the inflexible base load facilities have shutdown and start-up costs, forcing them to accept negative marginal returns in order to generate continuously. This has a lowering effect on electricity prices. Hagfors et al. (2016c) find that negative prices are mainly caused by high wind production at times when demand is low. Thus, negative price spikes occur mainly at night.

Reserve margin is a commonly considered supply side factor in the literature. It is defined as available supply minus demand. Bunn et al. (2016) argue that spot prices are sensitive to supply shocks such as plant outages, and that expectations of spot prices involve consideration of the reserve margin.

4. Data analysis

Our dependent variables are selected prices from EPEX observed between 1 January 2010 and 31 August 2016. The main reason for this choice is the Equalisation Mechanism Ordinance, which came into force on 1 January 2010. This act induced a significant increase in the use of renewable energy and caused large changes in the EPEX input mix. However, some of the data, like solar and power plant availability, are incomplete or not available for earlier time periods. The spot price data have hourly resolution, which means that we have 58,440 price observations. However, since each hour is a separate trading period, we treat the price data as 24 independent time series with 2,435 data points each. We have selected hours 3, 8, and 19 as the periods we model as representatives of hours with different dynamics.

Our selection of independent variables is based on our discussion in Section 3. The data set applied in this analysis consists of the variables shown in Table 1.2 and Table 1.3; Figure 1.1 shows the development of spot prices for hours 3, 8, and 19. We see occurrences of negative price spikes in hour 3 and positive spikes in hours 8 and 19. These hours clearly display different price characteristics due to the various demand conditions and the use of different technologies for electricity production. Table 1.4 gives more details about the properties of the various prices. All prices were found stationary using Dickey Fuller tests and we found significant serial correlation for several lags (not shown in the

Table 1.2 Data granularity for the dependent and independent variables used in our analysis. We apply hours 3, 8, and 19 with the associated forecasts in our analysis. The data period is from 1 January 2010 to 31 August 2016.

Variable	Daily	Hourly
Phelix spot price		X
Coal price	X	
Gas price	X	
Oil price	X	
CO_2 allowance price	X	
EU expected wind infeed		X
Expected solar (PV) infeed		X
Expected power plant availability (PPA)	X	
Expected demand		X

Table 1.3 Description of dependent and independent variables used in our analysis. We apply hours 3, 8, and 19 with the associated forecasts in our analysis. The data period is from 1 January 2010 to 31 August 2016.

Variable	Units	Description	Data Source
Spot price	EUR/ MWh	Market clearing price	European Energy Exchange: www.eex.com
Coal price	EUR/ 12,000 t	Latest available price (daily auctioned) of the front-month ARA futures contract before the electricity price auction takes place	European Energy Exchange: www.eex.com
Gas price	EUR/ MWh	Latest price of the NCG Day Ahead Natural Gas Spot Price on the day before the electricity price auction takes place	Bloomberg, ticker: EGTHDAHD Index
Oil price	EUR/bbl	Latest price of the active ICE Brent Crude futures contract on the day before the electricity price auction takes place	Bloomberg, ticker: CO1 Comdty
CO_2 price	EUR 0.01/ EUA 1,000 t CO_2	Latest available price of the EEX Carbon Index (Carbix), daily auctioned at 10:30 a.m.	European Energy Exchange: www.eex.com
Expected wind and PV infeed	MWh	Sum of expected infeed of wind electricity into the grid, published by German transmission systems operators in the late afternoon following the electricity price auction	Transmission system operators: www.50Hertz.com, www.amprion.de, www.transnetbw.de, www.tennettso.de
Expected PPA	MWh	Forecast of expected power plant availability production (voluntary publication) on the delivery day (daily granularity), published at 10:00 a.m.	European Energy Exchange and transmission energy operators: ftp://infoproducts.eex. com
Expected demand	MWh	Sum of the total vertical system load and actual wind infeed for the same hour on the last relevant delivery day	Transmission system operators: www.50Hertz.com, www. amprion.de, www.transnetbw.de, www.tennettso.de

table). The mean of the prices shows in general a falling trend. For the whole period, hours 8 and 19 have a significantly higher mean price (euro/MWh) than hour 3. Negative prices are found every year for hour 3 prices, with the lowest price of −221 euro/MWh for the year 2012. There is a downward trend in the absolute values of negative prices indicating that power companies

(a)

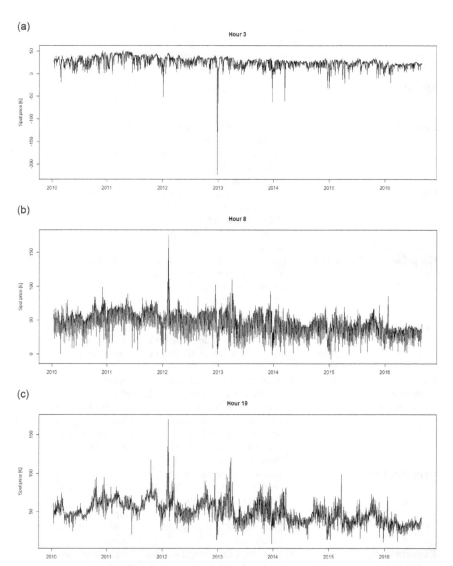

Figure 1.1 Development in selected hourly EPEX spot prices (hours 3, 8, 19) from 1 January 2010 to 31 August 2016

might have managed to improve negative spikes. There have also been minor changes in German energy policy over these years that might have had an effect. In hour 8 we detect negative prices in some years. In hour 19 there are (not surprisingly) no negative prices as this represents the hour with highest demand. Hour 8 has few positive spikes. Hours 8 and 19 have substantial positive price spikes in some years (although the trend is falling). There has in general been a falling trend of volatility for all prices. Hour 3 has negative skewness

Table 1.4 Descriptive statistics of EPEX spot prices hours 3, 8, and 19 measured in euros. The tables show the characteristics based on daily data each year from 1 January 2010 to 31 August 2016 (that is summary statistics are only given for part of 2016).

Hour 3	Median	Mean	Min	Max	Std.dev.	Skewness	Kurtosis
2010	29.83	27.63	−18.10	50.15	10.60	−0.77	3.47
2011	38.58	34.85	−0.10	51.08	10.71	−1.10	3.47
2012	30.08	26.21	−221.94	45.20	20.99	−8.11	86.69
2013	25.90	23.29	−62.03	39.67	10.78	−2.03	13.98
2014	23.98	21.14	−60.26	34.46	9.00	−3.09	23.16
2015	24.02	21.29	−31.41	34.92	9.21	−1.82	7.73
2016	20.10	18.48	−19.30	30.01	6.27	−1.99	8.95
Total	25.67	25.00	−221.90	51.08	13.10	−5.37	84.24

Hour 8	Median	Mean	Min	Max	Std.dev.	Skewness	Kurtosis
2010	51.55	50.07	1.06	98.71	14.66	−0.50	3.83
2011	60.63	57.44	−5.95	88.78	13.83	−1.18	5.10
2012	53.24	51.38	−0.09	175.55	19.35	1.15	10.20
2013	46.61	46.71	−0.98	109.36	18.14	−0.10	3.02
2014	41.03	39.65	0.05	72.94	13.81	−0.35	2.82
2015	40.46	38.85	−6.86	71.92	13.88	−0.43	3.05
2016	34.10	31.17	2.59	85.05	10.53	0.03	5.86
Total	46.37	45.76	−6.86	175.60	17.21	0.19	2.02

Hour 19	Median	Mean	Min	Max	Std.dev.	Skewness	Kurtosis
2010	50.85	53.52	24.76	95.00	10.78	0.92	4.15
2011	62.53	62.37	21.49	117.49	9.79	0.20	6.20
2012	55.00	56.39	13.70	169.90	15.85	1.87	12.79
2013	49.55	51.29	9.28	120.16	15.67	0.85	4.45
2014	42.44	44.20	14.34	81.51	11.56	0.67	3.73
2015	42.11	42.53	10.55	98.05	11.39	0.44	4.40
2016	33.15	33.04	11.79	70.03	6.99	0.75	6.74
Total	48.95	49.85	9.28	169.90	14.99	0.74	2.65

each year in prices, while hour 8 has negative skewed prices in some years and some years with positive prices. Hour 19 has positive skewness in prices in all years. The kurtosis is also high for all series. Extreme negative spikes in some periods make the kurtosis highest for hour 3. Figure 1.1 also illustrates this.

Table 1.5 displays descriptive statistics of the fundamental variables used in the analysis. Wind, solar, and demand all have hourly resolution, while coal, gas, oil, CO_2 prices, and PPA are given on a daily basis in the period 1 January 2010 to 31 August 2016. Table 1.6 presents the correlation between the spot price at the specific hour and the fundamentals. Wind and solar have a negative correlation on the electricity price as expected. Demand and fuel prices have a positive correlation as expected. Expected power plant availability has a positive correlation (as expected) with prices at hours 8 and 19. At hour 3 the effect is negligible. This might be because the supply capacity is usually in surplus in the night hours.

Table 1.5 Descriptive statistics of fundamental variables used in the analysis. Note that coal, gas, oil, CO_2, and PPA have a daily data granularity, and therefore show the same numbers for all hours. The calculations are based on daily data from EPEX from 1 January 2010 to 31 August 2016.

Hour 3	Median	Mean	Min	Max	Std.dev.	Skewness	Kurtosis
Wind	4491	6067	286	37322	5265	1.9	7.4
Solar	0.0	0.1	0.0	255.0	5.2	49.3	2433
Demand	31078	31219	19127	45071	3821	0.2	3.1
Coal	60.4	64.2	37.6	99.0	14.1	0.3	2.2
Gas	22.1	21.4	11.0	39.5	4.7	−0.3	2.7
Oil	45.3	40.4	15.0	56.7	10.1	−0.6	2.1
CO_2	7.2	8.5	2.7	16.8	3.8	0.8	2.3
PPA	55531	55323	40016	64169	4863	−0.2	2.1

Hour 8	Median	Mean	Min	Max	Std.dev.	Skewness	Kurtosis
Wind	4075	5875	229	35663	5399	1.8	6.9
Solar	2087	3011	0.0	11665	2849	0.8	2.6
Demand	48673	45193	22783	62594	7800	−0.8	2.3
Coal	60.4	64.2	37.6	99.0	14.1	0.3	2.2
Gas	22.1	21.4	11.0	39.5	4.7	−0.3	2.7
Oil	45.3	40.4	15.0	56.7	10.1	−0.6	2.1
CO_2	7.2	8.5	2.7	16.8	3.8	0.8	2.3
PPA	55531	55323	40016	64169	4863	−0.2	2.1

Hour 19	Median	Mean	Min	Max	Std.dev.	Skewness	Kurtosis
Wind	4473	6101	270	33522	5225	1.7	6.3
Solar	74.0	736	0.0	4730	1047	1.3	3.5
Demand	45947	45496	30768	60966	5840	−0.3	2.4
Coal	60.4	64.2	37.6	99.0	14.1	0.3	2.2
Gas	22.1	21.4	11.0	39.5	4.7	−0.3	2.7
Oil	45.3	40.4	15.0	56.7	10.1	−0.6	2.1
CO_2	7.2	8.5	2.7	16.8	3.8	0.8	2.3
PPA	55531	55323	40016	64169	4863	−0.2	2.1

Table 1.6 Correlation between spot prices and fundamental variables. The calculations are based on daily data from EPEX from 1 January 2010 to 31 August 2016.

Hour	Wind	Solar	Demand	Coal	Gas	Oil	CO_2	PPA
3	−0.571	−0.003	0.264	0.370	0.151	0.222	0.316	−0.074
8	−0.378	−0.224	0.699	0.441	0.300	0.321	0.308	0.132
19	−0.394	−0.368	0.538	0.553	0.425	0.427	0.336	0.182

5. Econometric methods and procedures

In this section, we describe how we implement and test quantile regression models as well as a set of benchmark models. We also explain our evaluation procedure for distributional forecasts, our variable selection approach, and our rolling window forecast approach.

We implement three different quantile regression models and three benchmark GARCH and CaViaR models:

- Traditional quantile regression (QR)
- Exponentially weighted quantile regression (EWQR)
- Exponentially weighted double kernel quantile regression (EWDKQR)
- GARCH (1,1) with skewed student-*t* distribution (GARCH-T)
- Symmetric absolute value CAViaR (SAV CAViaR)
- Asymmetric slope CAViaR (AS CaViaR).

5.1. Linear quantile regression

We start with the original quantile regression model by Koenker and Bassett (1978). This is given by

$$Q_\theta(lnP_{i,t+1}) = \beta_{i,0}^\theta + \sum_{n=1}^{N} \beta_{i,n}^\theta X_{n,t} \tag{5.1}$$

Here, $\theta \in \{1\%, 5\%, 10\%, 25\%, 50\%, 75\%, 90\%, 95\%, 99\%\}$ denotes the quantile, $i \in [0, 23]$ is the hour, and n indexes the set of explanatory variables x which has N elements. P is the price of electricity. The set of fundaments are from those described in Section 4 but will vary as we perform a variable selection procedure (this will be described later). The quantile coefficients are found by minimizing:

$$\min_{\beta_i^\theta} \sum_{t=1}^{T}(lnP_{i,T} - X_{i,t}\beta_i^\theta)(\theta - I(lnP_{i,T} \leq X_{i,t}\beta_i^\theta)) \tag{5.2}$$

$X_{i,t}$ is a vector of explanatory variables at time t and β_i^θ is a vector of regression coefficients. I() refers to an indicator function returning the value 1 or 0. We solve the minimization problem using the "quantreg" package in R.

5.2. Exponentially weighted quantile regression

By adding a weighting parameter λ to Equation 5.2, we get the exponentially weighted quantile regression by Taylor (2008b). λ decays exponentially, amounting to simple exponential smoothing of the cumulative distribution function. Thus, the EWQR minimization has the form

$$\min_{\beta_i^\theta} \sum_{t=1}^{T} \lambda^{T-t}(lnP_{i,T} - X_{i,t}\beta_i^\theta)(\theta - I(lnP_{i,T} \leq X_{i,t}\beta_i^\theta)) \tag{5.3}$$

Again, we solve the minimization using R's "quantreg" package. The value of λ determines how fast the weights decay. If the distribution changes rapidly, a relatively low value is needed to ensure that the model adapts swiftly. However, larger values may be necessary in the extreme quantiles to give significant weight to a higher number of observations. We follow Taylor's approach to optimize the λ-values. This is done by using a rolling window to produce one step-ahead quantile forecasts for the observations in the in-sample set, and selecting the λ that yields the minimum QR sum. This is the summation in the standard form of QR in Equation 5.2. Since λ depends on all parts of the model specification, we perform this optimization for all combinations of hours, quantiles, explanatory variables, and window sizes. We test a window of λ-values between 0.9 and 1, with a step size of 0.001.

5.3. Exponentially weighted double kernel quantile regression

We expand the exponentially weighted quantile regression model further to an exponentially weighted double kernel quantile regression following the approach of Taylor (2008b). In this model, we replace the observations $lnP_{i,t}$ from Equation 5.3 with a kernel function K_{h2}. Taylor argues that introducing kernels may allow faster decay of the exponentially weighting parameter, and consequently, better adaption to swift distribution changes. To perform the minimization, we use the "nlm" non-linear optimization solver in R.

5.4. Fully parametric GARCH models

In several studies investigating GARCH models for commodity VaR predictions, GARCH with a skewed student-t distribution performs significantly better than Gaussian GARCH (see for example Giot and Laurent (2003) and Fuss et al. (2010)). This is the reason why we only implement skewed student-t GARCH. For details of the model, see Giot and Laurent (2003). We first run a regression with $ln(P_t)$ as the dependent variable against a set of fundamentals. The residuals from this regression are then modeled by a skewed student-t GARCH. This model is then used for forecasting VaR (see Giot and Laurent (2003) for details). We use the "fGarch" package in R.

5.5. Conditional autoregressive value-at-risk models

The CAViaR models by Engle and Manganelli (2004) specify the evolution of a quantile over time as an autoregressive process. They derive expressions for four different CAViaR processes: symmetric absolute value, asymmetric slope, adaptive, and indirect GARCH (1,1). We use the first two as benchmarks, as Fuss et al. (2010)) found that these generally outperformed the others in predicting VaR. These models are estimated using a developed code in R.

5.6. Out-of-sample performance analysis

To test the predictive performance of the models, we use Kupiec's unconditional coverage (UC) test (1995), Christoffersen's conditional coverage (CC) test (1998), and the dynamic conditional quantile (DQ1 and DQ2) tests by Engle and Manganelli (2004). Alexander (2008b, d) gives a nice description on how these measures are used in risk management and backtesting of VaR models in practice.

5.7. Variable selection and forecasting approach

Variable selection is a crucial step in building a good prediction model (e.g., Diebold (2015)). Distributional forecasting is a complex process, and the standard goodness-of-fit tests are not sufficient. In Section 2, we saw evidence that fundamental variables affect specific hours and quantiles differently. As our target is forecasting, it is therefore necessary to perform variable selections for all combinations of hours and quantiles to take full advantage of modeling each quantile separately. To achieve high predictive power, variable selection should be based on the quality of the *association* between predictors and responses rather than causal relationships (see Shmueli (2010) and Diebold (2015) for more discussion. For each hour and quantile, we choose the combination of variables that yields the best SIC score[2] in-sample while also demanding that the model passes the critical out-of-sample tests.[3]

We apply a rolling window, which works as follows. If the window size is 365, observations [1, 365] are used for forecasting the VaR of observation 366. Next, we re-estimate the model with observations [2, 366] and forecast the VaR of observation 367, and so on. We test window sizes of 250, 365, 548, 730, and 913 days. The window that gives the best results for a given hour and quantile is chosen in each case.

6. Results

Tables 1.7, 1.8, and 1.9 list the predictive performance of the models presented in Section 5. As evaluation criteria, we use the UC-, CC-, and DQ tests and display the detailed results for hours 3, 8, and 19, respectively. Here, we only present the optimized model for each quantile and hour. That is, models that are optimized with window size and variable combinations for each hour and quantile.

It is difficult to draw a general conclusion about which model is performing best based on our results. The model with the highest predictive performance varies across both the distribution and the trading periods. Moreover, the four evaluation criteria favor different models in each case. We calculate the total number of rejected tests when we rate one model against another in Tables 1.10, 1.11, and 1.12 below.

In Table 1.10 we display the total number of test rejections per model. Based on this, we rate the EWQR as the best model overall; it outperforms both the other QR type models and the benchmarks in terms of test rejections. Another important observation is that clustering of exceedances is challenging to capture for all models. Again, EWQR is relatively the best model regarding the CC test but not with the more advanced DQ1 and DQ2 tests.

Next, we break down the analysis into performance in each hour and parts of the distribution. The results for each hour are summarized in Table 1.11. EWQR is performing best for hours 3 and 8 and third best for hour 19. For hour 19 SA CAViaR is performing best. An observation is also that hour 8 has a higher level of rejections in general than hour 3 and hour 19. In Table 1.12, we assess performance across the distribution. For risk management purposes, it is particularly important to consider accuracy in the tails. Thus, we divide the distribution into three parts: (1) the lower tail with quantiles 0.01%, 0.05% and 0.10%; (2) the mid-region with quantiles 0.25%, 0.50% and 0.75%; and (3) the upper tail with quantiles 0.90%, 0.95% and 0.99%. EWQR performs second in the

Table 1.7 Predictive performance in hour 3

	Quantile	Violations	P_UC	P_CC	P_DQ1	P_DQ2
QR	0.01	1.09E-02	8.01E-01	0.00E+00*	1.86E-01	2.61E-02*
	0.05	4.92E-02	9.25E-01	3.07E-01	1.32E-01	1.65E-01
	0.10	8.48E-02	1.61E-01	2.73E-01	6.11E-01	6.07E-01
	0.25	2.42E-01	6.22E-01	1.08E-01	7.81E-03*	1.21E-01
	0.50	5.62E-01	7.51E-04*	0.00E+00*	5.54E-31*	3.38E-02*
	0.75	7.44E-01	7.17E-01	0.00E+00*	2.46E-38*	2.16E-01
	0.90	8.88E-01	2.81E-01	3.61E-02*	5.28E-04*	3.75E-01
	0.95	9.51E-01	9.25E-01	6.71E-01	1.56E-04*	9.64E-01
	0.99	9.84E-01	1.11E-01	0.00E+00*	1.90E-04*	2.83E-02*
# Rejections			1	5	6	3
EWQR	0.01	1.37E-02	3.44E-01	0.00E+00*	4.95E-01	9.23E-02
	0.05	5.06E-02	9.39E-01	3.52E-01	1.85E-01	2.70E-01
	0.10	9.44E-02	6.10E-01	7.24E-01	7.26E-01	7.97E-01
	0.25	2.46E-01	8.14E-01	8.27E-01	1.41E-02*	1.50E-01
	0.50	4.77E-01	2.22E-01	0.00E+00*	1.14E-23*	8.24E-03*
	0.75	6.87E-01	1.17E-04*	0.00E+00*	5.96E-27*	7.97E-03*
	0.90	8.82E-01	1.21E-01	4.32E-02*	2.70E-02*	1.22E-01
	0.95	9.51E-01	9.25E-01	6.71E-01	1.56E-04*	9.64E-01
	0.99	9.82E-01	5.66E-02	7.74E-02	1.60E-01	4.90E-01
# Rejections			1	4	5	2
EWDKQR	0.01	6.84E-03	3.62E-01	0.00E+00*	1.00E+00	7.49E-02
	0.05	3.97E-02	1.84E-01	3.13E-01	8.41E-01	8.72E-01
	0.10	8.62E-02	2.03E-01	4.30E-01	4.58E-01	4.73E-01
	0.25	2.37E-01	4.02E-01	0.00E+00*	3.98E-43*	2.79E-10*
	0.50	4.90E-01	5.79E-01	4.45E-02*	3.44E-02*	3.83E-08*
	0.75	7.35E-01	3.40E-01	0.00E+00*	6.60E-85*	1.48E-26*
	0.90	9.53E-01	9.73E-08*	1.53E-07*	1.84E-01	4.63E-18*
	0.95	9.53E-01	6.62E-01	4.51E-11*	2.12E-25*	2.17E-12*
	0.99	9.96E-01	6.92E-02	0.00E+00*	1.00E+00*	2.29E-07*
# Rejections			1	7	4	6

	Quantile	Violations	P_UC	P_CC	P_DQ1	P_DQ2
GARCH	0.01	6.84E-03	3.62E-01	0.00E+00*	1.00E+00	1.80E-01
	0.05	6.29E-02	1.22E-01	3.03E-01	3.54E-01	5.66E-01
	0.10	1.07E-01	5.50E-01	5.09E-01	6.24E-01	9.45E-01
	0.25	2.38E-01	4.52E-01	7.26E-04*	1.49E-05*	4.28E-02*
	0.50	8.81E-01	0.00E+00*	0.00E+00*	7.93E-13*	1.46E-02*
	0.75	6.13E-01	3.33E-16*	0.00E+00*	3.60E-16*	2.03E-06*
	0.90	8.84E-01	1.52E-01	1.18E-01	3.11E-01	2.29E-09*
	0.95	9.49E-01	9.39E-01	7.62E-01	6.04E-02	1.37E-06*
	0.99	9.93E-01	3.62E-01	0.00E+00*	1.00E+00	2.07E-02*
# Rejections			2	5	3	6
Asym. slope CAViaR	0.01	1.37E-02	3.44E-01	1.74E-01	9.98E-01	3.13E-01
	0.05	5.75E-02	3.66E-01	3.86E-01	8.26E-01	2.71E-01
	0.10	9.44E-02	6.10E-01	1.32E-02*	1.24E-02*	2.59E-01
	0.25	2.28E-01	1.74E-01	2.20E-04*	7.02E-05*	9.86E-02
	0.50	5.27E-01	1.49E-01	7.05E-09*	6.33E-14*	1.72E-07*
	0.75	7.55E-01	7.48E-01	9.26E-04*	2.97E-11*	3.32E-06*
	0.90	9.21E-01	5.43E-02	5.29E-05*	5.49E-05*	3.99E-09*
	0.95	9.67E-01	2.34E-02*	1.79E-03*	1.30E-03*	5.79E-01
	0.99	9.86E-01	3.44E-01	0.00E+00*	1.21E-05*	2.64E-01
# Rejections			1	7	7	3
Sym. Abs. value CAViaR	0.01	1.09E-02	8.01E-01	1.89E-01	2.98E-03*	2.26E-01
	0.05	5.61E-02	4.58E-01	1.77E-01	1.26E-01	1.20E-01
	0.10	1.11E-01	3.38E-01	4.76E-03*	3.11E-02*	9.41E-01
	0.25	1.44E-01	1.82E-12*	0.00E+00*	1.09E-18*	2.30E-02*
	0.50	5.40E-01	2.90E-02*	0.00E+00*	2.47E-39*	1.59E-04*
	0.75	6.80E-01	2.05E-05*	0.00E+00*	6.18E-43*	4.10E-04*
	0.90	8.96E-01	7.22E-01	4.45E-01	5.17E-01	4.05E-09*
	0.95	9.52E-01	7.91E-01	8.11E-01	9.57E-01	2.12E-10*
	0.99	9.88E-01	5.44E-01	0.00E+00*	9.97E-01	3.06E-11*
# Rejections			3	5	5	6

The table displays the violation in percent, p-values of the unconditional coverage test (UC), the conditional coverage test (CC), and the two dynamic conditional quantile tests (DQ1 and DQ2), as described in Section 5. P-values highlighted with * are significant at the 5% level, which implies poor model calibration (under H0 we have a correct model). Window sizes and variable selection are optimized for each model as described in Section 5.

Table 1.8 Predictive performance in hour 8

Left panel:

	Quantile	Violations	P_UC	P_CC	P_DQ1	P_DQ2
QR	0.01	9.58E-03	9.08E-01	0.00E+00*	9.99E-01	2.73E-01
	0.05	3.15E-02	1.39E-02*	4.60E-02*	6.06E-01	9.98E-01
	0.10	7.52E-02	2.01E-02*	6.10E-02	1.96E-02*	6.43E-01
	0.25	2.54E-01	7.82E-01	6.66E-16*	9.75E-20*	2.52E-02*
	0.50	4.90E-01	5.79E-01	1.37E-14*	6.91E-49*	1.66E-01
	0.75	7.15E-01	3.35E-02*	3.26E-13*	6.64E-23*	5.32E-02
	0.90	9.18E-01	9.66E-02	6.16E-13*	1.30E-28*	1.41E-04*
	0.95	9.49E-01	9.39E-01	2.33E-15*	1.11E-42*	1.86E-05*
	0.99	9.96E-01	6.92E-02	0.00E+00*	1.00E+00	4.56E-01
# Rejections			3	8	6	3
EWQR	0.01	1.23E-02	5.44E-01	0.00E+00*	9.97E-01	3.30E-01
	0.05	4.79E-02	7.91E-01	9.35E-01	6.77E-01	6.50E-01
	0.10	9.85E-02	8.92E-01	3.08E-01	9.48E-04*	1.23E-01
	0.25	2.60E-01	5.38E-01	8.48E-10*	4.87E-10*	2.86E-01
	0.50	4.66E-01	6.98E-02	5.07E-12*	6.05E-52*	7.33E-03*
	0.75	7.10E-01	1.40E-02*	3.72E-10*	2.90E-15*	1.28E-03*
	0.90	9.12E-01	2.53E-01	2.63E-12*	7.48E-21*	4.84E-01
	0.95	9.44E-01	4.58E-01	7.71E-11*	7.32E-24*	1.44E-01
	0.99	9.86E-01	3.44E-01	0.00E+00*	7.70E-02	1.34E-04*
# Rejections			1	7	6	3
EWDKQR	0.01	1.50E-02	2.02E-01	1.37E-02*	9.01E-08*	4.42E-01
	0.05	5.20E-02	8.07E-01	7.50E-01	2.35E-04*	9.10E-01
	0.10	9.99E-02	9.90E-01	1.65E-06*	3.50E-07*	8.85E-01
	0.25	2.50E-01	9.83E-01	1.40E-02*	1.11E-59*	1.47E-01
	0.50	5.06E-01	7.39E-01	0.00E+00*	4.43E-29*	4.71E-01
	0.75	7.47E-01	8.48E-01	6.50E-07*	5.43E-08*	5.04E-08*
	0.90	9.06E-01	6.10E-01	2.55E-15*	3.80E-28*	3.67E-01
	0.95	9.53E-01	6.62E-01	3.49E-06*	2.82E-17*	4.76E-11*
	0.99	9.88E-01	5.44E-01	2.05E-01	7.89E-04*	9.62E-01
# Rejections			0	7	9	2

Right panel:

	Quantile	Violations	P_UC	P_CC	P_DQ1	P_DQ2
GARCH	0.01	1.37E-02	3.44E-01	0.00E+00*	5.08E-01	1.01E-03
	0.05	3.15E-02	1.39E-02*	4.60E-02*	2.53E-02*	1.52E-03
	0.10	7.66E-02	2.85E-02*	8.16E-03*	1.21E-01*	1.25E-01
	0.25	1.86E-01	3.72E-05*	4.86E-07*	1.08E-02	8.81E-02
	0.50	6.05E-01	1.35E-08*	1.66E-11*	2.79E-06	2.22E-08
	0.75	7.28E-01	1.69E-01	6.20E-06*	2.20E-06	2.17E-11
	0.90	8.77E-01	4.35E-02*	1.10E-02*	1.03E-01	4.04E-12
	0.95	9.44E-01	4.58E-01	4.21E-01	1.56E-01	5.50E-10
	0.99	9.89E-01	8.01E-01	0.00E+00*	1.38E-09	4.36E-05
# Rejections			5	8	5	7
Asym. slope CAViaR	0.01	3.83E-02	4.43E-09*	2.36E-08*	4.04E-09*	5.66E-03*
	0.05	8.62E-02	4.33E-05*	1.47E-05*	2.59E-12*	1.39E-01
	0.10	1.38E-01	1.07E-03*	5.48E-04*	5.51E-25*	1.59E-02*
	0.25	2.75E-01	1.23E-01	4.23E-07*	1.25E-05*	3.79E-02*
	0.50	4.47E-01	4.36E-03*	3.50E-06*	2.12E-57*	8.85E-16*
	0.75	6.51E-01	2.72E-09*	1.23E-12*	2.60E-29*	7.47E-08*
	0.90	8.73E-01	1.80E-02*	1.56E-09*	3.33E-20*	1.67E-03*
	0.95	9.36E-01	8.88E-02	2.36E-06*	6.59E-12*	7.45E-04*
	0.99	9.90E-01	9.08E-01	0.00E+00*	6.20E-02	5.99E-01
# Rejections			6	9	8	7
Sym. Abs. value CAViaR	0.01	1.78E-02	5.66E-02	0.00E+00*	7.79E-01	5.74E-02
	0.05	6.29E-02	1.22E-01	6.77E-02	3.68E-10*	2.44E-01
	0.10	9.85E-02	8.92E-01	1.64E-01	4.60E-13*	2.52E-02*
	0.25	2.60E-01	5.38E-01	2.50E-08*	1.24E-09*	1.74E-01
	0.50	4.40E-01	1.27E-03*	0.00E+00*	1.33E-65*	6.42E-04*
	0.75	6.59E-01	4.56E-08*	0.00E+00*	1.11E-33*	2.50E-04*
	0.90	9.02E-01	8.92E-01	4.12E-09*	8.98E-21*	5.26E-03*
	0.95	9.38E-01	1.66E-01	9.57E-06*	1.52E-12*	5.68E-03*
	0.99	9.90E-01	9.08E-01	0.00E+00*	6.20E-02	7.16E-01
# Rejections			2	7	7	5

The table displays the violation in percent, the p-values of the unconditional coverage test (UC), the conditional coverage test (CC), and the two dynamic conditional quantile tests (DQ1 and DQ2), as described in Section 5. P-values highlighted with * are significant at the 5% level, which implies poor model calibration (under H0 we have a correct model). Window sizes and variable selection are optimized for each model as described in Section 5.

Table 1.9 Predictive performance in hour 19

	Quantile	Violations	P_UC	P_CC	P_DQ1	P_DQ2
QR	0.01	1.23E-02	5.44E-01	0.00E+00*	3.24E-02*	9.21E-03*
	0.05	5.20E-02	8.07E-01	9.70E-01	2.80E-04*	5.39E-02
	0.10	9.58E-02	7.01E-01	9.22E-01	4.30E-04*	2.00E-01
	0.25	2.48E-01	8.81E-01	5.95E-01	1.06E-08*	5.55E-01
	0.50	4.99E-01	9.70E-01	4.95E-01	6.61E-01	1.34E-01
	0.75	7.55E-01	7.48E-01	1.31E-01	5.58E-01	3.70E-04*
	0.90	9.19E-01	7.30E-02	1.50E-03*	1.33E-02*	2.40E-01
	0.95	9.85E-01	4.18E-07*	7.84E-11*	5.81E-26*	8.27E-01
	0.99	9.96E-01	6.92E-02	0.00E+00*	1.00E+00	9.31E-01
# Rejections			1	4	6	2
EWQR	0.01	1.64E-02	1.11E-01	0.00E+00*	3.63E-01	2.58E-02*
	0.05	6.57E-02	6.32E-02	5.85E-02	5.40E-04*	5.44E-03*
	0.10	1.16E-01	1.52E-01	2.80E-01	1.91E-02*	9.33E-03*
	0.25	2.56E-01	7.17E-01	4.70E-01	4.32E-07*	4.05E-01
	0.50	5.03E-01	8.53E-01	7.07E-01	6.33E-01	7.39E-02
	0.75	7.36E-01	3.84E-01	1.18E-01	2.19E-01	2.38E-02*
	0.90	9.02E-01	8.92E-01	7.78E-02	6.55E-02	6.79E-02
	0.95	9.59E-01	2.52E-01	2.97E-10*	5.45E-24*	2.77E-01
	0.99	9.95E-01	1.78E-01	1.81E-02*	2.76E-08*	8.19E-01
# Rejections			0	3	5	4
EWDKQR	0.01	1.09E-02	8.01E-01	1.89E-01	1.70E-01	1.25E-01
	0.05	4.79E-02	7.91E-01	0.00E+00*	8.60E-02	3.97E-01
	0.10	9.71E-02	7.95E-01	9.66E-01	4.56E-03*	7.12E-02
	0.25	2.56E-01	7.17E-01	1.55E-15*	2.13E-18*	5.74E-01
	0.50	5.05E-01	7.96E-01	1.32E-01	2.24E-10*	2.71E-02*
	0.75	7.47E-01	8.48E-01	0.00E+00*	3.66E-41*	5.41E-01
	0.90	9.15E-01	1.61E-01	9.68E-02	5.92E-02	4.90E-02*
	0.95	9.70E-01	7.85E-03*	3.54E-04*	1.63E-04*	5.97E-01
	0.99	9.93E-01	3.62E-01	4.86E-02*	1.25E-04*	7.33E-01
# Rejections			1	5	6	2

	Quantile	Violations	P_UC	P_CC	P_DQ1	P_DQ2
GARCH	0.01	1.09E-02	8.01E-01	0.00E+00*	9.99E-01	2.84E-02*
	0.05	4.51E-02	5.40E-01	7.51E-01	8.82E-02	4.33E-01
	0.10	8.62E-02	2.03E-01	3.46E-01	4.85E-01	3.29E-01
	0.25	2.13E-01	2.01E-02*	8.09E-04*	3.14E-02*	4.67E-04*
	0.50	4.87E-01	4.82E-01	5.84E-02	1.10E-02*	7.33E-05*
	0.75	6.83E-01	4.19E-05*	2.65E-09*	9.73E-05*	3.65E-08*
	0.90	8.80E-01	7.41E-02	6.92E-02	2.52E-01	2.26E-05*
	0.95	9.45E-01	5.64E-01	7.28E-01	8.35E-01	2.39E-04*
	0.99	9.95E-01	1.78E-01	0.00E+00*	2.97E-08*	6.07E-01
# Rejections			2	4	4	6
Asym. slope CAViaR	0.01	2.33E-02	2.12E-03*	0.00E+00*	8.08E-01	2.41E-04*
	0.05	5.61E-02	4.58E-01	6.73E-02	1.55E-02*	4.35E-02*
	0.10	1.01E-01	9.12E-01	2.29E-01	2.75E-02*	6.87E-01
	0.25	2.68E-01	2.61E-01	4.36E-01	6.51E-08*	6.19E-01
	0.50	4.92E-01	6.84E-01	8.61E-01	8.03E-01	5.39E-02
	0.75	7.28E-01	1.69E-01	7.67E-02	1.87E-01	6.64E-05*
	0.90	9.15E-01	1.61E-01	9.68E-02	4.24E-01	1.42E-01
	0.95	9.48E-01	8.07E-01	2.89E-08*	9.87E-15*	6.05E-01
	0.99	9.85E-01	2.02E-01	5.59E-04*	6.51E-12*	9.58E-01
# Rejections			1	3	5	3
Sym. Abs. value CAViaR	0.01	1.37E-02	3.44E-01	0.00E+00*	1.34E-01	6.44E-01
	0.05	5.06E-02	9.39E-01	7.22E-01	2.96E-01	6.95E-01
	0.10	1.05E-01	6.33E-01	9.03E-02	2.60E-04*	4.84E-01
	0.25	2.76E-01	1.04E-01	2.00E-01	2.00E-06*	2.06E-01
	0.50	5.06E-01	7.39E-01	8.29E-01	7.46E-01	2.21E-02*
	0.75	7.35E-01	3.40E-01	3.04E-01	4.87E-01	3.42E-05*
	0.90	9.21E-01	5.43E-02	1.25E-01	3.55E-01	5.33E-02
	0.95	9.59E-01	2.52E-01	2.97E-10*	1.31E-24*	7.20E-01
	0.99	9.92E-01	6.15E-01	1.82E-03*	8.77E-18*	2.31E-01
# Rejections			0	3	4	2

The table displays the violation in percent, the p-values of the unconditional coverage test (UC), the conditional coverage test (CC), and the two dynamic conditional quantile tests (DQ1 and DQ2), as described in Section 5. P-values highlighted with * are significant at the 5% level, which implies poor model calibration (under H_0 we have a correct model). Window sizes and variable selection are optimized for each model as described in Section 5.

Table 1.10 Total number of test rejections per model over all quantiles and periods. The table displays the total number of test rejections per model at the 5% significance level. The numbers in parentheses give the maximum number of rejections. A high number of rejections indicates poor calibration. UC is the unconditional coverage test, CC is the conditional coverage test, and DQ1 and DQ2 are the two dynamic conditional quantile tests, as described in Section 5. The models are also described in Section 5.

	UC (27)	CC (27)	DQ1 (27)	DQ2 (27)	Total (108)
EWQR	2	14	16	9	41
QR	5	17	18	8	48
SAV CAViaR	5	15	16	13	49
EWDKQR	2	19	19	10	50
GARCH-T	9	17	12	19	57
AS CAViaR	8	21	18	12	59

Table 1.11 Total number of test rejections per hour. The table displays the total number of test rejections per model at the 5% significance level. The numbers in parentheses give the maximum number of rejections. A high number of rejections indicates poor calibration.

Rating	Model	Rejections	Rating	Model	Rejections
1	EWQR	12	1	EWQR	17
2	QR	15	2	EWDKQR	18
3	GARCH-T	16	3	QR	20
4	EWDKQR	18	4	SA CAViaR	21
5	AS CAViaR	18	5	GARCH-T	25
6	SA CAViaR	19	6	AS CAViaR	30
	Hour 3 (36)			Hour 6 (36)	

Rating	Model	Rejections
1	SA CAViaR	9
2	AS CAViaR	11
3	EWQR	12
4	QR	13
5	EWDKQR	14
6	GARCH-T	16
	Hour 19 (36)	

lower tail and best in the upper tail. In the mid-region it performs second best (which is of less interest regarding risk management). In general, it is harder to predict the lower tail than the upper tail. AS CAViaR performs worst for both tails.

We rate EWQR as the best model overall. This model has the fewest test rejections in total, and shows particularly good performance in the tails. This indicates that this model (although not perfect) is able to account for the changing market dynamics in Germany. The reason that EWQR generally outperforms EWDKQR might be due to that the latter suffers from overfitting (EWDKQR requires estimation of an additional parameter).

Table 1.12 Total number of test rejections in sections of the distribution. The table displays the total number of test rejections per model at the 5% significance level. The numbers in parentheses give the maximum number of rejections. A high number of rejections indicates poor calibration.

Rating	Model	Rejections	Rating	Model	Rejections
1	EWDKQR	8	1	QR	17
2	EWQR	9	2	EWQR	19
3	SA CAViaR	9	3	AS CAViaR	20
4	GARCH-T	11	4	EWDKQR	22
5	QR	12	5	SA CAViaR	25
6	AS CAViaR	17	6	GARCH-T	31
	Lower tail (36)			Mid-region (36)	

Rating	Model	Rejections
1	EWQR	13
2	GARCH-T	15
3	SA CAViaR	15
4	QR	19
5	EWDKQR	20
6	AS CAViaR	22
	Upper tail (36)	

7. Conclusion and further research

This paper has the objective of forecasting VaR for the German EPEX spot price using various sets of fundamentals and state-of-the-art models. VaR model analysis and forecasting for energy commodities remains an under-researched area despite the need for energy risk management among producers, consumers, and other participants in this market. We have focused on using fundamentals to capture the complex and non-linear response of supply and demand variables to the electricity price. Not only can fundamentals improve forecasting electricity price distributions (which is the main aim of this paper), but also help us to understand which risk drivers influence most at certain hours and certain quantiles.

We apply state-of-the-art models found to yield good results in other studies of commodity VaR forecasting. These are quantile regression, exponentially weighted quantile regression, exponentially weighted double kernel quantile regression, GARCH models with skewed *t* error distributions, and various CAViaR models. We optimize the use of exogenous variables by finding the best models in-sample using the SIC criterion as well as checking whether these models pass some of the out-of-sample tests for each hour and each quantile. This is motivated by evidence in the literature that the impact of fundamentals differs across the distribution and between trading periods. Our findings highlight the importance of variable selection, and show that in many cases it is as important as the choice of model.

We investigate hours 3, 8, and 19 in this study using daily prices and fundamental data from the period 1 January 2010 to 31 August 2016. The set of fundamentals we use are the coal price, gas price, oil price, CO_2 allowance price, expected wind infeed, expected solar infeed, expected power plant availability, and expected demand. In general we find that exponentially weighted quantile regression is the best model overall based on the total number of test rejections. This model is among the top performers for all trading periods, and performs particularly well in the outer quantiles. This is also an easy model to implement relative to the other models investigated in this study. Thus we recommend this model together with carefully selected fundamentals for given hours and quantiles when the aim is to forecast VaR for German electricity prices.

These insights can be applied by risk managers for a rigorous assessment of price risk distributions and how input variables impact price regions. An electricity producer that is able to understand what influences the price distribution will be able to improve the planning of the production mix during one day. On the other hand, policy makers who are concerned with increasing the use of renewables in electricity production can get a clearer view and understanding of their impact on the price formation process and the consequences for consumers and producers in society.

In this paper we have suggested the use of a quantile regression model using exponentially weighted moving average coefficients to account for the change in the production mix in Germany over the last years. A more robust model, taking into account time variation in parameters, would be to make a state space representation of a quantile regression model. Extreme tails are difficult to model and forecast by quantile regression models alone. Establishing a combination of a quantile regression model with an extreme value approximation of the very low and high quantiles could be a fruitful path for research. Finally, we encourage investigation of other electricity markets with different input mixes and compare our results with these markets. This is relevant for market coupling, trading strategies, and risk management for participants operating in several markets.

Notes

1 For example, the sensitivity of the electricity price to wind production is allowed to vary over the quantiles of the electricity prices in a static QR model but not over time. Since the share of wind production in Germany has increased a lot over the last few years, it is reasonable that the sensitivity for a given quantile also will change over time. This feature can be captured in a dynamic QR model.

2 SIC measures for quantile regression are described Koenker et al. (1994) and in Vinod (2010), chapter 2. For GARCH models, it is the standard SIC measure based on the likelihood function and number of parameters.

3 Details on which variables to include for each model, each hour, and each quantile as well as the optimal window size can be given by contacting the corresponding author.

Bibliography

AG Energibalanzen e.V., 2017. *Stromerzeugung nach Energietragern (Strommix) von 1990 bis 2016 (in MWh) Deutschland insgesamt.* URL: www.ag-energiebilanzen.de/28-0-Zusatzinformationen.

Alexander, C., 2008a. *Market Risk Analysis, Volume II, Practical Financial Econometrics*. John Wiley.

Alexander, C., 2008b. *Market Risk Analysis, Volume IV, Value-at-Risk Models*. John Wiley.

Behl, P., Claeskens, G., and Dette, H., 2014. Focused model selection in quantile regression. *Statistica Sinica* 24, 601–624.

Bollerslev, T., 1986. Generalized autoregressive conditional heteroskedasticity. *Journal of Econometrics* 31 (3), 307–327.

Bremnes, J., 2006. A comparison of a few statistical models for making quantile wind power forecasts. *Wind Energy* 9, 3–11.

Bunn, D., Andresen, A., Chen, D., and Westgaard, S., 2016. Analysis and forecasting of electricity price risks with quantile factor models. *The Energy Journal* 37 (2), 169–190.

Bystrom, H. N., 2005. Extreme value theory and extremely large electricity price changes. *International Review of Economics and Finance* 14 (1), 41–55.

Chan, K. F., and Gray, P., 2006. Using extreme value theory to measure value at risk for daily electricity spot prices. *International Journal of Forecasting* 22 (2), 283–300.

Chatfield, C., 2000. *Time-Series Forecasting*. Chapman & Hall/CRC.

Chen, D., and Bunn, D., 2010. Analysis of the nonlinear response of electricity prices to fundamental and strategic factors. *IEEE Transactions on Power Systems* 25 (2), 595–606.

Chen, M.-Y., and Chen, J.-E., 2002. Application of quantile regression to estimation of value at risk. *Review of Financial Risk Management* 1 (2), 15.

Christoffersen, P., 1998. Evaluating interval forecasts. *International Economic Review* 39, 841–862.

Clean Energy Wire, 2017. *Germany's Energy Consumption and Power Mix in Charts*. URL: www.cleanenergywire.org/search/site/factsheets

De Livera, A. M., Hyndman, R. J., and Snyder, R. D., 2011. Forecasting time series with complex seasonal patterns using exponential smoothing. *Journal of the American Statistical Association* 106 (496), 1513–1527.

Deng, S.-J., and Oren, S. S., 2006. Electricity derivatives and risk management. *Energy* 31 (6), 940–953.

Diebold, F., 2015. *Forecasting. Department of Economics*. University of Pennsylvania.

Engle, R., 1982. Autoregressive conditional heteroscedasticity with estimates of the variance of United Kingdom inflation. *Econometrica* 50 (4), 987–1007.

Engle, R., and Manganelli, S., 2004. Caviar conditional autoregressive value at risk by regression quantiles. *Journal of Business & Economic Statistics* 22 (4), 367–381.

EPEX Spot, 2017. *Renewable Energy: Increasingly Important Role in Europe*. URL: www.epexspot.com/en/renewables

Erni, D., 2012. *Day-Ahead Electricity Spot Prices – Fundamental Modelling and the Role of Expected Wind Electricity Infeed at the European Energy Exchange*. PhD dissertation, University of St. Gallen.

Federal Minsitry for Economic Affairs and Energy, 2017. *For a Future of Green Energy*. URL: www.bmwi.de/Redaktion/EN/Dossier/renewable-energy

Fleten, S. E., Huisman, R., Kilicz, M., and Pennings, E., 2015, Electricity futures prices: Time varying sensitivity to fundamentals. *Journal of Energy Markets* 18 (4), 1–21.

Frauendorfer, K., Paraschiv, F., and Schuerle, M., 2016. *Cross-border Effects of the German Electricity Market Fundamentals on the Swiss Electricity Prices*. Working paper.

Füss, R., Adams, Z., and Kaiser, D. G., 2010. The predictive power of value-at-risk models in commodity futures markets. *Journal of Asset Management* 11 (4), 261–285.

Garcia, R. C., Contreras, J., Van Akkeren, M., and Garcia, J. B. C., 2005. A GARCH forecasting model to predict day-ahead electricity prices. *IEEE Transactions on Power Systems* 20 (2), 867–874.

Gelper, S., Fried, R., and Croux, C., 2010. Robust forecasting with exponential and holt – winters smoothing. *Journal of Forecasting* 29, 285–300.

Giot, P., and Laurent, S., 2003. Market risk in commodity markets: A VaR approach. *Energy Economics* 25 (5), 435–457.

Gonzales, V., Contreras, J., and Bunn, D., 2012. Forecasting power prices using a hybrid fundamental-econometric model. *IEEE Transactions on Power Systems* 27 (1), 363–372.

Grothe, O., and Schnieders, J., 2011. Spatial dependence in wind and optimal wind power allocation: A copula-based analysis. *Energy Policy* 39, 4742–4754.

Gurrola-Perez, P., an Murphy, D., 2015. *Filtered Historical Simulation Value-at-Risk Models and Their Competitors*. Working Paper No. 525, Bank of England.

Hagfors, L. I., Bunn, D., Kristoffersen, E., Staver, T. T., and Westgaard, S., 2016b. Modelling the UK electricity price distributions using quantile regression. *Energy* 102, 231–243.

Hagfors, L. I., Kamperud, H. H., Paraschiv, F., Prokopczuk, M., Sator, A., and Westgaard, S., 2016c. Prediction of extreme price occurrences in the German day-ahead electricity market. *Quantitative Finance* 16 (2), 1929–1948.

Hagfors, L., Paraschiv, F., Molnar, P., and Westgaard, S., 2016a. Using quantile regression to analyse the effect of renewables on EEX price formation. *Renewable Energy and Environmental Sustainability* 1 (32).

Hartz, C., Mittnik, S., and Paolella, M., 2006. Accurate value at risk forecasting based on the normal GARCH model. *Computational Statistics and Data Analysis* 51 (4), 2295–2312.

Huisman, R., Michels, D., and Westgaard, S., 2015a. Hydro reservoir levels and power price dynamics. Empirical insight on the nonlinear influence of fuel and emission cost on Nord Pool day-ahead electricity prices. *Journal of Energy and Development* 40 (1 and 2), 149–187.

Huisman, R., Stradnicy, V., and Westgaard, S., 2015b. Renewable energy and electricity prices: Indirect empirical evidence from hydro power, *Applied Economics*, 1–16.

Jeon, J., and Taylor, J., 2013. Using caviar models with implied volatility for value at risk estimation. *Journal of Forecasting* 32, 62–74.

Jones, M., and Yu, K., 1998. Local linear quantile regression. *Journal of the American Statistical Association* 93, 228–237.

J.P. Morgan/Reuters, 1996. *RiskMetrics TM – Technical Document*. Tech. rep., Morgan Guaranty Trust Company, Reuters Ltd.

Kaminski, V., 2013. *Energy Markets*. Risk Books.

Karakatsani, N. V., and Bunn, D. W., 2008. Forecasting electricity prices: The impact of fundamentals and time-varying coefficients. *International Journal of Forecasting* 24, 764–785.

Keles, D., Scelle, J., Paraschiv, F., and Fichtner, W., 2016. Extended forecast methods for day- ahead electricity spot prices applying artificial neural networks. *Applied Energy* 162, 218–230.

Koenker, R., and Bassett Jr., G., 1978. Regression quantiles. *The Econometric Society* 46 (1), 33–50.

Koenker, R., Ng, P., and Portnoy, S., 1994. Quantile smoothing splines. *Biometrika* 81, 673–680.

Kuester, K., Mittnik, S., and Paoella, M., 2006. Value at risk prediction: A comparison of alternative strategies. *Journal of Financial Econometrics* 9 (2), 53–89.

Kupiec, P., 1995. Techniques for verifying the accuracy of risk measurement models. *Journal of Derivatives* 2, 173–184.

Lee, E. R., Noh, H., and Park, B. U., 2014. Model selection via bayesian information criterion for quantile regression models. *Journal of the American Statistical Association* 109 (505), 216–229.

Lundby, M., and Uppheim, K., 2011. *Fundamental Risk Analysis and Var Forecasts of the Nord Pool System Price*. Master's thesis, Norwegian University of Science and Technology (NTNU).

Maciejowska, K. et al., 2016. Probabilistic forecasting of electricity spot prices using factor quantile regression averaging. *International Journal of Forecasting* 37 (3), 957–965.

Maciejowska, K., and Weron, R., 2016. Short- and mid-term forecasting of baseload electricity prices in the UK: The impact of intra-day price relationships and market fundamentals. *IEEE Transactions on Power Systems* 31 (2), 957–965.

Maciel, L., Ballini, R., and Gomide, F., 2017. Evolving probabilistic fuzzy modelling and application in value at risk estimation. Working paper, Institute of Economics, University of Campinas, Brazil, 119–139.

Mirza, F., and Bergland, O., 2012. Transmission congestion and market power: The case of the Norwegian electricity market. *The Journal of Energy Markets* 5 (2), 59–88.

Mostafa, F., Dillon, T., and Chang, E., 2017. Computational intelligence applications to option pricing, volatility forecasting and value at risk. *Studies in Computational Intelligence* 697, 137–147.

Neupane, B., Woon, W. L., and Aung, Z., 2017. Ensemble prediction model with expert selection for electricity price forecasting. *Energies* 10 (1).

Nowotarski, J., and Weron, R., 2018. Recent advances in electricity price forecasting: A review of probabilistic forecasting. *Renewable and Sustainable Energy Reviews* 81 (Part 1), 1548–1568.

Paraschiv, F., Bunn, D., and Westgaard, S., 2016. *Estimation and Applications of Fully Parametric Multifactor Quantile Regression With Dynamic Coefficients*. University of St. Gallen, School of Finance Research.

Paraschiv, F., Erni, D., and Pietsch, R., 2014. The impact of renewable energies on EEX day- ahead electricity prices. *Energy Policy* 73, 196–210.

Paraschiv, F., and Hadzi-Mishev, R., 2016. Extreme value theory for heavy tails in electricity prices. *Journal of Energy Markets* 9 (2).

Reisch, L., and Micklitz, H., 2006. Consumers and deregulation of the electricity market in Germany. *Journal of Consum Policy* 29, 399–415.

Schwarz, G. et al., 1978. Estimating the dimension of a model. *The Annals of Statistics* 6 (2), 461–464.

Senera, E., Baronyana, S., and Menguturkb, L., 2012. Ranking the predictive performances of value-at-risk estimation methods. *International Journal of Forecasting* 28 (4), 849–873.

Sensfu, F., Ragwitz, M., and Genoese, M., 2008. Autoregressive conditional heteroscedasticity with estimates of the variance of United Kingdom inflation. *Energy Policy* 36, 3086–3094.

Shmueli, G., 2010. To explain or to predict? *Statistical Science* 25, 289–310.

Taylor, J. W., 2007. Forecasting daily supermarket sales using exponentially weighted quantile regression. *European Journal of Operational Research* 178 (1), 154–167.

Taylor, J. W., 2008a. Estimating value at risk and expected shortfall using expectiles. *Journal of Financial Econometrics*, 231–252.

Taylor, J. W., 2008b. Using exponentially weighted quantile regression to estimate value at risk and expected shortfall. *Journal of Financial Econometrics* 6 (3), 382–406.

Vinod, H. D., 2010, *Advances in Social Science Research Using R*. 23 Lecture Notes in Statistics, 196. New York: Springer-Verlag. doi:10.1007/978-1-4419-1764-5

Weron, R., 2014. Electricity price forecasting: A review of the state-of-the-art with a look into the future. *International Journal of Forecasting* 30, 1030–1081.

2 Forecasting crude oil price dynamics based on investor attention

Evidence from the ARMAX and ARMAX-GARCH models

Ting Yao and Yue-Jun Zhang

1. Introduction

Crude oil is a significant commodity and its price volatility often affects the macro-economic growth of the world, especially the giant oil importers (Zhang and Yao, 2016; Zhang and Zhang, 2015). Consequently, understanding the mechanism of crude oil pricing and forecasting crude oil prices have become crucial and hot issues in academia and practical cycles (Zhang and Wang, 2013; Narayan et al., 2014; Narayan and Wong, 2009). However, crude oil pricing is a complex process since crude oil has both political and financial properties. The changes of the psychological expectation and the concerns of investors in crude oil market are likely to cause significant shocks in crude oil prices (Kaiser and Yu, 2010; Vosen and Schmidt, 2012).

Unfortunately, investor attention is hard to observe and measure; consequently, indirect proxies are often used for measuring investor attention, such as extreme returns (Barber and Odean, 2008), trading volume (Hou et al., 2009), news and headlines (Narayan et al., 2016; Yuan, 2015; Drake et al., 2016), and price limits (Seasholes and Wu, 2007). These proxies are based on a common hypothesis that if the asset or stock is of extreme return or trading volume, or mentioned in news headline, investors have paid attention to it. However, the abnormal return or trading volume cannot guarantee investors' attention to it, and investors even never read the news in *The Wall Street* related to the asset or stock (Da et al., 2011). Hence, the proxies are usually biased and lagged. Specifically, on one hand, for the selection of indicators used for investor attention, the proxies are of strong subjectivity. On the other hand, most indicators are calculated through the statistical data, but they can hardly measure the investor attention in time.

Instead, according to the data submitted by the searching on Internet, we can track their needs, interests, and concerns (Ettredge et al., 2005). Under these circumstances, in this chapter we develop a direct and unbiased proxy for investor attention in the crude oil market by constructing the Google search volume index (GSVI) and then explore the relationship between investor attention and crude oil prices. Google search volume data are available in Google Trends (www.google.com/trends), a service provided by Google.

There are two reasons for us to choose the Google search volume as the measure of investor attention. First, Internet users are inclined to use search engines to collect information, and Google continues to be the most popular, especially in developed countries. Thus, the Internet search behaviors of the general population are most likely to be reflected by the search volume provided by Google. Second, the Google index proves a direct measure of the market attention. When we search oil in Google, we are undoubtedly concerned about it. Consequently, the aggregated Google search volume is a direct and unbiased measure of the market attention. In fact, some studies have confirmed this viewpoint. For instance, Da et al. (2011) argue that the search frequency in Google is a timely proxy for measuring the investor attention. Drake et al. (2012) claim that investors accept information through the Internet, and the Google searches can reflect investors' demand for public information. Da et al. (2015) construct the Financial and Economic Attitudes Revealed by Search (FEARS) index by counting the search volume related to household concerns.

In order to measure the investor attention in the crude oil market by aggregating the search volume, we need to understand how crude oil price can be searched by investors. To do this, we aggregate the search volumes of a series of key words related to "crude oil price", which are likely to be used by users for different search habits, and we proceed as follows. We input the primitive words "crude oil price" into Google Correlate (www.google.com/trends/correlate) and retrieve the top related words whose correlation coefficients with "crude oil price" are larger than 0.9. After filtering out the related words, we can acquire the search volumes of these words and construct the composite attention index by weighting the search volumes. There are many widely used weighting methods, such as the subjective weighting method, the information entropy theory, and the linear combination weighting method (Zhang and Hao, 2017). However, among these search volumes, some should be correlated with other search volumes, and among the widely used weighting methods, the Principle Component Analysis (PCA) is powerful in reducing the dependence of individual proxies. Meanwhile, the index constructed by individual proxies would behave almost the same as the index organized by PCA (Baker and Wurgler, 2007; DeFelice et al., 2015). Therefore, we apply the PCA approach to build a linear combination of the selected proxies, so as to construct the GSVI.

After obtaining the unbiased and direct proxy of the investor attention, we can further investigate the effect and predictive effect of investor attention on the international crude oil price applying some quantitative methods. In fact, there are several papers exploring the impact of Internet information on oil price shocks. For instance, Da et al. (2011) argue that the search frequency in Google is a timely proxy for measuring investor attention. Drake et al. (2012) claim that investors accept information through the Internet, and Google searches can reflect investors' demand for public information. Ji and Guo (2015) investigate the effect of oil-related events on oil price volatility using Internet search data. Meanwhile, the Google index can be utilized to study the mechanisms of asset prices and improve the forecasting performance of economic indicators (Choi and Varian, 2012; Narayan and Narayan, 2016). For example, Vicente et al. (2015) find that Internet search data can effectively improve the forecasting performance of unemployment. However, there is little literature that studies the predictive power of the Google index in the crude oil market.

Therefore, based on the unbiased and direct proxy of investor attention, this chapter aims to investigate the effect of the investor attention on WTI crude oil prices and explore whether investor attention can help improve the forecasting performance of WTI crude oil prices. Specifically, we first estimate ARMA and ARMA-GARCH models and then we estimate the ARMAX and ARMAX-GARCH models by incorporating the Google index to investigate the effect and predictive power of the investor attention on crude oil prices. The results show that the Google index has a negative impact on crude oil prices and the Google index cannot provide a better estimation or forecast for WTI crude oil prices.

The rest of this chapter is outlined as follows. Section 2 reviews the related literature. Section 3 details the data and methodology used in this chapter. Section 4 describes the empirical results and analysis. Section 5 concludes this chapter.

2. Literature review

2.1. Investor attention, the Google search volume index and crude oil prices

According to traditional asset pricing theory, the information is instantaneously incorporated into prices when it emerges. This assumption is based on the requirement that investors have adequate attention to the asset (Da et al., 2011). However, as Kahneman (1973) claims that investors have limited attention, which is a scarce cognitive resource. Huberman and Regev (2001) hold that the effect of new information on asset prices exists only when investors do pay attention to it. As a result, recent studies attempt to measure investor attention and investigate the effect of investors' limited attention on asset pricing statics as well as dynamics.

It is well documented that when information releases or price fluctuates largely, the volume increases (Bamber et al., 1997; Karpoff, 1987). For example, the volume of the stock reaches nearly six times of the usual volume in the minutes after Maria Bartiromo mentions a stock during the Midday Call on CNBC (Busse and Green, 2002). Guo et al. (2015) study the effect of investor attention using a unique data set of financial advisors' daily tweets. They construct the investor attention proxy based on tweets between individual investors and their advisors so that they can investigate the effect of investor attention on market price fluctuations. Based on the tweet data, they claim that investor attention increases on days that the price fluctuates sharper. Compared to small losses, small gains can catch more attention from investors. However, large losses seize more attention against large gains. Their findings provide support to the argument that asset return fluctuations are influenced by individual investor attention. Our findings provide evidence that daily equity return fluctuations are associated with individual investor attention.

Meanwhile, Andrei and Hasler (2015) theoretically and empirically prove that investor attention is the key determinant of asset prices. They show that when attention increases, asset return volatility and risk premia will also increase. They explain the intuition as follows. When investor attention is low, information cannot be incorporated into prices in a short time because investors need time for learning. As a result, low attention leads to low return volatility. In contrast, when investors pay much attention to new information, the new information can be immediately incorporated into prices by the attracted investors. Hence, high attention results in high return volatility. At the same time, since the volatility becomes high, investors need a high risk premium to withstand the high risk caused by high attention.

According to the Commodity Futures Trading Commission (CFTC), the main trading participants can be divided into commercial, noncommercial, and non-reporting traders based on their trading motivations. However, in financial studies, investors are often defined as institutional investors and individual investors.

As Barber and Odean (2008) hold that individual investors are net buyers of the attention-grabbing assets. As a result, there is a temporary positive pressure in price when individual investor attention increases. The influencing mechanism behind their argument can be interpreted as follows. Individual investors must choose from a large number of available alternatives in order to make a buying decision. In making a decision, investors choose from the options that they consider, but the options they consider are the assets to those already been paid attention by investors. But when they are making a selling decision, they can only choose from what they own. Meanwhile, Gervais et al. (2001) claim that increased visibility of an asset may attract new investors. This means that the fluctuation in investor attention often leads to net buying from these uninformed individual investors.

In order to measure the investor attention, many indirect proxies are used, such as extreme returns (Barber and Odean, 2008), trading volume (Hou et al., 2009), news and headlines (Narayan et al., 2016; Yuan, 2015; Drake et al., 2016), and price limits (Seasholes and Wu, 2007). These proxies are based on a common hypothesis that if the asset or stock is of extreme return or trading volume, or mentioned in news headline, investors have paid attention to it. However, the abnormal return or trading volume cannot guarantee investors' attention to it, and investors even never read the news in *The Wall Street* related to the asset or stock (Da et al., 2011).

In fact, as Huberman and Regev (2001) claim that the effect of new information on asset prices exists only when investors do pay attention to it. Under this circumstance, the Google search volume is proposed as a new and direct proxy for investor attention. For one thing, Internet users are inclined to use search engines to collect information, and Google continues to be the most popular, especially in developed countries. Thus, the Internet search behaviors of general population are most likely to be reflected by the search volume provided by Google. For another thing, the Google index proves a direct measure of the market attention. When we search oil in Google, we are undoubtedly concerned about it.

Furthermore, compared to institutional investors, individual investors are more likely to search for information related to crude oil market using the Google search engine. For the rational and relatively informed institutional investors, they recognize that buying the attention-grabbing assets is not a wise choice. They are aware that there may be bubble components in the assets of high attention. Because when the asset is associated with the attention-grabbing information, the price may be deviated from the fundamentals. The attention-grabbing information is not likely to influence the future performance, and the assets without highly abnormal attention may have better performance in the future and turn to be a better option. Odean (1998) argues that there are many investors who overvalue the information that catches their attention, and they are more likely to trade too much due to the overconfidence about the quality of their information, and finally result in trading irrationally. As a result, constructing the GSVI can help us to measure the individual investors' attention. Because when they are making a buying decision, they select the asset from the options grabbed their attention, and the attention can be captured by the Google search volume index. As a result, the GSVI is an accurate and direct proxy for investor attention, especially the individual investors' attention.

Recently, the GSVI has been recognized as the direct proxy of investor attention by scholars. Da et al. (2011) first propose the new measure of investor attention by aggregating the search volume in Google (Search Volume Index, SVI). They investigate the effect of the SVI based on the sample of Russell 3000 stocks ranging from 2004 to 2008. The empirical results show that the new proxy of investor attention by SVI is correlated with but different from the existing measures, such as extreme returns. What's more, the increase in SVI predicts positive stock returns in the next two weeks and the reversal stock returns within the year. Joseph et al. (2011) use the Google search volume as the proxy of the investor attention and investigate the effect of search intensity on abnormal returns and excessive trading volumes. The empirical results based on a series of S&P 500 firms over the period 2005–2008 indicate that, for weekly data, Google search volumes index predicts abnormal stock returns and trading volumes.

Similarly, according to the results of Barber and Odean (2008), a positive Abnormal Search Volume Index (ASVI) results in a positive price pressure in the short run and a reversed effect in the long run. What's more, for the stocks which obtain more investors' attention, the pressure induced by attention is stronger.

At the same time, the Google search volume is also used in the crude oil market. For instance, Ji and Guo (2015) collect the search query volumes for different areas from Google to investigate the influence of short- and long-run investor concerns on crude oil price volatility. The empirical results indicate the long-term equilibrium relationship between oil prices and long-run investor attention for oil prices and demand. Meanwhile, there is a significant and asymmetric influence of the short-run investor concern for the 2008 financial crisis and the Libyan war convulsion on oil price volatility.

2.2. Crude oil price forecasting

Crude oil price fluctuation is a complex system, since crude oil price is determined by a series of factors, including the fundamentals (i.e., supply and demand), geopolitics, US exchange rate, gold price, and so on. When the uncertainty of the crude oil price becomes larger, crude oil price forecasting becomes a hot and challenging topic. As a commodity, the traditional models for forecasting commodity prices are used for forecasting the price of international crude oil. However, crude oil does not only have commodity property, but it also has strong financial and political properties. The international crude oil price fluctuation is much more complex than other commodities. As a result, a variety of empirical models emerge for providing a relatively high forecasting accuracy.

(1) The generalized autoregressive conditional heteroskedasticity (GARCH) type models are widely used for forecasting crude oil market volatility due to their good performance in capturing the time-varying feature of high-frequency data (Wang and Wu, 2012). Wei et al. (2010) capture the volatility features of both Brent and West Texas Intermediate (WTI) crude oil markets by applying a series of linear and nonlinear GARCH-class models. They evaluate the forecasting performance using the superior predictive ability test and loss functions and find that no model can outperform all of the other models for either the Brent or the WTI market across different loss functions. However, the predictive power of the nonlinear GARCH-class models is larger than the linear ones.

Mohammadi and Su (2010) model and forecast the conditional mean and volatility of weekly crude oil prices upon the sample period from 2 January 1997 to 3 October 2009 using four GARCH type models (GARCH, EGARCH, APARCH, and FIGARCH). Specifically, the training period ranges from January 1997 to December 2008, while the testing period ranges from January 2009 to October 2009. The empirical results indicate that, in general, the APARCH model outperforms the others.

Wang and Wu (2012) forecast price volatility in energy market using both univariate and multivariate GARCH-class models. On one hand, they find the multivariate models display superior performance against univariate models in forecasting volatilities of individual. On the other hand, they forecast crack spread volatility and contrast the performance of univariate and multivariate models. Specifically, the multivariate models forecast the crack spreads for two oil prices, while univariate ones forecast the crack spreads directly. The empirical results show that univariate models allowing for asymmetric effects provides the forecasts with the greatest accuracy.

In order to investigate the effect of structural breaks and long memory in forecasting performance in energy market, Arouri et al. (2012) model and forecast the conditional volatility of oil spot and futures prices using a variety of GARCH-class models. The empirical results indicate that, first, five out of nine GARCH-based conditional volatility processes for energy prices display parameter instability. Second, there is evidence of the existence of long memory characteristic in all the series considered and the FIGARCH model fit the data with a higher goodness-of-fit. At the same time, the degree of volatility persistence can be significantly reduced after adjusting for structural breaks. Finally, the out-of-sample results show that, in general, the models which take the instability and long memory characteristics into consideration outperform against other models in forecasting energy price volatility.

Fong and See (2002) forecast crude oil price volatility using a generalized regime switching model that allows for abrupt changes in mean and variance, GARCH dynamics, basis-driven time-varying transition probabilities, and conditional leptokurtosis. Based on the empirical results, they conclude that regime switching models proved to be a useful tool for studying factors behind the evolution of volatility and forecasting oil futures volatility in short terms.

(2) Apart from the GARCH type models, the neural network method, the support vector machine (SVM) and the wavelet technique are also proved to be powerful forecasting models for international crude oil price series. Shin et al. (2013) propose a new forecasting model based on the neural network method and machine learning technique. The empirical results show that the new method provides significantly more accurate results compared with ANN, AR, SVM, and other methods. Zhang et al. (2008) introduce the ensemble empirical mode decomposition (EEMD) method to crude oil price analysis and forecast. In their empirical study, three crude oil price series with different time ranges and frequencies are selected. They first decompose the three price series into several independent intrinsic modes, from high to low frequency. Then they compose the several intrinsic modes into a fluctuating process. The three components represent a long-term trend, the short-term fluctuations, and the effect of a shock of a significant event, respectively. Finally, the empirical results show that the EEMD is a powerful technique for crude oil market analysis. What's more, the support vector regression (SVM) or ANN model can effectively forecast the short-term fluctuations and long-term trends, which are decomposed from the original crude oil price series.

Xie et al. (2006) propose a new forecasting method for crude oil prices based on the support vector machine (SVM). The empirical results show that SVM is a fairly good candidate for forecasting crude oil price series. El-Sebakhy (2009) proposes a new framework based on the support vector machine (SVM) technique for predicting the PVT properties of crude oil systems. In order to illustrate the performance of the newly proposed algorithm, the performance of the support vector machines regression performance is compared with that of the neural networks, nonlinear regression, and different empirical correlation techniques. The empirical results show that the performance of support vector machines is superior against most of the other models in both accuracy and reliability.

Shabri and Samsudin (2014) propose a new method for forecasting crude oil prices, which is based on integrating discrete wavelet transform and artificial neural networks (WANN) model. They use the discrete wavelet transform to decompose the original crude oil prices into an approximation series and several detailed series. Then the artificial neural network model is used for forecasting crude oil prices. The empirical results indicate that the WANN model is able to provide more accurate forecasting results than the individual ANN model. He et al. (2012) propose a forecasting model, i.e., the wavelet decomposed ensemble model, in order to provide more accurate forecasts for crude oil prices. The proposed model analyzes the dynamic underlying Data Generating Process at finer time ranges by utilizing the wavelet analysis. They introduce the simple averaging based ensemble to reduce the estimation bias resulting from the use of different wavelet families. Meanwhile, they filter the ensemble members dynamically based on their in-sample performance. The empirical results show that the proposed method provides a higher directional predictive accuracy against the benchmark models. Specifically, the proposed model can extract and capture the dynamic heterogeneous market microstructure correctly, and the accurate characterization results help to provide a superior performance in prediction.

(3) Given the complexity and time-varying characteristic of international crude oil price series, some new hybrid models are also proposed. Yu et al. (2008) propose an empirical mode decomposition (EMD)-based neural network ensemble learning paradigm for forecasting the world crude oil spot price. They first decompose the original crude oil price series into a few independent intrinsic mode functions (IMFs). Then they predict the tendencies of the nonlinear and time-varying components of crude oil prices by modeling the different IMFs using a three-layer feed forward neural network (FNN) model. Finally, they construct an ensemble output for the original crude oil price series by combining the predicted IMFs using an adaptive linear neural network (ALNN) model.

Similarly, Zhang et al. (2015) propose a novel hybrid method for crude oil price forecasting. First, the ensemble empirical mode decomposition (EEMD) method is used for decomposing the original international crude oil price into a small number of intrinsic mode functions (IMFs) and an error term. Then, they apply the least square support vector machine model, the particle swarm optimization (LSSVM – PSO) method and the generalized autoregressive conditional heteroskedasticity (GARCH) model to forecast the separate IMFs. Finally, the forecasted crude oil prices of different separate components are summed as the final forecasted results of the original crude oil prices.

Baumeister and Kilian (2015) investigate the advantage of constructing a combined model of six real-time econometric oil price forecasting models. They claim that the combined model provides more accurate forecasts at horizons up to 6 quarters or 18 months. The MSPE reduction is 12% and direction accuracy can be as high as 72%. They also claim the robustness of the gains in accuracy.

(4) What's more, financial economists have sought to identify variables that forecast crude oil market returns. Since the increasing link between financial market and oil market, the interest in the question of whether the incorporation of financial market variables can help to improve the forecasting accuracy of international crude oil price also increases. One of the merits of incorporating financial market information is that daily or weekly financial data can be used for predicting monthly crude oil prices. Baumeister et al. (2015) explore the

predictive ability of the financial market data using mixed-frequency models and show that among a series of high-frequency predictors, the cumulative changes in US crude oil inventories statistically significantly improves the forecast accuracy. They finally conclude that, ignoring the high-frequency financial information does not cause a typically large loss in forecasting monthly international crude oil price.

Economic literature suggests that there is a nonlinear relationship between inventory level and crude oil prices. Ye et al. (2006) investigate the predictive power of the low- and high-inventory variable in crude oil price forecasting. They define two nonlinear inventory variables, one for the low-inventory state and another for the high-inventory state, according to the monthly level of OECD crude oil inventories from post-1991 Gulf War to October 2003. According to the empirical findings, they conclude that the incorporation of the inventory variables does help to improve the fitting and forecasting accuracy of the crude oil price series.

Many oil industry analysts believe that the product spread, the difference between weighted refined product market prices and crude oil prices, can help predict the crude oil price. Accordingly, Baumeister et al. (2018) construct a series of alternative forecasting models based on product spreads and compare the forecasts with the traditional forecasting results. They find the most effective model is a time-varying parameter model of gasoline and heating oil spot price spreads, which proves to be a good complement to forecasting models based on fundamentals.

Motivated by empirical evidence on the effect of limited investor attention, in this chapter, we select the investor attention as the predictor. We construct the proxy of the investor attention by aggregating the searching volume using the PCA technique. By applying the ARMA, ARMAX, ARMA-GARCH, and ARMAX-GARCH models, we investigate the predictive power of investor attention. Finally, we evaluate the forecasting accuracy using several loss functions.

3. Data and methods

3.1. Data definitions

In this chapter, we examine whether the Google index can help to improve the forecasting performance of crude oil prices. We select the monthly WTI crude oil spot prices as research object and the sample period ranges from January 2004 to November 2016. Specifically, the training period ranges from January 2004 to December 2015 while the testing period ranges from January 2016 to November 2016 as forecasting horizon. WTI crude oil spot prices are obtained from the Energy Information Administration (EIA), USA. Crude oil price returns are calculated as the logarithmic difference of crude oil prices.

The investor attention is the exogenous variable in this chapter is denoted by the Google search volume index (GSVI), which is constructed based on the search volume data provided by Google Trends. Google Trends describes the searches for crude oil through Google, and the data are obtained from the Google Trends' service (www.google.com/trends). The values of the index are normalized by setting the value of the month with highest incidence as 100.

The trends of crude oil prices, returns, and volatilities are shown in Figure 2.1. We can find that from 2004 to 2007, crude oil price experienced a stably increase due to the development of world economic activity. In 2008, the abnormal demand shock driven by the financial crisis resulted in a strong fluctuation in crude oil price, i.e., the price dropped from 133.9 dollars per barrel to 39.1 dollars per barrel. Oil price volatility become large during this period. Thereafter, the world economy gradually recovered from the financial crisis, and crude oil price ran back to the pre-crisis level. However, when it comes to the end of 2014, the shale oil revolution occurred, at the same time, OPEC insisted not to cut the production. As a result, crude oil supply overtook demand, and crude oil price started to fall, specifically, during this period, crude oil price dropped from 105.8 dollars per barrel to 30.3 dollars per barrel and the volatility

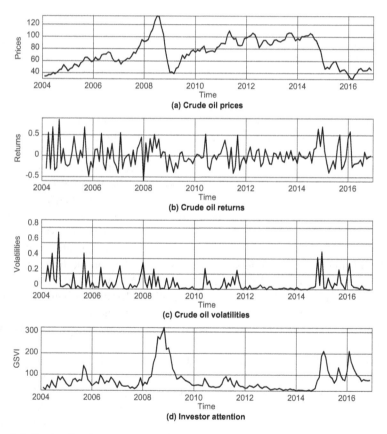

Figure 2.1 Crude oil prices, returns, volatilities, and investor attention

Table 2.1 Descriptive statistics for oil prices and returns[1]

	Price	*Return*
Mean	73.126	0.186
Max	73.740	21.387
Min	133.880	−33.198
Std. Dev.	30.320	9.202
Skewness	23.700	−0.850
Kurtosis	0.155	4.608
Jarque-Bera	5.653	35.121
	(0.059)	(0.000)
$Q(10)$	643.300	38.109
	(0.000)	(0.000)
$Q(20)$	689.880	45.064
	(0.000)	(0.000)
ADF	−2.733	−8.627
	(0.071)	(0.000)
PP	−2.466	−8.623
	(0.126)	(0.000)

Note: The *P* values are reported in the parentheses. Std. Dev. represents the standard deviation. Jarque-Bera is the statistics from Jarque and Bera (1980) test with a null hypothesis of a Gaussian distribution. ADF and PP denote statistics from the augmented Dickey and Fuller (1979) and Phillips and Perron (1988) unit root tests, respectively. The optimal lag length of the ADF test is determined by the Schwarz information criterion (SIC) (Schwarz, 1978). $Q(10)$ and $Q(20)$ denote the Ljung and Box (1978) statistics of the return series for up to 10th and 20th order serial correlation, respectively.

become large. The general review of crude oil price trend shows that crude oil price is extremely volatile. Modeling and forecasting crude oil dynamics are important for us to know the pricing mechanism and avoid market risk.

Accordingly, Table 2.1 displays the descriptive statistics of the price and return series. We check the stationary property of the WTI crude oil price and return series by conducting the augmented Dickey-Fuller (ADF) and Phillips-Perron (PP) unit root tests, and the results are shown in Table 2.1. As claimed by Hyndman and Athanasopoulos (2014), the properties of a stationary time series do not depend on the time at which the series is observed, and the value of non-stationary time series may be depending on the time you observe it. Hence, before proceed the ARMA and ARMA-GARCH models, we should check the stationary of the series. Specifically, according to both ADF and PP results, we can say that the price series is not stationary but the return series is stationary at the significance level of 1%. As a result, we take the return series in this chapter.

For the crude oil return series, the Jarque–Bera statistic shows that the null hypothesis of normality is rejected at the 1% significant level. It also has a relatively high excess kurtosis (4.6076) and a negative skewness (−0.8499). Meanwhile, the Ljung–Box statistic for serial correlation rejects the null hypothesis of no autocorrelation up to the 20th order and confirms serial autocorrelation in the crude oil returns.

3.2. Methods

(1) Principal component analysis approach

To construct the GSVI, we aggregate the Google search volumes generated by the top related words applying the principal component analysis (PCA). The PCA technique helps us transform the original search volume series into several new and uncorrelated variables, which are called the principal components (Wold et al., 1987; Gaitani et al., 2010).

In fact, each principal component is a linear combination of the original search volume series, and the amount of the information conveyed by each principal component is measured by its variance. All the principal components are arranged by the decreasing value of the variance, so the first principal component is the most informative and the last principal component proves the least.

Given that we select the top n correlated words, then we have the vector $\boldsymbol{a}(n \times 1)$ consisting in the search volumes generated by the top n correlated words. Our aim is to simplify the vector $\boldsymbol{a}(n \times 1)$ by reducing the dimensionality n to $k(k < n)$, and the new vector can be represented as $\boldsymbol{b}(k \times 1)$. The variable $b_j(j = 1, \cdots, k)$ in the new vector $\boldsymbol{b}$ is the linear combination of the n variables, and is known as principal components (Wold et al., 1987). The jth principal components b_j can be represented by Eq. (1).

$$b_j = \delta_{j1}a_1 + \delta_{j2}a_2 + \cdots + \delta_{jn}a_n \tag{1}$$

where $\delta_{jm}(m = 1, \cdots, n)$ is a constant denoting the eigenvalue of the mth principal component.

In this chapter, according to Gaitani et al. (2010), we select the number of principal components by examining the proportion of total variance explained by each component.

(2) ARMA-GARCH and ARMAX-GARCH models

After confirming the stationarity of crude oil price series, following Brooks and Tsolacos (1999) and De Wit and Van Dijk (2003), we can develop the Autoregressive Moving Average (ARMA) model to estimate the training samples and forecast the testing samples.

The WTI crude oil price series, y_t, which follows an ARMAX (p,q) model, can be defined as:

$$D(y_t, d) = c + \rho_1 \upsilon_t + \rho_2 \upsilon_{t-2} + \cdots + \rho_p \upsilon_{t-p} + \theta_1 \varepsilon_{t-1} + \theta_2 \varepsilon_{t-2} + \cdots + \theta_q \varepsilon_{t-q} \tag{2}$$

and with the incorporation of the investor attention, the WTI crude oil price series y_t can be defined as:

$$D(y_t, d) = c + \beta GI_t + \upsilon_t \tag{3}$$

$$\upsilon_t = \rho_1 \upsilon_t + \rho_2 \upsilon_{t-2} + \cdots + \rho_p \upsilon_{t-p} + \theta_1 \varepsilon_{t-1} + \theta_2 \varepsilon_{t-2} + \cdots + \theta_q \varepsilon_{t-q} \tag{4}$$

where the exogenous variable *GI* stands for the Google Index; meanwhile, the lag number of AR and MA terms are p and q, respectively.

The GARCH (m,s) model can be defined as:

$$a_t = \sigma_t \varepsilon_t; \quad \sigma_t^2 = \alpha_0 + \sum_{i=1}^{m} \alpha_i a_{t-i}^2 + \sum_{j=1}^{s} \tau_j \sigma_{t-j}^2 \tag{5}$$

There is not a standard criterion for evaluating the forecasting performance of different models. As Wei et al. (2010) claim that there is no loss function that evaluates the predictive ability of different models more appropriately. Hence, instead of making an evaluation based on a single criterion, we use four different widely used accurate statistics or loss functions as forecasting criteria, including ME (Mean Error), RMSE (Root Mean Squared Error), MAE (Mean Absolute Error), MPE (Mean Percent Error) and MAPE (Mean Absolute Percent Error).

$$ME = \frac{1}{n} \sum_{t=1}^{n} (r_t - \hat{r}_t) \tag{6}$$

$$RMSE = \sqrt{\frac{1}{n} \sum_{t=1}^{n} (r_t - \hat{r}_t)^2} \tag{7}$$

$$MAE = \frac{1}{n} \sum_{t=1}^{n} |r_t - \hat{r}_t| \tag{8}$$

$$MPE = \frac{1}{n} \sum_{t=1}^{n} \left(\frac{r_t - \hat{r}_t}{r_t} \right) \tag{9}$$

$$MAPE = \frac{1}{n} \sum_{t=1}^{n} \left| \frac{r_t - \hat{r}_t}{r_t} \right| \tag{10}$$

where n denotes the number of forecasting data; r_t and $\hat{r}_t$ are the actual values and forecasting values, respectively.

4. Empirical results and discussions

4.1. The construction of the GSVI

An important choice concern for constructing the GSVI is the identification of the attention to crude oil price. For the sake of different search habits and expressions, an Internet user is likely to search crude oil price using several related key words (such as "oil price" and "crude oil"). Hence, we select the primitive words as "crude oil price" (*cop*) and we search for the related words in Google Correlate (www.google.com/trends/correlate). We single out 11 related key words of which the correlation coefficient with "crude oil price" larger than 0.9. Specifically, the selected key words related to crude oil prices include "oil price" (*op*), "current oil prices" (*cops*), "price per barrel" (*ppb*), "bloomberg energy" (*be*), "oil price per barrel" (*oppb*), "current oil"(*co*), "crude oil chart" (*coc*), "crude oil" (*col*), "current crude oil" (*cco*), "current crude oil price" (*ccop*), and "current crude" (*cc*).

After downloading the Google search volume of these proxies, we use the principle component analysis (PCA) approach to exclude the idiosyncratic elements in the proxies. Specifically, we build a linear combination of the selected proxies using the PCA approach, so as to construct the GSVI. The eigenvalues and explained variances of each principal component are shown in Table 2.2 and the weights of the raw variables on each principal component are shown in Table 2.3.

In the PCA framework, each principal component is a linear combination, and the explained information of each principal component is reflected by the value of the variance. According to Wang (2015), we can select the principal components with their cumulatively explained proportion larger than 80% or with their eigenvalues above 1.00. In this chapter, according to the results shown in Table 2.2, there are 12 principal components in total, and the first principal component explains 87.41% of the sample variance of the variables, which is larger than 80%. Meanwhile, as shown in Table 2.2, only the eigenvalue of the first principal component is above 1.00. As a result, the first principle component is selected to be the Google Search Volume Index in crude oil market and the coefficients of the raw variables are determined according to the weights shown in Table 2.2.

The trends of the GSVI are shown in Figure 2.1, from which we can see that the investor attention fluctuated strongly during the 2008 financial crisis and from the end of 2014 to 2016, and the series stays stable at other periods. In fact, during the two periods, crude oil price fluctuated heavily and oil volatility is very large. Specifically, from the trend of the crude oil price shown in Figure 2.1, we can know that the crude oil price experienced a large drop in both 2008 and 2014. In 2008, the abnormal demand shock driven by the financial crisis resulted in a strongly fluctuation in crude oil price. In the end of 2014,

Table 2.2 Eigenvalues and explained variances of the principal components

Component	Eigenvalue	Proportion	Cumulative Proportion
1	10.4897	0.8741	0.8741
2	0.6034	0.0503	0.9244
3	0.4131	0.0344	0.9589
4	0.1566	0.0130	0.9719
5	0.1347	0.0112	0.9831
6	0.0603	0.0050	0.9881
7	0.0443	0.0037	0.9918
8	0.0384	0.0032	0.9950
9	0.0318	0.0026	0.9977
10	0.0183	0.0015	0.9992
11	0.0081	0.0007	0.9999
12	0.0014	0.0001	1

Table 2.3 The weights of the raw variables on principal components

Variable	Com1	Com2	Com3	Com4	Com5	Com6	Com7	Com8	Com9	Com10	Com11	Com12
cop	0.298	-0.164	0.298	-0.122	-0.093	-0.168	-0.295	0.046	-0.202	-0.076	-0.779	-0.051
op	0.296	-0.200	0.268	-0.247	-0.137	-0.040	-0.388	-0.096	-0.428	-0.172	0.588	0.042
cops	0.300	0.111	-0.239	0.120	-0.015	-0.154	0.436	-0.453	-0.187	-0.606	-0.069	0.016
ppb	0.284	0.453	0.111	0.380	-0.074	0.031	-0.129	0.028	-0.024	0.113	0.091	-0.720
be	0.274	0.403	0.315	-0.647	-0.021	-0.075	0.349	0.142	0.305	0.020	0.055	0.011
oppb	0.283	0.463	0.116	0.405	-0.068	0.040	-0.130	0.089	-0.047	0.123	0.001	0.694
co	0.286	0.072	-0.280	-0.151	0.863	0.124	-0.217	0.031	-0.058	0.023	-0.021	-0.005
coc	0.260	-0.471	0.534	0.358	0.272	0.174	0.393	0.066	0.163	0.025	0.087	-0.002
col	0.291	-0.223	-0.305	0.113	-0.039	-0.752	0.053	0.359	0.138	0.149	0.141	0.000
cco	0.299	-0.129	-0.244	-0.133	-0.175	0.190	0.294	-0.286	-0.332	0.685	-0.060	0.002
ccop	0.300	-0.169	-0.137	-0.013	-0.174	0.121	-0.353	-0.452	0.698	0.010	0.017	0.034
cc	0.292	-0.133	-0.352	-0.038	-0.284	0.526	0.044	0.578	0.012	-0.278	-0.025	-0.023

driven by the shale oil revolution and the decision of not reducing the production by OPEC, crude oil supply overtook demand, and the crude oil price started to sell. The general review of investor attention indicates that the investor attention is likely to increase following the large fluctuation of crude oil prices.

4.2. The estimation and forecast results

The estimation results for the ARMA, ARMAX, ARMA-GARCH, and ARMAX-GARCH models are shown in Table 2.4, from which we can find that the Google index has a negative effect on WTI crude oil prices. Specifically, the coefficients of the Google index in the ARMAX and ARMAX-GARCH models are −0.068 and −0.052, respectively, which are smaller than 0 at the significance level of 1%. This indicates that investor attention negatively affect WTI crude oil prices. This finding can be interpreted by the candidate explanations as follows. First, the price pressure theory as described in Barber and Odean (2008) can explain the negative price pressure in the long run. They find that the increased investor attention predicts temporary higher stock prices, but the prices get reversed in the long run (Barber and Odean, 2008). According to their research, individual investors are attention-grabbed net buyers and thus stock prices experience a temporary positive price pressure as the individual investor attention increases. However, when the excess returns cause price pressures, the demand of individual investors dissipates; resulting in the reverse in crude oil price.

Second, according to Da et al. (2011), the investor attention generated by the search volume reflects the attention of individual investors. However, the institutional investors are rational and not easily to be driven by psychological fluctuations, and the high market attention often leads rational institutional investors to be more conservative, so they are usually to realize that buying assets with high market attention is not the best choice (Edelen et al., 2016). They are conscious that the highly concerned asset is likely to experience abnormal increases in prices deviated from fundamentals, and there would be bubble compositions in the asset prices. As a result, they may make decisions contrary to the individual investors and impose a reverse pressure to crude oil price changes. The negative effect of investor attention on crude oil price is confirmed by the facts. For example, in December 2008, the investor attention began to drop, and in February 2009, WTI crude oil price began to increase. At that time, a large portion of investors were in a panic caused by the financial crisis in 2008, they were cautious and unwilling to concern crude oil price, and the attention-driven buying was reduced. Subsequently, the crude oil price gradually fluctuated around the fundamentals. Meanwhile, the rational institutional investors realized that the bubble compositions were reduced and there was an opportunity to make profits.

Meanwhile, from the estimation results shown in Table 2.4, we can find that the incorporation of the investor attention improves the estimation accuracy. Specifically, for the ARMA and ARMAX models, the value of R^2 of the ARMA model is larger than that of the ARMAX model, and the value of AIC of the ARMA model is smaller than that of the ARMAX model. Specifically, the values of R^2 of the

Table 2.4 The estimation results

Parameter	ARMA		ARMAX		ARMA-GARCH		ARMAX-GARCH	
	Coefficient	Probability	Coefficient	Probability	Coefficient	Probability	Coefficient	Probability
c			5.010	0.002	0.877	0.283	3.582	0.013
β			-0.068	0.000			-0.052	0.000
ρ_1	0.317	0.000			-0.834	0.000		
θ_1	0.247	0.000	0.223	0.009	1.040	0.000	0.181	0.041
θ_2			0.179	0.036	0.120	0.353	0.080	0.330
a_0					7.405	0.012	11.767	0.000
α_1					0.139	0.019	0.053	0.069
τ_1					1.403	0.000	1.718	0.000
τ_2					-0.633	0.000	-0.954	0.000
R^2	0.134		0.217		0.065		0.204	
AIC	7.141		7.054		7.093		7.004	

Table 2.5 The forecast performance for WTI crude oil returns

Model	ME	RMSE	MAE	MPE	MAPE
ARMA	2.487	10.203	8.274	95.125	95.125
ARMAX	4.696	10.905	8.400	112.465	125.342
ARMA-GARCH	1.142	10.317	8.489	40.121	123.226
ARMAX-GARCH	4.207	10.771	8.413	127.425	125.195

ARMA and ARMAX model are 0.134 and 0.217, respectively, while those of AIC are 7.141 and 7.054, respectively. Similarly, for the ARMA-GARCH and ARMAX-GARCH models, the value of R^2 of the ARMA-GARCH model is larger than that of the ARMAX-GARCH model, and the value of AIC of the ARMA-GARCH model is smaller than that of the ARMAX-GARCH model. Specifically, the value of R^2 of the ARMAX-GARCH is 0.204, which is larger than that of the ARMA-GARCH model (0.065); the value of AIC of the ARMAX-GARCH is 7.093, which is smaller than that of the ARMA-GARCH (7.004).

The forecast results are shown in Table 2.5, from which we can see that, in general, the incorporation of the investor attention fails to improve the forecast performance, i.e., according almost all the loss functions, the forecasting models without the investor attention are better than the models with the investor attention. Specifically, for the ARMAX models, the values of all the loss functions (i.e., the ME, RMSE, MAE, MPE and MAPE) are larger than those of the ARMA model. For example, the value of ME of ARMA is 2.487, which is much smaller than that of ARMAX (4.696). The MAPE of the ARMA is 95.125, but after incorporating the investor attention, the value rises up to 125.342. Similarly, for the ARMAX-GARCH model, expect for MAE, all the values of all the other loss functions are larger than those of ARMA-GARCH model. For example, the value of MAE of ARMA-GARCH is 8.489, which is larger than that of ARMAX-GARCH (8.413). The value of MPE of ARMA-GARCH is 40.121, but after the investor attention incorporated into the model, the value becomes much larger, i.e., 127.425.

According to the empirical results, there is a negative effect of the Google index on crude oil price returns; and there is no significant improvement on forecasting WTI crude oil price returns observed in the ARMAX and ARMAX-GARCH models when the Google index data is included.

4.3. Effect of using different construction forms of the GSVI

For the sake of different search habits and expressions, an Internet user is likely to search crude oil price using several related key words (such as "oil price" and "crude oil"). However, as for how many related key words should be considered, there is not a consensus. As a result, we construct two GSVIs using different number of related words to test the robustness. Specifically, we reconstruct the GSVI by weighting the search volume of the ten "top searches" related to the primitive words provided by Google Correlate, which is motivated by Da et al. (2015).

Table 2.6 Eigenvalues and explained variances of the principal components of different GSVI

Component	Eigenvalue	Proportion	Cumulative
1	8.6776	0.8678	0.8678
2	0.5788	0.0579	0.9256
3	0.3484	0.0348	0.9605
4	0.1564	0.0156	0.9761
5	0.1190	0.0119	0.9880
6	0.0476	0.0048	0.9928
7	0.0415	0.0041	0.9969
8	0.0213	0.0021	0.9990
9	0.0081	0.0008	0.9999
10	0.0014	0.0001	1

Table 2.7 The weights of the raw variables on principal components of different GSVI

Variable	Com1	Com2	Com3	Com4	Com5	Com6	Com7	Com8	Com9	Com10
cop	0.328	0.231	0.229	−0.117	−0.133	0.221	−0.296	−0.120	−0.776	−0.042
op	0.325	0.262	0.197	−0.240	−0.182	0.043	−0.534	−0.237	0.592	0.045
cops	0.328	−0.117	−0.301	0.111	−0.147	−0.336	0.272	−0.751	−0.061	0.022
ppb	0.316	−0.416	0.161	0.385	−0.026	0.037	−0.129	0.110	0.085	−0.717
be	0.306	−0.339	0.376	−0.640	−0.009	0.051	0.476	0.088	0.056	0.009
oppb	0.314	−0.426	0.169	0.410	−0.013	0.057	−0.133	0.146	0.003	0.694
co	0.314	−0.075	−0.400	−0.203	0.805	0.064	−0.205	0.021	−0.021	−0.004
coc	0.287	0.576	0.397	0.348	0.339	−0.184	0.382	0.075	0.089	0.000
col	0.317	0.210	−0.447	0.101	−0.273	0.654	0.313	0.163	0.139	0.000
cco	0.325	0.118	−0.325	−0.132	−0.299	−0.603	−0.078	0.541	−0.077	−0.002

The eigenvalue, explained proportion and cumulatively explained proportion of the principal components are shown in Table 2.7, from which we find that there are 10 principal components in total, and the first principal component explains 86.78% of the sample variance of the variables, which is larger than 80%. Meanwhile, only the eigenvalue of the first principal component is above 1.00. As a result, the first principle component is selected to be the Google Search Volume Index in crude oil market, and the coefficients of the raw variables are determined according to the weights shown in Table 2.8.

As can be seen from Table 2.8, the effect of the incorporation of the investor attention on the estimation accuracy is in line with that obtained from the former construction of GSVI. Specifically, from the estimation results shown in Table 2.9, we can find that, the incorporation of the investor attention improves the estimation accuracy. For the ARMA and ARMAX models, the value of R^2 of the ARMA model is larger than that of the ARMAX model, and the value of AIC of the ARMA model is smaller than that of the ARMAX model. Specifically, the value of R^2 of the ARMA model is 0.134 while that of the ARMAX model is 0.224, respectively; the value of AIC of the ARMA is 7.141 while that of the ARMAX is 7.046, respectively. Similarly, for the ARMA-GARCH and

Table 2.8 The estimation results of the models with different GSVI

Parameter	ARMA		ARMAX		ARMA-GARCH		ARMAX-GARCH	
	Coefficient	Probability	Coefficient	Probability	Coefficient	Probability	Coefficient	Probability
c			5.334	0.002	0.877	0.283	3.916	0.006
β			−0.078	0.000			−0.060	0.000
ρ_1					−0.834	0.000		
θ_1	0.317	0.000	0.221	0.009	1.040	0.000	0.177	0.044
θ_2	0.247	0.000	0.175	0.039	0.120	0.353	0.076	0.355
α_0					7.405	0.012	11.759	0.000
α_1					0.139	0.019	0.055	0.068
τ_1					1.403	0.000	1.711	0.000
τ_2					−0.633	0.000	−0.951	0.000
R^2	0.134		0.224		0.065		0.211	
AIC	7.141		7.046		7.093		6.997	

Table 2.9 The forecast performance of different GSVI for WTI crude oil returns

Model	ME	RMSE	MAE	MPE	MAPE
ARMA	2.487	10.203	8.274	95.125	95.125
ARMAX	4.816	10.936	8.428	120.960	134.143
ARMA-GARCH	1.142	10.317	8.489	40.121	123.226
ARMAX-GARCH	4.271	10.781	8.424	131.034	136.412

ARMAX-GARCH models, the value of R^2 of the ARMA-GARCH model is larger than that of the ARMAX-GARCH model, and the value of AIC of the ARMA-GARCH model is smaller than that of the ARMAX-GARCH model. Specifically, the value of R^2 of the ARMAX-GARCH is 0.211, which is larger than that of the ARMA-GARCH model (0.065); the value of AIC of the ARMAX-GARCH is 7.093, which is larger than that of the ARMA-GARCH (6.997).

The forecast results are shown in Table 2.9, from which we can see that, in general, the incorporation of the investor attention fails to improve the forecast performance, i.e., according almost all the loss functions, the forecasting models without the investor attention are better than the models with the investor attention. Specifically, for the ARMAX models, the values of all the loss functions (i.e., the ME, RMSE, MAE, MPE and MAPE) are larger than those of the ARMA model. For example, the value of ME of ARMA is 2.487, which is much smaller than that of ARMAX (4.816). The MAPE of the ARMA is 95.125, but after incorporating the investor attention, the value rises up to 120.960. Similarly, for the ARMAX-GARCH model, expect for MAE, all the values of all the other loss functions are larger than those of ARMA-GARCH model. For example, the value of MAE of ARMA-GARCH is 8.489, which is larger than that of ARMAX-GARCH (8.424). The value of MPE of ARMA-GARCH is 40.121, but after the investor attention incorporated into the model, the value becomes much larger, i.e., 131.034.

5. Conclusions and future work

In this chapter, we aim to investigate the effect and predictive power of the investor attention on crude oil price forecasting using the ARMA, ARMAX, ARMA-GARCH and ARMAX-GARCH models. The empirical results are obtained based on the sample period ranging from January 2004 to November 2016, and the main conclusions can be safely drawn as follows: (1) The investor attention has a negative impact on crude oil price returns. (2) The incorporation of the investor attention brings an improvement on the goodness-of-fit. (3) In general, the incorporation of investor attention fails to improve the forecasting performance in crude oil market, specifically, the forecasting performance becomes worse after the incorporation of the investor attention according to almost all the loss functions. (4) The robustness check by re-constructing the GSVI from the search volume of the ten "top searches" related to the primitive words provided by Google Correlate confirms that our empirical results are robust.

As for the future work, we can explore the relationship between Internet data and crude oil price forecasting by incorporating other kinds of Internet data, such as the news related with crude oil market.

Acknowledgments

We gratefully acknowledge the financial support from National Natural Science Foundation of China (nos. 71273028, 71322103 and 71774051), National Program for Support of Top-notch Young Professionals (no. W02070325), Changjiang Scholars Programme of the Ministry of Education of China (no. Q2016154), Hunan Youth Talent Program and China Scholarship Council (no. 201606135020).

Note

1 In order to guarantee that the coefficients in the ARMAX and ARMAX-GARCH models are significantly not zero, we set the value of crude oil returns by multiplying by 100.

Bibliography

Andrei D, Hasler M. Investor attention and stock market volatility. *The Review of Financial Studies* 2015; 28(1): 33–72.

Arouri MEH, Lahiani A, Lévy A, Nguyen DK. Forecasting the conditional volatility of oil spot and futures prices with structural breaks and long memory models. *Energy Economics* 2012; 34(1): 283–293.

Baker M, Wurgler J. Investor sentiment in the stock market. *Journal of Economic Perspectives* 2007; 21(2): 129–151.

Bamber LS, Barron OE, Stober TL. Trading volume and different aspects of disagreement coincident with earnings announcements. *Accounting Review* 1997; 575–597.

Barber BM, Odean T. All that glitters: The effect of attention and news on the buying behavior of individual and institutional investors. *Review of Financial Studies* 2008; 21(2): 785–818.

Baumeister C, Guérin P, Kilian L. Do high-frequency financial data help forecast oil prices? The MIDAS touch at work. *International Journal of Forecasting* 2015; 31(2): 238–252.

Baumeister C, Kilian L. Forecasting the real price of oil in a changing world: A forecast combination approach. *Journal of Business & Economic Statistics* 2015; 33(3): 338–351.

Baumeister C, Kilian L, Zhou X. Are product spreads useful for forecasting oil prices? An empirical evaluation of the Verleger hypothesis. *Macroeconomic Dynamics* 2018; 22(3): 562–580.

Brooks C, Tsolacos S. The impact of economic and financial factors on UK property performance. *Journal of Property Research* 1999; 16: 139–152.

Busse JA, Green TC. Market efficiency in real time. *Journal of Financial Economics* 2002; 65(3): 415–437.

Choi H, Varian H. Predicting the present with Google Trends. *Economic Record* 2012; 88: 2–9.

Da Z, Engelberg J, Gao P. In search of attention. *Journal of Finance* 2011; 66(5): 1461–1499.

Da Z, Engelberg J, Gao P. The sum of all fears investor sentiment and asset prices. *Review of Financial Studies* 2015; 28(1): 1–32.

DeFelice M, Alessandri A, Catalano F. Seasonal climate forecasts for medium-term electricity demand forecasting. *Applied Energy* 2015; 137: 435–444.

De Wit I, Van Dijk R. The global determinants of direct office real estate returns. *The Journal of Real Estate Finance and Economics* 2003; 26(1): 27.

Dickey DA, Fuller WA. Distribution of the estimators for autoregressive time series with a unit root. *Journal of the American Statistical Association* 1979; 74: 427–431.

Drake MS, Jennings J, Roulstone DT, Thornock JR. The comovement of investor attention. *Management Science* 2016; 63(9): 2773–3145.

Drake MS, Roulstone DT, Thornock JR. Investor information demand: Evidence from Google searches around earnings announcements. *Journal of Accounting Research* 2012; 50(4): 1001–1040.

Edelen RM, Ince OS, Kadlec GB. Institutional investors and stock return anomalies. *Journal of Financial Economics* 2016; 119(3): 472–488.

El-Sebakhy EA. Forecasting PVT properties of crude oil systems based on support vector machines modeling scheme. *Journal of Petroleum Science and Engineering* 2009; 64(1–4): 25–34.

Ettredge M, Gerdes J, Karuga G. Using Web-based search data to predict macroeconomic statistics. *Communications of ACM* 2005; 48(11): 87–92.

Fong WM, See KH. A Markov switching model of the conditional volatility of crude oil futures prices. *Energy Economics* 2002; 24(1): 71–95.

Gaitani N, Lehmann C, SantaMouris M, Mihalakakou G, Patargias P. Using principal component and cluster analysis in the heating evaluation of the school building sector. *Applied Energy* 2010; 87(6): 2079–2086.

Gervais S, Kaniel R, Mingelgrin DH. The high-volume return premium. *The Journal of Finance* 2001; 56(3): 877–919.

Guo T, Finke M, Mulholland B. Investor attention and advisor social media interaction. *Applied Economics Letters* 2015; 22(4): 261–265.

He K, Yu L, Lai KK. Crude oil price analysis and forecasting using wavelet decomposed ensemble model. *Energy* 2012; 46(1): 564–574.

Hou K, Xiong W, Peng L. *A Tale of Two Anomalies: The Implications of Investor Attention for Price and Earnings Momentum*. Working Paper, Ohio State University and Princeton University, 2009.

Huberman G, Regev T. Contagious speculation and a cure for cancer: A nonevent that made stock prices soar. *The Journal of Finance* 2001; 56(1): 387–396.

Hyndman RJ, Athanasopoulos G. Forecasting: Principles and practice. *OTexts* 2014: 291.

Jarque CM, Bera AK. Efficient tests for normality, homoscedasticity and serial independence of regression residuals. *Economics Letters* 1980; 6(3): 255–259.

Ji Q, Guo JF. Oil price volatility and oil-related events: An Internet concern study perspective. *Applied Energy* 2015; 137: 256–264.

Joseph K, Wintoki MB, Zhang Z. Forecasting abnormal stock returns and trading volume using investor sentiment: Evidence from online search. *International Journal of Forecasting* 2011; 27(4): 1116–1127.

Kahneman D. *Attention and Effort.* Vol. 1063. Englewood Cliffs, NJ: Prentice-Hall, 1973.

Kaiser M, Yu Y. The impact of Hurricanes Gustav and Ike on offshore oil and gas production in the Gulf of Mexico. *Applied Energy* 2010; 87: 284–297.

Karpoff JM. The relation between price changes and trading volume: A survey. *Journal of Financial and Quantitative Analysis* 1987; 22(1): 109–126.

Liang Q, Fan Y, Wei YM. A long-term trend forecasting approach for oil price based on wavelet analysis. *Chinese Journal of Management Science* 2005; 13(1): 30–36.

Ljung GM, Box GE. On a measure of lack of fit in time series models. *Biometrika* 1978; 65(2): 297–303.

Mohammadi H, Su L. International evidence on crude oil price dynamics: Applications of ARIMA-GARCH models. *Energy Economics* 2010; 32(5): 1001–1008.

Narayan PK, Ranjeeni K, Bannigidadmath D. New evidence of psychological barrier from the oil market. *Journal of Behavioral Finance* 2016; 18(4): 457–469.

Narayan PK, Sharma S, Poon WC, Westerlund J. Do oil prices predict economic growth? New global evidence. *Energy Economics* 2014; 41: 137–146.

Narayan PK, Wong P. A panel data analysis of the determinants of oil consumption: The case of Australia. *Applied Energy* 2009; 86: 2771–2775.

Narayan S, Narayan P. Are oil price news headlines statistically and economically significant for investors? *Journal of Behavioral Finance* 2017; 18: 258–270.

Odean T. Volume, volatility, price, and profit when all traders are above average. *The Journal of Finance* 1998; 53(6): 1887–1934.

Phillips PC, Perron P. Testing for a unit root in time series regression. *Biometrika* 1988; 75(2): 335–346.

Schwarz G. Estimating the dimension of a model. *The Annals of Statistics* 1978; 6(2): 461–464.

Seasholes MS, Wu G. Predictable behavior, profits, and attention. *Journal of Empirical Finance* 2007; 14(5): 590–610.

Shabri A, Samsudin R. Daily crude oil price forecasting using hybridizing wavelet and artificial neural network model. *Mathematical Problems in Engineering* 2014: 1–10.

Shin H, Hou T, Park K, Park CK, Choi S. Prediction of movement direction in crude oil prices based on semi-supervised learning. *Decision Support Systems* 2013; 55(1): 348–358.

Vicente MR, López-Menéndez AJ, PéRez R. Forecasting unemployment with internet search data: Does it help to improve predictions when job destruction is skyrocketing? *Technological Forecasting and Social Change* 2015; 92: 132–139.

Vosen S, Schmidt T. A monthly consumption indicator for Germany based on Internet search query data. *Applied Economics Letters* 2012; 19: 683–687.

Wang E. Benchmarking whole-building energy performance with multi-criteria technique for order preference by similarity to ideal solution using a selective objective-weighting approach. *Applied Energy* 2015; 146: 92–103.

Wang Y, Wu C. Forecasting energy market volatility using GARCH models: Can multivariate models beat univariate models? *Energy Economics* 2012; 34(6): 2167–2181.

Wei Y, Wang Y, Huang D. Forecasting crude oil market volatility: Further evidence using GARCH-class models. *Energy Economics* 2010; 32(6): 1477–1484.

Wold S, Esbensen K, Geladi P. Principal component analysis. *Chemometrics and Intelligent Laboratory Systems* 1987; 2(1–3): 37–52.

Xie W, Yu L, Xu S, Wang S. A new method for crude oil price forecasting based on support vector machines. In *International Conference on Computational Science*. Berlin, Heidelberg: Springer, 2006, 444–451.

Ye M, Zyren J, Shore J. Forecasting short-run crude oil price using high-and low-inventory variables. *Energy Policy* 2006; 34(17): 2736–2743.

Yu L, Wang S, Lai KK. Forecasting crude oil price with an EMD-based neural network ensemble learning paradigm. *Energy Economics* 2008; 30(5): 2623–2635.

Yuan Y. Market-wide attention, trading, and stock returns. *Journal of Financial Economics* 2015; 116(3): 548–564.

Zhang JL, Zhang YJ, Zhang L. A novel hybrid method for crude oil price forecasting. *Energy Economics* 2015; 49: 649–659.

Zhang X, Lai KK, Wang SY. A new approach for crude oil price analysis based on empirical mode decomposition. *Energy Economics* 2008; 30(3): 905–918.

Zhang YJ, Hao JF. Carbon emission quota allocation among China's industrial sectors based on the equity and efficiency principles. *Annals of Operations Research* 2017; 255: 117–140.

Zhang YJ, Wang ZY. Investigating the price discovery and risk transfer functions in the crude oil and gasoline futures markets: Some empirical evidence. *Applied Energy* 2013; 104: 220–228.

Zhang YJ, Yao T. Interpreting the movement of oil prices: Driven by fundamentals or bubbles? *Economic Modelling* 2016; 55: 226–240.

Zhang YJ, Zhang L. Interpreting the crude oil price movements: Evidence from the Markov regime switching model. *Applied Energy* 2015; 143: 96–109.

Part 2

International economics and finance

3 Contagion dynamics on financial networks*

Monica Billio, Roberto Casarin,
Michele Costola, and Lorenzo Frattarolo

1. Introduction

Given the relevance of the latest financial and sovereign crises, systemic events are now deeply analyzed by scholars and policy makers. As a matter of fact, the studies on the consequences of systemic risk are relevant both for the stability of the financial and banking system and in terms of diversification in an investor perspective [Das and Uppal, 2004]. As in Billio et al. [2012], we define systemic risk "any set of circumstances that threatens the stability of or public confidence in the financial system" where interconnectedness among financial institutions and markets represents a potential channel in propagation of shocks to the system [Billio et al., 2012, Diebold and Yilmaz, 2015]. Pairwise Granger causality tests have been used to extract the network of significant linkages among financial institutions and to find which ones are systemically important [Billio et al., 2012]. The question here is to compare the network defined over time (using pairwise Granger causality tests), to identify possible distortions, sources of systemic risk. Recently, entropy measures have been involved in systemic risk measurement for propagation of financial contagion [Paltalidis et al., 2015] and as early warning indicator for banking crises [Billio et al., 2016]. Billio et al. [2016] use the Shannon, Tsallis and Rényi entropies of the degree distribution of financial networks. While these measures revealed effective in predicting banking crisis, they take into account only the dispersion of the degree distribution. In this paper we propose an alternative entropy measure, the Von Neumann entropy, which is specifically designed for networks. The Von Neumann entropy has been widely used for the analysis of complex systems and it naturally arises from the relationship between network structure and density matrix of a state of a quantum system [for definition and references, see Garnerone et al., 2012]. Unfortunately, most of this literature has focused on undirected networks and has used both the adjacency matrix and the Laplacian matrix to obtain the association with a state of a quantum system. In any case, the analogy with a quantum system is not in any way essential to understand the remaining of the paper. Within the few works providing extensions of the Von Neumann entropy for undirected graphs to the case of directed graphs, Ye et al. [2014] certainly represents a relevant reference. The peculiarity of directed networks and in particular their asymmetry requires some care and redefinition of the Laplacian [Chung, 2005]. In particular, the combinatorial Laplacian for directed networks is formulated in terms of nodes out degree, the Perron vector of the transition matrix, that is related to eigenvector centrality, and can be soundly computed only for strongly connected components, and related to the circulation on the graph [Chung, 2005]. In this paper, we build on Ye et al. [2014] and propose an alternative definition of Von Neumann entropy for directed graphs which accounts for positive Laplacian matrix. We show that the new measures can be written as weighted sums of walks of the network and relate them to consensus dynamics.

This chapter is organized as follows. Section 2 introduces a notion of financial network and some background in graph theory. Section 3 reviews some methods of network extraction. Section 4 presents classical network measures and Section 5 discusses our new measures based on the notion of Von Neumann entropy while in Section 5.2, we discuss the role of the Diplacian in consensus dynamics and design an associated measure. Section 7 provides an empirical application.

2. Financial networks

A network can be defined as a set of vertices (or nodes) and arcs (or edges) between vertices. In financial networks, a node represents a financial institution (e.g., a bank, an insurance company, a financial agglomeration) and an edge has the interpretation of financial linkage between two institutions. In mathematical terms a network can be represented through the notion of graph and its properties. In the following sections we provide some background in graph theory useful for a better comprehension of the new indicators developed in this paper and of the analysis of financial networks. For further material on graph theory and random graph we refer the interested reader to Bollobás [1998] and Bollobás [2001]. See Jackson [2008] for an introduction to network theory in social sciences.

2.1. Graph theoretic foundation

A graph is defined as the ordered pair of sets $G = (V, E)$ where $V = \{1, ..., n\}$ is the set of vertices (or nodes) and $E \subset V \times V$ the set of edges (or arcs). The order of a graph is the number of vertices in V, that is the cardinality of V denoted with $|V|$. An (directed) edge between two nodes exists if there is a relationship between them and it can be identified as the (ordered) pair $\{u, v\}$ with $u, v \in V$. If there is no direction in the connection between nodes then an edge $\{u, v\}$ is an unordered pair of nodes and the graph G is said to be undirected, whereas if a direction exists, then each edge $\{u, v\}$ is defined as an ordered pair of nodes and the graph G is said to be directed graph (or digraph).

Assume for simplicity the graph $G = (V, E)$ is undirected. If $\{u, v\} \in E$ then u and v are adjacent vertices and they are incident with the edge $\{u, v\}$. For each node u, it possible to define its neighborhood as the set of nodes adjacent to u, that is $N_u = \{v \in V; \{u, v\} \in E\}$. The vertex adjacency structure of a n-order

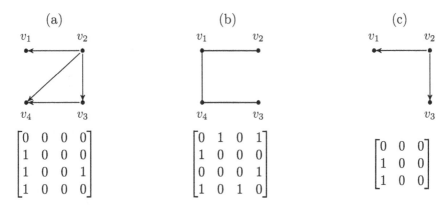

Figure 3.1 Panel (a): directed graph $G = (V, E)$ (top) with vertex set $V = \{v_1, v_2, v_3, v_4\}$ and edge set $E = \{e_1, e_2, e_3, e_4\}$, where $e_1 = \{v_2, v_1\}$, $e_2 = \{v_2, v_3\}$, $e_3 = \{v_2, v_4\}$, $e_4 = \{v_3, v_4\}$ and its adjacency matrix (bottom). Panel (b): undirected graph $G = (V, E)$ (top) with vertex set $V = \{v_1, v_2, v_3, v_4\}$ and edge set $E = \{e_1, e_2, e_3\}$, where $e_1 = \{v_1, v_2\}$, $e_2 = \{v_1, v_4\}$, $e_3 = \{v_3, v_4\}$ and its adjacency matrix (bottom). Panel (c): subgraph of the graph given in panel (a).

graph $G = (V, E)$ can be represented through a n-dimensional matrix A called adjacency matrix. Each element a_{uv} of the adjacency matrix is equal to 1 if there is an edge from institution u to institution v with $u, v \in V$, and 0 otherwise, where $u \neq v$, since self-loops are not allowed. If the graph is undirected then $a_{uv} = a_{vu}$, that is the adjacency matrix is symmetric.

As an example, Figure 3.1 includes two graphs, one directed (panel (a)) and the other undirected (panel (b)). The edges of the directed graph are $e_1 = \{v_2, v_1\}$, $e_2 = \{v_2, v_4\}$, $e_3 = \{v_2, v_3\}$ and $e_4 = \{v_3, v_4\}$ and its adjacency matrix is given in the second line of the same panel. The edges of the undirected graph are $e_1 = \{v_1, v_2\}$, $e_2 = \{v_1, v_4\}$, $e_3 = \{v_3, v_4\}$ and its adjacency matrix is given in the second line of the same panel.

In some applications it is useful to focus the analysis on a part of the graph. We say that $G' = (v', E')$ is a subgraph of G if $V' \subset V$ and $E' \subset E$. The subgraph can be induced by a subset of edges or by a subset of nodes. Panel (c) of Figure 3.1 shows, as an example, the subgraph of the directed graph reported in Panel (a). Given two subgraphs of G, $G_1 = (V_1, E_1)$ and $G_2 = (V_2, E_2)$, the graph union $G_3 = G_1 \cup G_2$ is defined as the graph $G_3 = (V_3, E_3)$ such that $V_3 = V_1 \cup V_2$ and $E_3 = \{\{u, v\} \in E; u, v \in V_3\}$. Note that $E_1 \cup E_2 \subset E_3$. The graph difference $G_3 = G_2 \backslash G_1$ with $V_1 \subset V_2$, is defined as the graph $G_3 = (V_3, E_3)$ such that $V_3 = V_2 \backslash V_1$ and $E_3 = \{\{u, v\} \in E; u, v \in V_3\}$.

2.2. Graph connectivity

The two extreme configurations of the connectivity structure of a n-order graph G are given by the graph with empty edge set, i.e., $|E| = 0$, which is called empty graph and denoted with E_n and the complete graph where each node is adjacent

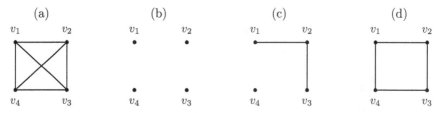

Figure 3.2 Example of complete graph K_4 (a), empty graph E_4 (b), path P_2 (c) and cycle C_4 (d)

to all other nodes in the graph. In this case, the cardinality of the edge set is maximal, i.e., $|E| = n(n - 1)/2$, and graph is denoted with K_n. Panels (a) and (b) of Figure 3.2 show an example of complete, K_4, and empty, E_4, graphs.

In the connectivity structure of a graph and in spreading of contagion in a network the cohesiveness and the indirect connections between nodes play a crucial role. The cohesiveness can be represented through the number and size of cliques or of communities. The notion of indirect connection can be made more precise through the definitions of walk, trail, path, circuit and cycle.

A clique $C \subset G$, is defined as an ordered pair of sets $C = (V_C, E_C)$ with $V_C \subset V$ and $E_C = \{\{u, v\} \in E; u, v \in V_C\}$ such that $m = |V_C| > 2$, $E_C = K_m$ and $C \cup \{w\}$ with $w \in G \backslash C$ is not complete.

A walk $W_{uv} = (v_0, e_1, \ldots , e_l, v_l)$ between two vertices u and v of G, called end-vertices, is identified by an alternating sequence of (not necessary distinct) vertices $V(W_{uv}) = \{v_0, v_1, \ldots , v_l\}$ and edges $E(W_{uv}) = \{e_1, \ldots , e_l\} \subset E$, with $e_1 = (v_0, v_1)$, $e_l = \{v_{l-1}, v_l\}$, and $v_0 = u$ and $v_l = v$. The number of edges $|E(W_{uv})| = l$ in a walk is called "walk length". A walk of length l is called l-walk and denoted with W_l. It is easy to show that the number of l-walks from node u to node v is equal to the (u, v)-th element of A^l that is equal to

$$\sum_{v_1=1}^{n}\sum_{v_2=1}^{n}\cdots\sum_{v_{l-1}=1}^{n} a_{uv_1} a_{v_2 v_3} \cdots a_{v_{l-1}v}. \tag{1}$$

If all edges are distinct then the walk is called a trail. A trail with coincident end-vertices is called a circuit (or closed trail). A walk W_l with $l \geq 3$ with $v_0 = v_l$ and vertices v_j, $0 < j < l$ distinct from each other and from v_0, is called cycle and denoted with C_l. An example of cycle C_4 is given in panel (d) of Figure 3.2.

A path P_{uv} between vertices u and v of G is a walk with distinct elements in its vertex set. A generic path of length l is denoted with l. The shortest-path P^*_{uv} between two vertices u and v is $\underset{l}{\min} \{P_{uv} = (v_0, e_1, \ldots, e_l, v_l), l \geq 1\}$ that is the path with the minimum length. An example of path P_2 is given in panel (c) of Figure 3.2. The notion of shortest path is relevant in spreading of contagion in financial networks. The average shortest path over pairs of nodes reflects the time a shock takes to spread out in the network. The lower the average shortest path is the higher will be speed of shocks transmission. Moreover, if a function of the losses is assigned as weight to the edges between nodes, then the shortest path can be used to provide a measures of the minimum loss following a transmission of shocks in the financial networks.

The notion of path allows us to introduce the definition of connected graph and some other basic graph structures. A graph is connected if for every pair of distinct vertices u and v there is a path from u to v. A maximal connected subgraph is a component of the graph. A cut-vertext is a vertex whose deletion increases the number of components. An edge is a bridge if its deletion increases the number of components. A graph without cycles is a forest or an acyclic graph. A tree is a connected forest.

Also, the notion of path can be used to define the distance between two nodes u and v, $d(u, v)$ as the length of the shortest path or geodesic between u and v. The notion of distance allows us to define the diameter of G, $\text{diam}(G)$ as the $\max_{u, v \in V} d(u, v)$ and the radius of G, $\text{rad}(G)$, as the $\min_u \max_v d(u, v)$. If the graph G is connected then there exists and integer $l > 0$ for which the (u, v)-th element of A^l is not equal to 0 for each pair (u, v) and the lowest integer l^* such that A^{l^*} is not equal to 0 for each pair of nodes is $\text{diam}(G)$. Thus the diameter is equal to the length of the longest shortest path in G.

Finally, note that it is possible to define graph measures using cycles rather than paths. The girth of a graph G, $\text{gir}(G)$, is the length of the shortest cycle in a network (set to infinity if there are no cycles) and the circumference, $\text{circ}(G)$, is the length of the largest cycle.

3. Network extraction

Financial linkages among all the institutions in the system are commonly unobservable, but they can be inferred from data by applying suitable econometric tools. In the following, we review some techniques used to extract financial networks from a panel of observations which contains, for each institution i, $i = 1, \ldots, n$, the time series of a variable of interest, y_{it}, $t = 1, \ldots, T$, such as financial returns, or realized volatility.

3.1. Pairwise and conditional Granger networks

Billio et al. [2012] proposed pairwise Granger causality between returns to extract the network of financial institutions. The adjacency matrix A is estimated using a Granger causality test on pairs of time series to detect the direction and propagation of the shocks among the two institutions considered. In the pairwise-Granger approach to network extraction, the following bivariate vector autoregressive model (VAR) of the order one is estimated

$$\begin{cases} y_{it} = \varphi_{10} + \varphi_{11} y_{it-1} + \varphi_{12} y_{jt-1} + \varepsilon_{it} \\ y_{jt} = \varphi_{20} + \varphi_{21} y_{it-1} + \varphi_{22} y_{jt-1} + \varepsilon_{jt} \end{cases} \tag{2}$$

$\forall i, j = 1, \ldots, n, i \neq j$, where ε_{it} and ε_{jt} are uncorrelated white noise processes. Then, a test for the existence of Granger causality is applied. The definition of causality implies, for $t = 1, \ldots, T$,

- if $\varphi_{12} \neq 0$ and $\varphi_{21} = 0$, y_{jt} causes y_{it} and $a_{ji} = 1$;
- if $\varphi_{12} = 0$ and $\varphi_{21} \neq 0$, y_{it} causes y_{jt} and $a_{ij} = 1$;
- if $\varphi_{12} \neq 0$ and $\varphi_{21} \neq 0$, there is a feedback relationship among y_{it} and y_{jt} and $a_{ij} = a_{ji} = 1$, where $a_{i, j}$ is the element in *ith* row and *jth* column of the adjacency matrix A.

The standard pairwise Granger causality approach deals only with bivariate time series and does not consider the conditioning on relevant covariates. In order to account for spurious causality effects, the model given above can be extended to include exogenous variables and endogenous variables at higher order lags. The maximum lag can be selected according to some criteria, such as AIC or BIC. The conditional Granger approach considers the conditioning on relevant covariates, however, with a higher number of variables relative to the number of data point, it encounters problems of over-parameterization, that leads to a loss of degrees of freedom and to inefficiency in correctly gauging the causal relationships.

3.2. Granger networks and graphical models

Ahelegbey et al. [2016a, b] proposed an alternative approach for network estimation based on graphical models. In their approach, the following structural VAR (SVAR) model is estimated,

$$
\begin{cases}
y_{1t} - \sum_{j=2}^{n} \gamma_{1j} y_{jt} = \sum_{j=1}^{n} \varphi_{1j} y_{jt-1} + \varepsilon_{1t} \\[2mm]
y_{2t} - \sum_{\substack{j=1 \\ j \neq 2}}^{n} \gamma_{2j} y_{jt} = \sum_{j=1}^{n} \varphi_{2j} y_{jt-1} + \varepsilon_{2t} \\[2mm]
\vdots \\[2mm]
y_{nt} - \sum_{j=1}^{n-1} \gamma_{nj} y_{jt} = \sum_{j=1}^{n} \varphi_{nj} y_{jt-1} + \varepsilon_{nt}
\end{cases}
\tag{3}
$$

where ε_{it}, $i = 1, \ldots, n$, are uncorrelated white noise processes, φ_{ij} are the autoregressive coefficients of the lagged dependence structure and γ_{ij} the structural coefficients of the contemporaneous dependence structure. In this approach two kind of networks are extracted: the undirected acyclic graph G_0 for the contemporaneous dependence and the directed graph G for the lagged dependence structure. To this aim, the coefficients are re-parametrized as $\gamma_{ij} = a_{0,ij} \gamma_{ij}^*$ where $a_{0,ij} \in \{0, 1\}$ is the element of the adjacency matrix of G_0 and $\varphi_{ij} = a_{ij} \varphi_{ij}^*$ where a_{ij} is an element of the adjacency matrix of G. Then the binary connectivity variables are estimated by applying a Markov-chain Monte Carlo search algorithm. For the contemporaneous dependence graph G_0 an acyclic constraint is used to identify the causal directions in the system and to produce an identifiable SVAR model.

3.3. Quantile Networks

In the quantile approach the network is extracted by using a pairwise quantile regression [e.g., see Adrian and Brunnermeier, 2016] at a given quantile level $q \in (0, 1)$,

$$\begin{cases} y_{it} = \varphi_{01} + \varphi_{11} y_{jt-1} + \varepsilon_{1t}, \\ y_{jt} = \varphi_{02}^* + \gamma_{21}^* y_{it} + \varphi_{21}^* y_{jt-1} + \varepsilon_{2t}^* \end{cases} \tag{4}$$

and

$$\begin{cases} y_{it} = \varphi_{01}^* + \gamma_{12}^* y_{jt} + \varphi_{11}^* y_{jt-1} + \varepsilon_{1t}^*, \\ y_{jt} = \varphi_{02} + \varphi_{21} y_{jt-1} + \varepsilon_{2t} \end{cases} \tag{5}$$

$\forall i, j = 1, \ldots, n$, $i \neq j$, where ε_{1t}^* and ε_{2t}^* are uncorrelated white noise processes.

- if $\gamma_{21}^* y_{it} \neq 0$ and $\gamma_{12}^* y_{jt} = 0$, y_{jt} is tail dependent from y_{it} and $a_{ij} = 1$, but not vice versa, $a_{ji} = 0$;
- if $\gamma_{21}^* y_{it} = 0$ and $\gamma_{12}^* y_{jt} \neq 0$, y_{it} is tail dependent from y_{jt} and $a_{ji} = 1$, but not vice versa, $a_{ij} = 0$;
- if $\gamma_{21}^* y_{it} \neq 0$ and $\gamma_{12}^* y_{jt} \neq 0$, y_{it} is a tail mutual independence among y_{it} and y_{jt} and $a_{ji} = a_{ij} = 0$.

The relationship between the financial institutions using the quantile regression is asymmetric which implies the network extracted can be represented as a directed graph with an asymmetric adjacency matrix. The approach given above can be extended to include more lags and further covariates to control for spurious linkages.

4. Classical network measures

In this section, we present the commonly used measures in network analysis. See also Newman [2010] for a review. The structure and connectivity features of a network can be characterized by means of some measures. Node-specific measures are evaluated at the node level and reveal the role of a node in the connectivity structure of the network and its relationship with the other nodes. Local measures can be used to identify systemically important financial institutions. Global measures aim to describe the connectivity structure or topological features of the network, and therefore can be used to analyze the stability and fragility of the financial system.

4.1. Node-specific measures (i.e. local measures)

In the undirected network, the degree indicates the number of adjacent nodes, that is the number of nodes to which the node is connected. If a_{uv} is the u-th row and v-th column element of the adjacency matrix A, then the degree is equal to

$$d_u = \sum_{v=1}^{n} a_{uv} \tag{6}$$

In directed graphs, for a given node i it is useful to define the number of edges directed from othr nodes to node i (in-degree) and from node i to other nodes (out-degree), and the total number of incident edges (total degree), that are

$$d_u^{out} = \sum_{v=1}^{n} a_{vu} \tag{7}$$

$$d_u^{in} = \sum_{v=1}^{n} a_{uv} \tag{8}$$

$$d_u^{tot} = d_u^{in} + d_u^{in} \tag{9}$$

The measures d_u^{out} and d_u^{in} are also known as in-degree and out-degree centrality measures and assess the centrality of a node in the network. They can be used to identify which are the nodes in the network spreading risk (spreaders) and which absorbing it (receivers).

While the degree measures how connected a node is, closeness account for connectivity patterns (such as paths and cycles) and indicates how easily a node can reach other nodes. The closeness centrality of a node u is defined as

$$\text{Clo}_u(G) = \frac{n-1}{\sum_{v \in V, v \neq u} l(u, v)} \tag{10}$$

where $l(u, v)$ is the length of the shortest path between u and v.

A measure related to the closeness is the betweenness centrality which indicates how relevant is a node in terms of connecting other nodes in the graph. Let $n(u, v)$ be the number of shortest paths P_{uv}^* from u to v, and $n_w(u, v) = |\{P_{uv}^*; w \in P_{uv}^*\}|$, i.e., the number of shortest paths from u to v going through the node w, then the betweenness centrality

$$\text{Bet}_w(G) = \sum_{u \neq v, w \notin \{u, v\}} \frac{n_w(u, v)/n(u, v)}{(n-1)(n-2)} \tag{11}$$

Bonacich [1987] introduced a measure of centrality for a undirected graph,[1] called eigenvector centrality, which accounts for the centrality of the neighbourhood of a given node. This measure describe the influence of a node in a network and is defined as

$$\lambda x_u = \sum_{v \in N_u} a_{uv} x_v,$$ (12)

where the score x_u is related by the score of its neighbourhood $N_u = \{v \in V; a_{uv} = 1\}$. It is easy to show that the score vector $\mathbf{x} = (x_1, \ldots , x_n)'$ satisfies the equation $A\mathbf{x} = \lambda \mathbf{x}$, where λ is an eigenvalue of the matrix A. Eigenvector centrality explains the propagation of economic shocks better than other measure as closeness and betweenness centrality since it accounts not only for the number of connections of each node with the adjacent nodes, but also for its weight and for the weights of the paths connecting the node to the other nodes of the graph.

Bonacich [2007] introduced a related centrality measure, the $c(\beta)$ centrality, defined as

$$c(\beta) = \sum_{j=1}^{\infty} \beta^{j-1} A^j \imath$$

with $|\beta| < 1/\lambda_1$ where longer paths are weighted less through higher powers of the discount parameter β. $\imath$ is the n-dimensional unit vector and λ_1 is the largest eigenvalue. This measure is a weighted sum over all possible paths connecting other vertices to each position. $c(\beta)$ centrality has the eigenvector centrality as limiting case for $\beta \rightarrow 1/\lambda_1$.

The $c(\beta)$ centrality is strictly related to another widely used measure, that is the Katz centrality. Katz [1953] proposed a node centrality measure which is a weighted sum of the walks of a given node neighbours, with weights driven by an attenuation parameter. The Katz centrality of the node u is defined as

$$x_u = \beta \sum_{v=1}^{n} a_{uv} x_v + \alpha$$ (13)

where $0 < \beta < 1$ is the attenuation parameter and α is an arbitrary term that avoids to consider in the centrality score all vertices with null degree. The parameter α is usually set to 1. Equation 13 can be written in matrix form: $\mathbf{x} = (I_n - \beta A)^{-1} \alpha \imath = (I_n + \beta A + \beta^2 A^2 + \ldots + \beta^k A^k + \ldots) \alpha \imath$ which shows how neighbours, and neighbours of neighbours affect the nodes centrality. Finally, note that the Katz centrality has as special cases the $c(\beta)$ centrality for $\alpha = 1$ and the Bonacich's centrality for $\alpha = 0$ and $\beta = 1/\lambda_1$.

4.2. Global measures

The density of a n-order graph is given by the ratio between the number of edges in the edge set E, denoted with $e(G)$, and the number of edges of the complete graph K_n. If the K_n graph is undirected the cardinality of the edge set is

$e(K_n) = n(n-1)/2$, if it is directed the cardinality is $e(K_n) = n(n-1)$. Thus the graph density is

$$\text{De} = \frac{e(G)}{K_n} \tag{14}$$

The density is null if G is the empty graph E_n and it is equal to one if G is the complete graph K_n. Density is a good indicator of the level of interconnectedness in a financial network. Nevertheless this measure relies on the adjacency of the nodes and does not consider indirect connectivity patterns such as paths and cycles.

A way to account for connectivity patterns is to analyze the cliquishness of a graph. Unfortunately, the clique structure can be very sensitive to slight changes in the graph and thus, a general procedure for extracting cliques can fail in finding the clique structure. A common way to measure cliquishness is to employ the average clustering coefficient of a n-order graph $G = (V, E)$, $\text{Cl}(G)$, which counts the fraction of fully connected triples of nodes out of the potential triples where at least two links are presents. In formulas, we have

$$\text{Cl}(G) = \frac{1}{n}\sum_{u=1}^{n} Cl_u(G) \tag{15}$$

where

$$\text{Cl}_u(G) = \frac{|\{(u',v') \in E; u' \neq v', u' \in N_u(G), v' \in N_u(G)\}|}{|\{(u',v') \in K_n; u' \neq v', u' \in N_u(K_n), v' \in N_u(K_n)\}|}$$

where $N_u(G)$ indicates the neighbourhood of a node u in G, and so if G is the complete graph K_n, $N_u(K_n)$ is of the set all the nodes different from u.

Assortativity can be defined as the difference between the number of edges among vertexes having the same characteristics and therefore belonging to the same class, and the expected number of edges among these vertexes if the attachment were purely random [Newman, 2002, 2003]. Let m_i be the class of the vertex i, and n_m the number of classes in the network. In a directed network, the number of edges among the vertexes of the same class is

$$\sum_{u,v \in V} a_{uv}\delta_{m_u m_v}, \tag{16}$$

where δ_{xy} is the Kronecker delta.[2] Assuming a random graph, the expected number of edges among vertices of the same class is equal to

$$\sum_{u,v \in V} \frac{d_u^{out} d_v^{in}}{e(G)} \delta_{m_u m_v}, \tag{17}$$

where d_u^{out} and d_v^{in} denote the nodes out- and in-degree. Thus, the assortativity measure of the graph $G = (V, E)$ can be defined as

$$Q = \frac{1}{e(G)}\left(e(G) - \frac{d_u^{out} d_v^{in}}{e(G)}\delta_{m_u m_v}\right). \tag{18}$$

The maximum assortativity value Q_{max} is attained when all edges of E are adjacent to all vertices of the same category, so

$$Q_{max} = \frac{1}{e(G)}\left(e(G) - \sum_{u,v \in V} \frac{d_u^{out} d_v^{in}}{e(G)} \delta_{m_u m_v} \right). \tag{19}$$

If $0 < Q \leq Q_{max}$ the nodes have an homophily behavior and if Q/Q_{max} is close to zero there is any preferential attachment of the nodes and the network is a random graph. If $-Q_{max} \leq Q < 0$ the nodes exhibit disassortative patterns, in sense that it is likely that a given node is connected to nodes in a different class.

The assortativity measure is very important in systemic risk analysis because it allows to detect clusters in the network that can be useful to block the shocks propagation in some circumstances as a firewall. The assortativity can be also applied to the vertex degree in order to capture the tendency of each node to connect with vertices having similar or different degree. This measure is able to detect a core-periphery structure of the graph when the assortativity coefficient is high. Let e_{jk} be the edges fraction connecting vertices of degree j to vertexes of degree k, q_j^{out} and q_j^{in} the probabilities to have an excess in-degree, out-degree,[3] respectively, equal to j and σ_q^{out} and σ_q^{in} standard deviation of the degree distributions of q_j^{out} and q_j^{in}, respectively. Then, following Newman [2003], the assortativity by degree for directed graphs is defined as

$$r = \frac{\sum_{jk} jk(e_{jk} - q_j^{in} q_k^{out})}{\sigma_{in} \sigma_{out}}. \tag{20}$$

Assortativity can be similarliy defined for undirected graph [see Newman, 2003].

5. Entropy measures

5.1. Von Neumann entropy for directed graph

Following Ye et al. [2014], we introduce a Markov chain process on the graph with transition matrix P with entries

$$p_{uv} = \begin{cases} \frac{1}{d_u^{out}} a_{uv} & \text{if } \{u,v\} \in E \\ 0 & \text{otherwise.} \end{cases}$$

Let $D = diag\{(d_1^{out}, d_2^{out}, \ldots, d_n^{out})\}$ then P can be in written in the matrix form: $P = D^{-1}A$. Additionally, given the vector φ of the ergodic probability of the Markov chain associated to P,[4] we define the diagonal matrix $\varphi = diag\{\varphi\}$ and the Laplacian [Chung, 2005] for undirected graphs:

$$L_1 = I_n - \frac{\varphi^{1/2} P \varphi^{-1/2} + \varphi^{-1/2} P' \varphi^{1/2}}{2} \tag{21}$$

$$L_2 = \varphi - \frac{\varphi P + P'\varphi}{2} \qquad (22)$$

where I_n is the identity matrix. L_1 can be related to a random walk onto the graph starting at a given node chosen with uniform probability while L_2 to a random walk starting at a node chosen according to the ergodic probability vector φ. In fact, those Laplacians can be interpreted as the Laplacians for an equivalent weighted undirected graph obtained by changing the weights of the starting graph but not its connectivity [Boley et al., 2011]. The difference among the two is in the equivalent ergodic probabilities that are uniform in the L_1 and again equal to φ for L_2. In this line, L_1 is largely driven by long-run effects with respect to L_2.

The induced L_i by the directed graph is symmetric but not positive definite and consequently, it is not suitable to be used as a proper density matrix [Braunstein et al., 2006]. Using the results in Braunstein et al. [2006] and Garnerone et al. [2012], we obtain a density matrix ρ, based on the Laplacian but corrected for directed graphs. A proper density matrix, ρ, is a symmetric positive definite matrix with unitary trace. The functional form of the density matrix describes the correspondence of the graph to a given quantum system. In Passerini and Severini [2009] for undirected graphs, the density matrix is defined as the Laplacian normalized by its trace while Ye et al. [2014] generalizes the same construction for directed graphs,

$$\rho_{Li} = \frac{L_i}{\text{trace}(L_i)}. \qquad (23)$$

Formally, any positivity preserving transformation of the Laplacian could provide a proper density matrix ρ. In this regard, we consider the exponential function as an alternative transformation,

$$\rho_{Ei} = \frac{\exp(L_i)}{\text{trace}(\exp(L_i))}. \qquad (24)$$

The linear transformation takes into consideration only the 1-step walk probability which can be viewed as the short run effect of propagation in the network. Differently, the exponential considers all the possible walk probabilities which are weighted by the inverse of the factorial of the walk length. Thus, it can be interpreted as the long run effect of propagation. According to the random walk interpretation of the two Laplacians, we do not expect large differences among $\rho(L_1)$ and $\rho(E_1)$. Given the density matrix ρ, we can measure the complexity of the network using the Von Neumann entropy,

$$S(\rho) = -\text{trace}(\rho \log(\rho)), \qquad (25)$$

which is equivalent to the Shannon entropy of the eigenvalues of ρ,

$$S(\rho) = -\sum_{i=1}^{n} \lambda_i^{\rho} \log\left(\lambda_i^{\rho}\right). \tag{26}$$

and is bounded [Passerini and Severini, 2009],

$$S(\rho) \leq -\log(n). \tag{27}$$

For undirected graphs and ρ_{Li} the maximum entropy is associated with the complete graph [Passerini and Severini, 2009]. For directed graphs, linear density matrix and the Laplacians L_1, Ye et al. [2014] show that the maximum value of entropy is associated with the star graph according to the quadratic approximation.

5.2. A Von Neumann entropy decomposition

We present some preliminary results which will be used to state some properties of the Von Neumann entropy proposed in this paper. Let L be one the two Laplacian matrices L_i, $i = 1, 2$, then the following results hold.

Theorem 1 *The following property holds for the Laplacian L*

- *For $L = L_1$*

$$tr(L^m) = n + \sum_{k=0}^{m-1}\sum_{l=0}^{m-k} \omega_{lk}\, tr(R^{(lk)}) \tag{28}$$

$m = 0, 1, 2, \ldots$, where

$$\omega_{lk} = \binom{m}{k}(-2)^{m-k}\binom{m-k}{l}$$

are weights and $R^{(lk)}$ is a matrix with the (i, j)-th element

$$R_{ij}^{(lk)} = \sum_{h=1}^{n} W_{ih}^{(l)} W_{jh}^{(m-k-l)} \frac{\varphi_i}{\varphi_h}$$

with

$$W_{ij}^{(q)} = \sum_{i_2 \cdots i_q} \prod_{r=1}^{q} a_{i_r\, i_{r+1}} \frac{1}{d_{i_r}^{in}}$$

where $i_1 = i$ and $i_{q+1} = j$, $q = 0, 1, \ldots, n-1$ the length of the walk and $d_{i_r}^{in}$ is defined in Equation 8.

- *For $L = L_2$*

$$tr(L^m) = \sum_{i=1}^{n} \varphi_i^m + \sum_{k=0}^{m-1} \omega_k\, tr(R^{(k)}) \tag{29}$$

$m = 0, 1, 2, \ldots$, *where*

$$\omega_k = \binom{m}{k}(-2)^{-(m-k)}$$

are weights, $R^{(k)} = \varphi^k W^{(m-k)}$, and $W^{(q)}$ is a matrix with the (i, j)-th element

$$W_{ij}^{(q)} = \sum_{i_2 \cdots i_q} \prod_{r=1}^{q} \left(\frac{\varphi_{i_r}}{d_{i_r}^-} a_{i_r i_{r+1}} + a_{i_{r+1} i_r} \frac{1}{\varphi_{i_{r+1}} d_{i_{r+1}}^-} \right)$$

with $i_1 = i$ and $i_{q+1} = j$.

Proof. See Appendix A.

In the theorem given above the matrices $W^{(q)}$ have an interpretation in terms of path of random walk on a network. More specifically, for $L = L_1$ $W_{ij}^{(q)}$ is the transition q steps forward in time starting in i at time 1 and arriving in j at time $(q + 1)$. Whereas for $L = L_2$ $W_{ij}^{(q)}$ is the transition q steps forward and q steps backward in time, starting in i at time 0 and arriving in j at time $2q$.

We show that the Von Neumann entropy based on the transformed Laplacian accounts for various features of the associated graph. We focus on the numerator of Eq. 24

$$\exp\{L_i\} = \sum_{m=0}^{\infty} \frac{1}{m!} L_i^m \tag{30}$$

where $m!$ is factorial. It can be approximated by

$$\tilde{L}_i^{(M)} = \sum_{m=0}^{M} \frac{1}{m!} L_i^m \tag{31}$$

with $M < \infty$. Then, the Von Neumann entropy S given in equation 25 can be approximated as

$$S_i^{(M)}(\lambda) = \frac{1}{n} \mathrm{tr}(L_i^{(M)}) - \frac{1}{n^2} \mathrm{tr}((L_i^{(M)})^2) \tag{32}$$

Proof. See Appendix A.

Theorem 2 *The approximated quadratic Von Neumann entropy for various degrees of approximation can be written as*

- *For M = 1*

$$S^{(M)}(\lambda_1) = 2 - \frac{3}{n} - \frac{1}{4n^2} tr((P')^2) - \frac{2}{n^2} tr(\varphi P \varphi^{-1} P') - \frac{1}{n^2} tr(P^2))$$

$$S^{(M)}(\lambda_2) = 1 - \frac{2}{n^2} + \left(\frac{1}{n} - \frac{2}{n^2}\right)(tr(P(\varphi + \varphi^{-1})/2))$$

$$- \frac{1}{n^2}\left(\sum_{i=1}^{n}\varphi_i^2 + \frac{1}{4}(tr((\varphi P)^2) + tr((P'\varphi^{-1})^2) + tr(P'P) + tr(PP')) - tr(\varphi^2 P)\right)$$

- *For M = 2*

$$S^{(M)}(\lambda_1) = 2 - \frac{25}{4n} - \frac{1}{n^2}\left(\sum_{k=0}^{3}\sum_{l=0}^{4-k}\tilde{\omega}_{lk} tr(R^{(lk)})\right)$$

$$S^{(M)}(\lambda_2) = 2 - \frac{3}{n} - \frac{1}{n^2}\sum_{k=0}^{3}\tilde{\omega}_k tr(R^{(k)})$$

where $R^{(lk)}$ and $R^{(k)}$ have been defined in Theorem 1.

Note that our quadratic entropy for the case $M = 1$ has an analytical relationship with the quadratic entropy $S_Q = n^{-1}tr(L_1) - n^{-2}tr(L_1)$ of Ye et al. [2014] as stated in the following.

Corollary 1

$$S_1 - S_Q = 1 - \frac{3}{n} \tag{33}$$

Proof. See Appendix A.

6. Diplacian and convergence rate to distributed consensus

In the computation of the Von Neumman entropy we considered a symmetrized version of the Laplacian matrix for directed graphs. This choice, as pointed out in two recent papers, could hamper the comprehension of several important aspect related to diffusion on the graph [Boley et al., 2011, Li and Zhang, 2012]. In particular, we investigate the relationship between the eigenvalues of the diplacian introduced in Li and Zhang [2012]. The Diplacian is defined as

$$\Gamma = \varphi^{1/2}(I - P)\varphi^{-1/2}$$

and the rate of convergence of autonomous agents on the network to a consensus [Olfati-Saber et al., 2007]. The application of those techniques to financial networks could be understood as measuring the structural speed of coordination so that a low rate implies persistence of disagreement in the market that in line with

Carlin et al. [2014] is "magnified when major events occur in financial markets". Our approach considers a limited communication network see [see Parikh and Krasucki, 1990] among agents, proxied by the causality relationship between those stocks returns. The convergence to a final group decision is then a convergence to the consensus of investors, trading in different stocks, on common Arrow-Debreu securities prices. Consequently, we propose the persistence of disagreement as a general proxy for the presence of market frictions. Consider a graph with adjacency matrix A and elements a_{ij} and with out-degree diagonal matrix D with non zero elements d_i^{out}. We investigate the following discrete time multi-agent dynamical system on the network:

$$x_{it} = x_{it} + \frac{1}{2d_i^{out}} \sum_{j=1}^{n} a_{ij} (x_{jt} - x_{it}) \tag{34}$$

Similar systems, pioneered by DeGroot [1974], are considered in models of belief evolution of bounded rational agents, with the bounded rationality motivated by a persuasion bias [DeMarzo et al., 2003, Golob and Jackson, 2010]. The closer analogue to our approach is the one considered in the Theorem 2 of Olfati-Saber et al. [2007] and can be rewritten in vectorial form as

$$\mathbf{x}_t = \frac{1}{2} I_n + \frac{1}{2}(I_n - D^{-1}(D-A))\mathbf{x}_{t-1} = P_L X_{t-1}$$

Where $\mathbf{x}_t = (x_{it}, \dots, x_{nt})$ is the state vector of the agents $P = D^{-1}A$ is the transition probability matrix of the Markov chain associated with random walks on G, where at each vertex i, a random walk has probability $p_{ij} = a_{ij}/d_i^{out}$ of transiting from vertex i to vertex j and $P_L = (I_n - P)$ corresponds to the transition matrix of the lazy random walk introduced in Chung [2005] and further studied in Li and Zhang [2012]. Using their results, if the graph is strongly connected, P_L is irreducible and aperiodic, so that Perron-Frobenious theorem applies and we can easily adapt Theorem 2 of Olfati-Saber et al. [2007], being sure that the system converge to a consensus with group decision value $\varphi' \mathbf{x}_0$. The group decision is a conserved quantity of the dynamics:

$$\varphi' \mathbf{x}_t = \varphi' P_L \mathbf{x}_{t-1} \varphi' \mathbf{x}_{t-1} = \alpha,$$

$$\alpha \in \mathbb{R}.$$

Consequently, we can define a disagreement vector and its dynamics

$$\xi_t = \mathbf{x}_t - \alpha \mathbf{1}$$

$$\xi_t = P_L \xi_{t-1}$$

The disagreement dynamics allows us to study speed of convergence to this decision value. We exploit the theoretical results on lazy random walks on strongly connected directed graphs due to Chung [2005] and Li and Zhang [2012]. In particular in Li and Zhang [2012] the decomposition of the Diplacian Γ in its symmetric and asymmetric part is introduced

$$\Gamma = L + \Delta,$$

$$L = \frac{\Gamma + \Gamma'}{2} \tag{35}$$

$$\Delta = \frac{\Gamma - \Gamma'}{2} \tag{36}$$

In the following theorem the convergence rate is expressed in terms of λ_2 the second smallest eigenvalue of L and of the second largest singular value $\sigma_{n-1}(I_n - L)$ of $I_n - L$ and the largest singular value $\sigma_n(\Delta)$ of the skew-symmetric part of the diplacian Δ.

Theorem 3 *Consider the discrete-time system introduced in (34) on a a strongly connected directed network. A consensus is globally exponentially reached according to*

$$\| \xi_t \| \leq \exp\left\{ \frac{1}{2}\left[\log\left(\frac{\max(\varphi)}{\min(\varphi)} \right) + \log(\mu)t \right] \right\} \| \xi_0 \|$$

$$\mu = \frac{3}{4} - \frac{\lambda_2}{2} + \frac{(\sigma_{n-1}(I_n - L) + \sigma_n(\Delta))^2}{4}.$$

where μ is the disagreement persistence index, measuring the convergence rate to consensus.

Proof. See Appendix A.

Li and Zhang [2012] show that for symmetric adjacency matrices, i.e., for undirected graphs, $\sigma_n(\Delta) = 0$ and they propose it as a measure of asymmetry (directedness). Moreover they underline that in this case

$$\mu = 1 - \frac{\lambda_2}{2}$$

a bound previously derived in Chung [2005].

The expression in Theorem 3 implies a slower convergence if the graph is directed and shows an initial magnifing effect of the heterogeneity of importance of the nodes in the group decision. The latter effect is not present for directed balanced graphs i.e., for directed graphs that have row and column sum equal, because in that case the group decision is the average of the initial state vector. Going further, if we assume an initial disagreement vector of unitary norm we can evaluate the time needed to reach consensus. In fact, for each

$\epsilon > 0$, we have $\|\boldsymbol{\xi_t}\| \leq \epsilon$ in a time

$$t \leq \frac{2\log\left(\epsilon\right) - \log\left(\dfrac{\max\left(\varphi\right)}{\min\left(\varphi\right)}\right)}{\log\mu}$$

In the empirical result section we will evaluate μ on the giant strongly connected component and multiply it by a weight proportional to the size of the component in order to take into consideration the impact of the number of coordinated agents.

7. Empirical analysis

7.1. Data description

The dataset is composed by the daily closing price series for the European financial institutions (active and dead) from 29th December 1999 to 16th January 2013. We analyze a total of 437 European financial institutions according to the Industrial Classification Benchmark (ICB). We select the MSCI Europe index as the proxy for the market index, which covers the 15 European countries where the financial institutions are based. To estimate dynamic Granger networks, we use a rolling window approach [e.g., see Billio et al., 2012, Diebold and Yılmaz, 2014, Zivot and Wang, 2003] with a window size of 252 daily observations, that is approximately one year.[5]

The rolling-window estimations have been parallelized and implemented in Matlab. It takes approximately 72 hours on the SCSCF (Sistema di Calcolo Scientifico Ca' Foscari) cluster multiprocessor system which consists of 4 nodes; each comprises four Xeon E5-4610 v2 2.3GHz CPUs, with 8 cores, 256GB ECC PC3-12800R RAM, Ethernet 10Gbit, 20TB hard disk system with Linux.

The sequence of adjacency matrices of the directed graph extracted with the pairwise Granger approach is represented in Figure 3.3 (a weekly sampling frequency has been used for expository purposes). Boxes highlight the adjacency matrix at a given date. In each box dots represent directed edges between nodes.

The question here is to compare the network defined over time, to identify possible distortions and sources of systemic risk. Figure 3.4 shows the graphs of four financial networks extracted in January 2001 (Panel a), August 2004 (Panel b), October 2008 (Panel c), and March 2012 (Panel d). The size of the nodes is proportional to the node degree. For expository purposes nodes with a degree lower then a given threshold have been removed (see caption of Figure 3.4). From a visual inspection, the graphs in panel (a) and (b) exhibit a lower number of edges then the graphs in panel (b) and (d), which reflects a higher level of financial interconnectedness. The node brightness from black to gray reflects the node eigenvector centrality. Gray indicates a large centrality level, black a low centrality. A more precise description of the four networks can be achieved by applying the network measures discussed in the previous section.

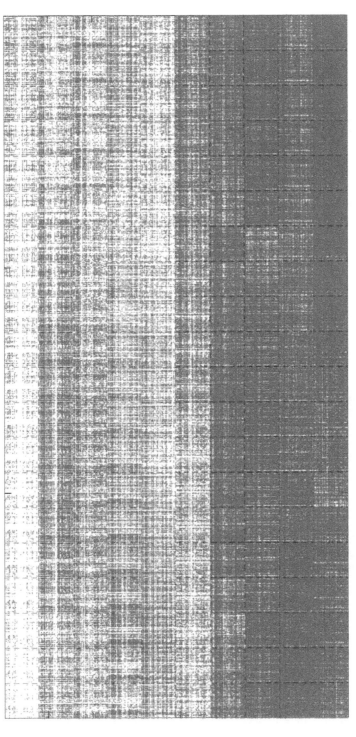

Figure 3.3 Sequence of adjacency matrices from 29th December 1999 to 16th January 2013 (re-sampled at weekly frequency for expository purposes). The boxes highlight the adjacency matrix at a given week. In each box dots represent directed edges between nodes.

(a)   (b)

(c)   (d)

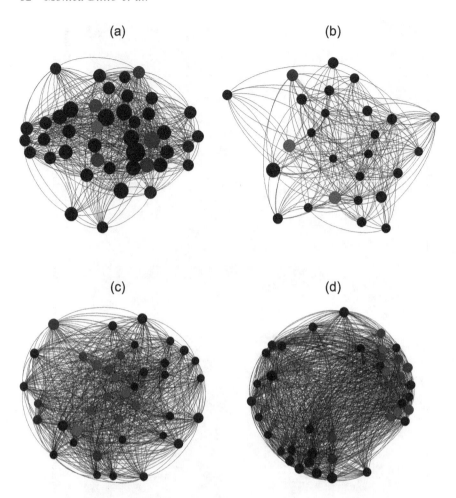

Figure 3.4 Financial networks extracted in January 2001 (a), August 2004 (b), October
2008 (c), and March 2012 (d). The size of the nodes are proportional to the
node degree. For expository purposes, nodes with a degree lower than 70 (a),
90 (b), 300 (c), and 350 (d) have been removed. The difference in threshold
is due to different network density. The node color from black to gray reflects
the node eigenvector centrality. Gray indicates a large centrality level, black
a low centrality.

Table 3.1 shows the network measures for the four networks depicted in
Figure 3.5. Panels (a) and (b) refer to two tranquil periods whereas (c) and (d)
refer to instability periods due to the global financial and European sovereign
debt crises.

A comparison of statistics in panels (a) and (b) with the one in panels (c) and
(d) reveals that the level of connectivity changes during periods of instability.
More specifically, the number of direct connections increases, since the

Table 3.1 Network statistics for the four financial networks in Figure 3.4 extracted in January 2001 (Panel a), August 2004 (Panel b), October 2008 (Panel c), and March 2012 (Panel d). Average degree (AD), average in-degree (AID), density (De), diameter (Di), radius (Ra), average path length (APL), number of weakly and strongly connected components (WCC and SCC), average clustering coefficient (ACluCoe), average closeness centrality (ACloCen), average betweenness centrality (ABetCen), average eigenvector centrality (AEigCen), the Von Neumann entropies for the linear, i.e., $S(\rho_{L_1})$ and $S(\rho_{L_2})$, and exponential, i.e., $S(\rho_{E_1})$ and $S(\rho_{E_2})$, functional forms using the two Laplacians L_1 and L_2 and the disagreement persistence index (μ).

	AD	AID	De	Di	Ra	APL
Panel (a)	55.065	27.53	0.149	4	3	2.001
Panel (b)	47.517	23.758	0.161	4	3	2.008
Panel (c)	213.935	106.967	0.291	3	2	1.731
Panel (d)	257.636	128.812	0.356	3	2	1.652

	WCC	SCC	ACluCoe	ACloCen	ABetCen	AEigCen
Panel (a)	1	1	0.181	0.503	185.134	0.332
Panel (b)	1	1	0.232	0.505	149.196	0.236
Panel (c)	1	2	0.377	0.586	267.54	0.272
Panel (d)	1	1	0.417	0.6145	236	0.3077

	$S(\rho_{L_1})$	$S(\rho_{L_2})$	$S(\rho_{E_1})$	$S(\rho_{L_2})$	μ
Panel (a)	−50.4660	−720.6452	−10.8064	−0.0065	0.3341
Panel (b)	−49.9492	−1238.3541	−10.3041	−0.0223	0.2450
Panel (c)	−16.0168	−1421.1440	−3.2444	−0.0041	0.5296
Panel (d)	−11.6902	−673.3415	−2.1504	−0.0014	0.4500

average degree and density for (a) and (b) are lower than (c) and (d). Also the number of indirect connections increases, since the network diameter, that is the longer shortest path, is 4 in (a) and (b) and 3 in (c) and (d). The decrease in the diameter indicates that a financial shock propagates faster in (c) and (d) than in (a) and (b). This is supported also by the average path length (APL) which is larger in (a) and (b) with respect to (c) and (d) (see Table 3.1. The same applies to the average cluster coefficient (ACluCoe), average closeness centrality (ACloCen) and average betweenness centrality (ABetCen). Finally, the increase of the (log) Von Neumann entropies and the disagreement persistence index (μ) in (c) and (d) with respect than to (a) and (b) indicates a more complex topology of the network.

Figure 3.5 reports the Von Neumann entropies evaluated over the sequence of inferred networks of Figure 3.3. In the different panels, we have the Von Neumann entropies for the linear, i.e., $S(\rho_{L_1})$ and $S(\rho_{L_2})$, and exponential, i.e., $S(\rho_{E_1})$ and $S(\rho_{E_2})$, functional forms using the two Laplacians L_1 and L_2. Given the first Laplacian, L_1, the dynamic of the linear $S(\rho_{L_1})$ (top-left panel) and the exponential $S(\rho_{E_1})$ (bottom-left panel) are almost identical. The second Laplacian provides different dynamics in the linear $S(\rho_{L_2})$ entropy and

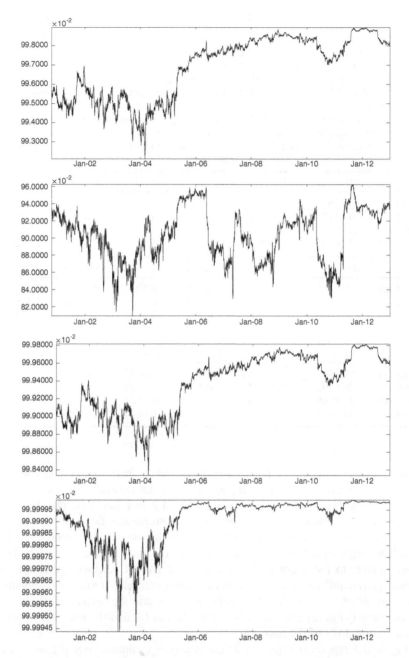

Figure 3.5 Von Neumann entropies of the Granger network of European financial institutions during 2000–2014. First panel: $S(\rho_{L_1})$ indicates the Von Neumann entropy with the linear functional form and Laplacian L_1. Second panel: $S(\rho_{L_2})$ indicates the Von Neumann entropy with the linear functional form and Laplacian L_2. Third panel: $S(\rho_{E_1})$ indicates the Von Neumann entropy with the exponential functional form and Laplacian L_1. Fourth panel: $S(\rho_{E_2})$ indicates the Von Neumann entropy with the exponential functional form and Laplacian L_2.

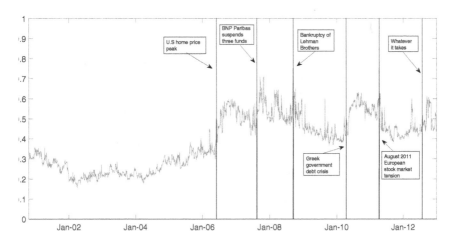

Figure 3.6 Disagreement persistence index (μ) of the Granger Network of European financial institutions during 2000–2014.

the exponential one $S(\rho_{E_2})$. While the Von Neumann entropies depict a structural change in the European financial system starting from 2006, the disagreement persistence index (μ) reported Figure 3.6 seems to capture some well-known events which provoked turbulences and stress in the financial system. In fact, the indicator signals a first level of stress in mid-2006 when the U.S. market price reaches its peak and there are some tensions in the financial market due to rising of the interest rates. The second signal is located at the beginning of the global financial crisis in August 2007 when BPN Paribas suspends three funds due to the subprime mortgage sector large decline and the inability by the fund managers to determine their market value. The level of the indicator remains at its higher levels during the crisis and slowly declines after the peak in the correspondence of the bankruptcy of Lehman Brothers on 15th September 2008. The beginning of the European sovereign debt crisis is captured by the a new rise of the disagreement persistence index occurred in April 2010 with the Greece government debt crisis and the downgrade of Greek bonds to junk status. The persistence of the high level of the indicator culminated with the peak in August 2011 in the correspondence of the euro market fall due the contagion to the peripheral countries such as Italy and Spain. Then, the index decreases with some short spikes before and immediately after the ECB's asset purchase program.

7.2. Early warning indicators

As in Billio et al. [2016], we observe a persistence in the dynamics of entropy and thus we test the ability of the Von Neumann entropy and the disagreement persistence index as early warning indicators in nowcasting banking crises. An early warning system issues a signal in case the likelihood of a crisis crosses a specified threshold [Demirgüç-Kunt and Detragiache, 1999]. In this regard, we select as the European banking crisis indicator the one presented in Babecký et al. [2014] and Alessi and Detken [2014a] which represents one of the target variables monitored by European Systemic Risk Board (ESRB). The indicator identifies significant signs of financial distress in the banking system as evidenced bank runs in relevant institutions or losses in the banking system (nonperforming loans above 20% or bank closures of at least 20% of banking system assets), or significant public intervention in response to or to avoid the realization of losses in the banking system. As stated in Billio et al. [2016], we define an indicator on European basis to be used in the early warning system since the crisis indicator is given on a per-country basis,

$$C_t = \begin{cases} 1 & \text{if more than one country is in crisis at time } t \\ 0 & \text{otherwise.} \end{cases} \tag{37}$$

The banking crisis indicator in Alessi and Detken [2014a] has its last record in December 2012 and thus we consider the period from is from October 2000 to December 2012. Since the crisis indicator is at a quarterly frequency and networks are extracted from daily returns, we assume that the daily crisis indicator is equal to 1 for all days in a given quarter, if the quarterly indicator equals 1 for that quarter [see Billio et al., 2016]. Consequently, we make use of the logistic model with Von Neumann entropies and the disagreement persistence index as covariates. As comparison, we include the DCI [Billio et al., 2012], that is the density of the network (De) defined in Equation 14, and the Shannon entropy (H) of the degree distribution as proposed in Billio et al. [2016].

Hence, we set the following logistic regression model,

$$\mathbb{P}(C_t = 1|S_t) = \Phi(\beta_0 + \beta_1 S_t), \tag{38}$$

$t = 1, \dots, T$, where $\Phi(x) = 1/(1 + \exp(-x))$ is the logistic function and S_t is an early warning indicator. The estimation results from the logit specification are presented in Table 3.2. All indicators are significant at 1% confidence level. All the Von Neumann entropies (except for the one with the linear functional form and the second Laplacian) and the disagreement persistence index provide better estimates in terms of Adjusted-R-squared, AIC and BIC criteria with respect to the DCI and Shannon Entropy. In particular, the Von Neumann entropy with the exponential functional form and Laplacian L_1 shows the best fitting with an adjusted-R-squared of 0.34. The corresponding estimated response variables are reported in Figure 3.7. Von Neumann entropies with exponential functional form together Laplacian L_1 (solid line) and with linear functional form together with Laplacian L_2 (dashed line), $S(\rho_{E1})$ and $S(\rho_{L2})$, respectively, provide the best fit with the actual crises indicator (stepwise red

Table 3.2 Logit specification where the dependent variable is the banking crisis indicator from Alessi and Detken [2014a] and the explanatory variables are from the European Granger Network (columns): 1) Dynamic causality index (DCI) as proposed in Billio et al. [2012]; 2) Shannon entropy on In-Out degree (H) as in Billio et al. [2016]; 3) $S(\rho_{L_1})$ indicates the Von Neumann entropy with the linear functional form and Laplacian L_1; 4) $S(\rho_{L_2})$ indicates the Von Neumann entropy with the linear functional form and Laplacian L_2; 5) $S(\rho_{E_1})$ indicates the Von Neumann entropy with the exponential functional form and Laplacian L_1; 6) $S(\rho_{E_2})$ indicates the Von Neumann entropy with the exponential functional form and Laplacian L_2 and 7) μ indicates the disagreement persistence. Significance level: 1% (***). Standard errors in parentheses. The number of observations are 3,187.

	DCI	H	$S(\rho_{L1})$	$S(\rho_{L2})$	$S(\rho_{E1})$	$S(\rho_{E1})$	μ
β_0	0.54***	−22.35***	−1009***	−3.11***	−4717***	−2838741***	4.25***
	(0.13)	(1.29)	(36.78)	(1.07)	(173.74)	(134373)	(0.16)
β_1	−4.10***	25.16***	1012***	3.22***	4719***	2838742***	10.25***
	(0.70)	(1.47)	(36.87)	(1.19)	(173.83)	(134373)	(0.37)
Adj-R²	0.01	0.010	0.33	0.010	0.32	0.34	0.28
AIC	4356	4054	3149	4383	3208	3068	3360
BIC	4368	4066	3162	4395	3220	3080	3372

line) defined in Equation 37. It is worth noting that the estimated response variable in all the logit model specifications returns a high probability level of crisis in correspondence of the European sovereign debt crisis after a recovery from the global financial crisis in 2007 and 2008.

7.3. EWI evaluation and loss function

In the previous section we compare the models by applying some goodness of fit statistical measures. In practice an economic comparison is needed, especially when policymakers are interested using early warning signals to detect vulnerabilities in the financial system according to the indicators of interest (i.e., banking crises). For detecting crisis events using information from indicator C_t, we use $\hat{\Phi}_t = \Phi(\hat{\beta}_0 + \hat{\beta}_1 S_t)$, the predicted probability of crisis returned by the logit model. Then, the predicted probability is turned into a binary prediction, which takes the value of 1 if $\hat{\Phi}_t$ exceeds a specified threshold c and 0 otherwise, i.e.,

$$\hat{C}_t = \begin{cases} 1 & \text{if } \hat{\Phi}_t \geq c, \\ 0 & \text{otherwise.} \end{cases} \tag{39}$$

We set the threshold $c = 0.50$.[6] The key aspect of these models is the forecast evaluation and therefore the quality of the issued signals. In fact, policymakers aim to distinguish for two type of potential errors: the missed crisis (type 1 error) and the false signal of crisis (type 2 error). Therefore, the pairs of values of the actual and predicted crisis $(C_t, \hat{C}_t)$ can form four possible

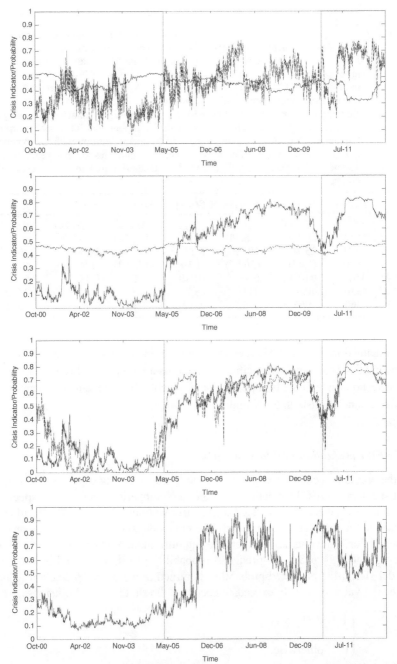

Figure 3.7 Overview of the actual (stepwise red lines) defined in Equation 37 and the estimated response variable over time: (*first panel*) Dynamic causality index (DCI, solid line) as proposed in Billio et al. [2012] and Shannon entropy on In-Out degree (dashed line) as in Billio et al. [2016]; (*second panel*) Von Neumann entropies with linear functional form and Laplacian L_1 (solid line) and Laplacian L_2 (dashed line); (*third panel*) Von Neumann entropies with exponential functional form and Laplacian L_1 (solid line) and Laplacian L_2 (dashed line) and (*fourth panel*) μ indicates the Disagreement persistence (solid line).

	Crisis ($C_t = 1$)	Not crisis ($C_t = 0$)
Signal issued ($\hat{C}_t = 1$)	Correct signal *(true positive, TP)*	False alarm *(false positive, FP)*
No signal issued ($\hat{C}_t = 0$)	Missed crisis *(false negative, FN)*	Correct no signal *(true negative, TN)*

Figure 3.8 The contingency matrix for the crises indicator C_t and the binary predictor $\hat{C}_t$. The type 1 error (T_1) represents the share of missed crises on the total crises, $FN/(TP + FN)$, while the type 2 error (T_2) represents the share of issued false alarms on the total tranquil periods, $FP/(TN+ FP)$. The percentage of correctly predicted indicators is the correct signal (TP) and no signal (TN) over the possible situations.

combinations: both equal to 1 or 0, or different. We can represent those values into a contingency matrix [see Alessi and Detken, 2014b, Duca and Peltonen, 2013, Holopainen and Sarlin, 2016, Sarlin, 2013] which describes this relationship as reported in Figure 3.8.

The type 1 error (T_1) represents the share of missed crises on the total crises,

$$\frac{FN}{TP + FN}, \tag{40}$$

while the type 2 error (T_2) represents the share of issued false alarms on the total tranquil periods,

$$\frac{FP}{TN + FP}. \tag{41}$$

The percentage of correctly predicted indicators is the correct signal (TP) and correct no signal (TN) over the total realizations. We evaluate the impact of the two type of errors using a loss function. In this regard, we adopt the one proposed by Alessi and Detken [2014b] L which is simple to implement and robust to small perturbations,

$$L(\theta) = \theta T_1 + (1 - \theta)T_2, \tag{42}$$

where θ is the relative risk aversion parameter of the decision maker among type 1 and type 2 errors. If $\theta > 0.5$, the aversion is greater for missing a crisis (false negative) than a false alarm (false positive). As suggested by Alessi and Detken [2014b], we set θ equal to 0.5 since it is uncommon to have preferences for values above this value among the financial stability community. If the binary predictor performs perfectly the value of the loss function is 0. Conversely, the worst it performs the more is close to 1. Other robust methods such as the ROC curve can be used to evaluate the TP and TN by varying the threshold [e.g., see Drehmann and Juselius, 2014]. Table 3.3 reports the results of the predicted crises specified according to the contingency matrix. Results show the goodness of the Von Neumann entropies and the disagreement persistence index with respect to the DCI and the Shannon entropy on the In-Out degree.

Table 3.3 Percentage of correctly predicted banking crises with the logit models using: a) Dynamic causality index (DCI) as proposed in Billio et al. [2012]; b) Shannon entropy on In-Out degree as in Billio et al. [2016]; c) $S(\rho_{L_1})$ indicates the Von Neumann entropy with the linear functional form and Laplacian L_1; d) $S(\rho_{L_2})$ indicates the Von Neumann entropy with the linear functional form and Laplacian L_2; e) $S(\rho_{E_1})$ indicates the Von Neumann entropy with the exponential functional form and Laplacian L_1; f) $S(\rho_{E_2})$ indicates the Von Neumann entropy with the exponential functional form and Laplacian E_2 and g) μ indicates the disagreement persistence index. Banking crisis indicators are defined as more than one countries on crisis. The data are from Alessi and Detken [2014a]. T_1 and T_2 represent the share of missed crises on the total crises ($FN/(TP + FN)$) and the share of issued false alarms on the total tranquil periods ($FP/(TN + FP)$), respectively. The percentage of correctly predicted indicators is the correct signal (TP) and no signal (TN) over the possible situations. $L(\theta)$ is the loss function and θ represents the relative risk aversion parameter of the decision maker among type 1 and type 2 errors.

	DCI	H	$S(\rho_{L_1})$	$S(\rho_{L_2})$	$S(\rho_{E_1})$	$S(\rho_{E_2})$	μ
correctly predicted	0.59	0.67	0.78	0.48	0.79	0.80	0.71
TP	0.31	0.31	0.41	0.23	0.41	0.43	0.34
TN	0.29	0.36	0.37	0.25	0.38	0.37	0.37
FP	0.26	0.19	0.18	0.30	0.17	0.18	0.18
FN	0.14	0.14	0.04	0.22	0.04	0.02	0.11
T_1	0.32	0.31	0.09	0.49	0.10	0.05	0.24
T_2	0.48	0.34	0.33	0.54	0.30	0.33	0.33
$L(\theta = 0.5)$	0.40	0.33	0.21	0.51	0.20	0.19	0.28
$L(\theta = 0.4)$	0.42	0.33	0.23	0.22	0.22	0.22	0.29
$L(\theta = 0.3)$	0.43	0.33	0.26	0.53	0.24	0.25	0.30

In particular, the Von Neumann entropy with the exponential functional form and Laplacian L_2, $S(\rho_{E_2})$, shows the lowest value in the loss function (0.19) with the highest true positive (TP) and the lowest false negative (FN) values. Moreover, the Von Neumann entropy with the exponential functional form and the Laplacian L_2 shows the lowest type 2 errors (T_2) while the exponential one with Laplacian L_1 shows the lowest type 1 errors (T_1). Since $S(\rho_{E_2})$ has a higher T_1 but a lower T_2 with respect to the $S(\rho_{E_1})$, if we set a lower value for θ, the loss function penalizes more T_2 errors and consequently $S(\rho_{E_1})$. By selecting $\theta = 0.4$, both the Von Neumann entropies with the exponential functional form perform equally well, while for values below or equal to 0.3 the entropy with the Laplacian L_1 performs better.

8. Conclusion

In this paper, we provide a graph theoretic background for the analysis of financial networks and review some technique recently proposed for the extraction of financial networks. We develop new measures of network connectivity based on the notion of Von Neumann entropy and show that they account for global connectivity patterns given by paths and walks of the network. We apply the new measures to a sequence of inferred pairwise-Granger networks. In the application, we show how to use the proposed measures to achieve effective immunization of the financial system from the spread of contagion. Finally, we show that entropy measures can be successfully employed to generate early warning signals for banking crises.

Notes

* We thank the conference participants at the International Conference on Econometrics and Statistics (EcoSta 2017) in Hong Kong, the 10th CSDA International Conference on Computational and Financial Econometrics (CFE 2016) in Seville (Spain) and the Mathematical and Statistical Methods for Actuarial Sciences and Finance (MAF 2016) in Paris (France) for their helpful comments. Michele Costola acknowledges financial support from the Marie Skłodowska-Curie Actions, European Union, Seventh Framework Program HORIZON 2020 under REA grant agreement n. 707070. He also gratefully acknowledges research support from the Research Center SAFE, funded by the State of Hessen initiative for research LOEWE. The computation has been performed using Matlab through the SCSCF (Sistema di Calcolo Scientifico Ca' Foscari) cluster.
1 The concept of the eigenvector centrality could be applied to the directed network, but since the adjacency matrix is not symmetric the right and the left eigenvector are different.
2 The Kronecker delta δ_{xy} is a function of two variables which is equal to 1 if they are equal and 0 otherwise.
3 As calculated in Equation 6 above.
4 φ satisfies the equation: $\varphi P = \lambda \varphi$, where λ is the associated eigenvalue and $\sum_{i=1}^{n} \varphi_i = 1$.
5 The rolling-window estimations have been parallelized and implemented in Matlab. It takes approximately 72 hours on the SCSCF (Sistema di Calcolo Scientifico Ca' Foscari) cluster multiprocessor system which consists of 4 nodes; each comprises

four Xeon E5-4610 v2 2.3GHz CPUs, with 8 cores, 256GB ECC PC3-12800R RAM, Ethernet 10Gbit, 20TB hard disk system with Linux.
6   As defined in Equation 17 in Billio et al. [2016].

Bibliography

Adrian, T., and Brunnermeier, M. K. (2016). Covar. *The American Economic Review*, 106(7):1705–1741.

Ahelegbey, D. F., Billio, M., and Casarin, R. (2016a). Bayesian graphical models for structural vector autoregressive processes. *Journal of Applied Econometrics*, 2(31):357–386.

Ahelegbey, D. F., Billio, M., and Casarin, R. (2016b). Sparse graphical multivariate autoregression: A Bayesian approach. *Annals of Economics and Statistics*, 123(124):1–30.

Alessi, L., and Detken, C. (2014a). *Identifying Excessive Credit Growth and Leverage*. ECB Working Paper, N. 1723.

Alessi, L., and Detken, C. (2014b). On policymakers' loss functions and the evaluation of early warning systems: Comment. *Economics Letters*, 124(3):338–340.

Babecky, J., Havranek, T., Mateju, J., Rusnák, M., Smidkova, K., and Vasicek, B. (2014). Banking, debt and currency crises: Early warning indicators for developed countries: Stylized facts and early warning indicators. *Journal of Financial Stability*, 15(C):1–17.

Billio, M., Casarin, R., Costola, M., and Pasqualini, A. (2016). An entropy-based early warning indicator for systemic risk. *Journal of International Financial Markets, Institutions and Money*, 45:42–59.

Billio, M., Getmansky, M., Lo, A. W., and Pelizzon, L. (2012). Econometric measures of connectedness and systemic risk in the finance and insurance sectors. *Journal of Financial Economics*, 104(3):535–559.

Boley, D., Ranjan, G., and Zhang, Z.-L. (2011). Commute times for a directed graph using an asymmetric laplacian. *Linear Algebra and Its Applications*, 435(2):224–242.

Bollobás, B. (1998). *Modern Graph Theory*. Springer.

Bollobás, B. (2001). *Random Graphs*. Cambridge University Press.

Bonacich, P. (1987). Family and centrality: A family of measures. *American Journal of Sociology*, 92(5):1170–1182.

Bonacich, P. (2007). Some unique properties of eigenvector centrality. *Social Networks*, 29:555–564.

Braunstein, S. L., Ghosh, S., and Severini, S. (2006). The laplacian of a graph as a density matrix: a basic combinatorial approach to separability of mixed states. *Annals of Combinatorics*, 10(3):291–317.

Carlin, B. I., Longsta, F. A., and Matoba, K. (2014). Disagreement and asset prices. *Journal of Financial Economics*, 114(2):226–238.

Chung, F. (2005). Laplacians and the cheeger inequality for directed graphs. *Annals of Combinatorics*, 9(1):1–19.

Das, S. R., and Uppal, R. (2004). Systemic risk and international portfolio choice. *The Journal of Finance*, 59(6):2809–2834.

DeGroot, M. H. (1974). Reaching a consensus. *Journal of the American Statistical Association*, 69(345):118–121.

DeMarzo, P. M., Vayanos, D., and Zwiebel, J. (2003). Persuasion bias, social influence, and unidimensional opinions. *The Quarterly Journal of Economics*, 118(3):909–968.

Demirgüç-Kunt, A., and Detragiache, E. (1999). *Monitoring Banking Sector Fragility: A Multivariate Logit Approach With an Application to the 1996–97 Banking Crises*. World Bank Policy Research Working Paper, N. 2085.

Diebold, F. X., and Yılmaz, K. (2014). On the network topology of variance decom positions: Measuring the connectedness of financial firms. *Journal of Econometrics*, 182(1):
119–134.

Diebold, F. X., and Yilmaz, K. (2015). *Financial and Macroeconomic Connectedness: A
Network Approach to Measurement and Monitoring*. Oxford University Press.

Drehmann, M., and Juselius, M. (2014). Evaluating early warning indicators of banking
crises: Satisfying policy requirements. *International Journal of Forecasting*, 30(3):759–
780.

Duca, M. L., and Peltonen, T. A. (2013). Assessing systemic risks and predicting systemic
events. *Journal of Banking & Finance*, 37(7):2183–2195.

Garnerone, S., Giorda, P., and Zanardi, P. (2012). Bipartite quantum states and random
complex networks. *New Journal of Physics*, 14(1):013011.

Golob, B., and Jackson, M. O. (2010). Naive learning in social networks and the wisdom
of crowds. *American Economic Journal: Microeconomics*, 2(1):112–149.

Holopainen, M., and Sarlin, P. (2016). *Toward Robust Early-Warning Models: A Horse
Race, Ensembles and Model Uncertainty*. ECB Working Paper, N. 1900.

Jackson, M. O. (2008). *Social and Economic Networks*. Princeton University Press.

Katz, L. (1953). A new status index derived from sociometric analysis. *Psychometrika*,
18(1):39–43.

Li, Y., and Zhang, Z.-L. (2012). Digraph laplacian and the degree of asymmetry. *Internet
Math.*, 8(4):381–401.

Newman, M. E. (2002). Assortative mixing in networks. *Physical Review Letters*, 89(20):
208701.

Newman, M. E. (2003). Mixing patterns in networks. *Physical Review E*, 67(2):026126.

Newman, M. E. (2010). *Networks: An introduction*. Oxford University Press.

Olfati-Saber, R., Fax, J. A., and Murray, R. M. (2007). Consensus and cooperation in net-
worked multi-agent systems. *Proceedings of the IEEE*, 95(1):215–233.

Paltalidis, N., Gounopoulos, D., Kizys, R., and Koutelidakis, Y. (2015). Transmission
channels of systemic risk and contagion in the european financial network. *Journal
of Banking & Finance*, 61:S36–S52.

Parikh, R., and Krasucki, P. (1990). Communication, consensus, and knowledge. *Journal
of Economic Theory*, 52(1):178–189.

Passerini, F., and Severini, S. (2009). Quantifying complexity in networks: The Von Neu
mann entropy. *International Journal of Agent Technologies and Systems*, 1(4):58–67.

Sarlin, P. (2013). On policymakers' loss functions and the evaluation of early warning
systems. *Economics Letters*, 119(1):1–7.

Ye, C., Wilson, R. C., Comin, C. H., Costa, L. D. F., and Hancock, E. R. (2014). Approx
imate Von Neumann entropy for directed graphs. *Physical Review E*, 89(5):052804.

Zivot, E., and Wang, J. (2003). *Modelling Financial Time Series With S-Plus*. Springer.

Appendix A

Proofs of the results in the paper

A.1. Proof of theorem 1

- Let $L = L_1$, $B = \varphi^{1/2}P\varphi^{-1/2}$ and $C = \varphi^{-1/2}P'\varphi^{1/2}$. Note that

$$B^l C^{r-l} = \underbrace{(\varphi^{1/2}P\varphi^{-1/2} \cdots \varphi^{1/2}P\varphi^{-1/2})}_{l \text{ times}}\underbrace{(\varphi^{-1/2}P'\varphi^{1/2} \cdots \varphi^{-1/2}P'\varphi^{1/2})}_{r-1 \text{ times}}$$

$$= \varphi^{1/2}P'\varphi^{-1/2}\varphi^{-1/2}(P')^{r-l}\varphi^{1/2} = \varphi^{1/2}P'\varphi^{-1}(P')^{r-l}\varphi^{1/2}$$

then

$$\operatorname{tr}(L^m) = \operatorname{tr}(I^m) + \sum_{k=0}^{m-1}\binom{m}{k}(-2)^{-(m-k)}\operatorname{tr}((B+C)^{m-k})$$

$$= n + \sum_{k=0}^{m-1}\binom{m}{k}(-2)^{-(m-k)}\sum_{l=0}^{m-k}\binom{m-k}{l}\operatorname{tr}(P'\varphi^{-1}(P')^{m-k-l}\varphi) \tag{43}$$

The results follows by considering that the (i, j)-th element of P^q is equal to the (j, i)-th element of $(P')^q$ which is

$$W_{ij}^{(q)} = \sum_{i_2} \cdots \sum_{i_q}\prod_{r=1}^{q}P_{i_r i_{r+1}} = \sum_{i_2 \cdots i_q}\prod_{r=1}^{q}a_{i_r i_{r+1}}\frac{1}{d_{i_r}^-}$$

where $i_1 = i$ and $i_{q+1} = j$, and by applying the definition of trace

$$\operatorname{tr}(P'\varphi^{-1}(P')^{r-l}\varphi) = \sum_{i=1}^{n}\sum_{h=1}^{n}W_{ih}^{(l)}W_{ih}^{(r-l)}\varphi_i\varphi_h^{-1}$$

- Let $L = L_2$ and $B = \varphi P + P'\varphi^{-1}$, then

$$\operatorname{tr}(L^m) = \operatorname{tr}(\varphi^m) + \sum_{k=0}^{m-1}\binom{m}{k}(-2)^{-(m-k)}\operatorname{tr}(\varphi^k B^{m-k}) \tag{44}$$

Let $R^{(k)} = \varphi^k B^{m-k}$ with (i, j)-th element

$$(\varphi^k B^{m-k})_{ij} = \varphi_i^k W_{ij}^{(m-k)}$$

where

$$W_{ij}^{(q)} = \sum_{i_2=1}^{n} \cdots \sum_{i_q=1}^{n} \prod_{r=1}^{q} \left(\frac{\varphi_{i_r}}{d_{i_r}^-} a_{i_r i_{r+1}} + a_{i_{r+1} i_r} \frac{1}{\varphi_{i_{r+1}} d_{i_{r+1}}^-} \right)$$

is the (i, j)-th element of $W^{(q)} = B^q$ one obtains

$$\text{tr}(L^m) = \sum_{i=1}^{n} \varphi_i^m + \sum_{k=0}^{m-1} \binom{m}{k} (-2)^{-(m-k)} \text{tr}(R^{(k)}) \tag{45}$$

A.2. Proof of theorem 2

Note that the Von Neumann entropy can be rewritten in terms of trace of the Laplacian, that is

$$S^{(M)}(\lambda_i) = \frac{1}{n} \text{tr}(\tilde{L}_i^{(M)}) - \frac{1}{n^2} \text{tr}((\tilde{L}_i^{(M)})^2) \tag{46}$$

where λ_i is the vector of eigenvalues of $\tilde{L}_i^{(M)}$.

By replacing $L_1^{(M)}$ by its definition with $M = 1$ and by applying the results in Theorem 1 one obtains

$$S^{(M)}(\lambda_1) = \frac{1}{n} \text{tr}(I + L_1) - \frac{1}{n^2} \text{tr}((I + L_1)^2)$$

$$= 2 - \frac{3}{n} - \frac{1}{n^2} \text{tr}(L_1^2) \tag{47}$$

$$= 2 - \frac{3}{n} - \frac{1}{n^2} \left(\frac{1}{4} (\text{tr}(P') + 2\text{tr}(\varphi P \varphi^{-1} P') + \text{tr}(P^2)) - 2\frac{1}{2} (\text{tr}(P') + \text{tr}(P)) \right)$$

$$= 2 - \frac{3}{n} - \frac{1}{4n^2} (2\text{tr}(P^2) + 2\text{tr}(\varphi P \varphi^{-1} P')) \tag{48}$$

by using the fact that $\text{tr}(P') = \text{tr}(P) = 0$ since the transition matrix P has zero elements on the main diagonal. This entropy can be decomposed further using out- and in-degree of the node following Ye et al. [2014].

For $L_2^{(M)}$ we have instead

$$S^{(M)}(\lambda_2) = \frac{1}{n} \text{tr}(I + L_1) - \frac{1}{n^2} \text{tr}((I + L_1)^2)$$

$$= 1 - \frac{2}{n^2} + \left(\frac{1}{n} - \frac{2}{n^2} \right) (\text{tr}(P(\varphi + \varphi^{-1})/2)) \tag{49}$$

$$- \frac{1}{n^2} \left(\sum_{i=1}^{n} \varphi_i^2 + \frac{1}{4} (\text{tr}((\varphi P)^2) + \text{tr}((P'\varphi^{-1})^2) + \text{tr}(P'P) + \text{tr}(PP')) - \text{tr}(\varphi^2 P) \right)$$

By replacing $L_1^{(M)}$ by its definition with $M = 2$ and by applying the results in Theorem 1 one obtains

$$S^{(M)}(\lambda_1) = \frac{1}{n}\mathrm{tr}(I + L_1 + L_1^2) - \frac{1}{n^2}\mathrm{tr}\left(I + 2L_1 + L_1^2 + \frac{3}{2}L_1^3 + \frac{1}{4}L_1^4\right)$$

$$= 2 - \frac{3}{n} - \frac{2}{n^2}\mathrm{tr}(L_1^2) - \frac{1}{n^2}\mathrm{tr}(L_1^3) - \frac{1}{4n^2}\mathrm{tr}(L_1^4)$$

$$= 2 - \frac{3}{n} - \frac{2}{n^2}\sum_{k=0}^{1}\sum_{l=0}^{2-k}\omega_{lk}\mathrm{tr}(R^{(lk)}) - \frac{1}{n^2}\sum_{k=0}^{2}\sum_{l=0}^{3-k}\omega_{lk}\mathrm{tr}(R^{(lk)}) - \frac{1}{4n^2}\mathrm{tr}(\sum_{k=0}^{3}\sum_{l=0}^{4-k}\omega_{lk}\mathrm{tr}(R^{(lk)}))$$

$$= 2 - \frac{25}{4n} - \frac{1}{n^2}\left(\sum_{k=0}^{3}\sum_{l=0}^{4-k}\tilde{\omega}_{lk}\mathrm{tr}(R^{(lk)})\right)$$

$$\tag{50}$$

with

$$\tilde{\omega}_{00} = \frac{13}{4}\omega_{00}, \ \tilde{\omega}_{10} = \frac{13}{4}\omega_{10}, \ \tilde{\omega}_{20} = \frac{13}{4}\omega_{20}, \ \tilde{\omega}_{30} = \frac{5}{4}\omega_{30}, \ \tilde{\omega}_{40} = \frac{1}{4}\omega_{40}$$

$$\tilde{\omega}_{01} = \frac{13}{4}\omega_{01}, \ \tilde{\omega}_{11} = \frac{13}{4}\omega_{11}, \ \tilde{\omega}_{21} = \frac{5}{4}\omega_{21}, \ \tilde{\omega}_{31} = \frac{1}{4}\omega_{31}$$

$$\tilde{\omega}_{02} = \frac{5}{4}\omega_{02}, \ \tilde{\omega}_{12} = \frac{5}{4}\omega_{12}, \ \tilde{\omega}_{22} = \frac{1}{4}\omega_{22}$$

$$\tilde{\omega}_{03} = \frac{1}{4}\omega_{03}, \ \tilde{\omega}_{13} = \frac{1}{4}\omega_{13}$$

where we used $\mathrm{tr}(L_1) = n$.

By replacing $L_2^{(M)}$ by its definition with $M = 2$ and by applying the results in Theorem 1 one obtains

$$S^{(M)}(\lambda_2) = 2 - \frac{3}{n} - \frac{2}{n^2}\mathrm{tr}(L_2^2) - \frac{1}{n^2}\mathrm{tr}(L_2^3) - \frac{1}{4n^2}\mathrm{tr}(L_2^4)$$

$$= 2 - \frac{3}{n} - \frac{2}{n^2}\left(\sum_{i=1}^{n}\varphi_i^2 + \sum_{k=0}^{1}\omega_k\mathrm{tr}(R^{(k)})\right) - \frac{1}{n^2}\left(\sum_{i=1}^{n}\varphi_i^3 + \sum_{k=0}^{2}\omega_k\mathrm{tr}(R^{(k)})\right)$$

$$- \frac{1}{4n^2}\left(\sum_{i=1}^{n}\varphi_i^4 + \sum_{k=0}^{3}\omega_k\mathrm{tr}(R^{(k)})\right)$$

$$= 2 - \frac{3}{n} - \frac{1}{n^2}\sum_{k=0}^{3}\tilde{\omega}_k\mathrm{tr}(R^{(k)})$$

$$\tag{51}$$

with

$$\tilde{\omega}_0 = \frac{13}{4}\omega_0, \ \tilde{\omega}_1 = \frac{13}{4}\omega_1, \ \tilde{\omega}_2 = \frac{5}{4}\omega_2, \ \tilde{\omega}_3 = \frac{1}{4}\omega_3$$

A.3. Proof of corollary 1

Consider $S^{(M)}(\lambda_1)$ given in Equation 25 with $M = 1$, and note that $\mathrm{tr}(L_1) = n$, then

$$S^{(1)}(\lambda_1) - S_Q = 2 - \frac{3}{n} - \frac{1}{n^2}\mathrm{tr}(L_1^2) - \left(\frac{1}{n}\mathrm{tr}(L_1) - \frac{1}{n^2}\mathrm{tr}(L_1^2)\right) = 1 - \frac{3}{n} \qquad (52)$$

A.4. Proof of theorem 3

In order to prove Theorem 3 we need the following lemma

Lemma 1 Given the matrix $M = \varphi^{1/2}P_L\varphi^{-1/2}$ we have

$$\max_{\varphi'\mathbf{v}=0} \frac{\mathbf{v}'P_L'\varphi P_L\mathbf{v}}{\mathbf{v}'\varphi\mathbf{v}} = \max_{\varphi^{1/2}\mathbf{u}=0} \frac{\mathbf{u}'M'M\mathbf{u}}{\mathbf{u}'\mathbf{u}} \leq \mu$$

Proof.

$$\max_{\varphi'\mathbf{v}=0} \frac{\mathbf{v}'P_L'\varphi P_L\mathbf{v}}{\mathbf{v}'\varphi\mathbf{v}} = \max_{\varphi\varphi^{-1/2}\varphi^{1/2}\mathbf{v}=0} \frac{\mathbf{v}'\varphi^{1/2}\varphi^{-1/2}P_L'\varphi^{1/2}\varphi^{1/2}P_L\varphi^{-1/2}\varphi^{1/2}\varphi^{1/2}\mathbf{v}}{\mathbf{v}'\varphi^{1/2}\varphi^{1/2}\mathbf{v}}$$

$$= \max_{\varphi^{1/2}\mathbf{u}=0} \frac{\mathbf{u}'M'M\mathbf{u}}{\mathbf{u}'\mathbf{u}}$$

According to Chung [2005] we can bound the last term using the second eigenvalue λ_2 of the symmetrized Laplacian L

$$\max_{\varphi^{1/2}\mathbf{u}=0} \frac{\mathbf{u}'M'M\mathbf{u}}{\mathbf{u}'\mathbf{u}} \leq 1 - \frac{\lambda_2}{2}$$

Li and Zhang [2012] give a tighter bound:

$$\max_{\varphi^{1/2}\mathbf{u}=0} \frac{\mathbf{u}'M'M\mathbf{u}}{\mathbf{u}'\mathbf{u}} \leq \frac{3}{4} - \frac{\lambda_2}{2} + \frac{(\sigma_{n-1}(I_n - L) + \sigma_n(\Delta))^2}{4}$$

In addition, using the primitivity of P and the results in theorem 4.3 in Li and Zhang [2012], $\mu < 1$.

$\square$

To show the results in Theorem 3, we note that

$$\varphi'\xi_t = \varphi'\mathbf{x}_t - \alpha\varphi'\mathbf{1} = 0 \qquad (53)$$

So the disagreement vector satisfies, at any time, the constraint imposed on the maximization of the quotient in Lemma 1.

Let $V(t) = \xi_t'\varphi\xi_t$ a candidate Lyapunov function for the system (34). It is a valid candidate because it is well known that the Perron vector φ is strictly positive and so $V(t) = 0$ if and only if ξ_t is equal to the zero vector. Then a bound on

$V(t + 1)$ is easily obtained using Lemma 1:

$$
\begin{aligned}
V(t+1) & = \xi'_{t+1}\varphi\xi_{t+1} = \xi'_t P'_L \varphi P_L \xi_t \\
& \leq \mu\xi'_t\varphi\xi_t \\
& \leq \mu V(t)
\end{aligned}
$$

since $\mu < 1$ the system is asymptotically stable. Accordingly we have

$$
\min(\varphi)\xi'_t\xi_t \leq \xi'_t\varphi\xi_t \leq \mu^t\xi'_0\varphi\xi_0 \leq \max(\varphi)\mu^t\xi'_0\xi_0
$$

from which the result follows.

4 Quantifying informational linkages in a global model of currency spot markets

Matthew Greenwood-Nimmo, Viet Nguyen, and Yongcheol Shin

1. Introduction

Among the most influential papers studying the transmission of information between financial markets is that of Engle, Ito, and Lin (1990), which likens the transmission of volatility between markets to a *meteor shower*. Subsequent studies of volatility transmission across currency markets in a similar vein include Fung and Patterson (1999), Melvin and Melvin (2003) and Cai, Howorka, and Wongswan (2008). The considerable weight of evidence of volatility transmission across markets is highly suggestive of underlying informational linkages between markets. However, the study of volatility transmission alone cannot shed light on the mechanisms by which trading information in one market affects prices in another.

The microstructure literature has opened new avenues to model these informational linkages directly. This literature exploits information about the trading process to develop microstructure exchange rate models with superior in- and out-of-sample performance to the class of macro exchange rate models. In a seminal contribution, Evans and Lyons (2002b) develop a static portfolio shifts model that explains how trading activity affects price determination in a currency market. Evans and Lyons (2002a) subsequently extend this model into a multi-currency setting to explain how trading activity in one market can influence prices in other markets, thereby shedding new light on the mechanism of cross-market linkages. Within this framework, the order flow (defined as the number of buyer-initiated orders less the number of seller-initiated orders) plays an important role, as it conveys public information about fundamentals as well as traders' private information or beliefs about fundamentals (Evans and Lyons, 2002b; Evans and Lyons, 2008; Love and Payne, 2008).

The portfolio shifts models represent an important benchmark in the literature and have been widely applied in recent studies, including those of Berger, Chaboud, Chernenko, Howorka, and Wright (2008), Rime, Sarno, and Sojli (2010) and Daníelsson, Luo, and Payne (2012). Nevertheless, the Evans and Lyons approach suffers from one principal limitation, namely that price-order flow interactions and cross-market linkages are addressed only in a static setting under the strong assumptions of continuous market equilibrium and unidirectional causality running from order flow to price. In practice, however, it is widely documented that the collective action of imperfectly informed noise traders may frequently cause the market to under- or over-react with respect to fundamentals and that various risks in the financial markets and/or synchronization problems may limit the arbitrage of rational traders (e.g., DeLong, Shleifer, Summers, and Waldmann, 1990; Barberis, Shleifer, and Vishny, 1998; Abreu and Brunnermeier, 2002). Consequently, we may observe persistent mispricing and significant episodes of market disequilibrium.

We contribute to the literature on currency market linkages by deriving a dynamic error correction representation of the Evans and Lyons (2002a) multi-currency portfolio shifts model. Our model explicitly addresses the concern raised by Sager and Taylor (2006) that dealers may find themselves holding overnight imbalances as a result of mispricing. We then develop a well-specified empirical analogue of our dynamic multi-currency portfolio shifts model using the global vector autoregressive (GVAR) framework advanced by Pesaran, Schuermann, and Weiner (2004) and Dees, di Mauro, Pesaran, and Smith (2007). The GVAR model is built by combining market-specific VAR models using so-called link matrices, which contain granular weights used in the construction of cross-sectional averages of the market-specific data.

The GVAR framework is uniquely well suited to the analysis of informational linkages across markets. By virtue of its vector autoregressive form combined with its ability to exploit the panel structure of the price and trading data across markets, the GVAR model explicitly accounts for the dynamic interactions between prices and order flows simultaneously and across all of the currency markets in the system. Specifically, the GVAR model captures the interactions across currency markets through two distinct channels: (i) the price and order flow in market i depend directly on the contemporaneous and lagged values of the weighted average order flow from the other markets in the system, $j \neq i$; and (ii) the weak correlation of shocks across different currency markets. This structure allows for an explicit treatment of the effect of trading information in one market on the prices and order flows observed in other markets.

Our GVAR model significantly extends the frontier demarcated by the existing empirical literature in a number of directions. Unlike the majority of the dynamic literature, which deduces information about the underlying linkages among markets via the analysis of volatility spillovers (e.g., Fung and Patterson, 1999; Melvin and Melvin, 2003), we directly model the dynamic linkages between prices and order flows in a framework that is firmly rooted in the theoretical work of Evans and Lyons (2002b). Of the existing dynamic models, ours is most closely related to that of Cai et al. (2008), which studies the transmission of information between five different trading centres (Asia Pacific, the Asia–Europe overlap, Europe, the Europe–America overlap, and America). They estimate separate VAR models for a variety of different informational proxies including both volatility and the order flow. In this way, they find that local information (i.e., within-region) tends to dominate spillovers between regions in terms of economic significance. However, our model differs from theirs in two crucial respects. First, since Cai et al. estimate separate VAR models for each of their informational proxies, their approach cannot illuminate the linkage between price and order flow, which is central to the portfolio shifts model of Evans and Lyons (2002b). Second, and on a closely related note, Cai et al.'s analysis is based on the trading of the same currency pair (e.g., trading the dollar versus the yen) across different regional trading centres. As such, their model cannot address spillovers *between* currency pairs, which is essential if one wishes to capture the rebalancing of investor portfolios in response to shocks and to uncover how trading in one currency may affect prices and order flows in another.

Our framework is also considerably more general than the static models employed by Evans and Lyons (2002a) and more recently by Daníelsson et al. (2012). Both of these studies analyze a separate single equation model for each market in their respective datasets, where the price of currency i is assumed to depend on both the order flow for currency i and the order flows for other currencies $j \neq i$. At an elementary level, unlike the dynamic models discussed above, static models must inherently abstract from the possibility that prices may not fully adjust to reflect new information within the trading day. More subtly, however, the use of a single-equation framework implies that the trading information from all markets – including the domestic market – is exogenous, which reduces the scope for contemporaneous interactions among markets. For example, such a model cannot directly account for the possibility that foreign order flows may induce local order flows that, in turn, may affect prices. By contrast, the GVAR model distinguishes between within-market information (which is treated as endogenous) and between-market information (which is treated as weakly exogenous). Weak exogeneity testing strongly supports the validity of this distinction in our dataset. Thus, the GVAR model enjoys a number of methodological advantages relative to the approaches that have been adopted in the existing literature. In particular, it allows the modeler to account for both the *direct association* between prices and order flows as well as the *dynamic interactions* among prices and order flows in all currency markets. At the time of writing, we are unaware of any existing studies that have addressed both of these issues.

Given that the GVAR model is essentially a large VAR model, it can be readily transformed into its vector moving average form, based on which it is straightforward to apply all of the standard tools of dynamic analysis, including impulse response analysis and forecast error variance decomposition. Furthermore, we demonstrate that the connectedness methodology developed by Diebold and Yilmaz (2009, 2014) can be applied to explore the network topology of a simple GVAR model such as ours without difficulty. Using these tools, and adopting the terminology of Engle et al. (1990), we evaluate the importance of heatwave (within-market or local) effects and meteor shower (between-market or foreign) effects for each of the markets in our sample. Moreover, by comparing the strength of the meteor shower from market j to market i against the heatwave effect in market i, we develop a novel data-driven method to identify leader-recipient relationships between pairs of markets. Finally, by studying the trading patterns across all markets following local currency selling pressure in the *i*-th market, we are able to identify safe haven currencies with respect to currency *i* in a data-driven manner.[1]

Our GVAR model allows us to map out the complex network of interlinkages among the currency markets in the Evans and Lyons dataset in considerable detail for the first time. Our results unambiguously confirm the central contention of the order flow literature – order flow is an important determinant of the price. Furthermore, in keeping with the literature on information transmission across markets, we find that the order flow in market *j* exerts a non-negligible influence on the trading behaviors and prices observed in other markets, particularly if market *j* is a large, heavily-traded and liquid market (Daníelsson et al., 2012).

Our dataset is drawn from the classic order flow dataset of Evans and Lyons (2002a, b), which has subsequently underpinned notable papers by Cao, Evans, and Lyons (2006), Evans and Lyons (2008) and Sager and Taylor (2008), among others. Our dataset contains daily observations over the four-month period May–August 1996 on both the bilateral spot exchange rate against the dollar and the order flow in eight currency markets: the Deutsche mark (DEM), the British pound (GBP), the Japanese yen (JPY), the Swiss franc (CHF), the French franc (FRF), the Belgian franc (BEF), the Italian lira (ITL) and the Dutch guilder (NLG). By working with Evans and Lyons' seminal dataset, we achieve direct comparability of our results against a large and influential body of existing order flow literature, which therefore provides us with a natural benchmark against which to gauge our findings. Therefore, although our analysis here focuses on a historial dataset, we emphasize that our approach can be applied without limitation to any panel dataset containing price and order flow information.

Our results can be broken down into five principal findings. First, we find that error correction is not instantaneous and that disequilibrium can persist beyond the day in which a shock occurs. Static models are inherently unable to accommodate such behavior and therefore omit an important aspect of information integration within and between currency markets. Hence, we concur with Sager and Taylor (2006) that future theoretical work should strive to account for overnight portfolio imbalances and that empirical research should accommodate partial adjustment.

Second, in contrast to Cai et al. (2008), we find that, while heatwave effects are important, they are by no means the dominant factor influencing global currency markets. At the one-day ahead horizon, heatwave effects account for between 13% and 80% of the forecast error variance of prices across markets, with the remainder due to meteor showers. However, the equivalent range at the five-days ahead horizon is 12%–70%, with six out of eight markets recording a heatwave effect of less than 35%. Hence, our results are strongly consistent with Evans and Lyons (2002a) and Daníelsson et al. (2012), both of which conclude that informational linkages between markets play an important role in price determination.

Third, we find that the smaller markets in our sample (BEF, FRF, ITL, NLG) behave quite differently than the deeper and more liquid markets (DEM, GBP, JPY, CHF). Specifically, among the smaller markets, we find that the influence of within-market order flows is much weaker and the role of meteor showers much greater. Furthermore, the meteor shower effects arising from the smaller markets are generally rather weak. This suggests that the larger markets exert a dominant influence in the global foreign exchange market. This leads directly to our fourth main result – the meteor showers from the Deutsche mark and the yen are so strong that they exceed the heatwave effect in the markets for the Belgian franc, the French franc, the Swiss franc, and the Dutch guilder. We therefore conclude that there exists a leader-recipient relationship between the Deutsche mark/yen and each of these four markets. Interestingly, while the influence of shocks to the Deutsche mark on other currencies is immediate and profound, the meteor shower effects from the yen are relatively muted initially before they gradually intensify. This perhaps reflects delays in the transmission of news regarding fundamentals from Japan to the market in London given the time zone difference as well as the available communications technologies in 1996.

Finally, by innovative use of impulse response analysis, we are able to indirectly identify safe haven currencies with respect to each market in our sample. Since our model is based on that of Evans and Lyons, which does not explicitly include risk measures, we cannot directly evaluate the safe haven effect and so instead we develop a mechanism that is consistent with the move towards a safe haven currency in the wake of an adverse shock. Specifically, we consider that currency j is a safe haven for currency i if buying pressure for currency j intensifies following an adverse shock to currency i that is associated with excess sales of currency i. Therefore, for each of the eight markets in our sample, we investigate the effect of local currency selling pressure and identify the safe haven as that market which experiences the strongest cumulative local currency buying pressure over the next five trading days. On this basis, we find that the dollar and the yen are the main safe havens for the European currencies, while the dollar and pound are safe havens for the yen.

This paper proceeds in six sections as follows. Section 2 provides a brief summary of the multi-currency portfolio shifts (MPS) model of Evans and Lyons (2002a) and develops an empirical framework within which to estimate the MPS model in a dynamic setting with a potentially large number of markets. Section 3 reviews the properties of the dataset and presents the core estimation results for the GVAR model. Section 4 analyzes the connectedness of the global system using the methodology developed by Diebold and Yilmaz (2009, 2014) in order to measure the strength of meteor shower effects and to identify leader-recipient relationships among the markets. Section 5 analyzes impulse response functions in order to identify market-specific safe haven currencies. Finally, Section 6 concludes.

2. A global model of currency spot markets

2.1. The multi-currency portfolio shifts (MPS) model

The MPS model extends the single-market portfolio shifts model advanced by Evans and Lyons (2002a) by explicitly incorporating the linkages among currency markets. Evans and Lyons (2002b) examine a pure dealership-type exchange economy with T trading days indexed by t and $K + 1$ assets (currencies), where one asset is riskless (i.e., its gross returns are normalized to 1) and the other K risky assets have stochastic payoffs. Agents buy and sell the riskless asset for risky assets so there are K asset markets for K risky assets. Buying pressure for the i-th risky asset signals decreasing risk exposure of that asset. The MPS model is given by:

$$\Delta P_t = \Delta R_t + \Lambda \Delta Q_t, \tag{1}$$

where $\Delta P_t = (\Delta P_{1t}, \ldots, \Delta P_{Kt})'$ is a $K \times 1$ vector of price changes in which P_{it} denotes the price of asset i relative to the riskless asset, $\Delta R_t = (\Delta R_{1t}, \ldots, \Delta R_{Kt})'$ is a $K \times 1$ vector of payoff increments for the risky assets, $\Delta Q_t = (\Delta Q_{1t}, \ldots, \Delta Q_{Kt})'$ is a $K \times 1$ vector of order flows and Λ is a $K \times K$ matrix capturing the price impacts of order flows. In the general case in which Λ is non-diagonal, the price change of asset i is jointly determined by the trading in market i as well as the trading in the remaining $K - 1$ markets. The MPS model therefore explicitly accounts for information integration among currency markets, as the linkage between the price in one market and the order flows in other markets is directly modeled.

The MPS model (1) is based on the assumption that all market participants are rational and thus all markets clear at the end of each trading day. In this setting, the long-run relationship between exchange rates (prices) and order flows can be expressed as follows:

$$P_t = R_t + \Lambda Q_t, \tag{2}$$

where P_t, R_t and Q_t are the cumulative representations of ΔP_t, ΔR_t and ΔQ_t, respectively. However, a number of studies have documented pervasive evidence of persistent mispricing in financial markets due to the presence of noise traders and the limits of arbitrage (DeLong et al., 1990; Barberis et al., 1998; Abreu and Brunnermeier, 2002).[2] Under the Evans and Lyons (2002b) portfolio shifts framework, persistent mispricing implies that the market may not clear at the end of each trading day. Therefore, Sager and Taylor (2006) stress that micro exchange rate models that correspond closely to the real world should allow for the possibility that dealers hold overnight imbalances, as one cannot simply assume that customers always absorb dealers' daily inventories. Where the market-clearing assumption cannot be maintained, then (2) can be generalized to:

$$P_t = R_t + \Lambda Q_t + \xi_t,\tag{3}$$

where $\xi_t = (\xi_{1t}, \ldots, \xi_{Kt})'$ is a $K \times 1$ vector of error correction terms which capture the aggregate overnight inventory imbalances (if any) of the dealers in the K markets at the end of day t due to mispricing. Therefore, if mispricing persists beyond a trading day, then (1) is misspecified due to the omission of the error-correction term, ξ_t.

2.2. Country-specific modeling

Under the assumption that the public information increments, R_t, are directly impounded into prices and have no effect on order flows, the relationship between price and order flow in currency market i – that is, the i-th equation of (3) – can be written as follows:

$$P_{it} = \lambda_i Q_{it} + \lambda_i^{*'} Q_{it}^* + \xi_{it},\tag{4}$$

where λ_i is the long-run (equilibrium) impact of the order flow in the i-th market on the price of asset i, $\mathbf{Q}_{it}^* = (Q_{1t}, \ldots, Q_{i-1,t}, Q_{i+1,t}, \ldots, Q_{Kt})'$ is a $(K-1) \times 1$ vector recording the order flows in the remaining $K-1$ currency markets, $\lambda_i^* = (\lambda_1, \ldots, \lambda_{i-1}, \lambda_{i+1}, \ldots, \lambda_K)$ is a $(K-1) \times 1$ vector of parameters capturing the long-run price impacts of these $K-1$ foreign order flows on the price of asset i and ξ_{it} is the aggregated inventory imbalance of the dealers in market i.

Estimating a dynamic form of (3) as a vector autoregression is infeasible with available datasets due to the curse of dimensionality. With K markets in which we observe both the price and the order flow, the dimension of the p-th order VAR model would be $2K(2Kp + 1)$. To overcome this issue, we estimate a set of K market-specific VAR models, each of which does not include the $K-1$ foreign order flows directly but rather a weighted average of these foreign order flows. The aggregate foreign order flow with respect to market i is defined as $Q_{it}^* = \sum_{j=1}^{K} w_{ij} Q_{jt}$, where $w_{ij} \geq 0$ are the set of granular weights which satisfy $\sum_{j=1}^{K} w_{ij} = 1$ and $w_{ii} = 0$. The weight assigned to each market depends on its relative trading volume within the global currency market, with greater weight attached to more heavily traded markets which are likely to play a greater role in information dissemination. Specifically, the w_{ij}'s are calculated as follows:

$$w_{ij} = \frac{V_j}{\sum_{j=1}^{K} V_j - V_i} \text{ with } V_j = \sum_{t=1}^{T} |\Delta Q_{jt}| \text{ and } V_i = \sum_{t=1}^{T} |\Delta Q_{it}| \text{ for } i,j = 1, \ldots, K,$$

where ΔQ_{it} and ΔQ_{jt} are the order flows in the i-th and j-th markets, respectively. Consequently, w_{ij} is the share of the aggregate excess orders (buying and selling) from market j over the sample period ($\sum_{t=1}^{T} |\Delta Q_{jt}|$) in the total excess orders from all markets less market i $(\sum_{j=1}^{K} \sum_{t=1}^{T} |\Delta Q_{jt}| - \sum_{t=1}^{T} |\Delta Q_{it}|)$.[3] We therefore modify (4) as follows:

$$P_{it} = \lambda_i Q_{it} + \lambda_i^* Q_{it}^* + \xi_{it}, \tag{5}$$

where λ_i^* captures the price impact of the weighted-average foreign order flow. Embedding the long-run relationship, (5), into an otherwise unrestricted VAR(p) model and assuming that Q_{it}^* is weakly exogenous, we obtain the following market-specific VECM model:

$$\Delta X_{it} = \Lambda_i \Delta Q_{it}^* + \alpha_i \beta_i' Z_{i,t-1} + \sum_{j=1}^{p-1} \Gamma_{ij} \Delta Z_{i,t-j} + \varepsilon_{it}, \tag{6}$$

where $X_{it} = (P_{it}, Q_{it})'$ is a 2×1 vector of endogenous variables containing the price and order flow for market i, $Z_{it} = (X_{it}', Q_{it}^*)'$, $\beta_i = (1, \lambda_i, \lambda_i^*)$ is a 3×1 vector of cointegrating parameters, α_i is a 2×1 vector of adjustment parameters, $\xi_{it} = \beta_i' Z_{it}$, the dimensions of dynamic parameter matrices Λ_i and Γ_{ij} are 2×1 and 2×3, respectively and ε_{it} is a 2×1 vector of residuals, which are serially uncorrelated and are allowed to be weakly cross-sectionally dependent.[4]

Using the market-specific model (6), we can directly account for the observation of Fung and Patterson (1999) that major and minor currencies play different informational roles, being either leaders or recipients. Note that (6) also allows for the presence of feedback trading through the parameters of the order flow equation and via free estimation of the covariance matrix, which allows for the possibility that price and order flow shocks may be correlated. This is an important feature of the model in light of the compelling evidence of feedback trading in financial markets (e.g., Hasbrouck, 1991; Cohen and Shin, 2003) and the observation of Daníelsson and Love (2006) that, unless the data are sampled at the highest possible frequency, then contemporaneous feedback trading may be observed.

2.3. The global model

The inclusion of the foreign order flow variables in the market-specific VAR models explicitly accommodates linkages among the currency markets. With the K estimated market-specific VAR models in hand, it is straightforward to combine them into the global VAR model. First, note that (6) can be rewritten equivalently as:

$$A_{i0} Z_{it} = A_{i1} Z_{i,t-1} + A_{i2} Z_{i,t-2} + \ldots + A_{i,p} Z_{i,t-p} + \varepsilon_{it}, \tag{7}$$

where $A_{i0} = (I_2, -\Lambda_i)$, $A_{i1} = A_{i0} + \alpha_i \beta_i' + \Gamma_{i1}$, $A_{ij} = \Gamma_{i,j+1} - \Gamma_{i,j}$ for $j = 2, \ldots, p - 1$, and $A_{ip} = -\Gamma_{ip}$. Now, we define the $m \times 1$ vector of global variables $X_t = (X_{1t}', \ldots, X_{Kt}')'$, where $X_{it} = (P_{it}, Q_{it})'$ and $m = 2K$. It is possible to express Z_{it} compactly as:

$$Z_{it} = W_i X_t, \quad i = 1, \ldots, K, \tag{8}$$

where W_i is the $(2+1) \times 2K$ link matrix. Careful construction of the link matrices is critical in the development of the GVAR model. We construct the W_i's as follows:

$$\underset{(2+1) \times 2K}{W_i} = \begin{pmatrix} O_{i1} & O_{i2} & O_{i3} & \cdots & O_{iK} \\ W_{i1} & W_{i2} & W_{i3} & \cdots & W_{iK} \end{pmatrix}, \quad i = 1, \ldots, K,$$

where:

$$\{O_{ij}\}_{j=1}^{K} = \begin{cases} \begin{bmatrix} 0 & 0 \\ 0 & 0 \end{bmatrix} & \text{if } j \neq i \\ I_2 & \text{if } j = i \end{cases}, \quad \{W_{ij}\}_{j=1}^{K} = \begin{bmatrix} 0 & w_{ij} \end{bmatrix}, \quad i = 1, \ldots, K,$$

and w_{ij} is the weight assigned to market j in creating the weighted-average foreign order flow variable from the perspective of market i.[5] Using (8) in (7) and stacking the results we obtain:

$$H_0 X_t = H_1 X_{t-1} + \cdots + H_p X_{t-p} + \varepsilon_t, \tag{9}$$

where $\varepsilon_t = (\varepsilon'_{1t}, \varepsilon'_{2t}, \cdots, \varepsilon'_{Kt})'$ and $H_j = (W'_1 A'_{1j}, W'_2 A'_{2j}, \cdots, W'_K A'_{Kj})'$ for $j = 0$, 1, ... , p. The reduced-form GVAR is finally obtained as:

$$X_t = G_1 X_{t-1} + G_2 X_{t-2} + \cdots + G_p X_{t-p} + \zeta_t, \tag{10}$$

where $G_j = H_0^{-1} H_j, j = 1, \ldots, p$ and $\zeta_t = H_0^{-1} \varepsilon_t$. Following the convention in the GVAR literature, we allow the market-specific shocks to be weakly correlated across markets such that $E(\varepsilon_{it}\varepsilon'_{jt}) = \Sigma_\varepsilon$ for $t = t'$ and 0 otherwise. Hence, the covariance matrix of ζ_t in (10) can be expressed as $\Sigma_\zeta = E(\zeta_t \zeta'_t) = H_0^{-1} \Sigma_\varepsilon H_0^{-1'}$. This is an important feature of the global model as it accommodates contemporaneous feedback trading across markets, because shocks to the equation for ΔP_{it} can have contemporaneous effects on ΔQ_{it} and ΔQ_{jt} for $j \neq i$.

The GVAR model in (10) links the K currency markets together in a coherent and flexible manner. The model accommodates informational linkages among currency markets through two distinct channels: (i) direct dependence of the domestic price and order flow on the weighted average foreign order flow and its lagged values; and (ii) non-zero contemporaneous dependence of shocks across markets. The first channel represents the direct impact of trading information in the $K-1$ foreign markets on the trading activity and price in market i. By contrast, the second channel accounts for the contemporaneous linkage of shocks across markets and is therefore of particular interest when one seeks to model spillover effects.

2.4. Dynamic analysis of the global model

In the context of the multi-currency portfolio shifts framework, we are princi-
pally interested in evaluating the following:

(i)   The *heatwave* effect, defined as the impact of a shock emanating from
market i on the price and order flow in the same market (see Engle et
al., 1990, for a discussion based on sequences of volatile trading days
within a given market).

(ii) The *meteor shower* effect, defined as the impact of a shock emanating
from market j on the price and order flow of another market $i \neq j$ (see
Engle et al., 1990, on the transmission of volatility between markets). A
meteor shower is simply a spillover between markets so we shall
henceforth use these terms interchangeably.

(iii) The *leader–recipient* relationship. If the spillover from market j to the
price in market i dominates the effect of both price and order flow shocks
in market i on the price in market i, then market j is a leader and market i
a recipient (see Fung and Patterson, 1999 for a related approach based on
the error variance decomposition of a small VAR model).[6]

(iv) The *safe haven currency* hypothesis.[7] Currency j is considered a safe
haven with respect to currency i if selling pressure for currency i results
in buying pressure for currency $j \neq i$. While this definition does not
directly imply increased risk of currency i, we argue that it is consistent
with investors rebalancing their portfolios in favor of currency j to
mitigate their exposure to risks arising from currency i. Specifically,
currency j is considered to have a lower risk exposure following a shock
that leads to a depreciation of currency i.

Since the GVAR model is still a VAR model, all of the standard tools for the
dynamic analysis of VAR models can be employed. While it is technically possible to structurally identify shocks in a GVAR model (particularly by means of sign
restrictions which permit set identification; see, for example, Cashin et al., 2014),
the large majority of existing studies have not attempted to do so due to the difficulties associated with achieving an uncontroversial structure in a multi-market
setting. Similarly, reliance on a Wold causal identification scheme is acutely problematic in the setting of a GVAR model, as it carries the implication that markets
respond to one-another sequentially. Therefore, we follow the standard approach
in the GVAR literature and employ generalized impulse response functions
(GIRFs) and generalized forecast error variance decompositions (GFEVDs),
which are based on non-orthogonalized shocks (Pesaran and Shin, 1998). This
is a natural choice given that market participants trade at high frequency and so
one would naturally expect to observe non-negligible correlation of shocks
across markets when working with daily data (Daníelsson and Love, 2006).

It is natural to model the first three effects using the connectedness methodology advanced by Diebold and Yilmaz (2009, 2014). This technique involves the

construction of a weighted directed network on the basis of forecast error variance decompositions. The proportion of the h-step-ahead forecast error variance
of variable i explained by shocks originating within (outside) market i is a
natural measure of the heatwave (meteor shower) effect. The GVAR model in
(10) is first recast in its Wold representation as follows:

$$X_t = \sum_{j=0}^{\infty} B_j \zeta_{t-j}, \tag{11}$$

where the B_j's are evaluated recursively as:

$$B_j = G_1 B_{j-1} + G_2 B_{j-2} + \cdots + G_{p-1} B_{j-p+1}, \ j = 1, \cdots, \text{ with } B_0 = I_m, \ B_j$$
$$= 0 \text{ for } j < 0.$$

Following Pesaran and Shin (1998), the h-step ahead GFEVD is written as
follows:

$$\varphi_{j \leftarrow i}^{(h)} = \frac{\sigma_{\varepsilon,ii}^{-1} \sum_{\ell=0}^{h} \left(e_j' B_\ell H_0^{-1} \Sigma_\varepsilon e_i\right)^2}{\sum_{\ell=0}^{h} e_j' B_\ell H_0^{-1} \Sigma_\varepsilon H_0^{-1'} B_\ell' e_j} = \frac{\sigma_{\varepsilon,ii}^{-1} \sum_{\ell=0}^{h} \left(e_j' B_\ell H_0^{-1} \Sigma_\varepsilon e_i\right)^2}{\sum_{\ell=0}^{h} e_j' B_\ell \Sigma_\zeta B_\ell' e_j} \tag{12}$$

for $i, j = 1, \ldots, m$, where e_i is an $m \times 1$ selection vector whose i-th element is
unity with zeros elsewhere and e_j is an $m \times 1$ selection vector whose j-th element
is unity with zeros elsewhere. $\sigma_{\varepsilon,ii}$ denotes the standard deviation of the residuals
in the equation for variable i in the GVAR model. Note that $\varphi_{j \leftarrow i}^{(h)}$ denotes the contribution of a one standard error shock to variable i to the h-step forecast error
variance (FEV) of variable j. Due to the non-orthogonal structure of Σ_ε, the forecast error variance contributions need not sum to 100% across i. Diebold and
Yilmaz (2014) therefore normalize $\varphi_{j \leftarrow i}^{(h)}$ as follows:

$$\phi_{j \leftarrow i}^{(h)} = 100 \left(\frac{\varphi_{j \leftarrow i}^{(h)}}{\sum_{i=1}^{m} \varphi_{j \leftarrow i}^{(h)}}\right),$$

such that $\sum_{i=1}^{m} \phi_{j \leftarrow i}^{(h)} = 100$ and $\sum_{j,i=1}^{m} \phi_{j \leftarrow i}^{(h)} = 100m$. To demonstrate the computation of the spillover and heatwave effects via the Diebold–Yilmaz method,
consider the simplest possible setting with two markets ($K = 2$) and hence
$m = 2K = 4$ variables in total, in the order of $P_{1,t}, Q_{1,t}, P_{2,t}, Q_{2,t}$. As such,
at any forecast horizon h, the forecast error variance contributions can be

cross-tabulated as follows:

$$
\mathbb{C}^{(h)} = \begin{bmatrix}
\phi^{(h)}_{P_1 \leftarrow P_1} & \phi^{(h)}_{P_1 \leftarrow Q_1} & \phi^{(h)}_{P_1 \leftarrow P_2} & \phi^{(h)}_{P_1 \leftarrow Q_2} \\
\phi^{(h)}_{Q_1 \leftarrow P_1} & \phi^{(h)}_{Q_1 \leftarrow Q_1} & \phi^{(h)}_{Q_1 \leftarrow P_2} & \phi^{(h)}_{Q_1 \leftarrow Q_2} \\
\phi^{(h)}_{P_2 \leftarrow P_1} & \phi^{(h)}_{P_2 \leftarrow Q_1} & \phi^{(h)}_{P_2 \leftarrow P_2} & \phi^{(h)}_{P_2 \leftarrow Q_2} \\
\phi^{(h)}_{Q_2 \leftarrow P_1} & \phi^{(h)}_{Q_2 \leftarrow Q_1} & \phi^{(h)}_{Q_2 \leftarrow P_2} & \phi^{(h)}_{Q_2 \leftarrow Q_2}
\end{bmatrix}
\tag{13}
$$

Note that (13) is structured such that the total h-step ahead FEV of the i-th variable in the system is decomposed into the elements of the i-th row of $\mathbb{C}^{(h)}$. Meanwhile, the contributions of the i-th variable to the h-step ahead FEV of all variables in the system are contained in the i-th column of $\mathbb{C}^{(h)}$. Therefore, based on (13) and following Diebold and Yilmaz (2009, 2014), the aggregate h-step ahead heatwave and spillover indices, denoted $H^{(h)}$ and $S^{(h)}$, respectively, can be computed as follows:

$$
H^{(h)} = \frac{1}{m}\,\text{trace}\left(\mathbb{C}^{(h)}\right) \quad \text{and} \quad S^{(h)} = \frac{1}{m}\left(\mathbf{e}'\mathbb{C}^{(h)}\mathbf{e} - \text{trace}\left(\mathbb{C}^{(h)}\right)\right),
\tag{14}
$$

where $\mathbf{e}$ is an $m \times 1$ vector of ones. By construction, $H^{(h)} + S^{(h)} = 100$. Furthermore, with some simple algebra we are able to evaluate heatwave and meteor shower effects at the *market level* as opposed to the variable level (via $\mathbb{C}^{(h)}$) or the systemwide aggregate level (via $H^{(h)}$ and $S^{(h)}$). To see this, note that:

$$
\begin{aligned}
H^{(h)}_{1 \leftarrow 1} &= \frac{1}{K}\left(\phi^{(h)}_{P_1 \leftarrow P_1} + \phi^{(h)}_{P_1 \leftarrow Q_1} + \phi^{(h)}_{Q_1 \leftarrow P_1} + \phi^{(h)}_{Q_1 \leftarrow Q_1}\right), \\
H^{(h)}_{2 \leftarrow 2} &= \frac{1}{K}\left(\phi^{(h)}_{P_2 \leftarrow P_2} + \phi^{(h)}_{P_2 \leftarrow Q_2} + \phi^{(h)}_{Q_2 \leftarrow P_2} + \phi^{(h)}_{Q_2 \leftarrow Q_2}\right), \\
S^{(h)}_{1 \leftarrow 2} &= \frac{1}{K}\left(\phi^{(h)}_{P_1 \leftarrow P_2} + \phi^{(h)}_{P_1 \leftarrow Q_2} + \phi^{(h)}_{Q_1 \leftarrow P_2} + \phi^{(h)}_{Q_1 \leftarrow Q_2}\right), \\
S^{(h)}_{2 \leftarrow 1} &= \frac{1}{K}\left(\phi^{(h)}_{P_2 \leftarrow P_1} + \phi^{(h)}_{P_2 \leftarrow Q_1} + \phi^{(h)}_{Q_2 \leftarrow P_1} + \phi^{(h)}_{Q_2 \leftarrow Q_1}\right),
\end{aligned}
\tag{15}
$$

where $H^{(h)}_{1 \leftarrow 1}$ ($H^{(h)}_{2 \leftarrow 2}$) denotes the heatwave effect within market 1 (market 2) and $S^{(h)}_{1 \leftarrow 2}$ ($S^{(h)}_{2 \leftarrow 1}$) denotes the meteor shower effect from market 2 to market 1 (from market 1 to market 2). Note that $H^{(h)}_{1 \leftarrow 1} + S^{(h)}_{1 \leftarrow 2} = 100$ and $H^{(h)}_{2 \leftarrow 2} + S^{(h)}_{2 \leftarrow 1} = 100$ by construction. With these definitions in place, the net connectedness between market 1 and market 2 can be defined as follows:

$$
N^{(h)}_1 = S^{(h)}_{2 \leftarrow 1} - S^{(h)}_{1 \leftarrow 2} \quad \text{and} \quad N^{(h)}_2 = S^{(h)}_{1 \leftarrow 2} - S^{(h)}_{2 \leftarrow 1}.
\tag{16}
$$

Note that in this simple case with two markets, $N_1^{(h)} = -N_2^{(h)}$ by construction. In a more general setting with K markets, the sign of $N_i^{(h)}$ indicates whether market i is a net transmitter of shocks to the system ($N_i^{(h)} > 0$) or a net receiver of shocks from the system ($N_i^{(h)} < 0$). Using these market-level connectedness measures, we can examine the relative importance of within-market (heatwave) and cross-market (meteor shower/spillover) information in explaining the trading activity and price movements in each currency market. By extension, the case where one is interested in spillovers between *groups of markets* (e.g., major versus minor markets) is conceptually analogous and computationally straightforward.

Finally, we can analyze the safe-haven currency hypothesis by means of generalized impulse response analysis. Recall that we identify currency j as a safe haven with respect to currency i if an adverse shock to currency i leads investors to move away from currency i in favor of currency j. That is, currency j is a safe haven with respect to currency i if selling pressure for currency i results in buying pressure for currency j. Therefore, by analyzing the directional impact of local currency selling pressure in one currency market on trading activities and prices in other markets, we can observe how investors switch between currencies in the wake of a shock and, therefore, which currencies act as safe havens.

3. Empirical results

3.1. The dataset

We employ the dataset used by Evans and Lyons (2002a), which contains daily data on direct interdealer trading for 82 trading days over the four-month period from 1 May to 31 August 1996. The data is drawn from the Reuters D2000-1 platform and covers trades in the following eight currency spot markets against the US dollar: the German mark (DEM), the British pound (GBP), the Japanese yen (JPY), the Swiss franc (CHF), the French franc (FRF), the Belgian franc (BEF), the Italian lira (ITL), and the Dutch guilder (NLG).[8] In each case, trades are defined such that investors buy and sell the US dollar for other currencies. Thus, in order to convert holdings of Japanese yen into pounds, for example, an investor must first sell the yen to buy the dollar and then sell the dollar to buy the pound.

Table 4.1 presents basic summary statistics for each market. The change in the spot rate of the nominated currency against the dollar, ΔP_{it}, is the log change in the purchase transaction price between 4:00 p.m. Greenwich Mean Time (GMT) on day t and 4:00 p.m. on day $t - 1$. When day t is a Monday, the day $t - 1$ price is the previous Friday's price. The daily order flow measured in thousands of orders, ΔQ_{it}, is the difference between the number of buyer-initiated trades (positively signed) and seller-initiated trades (negatively signed) from 4:00 p.m. GMT on day $t - 1$ to 4:00 p.m. on day t. Hence, for the i-th market, $\Delta Q_{it} > 0$

Table 4.1 Summary trading statistics

Market	$\sum \Delta Q_{it}^-$	$\sum \Delta Q_{it}^+$	$\sum \Delta Q_{it}$	$\sum |\Delta Q_{it}|$	$\sum \Delta P_{it}$	$\rho(P_{it}, Q_{it}^*)$	$\rho(P_{it}, Q_{it}^*)$	$\rho(Q_{it}, Q_{it}^*)$
DEM	−4.343	4.326	−0.017	8.669	−0.037	0.779	−0.528	−0.263
GBP	−1.082	2.162	1.080	3.244	−0.043	−0.501	−0.312	0.108
JPY	−1.954	4.907	2.953	6.861	0.033	0.769	−0.248	−0.567
CHF	−3.011	1.565	−1.446	4.576	−0.041	0.711	−0.256	−0.628
FRF	−0.919	0.894	−0.025	1.813	−0.022	0.889	0.041	0.218
BEF	−0.151	0.403	0.252	0.554	−0.035	−0.830	−0.016	0.531
ITL	−0.421	0.529	0.108	0.950	−0.035	−0.697	−0.349	0.427
NLG	−0.287	0.132	−0.155	0.419	−0.036	0.939	−0.009	−0.274

Notes: Each exchange rate is bilateral vis-à-vis the US dollar. For each market, $\sum \Delta Q_{it}^-$ (in thousands) denotes the total USD-selling orders over the sample period, $\sum \Delta Q_{it}^+$ (in thousands) the total USD-buying orders, $\sum \Delta |Q_{it}|$ the total trading orders, $\sum \Delta Q_{it}$ the net trading orders and $\sum \Delta P_{it}$ the aggregate price change over the sample period. Following Evans and Lyons (2002a), P_{it} is expressed in logarithmic form while Q_{it} and Q_{it}^* are cumulative order flows measured in thousands of orders. Q_{it}^* is defined as in subsection 2.2. $\rho_{(i,j)}$ denotes the correlation between $i,j \in (P_{it}, Q_{it}, Q_{it}^*)$.

indicates selling pressure of currency i (i.e., net dollar buying) and $\Delta Q_{it} < 0$ indicates buying pressure of currency i (net dollar selling). In all cases, unit root tests indicate that P_{it} and Q_{it} are difference stationary; results are available on request.

The eight markets that we consider divide naturally into two groups according to the volume of total excess trades, $\sum |\Delta Q_{it}|$. The more heavily traded group is composed of the DEM, JPY, CHF and GBP markets, in descending order of trade volume. These may be considered the major markets in our sample and the remainder (FRF, ITL, BEF, NLG) may be viewed as the minor markets. The sum of the excess trades in the major markets during our sample period exceeds that for the minor markets by a factor of five, with the respective totals standing at 23,350 and 4,686. As explained above, we employ the total excess trades in each market to compute the weighting matrix required to construct the market-specific weakly exogenous foreign order flow variables (the Q_{it}^*'s). The resulting weight matrix is recorded in Table 4.2. The weights reveal the importance of the four major markets identified above and of the DEM and JPY markets in particular. The importance of the Deutsche mark reflects its importance as an investment currency while the weight attached to the yen is a manifestation of the yen carry trade to a large degree (Gagnon and Chaboud, 2007).

Over the time period spanned by our sample, the yen depreciated mildly while all of the other currencies appreciated. This pattern is clearly visible in Figures 4.1(a)–(h), which plot both the log exchange rate and the cumulative order flow for each country. In all cases except the relatively illiquid BEF market, large movements in cumulative order flow are associated with large movements in the exchange rate, in keeping with the predictions of the MPS model. In five markets (DEM, JPY, CHF, FRF and NLG), the price and local order flow

Table 4.2 Matrix of weights used to construct foreign order flows

	DEM	GBP	JPY	CHF	FRF	BEF	ITL	NLG
DEM	0.000	0.176	0.373	0.248	0.098	0.030	0.052	0.023
GBP	0.364	0.000	0.288	0.192	0.076	0.023	0.040	0.018
JPY	0.429	0.160	0.000	0.226	0.090	0.027	0.047	0.021
CHF	0.385	0.144	0.305	0.000	0.081	0.025	0.042	0.019
FRF	0.343	0.128	0.271	0.181	0.000	0.022	0.038	0.017
BEF	0.327	0.122	0.259	0.172	0.068	0.000	0.036	0.016
ITL	0.332	0.124	0.263	0.175	0.069	0.021	0.000	0.016
NLG	0.325	0.122	0.257	0.172	0.068	0.021	0.036	0.000

Notes: The (i,j)-th element of the weight matrix, w_{ij}, is calculated as $w_{ij} = \frac{V_j}{\sum_{j=1}^{K} V_j - V_i}$, for $i,j = 1,...,K$, where $V_j = \sum_{t=1}^{T} |\Delta Q_{jt}|$, $V_i = \sum_{t=1}^{T} |\Delta Q_{it}|$ and ΔQ_{it} and ΔQ_{jt} are the order flows in the i-th and j-th markets, respectively. As such, w_{ij} is the share of the aggregate excess orders (buying and selling) from market j over the sample period ($\sum_{t=1}^{T} |\Delta Q_{jt}|$) in the total excess orders from all markets less market i ($\sum_{j=1}^{K} \sum_{t=1}^{T} |\Delta Q_{jt}| - \sum_{t=1}^{T} |\Delta Q_{it}|$).

series show relatively close comovement, which is reflected in the strong positive correlations reported in the seventh column of Table 4.1. This may be viewed as a normal situation, as excess local currency selling orders lead to a depreciation of the local currency. Meanwhile, we observe a negative association between price and local order flow in the GBP, BEF and ITL markets, where the respective currencies gradually appreciate against the dollar in spite of a prolonged sequence of excess local currency selling orders in these markets.

Two further features of the data are apparent in Figure 4.1. First, there are notable similarities in the trading patterns and particularly in the prices of the continental European currencies. On an informal level, this is suggestive of either a common risk exposure of the European currencies or of a leader-recipient relationship among them. By contrast, the trading activities and price movements observed in the JPY market differ substantially from the European currency markets. To a lesser extent, this is also true of the market for GBP. This raises the possibility that traders may be able to exploit the yen and/or pound as safe havens relative to the continental European currencies. These initial conjectures will be formally scrutinized below.

3.2. VECM estimation results

The Johansen Trace and Maximum Eigenvalue tests provide mixed support for cointegration. Specifically, there is evidence of one cointegrating relationship in the CHF, BEF, NLG, and GBP markets but not in the other cases (test results are available on request). A similar result is recorded by Boyer and van Norden (2006), who test for market-specific cointegration between the exchange rate and cumulative order flow in a VAR framework using the same dataset we employ here. The authors conclude that failure to resoundingly

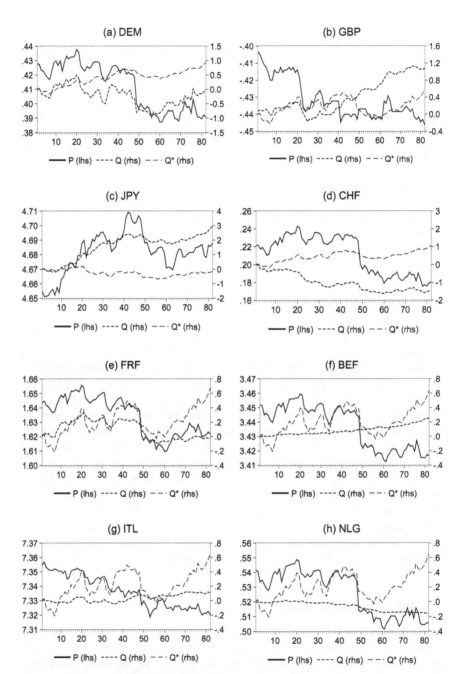

Figure 4.1 Price and cumulative order flow data by market

Notes: The labels on the horizontal time axis represent trading days 1 to 82. P_{it} denotes the natural logarithm of the exchange rate. Q_{it} denotes the cumulative local order flow in the named market, measured in thousands of trades. Q_{it}^* denotes the foreign cumulative order flow from the perspective of the named market, measured in thousands of trades.

Table 4.3 Westerlund panel cointegration test results

Statistic	Value	z-value	p-value
G_τ	−3.15	−2.09	0.02
G_α	−18.14	−1.74	0.04
P_τ	−8.29	−2.01	0.02
P_α	−15.57	−2.13	0.02

Notes: The Westerlund cointegration test is based on a panel error correction model (with an intercept and a time trend) for the null hypothesis that there is no cointegration between P_{it}, Q_{it} and Q_{it}^*. P_τ and P_α are the test statistics for the null of no cointegration against the alternative that the panel is cointegrated as a whole. G_τ and G_α are the test statistics for the null of no cointegration against the alternative that at least one unit in the panel is cointegrated.

detect a cointegrating relationship does not imply the absence of such a relationship. In practice, testing for market-specific cointegration will inevitably be difficult in the current context due to the relatively low power of traditional cointegration tests in small samples. To achieve higher power, we therefore make use of the panel structure of our dataset, which allows us to exploit both the time-variation and the cross-section variation in our sample. Table 4.3 records the results of the panel cointegration tests devised by Westerlund (2007), which provide overwhelming evidence of cointegration between P_{it}, Q_{it} and Q_{it}^* at the panel level.

Although rejecting the null hypothesis of no cointegration in a panel does not confirm the existence of cointegration in each cross-section unit, we will proceed on the basis that there exists a single cointegrating vector between the three variables P_{it}, Q_{it}, and Q_{it}^* in each market. It is straightforward to verify whether this assumption yields a dynamically stable error correction model by inspecting the persistence profile of the cointegrating vector with respect to a systemwide shock, as in Figure 4.2. The figure plots the persistence profiles alongside 90% bootstrap intervals. Throughout this paper, we employ the non-parametric sieve bootstrap detailed in Dees et al. (2007, especially Supplement A) based on 10,000 stable iterations. From the figure, we see that the persistence profile converges to equilibrium swiftly in each case, with the effect of the shock typically dying away to zero after 4 to 8 days. Furthermore, with the exception of the market for the Swiss franc where we observe some mild noise, adjustment is smooth. As stressed by Pesaran and Shin (1996), the absence of excess persistence and the smooth adjustment reflected in the persistence profiles indicates that the long-run relationships embedded in the market-specific models are valid and well-specified.

We estimate each market-specific VECM including a constant and a restricted time trend. The i-th market-specific model includes p_i lags of $\mathbf{Z}_{it} = \left(\mathbf{X}'_{it}, Q_{it}^*\right)'$, where p_i is chosen from the set (2, 3, 4, 5) using the Akaike Information Criterion, as documented in Table 4.4. The market specific models achieve a very good fit to the data relative to the class of macro exchange rate models, with $\bar{R}^2$s in the range 10% to 80%. Furthermore, specification tests reveal that the models are dynamically stable and well-specified. Detailed results are available on request.

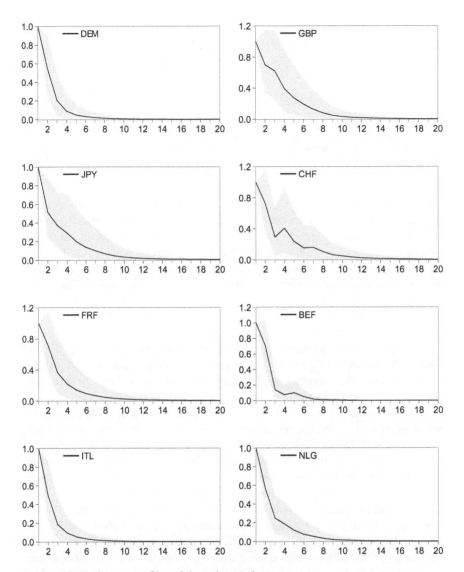

Figure 4.2 Persistence profiles of the cointegrating vectors

Notes: The horizontal axis records the horizon in trading days, while the vertical axis records the response of the cointegrating vector to a systemwide shock. The response is normalized to unity on impact. In a stable and well-specified model, the persistence profiles will die away to zero smoothly and rapidly. See Pesaran and Shin (1996) for further details. The 90% bootstrap interval is shaded in each case.

Table 4.4 Key parameters of the market-specific VECMs

		DEM	GBP	JPY	CHF	FRF	BEF	ITL	NLG
(a) Lag Order	p_i	2	3	2	4	2	2	2	2
(b) LR Coefs	$P_{i,t-1}$	1.000	1.000	1.000	1.000	1.000	1.000	1.000	1.000
	$Q_{i,t-1}$	-0.401	-1.818**	-2.452*	2.508	-6.495	14.644*	-2.845	-39.804**
	$Q^*_{i,t-1}$	-3.230**	0.483	-2.051	-6.413	-0.375	-4.639*	-0.935***	-0.098
(c) Adj. Coefs	$\xi^P_{i,t-1}$	-0.001*	-0.001*	-0.001**	-0.001*	0.000 ***	-0.001*	-0.001**	0.000
	$\xi^Q_{i,t-1}$	-0.042**	-0.009	-0.010	-0.015**	0.005***	-0.001	-0.003	-0.003*

Notes: The lag order is selected using the Akaike Information Criterion. The reported values of the long-run (LR) coefficients are normalized on $P_{i,t-1}$ and are then multiplied by 100 to ease their interpretation (e.g., a dollar buying (positive) shock of 100 trades in the GBP/USD market causes a long-run pound depreciation against the US dollar of 1.82%). Significance at the 10%, 5% and 1% levels is denoted by *, ** and ***. Recall that the significance of the adjustment coefficients indicates the significance of the error correction terms $\xi_{it} = \boldsymbol{\beta}'_i \boldsymbol{Z}_{it}$ in equation (6) with $\xi_{it} = \left(\xi^P_{i,t}, \xi^Q_{i,t} \right)'$.

The long-run parameters recorded in Table 4.4 indicate the expected positive relationship between the exchange rate and the local order flow, Q_{it}, in the majority of markets. That is, our results show that selling the i-th currency in favor of the dollar causes the i-th currency to depreciate against the dollar. The notable exception is the BEF market, where we find a negative long-run association. This is not unexpected given the negative correlation between the exchange rate and the local order flow in the BEF market observed in the data and documented in Table 4.1. Furthermore, it is consistent with Evans and Lyons (2002a), who establish a comparable result and suggest that the market for the Belgian franc is a recipient and, therefore, that the price of the Belgian franc is not predominantly determined by local (within-market) trading information. This observation is certainly borne out by the coefficient on the foreign order flow, Q_i^*, which is large and significant for the BEF market.

Looking at the long-run coefficients on Q_i^* across all eight market-specific models, we see a considerable degree of heterogeneity in their magnitude, indicating varying degrees of sensitivity to conditions in foreign markets. In general, our coefficient estimates reveal that the long-run price impact of both domestic and foreign order flows is stronger in the smaller and less liquid markets, where a given volume of trading conveys more information. This effect has been well documented in the microstructure literature (Kyle 1985). Setting the scale differences aside, the sign of the coefficient on foreign order flow is positive in the large majority of cases, indicating that aggregate dollar-buying pressure in foreign currency markets is typically associated with a depreciation of the local currency against the dollar. This is an intuitively reasonable result, as an aggregate increase in demand for the dollar will tend to cause it to appreciate against a basket of currencies.

The error correction coefficients reported in Table 4.4 convey a great deal of information about the dynamic adjustment of both prices and order flows. With the exception of the market for the Dutch guilder, the error correction coefficients in the price equations are negative, indicating that disequilibrium errors are corrected in subsequent trading periods. The market for the guilder is the smallest and least liquid in our sample, so it is likely that a significant and negative error correction term would be uncovered with more data. The speed of error correction is relatively slow in all models, which is consistent with the prevalence of persistent mispricing discussed in subsection 2.1. Nevertheless, we observe relatively rapid convergence of the impulse response functions and forecast error variance decompositions employed below due to the joint influence of the error correction terms and the coefficients on lagged first differences in the market-specific VECMs. Finally, while the error correction parameters in the order flow equations may take either positive or negative values in our model, we find that they are typically negative, indicating that feedback trading will tend to correct deviations from equilibrium. Interestingly, the error correction terms in the major markets are considerably larger than in the minor markets, indicating that traders respond to disequilibrium more rapidly in these more liquid markets.

4. Market connectedness and spillover analysis

Figure 4.3 presents the systemwide heatwave and spillover indices defined in (14) over horizons $h = 1,2,...,10$. At the systemwide level, heatwave effects are initially marginally dominant, accounting for just over 50% of the 1-step-ahead FEV, with spillovers accounting for the remainder. However, as the horizon increases, the heatwave effects gradually diminish, reflecting the rapid integration of within-market information via the trading process. As a result, after one trading week, meteor shower effects account for more than 60% of the systemwide FEV. This simple exercise highlights the importance of informational linkages among global currency markets and provides the backdrop against which the remainder of our analysis is conducted.

Table 4.5 presents the one-step ahead 16×16 connectedness matrix, $\mathbb{C}^{(1)}$, in the form of a heat map. Note that the elements of the 2×2 blocks lying on the prime diagonal collect the within-market (or local) information. For each of these 2×2 blocks, the elements on the diagonal measure heatwave effects while the off-diagonal elements capture the linkage between price and local order flow. Meanwhile the off-diagonal blocks relate to meteor shower effects across markets.

Although heatwave effects are largely dominant in the aggregate at $h = 1$ (as noted above), there is nevertheless some significant variation. In particular, looking at the diagonal blocks of Table 4.5, we find an interesting distinction between the major markets (DEM, GBP, JPY, and CHF) and the smaller markets. Specifically, the heatwave effects are generally weaker among the smaller markets and the average spillover from Q_{it} to P_{it} at $h = 1$ is considerably weaker in this group. This implies that prices in the smaller markets are more sensitive to foreign order flows than prices in the larger markets. For example, the meteor shower effect from the DEM exchange rate to the BEF exchange rate (26.4%) significantly exceeds the heatwave effect of the BEF exchange rate (12.4%). A similar phenomenon is observed for both the FRF and NLG

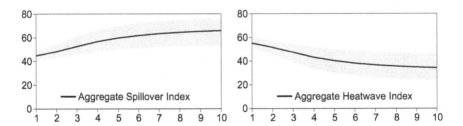

Figure 4.3 Aggregate spillover and heatwave indices

Notes: The horizontal axis records the horizon in trading days, while the vertical axis is measured in percent. The aggregate heatwave and spillover indices, $H^{(h)}$ and $S^{(h)}$ respectively, are computed following equation (14) for horizons one to ten. Note that $H^{(h)} + S^{(h)} = 100 \; \forall h$. The 90% bootstrap interval is shaded in each case.

Table 4.5 Bootstrapped connectedness among variables, one-day ahead

	DEM P	DEM Q	GBP P	GBP Q	JPY P	JPY Q	CHF P	CHF Q	FRF P	FRF Q	BEF P	BEF Q	ITL P	ITL Q	NLG P	NLG Q
DEM P	33.9 (26.7,40.6)	18.3 (8.7,28.1)	1.2 (0.0,3.5)	0.8 (0.0,2.7)	4.4 (0.6,10.3)	3.8 (0.3,10.2)	8.6 (4.4,13.1)	1.9 (0.1,4.8)	8.7 (4.0,13.2)	1.0 (0.0,3.4)	7.3 (3.4,11.2)	0.4 (0.0,1.6)	1.6 (0.0,4.3)	0.6 (0.0,2.2)	6.9 (2.8,10.9)	0.4 (0.0,1.7)
DEM Q	30.4 (19.0,38.4)	58.8 (49.7,68.5)	0.7 (0.0,2.5)	1.3 (0.0,4.1)	0.7 (0.0,2.8)	1.6 (0.0,6.3)	0.5 (0.0,1.9)	1.1 (0.0,3.7)	0.8 (0.0,2.9)	0.7 (0.0,2.7)	0.6 (0.0,2.1)	0.5 (0.0,1.9)	0.5 (0.0,2.1)	0.7 (0.0,2.6)	0.6 (0.0,2.4)	0.4 (0.0,1.7)
GBP P	6.7 (1.5,13.2)	6.5 (1.1,13.7)	54.2 (43.1,65.5)	14.3 (5.5,23.7)	1.8 (0.0,6.2)	2.2 (0.0,7.4)	1.9 (0.0,6.0)	0.7 (0.0,2.7)	2.7 (0.0,7.4)	0.8 (0.0,2.9)	2.5 (0.0,6.8)	1.0 (0.0,3.6)	1.5 (0.0,5.2)	1.1 (0.0,3.9)	1.0 (0.0,3.4)	1.1 (0.0,4.0)
GBP Q	1.9 (0.0,5.5)	2.9 (0.1,7.2)	15.5 (6.8,24.2)	59.5 (48.6,71.4)	2.8 (0.1,7.6)	3.8 (0.2,8.9)	0.7 (0.0,2.8)	1.8 (0.0,5.7)	1.1 (0.0,3.8)	0.9 (0.0,3.4)	0.9 (0.0,3.2)	2.3 (0.0,6.1)	1.2 (0.0,4.5)	1.7 (0.0,5.5)	0.7 (0.0,2.5)	2.2 (0.0,7.0)
JPY P	0.7 (0.0,2.6)	0.9 (0.0,2.8)	4.0 (0.1,10.0)	2.1 (0.0,6.0)	54.7 (46.6,62.9)	25.6 (16.8,33.1)	3.2 (0.1,8.4)	0.7 (0.0,2.6)	0.9 (0.0,3.2)	0.9 (0.0,3.4)	0.6 (0.0,2.2)	2.3 (0.0,6.2)	1.2 (0.0,4.5)	0.8 (0.0,2.9)	1.0 (0.0,3.7)	0.7 (0.0,2.8)
JPY Q	2.6 (0.5,4.9)	3.2 (0.8,5.8)	0.8 (0.0,2.7)	3.4 (0.5,7.2)	22.5 (14.3,29.9)	53.2 (44.9,62.6)	0.7 (0.0,2.4)	1.6 (0.0,4.7)	1.9 (0.0,5.0)	0.5 (0.0,2.0)	2.5 (0.0,6.0)	2.2 (0.0,5.6)	0.5 (0.0,2.0)	0.7 (0.0,2.5)	2.6 (0.2,6.2)	0.6 (0.0,2.2)
CHF P	21.7 (14.1,29.0)	12.5 (4.0,22.2)	1.3 (0.0,4.1)	0.6 (0.0,2.1)	8.0 (1.9,15.8)...	7.6 (1.9,15.8)...	21.4 (14.9,28.6)	3.7 (0.7,7.9)	7.8 (3.3,12.4)	0.6 (0.0,2.1)	5.3 (1.5,9.4)	0.5 (0.0,1.8)	2.7 (0.2,6.1)	1.0 (0.0,3.3)	4.8 (1.1,8.8)	0.5 (0.0,1.9)
CHF Q	11.0 (3.3,19.1)	14.4 (5.1,24.5)	0.8 (0.0,2.9)	2.4 (0.0,7.5)	3.3 (0.3,8.1)	3.5 (0.5,8.5)	6.3 (1.0,13.2)	49.4 (35.9,62.9)	0.9 (0.0,3.1)	1.2 (0.0,4.5)	0.7 (0.0,2.9)	0.7 (0.0,2.7)	0.9 (0.0,3.4)	1.2 (0.0,4.4)	0.9 (0.0,3.1)	2.2 (0.0,6.9)
FRF P	23.6 (17.8,29.5)	14.6 (7.2,22.8)	1.8 (0.0,5.0)	1.2 (0.0,3.6)	2.8 (0.1,8.0)	4.0 (0.1,11.1)	8.3 (4.3,12.4)	1.5 (0.1,3.7)	18.9 (14.3,23.7)	2.5 (0.2,5.6)	7.1 (3.3,10.8)	0.5 (0.0,2.0)	3.5 (0.5,7.2)	1.2 (0.0,3.4)	7.7 (3.5,11.8)	0.8 (0.0,2.6)
FRF Q	12.4 (4.3,20.2)	15.6 (7.4,24.4)	0.6 (0.0,2.5)	1.6 (0.0,5.4)	4.8 (0.7,10.9)	6.6 (1.4,14.3)	0.8 (0.0,2.8)	0.9 (0.0,3.4)	5.7 (0.6,11.3)	46.6 (32.3,62.2)	1.5 (0.0,4.8)	0.8 (0.0,2.9)	1.5 (0.0,5.2)	1.0 (0.0,3.6)	3.2 (0.1,7.6)	1.1 (0.0,4.4)
BEF P	26.4 (18.8,33.4)	20.6 (11.6,29.8)	1.9 (0.0,5.1)	1.2 (0.0,3.8)	5.0 (0.3,11.1)	6.7 (1.4,13.2)	6.0 (2.5,9.9)	0.8 (0.0,2.8)	6.6 (2.3,11.1)	1.0 (0.0,3.4)	12.4 (7.8,17.1)	0.7 (0.0,2.5)	3.1 (0.3,7.0)	1.0 (0.0,3.2)	5.1 (1.3,9.2)	0.5 (0.0,1.8)
BEF Q	0.9 (0.0,3.4)	1.4 (0.0,5.2)	1.3 (0.0,4.5)	2.2 (0.0,6.1)	3.2 (0.1,8.2)	5.1 (0.6,12.0)	1.7 (0.0,5.5)	0.9 (0.0,3.5)	2.8 (0.1,6.9)	1.4 (0.0,4.7)	5.2 (0.6,10.8)	65.9 (51.9,79.9)	0.7 (0.0,2.6)	1.0 (0.0,3.7)	1.9 (0.0,5.5)	0.9 (0.0,3.4)
ITL P	9.2 (2.5,16.4)	7.3 (1.3,15.2)	1.4 (0.0,4.7)	0.6 (0.0,2.3)	4.4 (0.3,10.4)	6.1 (0.9,13.5)	4.6 (1.1,8.7)	1.3 (0.0,4.0)	5.9 (1.4,10.5)	1.1 (0.0,3.9)	5.6 (0.9,11.0)	0.5 (0.0,1.8)	37.4 (27.3,48.8)	11.3 (4.1,19.7)	4.9 (1.0,9.2)	0.6 (0.0,2.3)
ITL Q	2.9 (0.1,7.4)	2.0 (0.0,6.2)	1.4 (0.0,4.6)	2.2 (0.0,7.0)	4.3 (0.6,9.7)	3.4 (0.4,8.6)	2.0 (0.0,5.7)	1.9 (0.0,5.9)	2.4 (0.0,6.4)	1.0 (0.0,3.8)	1.6 (0.0,5.4)	0.7 (0.0,2.5)	15.1 (6.1,24.1)	51.8 (40.7,62.8)	1.8 (0.0,5.3)	2.6 (0.0,7.7)
NLG P	23.9 (17.7,30.1)	15.1 (7.4,23.6)	1.0 (0.0,3.1)	0.8 (0.0,2.8)	1.5 (0.0,5.8)	3.4 (0.9,7.0)	6.8 (3.1,10.4)	2.1 (0.2,4.9)	9.5 (5.1,13.6)	2.1 (0.0,5.1)	7.1 (3.5,10.7)	0.4 (0.0,1.6)	3.5 (0.7,6.8)	1.1 (0.0,3.2)	17.6 (13.0,22.4)	1.2 (0.0,3.5)
NLG Q	3.7 (0.1,9.6)	3.5 (0.1,9.2)	1.1 (0.0,3.8)	2.0 (0.0,6.6)	1.5 (0.0,5.8)	3.4 (0.9,7.0)	1.3 (0.0,4.3)	2.1 (0.0,6.9)	2.9 (0.0,8.0)	1.2 (0.0,4.7)	1.3 (0.0,4.4)	1.2 (0.0,4.4)	1.0 (0.0,3.8)	2.9 (0.1,8.2)	4.3 (0.1,10.6)	66.7 (51.8,80.1)

Notes: The connectedness matrix is computed using normalized generalized forecast error variance decompositions following Diebold and Yilmaz (2014). Each row sums to 100% by construction. The depth of shading reflects the strength of the associated heatwave/spillover effect, with darker shading indicating a stronger effect. Values reported are empirical means with the corresponding 90% empirical confidence interval shown in rounded parentheses below. We employ a non-parametric sieve bootstrap based on 10,000 stable iterations. For more information about the sieve bootstrap procedure, see Dees et al. (2007), especially Supplement A.

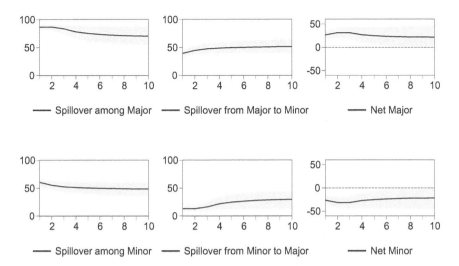

Figure 4.4 Spillover and heatwave indices for major and minor markets

Notes: The horizontal axis records the horizon in trading days, while the vertical axis is measured in percent. The major markets are DEM, GBP, JPY, and CHF while the minor markets are FRF, BEF, ITL, and NLG. The decomposed spillover indices reported here are computed following the method described in equation (15). In each case, the net connectedness is computed following equation (16). Note that the values of *net major* are equal in magnitude but of opposite sign to the values of *net minor* by construction. The 90% bootstrap interval is shaded in each case.

markets. Meanwhile, as expected, the meteor shower effects from the minor markets to the major markets are negligible in all cases.

In light of the apparent differences in the behavior of the major and minor markets, Figure 4.4 presents an aggregated representation of the spillovers between these two groups over ten trading days. The contrast between the two groups is stark. First, note that heatwave effects and spillovers among the major markets account for almost 90% of the FEV in these markets at $h = 1$ and for approximately 75% at $h = 10$. This indicates that trading activity and prices in the major markets are largely unaffected by conditions in the minor markets. Meanwhile, spillovers from the major markets to the minor markets account for approximately 50% of the FEV of the minor markets on average across all horizons. As a result, the major markets record strong positive net connectedness with respect to the system as a whole, reflecting the importance of shocks in the major markets for global currency trading.

It is important to note, however, that price and order flow innovations in the DEM market are also key factors influencing the price of the Swiss franc at $h = 1$. Similarly, we observe considerable spillovers from the yen to the Swiss franc. This implies that significant meteor shower effects are not felt only by the smaller markets but also occur among the major markets. Fung and Patterson (1999) also find a close linkage among currency futures markets for DEM, GBP, JPY, and CHF. In particular, they find that volatilities in the DEM, GBP, and JPY markets explain up to 90% of the volatility in the CHF market, contributing around 30% each. Collectively, the importance of shocks to the Deutsche mark at the one-day ahead horizon is suggestive of a leader-recipient relationship between the Deutsche mark and the other continental European currencies, an observation to which we will shortly return. However, we also observe non-negligible spillovers from the CHF, FRF, BEF, and NLG exchange rates to the DEM exchange rate, which suggests that the European markets may also share some common risk exposure.

Table 4.6 presents a similar heat map at the five-days ahead horizon. While we still observe non-negligible heatwave effects, they are considerably weaker than in the one-day ahead case. By contrast, the meteor shower effects are much stronger. The key difference between Tables 4.5 and 4.6 lies in the relative magnitude of meteor shower effects coming from the DEM and JPY markets. At the one-day ahead horizon, the Deutsche mark was by far the dominant currency. However, at $h = 5$, this dominance is challenged by the yen. This shift arises because spillovers from the Deutsche mark tend to subside as the horizon increases while spillovers from the yen intensify at longer horizons. This suggests that while information from the market for the Deutsche mark is immediately impounded into the trading activity and prices of the other markets, information from the yen market is impounded more gradually.

The different informational roles of the Deutsche mark and the Japanese yen markets can be seen clearly in Table 4.7, which identifies the foreign market that exerts the strongest leadership effect with respect to each market in the system. To measure the strength of the leadership effect experienced by the i-th market at the h-day ahead horizon, we compute the following:

$$L_{i \leftarrow j}^{(h)} = \left(\phi_{P_i \leftarrow P_j}^{(h)} + \phi_{P_i \leftarrow Q_j}^{(h)} \right) - \left\{ \phi_{P_i \leftarrow P_i}^{(h)} + \phi_{P_i \leftarrow Q_i}^{(h)} \right\} \tag{17}$$

for $j = 1, \ldots, K, j \neq i$. The terms in rounded parentheses measure the meteor shower effect from market j to the price in market i, while the terms in braces measure the effect of local information on the price in market i. Hence, if $L_{i \leftarrow j}^{(h)} > 0$ then market j leads market i at horizon h. For each market i, Table 4.7 records the leader as the market j for which $L_{i \leftarrow j}^{(h)} > 0$ is maximized. The growing importance of shocks to the yen at longer horizons is readily apparent.

Careful consideration of the heat maps in Tables 4.5 and 4.6 provides one final insight. The price and order flow in the markets for both the Japanese yen and the British pound are largely determined by their domestic innovations. This suggests that these two markets may be insulated to some extent from shocks in the continental European markets. As such, it is likely that investors may view them as safe havens following adverse shocks to the European markets. Formal evaluation of the safe haven hypothesis requires directional information from impulse response analysis and will be conducted in the next section.

Table 4.6 Bootstrapped connectedness among variables, five-days ahead

	DEM P	DEM Q	GBP P	GBP Q	JPY P	JPY Q	CHF P	CHF Q	FRF P	FRF Q	BEF P	BEF Q	ITL P	ITL Q	NLG P	NLG Q
DEM P	17.4 (9.5,29.3)	12.9 (3.1,32.8)	1.4 (0.1,3.8)	1.8 (0.1,6.3)	11.7 (1.8,25.3)	17.9 (2.5,33.6)	7.7 (3.3,13.4)	2.1 (0.3,6.2)	7.5 (3.3,12.4)	1.0 (0.1,3.0)	7.3 (2.9,12.4)	1.0 (0.1,3.0)	1.7 (0.3,3.9)	0.9 (0.1,2.7)	6.8 (2.6,11.9)	0.9 (0.1,2.9)
DEM Q	12.5 (4.5,26.8)	29.2 (7.1,57.0)	1.2 (0.1,3.7)	1.7 (0.1,5.9)	3.1 (0.2,10.9)	6.5 (0.2,20.0)	9.9 (1.4,17.7)	1.1 (0.1,3.6)	9.2 (1.1,16.3)	0.9 (0.1,3.1)	10.2 (1.2,17.1)	1.1 (0.1,3.6)	2.1 (0.1,5.3)	1.0 (0.1,3.2)	9.3 (1.0,16.3)	1.0 (0.1,3.3)
GBP P	6.3 (1.9,12.2)	5.6 (1.2,13.1)	32.1 (16.9,47.3)	23.6 (7.7,38.9)	2.8 (0.4,7.6)	4.7 (0.5,13.8)	4.8 (1.0,10.1)	1.2 (0.1,3.8)	4.1 (0.8,8.9)	1.0 (0.1,3.2)	4.1 (0.8,9.0)	0.9 (0.1,2.8)	1.8 (0.3,4.4)	1.3 (0.2,3.2)	4.0 (0.5,9.5)	1.9 (0.1,5.8)
GBP Q	1.9 (0.2,5.0)	2.7 (0.3,7.6)	15.3 (3.7,30.0)	57.0 (43.2,70.2)	2.5 (0.1,7.4)	3.1 (0.3,9.3)	2.0 (0.1,6.4)	1.8 (0.0,5.8)	1.6 (0.1,5.0)	0.9 (0.0,3.4)	1.9 (0.1,5.2)	1.9 (0.1,5.5)	1.9 (0.1,6.1)	1.7 (0.0,5.5)	1.6 (0.1,5.5)	2.5 (0.0,7.7)
JPY P	2.9 (0.3,7.3)	2.4 (0.1,7.4)	2.6 (0.2,6.9)	1.7 (0.1,4.9)	37.6 (21.1,52.6)	31.9 (16.4,41.6)	3.0 (0.6,7.4)	0.9 (0.0,3.2)	3.5 (0.4,8.6)	0.9 (0.0,2.8)	4.0 (0.5,9.3)	2.4 (0.2,5.9)	0.9 (0.1,2.9)	0.9 (0.0,3.1)	3.6 (0.4,9.1)	0.9 (0.0,3.0)
JPY Q	5.0 (1.0,9.5)	3.7 (0.5,7.8)	1.1 (0.0,3.6)	2.3 (0.2,5.6)	22.0 (7.5,36.2)	43.6 (33.9,53.5)	2.3 (0.1,6.9)	1.3 (0.0,4.1)	4.0 (0.5,8.9)	1.2 (0.0,3.9)	4.8 (0.9,9.9)	2.2 (0.1,5.5)	0.7 (0.0,2.6)	0.7 (0.0,2.4)	4.6 (0.5,10.4)	0.6 (0.0,2.2)
CHF P	11.0 (5.1,19.0)	9.7 (1.7,26.8)	1.4 (0.1,3.9)	1.6 (0.1,5.8)	12.3 (5.2,25.6)	19.6 (4.6,34.2)	11.9 (6.4,18.0)	2.7 (0.6,7.5)	8.0 (3.1,13.3)	1.0 (0.1,3.1)	8.1 (2.8,14.0)	1.2 (0.1,3.4)	2.1 (0.5,4.5)	1.0 (0.1,2.9)	7.5 (2.5,13.4)	1.0 (0.1,3.0)
CHF Q	6.6 (2.3,12.6)	6.2 (0.9,18.9)	1.4 (0.1,4.4)	2.4 (0.1,7.8)	4.5 (0.2,13.3)	7.6 (0.2,19.9)	10.6 (3.8,19.1)	24.3 (6.8,48.7)	9.8 (2.4,16.6)	1.8 (0.1,5.7)	9.3 (2.2,15.7)	1.3 (0.1,3.4)	2.4 (0.4,6.0)	1.0 (0.1,3.1)	8.2 (1.7,14.5)	2.8 (0.2,7.6)
FRF P	14.3 (7.7,23.3)	12.7 (3.3,29.0)	2.0 (0.2,5.5)	2.6 (0.1,8.5)	10.0 (1.4,22.5)	15.1 (1.8,31.4)	7.4 (3.3,13.1)	2.0 (0.2,6.1)	11.7 (6.1,18.4)	3.5 (0.4,9.6)	6.3 (2.5,11.6)	0.8 (0.1,2.6)	2.7 (0.6,5.8)	1.6 (0.1,4.6)	6.2 (2.6,11.0)	1.0 (0.1,3.0)
FRF Q	8.6 (2.6,18.9)	12.9 (2.5,31.2)	1.3 (0.1,4.6)	2.9 (0.1,9.5)	9.3 (0.8,23.7)	15.0 (1.1,34.1)	4.1 (0.6,11.3)	1.4 (0.1,5.0)	6.2 (1.6,13.7)	24.9 (8.0,46.3)	4.1 (0.5,11.2)	0.9 (0.0,3.1)	1.7 (0.2,4.8)	1.5 (0.1,4.9)	3.9 (0.8,9.5)	1.3 (0.1,4.5)
BEF P	12.6 (6.7,20.3)	12.2 (2.7,30.9)	1.7 (0.2,4.6)	2.6 (0.1,8.6)	8.7 (1.4,21.0)	16.3 (3.0,31.3)	8.9 (3.2,15.7)	2.1 (0.2,6.3)	8.7 (3.4,14.3)	1.1 (0.1,3.3)	10.2 (5.1,15.2)	1.4 (0.1,4.7)	2.6 (0.6,5.2)	1.0 (0.1,3.0)	8.7 (2.9,14.7)	1.3 (0.1,4.0)
BEF Q	3.6 (0.5,8.2)	1.6 (0.1,5.1)	1.4 (0.1,4.1)	1.3 (0.1,4.0)	5.4 (0.7,12.4)	9.3 (2.7,17.1)	4.9 (0.8,10.0)	0.8 (0.0,2.7)	7.0 (1.6,12.2)	1.4 (0.1,4.1)	11.5 (2.8,19.4)	43.0 (26.1,63.3)	0.9 (0.1,4.1)	0.9 (0.0,3.0)	5.8 (1.0,11.2)	0.7 (0.0,2.3)
ITL P	7.6 (2.8,13.1)	6.2 (1.1,16.4)	1.4 (0.1,4.0)	1.4 (0.1,4.6)	6.9 (1.0,16.1)	12.4 (2.7,23.7)	3.5 (0.7,8.5)	1.6 (0.1,4.9)	6.5 (2.4,11.1)	1.1 (0.1,3.1)	6.7 (2.4,11.6)	0.9 (0.1,2.8)	22.2 (10.8,35.9)	11.4 (3.1,23.5)	6.1 (2.1,10.7)	1.3 (0.1,3.9)
ITL Q	3.7 (0.7,8.5)	2.1 (0.2,6.3)	1.3 (0.1,4.3)	3.3 (0.1,10.0)	6.2 (0.7,14.9)	10.1 (1.6,20.4)	3.5 (0.7,8.5)	1.8 (0.1,5.9)	3.5 (0.7,8.4)	1.0 (0.0,3.3)	4.3 (0.6,10.5)	0.9 (0.0,2.9)	8.7 (2.3,20.7)	42.2 (22.3,59.6)	3.6 (0.6,8.9)	3.8 (0.2,9.9)
NLG P	14.9 (8.0,23.7)	12.7 (3.5,28.1)	1.5 (0.1,4.2)	1.9 (0.1,6.6)	11.0 (1.9,24.0)	13.7 (1.3,29.7)	6.5 (2.8,11.9)	2.4 (0.3,7.0)	7.1 (3.3,11.5)	1.8 (0.2,4.4)	5.7 (2.4,9.9)	1.0 (0.1,3.0)	2.8 (0.7,6.0)	1.4 (0.1,4.1)	12.4 (5.9,20.5)	3.3 (0.2,9.4)
NLG Q	7.2 (1.0,16.9)	8.2 (0.9,21.8)	1.1 (0.1,3.4)	1.6 (0.1,4.7)	7.5 (0.5,19.6)	11.8 (0.8,29.0)	2.4 (0.3,6.2)	1.6 (0.2,4.7)	4.2 (0.5,10.3)	1.2 (0.1,3.6)	2.4 (0.2,6.5)	1.2 (0.0,4.0)	1.7 (0.1,4.9)	1.5 (0.2,4.4)	8.7 (1.0,18.1)	37.6 (19.2,58.4)

Notes: The connectedness matrix is computed using normalized generalized forecast error variance decompositions following Diebold and Yilmaz (2014). Each row sums to 100% by construction. The depth of shading reflects the strength of the associated heatwave/spillover effect, with darker shading indicating a stronger effect. Values reported are empirical means with the corresponding 90% empirical confidence interval shown in rounded parentheses below. We employ a non-parametric sieve bootstrap based on 10,000 stable iterations. For more information about the sieve bootstrap procedure, see Dees et al. (2007), especially Supplement A.

Table 4.7 Leader-recipient relationships

Market	One Day Ahead		Five Days Ahead	
	Leader	Magnitude	Leader	Magnitude
DEM	–	–	–	–
GBP	–	–	–	–
JPY	–	–	–	–
CHF	DEM	9.10	JPY	17.29
FRF	DEM	16.83	DEM	11.81
BEF	DEM	33.89	JPY	13.31
ITL	–	–	–	–
NLG	DEM	20.21	DEM	11.93

Notes: For the i-th market, magnitude is defined as $L_{i \leftarrow j}^{(h)} = \left(\phi_{P_i \leftarrow P_j}^{(h)} + \phi_{P_i \leftarrow Q_j}^{(h)} \right) - \left\{ \phi_{P_i \leftarrow P_i}^{(h)} + \phi_{P_i \leftarrow Q_i}^{(h)} \right\}$ for $j = 1,...,K, j \neq i$. The terms in rounded parentheses measure the spillover from market j to the price in market i, while the terms in braces measure the effect of local information (price and order flow in market i) on the price in market i. Hence, if $L_{i \leftarrow j}^{(h)} > 0$ then there is a leader-recipient relationship between markets i and j, where j is the leader. The market identified as the leader in each case is that market j for which $L_{i \leftarrow j}^{(h)}$ is maximized. Where no leader is identified then $L_{i \leftarrow j}^{(h)} \leq 0 \ \forall j \in (1,...,K)$, $j \neq i$.

5. Impulse response analysis

To further examine the linkages among currency markets, we conduct two counterfactual exercises based on generalized impulse response analysis with respect to adverse shocks in the order flow equations of selected market-specific models. The order flow is often used in the micro exchange rate literature to proxy for publicly unavailable information, which will be impounded into the exchange rate through the trading process. Hence, our counterfactual exercises trace the information integration process within and between currency markets given the arrival of news in a designated market. Significantly, and unlike the body of existing research, our GVAR model allows us to observe not only the price movement across markets following a given shock but also the order flows that drive this movement. Hence, our analysis will yield detailed insights into the dynamic interactions between the markets and thereby provide new insights into the leader-recipient and safe haven hypotheses in a manner that was hitherto infeasible.

Specifically, we analyze impulse responses following a positive shock to the order flow equation in the DEM market and in the JPY market. These shocks represent local currency selling pressure in the respective markets; that is, traders are selling either the Deutsche mark or the yen to buy the dollar. They may then liquidate their dollar position in favor of another currency. Our focus on shocks to the Deutsche mark and the yen is natural in light of the preceding analysis, which has shown that these markets are not only the most liquid in our sample but that they also exert a dominant effect over many other markets in the system. Furthermore, it is consistent with the focus of the seminal paper of Evans and Lyons (2002b), which studies the importance of order flow information as a determinant of the exchange rate in the Deutsche mark/dollar and yen/dollar markets using data of the same vintage that we employ here.

5.1. Deutsche mark selling pressure in the DEM/USD market

Figure 4.5 reports the first difference of the impulse responses following a shock of one standard deviation in the DEM order flow equation, which amounts to 110.79 excess Deutsche mark selling orders in the DEM market. By working with the first difference of the impulse response function, we are able to frame our discussion naturally in terms of order flows and price changes as opposed to cumulative order flows and price levels. The figure reveals that Deutsche mark selling pressure exerts strong heatwave effects. Furthermore, trading activity in the DEM market persists beyond the day in which the shock occurs and leads to a significant depreciation of the mark vis-à-vis the dollar.

Importantly, we also observe strong meteor-shower effects in the sense that an adverse shock in the DEM market causes portfolio shifts involving a number of other currencies, including both major and minor markets. This is a reflection of the intricate network of connections among markets identified using connectedness analysis in the preceding section. In particular, we see that Deutsche mark selling pressure is associated with considerable local currency selling pressure in the GBP, CHF, and FRF markets. This indicates that traders may consider the

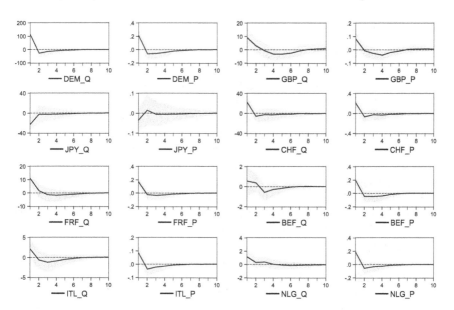

Figure 4.5 GIRFs with respect to Deutche mark selling pressure

Notes: The horizontal axis shows the horizon in trading days, while the vertical axis measures the reponse of the named variable to the Deutsche mark selling pressure in the DEM market. Price responses are measured in percent, while the order flow responses are measured in trades. The 90% bootstrap interval is shaded in each case.

Deutsche mark, the pound, the Swiss franc and the French franc to share similar risk exposures. Furthermore, we see that trading activity in these markets also continues on the day after the shock occurs, indicating that traders' portfolio shifts occur in a gradual fashion, in part due to the limits of arbitrage and informational asymmetries.

A further meteor shower effect is of particular interest, namely that from the DEM market to the JPY market. In response to local currency selling pressure in the DEM market, the JPY market experiences considerable yen buying pressure, as some investors convert positions from the Deutsche mark to the yen. This, in turn, leads to a marked appreciation of the yen. Recall that we define currency j as a safe haven from the perspective of currency i if selling pressure for currency i triggers buying pressure for currency j. Therefore, our analysis reveals that investors regard the yen as a safe haven currency relative to the mark.[9] This finding is consistent with Evans and Lyons (2002a), who find that Deutsche mark selling pressure leads to an appreciation (albeit insignificant) of the yen against the dollar.

Finally, we observe either negligible or insignificant trading responses in the BEF, ITL, and NLG markets. Nevertheless, each of these currencies experiences a significant depreciation against the dollar, with a pattern that closely mimics that described by the Deutsche mark. This is highly suggestive of a leader-recipient effect among the European currency markets — in keeping with our connectedness analysis — in which the Deutsche mark is the dominant currency.

5.2. Yen selling pressure in the JPY/USD market

We now consider a selling pressure shock of one standard deviation in the JPY market, which equates to 94.62 excess yen selling orders. Recall that interest rates in Japan were set close to zero from the end of 1995, creating a significant negative interest rate differential against most other major economies. As of 1996Q3, the interbank rate in Japan was 0.46%, relative to 5.31% in the US, 3.2% in Germany, 5.79% in the UK and 1.89% in Switzerland.[10] It is well known that these interest rate differentials fueled a sizeable yen carry trade (Gagnon and Chaboud, 2007; Burnside, Eichenbaum, and Rebelo, 2007;, Brunnermeier, Nagel, and Pedersen, 2009). Hence, over our sample period (May 1996–August 1996), a yen selling pressure shock in the JPY/USD market mimics the conversion of borrowed funds denominated in yen into investments denominated in dollars or other currencies.

In keeping with the results of connectedness analysis presented above, Figure 4.6 shows that yen selling pressure in the JPY market exerts a strong heatwave effect that is somewhat persistent, with significant feedback trading activity continuing for two days. The Japanese shock also exerts notable meteor shower effects, resulting in modest local currency selling pressure in most other currency markets. The notable exception is the GBP market, which experiences pronounced pound buying pressure. This is consistent with the carry trade mechanism discussed above, as the pound offers the highest yield among any of the major markets in our sample. However, given that the volume of excess yen

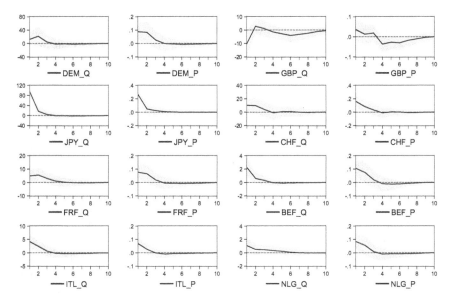

Figure 4.6 GIRFs with respect to yen selling pressure

Notes: The horizontal axis shows the horizon in trading days, while the vertical axis measures the reponse of the named variable to the yen selling pressure in the JPY market. Price responses are measured in percent, while the order flow responses are measured in trades. The 90% bootstrap interval is shaded in each case.

selling orders amounts to 113.39 at the five day horizon while the volume of excess pound buying orders is just 10.39 over the same period, it is clear that the yen–pound carry trade only accounts for a small proportion of the portfolio shift in the wake of the shock. Much of the remainder is likely to be invested in dollar-denominated assets to exploit the yen–dollar carry trade. Furthermore, since an adverse shock to the yen causes both dollar and pound buying pressure, it follows that the latter are safe havens with respect to the yen.

The shock causes some apparent movement in the pound exchange rate, although it is marginally insignificant at the 90% level. A careful examination of the trading data in the GBP market (plotted in Figure 4.1(b)) suggests that the price and cumulative order flow in this market do not always move in the same direction over our sample period. This is also apparent from Table 4.1, which reveals that the pairwise correlations between P_{it}, Q_{it}, and Q_{it}^* are considerably weaker than in most other markets. Evans and Lyons (2002a) also document that order flows in the JPY market have a negligible impact on the pound. Nevertheless, the shock generates an immediate and significant depreciation of all the remaining currencies against the dollar as it creates simultaneous local currency selling pressures (i.e., dollar buying pressures) in these markets. This confirms our earlier finding that the yen acts as a leader with respect to many European markets, particularly at longer horizons. A similar although somewhat narrower result is reported by Evans and Lyons (2002a). They find that selling pressure in the JPY/USD market is associated with a significant depreciation of not just the yen but also of the Swiss franc. The ability of our GVAR model to detect a greater number of significant responses than the Evans and Lyons model rests in its construction, which takes full account of informational linkages across markets in a dynamic setting in which all variables are globally endogenous.

5.3. Identifying safe haven currencies

Our analysis of the GIRFs above confirms that currency spot markets are intricately linked. Overall, we find that both the Deutsche mark and the yen play a major informational role in the global system, leading other markets. We also see that the impulse responses tend to converge to zero between one and two days after the initial shock, which suggests that cross-market information is integrated into prices with a modest lag. Finally, by studying the direction of meteor shower effects – which is often absent from existing studies – we are able to identify safe haven currencies with respect to market-specific shocks. In this way, we find that the yen and the dollar are safe havens with respect to the Deutsche mark, while the pound and the dollar are safe havens for yen investors.

By extending our analysis to consider adverse shocks to each market in our sample, we are able to identify safe havens for every market. Table 4.8 identifies as a safe haven the market which experiences the largest cumulative negative order flow (i.e., local currency buying pressure) in the five trading days following an adverse shock to a chosen market. A striking pattern emerges among the major markets: the yen is an important safe haven for each of the major markets, while the pound provides a safe haven for the yen, as seen earlier. Turning to the smaller markets, the pattern is less clear, although it is interesting to note that, in all cases, the safe haven identified using our method is one of the major currencies. This is an intuitively pleasing result. Furthermore, across all eight markets, it is clear that the yen and the pound (as well as the dollar) are the dominant safe havens for the continental European currencies, reflecting their importance for

Table 4.8 Safe haven currencies by market

Shock Origin	Size of Shock	Safe Haven	5 Day Response
DEM	110.79	JPY	−31.17
GBP	44.15	JPY	−18.94
JPY	94.62	GBP	−10.39
CHF	41.53	JPY	−11.99
FRF	18.77	JPY	−16.93
BEF	7.15	GBP	−7.37
ITL	12.90	DEM	−11.72
NLG	5.57	CHF	−17.30

Notes: In each case, the safe haven market is that market which experiences the strongest cumulative negative order flow in the five trading days following the initial adverse shock to the named originating market. The five-day cumulative responses are recorded in the final column and the size of the original shock is reported in the second column. The unit of measurement is net orders.

investors wishing to manage their exposure to risks arising from European shocks through diversification.

6. Concluding remarks

We develop a global model of currency spot markets using the Global VAR framework originated by Pesaran et al. (2004) and Dees et al. (2007). Our model represents a significant extension of the multi-currency portfolio shifts model of Evans and Lyons (2002a). As an error correction model, our GVAR explicitly accounts for persistent mispricing and for the possibility that dealers may hold overnight imbalances. Furthermore, as a dynamic model, it is able to trace the complex interactions between prices and order flows over time. Finally, by virtue of its dynamic panel structure, our model can analyze the interactions among variables both within a given market and also across markets. Hence, our approach can shed light on how trading activity in a chosen market may affect the trading activity and price in all other markets in the system in both the short- and the long-run. Therefore, our model offers a singularly rich framework to explore the intricate network of relationships underlying the global currency market. Such a level of detail has not been achieved by existing studies to date.

Working with the classic order flow dataset of Evans and Lyons (2002a, b), we map out a complex network of interlinkages among the eight currency markets in our sample. Our results can be broken down into five principal findings. First, our results indicate that adjustment to equilibrium following a shock is not necessarily completed within a single trading day, underscoring the necessity for future applied and theoretical work to account for overnight imbalances and persistent mispricing (Sager and Taylor, 2006). Second, we find that while heatwave effects are important, they are by no means the dominant factor influencing global currency markets. Meteor shower effects account for more than 60% of the forecast error variance in the system at the five-days ahead horizon. Third, we find that the minor markets (BEF, FRF, ITL, NLG) behave quite differently than the major markets (DEM, GBP, JPY, CHF) in the sense that the price in the minor markets is considerably more sensitive to meteor shower effects. Fourth, we find that the meteor showers from the Deutsche Mark and the Yen are so strong that they exert a leadership effect with respect to the minor markets as well as the Swiss franc. Interestingly, while the influence of shocks to the Deutsche mark on other currencies is immediate and profound, meteor showers from the yen are initially muted but gradually intensify. This perhaps reflects delays in the transmission of news regarding fundamentals from Japan to the physical marketplace in London given the time zone difference as well as the available communications technologies in 1996. Finally, by innovative use of impulse response analysis, we identify safe haven currencies with respect to each market in our sample. The dollar and the yen are the main safe havens for the European currencies, while the dollar and pound are safe havens for the yen.

Our work draws attention to the intricate linkages that exist between currency markets. As such, it offers a rich vein for continuing research which may, in time, shed light on some of the celebrated paradoxes of exchange rate research. Work toward a more complete understanding of these linkages is not only important for improving exchange rate modeling itself but is also likely to yield major gains in forecasting performance.

Acknowledgments

We are indebted to Heather Anderson, Tony Garratt, Guay Lim, Hashem Pesaran, and Kevin Reilly for their many helpful comments and suggestions and to Martin Evans for sharing the dataset. This paper has benefited greatly from the thoughtful discussion of participants at the China Meeting of the Econometric Society (Xiamen, June 2014), the Workshop of the Australasian Macroeconomics Society (Melbourne, July 2014), the ECB's Workshop on Modelling Cross-Border Financial Channels: A GVAR Perspective (Frankfurt, November 2014), the Inaugural Conference on Recent Developments in Financial Econometrics and Applications (Geelong, December 2014), the 41st Annual Conference of the Eastern Economic Association (New York, February 2015), the 2016 Australasian Meeting of the Econometric Society (Sydney, July 2016) and of participants in research seminars at the University of Melbourne and the Reserve Bank of New Zealand. Any remaining errors or omissions are the sole responsibility of the authors.

Notes

1 Subsection 2.4 provides a detailed definition of the safe haven currency hypothesis. See Kaul and Sapp (2006) and Ranaldo and Soderlind (2007) as good examples of the safe haven currency literature.
2 For example, DeLong et al. (1990) argue that persistent mispricing arises because of noise trader risk which deters arbitrageurs from taking large positions, while Abreu and Brunnermeier (2002) discuss the importance of the synchronization problem which arises due to the dispersion of opinions among arbitrageurs.
3 In principle, one can employ time-varying weights in the construction of the weakly exogenous variables. However, given the relatively short period spanned by our dataset (82 trading days), we do not pursue this option.
4 Section 2.3 provides more information about the covariance matrix of ε_{it} in a global setting.
5 In our application, with eight markets, the dimension of W_i is 3×16.
6 Note that our concept of the leader-recipient relationship differs significantly from that of Sapp (2002), who examines price leadership from the institutional perspective by studying which institutions incorporate information into their quoted prices first.
7 We note in passing that safe haven currency effects have been somewhat neglected in the literature. Ranaldo and Soderlind (2007, p. 25) define a safe haven currency as one which "benefits from negative exposure to risky assets and appreciates when market risk and illiquidity increase". They find that the Swiss franc, the yen and, to some extent, the euro appreciate against the US dollar when US equity prices decrease and when US bond prices and foreign exchange trading volatility increase, suggesting

that they exhibit safe haven attributes. Meanwhile, Kaul and Sapp (2006) study safe haven trading in the EUR/USD spot and forward markets around Y2K and find that investors channeled their funds into the dollar in the months preceding December 1999 and well into January 2000, suggesting that the dollar was considered the principal safe haven currency as Y2K concerns grew.

8 Additional trading data for the Danish kroner was excluded due to two missing observations (27 May and 12 July 1996). This is not a significant omission as this market is neither particularly deep nor liquid during our sample period.

9 Our analysis indicates that the dollar is also a safe haven with respect to the Deutsche mark given that our dataset contains information on bilateral exchange rates vis-à-vis the dollar and that local currency selling pressure in the i-th market is equivalent to dollar buying pressure in that market.

10 Data are sourced from the 'Interbank Money Rate' series in the IMF's International Financial Statistics.

Bibliography

Abreu, D. and M. K. Brunnermeier (2002): "Synchronization Risk and Delayed Arbitrage," *Journal of Financial Economics*, 66, 341–360.

Barberis, N., A. Shleifer, and R. Vishny (1998): "A Model of Investor Sentiment," *Journal of Financial Economics*, 49, 307–343.

Berger, D. W., A. P. Chaboud, S. V. Chernenko, E. Howorka, and J. Wright (2008): "Order Flow and Exchange Rate Dynamics in Electronic Brokerage System Data," *Journal of International Economics*, 75, 93–109.

Boyer, M. M. and S. van Norden (2006): "Exchange Rates and Order Flow in the Long Run," *Finance Research Letters*, 3, 235–243.

Brunnermeier, M. K., S. Nagel, and L. H. Pedersen (2009): "Carry Trades and Currency Crashes," Nber Working Paper 14473, National Bureau of Economic Research.

Burnside, C., M. Eichenbaum, and S. Rebelo (2007): "The Returns to Currency Speculation in Emerging Markets," *American Economic Review*, 97, 333–338.

Cai, F., E. Howorka, and J. Wongswan (2008): "Informational Linkage Across Trading Regions: Evidence From Foreign Exchange Markets," *Journal of International Money and Finance*, 27, 1212–1243.

Cao, H. H., M. Evans, and R. K. Lyons (2006): "Inventory Information," *The Journal of Business*, 79, 325–364.

Cashin, P., K. Mohaddes, M. Raissi, and M. Raissi (2014): "The Di erential E ects of Oil Demand and Supply Shocks on the Global Economy," *Energy Economics*, in press.

Cohen, B. H. and H. S. Shin (2003): "Positive Feedback Trading Under Stress: Evidence From the US Treasury Securities Market," BIS Working Paper 122, Bank for International Settlements.

Daníelsson, J. and R. Love (2006): "Feedback Trading," *International Journal of Finance & Economics*, 11, 35–53.

Daníelsson, J., J. Luo, and R. Payne (2012): "Exchange Rate Determination and Inter-Market Order Flow E ects," *European Journal of Finance*, 18, 823–840.

Dees, S., F. di Mauro, M. H. Pesaran, and L. V. Smith (2007): "Exploring the International Linkages of the Euro Area: A Global VAR Analysis," *Journal of Applied Econometrics*, 22, 1–38.

DeLong, J. B., A. Shleifer, L. H. Summers, and R. J. Waldmann (1990): "Noise Trader Risk in Financial Markets," *Journal of Political Economy*, 98, 703–738.

Diebold, F. and K. Yilmaz (2009): "Measuring Financial Asset Return and Volatility Spill-overs, With Application to Global Equity Markets," *Economic Journal*, 119, 158–171.

——— (2014): "On the Network Topology of Variance Decompositions: Measuring the Connectedness of Financial Firms," *Journal of Econometrics*, in press.

Engle, R. F., T. Ito, and W.-L. Lin (1990): "Meteor Showers or Heat Waves? Heteroske-dastic Intra-daily Volatility in the Foreign Exchange Market," *Econometrica*, 58, 525–524.

Evans, M. D. D. and R. K. Lyons (2002a): "Informational Integration and FX Trading," *Journal of International Money and Finance*, 21, 807–831.

——— (2002b): "Order Flow and Exchange Rate Dynamics," *Journal of Political Economy*, 110, 170–180.

——— (2008): "How Is Macro News Transmitted to Exchange Rates?" *Journal of Financial Economics*, 88, 26–50.

Fung, H.-G. and G. A. Patterson (1999): "Volatility Linkage Among Currency Futures Markets During US Trading and Non-trading Periods," *Journal of Multinational Financial Management*, 9, 129–153.

Gagnon, J. E. and A. P. Chaboud (2007): "What Can the Data Tell Us About Carry Trades in Japanese Yen?" *International Finance Discussion Papers 899*, Board of Governors of the Federal Reserve System.

Hasbrouck, J. (1991): "Measuring the Information Content of Stock Trades," *Journal of Finance*, 46, 179–207.

Kaul, A. and S. Sapp (2006): "Y2K Fears and Safe Haven Trading of the U.S. Dollar," *Journal of International Money and Finance*, 25, 760–779.

Kyle, A. S. (1985): "Continuous Auctions and Insider Trading," *Econometrica*, 53, 1315–1335.

Love, R. and R. Payne (2008): "Macroeconomic News, Order Flows, and Exchange Rates," *Journal of Financial and Quantitative Analysis*, 43, 467–488.

Melvin, M. and B. P. Melvin (2003): "The Global Transmission of Volatility in the Foreign Exchange Market," *The Review of Economics and Statistics*, 85, 670–679.

Pesaran, M. H., T. Schuermann, and S. M. Weiner (2004): "Modeling Regional Interde-pendencies Using a Global Error-Correcting Macroeconometric Model," *Journal of Business and Economic Statistics*, 22, 129–162.

Pesaran, M. H. and Y. Shin (1996): "Cointegration and Speed of Convergence to Equilib-rium," *Journal of Econometrics*, 71, 117–143.

——— (1998): "Generalized Impulse Response Analysis in Linear Multivariate Models," *Economics Letters*, 58, 17–29.

Ranaldo, A. and P. Soderlind (2007): "Safe Haven Currencies," Working Papers, Swiss National Bank.

Rime, D., L. Sarno, and E. Sojli (2010): "Exchange Rate Forecasting, Order Flow and Macroeconomic Information," *Journal of International Economics*, 80, 72–88.

Sager, M. J. and M. P. Taylor (2006): "Under the Microscope: The Structure of the Foreign Exchange Market," *International Journal of Finance and Economics*, 11, 81–95.

——— (2008): "Commercially Available Order Flow Data and Exchange Rate Move-ments: Caveat Emptor," *Journal of Money, Credit and Banking*, 40, 583–625.

Sapp, S. G. (2002): "Price Leadership in the Spot Foreign Exchange Market," *Journal of Financial and Quantitative Analysis*, 37, 425–448.

Westerlund, J. (2007): "Testing for Error Correction in Panel Data," *Oxford Bulletin of Economics and Statistics*, 69, 709–748.

5 Smooth break, non-linearity, and speculative bubbles

New evidence of the G7 stock markets

Shyh-Wei Chen and Zixiong Xie

1. Introduction

A lot of studies have devoted much effort to the issue of bubble detecting in the financial literature by using the present value model. One avenue to examine the relationship between the stock prices and dividends over the long term is employing the linear unit root and cointegration tests, panel unit root and panel cointegration framework. If the stock prices and dividends exhibit a long-run relationship as evidenced by a cointegrating vector, then they serve as evidence against the existence of bubbles in the stock prices (see, for example, Diba and Grossman, 1988; Brooks and Katsaris, 2003). This is because, theoretically, the present value model argues that stock prices are determined by the discounted value of the future expected dividends (e.g., Campbell and Shiller, 1987; Campbell et al., 1997; Cochrane, 2001). If stock prices and dividends are integrated processes of order one, together with the assumption of a time-invariant discount rate, then the present value model predicts that there is a long-run equilibrium (cointegration) relationship between stock prices and dividends. Besides, if the present value model is valid, and assuming a time-varying discount rate instead of a constant one, then the logarithm of the dividend yield (i.e., the difference between the logarithm of the dividend and stock price) follows a stationary process (Diba and Grossman, 1988a; Campbell and Shiller, 1988a, 1988b).

The other avenue to examine this issue is adopting the non-linear model (van Norden, 1996; van Norden and Vigfusson, 1998; Bohl, 2003; Bohl and Siklos, 2004; Kanas, 2005; Brooks and Katsaris, 2003; McMillan, 2007a; Nunes and Da Silva, 2008; Shi, 2013). A good reason to explain this line of research is due to the following statement in Campbell, Lo and MacKinlay (1997, p. 260): "Empirically, there is little evidence of explosive behavior in these series. A caveat is that stochastic bubbles are *non-linear*, so standard linear methods may fail to detect the explosive behavior of the conditional expectation in these models." Theoretically, the rationale for such non-linearity comes from several factors including the presence of stochastic speculative bubbles (Blanchard and Watson, 1982; West, 1987; Evans, 1991; Charemza and Deadman, 1995), the behavior of noise traders (Kirman, 1991, 1993; Shleifer, 2000) or fads (Shiller, 1981), the presence of an intrinsic bubble (Driffill and Sola, 1998), and transaction costs (Kapetanios, Shin, and Snell, 2006).

Many studies (see, e.g., Froot and Obstfeld, 1991; Balke and Wohar, 2002; Bohl and Siklos, 2004; Jahan-Parvar and Waters, 2010) argue that stock prices and dividends remain in a long-run common trend path but that substantial deviation from this common behavior can occur. Such deviations could imply *non-linear* dynamics within the price-dividend relationship. An important explanation to account for the bubble-like behavior in the logarithm of the dividend yield is the presence of transaction costs (e.g., Kapetanios, Shin, and Snell, 2006). The rationale for this view is that when the logarithm of the dividend yield is close to its mean (equilibrium) then it exhibits a random walk behavior, while once the deviations from the mean become large, then its behavior is characterized by mean reversion. Thus, a linear approach, which would essentially average across the two regimes, would be inclined to find non-stationary behavior. Empirically, this type of non-linearity is well-characterized by the exponential smooth transition (ESTR) function (Kapetanios et al., 2003) and is therefore labeled *size non-linearity* (McMillan, 2008, p. 593). For existing evidence of the present value model with transaction costs by using the ESTR approach, readers are referred to, for example, Ryan (2006), McMillan (2004, 2006, 2007a), and McMillan and Wohar (2009) for the details.[1]

The second culprit to account for the deviation from the present value model is that the logarithm of the dividend yield has undergone a *structural break* or level shift. With respect to a structural break, this can arise through either a shift in the dividend growth rate or as a result of a change in the discount rate. Some authors have emphasized the importance of a structural break in testing of the validity of the prevent value model. For example, Bohl and Siklos (2004, p. 209) point out that "if we take as given the long-run validity of the present value model, the low power of unit root tests in particular, nonlinearities, *structural breaks* and/or outliers are possible candidates for the mixed findings." McMillan and Wohar (2010) also emphasize that it is important to consider the time variation in the mean parameter or level shifts, and hence structural breaks within the data, perhaps due to policy regime or macroeconomic shocks. Previous studies such as Sollis (2006), McMillan (2007a, 2009a, 2009b), Cerqueti and Costantini (2011), Homm and Breitung (2012), and Esteve et al. (2013) highlight the importance of a structural break and devote their efforts to examine the rational bubble hypothesis by allowing explicitly for a level shift or endogenous structural break.

The aim of this paper is to re-examine the importance of non-linearity and smooth break, respectively, in explaining the bubble-like behavior in the logarithm of the dividend yields for the group of seven (G7) stock markets. To this end, we adopt the following non-linear unit root tests in this study. First, we use the logistic trend function that allows for a smooth break in the trend, championed by Leybourne et al. (1998), to model a gradual break in the logarithm of the dividend yield by reason of policy announcements or financial shocks. The reason for us to model a smooth break in the trend is on the basis of Leybourne and Mizen (1999): "when considering aggregate behavior, the time path of structural changes in economic series is likely to be better captured by a model whose deterministic component permits gradual rather than instantaneous adjustment."

Second, we employ the exponential smooth transition autoregressive (ESTAR) unit root tests, proposed by Kapetanios et al. (2003), Kilic (2011), and Park and Shintani (2005, 2016), because these tests have been proven to be powerful methods to characterize non-linearity of data. The ESTAR non-linear behavior implies that there is a central region where the logarithm of the dividend yield behaves as a unit root whereas for values outside the central regime, the variable tends to revert to the equilibrium. In other words, the ESTAR function implies that the speed of mean reversion will be faster when the logarithm of the dividend-price ratio is far from the attractor point of zero, whereas it behaves as a unit root process (or a random walk) when it is close to it.

Third, we begin to adopt Leybourne et al.'s (1998) smooth transition augmented Dickey-Fuller test (hereafter LNV-ADF) to model a smooth break in the trend. Next, in order to capture the presence of a smooth break in the trend and non-linearity in the dividend yield simultaneously, we employ a two-step testing strategy: first estimating non-linear trend and then applying various non-linear unit root tests without a deterministic component. The idea of this procedure is in line with Leybourne et al. (1998), Sollis (2004), and Cook and Vougas (2009). As such, in the first step, we adopt the logistic smooth transition model proposed by Leybourne et al. (1998) to model the non-linear trend that stems from a structural break. This non-linear trend permits the possibility of a smooth transition between two different trend paths over time. In the second step, we test for a unit root on the residuals of step one. If the non-linearity stems from the presence of transaction cost, then we assume that the adjustment speed is asymmetric and follows an exponential smooth transition autoregressive process. That is, we take account of the possibility of a smooth break and non-linearity at the same time.

As compared to the literature, the contributions of this study are twofold. First, we evaluate the importance of non-linearity and smooth break in detecting speculative bubbles by employing various advanced non-linear econometric methods. These non-linear tests have been proven to be more powerful than the traditional linear approaches in the literature. Second, although recent studies (e.g., Bohl and Siklos, 2004; McMillan, 2006, 2007a, 2009a, 2009b; Jahan-Parvar and Waters, 2010; McMillan and Wohar, 2010, to name but a few) have pointed out the importance of the non-linearity and structural break in explaining the bubble-like behavior in the logarithm of the dividend yield, however, each of the two properties has largely been examined in isolation. This study fills this gap. We not only examine the importance of non-linearity and smooth break, respectively, in explaining the bubble-like behavior in the logarithm of the dividend yields, but also consider a model that is capable of capturing these non-linear characteristics of the logarithm of the dividend yields at the same time.[2]

The remainder of this paper is organized as follows. Section 2 reviews the theoretical foundation of the relation between a non-linear asset price and dividend. Section 3 reviews some newly-developed methods in detecting financial bubbles. Section 4 introduces the econometric methodologies that we employ in this paper. Section 5 describes the data and discusses the empirical test results. Section 6 presents the conclusions that we draw from this research.

2. A quick review of the present value model

Define the net simple return on a stock as

$$R_{t+1} = \frac{P_{t+1} - P_t + D_{t+1}}{P_t} = \frac{P_{t+1} + D_{t+1}}{P_t} - 1, \tag{1}$$

where R_{t+1} denotes the return on the stock held from time t to $t+1$ and D_{t+1} is the dividend in period $t+1$. The subscript $t+1$ denotes the fact that the return only becomes known in period $t+1$. Campbell et al. (1997) show that stock price (P_t) is the sum of the following two components:

$$P_t = E_t \left[\sum_{i=1}^{k} \left(\frac{1}{1+R_{t+i}} \right)^i D_{t+i} \right] + E_t \left[\left(\frac{1}{1+R_{t+k}} \right)^k P_{t+k} \right], \tag{2}$$

where D_t is the dividend in period t.

Further, the presence of time-varying expected stock returns has led to a non-linear relation between prices and returns. Campbell and Shiller (1988a) suggest a loglinear approximation of Equation (1) and derive the following logarithm dividend-price ratio yields after several manipulations

$$d_t - p_t = -\frac{\alpha}{1-\lambda} + E_t \left[\sum_{j=0}^{\infty} \lambda^j [-\Delta d_{t+1+j} + r_{t+1+j}] \right], \tag{3}$$

where the lower case letters p, d, and r denote the logarithm of prices, dividends, and the discount rate, respectively. The symbols λ and α denote linearization parameters which are $\lambda = 1/[\exp{(\overline{d-p})}]$ and $\alpha = -\log(\lambda) - (1-\lambda)\log(1/\lambda - 1)$. According to (3), if asset prices (p_t) and real dividends (d_t) follow integrated processes of order one, and no bubbles are present, the logarithm asset price and the logarithm dividends are cointegrated with the cointegrating vector $(1, -1)$ and the logarithm dividend-price ratio ($d_t - p_t$) is a stationary process under no rational bubble restriction. On the contrary, the presence of a unit-root in the logarithm dividend-price ratio is consistent with rational bubbles in asset markets. Intuitively, Eq. (3) states that if dividends are expected to grow, then current prices will be higher and the dividend-price ratio will be low, while if the future discount rate is expected to be high, then current prices will be low and the dividend-price ratio will be high (McMillan, 2007a).

3. A brief review of new developments in testing for rational bubbles

Recently, researchers have been interested in applying several newly-developed methods in order to detect financial bubbles. In this section, we briefly review some of these new approaches as follows.[3] First, Phillips, Wu, and Yu (2011, hereinafter PWY) and Phillips, Shi, and Yu (2015, hereinafter PSY) have proposed a new bubble detection strategy based on recursive and rolling ADF unit root tests (sup-ADF) that enable us to detect bubbles in the data and to date-stamp their occurrence. These types of tests use a right tail variation of the Augmented Dickey-Fuller unit root test wherein the null hypothesis is of a unit root and the alternative is of a mildly explosive process. For applications of the PWY and PSY to detect bubbles in the different asset markets, readers are referred to, for example, Gutierrez (2011), Yiu, Yu and Jin (2013), Engsted, Hviid and Pedersen (2016), Fantazzini (2016), Escobari and Jafarinejad (2016), and Chen and Xie (2017). However, as noted by Adämmer and Bohl (2015, p. 69), this approach cannot answer the question of dependencies between different prices and fundamentals since the sup-ADF test investigates whether prices are temporarily mildly explosive.

Second, some researchers have tried to detect bubbles by using the Bayesian approach in the literature. See, for example, Li and Xue (2009), Miao, Wang and Xu (2014), Fulop and Yu (2014), and Shi and Song (2016), to name just a few studies. The Bayesian approach can extend the bubble testing by using good prior information or providing more flexible extensions to the model. Fulop and Yu (2014) propose a new regime switching model with two regimes, a normal regime and a bubble regime. To estimate the model they use a sequential Bayesian simulation method that allows for real time detection of bubble origination and conclusion. Shi and Song (2016) propose a new infinite hidden Markov model to integrate the detection, date stamping, and estimation of bubble behaviors in a coherent Bayesian framework. As for hypothesis testing problem (the bubble case is a special case), it is known that there are some problems in Bayesian hypothesis testing. Bayes factor (BF) is the dominant statistic for Bayesian hypothesis testing (Kass and Raftery, 1995; Geweke, 2007). One serious drawback is that they are not well defined when using an improper prior. Another drawback is computational. The calculation of BF generally requires the evaluation of marginal likelihoods. In many models, the marginal likelihoods may be difficult to compute. Readers are referred to Li and Yu (2012), Li et al. (2014), and Li et al. (2015) for detailed discussions.

Third, Watanabe, Takayasu, and Takayasu (2007a, 2007b) introduce a mathematical criterion defining the bubbles or the crashes in financial market price fluctuations by considering the "exponential fitting" of the given data. By applying this criterion, it can automatically extract the periods in which bubbles and crashes are identified. However, it cannot tell when a bubble will stop. For example, Balcilar et al. (2014) apply the "exponential fitting" to identify bubbles in oil prices. Michaelides, Tsionas, and Konstantakis (2016) propose a rigorous and robust mathematical and econometric framework for the detection of bubbles, which is structured upon Artificial Neural Networks (ANN), which are perfectly capable of capturing any neglected non-linearity. Their paper is the first one in the relevant literature by employing the ANN to capture neglected nonlinearities in bubbles. In this study, we stick to adopting the classical statistical methods to detect bubble not only because the unit toot tests are well-known in the literature, but also easy to compute.

4. Econometric methodology

4.1. Smooth break and the LNV-ADF unit root test

As mentioned in the Introduction, non-linearity may affect a variable in the form of *structural changes* in the deterministic components. That is, a broken time trend is a particular case of a non-linear time trend. In order to take account of the possibility of non-linear trends, we apply the Leybourne et al. (1998) (LNV hereinafter) non-linear trend modeling approach. Leybourne et al. (1998) develop a unit root test against the alternative hypothesis of stationarity around a logistic smooth transition non-linear trend. It is appealing as it permits structural shifts to occur gradually over time. Let term $y_t = d_t - p_t$ denote the logarithm of the dividend yield or the logarithm of the dividend-price ratio. Leybourne et al. (1998) consider three logistic smooth transition regression models:

$$\text{Model A} \quad y_t = \alpha_1 + \alpha_2 S_t(\gamma, \tau) + v_t, \tag{4}$$

$$\text{Model B} \quad y_t = \alpha_1 + \beta_1 t + \alpha_2 S_t(\gamma, \tau) + v_t, \tag{5}$$

$$\text{Model C} \quad y_t = \alpha_1 + \beta_1 t + \alpha_2 S_t(\gamma, \tau) + \beta_2 t S_t(\gamma, \tau) + v_t, \tag{6}$$

where v_t is a zero mean I(0) process and $S_t(\gamma, \tau)$ is the logistic smooth transition function, based on a sample of size T,

$$S_t(\gamma, \tau) = [1 + \exp\{-\gamma(t - \tau T)\}]^{-1}, \quad \gamma > 0, \tag{7}$$

which controls the transition between regimes. The interpretation of the parameter of $S_{\tau T}(\gamma, \tau)$ is as follows. The parameter τ is the parameter determining the fraction of the sample at which the transition occurs. Since for $\gamma > 0$, we have $S_{-\infty}(\gamma, \tau) = 0$, $S_{+\infty}(\gamma, \tau) = 1$, and $S_{\tau T}(\gamma, \tau) = 0.5$. The speed of transition is determined by the parameter γ. If γ is small, then $S_t(\gamma, \tau)$ takes a long period of time to traverse the interval (0,1), and in the limiting case with $\gamma = 0$, $S_t(\gamma, \tau) = 0.5$ for all t. On the other hand, for large values of γ, $S_t(\gamma, \tau)$ traverse the interval (0,1) very rapidly, and as γ approaches $+\infty$ this function changes value from 0 to 1 instantaneously at time $t = \tau T$. If v_t is a zero-mean I(0) process, then in Model A y_t is stationary around a mean which changes from the initial value α_1 to the final value $\alpha_1 + \alpha_2$. Model B is similar, with the intercept changing from α_1 to $\alpha_1 + \alpha_2$, but it allows for a fixed slope term. In Model C, in addition to the change in intercept from α_1 to $\alpha_1 + \alpha_2$, the slope also changes simultaneously, and with the same speed of transition, from β_1 to $\beta_1 + \beta_2$.

The null hypothesis and alternative hypothesis are as follows:

$$H_0 \quad y_t = \mu_t, \quad \mu_t = \mu_{t-1} + \varepsilon_t, \quad \mu_0 = \psi, \tag{8}$$

$$H_1 \quad \text{Model A, Model B or Model C,} \tag{9}$$

or

$$H_0 \quad y_t = \mu_t, \quad \mu_t = \kappa + \mu_{t-1} + \varepsilon_t, \quad \mu_0 = \psi, \tag{10}$$

$$H_1 \quad \text{Model B or Model C.} \tag{11}$$

LNV suggests a two-step testing strategy, first estimating Eqs. (4)–(7) by non-linear least squares, and then applying an ADF test with no deterministic component to the resulting residual as follows:

$$\Delta \hat{v}_t = \hat{\rho} \hat{v}_{t-1} + \sum_{i=1}^{k} \hat{\delta}_i \Delta \hat{v}_{t-i} + \hat{\eta}_t, \tag{12}$$

where the lagged difference terms are included to account for any stationary dynamics in ε_t. The statistics are labeled s_α, $s_{\alpha(\beta)}$, and $s_{\alpha\beta}$, corresponding to Models A to C, respectively. The critical values of the LNV-ADF statistics are obtained from Table 1 of Leybourne et al. (1998).

4.2. Non-linearity and the ESTAR-type approaches

We are interested in modeling the transition between two regimes given by the unit root regime $y_t = y_{t-1} + \eta_t$ and the mean-reverting regime $y_t = (1 + \varphi)y_{t-1} + \eta_t$ with $\varphi < 0$. The unit root regime represents no adjustment movement, while the mean-reverting regime represents linear adjustment towards long-run equilibrium. We consider the transition function $F(\gamma, z_t)$ as a the weighted average of the two regimes. The resulting model is given by

$$y_t = (1 - F(\gamma, z_t))y_{t-1} + F(\gamma, z_t)(1 + \phi)y_{t-1} + \eta_t, \tag{13}$$

which is equivalent to

$$\Delta y_t = \phi y_{t-1} F(\gamma, z_t) + \eta_t, \tag{14}$$

with $\phi < 0$. The transition parameter γ determines the speed of transition between two extreme regimes and z_t represents the transition variable. As noted by Park and Shintani (2005, 2016), with various choices of the transition function $F(\gamma, z_t)$, the model (14) can represent a wide class of non-linear partial adjustment AR models with a state dependent speed of adjustment. If $\phi = 0$, there is only a single regime with a unit root that represents no adjustment towards long-run equilibrium. For this reason, it is of interest to test the null hypothesis $H_0 : \phi = 0$ against the alternative hypothesis $H_1 : \phi < 0$. The model (14) encompasses a variety of non-linear AR models with a long-run equilibrium.[4]

In order to take account of the possibility of asymmetric speed of adjustment towards equilibrium (i.e., size non-linearity), we assume that the adjustment speed is non-linear and follows an *exponential smooth transition autoregressive* (ESTAR) process. Park and Shintani (2005, p. 5) writes "The ESTAR model is often used when the economic agent can have arbitrage opportunities by facing deviation from the long run equilibrium in either directions. In such a case, unit root regime becomes an inner regime, and mean-reverting regime becomes two outer regime." In particular, Kilic (2011) utilizes the lagged difference of dependent variable as the transition variable, i.e., $F(\gamma, z_t) = 1 - \exp(-\gamma(\Delta y_{t-1})^2)$ and $z_t = \Delta y_{t-1}$. Kapetanios et al. (2003) and Park and Shintani (2005, 2016) adopt the lagged level of dependent variable as the transition variable under the alternative, i.e., $F(\gamma, z_t) = 1 - \exp(-\gamma y_{t-1}^2)$ and $z_t = y_{t-1}$. That is, we consider three specifications as shown in Eqs. (15) to (17) as follows:

$$\Delta y_t = \phi y_{t-1}[1 - \exp(-\gamma(\Delta y_{t-1})^2)] + \sum_{i=1}^{k} \delta_i \Delta y_{t-i} + \eta_t, \tag{15}$$

$$\Delta y_t = \psi y_{t-1}[1 - \exp(-\gamma y_{t-1}^2)] + \sum_{i=1}^{k} \delta_i \Delta y_{t-i} + \eta_t, \tag{16}$$

$$\Delta y_t = \lambda y_{t-1}^3 + \sum_{i=1}^{k} \delta_i \Delta y_{t-i} + \eta_t, \tag{17}$$

where $\gamma > 0$ and the lagged terms of Δy_{t-i} is added to regressions to assure the error term η_t is a white noise. This implies that the logarithm of the dividend yield may be a unit root process in inner regime, but a stationary process when the logarithm of the dividend yield reaches the outer regime. Eqs. (15) to (17) correspond to the unit root tests developed by Kilic (2011), Park and Shintani (2005, 2016), and Kapetanios et al. (2003), respectively.

Equations (15) to (17) allow testing for a unit root against a non-linear alternative. In particular in the model suggested by Kilic (2011) the transition parameter γ determines the speed of transition between two extreme regimes. The exponential transition function $F(\gamma, \Delta y_{t-1})$ is bounded between zero and unity with Δy_{t-1} being the transition variable that determines the regime. The use of Δy_{t-1} as a transition variable ensures that the transition variable is not highly persistent. At the extremes of $F(\gamma, \Delta y_{t-1}) = 0$ and $F(\gamma, \Delta y_{t-1}) = 1$ the smooth transition model (15) is linear and the corresponding AR(1) models are given by $y_t = y_{t-1} + \eta_t$ and $y_t = (1 + \phi)y_{t-1} + \eta_t$, respectively.

To test the null unit root hypothesis $H_0 : \phi = 0$ against the alternative hypothesis $H_1 : \phi < 0$ of Eq. (15), we follow Kilic (2011) and use the following *t*-statistic:

$$\inf_{\gamma \in \Gamma_T} \hat{t}_{\phi=0}(\gamma) = \inf_{\gamma \in \Gamma_T} \frac{\hat{\phi}(\gamma)}{\widehat{se}(\hat{\phi}(\gamma))}, \tag{18}$$

which is the infimum of *t*-ratios in model (15) taken over all possible values of $\gamma \in \Gamma_T$, where $\Gamma_T = [\underline{\gamma}_T, \bar{\gamma}_T] = \left[\frac{1}{100 s_{zT}}, \frac{100}{s_{zT}}\right]$, where s_{zT} is the sample standard deviation of $z_t = \Delta y_{t-1}$. The scale parameter γ in the ESTAR model is searched over the fixed interval normalized by the sample standard deviation of the transition variable z_t (see, e.g., van Dijk et al., 2002). Because z_t is a stationary process, this choice yields a well-defined limit lower and upper bounds for the parameter space and hence a well-defined limit parameter space. We label this test the inf-Kilic test. The critical values of the inf-Kilic test are obtained from Table 1 of Kilic (2011).

Using Eq. (16), Park and Shintani (2005, 2016) develop a unit root test (H_0 : $\phi = 0$) against a general transition AR model (H_1 : $\phi < 0$) that uses, unlike Kilic (2011), y_{t-1} as transition variable instead of Δy_{t-1}. Park and Shintani (2005, 2016) construct the test based on the extremum over the region for the parameter γ, which is not identified under the null hypothesis of a unit root. The test can be implemented as follows. Let Γ_n denote a random sequence of parameter spaces given for each n as functions of the sample ($y_1, \dots, y_n$). For each $\gamma \in \Gamma_n$, one obtains the *t*-statistic for ψ in (16),

$$T_n(\gamma) = \frac{\hat{\psi}(\gamma)}{\widehat{se}(\hat{\psi}(\gamma))},$$

where $\hat{\psi}(\gamma)$ is the least squares estimate and $\widehat{se}(\hat{\psi}(\gamma))$ is the corresponding standard error. The inf-*t* test is then defined as

$$T_n = \inf_{\gamma \in \Gamma_n} T_n(\gamma), \tag{19}$$

which is the infimum of *t*-ratios in model (16) taken over all possible values of $\gamma \in \Gamma_n$. Similar to Park and Shintani (2005, 2016), we consider $\gamma \in [10^{-1}, 10] \times P_n$, where $P_n = (\sum_{t=1}^{n} y_{t-1}^2)^{-1/2}$. We label this test the inf-PS test and the critical values of the inf-PS test are obtained from Tables 1–2 of Park and Shintani (2005) or from Table 2 of Park and Shintani (2016).

Kapetanios et al. (2003) develop a test for the null hypothesis of a unit root against an alternative of a non-linear but globally stationary smooth transition autoregressive process. Kapetanios et al. (2003) circumvent the problem caused by lack of identification of parameters under the null hypothesis by using a Taylor series expansion of the non-linear model around the parameter value under the null. The Kapetanios et al. (2003) unit root test is in fact a linearized version of the Kilic (2011) test that uses, like Park and Shintani (2005, 2016),

y_{t-1} as transition variable. The null hypothesis to be tested with Eq. (17) is $H_0 : \lambda = 0$ (unit root in outer regime) against the alternative of $H_1 : \lambda < 0$ (stationarity in outer regime). Specifically, the test is obtained with the following t-statistic:

$$t = \frac{\hat{\lambda}}{\hat{se}(\hat{\lambda})}, \tag{20}$$

We refer to this test as the KSS non-linear augmented Dickey-Fuller test and label it the KSS test. The critical values are obtained from Table 1 of Kapetanios et al. (2003).

Finally, in order to test for the null hypothesis of a unit root of the dividend-price ratio against the alternative hypothesis that encompasses smooth break and size non-linearity at the same time, we replace y_t in Eqs. (15)–(17) with the residuals $\hat{v}_t$ from Eqs. (4)–(7). That is, in the first step we estimate Eqs. (4)–(7) by non-linear least squares, and in the next step we apply Eqs. (18), (19) and (20) to the resulting residuals. We label these LNV-ESTAR-type unit root tests the LNV-inf-Kilic, LNV-inf-PS, and LNV-KSS statistics, respectively. The critical values of the LNV-inf-Kilic, LNV-inf-PS, and LNV-KSS statistics can be obtained from Table 1 of Chen and Xie (2015).

5. Data and results

5.1. Data description and preliminary data analysis

Monthly data on the dividend yield for the G7 stock markets, namely, Canada (S&P/TSX composite index, TTOCOMP), France (CAC 40), Germany (DAX 30), Italy (FTSE Italy), Japan (Nikkei 500), the UK (FTSE 100), and the US (S&P 500), are used in the analysis. The original data were obtained from the datastream. The sample periods were determined primarily based on the availability of the data. They are 1973:m6–2016:m4 for the TTOCOMP, 1988m1–2016m5 for the CAC 40, 1973:m1–2016:m5 for the DAX 30, and 1986m2–2016m4 for the FTSE Italy, 1991:m1–2015:m5 for the Nikkei 500, 1985:m12–2016:m4 for the FTSE 100, and 1973:m1–2016:m4 for the S&P 500.

Some descriptive statistics of the changes in the logarithms of the dividend yields are outlined in Table 5.1, which details the first four moments of each series and presents tests for normality and serial correlation. Several interesting facts are found from Table 5.1. First, with the exceptions of Germany (DAX 30) and the UK (FTSE 100), the coefficients of skewness for all of the changes in the logarithms of the dividend yields are positive, implying that returns are flatter to the right compared to the normal distribution. Second, with the exceptions of France (CAC 40) and Italy (FTSE Italy), the coefficients of excess kurtosis for all of the changes in the logarithms of the dividend yields are much higher than zero, indicating that the empirical distributions of these samples have fat tails. The coefficients of skewness and excess kurtosis reveal non-

Table 5.1 Summary statistics

	Changes in the logarithms of the dividend yields						
	Mean	S.D.	SK	EK	JB	LB(24)	ARCH(4)
Canada	< 0.001	0.050	0.954	3.587	353.760**	30.541	1.684
France	0.001	0.071	−0.199	4.229	255.723**	27.156	0.153
Germany	< −0.001	0.065	0.723	2.124	143.088**	31.174	3.317
Italy	0.002	0.086	−0.196	1.479	35.326**	18.512	2.960
Japan	0.003	0.062	0.119	0.843	9.763**	36.242*	1.849
the UK	< −0.001	0.050	0.383	4.847	356.239**	21.648	1.356
the US	< 0.001	0.045	0.490	2.279	133.157**	19.314	4.888**

(1) *, **, *** denote significance at the 10%, 5% and 1%, respectively. (2) Mean and S.D. refer to the mean and standard deviation, respectively. (3) SK is the skewness coefficient. (4) EK is the excess kurtosis coefficient. (5) JB is the Jarque-Bera statistic. (6) LB(24) is the Ljung-Box Q statistic calculated with 24 lags. (7) ARCH(4) is the ARCH test calculated with four lags on raw returns. (8) '< 0.001' indicates that the number is less than 0.001.

normality in the data. This is confirmed by the Jarque-Bera normality test as shown in Table 5.1. Third, the Ljung-Box Q-statistics, LB(24), indicate that significant autocorrelation exists only for the changes in the logarithms of the dividend yields of the Nikkei 500 (Japan). We also report a standard ARCH test for the changes in the logarithms of the dividend yields. For example, the test results indicate that a significant ARCH effect exists only for the S&P 500 (US), but not for the cases of the Canada (TTOCOMP), France (CAC 40), Germany (DAX 30), Italy (FTSE Italy), Japan (Nikkei 500), and the UK (FTSE 100).

5.2. Results of the linear unit root tests

By following the recommendation of Bohl and Siklos (2004), we adopt the unit root test approach to examine the stationarity of the logarithm of the dividend yield.[5] As a preliminary analysis, we apply a number of linear unit root tests to determine the order of integration of the logarithm of the dividend yield. We consider the Augmented Dickey-Fuller (ADF) test, as well as the ADF-GLS test of Elliott et al. (1996) in this study. Vougas (2007) highlights the usefulness of the Schmidt and Phillips (1992) (SP hereinafter) unit root test in empirical study. Therefore, we also employ it in this study. These authors propose some modifications of existing linear unit root tests in order to improve their power and size. For the ADF and ADF-GLS tests, an auxiliary regression is run with an intercept and a time trend. To select the lag length (k), we use the 't-sig' approach proposed by Hall (1994). That is, the number of lags is chosen for which the last included lag has a marginal significance level that is less than the 10% level.

The results of applying these tests are reported in the left panel of Table 5.2. We find that, for all countries, the null hypothesis of a unit root cannot be rejected at the 10% significance level for the ADF statistics. Based on the well-known low-power problem of the ADF test, we turn our attention to

Table 5.2 Results of the linear unit root tests – the logarithm of the dividend yields

	Linear trend				Quadratic trend and breaks tests		
	ADF	SP(1)	DF-GLS	KPSS	SP(2)	LP, Model C	LP, Model C
Canada	−1.966	−1.516	−1.599	1.518**	−1.938	−5.428**	−6.380
France	−2.826	−3.093**	−3.061**	0.505**	−3.161	−4.381	−5.131
Germany	−1.854	−2.254	−2.211	1.783**	−2.723	−4.538	−5.808
Italy	−2.579	−2.281	−2.130	0.501**	−2.133	−3.706	−5.404
Japan	−2.344	−2.069	−1.904	0.628**	−2.565	−5.128**	−5.406
the UK	−2.169	−2.203	−2.053	0.898**	−2.543	−3.982	−5.333
the US	−2.286	−1.186	−1.164	1.196**	−1.548	−4.324	−5.604

(1) *, **, *** denote significance at the 10%, 5% and 1%, respectively. (2) ADF, SP(1), and DF-GLS denote the augmented Dickey-Fuller test, Schmidt-Phillips τ test with linear trend, and Elliott et al. (1996) DF-GLS test, respectively. (3) SP(2), ZA, and LP denote the Schmidt-Phillips τ test with quadratic trend, Zivot and Andrews (1992) and Lumsdaine and Papell (1997) tests, respectively. (4) The 5% critical values for the ADF, SP(1), and DF-GLS tests are −3.43, −3.04, and −2.89, respectively. (5) The 5% critical values for the SP(2), ZA, and LP tests are −3.55, −5.08, and −6.75, respectively.

other statistics. With the exception of France (CAC 40), the results from the DF-GLS (see Elliott et al., 1996) and the SP(1) test (see Schmidt and Phillips, 1992), with parametric correction, cannot reject the unit root hypothesis with a linear trend at the 5% significance level.[6] The results from the SP(2) test suggest that the null hypothesis of a unit root cannot be rejected for all markets, suggesting that the logarithm of the dividend-price ratios for all markets are non-stationary processes. Based on the linear unit root test results, the presence of a unit root in the logarithm of the dividend yield is consistent with the rational bubble in the G7 stock markets. We also execute the KPSS (Kwiatkowski, Phillips, Schmidt and Shin, 1992) test to see how the unit root results would differ. The null hypothesis of the KPSS test assumes that the series is I(0). Therefore, rejection of the null hypothesis is indicative of the series follows I(1) process. The results of the KPSS test echo the ADF and SP(2) tests as shown in Table 5.2. It is clear that our empirical results are quite robust based on these traditional linear unit root tests.

As Perron (1989) pointed out, in the presence of a structural break, the power to reject a unit root decreases if the stationarity alternative is true and the structural break is ignored. To address this, we use Zivot and Andrews' (1992) sequential one trend break model and Lumsdaine and Papell's (1997) two trend breaks model to investigate the order of the empirical variables. We use the 't-sig' approach proposed by Hall (1994) to select the lag length (k). We set $k_{max} = 12$ and use the approximate 10% asymptotic critical value of 1.60 to determine the significance of the t-statistic on the last lag. We use the 'trimming region' [0.10T, 0.90T] and select the break point endogenously by choosing the value of the break that maximizes the ADF t-statistic. We report the results in the right panel of Table 5.2. With the exceptions of Canada and Japan, the results suggest that the null hypothesis of a unit root cannot be rejected at the 5% significance level based on the ZA and LP unit root tests, indicating that the logarithm of the dividend-price ratios are non-stationary in their respective levels. These findings fully echo those obtained from the linear unit roots and, again, are in favor of the rational bubble hypothesis.

Lee and Strazicich (2003) show that the ZA and LP unit root tests, which do not allow for a break under the null hypothesis, suffer from severe spurious rejections in finite samples when a break is present under the null hypothesis. The root of the problem of spurious rejections is that the parameters of the test regression have different interpretations under the null and alternative hypotheses, which is crucial since the parameters have implications for the selection of the structural break date. Following Schmidt and Phillips (1992), Popp (2008), and Narayan and Popp (2010, hereinafter NP) propose a new endogenous structural break unit root test by formulating the data-generating process (DGP) as an unobserved components model to avoid the above problem. Narayan and Popp (2013) show that the NP test has better size properties and identifies the breaks more accurately than its main two-break unit root rivals; namely, the Lumsdaine and Papell (1997) and Lee and Strazicich (2003) tests. In this study, we also test for a unit root for the logarithms of the dividend yields by employing Popp's (2008) one-break and Narayan and Popp's (2010) two-break unit root tests. We consider Model 1 (two breaks in the intercept) and Model 2 (two breaks in the intercept and trend) and extract appropriate critical values from Popp (2008) and Narayan and Popp (2010), respectively. We report the Popp (2008) and the NP test results for the logarithms of the dividend yields in Tables 5.3 and 5.4, respectively.

Beginning with the Popp (2008) one-break test (Table 5.3), we find that we are unable to reject the unit root null hypothesis for the logarithms of the dividend yields of all stock markets at the 5% significance level or better. In the case of the NP test (Table 5.4), with the exception of Canada, the null hypothesis of a unit root cannot be rejected at the 5% level for the M1 and M2 models. The results from the Popp (2008) and the NP tests echo the results of the linear unit root tests and the ZA and LP tests, suggesting that any shock has a permanent effect on the dividend yields.

In order to validate the non-linear unit root used in this paper, we conduct several non-linearity tests for these dividend yields. Psaradakis and Spagnolo (2002) examine the relative performance of some popular non-linearity tests. The non-linearity tests considered include the RESET-type tests, the Keenan test, the Tsay test, the McLeod-Li test, the BDS test, the White dynamic information matrix test, and the neural network test.[7] We adopt these statistics to examine whether any non-linearity exists in the dividend yields. The results are reported in Table 5.5, which shows that some of the p-values of these non-linear tests are below the 10% significance level or better for all dividend yields considered in this paper, indicating that the dividend yields of the G7 countries are characterized by non-linearity.

We also test for non-linearity by using Harvey et al.'s (2008) test. These authors propose a test with the same limiting distribution, regardless of whether the

Table 5.3 Results of the Popp one-break unit root test

	M1		M2	
	Test statistic	TB1	Test statistic	TB1
Canada	−2.108	1987m9	−2.712	1987m9
France	−2.734	2004m12	−2.680	2004m12
Germany	−3.508	2005m3	−3.499	2005m3
Italy	−2.057	2009m4	−1.984	2009m4
Japan	−2.834	2008m9	−2.841	2008m9
the UK	−2.450	1997m12	−3.310	1997m12
the US	−2.589	1987m9	−2.077	1987m9

(1) *, **, *** denote significance at the 10%, 5%, and 1% levels, respectively.

Table 5.4 Results of the NP two-break unit root test

	M1			M2		
	Test statistic	TB1	TB2	Test statistic	TB1	TB2
Canada	−1.484	1987m9	1998m6	−5.126**	1987m9	1998m6
France	−2.786	2004m12	2009m2	−2.965	2004m12	2009m2
Germany	−3.648	1999m7	2005m3	−3.669	1999m7	2005m3
Italy	−2.697	2004m2	2009m4	−3.296	2004m2	2009m4
Japan	−3.710	2006m4	2008m9	−4.476	2006m4	2008m9
the UK	−2.200	1997m12	2009m7	−3.941	1997m12	2009m7
the US	−1.225	1987m9	1998m7	−2.077	1987m9	1998m7

(1) *, **, *** denote significance at the 10%, 5%, and 1% levels, respectively.

Table 5.5 p-values for a number of non-linear tests

	Canada	France	Germany	Italy	Japan	the UK	the US
RESET1	0.032	0.005	0.020	< 0.001	< 0.001	0.058	0.091
RESET2	0.032	0.005	0.020	< 0.001	0.001	0.058	0.091
KEENAN	0.053	0.029	0.198	0.031	0.004	0.038	0.149
TSAY	0.052	0.029	0.198	< 0.001	0.008	0.038	0.148
MCLEOD	< 0.001	0.004	< 0.001	< 0.001	< 0.001	< 0.001	< 0.001
BDS	< 0.001	0.061	< 0.001	< 0.001	< 0.001	< 0.001	< 0.001
WHITE1	0.175	0.056	0.571	< 0.001	0.197	0.363	0.750
WHITE2	< 0.001	< 0.001	< 0.001	< 0.001	< 0.001	< 0.001	0.004
NEURAL1	0.076	0.073	0.102	0.017	< 0.001	0.058	0.185
NEURAL2	0.087	0.076	0.133	< 0.001	< 0.001	0.060	0.240

(1) RESET1: Ramsey and Schmidt (1976). (2) RESET 2: Thursby and Schmidt (1977). (3) KEENAN: Keenan (1985). TSAY: Tsay (1986). (4) MCLEOD: McLeod and Li (1983). (5) BDS: Brock et al. (1996). (6) WHITE1 and WHITE2 are White's (1987) information matrix tests. (7) NEURAL1 and NEURAL2 are the neural network proposed by White (1989a, b). (8) < 0.001 indicates that the number is less than 0.001.

variable is I(0) or I(1). The new test is referred to as W_λ and is distributed as a $\chi^2(2)$. We display the results of applying the W_λ test in Table 5.6. From the second column, we can see that the null of linearity is rejected at the conventional significance level only for the case of France. The results are not surprising

Table 5.6 Results of the W_λ linearity test

Country	W_λ	$W^*_{10\%}$	$W^*_{5\%}$	$W^*_{1\%}$
Canada	1.63	11.07	11.15	11.29
France	11.76**	9.28	9.33	9.41
Germany	1.57	9.36	9.40	9.49
Italy	49.16	82.91	83.31	84.03
Japan	0.92	15.73	15.90	16.20
the UK	7.22	11.88	11.95	12.07
the US	0.29	5.74	5.79	5.90

(1) *, **, *** denote significance at the 10%, 5%, and 1% levels, respectively.

because the W_λ statistic is comprised of a simple data dependent weighted average of two Wald test statistics: one that is efficient when the data are generated by an I(0) process and a second that is efficient when the data are I(1). It may, however, suffer from a loss of power when the true data generating process is simply a stationary process.

5.3. Results of the LNV-ADF approach

In order to take the possibility of non-linear trends into consideration, we apply the logistic smooth transition unit root test, championed by Leybourne et al. (1998), in this study. This approach permits a structural shift to occur gradually over time instead of instantaneously. Following the two-step procedure described in Section 3.1, we first fitted the logistic smooth transition model to the dividend yields of the G7. Figure 5.1 collects the time series plots of the dividend yields (black line) and the estimated logistic smooth transition functions (gray line) of Model C for the G7 countries. It is clear that the estimated logistic smooth transition trends mimic the raw data very well.

We then proceed to Step 2 of our testing procedures and obtain the residuals from the logistic smooth function and apply the LNV-ADF test where we assume that mean reversion follows a linear process. The optimal lag order of the ADF regression is selected by the Bayesian information criterion (BIC). We summarize the test results of the LNV-ADF statistic in Table 5.7. Based on the s_α, $s_{\alpha(\beta,)}$, and $s_{\alpha\beta}$ statistics, it is found that in Canada, Germany, Italy, and Japan, the null hypothesis of a unit root is rejected at least at the 10% significance level or better, indicating that the dividend yields of these countries are stationary processes around a logistic smooth transition non-linear trend.

5.4. Results of the ESTAR approach

We summarize the results of the ESTAR-type unit root tests in Tables 5.8–5.10. The results from Kilic's (2011) test indicate that, with the exceptions of Germany and the UK, the null hypothesis of a unit root is rejected at the 10% significance

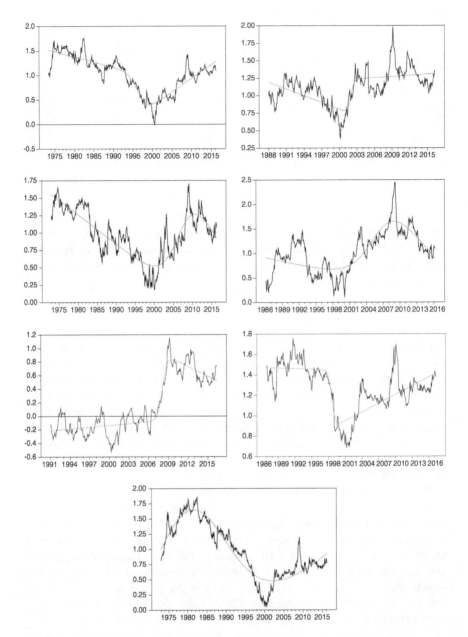

Figure 5.1 The logarithm of the dividend yield (black line) and the fitted logistic smooth transition function (gray line) for Leybourne et al. (1998) Model C. The order of countries from left to right are stock markets of Canada, France, Germany, Italy, Japan, the UK, and the US.

Table 5.7 Results of the LNV-ADF unit root test

Country	LNV-ADF		
	S_α	$S_{\alpha(\beta)}$	$S_{\alpha\alpha}$
Canada	−2.744	−4.602**	−5.069**
France	−2.779	−3.844	−4.147
Germany	−2.895	−4.687**	−4.697*
Italy	−3.356	−4.291*	−4.294
Japan	−3.887*	−3.879	−4.058
the UK	−2.732	−3.711	−3.775
the US	−3.238	−3.673	−3.453
10% cv	−3.797	−4.277	−4.552
5% cv	−4.013	−4.565	−4.825
1% cv	−4.685	−5.141	−5.420

(1) *, **, *** denote significance at the 10%, 5%, and 1% levels, respectively. (2) LNV-ADF denotes the non-linear unit root test proposed by Leybourne et al. (1998). (3) The critical values for the LNV-ADF statistics are obtained from Leybourne et al. (1998).

Table 5.8 Results of the inf-Kilic unit root test

Country	inf-Kilic		
	Raw data	Demeaned	Demeaned and Detrended
Canada	−0.780	−1.448	−2.288*
France	−1.535	−2.608**	−2.989**
Germany	−0.199	−1.737	−1.603
Italy	−3.179***	−4.343***	−4.309***
Japan	−0.997	−1.518	−2.455*
the UK	−0.838	−1.465	−1.372
the US	−1.645*	−0.969	−2.161
10% cv	−1.57	−2.05	−2.23
5% cv	−1.90	−2.37	−2.57
1% cv	−2.59	−2.98	−3.19

(1) *, **, *** denote significance at the 10%, 5%, and 1% levels, respectively. (2) The critical values for the inf-Kilic statistics are obtained from Kilic (2011).

level and in favor of non-linearity of the dividend yields. However, the hypothesis of a unit root can be rejected in the cases of Germany, Italy, and Japan at the 10% significance level based on Park and Shintani's (2005, 2016) test.[8] When we turn to the KSS test, rejection of the null of a unit root occurs in four cases at the conventional significance level with the exception of Canada, the UK, and the US.

Overall, the results from the ESTAR-type tests point to the rejection of the null hypothesis of a unit root ($H_0 : \phi = 0$) against the alternative of a globally stationary ESTAR process ($H_1 : \phi > 0$) for six of G7 countries. This implies that size non-linearity is an important feature to the logarithms of the dividend yields of

Table 5.9 Results of the inf-PS unit root test

Country	Raw data	Demeaned	Demeaned and Detrended
Canada	−1.057	−2.122	−2.109
France	−0.748	−2.287	−2.744
Germany	−1.373	−2.831*	−3.071*
Italy	−1.387	−2.836*	−3.189*
Japan	−1.904*	−1.763	−2.994
the UK	−0.928	−1.994	−2.026
the US	−0.902	−1.670	−2.312
10% cv	−1.807	−2.589	−3.016
5% cv	−2.126	−2.889	−3.308
1% cv	−2.730	−3.469	−3.817

(1) *, **, *** denote significance at the 10%, 5%, and 1% levels, respectively. (2) The critical values for the inf-PS statistics are obtained via Monte Carlo simulation.

Table 5.10 Results of the KSS unit root test

Country	KSS		
	Raw data	Demeaned	Demeaned and Detrended
Canada	−1.116	−3.372	−2.335
France	−1.255	−2.885*	−3.038
Germany	−1.405	−2.839*	−3.079
Italy	−1.483	−2.712*	−3.045
Japan	−1.388	−2.061	−3.168*
the UK	−1.175	−2.047	−1.973
the US	−0.934	−1.679	−2.302
10% cv	−1.92	−2.66	−3.13
5% cv	−2.22	−2.93	−3.40
1% cv	−2.82	−3.48	−3.93

(1) *, **, *** denote significance at the 10%, 5%, and 1% levels, respectively. (2) The critical values for the KSS statistics are obtained from Kapetanios et al. (2003).

Canada, France, Germany, Italy, Japan, and the US. The existence of transaction costs in stock markets favors a non-linear mean-reverting process in stock markets. However, depending on the realization of Δy_{t-1}, the quantity $\phi F(\gamma, \Delta y_{t-1}) = 1 - \exp(-\gamma(\Delta y_{t-1})^2)$ [Eq. (15)] can be arbitrarily close to zero during some periods. This basically means that we still have episodes of rationale bubbles under the alternative hypothesis, which are followed by episodes of mean reversion. As such, a stationary model that is capable of generating bubbles with a built-in mechanism to return back to a mean reverting dynamics.[9]

5.5. Results of the LNV-ESTAR-type approaches

Finally, we test for the null hypothesis of a unit root against the alternative of a smooth break and size non-linearity at the same time. The size non-linearity which is related to the possibility of asymmetric speed of adjustment towards equilibrium. That is, the further the dividend yield deviates from its fundamental equilibrium, the faster will be the speed of mean reversion. We adopt a two-step testing strategy, which is a combination of the LNV and ESTAR-type unit root tests as outlined in Section 4. In the first step, we estimate Eqs. (4)–(6) to model the non-linear trend that stems from a smooth break. In the second step, we test for a ESTAR-type unit root on the residuals of step one by estimating Eqs. (15)–(17). Then we calculate the test statistics (18), (19) and (20), respectively. The critical values of the three tests are obtained via Monte Carlo simulation. We label these tests the LNV-inf-Kilic, LNV-inf-PS, and LNV-KSS tests and report the empirical results in Tables 5.11, 5.12, and 5.13, respectively.

The results from the LNV-inf-Kilic test indicate that we can reject the null in five cases at the 10% significance level or better. These are the countries for which we rejected a unit root using the LNV-ADF test plus Italy and the US but minus Japan. When we turn to the LNV-inf-PS test, rejection of the null of a unit root occurs in six cases with the exception of the UK. The results from the LNV-KSS test show that we can reject the null hypothesis of a unit root at the 10% significance level or better for all G7 countries.[10]

In sum, the results point to the rejection of the null hypothesis of a unit root against the alternative of a globally stationary ESTAR process around a non-linear deterministic trend in all G7 countries. Again, this implies that non-linearity and a smooth break are indispensable features of the dividend yields of the G7 stock markets. Figure 5.2 summarizes the plots of the transition function of LNV-inf-Kilic test for Models C. These plots show that the speed of transition between the inner and outer states is quick for the majority of countries, making it close to a threshold process for countries like Germany and the UK.

Table 5.11 Results of the LNV-inf-Kilic unit root test

	LNV-inf-Kilic		
Country	Model A	Model B	Model C
Canada	−3.057	−4.664**	−4.970**
France	−3.641*	−3.929	−3.660
Germany	−3.115	−5.282***	−5.313**
Italy	−4.080**	−4.713**	−4.514*
Japan	−3.327	−3.341	−3.410
the UK	−2.714	−3.462	−3.481
the US	−4.851***	−5.760***	−6.138**
10% cv	−3.636	−4.014	−4.401
5% cv	−3.981	−4.299	−4.738
1% cv	−4.678	−4.837	−5.360

(1) *, **, *** denote significance at the 10%, 5%, and 1% levels, respectively. (2) The critical values for the LNV-inf-Kilic statistics are obtained via Monte Carlo simulation.

Table 5.12 Results of the LNV-inf-PS unit root test

| Country | LNV-inf-PS | | |
	Model A	Model B	Model C
Canada	−3.441	−4.872**	−6.466***
France	−3.375	−4.581**	−4.219
Germany	−2.411	−5.444***	−5.370***
Italy	−4.593**	−5.210***	−4.432*
Japan	−4.323**	−3.976	−4.404*
the UK	−2.939	−3.837	−4.114
the US	−3.720*	−5.247***	−4.431*
10% cv	−3.620	−4.005	−4.344
5% cv	−3.999	−4.332	−4.665
1% cv	−4.697	−5.012	−5.348

(1) *, **, *** denote significance at the 10%, 5%, and 1% levels, respectively. (2) The critical values for the LNV-inf-PS statistics are obtained via Monte Carlo simulation.

Table 5.13 Results of the LNV-KSS unit root test

| Country | LNV-KSS | | |
	Model A	Model B	Model C
Canada	−2.833	−3.760	−4.143*
France	−3.292	−4.551**	−3.235
Germany	−2.938	−4.979**	−4.877**
Italy	−3.138	−3.621	−4.330**
Japan	−3.557*	−3.482	−3.909
the UK	−2.658	−4.088**	−3.464
the US	−3.298	−3.853*	−3.423
10% cv	−3.475	−3.766	−4.001
5% cv	−3.834	−4.074	−4.317
1% cv	−4.427	−4.650	−5.030

(1) *, **, *** denote significance at the 10%, 5%, and 1% levels, respectively. (2) The critical values for the LNV-KSS statistics are obtained via Monte Carlo simulation.

6. Concluding remarks

The purpose of this study is to investigate the issue of non-stationarity in the logarithm of the dividend yield of the G7 countries. If the null hypothesis of a unit root cannot be rejected, then it is in favor of the rational bubble in that market. However, the presence of this bubble-like behavior in the logarithm of the dividend yield could be owing to transaction cost (Kapetanios, Shin, and Snell, 2006) and structural break (McMillan, 2007a; 2009a; 2009b). As such, we examine the bubble-like behavior in the logarithm of the dividend yield of the G7 stock markets under the assumptions of non-linearity and a smooth break in the trend, respectively. To this end, we adopt the ESTAR-type and the LNV-ADF unit root tests in this study, respectively.

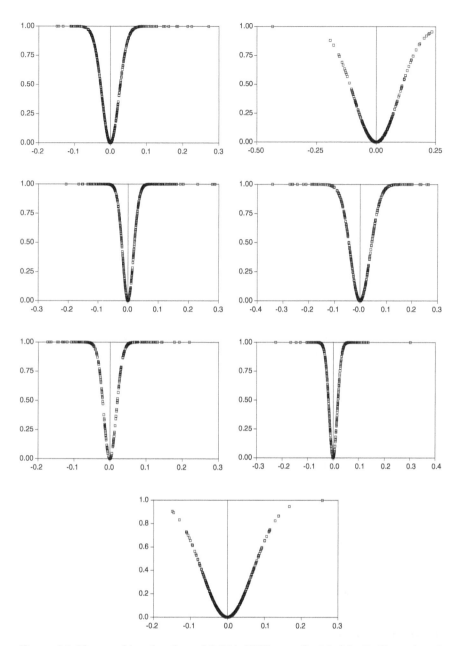

Figure 5.2 The transition function of INV-inf-Kilic test for Models C. The order of countries from left to right are\stock markets of Canada, France, Germany, Italy, Japan, the UK, and the US.

Table 5.14 Summary of various non-linear unit root tests

Country	AsyAdj ESTAR	One SB LNV-ADF	Popp test	One SB and AsyAdj LNV-ESTAR
Canada	yes	yes	no	yes
France	yes	no	no	yes
Germany	yes	yes	no	yes
Italy	yes	yes	no	yes
Japan	yes	yes	no	yes
the UK	no	no	no	yes
the US	yes	no	no	yes

(1) The term "AsyAdj" indicates non-linearity stems from asymmetric speed of adjustment (size non-linearity). (2) The term "SB" indicates non-linearity stems from structural break. (3) The term "no" indicates that the null of a unit root is not rejected and in favor of non-stationary process. (4) The term "yes" indicates that the null of a unit root is rejected and in favor of non-linear stationary process.

For the benefit of readers, we summarize our empirical results in Table 5.14. This study reaches the following key conclusions. First, by using a number of univariate unit root tests, the dividend yields of the G7 countries are characterized by the I(1) processes. Second, the results of the LNV-ADF test show that the dividend yields of these countries are stationary processes around a non-linear trend. Moreover, with the exception of the UK, the empirical evidence obtained for the ESTAR-type unit root tests favor a globally stationary ESTAR process in the dividend yield of the G7 countries, implying that the further the dividend yield deviates from its equilibrium, the faster will be the speed of mean reversion. Third, the Leybourne et al. (1998) test indicates that the dividend yield is a stationary process after taking account of the non-linear trend. Our empirical results echo the findings of, to name a few studies, Ryan (2006), McMillan and Wohar (2009), Sollis (2006), and McMillan (2006, 2007a, 2009a, 2009b).

All in all, this paper provides solid evidence that the logarithms of the dividend yields of the G7 countries are mean-reverting processes after considering the properties of non-linearity and a smooth break. The empirical results of this study justufy that a stationary model that is capable of generating bubbles with a built-in mechanism to return back to a mean reverting dynamics. Hence, an adequate assessment of the persistence of shocks to the dividend yield should account for the inherent non-linearity or smooth break in the data.

Acknowledgments

We would like to thank the editor, Professor Sophie Saglio, and two anonymous referees for helpful comments and suggestions. We thank Professor Paresh Kumar Narayan and Professor Stephen Popp for providing us with the Gauss code for conducting the Narayan and Popp (2010) unit root test. We also thank An-Chi Wu for her assistance in collecting the data used in this paper.

Financial support from the Ministry of Science and Technology (MOST 105-2410-H-029-002) is gratefully acknowledged. The usual disclaimer applies.

Notes

1 Alternatively, several researchers (Caporale and Gil-Alana, 2004; Cuñado et al., 2005; Koustas and Serletis, 2005) argue that the price-dividend ratio exhibits fractional integration such that it is characterized by long memory, while the series is ultimately mean-reverting. It is of interest to notice that "while the fractional integration approach may provide for statistical modeling of the data it provides no economic rationale for this behavior" (McMillan, 2007a, p. 801).
2 A byproduct of this paper is that we provide a brief review of new developments in testing for rational bubbles.
3 Readers are referred to Gürkaynak (2008) for a good survey on traditional approaches in testing for rational bubbles.
4 Readers are referred to page 4 of Park and Shintani (2005) for details.
5 Bohl and Siklos (2004, p. 212) emphasize two important advantages of the stationary test. First, the stationary test does not involve the estimation of an unknown cointegrating parameter and, second, measurement problems associated with deflating nominal stock prices and dividends by some price index do not occur.
6 The terms SP(1) and SP(2) denote the Schmidt-Phillips τ tests with a linear and quadratic trend, respectively.
7 Readers are referred to Psaradakis and Spagnolo (2002) for detailed descriptions of these tests.
8 We obtain critical values of Park and Shintani's (2005, 2016) test for the raw data, demeaned data, and demeaned and detrended data via Monte Carlo simulation.
9 We are very grateful to an anonymous referee for pointing this out to us.
10 The simulation results of Choi and Moh (2007) and Kilic (2011) show that the tests of Park and Shintani (2005, 2016) and Kilic (2011) are more powerful relative to the test of Kapetanios et al. (2003).

Bibliography

Adämmer, P. and Bohl, M. T. (2015), Speculative bubbles in agricultural prices, *The Quarterly Review of Economics and Finance*, 55, 67–76.
Balcilar, M., Gupta, R., Jooste, C. and Wohar, M. E. (2016), Periodically collapsing bubbles in the South African stock market, *Research in International Business and Finance*, 38, 191–201.
Balke, N. S. and Wohar, M. E. (2002), Low frequency movements in stock prices: A state-space decomposition, *Review of Economics and Statistics*, 84, 649–667.
Blanchard, O. J. and Watson, M. (1982), Bubbles, rational expectations, and financial markets. In P. Wachtel (Ed.), *Crises in the Economic and the Financial Structure* (pp. 295–315). Lexington: Lexington Books.
Bohl, M. T. (2003), Periodically collapsing bubbles in the US stock market? *International Review of Economics and Finance*, 12, 385–397.
Bohl, M. T. and Siklos, P. L. (2004), The present value model of US stock prices redux: A new testing strategy and some evidence, *Quarterly Review of Economics and Finance*, 44, 208–223.
Brooks, C. and Katsaris, A. (2003), Rational speculative bubbles: An empirical investigation of the London stock exchange, *Bulletin of Economic Research*, 55, 319–346.

Campbell, J. Y., Lo, A. W. and MacKinlay, A. C. (1997), *The Econometrics of Financial Markets*, Princeton University Press.

Campbell, J. Y. and Shiller, R. J. (1987), Cointegration and tests of present value models, *Journal of Political Economy*, 95 (5), 1062–1088.

Campbell, J. Y. and Shiller, R. J. (1988a), The dividend-price ratio and the expectations of future dividends and discount factors, *Review of Financial Studies*, 1, 195–228.

Campbell, J. Y. and Shiller, R. J. (1988b), Stock prices, earnings and expected dividends, *Journal of Finance*, 43, 661–676.

Caporale, G. M. and Gil-Alana, L. A. (2004), Fractional cointegration and tests of present value models, *Review of Financial Economics*, 13, 245–258.

Cerqueti, R. and Costantini, M. (2011), Testing for rational bubbles in the presence of structural breaks: Evidence from nonstationary panels, *Journal of Banking and Finance*, 35, 2598–2605.

Charemza, W. W. and Deadman, D. F. (1995), Speculative bubbles with stochastic explosive roots: The failure of unit root testing, *Journal of Empirical Finance*, 2, 153–163.

Chen, S.-W. and Xie, Z. (2015), Testing for current account sustainability under assumptions of smooth break and non-linearity, *International Review of Economics and Finance*, 38, 142–156.

Chen, S.-W. and Xie, Z. (2017), Detecting speculative bubbles under considerations of the sign asymmetry and size non-linearity: New international evidence, *International Review of Economics and Finance*, 52, 188–209.

Choi, C.-Y. and Moh, Y.-K. (2007), How useful are tests for unit-root in distinguishing unit-root processes from stationary but non-linear processes? *Econometrics Journal*, 10, 82–112.

Cook, S. and Vougas, D. (2009), Unit root testing against an ST-MTAR alternative: Finite-sample properties and an application to the UK housing market, *Applied Economics*, 41, 1397–1404.

Cuñado, J., Gil-Alana, L. A. and Perez de Gracia, F. (2005), A test for rational bubbles in the NASDAQ stock index: A fractionally integrated approach, *Journal of Banking and Finance*, 29, 2633–2654.

Diba, B. T. and Grossman, H. I. (1988), Explosive rational bubbles in stock prices? *American Economic Review*, 78, 520–530.

Driffill, J. and Sola, M. (1998), Intrinsic bubbles and regime switching, *Journal of Monetary Economics*, 42, 357–373.

Elliott, G., Rothenberg, T. J. and Stock, J. H. (1996), Efficient tests for an autoregressive unit root, *Econometrica*, 64, 813–836.

Enders, W. and Granger, C. W. J. (1998), Unit-roots tests and asymmetric adjustment with an example using the term structure of interest rates, *Journal of Business and Economic Statistics*, 16, 304–311.

Enders, W. and Siklos, P. L. (2001), Cointegration and threshold adjustment, *Journal of Business and Economic Statistics*, 19, 166–176.

Engsted, T., Hviid, S. J. and Pedersen, T. Q. (2016), Explosive bubbles in house prices? Evidence from the OECD countries, *Journal of International Financial Markets, Institutions and Money*, 40, 14–25.

Escobari, D. and Jafarinejad, M. (2016), Date stamping bubbles in real estate investment trusts, *The Quarterly Review of Economics and Finance*, 60, 224–230.

Esteve, V., Navarro-Ibáñez, M. and Prats, M. A. (2013), *The Present Value Model of U.S. Stock Prices Revisited: Long-run Evidence With Structural Breaks, 1871–2010*, Working Paper.

Evans, G. W. (1991), Pitfalls in testing for explosive bubbles in asset prices, *American Economic Review*, 81, 922–930.

Fantazzini, D. (2016), The oil price crash in 2014/15: Was there a (negative) financial bubble? *Energy Policy*, 96, 383–396.

Froot, K. A. and Obstfeld, M. (1991), Intrinsic bubbles: The case of stock prices, *American Economic Review*, 1189–1214.

Fulop, A. and Yu, J. (2014), *Bayesian Analysis of Bubbles in Asset Prices*, Working Paper.

Geweke, J. (2007), Bayesian model comparison and validation, *American Economic Review*, 97, 60–64.

Gürkaynak, R. S. (2008), Econometric tests of asset price bubbles: Taking stock, *Journal of Economic Survey*, 22, 166–186.

Gutierrez, L. (2011), Bootstrapping asset price bubbles, *Economic Modelling*, 28, 2488–2493.

Hall, A. D. (1994), Testing for a unit root in time series with pretest data based model selection, *Journal of Business and Economic Statistics*, 12, 461–470.

Harvey, D. I., Leybourne, S. J. and Xiao, B. (2008), A powerful test for linearity when the order of integration is unknown, *Studies in Non-Linear Dynamics and Econometrics*, 12 (3), article 2.

Homm, U. and Breitung, J. (2012), Testing for speculative bubbles in stock markets: A comparison of alternative methods, *Journal of Financial Econometrics*, 10, 198–231.

Jahan-Parvar, M. R. and Waters, G. A. (2010), Equity price bubbles in the Middle Eastern and North African financial markets, *Emerging Markets Review*, 11, 39–48.

Kanas, A. (2005), Non-linearity in stock price-dividend relation, *Journal of International Money and Finance*, 24, 583–606.

Kapetanios, G., Shin, Y. and Snell, A. (2003), Testing for a unit root in the non-linear STAR framework, *Journal of Econometrics*, 112, 359–379.

Kapetanios, G., Shin, Y. and Snell, A. (2006), Testing for cointegration in non-linear STAR error-correction models, *Econometric Theory*, 22, 279–303.

Kass, R. E. and Raftery, A. E. (1995), Bayes factors, *Journal of the American Statistical Association*, 90, 773–795.

Keenan, D. M. (1985), A Tukey nonadditivity-type test for time series non-linearity, *Biometrika*, 72, 39–44.

Kilic, R. (2011), Testing for a unit root in a stationary ESTAR process, *Econometric Reviews*, 30 (3), 274–302.

Kirman, A. P. (1991), Epidemics of opinion and speculative bubbles in financial markets. In M. P. Taylor (Ed.), *Money and Financial Markets* (pp. 354–368). Cambridge: Basil Blackwell.

Kirman, A. P. (1993), Ants, rationality, and recruitment, *Quarterly Journal of Economics*, 108, 137–156.

Koustas, Z. and Serletis, A. (2005), Rational bubbles or persistence deviation from market fundamentals? *Journal of Banking and Finance*, 29, 2523–2539.

Leybourne, S. and Mizen, P. (1999), Understanding the disinflations in Australia, Canada and New Zealand using evidence from smooth transition analysis, *Journal of International Money and Finance*, 18, 799–816.

Leybourne, S., Newbold, P. and Vougas, D. (1998), Unit roots and smooth transitions, *Journal of Time Series Analysis*, 19, 83–98.

Li, W. and Xue, H. (2009), A Bayesian's bubble, *The Journal of Finance*, 64(6), 2665–2701.

Li, Y., Liu, X., and Yu, J. (2015), Bayesian chi-square test for hypothesis testing, *Journal of Econometrics*, 189(1), 54–69.

Li, Y., Zeng, T. and Yu, J. (2014), A new approach to Bayesian hypothesis testing, *Journal of Econometrics*, 178(3), 602–612.

Lumsdaine, R. L., and Papell, D. H. (1997), Multiple trend breaks and the unit root hypothesis, *Review of Economics and Statistics*, 79, 212–218.

McMillan, D. G. (2004), Non-linear predictability of short-run deviations in UK stock market returns, *Economics Letters*, 84, 149–154.

McMillan, D. G. (2006), The price-dividend ratio and limits to arbitrage: Evidence from a time-varying ESTR model, *Economics Letters*, 91, 408–412.

McMillan, D. G. (2007a), Bubbles in the dividend-price ratio? Evidence from an asymmetric exponential smooth-transition model, *Journal of Banking and Finance*, 31, 787–804.

McMillan, D. G. (2007b), Structural breaks in financial ratios: Evidence for nine international markets, *Applied Financial Economics Letters*, 3, 381–384.

McMillan, D. G. (2008), Non-linear cointegration and adjustment: An asymmetric exponential smooth-transition model for US interest rates, *Empirical Economics*, 35, 591–606.

McMillan, D. G. (2009a), Are share prices still too high? *Research in International Business and Finance*, 23, 223–232.

McMillan, D. G. (2009b), Revisiting dividend yield dynamics and returns predictability: Evidence from a time-varying ESTR model, *The Quarterly Review of Economics and Finance*, 49, 870–883.

McMillan, D. G. and Speight, A. E. H. (2006), Non-linear long horizon returns predictability: Evidence from six south-east Asian markets, *Asia-Pacific Financial Markets*, 13, 95–111.

McMillan, D. G. and Wohar, M. (2009), Stock return predictability and dividend-price ratio: A non-linear approach, *International Journal of Finance and Economics*, 15, 351–365.

McMillan, D. G. and Wohar, M. (2010), UK stock market predictability: Evidence of time variation, *Applied Financial Economics*, 23 (12), 1043–1055.

Miao, J., Wang, P. and Xu, Z. (2014), *A Bayesian DSGE Model of Stock Market Bubbles and Business Cycles*, Working Paper.

Michaelides, P. G., Tsionas, E. G. and Konstantakis, K. N. (2016), Non-linearities in financial bubbles: Theory and Bayesian evidence from S&P500, *Journal of Financial Stability*, 24, 61–70.

Narayan, P. K. and Popp, S. (2010), A new unit root test with two structural breaks in level and slope at unknown time, *Journal of Applied Statistics*, 37, 1425–1438.

Narayan, P. K. and Popp, S. (2013), Size and power properties of structural break unit root tests, *Applied Economics*, 45, 721–728.

Nunes, M. and Da Silva, S. (2008), Explosive and periodically collapsing bubbles in emerging stock markets, *Economics Bulletin*, 3 (46), 1–18.

Park, J. Y. and Shintani, M. (2005), *Testing for a Unit Root Against Smooth Transition Autoregressive Models*, Working Paper.

Park, J. Y. and Shintani, M. (2016), Testing for a unit root against smooth transition autoregressive models, *International Economic Review*, 57, 635–663.

Perron, P. (1989), The great crash, the oil price shock, and the unit root hypothesis, *Econometrica*, 57, 1361–1401.

Phillips, P. C. B., Shi, S.-P. and Yu, J. (2015), Testing for multiple bubbles: Historical episode of exuberance and the collapse in the S& P 500, *International. Economic Review*, 56, 1043–1078,

Phillips, P. C. B., Wu, Y. and Yu, J. (2011), Explosive behavior and the Nasdaq bubble in the 1990s: When does irrational exuberance have escalated asset values? *International Economic Review*, 52, 201–226.

Popp, S. (2008), New innovational outlier unit root test with a break at an unknown time, *Journal of Statistical Computation and Simulation*, 78, 1145–1161.

Ryan, G. (2006), *Non-Linearities in the Present Value Model of Stock Prices; Enhanced Estimation and Forecasting Using Exponential Smooth Transition Autoregressive Models: A Multi-Country Analysis*, Working Paper, University College Cork.

Schmidt, P. and Phillips, P. C. B. (1992), LM test for a Unit Root in the presence of deterministic trends, *Oxford Bulletin of Economics and Statistic*, 54, 257–276.

Shi, S.-P. (2013), Specification sensitivities in the Markov-switching unit root test for bubbles, *Empirical Economics*, 45, 697–713.

Shi, S.-P. and Song, Y. (2016), Identifying speculative bubbles with an infinite hidden Markov model, *Journal of Financial Econometrics*, 14, 159–184.

Shleifer, A. (2000), *Inefficient Markets, An Introduction to Behavioral Finance*. Oxford: Oxford University Press.

Sollis, R. (2004), Asymmetric adjustment and smooth transitions: A combination of some unit root tests, *Journal of Time Series Analysis*, 25, 409–417.

Sollis, R. (2006), Testing for bubbles: An application of tests for change in persistence, *Applied Financial Economics*, 16, 491–498.

van Dijk, D., Teräsvirta, T. and Franses, P. H. (2002), Smooth transition autoregressive models: A survey of recent developments, *Econometric Reviews*, 21 (1), 1–47.

van Norden, S. (1996), Regime switching as a test for exchange rate bubbles, *Journal of Applied Econometrics*, 11, 219–251.

van Norden, S. and Schaller, H. (1999), Speculative behavior, regime switching and stock market crashes. In Philip Rothman (Ed.), *Non-Linear Time Series Analysis of Economic and Financial Data* (pp. 321–356). Boston: Kluwer.

Vougas, D. V. (2007), Is the trend in post-WW II US real GDP uncertain or non-linear? *Economics Letters*, 94, 348–355.

Watanabe, K., Takayasu, H. and Takayasu, M. (2007a), Extracting the exponential behaviors in the market data, *Physica A*, 382, 336–339.

Watanabe, K., Takayasu, H. and Takayasu, M. (2007b), A mathematical definition of the financial bubbles and crashes, *Physica A*, 383, 120–124.

West, K. D. (1987), A specification test for speculative bubbles, *Quarterly Journal of Economics*, 102, 553–580.

Yiu, M. S., Yu, J. and Jin, L. (2013), Detecting bubbles in Hong Kong residential property market, *Journal of Asian Economics*, 28, 115–124.

Zivot, E. and Andrews, D. W. K. (1992), Further evidence on the great crash, the oil-price shock and the unit root hypothesis, *Journal of Business and Economic Statistics*, 10, 251–270.

6   The Continuum-GMM estimation

Theory and application

Rachidi Kotchoni and Marine Carrasco

1. Introduction

Many econometrics models are naturally specified in terms of their characteristic function (CF) as their densities are unknown in closed form. This is the case for most stable distributions[1] and discretely sampled continuous-time processes.[2] For some models, the density takes the form of an infinite mixture (e.g., autoregressive Gamma processes; see Gourieroux and Jasiak, 2005) or an integral (e.g., variance Gamma processes; see Madan and Seneta, 1990). For other models, the density has a rather simple analytical expression but the likelihood function is numerically ill-behaved in finite sample (e.g., finite mixtures). In these models, parameter estimation may be done via the continuum of moment conditions that is obtained by taking the difference between the theoretical and empirical CF. As there is a one-to-one relationship between the CF and the probability distribution function of a random variable, an inference procedure based on the CF has the potential to be as efficient as one that is based on the likelihood function.

Indeed, many authors have relied on the CF to conduct parametric inference in various contexts. For instance, Paulson et al. (1975) used a weighted modulus of the difference between the theoretical CF and its empirical counterpart to estimate the parameters of a stable distribution. Feuerverger and Mureika (1977) studied the convergence properties of the empirical CF and suggested that it may be useful for tackling numerous statistical problems. Since then, various GMM-like estimators that are based on the CF have been advocated by several authors, including Feuerverger and McDunnough (1981a, 1981b, 1981c), Carrasco and Florens (2000), Singleton (2001), Jiang and Knight (2002), Knight and Yu (2002), Chacko and Viceira (2003), Yu (2004), and Carrasco, Chernov, Florens, and Ghysels (2007).

The Continuum-GMM (CGMM) procedure of Carrasco and Florens (2000) closely mimics the efficient two-step GMM of Hansen (1982). It is obtained by minimizing a quadratic form in a Hilbert space that spans the continuum of moment condition of interest. As the standard GMM estimator, it is implemented in two steps, the first step leading to a consistent estimator and the second step delivering an efficient estimator. The objective function of the efficient CGMM is a quadratic form with metrics K^{-1}, where K is the asymptotic covariance operator associated with the continuum of moment conditions of interest. To obtain a feasible second-step CGMM estimator, one has to replace K by a sample analogue K_T, where T is the sample size. However, K_T is not invertible and its limit as T goes to infinity, K, is not continuous. To circumvent this difficulty, Carrasco and Florens (2000) use a regularized inverse of the form $K_{\lambda T}^{-1} = \left(K_T^2 + \lambda I\right)^{-1} K_T$, where I is the identity operator and λ is a regularization parameter. The resulting estimator is root-T consistent and asymptotically normal for any fixed λ. Asymptotic efficiency is obtained by letting T go to infinity and λ go to zero at a specific rate.

This chapter reviews the theory underlying the CGMM procedure, discusses the properties of the CGMM estimator, and presents numerical algorithms for its implementation. An empirical application is proposed where a Variance Gamma model is fitted to the monthly increments of the USD/GBP exchange rates. This model is appealing for exchange rates because it features both mean reversion and heteroskedasticity. However, it has limited scope as it specifies the latent variance of the exchange rate increments as an independent and identically distributed (IID) process. Consequently, time varying predictions of the variance can only be obtained as its expectation conditional on the ex-post realizations of exchange rate increments. We find that these posterior variances are poor predictions of the monthly realized variances inferred from daily data. A model that specifies the variance as a dependent process should deliver better forecasts than the Variance Gamma model considered here.

The remainder of the presentation is organized as follows. In Section 2, we show how to construct a continuum of moment conditions in five different contexts. Section 3 presents a review of estimation methods that are based on the CF. In Section 4, we review the construction of the objective function of the CGMM procedure and discuss the asymptotic properties of the CGMM estimator. In Section 5, we discuss the selection of the regularization parameter, λ, in practice. Section 6 presents other implementation issues and proposes algorithmic solutions. Section 7 presents the empirical application and Section 8 concludes. A short appendix presents the derivation of the prediction formula inferred from the variance Gamma process for the latent variance process.

2. Moment conditions based on the characteristic function

This section presents five empirically relevant situations that motivate the use of a continuum of moment condition for parametric estimation. Although most cases involve the use of a CF, an important example concerns the conversion of a conditional moment restriction into a continuum of unconditional moment restrictions.

2.1. Finite mixtures

Consider a random variable y_t that may have been generated by a distribution $f_j(y_t, \theta_j)$ with probability $\omega_j, j = 1, \ldots, J$. These distributions can be viewed as linked with a discrete state variable $s_t \in \{1, \ldots, J\}$ so that:

$$\Pr(s_t = j) = \omega_j, \ j = 1, \ldots, J, \ \text{and} \ f(y_t | s_t = j) = f_j(y_t, \theta_j).$$

Under this convention, the marginal density of y is given by:

$$f(y_t) = \sum_{j=1}^{J} \omega_j f_j(y_t, \theta_j).$$

Assuming independence over time, the sample log-likelihood of $y_1, \ldots, y_T$ is:

$$\mathcal{L}(\theta) = \sum_{t=1}^{T} \log \left(\sum_{j=1}^{J} \omega_j f_j(y_t, \theta_j) \right). \tag{1}$$

where θ collects all the parameters.

The log-likelihood function above may not be globally concave because of the summation across states inside the logarithm. Moreover, when $f_j(y_t, \theta_j)$ is Gaussian, $\mathcal{L}(\theta)$ can be unbounded in finite sample. This occurs when the variance of y_t in one of the regimes eventually take a very small value during the numerical iterations of the likelihood maximization algorithm. However, the CF of y_t is always bounded in modulus. We have:

$$E(\exp(i\tau y_t)) = \sum_{j=1}^{J} \omega_j \varphi_j(\tau, \theta_j) \equiv \varphi(\tau, \theta), \ \tau \in \mathbb{R}.$$

where $\varphi_j(\tau, \theta_j) = E(\exp(i\tau y_t) | s_t = j)$ is a regime specific CF and i is the imaginary number such that $i^2 = -1$.

The following moment function is easily deduced from this CF:

$$h_t(\tau, \theta) = \exp(i\tau y_t) - \varphi(\tau, \theta), \ \text{for all} \ \tau \in \mathbb{R}. \tag{2}$$

Indeed, $E(h_t(\tau, \theta)) = 0$ for all $\tau \in \mathbb{R}$. Inference procedures that are based on the CF can take advantage of the fact that $h_t(\tau, \theta)$ is bounded. Indeed:

$$|h_t(\tau, \theta)|^2 = |\exp(i\tau y_t) - \varphi(\tau, \theta)|^2 \leq |\exp(i\tau y_t)|^2 + |\varphi(\tau, \theta)|^2 \leq 2$$

for all τ and θ.

2.2. Stable distributions

The stable distribution has been introduced in finance in an effort to fit the asymmetry and fat tail observed empirically in the distributions of assets returns (Mandelbrot, 1963; McCulloch, 1986). A random variable Z_t is said to follow the standard α-stable distribution if and only if its CF is given by:

$$E[\exp(i\tau Z_t)] = \exp\{-|\tau|^\alpha[1 + \text{sign}(\tau)i\beta g(\tau, \alpha)]\}, \tag{3}$$

where $\alpha \in (0, 2]$ is a stability parameter that controls the tail behavior, $\beta \in [-1, 1]$ is a skewness parameter, $g(\tau, \alpha) = -\tan \frac{\alpha\pi}{2}$ if $\alpha \neq 1$ and $g(\tau, \alpha) = \frac{2}{\pi} \ln |\tau|$ if $\alpha = 1$.

A random variable y_t follows a general α-stable distribution if and only if it is linked to a standard α-stable random variable Z_t through:

$$y_t = \begin{cases} \sigma Z_t + \mu, & \alpha \neq 1 \\ \sigma Z_t + \mu + \dfrac{2}{\pi} \beta \sigma \ln \sigma, & \alpha = 1 \end{cases}.$$

The moments of order larger than α do not exist for the stable distribution when $\alpha < 2$. When $\alpha = 2$, all moments exist but the asymmetry parameter β is not identified.

Closed form expressions for stable densities are available only in a few cases. For example, $\alpha = 2$ leads to the normal distribution $N(\alpha, 2\sigma^2)$ whereas $\alpha = 1$ and $\beta = 0$ leads to Cauchy distributions. Levy distributions are obtained by letting $\alpha = 1/2$ and $\beta = 1$. The density for the case $\alpha = 1/2$ and $\beta = -1$ can be deduced from the previous one via an identity (see Zolotarev, 1986; Weron, 1996). However, the knowledge of the likelihood function at isolated values of the parameter space is not helpful when one is trying to fit the model to real data. This difficulty has often led some empirical researchers to rely on numerical approximations of the likelihood of the stable distribution. For example, McCulloch (1998) discusses an approximate maximum likelihood procedure for symmetric stable distributions while Nolan (1997) proposes a numerical procedures for $\alpha > 0.1$. Mittnik et al. (1999) and Paolella (2007) use Fast Fourier Transform to approximate the likelihood function while quantile methods are advocated in McCulloch (1986).

As argued in Kotchoni (2012), the parameters of a stable distribution can be estimated using a CF-based continuum of moment condition of the form $E(h_t(\tau, \theta)) = 0$ for all $\tau \in \mathbb{R}$, where:

$$h_t(\tau, \theta) = \exp(i\tau y_t) - \varphi(\tau, \theta), \quad \tau \in \mathbb{R}.$$

where $\varphi(\tau, \theta) = E[\exp(i\tau y_t)]$ and $\theta = (\alpha, \beta, \sigma, \mu)$. The CF of y_t is given by:

$$E[\exp(i\tau y_t)] = \exp\{i\mu\tau - |\sigma\tau|^\alpha [1 + i\beta \text{sign}(\tau)g(\tau, \alpha)]\}, \tag{4}$$

where μ is a location parameter and σ is the scale parameter. Kotchoni (2012) performed a simulation study based on an AR(1) model with stable innovations and found that the CGMM estimator significantly outperforms a GMM estimator based on a discrete subset of moment conditions.

2.3. Discretely sampled continuous-time processes

Similarly to stable distributions, discretely sampled continous-time processes are more naturally characterized by their CFs rather by their densities. For example, consider the following stochastic differential equation specified for the short-term nominal interest rate:

$$dx_t = \mu(y_t)dt + \sigma(y_t)dW_t,$$

where y_t denotes an interest rate process, $\mu(y_t)$ is a drift function, $\sigma(y_t)$ is an instantaneous volatility function and W_t is a standard Brownian motion.

The transition density of discretely sampled observations from this model is known only in the special case of a Cox, Ingersoll and Ross (1985) model, that is, when $\mu(y_t) = \kappa(\rho - y_t)$ and $\sigma(y_t) = \sigma\sqrt{y_t}$. In this case, the conditional density of y_t given $y_{t-\delta}$ ($\delta > 0$) can be represented as an infinite mixture of Gamma densities with Poisson weights:

$$f(y_t|y_{t-\delta}) = \sum_{j=0}^{\infty} p_j \frac{y_t^{j+q-1} c^{j+q}}{\Gamma(j+q)} \exp(-cy_t), \tag{5}$$

where $c = \frac{2\kappa}{\sigma^2(1-\exp(-\delta\kappa))}$, $q = \frac{2\kappa\rho}{\sigma^2}$, $p_j = \frac{(c\exp(-\delta\kappa)y_{t-\delta})^j}{j!} \exp(-c\exp(-\delta\kappa)y_{t-\delta})$ and $\Gamma()$ is Euler's Gamma function[3] (see Devroye, 1986; Singleton, 2001). The parameter κ captures the strength of the mean reversion in the interest rate process, ρ is the long run value around which the interest rate process oscillates along the business cycles while σ captures the instantaneous volatility of the interest rate process.

The infinite mixture of densities given above will have to be truncated for the purpose of performing maximum likelihood. However, imprecise estimations of these parameters may have dramatic implications for the valuation of interest rate sensitive assets, the prediction of the term structure of the market risk premium and the assessment of interest rate risk. Contrasting with the infinite mixture (5), the conditional CF of the CIR model has a simple closed form expression given by:

$$\varphi(\tau, \theta; y_{t-\delta}) \equiv E(\exp(i\tau y_t)|y_{t-\delta}) = (1 - i\tau/c)^{-q} \exp\left(\frac{i\tau \exp(-\delta\kappa)y_{t-\delta}}{1 - i\tau/c}\right), \tag{6}$$

with $\theta = (\kappa, \rho, \sigma)'$. Moreover, the CF is available in closed form for more sophisticated affine-jump diffusions (Jiang and Knight, 2002) and stochastic volatility models (Yu, 2004).

Carrasco and Kotchoni (2017) study the performance of the CGMM by simulation based on the CIR model. The moment function that they consider is:

$$h_t(\tau, \theta) = (\exp(ir_1 y_t) - \varphi(r_1, \theta; y_{t-1})) \exp(ir_2 y_{t-1}), \quad \tau = (r_1, r_2)' \in \mathbb{R}^2.$$
(7)

where $\varphi(r_1, \theta; y_{t-1}) = E[\exp(ir_1 y_t)|y_{t-1}]$ and $\theta = (\kappa, \rho, \sigma)$. Here, $\exp(ir_2 y_{t-1}), r_2 \in \mathbb{R}$ is being used as a continuum of instruments. Carrasco, Florens, Chernov, and Ghysels (2007) showed that this set of instruments is optimal given that the process y_t is Markov.

2.4. Weakly dependent processes

The first two examples of CF-based continuum of moment conditions given above deal with IID models while the third example deals with Markov data. In all three examples, the moment function $h_t(\tau, \theta)$ is uncorrelated over time. Indeed, $h_t(\tau, \theta)$ is IID in the first two cases and a Martingale Difference Sequence in the third case. These cases can easily be extended to account for a type of heteroskedasticity that leaves the observations uncorrelated over time.

When y_t is non-Markov but weakly dependent, its distribution conditional on the past depends on its whole past history. In this case, one has to truncate the history of y_t to J lags by relying on the joint CF of $(y_t, y_{t-1}, \dots, y_{t-J+1})$. This leads to the moment function:

$$h_t(\tau, \theta) = \exp(i\tau' Y_t) - E^\theta(\exp(i\tau' Y_t)), \quad \tau \in \mathbb{R}^J,$$
(8)

where $Y_t = (y_t, y_{t-1}, \dots, y_{t-J+1})'$. The number of lags J must be large enough to guarantee that the parameters of the model are all identified. Moment functions of type (8) are correlated over time.

A CGMM procedure based on the continuum of moment condition (8) is roughly equivalent to the estimator that maximizes the sample conditional likelihood of y_t given J lags. As y_t is non-Markov, the larger J the more efficient the CGMM estimator. In practice, the quest for efficiency must be balanced with the computing cost. For more discussion on this point, see Jiang and Knight (2002), Yu (2004), and Carrasco, Florens, Chernov, and Ghysels (2007).

2.5. Conditional moment restrictions

Many prominent economic theories lead to testable implications that can be summarized into a set of conditional moment restrictions. Examples of such theories include the consumption capital asset pricing model and dynamic stochastic general equilibrium model. It is customary to convert conditional moment restrictions into a few number of unconditional moment restrictions for the purpose of parameter estimation using selected instruments. However, this approach entails a loss of information given that a conditional moment restriction is equivalent to an infinite number of unconditional moment restrictions. Interestingly, a conditional moment restriction can always be converted into a continuum of moment conditions with same information content (Bierens, 1982).

For example, consider the following conditional moment restriction:

$$E[f(y, \theta)|x] = 0, \tag{9}$$

where y and x are random variables. Dynamic Stochastic General Equilibrium models often lead to first order optimality conditions that are of this form (see Cochrane, 2009). This conditional moment restriction is equivalent to an infinite number of moment conditions since:

$$E[f(y, \theta)g(x)] = 0, \text{ for all possible function } g. \tag{10}$$

For specific classes of functions g, the set of unconditional moment restrictions (10) is equivalent to the conditional moment restriction (9).

For instance, Bierens (1982) and Lavergne and Patilea (2008) used the following type of continuum of moment condition:

$$E[f(y, \theta) \exp(i\tau'x)] = 0, \text{ for all } \tau \in \mathbb{R}^{\dim(x)}, \tag{11}$$

whereas Dominguez and Lobato (2004) propose:

$$E(f(y, \theta)1(x < \tau)) = 0, \tau \in \mathbb{R}^q \tag{12}$$

The type of continuum of moment condition used in this paper is closer to (11), being complex-valued. If the information content of the conditional moment restriction (9) is equivalent to that of the likelihood of y given x, an estimator based on (11) has the potential to be as efficient as the estimator that maximized this conditional likelihood.

In the particular case of asset pricing models (e.g., Consumption Capital Asset Pricing Model), the first order optimality conditions take the form:

$$E\left[m_{t+1}(\theta)\left(r_{i,t+1} - r_{f,t+1}\right)|I_t\right] = 0, \text{ for all } i = 1, ..., N. \tag{13}$$

where $m_{t+1}(\theta)$ is a stochastic discount factor, $r_{i,t+1}$ and $r_{f,t+1}$ are respectively the return on a risky asset and the risk free rate for period $[t, t+1]$ and I_t is the information set of the investor (see Cochrane, 2009). Following the same intuition as previously, one may consider using the following continuum of moment condition for the estimation of the asset pricing model:

$$E\left[m_{t+1}(\theta)\left(r_{i,t+1} - r_{f,t+1}\right) \exp(i\tau'X_t)\right] = 0, \text{ for all } \tau \in \mathbb{R}^{\dim(X_t)}. \tag{14}$$

for $i = 1, ..., N$, where X_t is a vector summarizing the investor's information set at time t. A suggestion is to restrict (14) to one continuum of moment condition by focusing on the market portfolio only.

3. Review of estimation methods based on the CF

Different approaches have been employed in the literature to estimate a vector of parameters θ_0 from a CF-based continuum of moment conditions (or moment function) $h_t(\tau, \theta), \tau \in \mathbb{R}^d$.[4] The simplest of these approaches consists of applying the GMM procedure to a discrete subset of moment conditions obtained by evaluating $h_t(\tau, \theta)$ at several points $\{\tau_1, \tau_2, \dots, \tau_q\}$ in $\mathbb{R}^d$ (see Feuerverger and McDunnough, 1981b; Singleton, 2001; Chacko and Viceira, 2003). This approach yields a vector of moment conditions of the following type:

$$g_t(\theta) = \left(\mathrm{Re}h_t(\tau_1, \theta), \dots, \mathrm{Re}h_t(\tau_q, \theta), \mathrm{Im}h_t(\tau_1, \theta), \dots, \mathrm{Im}h_t(\tau_q, \theta) \right)'. \qquad (15)$$

Typically, GMM estimators are obtained by minimizing a quadratic form of $\hat{g}(\theta) = \frac{1}{T}\sum_{t=1}^{T} g_t(\theta)$ with respect to θ.

The efficient GMM estimator of Hansen (1982) is given by:

$$\hat{\theta}^*_{\mathrm{GMM}} = \arg\min_{\theta} \hat{g}(\theta)' S^{-1} \hat{g}(\theta), \qquad (16)$$

where $\hat{g}(\theta) = \frac{1}{T}\sum_{t=1}^{T} g_t(\theta)$ and S is the asymptotic covariance matrix of $g_t(\theta_0)$, that is:

$$S = \lim_{T\to\infty} Var\left[\sqrt{T}\hat{g}(\theta_0) \right] = \Gamma_0 + \sum_{j=1}^{\infty} \left(\Gamma_j + \Gamma_j' \right), \qquad (17)$$

with $\Gamma_j = E[g_t(\theta_0)g_{t-j}(\theta_0)']$. However, $\hat{\theta}^*_{\mathrm{GMM}}$ is unfeasible as S is generally unknown.

If $g_t(\theta)$ is uncorrelated over time, the asymptotic covariance matrix of $g_t(\theta_0)$ reduces to $S = \Gamma_0$ and is therefore estimated by:

$$\hat{S} = \frac{1}{T}\sum_{t=1}^{T} g_t\left(\hat{\theta}^1\right) g_t\left(\hat{\theta}^1\right)', \qquad (18)$$

where $\hat{\theta}^1$ is a consistent first step estimator of θ_0. Such an estimator is given by:

$$\hat{\theta}^1 = \arg\min_{\theta} \| \hat{g}(\theta) \|^2. \qquad (19)$$

When $g_t(\theta)$ is autocorrelated, the suitable estimator of S takes the form:

$$\hat{S} = \hat{\Gamma}_0 + \sum_{j=1}^{J} w\left(\frac{j}{J}\right) \left(\hat{\Gamma}_j + \hat{\Gamma}_j' \right), \qquad (20)$$

where $\hat{\Gamma}_j = \frac{1}{T}\sum_{t=1}^{T} g_t\left(\hat{\theta}^1\right) g_{t-j}\left(\hat{\theta}^1\right)'$, $w(x)$ is a positive and decreasing kernel function on $[0, 1]$ satisfying $w(0) = 1$ and $w(1) = 0$ and J is a bandwidth that must be selected by the econometrician. Intuitively, the optimal bandwidth is increasing in the degree of persistence of $g_t(\theta)$ as well as in the sample size T. See Newey and West (1987) and Andrews and Monahan (1992) for more details on the properties of $\hat{S}$.

The feasible version of $\hat{\theta}^*_{\text{GMM}}$, commonly referred to as the "two-step efficient GMM estimator," is given by:

$$\hat{\theta}_{\text{GMM}} = \arg\min_{\theta} \hat{g}(\theta)' \hat{S}^{-1} \hat{g}(\theta). \tag{21}$$

Hansen (1982) showed that $\hat{\theta}_{\text{GMM}}$ and $\hat{\theta}^*_{\text{GMM}}$ are asymptotically equivalent, meaning that $\hat{\theta}_{\text{GMM}}$ is asymptotically efficient within the family of GMM estimators that are based on $g_t(\theta)$. However, $\hat{\theta}_{\text{GMM}}$ remains inefficient in the sense that it only utilizes a portion of the information content of the continuum of moment conditions at hand.

Feuerverger and McDunnough (1981b) claim that the asymptotic variance of $\hat{\theta}_{\text{GMM}}$ can be made arbitrarily close to the Cramer-Rao bound by selecting the grid $(\tau_1, \ldots, \tau_q)$ sufficiently refined and extended in $\mathbb{R}^d$ as T goes to infinity. However, the asymptotic covariance matrix of the moment conditions, S, becomes singular as one refines and extends the grid. Indeed, the discrete set of moment conditions converges to the continuous moment function $h_t(\tau, \theta)$, $\tau \in \mathbb{R}^d$ while the matrix S converges to the covariance operator associated with that moment function. This suggests that the GMM based on discretization is better handled in a Hilbertian functional space as $q \to \infty$.

GMM procedures that continuously match the empirical CF to its theoretical counterpart are studied in Press (1972), Paulson et al. (1975), Thorton and Paulson (1977), and more recently in Yu (2004). The corresponding estimators are generally of the form:

$$\arg\min_{\theta} \int |h_t(\tau, \theta)|^2 \pi(\tau) d\tau, \tag{22}$$

where $\pi(\tau)$ is continuous weighting function. As shown by Yu (2004, p. 98), these procedures are less efficient than the maximum likelihood.

When the moment function is deduced from a conditional CF, it is necessary to *instrument* it in order to guaranty the identification of θ_0. The moment function therefore take the form:

$$h_t(\tau, \theta) = \left(\exp\left(i\tau' y_{t+1}\right) - E\left[\exp\left(i\tau' y_{t+1}\right) | y_t\right] \right) w(\tau, y_t), \tau \in \mathbb{R}^d, \tag{23}$$

where $\left\{ w(\tau, y_t), \tau \in \mathbb{R}^d \right\}$ is a continuum of instruments. Singleton (2001) shows that the estimator defined by Equation (22) based on such a moment function achieves the maximum likelihood efficiency when the continuum of instruments is of the following form:

$$w(\tau, y_t) = \frac{1}{2\pi} \int \exp\left(i\tau' y_{t+1}\right) \frac{\partial \mathcal{L}(\theta, y_{t+1}|y_t)}{\partial \theta} dy_{t+1}, \tau \in \mathbb{R}^d, \tag{24}$$

where $\mathcal{L}(\theta, y_{t+1}|y_t)$ is the log-likelihood of y_{t+1} conditional on y_t. In most cases of practical interest, these optimal instruments cannot be computed as the conditional likelihood is unknown.

Carrasco and Florens (2000) proposed a two-step GMM procedure that avoids the discretization of the CF-based continuum of moment conditions. Interestingly, their procedure achieves the maximum likelihood efficiency and it can be implemented without knowing the conditional likelihood function of the data. This procedure is presented in detail in the next section.

4. Derivation and properties of the CGMM estimator

This section presents the CGMM estimator and its asymptotic properties. The first subsection presents the objective function that the CGMM estimator minimizes. The second subsection presents the consistency and asymptotic normality of the CGMM estimator. In the third subsection, we discuss the higher order bias and variance of the CGMM estimator.

4.1. The CGMM estimator

For the sake of generality, we assume that y_t is a d-dimensional random vector. We consider the following CFs:

$$\varphi(\tau, \theta) = E(\exp(i\tau' y_t)), \quad \tau \in \mathbb{R}^d \text{ if } y_t \text{ is IID,}$$
$$\varphi(r, \theta; y_{t-1}) = E(\exp(ir' y_t)|y_{t-1}), \quad r \in \mathbb{R}^d \text{ if } y_t \text{ is Markov and}$$
$$\varphi(\tau, \theta) = E^\theta(\exp(i\tau' Y_t)), \quad \tau \in \mathbb{R}^{dJ} \text{ if } y_t \text{ is non-Markov.}$$

where $Y_t = (y_t', y_{t-1}', \dots, y_{t-J+1}')'$. In the IID and non-Markov cases, the moment function is written as:

$$h_t(\tau, \theta) = \exp(i\tau' Y_t) - \varphi(\tau, \theta) \tag{25}$$

whereas in the Markov case we have:

$$h_t(\tau, \theta) = (\exp(ir_1 y_t) - \varphi(r_1, \theta; y_{t-1})) \exp(ir_2 y_{t-1}), \quad \tau = (r_1, r_2). \tag{26}$$

If the starting point is a conditional moment restriction of the form $E[f(y_t, \theta)|x_t] = 0$, then we let:

$$h_t(\tau, \theta) = f(y_t, \theta) \exp(i\tau' x_t), \quad \text{for all } \tau \in \mathbb{R}^q \tag{27}$$

where $q = \dim(x_t)$. Note that $h_t(\tau, \theta)$ is correlated over time in the non-Markov case while it is uncorrelated in the other cases.

The objective function of the CGMM is a quadratic form that is defined on the Hilbert space of square integrable functions with respect to a well-chosen measure π on $\mathbb{R}^d$, denoted $L^2(\pi)$. We have:

$$L^2(\pi) = \{f : \mathbb{R}^d \to \mathbb{C} | \int f(\tau)\overline{f(\tau)}\pi(\tau)d\tau < \infty\}, \tag{28}$$

where $\overline{f(\tau)}$ denotes the complex conjugate of $f(\tau)$. For simplicity, π may be taken as a probability density function on $\mathbb{R}^d$. As $|h_t(., \theta)|^2 \leq 2$ for all $\theta \in \Theta$, the function $h_t(., \theta)$ belongs to $L^2(\pi)$ for all $\theta \in \Theta$ and for any finite measure π.

We consider the following scalar product on $L^2(\pi) \times L^2(\pi)$:

$$\langle f, g \rangle = \int f(\tau)\overline{g(\tau)}\pi(\tau)d\tau.$$

Based on this notation, the efficient CGMM estimator of Carrasco and Florens (2000) is given by:

$$\hat{\theta} = \arg\min_{\theta} \left\langle K^{-1}\hat{h}_T(., \theta), \hat{h}_T(., \theta) \right\rangle. \tag{29}$$

where $\hat{h}_T(\tau, \theta) = \frac{1}{T}\sum_{t=1}^{T} h_t(\tau, \theta)$ and K is the asymptotic covariance operator associated with the moment function. Namely, K is an integral operator that satisfies:

$$Kf(\tau_2) = \int_{-\infty}^{\infty} k(\tau_1, \tau_2)f(\tau_1)\pi(\tau_1)d\tau_1, \quad \text{for any } f \in L^2(\pi),$$

where $k(\tau_1, \tau_2)$ is the kernel of K. The expression of $k(\tau_1, \tau_2)$ is given by:

$$k(\tau_1, \tau_2) = E\left[h_t(\tau_1, \theta)\overline{h_t(\tau_2, \theta)}\right]$$
$$+ \sum_{j=1}^{\infty} E\left[h_t(\tau_1, \theta)\left(\overline{h_{t-j}(\tau_2, \theta)} + \overline{h_{t+j}(\tau_2, \theta)}\right)\right]. \tag{30}$$

When $h_t(\tau_1, \theta)$ is uncorrelated, $k(\tau_1, \tau_2)$ reduces to:

$$k(\tau_1, \tau_2) = E\left(h_t(\tau_1, \theta)\overline{h_t(\tau_2, \theta)}\right). \tag{31}$$

Like Hansen's (1982) GMM estimator, the CGMM estimator must be implemented in two steps. In the first step, one estimates K by a sample analogue K_T based on a consistent first step estimator of θ. Such an estimator is given by:

$$\hat{\theta}_T^{(1)} = \arg\min_\theta \left\langle \hat{h}_T(.,\theta), \hat{h}_T(.,\theta) \right\rangle.$$

The feasible second step CGMM estimator is then obtained as:

$$\hat{\theta}_T(\lambda) = \arg\min_\theta \left\langle K_{\lambda T}^{-1} \hat{h}_T(.,\theta), \hat{h}_T(.,\theta) \right\rangle, \tag{32}$$

where $K_{\lambda T}^{-1}$ is a regularized inverse of K_T. In this paper, we consider:

$$K_{\lambda T}^{-1} = \left(K_T^2 + \lambda I \right)^{-1} K_T.$$

When the data generating process is IID or Markov, it is straightforward to estimates $k(\tau_1, \tau_2)$ by:

$$k_T(\tau_1, \tau_2, \hat{\theta}_T^1) = \frac{1}{T} \sum_{t=1}^T h_t(\tau_1, \hat{\theta}_T^1) \overline{h_t(\tau_2, \hat{\theta}_T^1)}. \tag{33}$$

In the specific case of IID data, the first step estimator of θ can be bypassed by considering:

$$k_T(\tau_1, \tau_2) = \frac{1}{T} \sum_{t=1}^T \left(\exp\left(i\tau_1' x_t\right) - \hat{\varphi}_T(\tau_1) \right) \overline{\left(\exp\left(i\tau_2' x_t\right) - \hat{\varphi}_T(\tau_2) \right)}. \tag{34}$$

where $\hat{\varphi}_T(\tau_1) = \frac{1}{T} \sum_{t=1}^T \exp\left(i\tau_1' x_t\right)$.

When the data are non-Markov, $k(\tau_1, \tau_2)$ may be estimated as in Newey and West (1987) or Andrews and Monahan (1992) using:

$$\begin{aligned}
\hat{k}_T(\tau_1, \tau_2, \hat{\theta}_T^1) = &\frac{1}{T} \sum_{t=1}^T h_t(\tau_1, \hat{\theta}_T^1) \overline{h_t(\tau_2, \hat{\theta}_T^1)} \\
&+ \sum_{j=1}^J \omega\left(\frac{j}{J}\right) \sum_{t=1}^T h_t(\tau_1, \hat{\theta}_T^1) \left(\overline{h_{t-j}(\tau_2, \hat{\theta}_T^1)} + \overline{h_{t+j}(\tau_2, \hat{\theta}_T^1)} \right),
\end{aligned} \tag{35}$$

where J is a bandwidth and $\omega : [0, 1] \to [0, 1]$ is a positive and decreasing kernel function from such that $\omega(0) = 1$ and $\omega(1) = 0$. An example of kernel function (the Bartlett kernel) is given by $\omega(x) = 1 - x$.

A regularized inverse is needed in (32) because the empirical operator K_T is degenerate and non invertible. The problem is worsened by the fact that the inverse of K (i.e., the theoretical counterpart of K_T) exists only on a dense subset of $L^2(\pi)$. Moreover, the integral equation $Kf = g$ is ill-posed in the sense that when $f \equiv K^{-1}g$ exists, a small perturbation in g may lead to an arbitrarily large variation in f (see Carrasco, Florens and Renault, 2007). Regularization permits to elude this problem while allowing $K_{\lambda T}^{-1}f$ to exist for all f in $L^2(\pi)$.

The remainder of the current section is rather theoretical as it is devoted to the asymptotic properties of the CGMM estimator. Practical issues regarding the implementation of the CGMM estimator are discussed in subsequent sections.[5]

4.2. Consistency and asymptotic normality

Carrasco and Kotchoni (2017) study the properties of CGMM estimators when the continuum of moment conditions are based on the CF of an IID or a Markov model and under the following assumptions:

Assumption 1: The measure π is strictly positive on $\mathbb{R}^d$ and admits all its moments.

Assumption 2: The equation

$$E^{\theta_0}(h_t(\tau,\theta)) = 0 \text{ for all } \tau \in \mathbb{R}^d, \pi - \text{almost everywhere,}$$

has a unique solution θ_0 which is an interior point of a compact set denoted Θ, where E^{θ_0} is the expectation operator under the true model and $h_t(\tau, \theta)$ is given by (25) in the IID case or (26) in the Markov case.

Assumption 3: (*i*) $h_t(\tau, \theta)$ is three times continuously differentiable with respect to θ. Furthermore, (*ii*) the first two derivatives of $h_t(\tau, \theta)$ with respect to θ satisfy:

$$\frac{1}{T}\sum_{t=1}^{T}\frac{\partial h_t(\tau,\theta)}{\partial \theta_j} - E\left(\frac{\partial h_t(\tau,\theta)}{\partial \theta_j}\right) = O_p(T^{-1/2}) \text{ and}$$

$$\frac{1}{T}\sum_{t=1}^{T}\frac{\partial^2 h_t(\tau,\theta)}{\partial \theta_j \partial \theta_k} - E\left(\frac{\partial^2 h_t(\tau,\theta)}{\partial \theta_j \partial \theta_k}\right) = O_p(T^{-1/2}),$$

for all j and k.[6]

Assumption 4: (*i*) $E^{\theta_0}(h_T(\tau,\theta)) \in F_\beta$ for all $\theta \in \Theta$ and for some $\beta \geq 1$, where

$$\Phi_\beta = \{f \in L^2(\pi) \text{ such that } \| K^{-\beta}f \| < \infty\}. \tag{36}$$

Furthermore, (*ii*) the first two derivatives of $E^{\theta_0}(h_T(\tau,\theta))$ with respect to θ belong to Φ_β for all θ in a neighborhood of θ_0 and for the same β as above.

Assumption 5: (*i*) The random variable y_t is stationary Markov and satisfies $y_t = D(y_{t-1},\theta_0,\varepsilon_t)$ where $D(y_{t-1},\theta^0,\varepsilon_t)$ is three times continuously differentiable with respect to θ^0 and ε_t is a IID white noise whose distribution is known and does not depend on θ^0. Furthermore, (*ii*) the gradient $G(\tau,\theta;\theta^0) = E\left(\frac{\partial h_t(\tau,\theta;\theta^0)}{\partial\theta}\right)$ and covariance operator K are continuously differentiable with respect to θ^0, where $h_t(\tau,\theta;\theta^0)$ is a moment function evaluated at parameter value θ but using data that are generated by θ^0.

Assumption 1 implies that the scalar product $\langle .,. \rangle$ underlying the objective function of the CGMM is well-defined and bounded. Assumption 2 imposes the global identification of θ. Assumption 3(i) ensures some smoothness proper-ties for $\hat{\theta}_T(\lambda)$ while Assumption 3(ii) requests that the Gradient and Hessian of the moment function converge in probability to their theoretical counterparts.

Assumption 4 guarantees that $E^{\theta_0}(h_T(\tau,\theta))$ lies the range of K: there exists g in $L^2(\pi)$ such that $E^{\theta_0}(h_T(\tau,\theta)) = Kg$. The largest real number β such that $f \in \Phi_\beta$ in Assumption 4 is the level of regularity of f with respect to K. The larger β is, the better f is approximated by a linear combination of the eigenfunctions of K associated with the largest eigenvalues. Because $Kf(.)$ involve a d-dimensional integration, β may be affected by both the dimensionality of the index τ and the smoothness of f.

Assumption 5-(i) implies that the data can be simulated upon knowing how to draw from the distribution of ε_t. It is satisfied for all random variables that can be written as a location parameter plus a scale parameter times a standardized rep-resentative of the family of distribution. Examples include the exponential family and the stable distribution. An IID model is a special case of Assumption 5 where $D(y_{t-1}, \theta_0, \varepsilon_t)$ takes the simpler form $D(\theta_0, \varepsilon_t)$. Note that the function $D(y_{t-1}, \theta_0, \varepsilon_t)$ may not be explicitly available in analytical form. For instance, the relation $y_t = D(y_{t-1}, \theta_0, \varepsilon_t)$ can be the numerical solution of a general equi-librium asset pricing model (e.g., as in Duffie and Singleton, 1993).

By Assumptions 3 and 5-(i), $\frac{\partial \hat{h}_T(\tau,\theta;\theta^0)}{\partial \theta}$ is twice continuously differentiable with respect to θ^0 while the kernel $k_T(\tau_1, \tau_2, \hat{\theta}^1)$ is three times continuously differenti-able with respect to θ^0. Therefore, the differentiability requirement of Assump-tion 5-(ii) holds for the empirical gradient $G_T(\tau,\theta;\theta^0) = \frac{\partial \hat{h}_T(\tau,\theta;\theta^0)}{\partial \theta}$ and the empirical covariance operator K_T. Assumption 5-(ii) extends this differentiability to the probability limits $G(\tau, \theta;\theta^0)$ and K.

Carrasco and Kotchoni (2017) establish the following result under the previ-ous assumptions.

Theorem 1 *Under Assumptions 1 to 5, the CGMM estimator is consistent and satisfies*:

$$T^{1/2}\left(\hat{\theta}_T(\lambda) - \theta_0\right) \xrightarrow{L} N(0, I_{\theta_0}^{-1}).$$

as T and $\lambda T^{1/2}$ go to infinity and λ goes to zero, where $I_{\theta_0}^{-1}$ denotes the inverse of the Fisher Information Matrix.

Theorem 1 stipulates that the CGMM estimator is consistent, asymptotically normal and efficient. Moreover, the asymptotic distribution does not depend on the regularization parameter λ nor on the measure π used to build the objec-tive function. A more general statement of this result is provided in Proposition 3.2 of Carrasco, Chernov, Florens, and Ghysels (2007). Due to Assumption 5-(i), non-Markov processes do not share the result of Theorem 1. This assump-tion can be modified to include non-Markov processes by letting $y_t = D(\chi_{t-1}, \theta_0, \varepsilon_t)$, where χ_{t-1} is a finite dimensional state variable summarizing the past history of y_t. Under the modified assumption, consistency and asymptotic normality stills hold. However, asymptotic efficiency is no longer guaranteed because the moment function used in the non-Markov case is deduced from a truncated information set and not on the density of y_t conditional on its entire history. See Proposition 4.3 of Carrasco, Chernov, Florens, and Ghysels (2007).

4.3. Stochastic expansion and approximate MSE

According to Theorem 1, any sequence of regularization parameters of type $\lambda_T = cT^{-a}$ with $c > 0$ and $0 < a < 1/2$ leads to an efficient CGMM estimator. Among the admissible convergence rates, we would like to find the one that minimizes the trace of the Mean Square Error matrix of the CGMM estimator for a given sample size T:

$$MSE(\lambda, \theta_0) = E\left[T\left(\hat{\theta}_T(\lambda) - \theta_0\right)\left(\hat{\theta}_T(\lambda) - \theta_0\right)'\right], \tag{37}$$

Unfortunately, there is no theoretical basis for claiming that $MSE(\lambda, \theta_0)$ is finite for any data generating process and any sample size. Indeed, the large sample properties of GMM-type estimators like $\hat{\theta}_T(\lambda)$ are well-known but their finite sample properties can be established only in special cases. In particular, the MSE of $\hat{\theta}_T(\lambda)$ can be infinite in finite samples even though $\hat{\theta}_T(\lambda)$ is consistent for θ_0.

To hedge against situations where $MSE(\lambda, \theta_0)$ is infinite in finite sample, we consider approximating the MSE of $\hat{\theta}_T(\lambda)$ by that of the leading terms of its stochastic expansion. Our goal is to examine the nature of the dependence of the higher order variance and bias of the CGMM estimator on the regularization parameter λ. The higher order properties of GMM-type estimators have been studied by Rothenberg (1983, 1984), Koenker et al. (1994), Rilstone et al. (1996), and Newey and Smith (2004). For estimators derived in the linear simultaneous equation framework, examples include Nagar (1959), Buse (1992), and Donald and Newey (2001). The approach followed by Carrasco and Kotchoni (2017) is similar to Nagar (1959) and in particular, Donald and Newey (2001), who select the number of instruments to include in a linear instrumental variable model by minimization of an AMSE criterion.

Carrasco and Kotchoni (2017) derived and expansion of $\hat{\theta}_T(\lambda) - \theta_0$ that is of the following form for both the IID and Markov cases:

$$\hat{\theta}_T(\lambda) - \theta_0 = \Delta_1 + \Delta_2 + \Delta_3 + o_p\left(\lambda^{-1}T^{-1}\right) + o_p\left(\lambda^{\min\left(1,\frac{2\beta-1}{2}\right)}T^{-1/2}\right), \tag{38}$$

where

$$\Delta_1 = O_p(T^{-1/2}),$$
$$\Delta_2 = O_p\left(\lambda^{\min\left(1,\frac{2\beta-1}{2}\right)}T^{-1/2}\right) \text{ and}$$
$$\Delta_3 = O_p\left(\lambda^{-1}T^{-1}\right)$$

See Appendix B of Carrasco and Kotchoni (2017) for details.[7] Carrasco and Kotchoni (2017) used this expansion to calculate an Approximate MSE (AMSE) for $\hat{\theta}_T(\lambda)$ and establish results on the optimal regularization parameter.

The following result is established in Carrasco and Kotchoni (2017) for the IID and Markov cases when the moment function is deduced from a CF.

Theorem 2 *Assume that Assumptions 1 to 5 hold. Then we have*:

(i) *The AMSE matrix of $\hat{\theta}_T(\lambda)$ up to order $O(\lambda^{-1}T^{-1/2})$ is decomposed as the sum of the squared bias and variance*:

$$AMSE(\lambda, \theta_0) = TBias * Bias' + TVar$$

where

$$
\begin{aligned}
TBias * Bias' &= O(\lambda^{-2}T^{-1}), \\
TVar &= I_{\theta_0}^{-1} + O\left(\lambda^{\min\left(2,\frac{2\beta-1}{2}\right)}\right) + O(\lambda^{-1}T^{-1/2}).
\end{aligned}
$$

as $T \to \infty$, $\lambda^2 T \to \infty$ and $\lambda \to 0$.

(ii) *The λ that minimizes the trace of AMSE (λ, θ_0), denoted $\lambda_T \equiv \lambda_T(\theta_0)$, satisfies*:

$$\lambda_T = O\left(T^{-\max\left(\frac{1}{6},\frac{1}{2\beta+1}\right)}\right).$$

First, note that the expansion is consistent with the condition of Theorem 1 since the optimal regularization parameter satisfies: $\lambda_T \to 0$ and $\lambda_T^2 T \to \infty$. Second, we have a trade-off between a term that is decreasing in λ and another that is increasing in λ. The squared bias term is dominated by two higher order variance terms whose rates of convergence are equated to obtain the optimal rate for the regularization parameter. The same situation happens for the Limited Information Maximum Likelihood estimator for which the bias is also dominated by variance terms (see Donald and Newey, 2001). Third, note that the rate of convergence for the $O\left(\lambda^{\min\left(2,\frac{2\beta-1}{2}\right)}\right)$ variance term does not improve for $\beta > 2.5$. This is due to a property of Tikhonov regularization that is well documented in the literature on inverse problems, see e.g., Carrasco, Florens, and Renault (2007).

It follows from Theorem 2 that the optimal regularization parameter λ_T is necessarily of the form:

$$\lambda_T = cT^{-g(\beta)}, \tag{39}$$

for some positive function c that does not depend on T and a positive function $g(\beta)$ that satisfies $\max\left(\frac{1}{6},\frac{1}{2\beta+1}\right) \leq g(\beta) < 1/2$. As the derivations of Theorem 2 all rely on big $O()$ approximation, the optimal λ_T can go to zero slightly faster than $T^{-\max\left(\frac{1}{6},\frac{1}{2\beta+1}\right)}$ but slower than $T^{-1/2}$.

From Appendix B of Carrasco and Kotchoni (2007), we have:

$$\hat{\theta}_T(\lambda) - \theta_0 \simeq \Delta_T(\lambda, \theta_0),$$

with

$$\begin{aligned}
\Delta_T(\lambda, \theta_0) = &- W_0^{-1}(\theta_0)\left\langle K_{\lambda T}^{-1} G(., \theta_0), \hat{h}_T(., \theta_0)\right\rangle \\
&+ W_0^{-1}(\theta_0)[\langle K_{\lambda T}^{-1} G(., \theta_0), G(., \theta_0)\rangle \\
&- W_0(\theta_0)] W_0^{-1} \Psi_{T,0}(\theta^0),
\end{aligned} \tag{40}$$

where

$$\begin{aligned}
G(\tau, \theta_0) &= P\lim \frac{1}{T} \sum_{t=1}^{T} \frac{\partial h_t(\tau, \theta_0)}{\partial \theta}, \\
C_{T,0}(\theta_0) &= \operatorname{Re}\left\langle K^{-1} G(., \theta_0), \hat{h}_T(., \theta_0)\right\rangle \text{ and} \\
W_0(\theta_0) &= \langle K^{-1} G(., \theta_0), G(., \theta_0)\rangle.
\end{aligned}$$

The AMSE of $\hat{\theta}_T(\lambda)$ coincides with the exact MSE of Δ_T. The trace of the MSE matrix of Δ_T is given by:

$$\Sigma_T(\lambda, \theta_0) = E\left[T\| \Delta_T(\lambda, \theta_0) \|^2\right]. \tag{41}$$

This quantity is always finite and its limit as $T \to \infty$ coincides with the trace of the approximate MSE matrix of $\hat{\theta}_T(\lambda)$. Hence, the optimal λ can be selected by minimizing an estimate of the MSE of $\Delta_T(\lambda, \theta_0)$, as explained in the next section.

5. Selection of the regularization parameter

The CGMM estimator is consistent for any reasonable choice of the regularization parameter λ_T. In most applications, an arbitrary choice of λ_T between 10^{-6} and 10^{-2} would work quite well. However, an arbitrary choice is not advised if the spectrum of the empirical covariance operator is severely discontinuous. In order to approximate the efficient CGMM as accurately as possible, two approaches may be used. The first method is a naive parametric bootstrap that is quite easy to implement while the second approach combines a parametric bootstrap and the stochastic expansion presented earlier. We briefly review these two methods below.

5.1. Naive bootstrap

The naive bootstrap approach assumes without formal proof that the MSE of $\hat{\theta}_T(\lambda)$ is finite. If θ_0 were known, the optimal regularization parameter would be:

$$\lambda_T(\theta_0) = \operatorname*{arg\,min}_{\lambda \in [0,1]} E\left[T\| \hat{\theta}_T(\lambda) - \theta_0 \|^2 \right].$$

where $\hat{\theta}_T(\lambda)$ is computed using a sample of size T generated by θ_0. The multiplication by T inside the expectation operator ensures that this objective function is $O(1)$ as $T \to \infty$. In the current context, it is useful to make the dependence of $\hat{\theta}_T(\lambda)$ on θ_0 explicit by writing:

$$\lambda_T(\theta_0) = \operatorname*{arg\,min}_{\lambda \in [0,1]} E\left[T\| \hat{\theta}_T(\lambda; \theta_0) - \theta_0 \|^2 \right], \tag{42}$$

This objective function is nothing but the trace of the MSE matrix of $\hat{\theta}_T(\lambda; \theta_0)$.

To approximate this MSE, assume that we can draw samples of size T from the true data generating process of $\{y_t\}$, and let $\hat{\theta}_T^j(\lambda; \theta_0)$ denote the CGMM estimator of θ_0 computed using the jth independently simulated sample. A good estimator of the MSE is given by:

$$\frac{T}{M} \sum_{j=1}^{M} \| \hat{\theta}_T^j(\lambda; \theta_0) - \theta_0 \|^2.$$

The Law of Large Numbers ensures that this criterion converges to its expected value as $M \to \infty$. Note that this simulation can be replaced by an appropriate resampling method, in which case $\hat{\theta}_T^j(\lambda; \theta_0)$ becomes the CGMM estimator inferred from the jth bootstrap sample. In the current context, bootstrap samples are obtained by resampling the set of moment conditions $\left\{ h_t(\tau, \theta), \tau \in \mathbb{R}^d \right\}_{t=1}^{T}$ in the time domain.

If θ_0 were known, (42) would suggest an estimator of $\lambda_T(\theta_0)$ of the form:

$$\hat{\lambda}_{TM}(\theta_0) = \operatorname*{arg\,min}_{\lambda \in [0,1]} \frac{T}{M} \sum_{j=1}^{M} \| \hat{\theta}_T^j(\lambda; \theta_0) - \theta_0 \|^2.$$

As θ_0 is unknown, a feasible approach consists of replacing θ_0 with a consistent first step estimator $\hat{\theta}^1$. This leads to estimate the optimal regularization parameter as:

$$\hat{\lambda}_{TM}\left(\hat{\theta}^1\right) = \operatorname*{arg\,min}_{\lambda \in [0,1]} \frac{T}{M} \sum_{j=1}^{M} \| \hat{\theta}_T^j(\lambda; \hat{\theta}^1) - \hat{\theta}^1 \|^2. \tag{43}$$

Hence, the optimal feasible CGMM estimator is $\hat{\theta}_T\left(\hat{\lambda}_{TM}\left(\hat{\theta}^1\right); \theta_0\right)$, i.e., the second step estimator of θ_0 computed with the actual data by using the point estimate of the optimal regularization parameter $\hat{\lambda}_{TM}\left(\hat{\theta}^1\right)$. The MSE must be simulated using common random numbers in order to eliminate the impact of the integration error when comparing the MSE across the different values of λ (see Kotchoni, 2012).

The naive parametric bootstrap is quite easy to implement. Unfortunately, the theoretical properties of $\hat{\lambda}_{TM}\left(\hat{\theta}^1\right)$ cannot be established as we do not know whether the theoretical counterpart of the feasible objective function is finite. If one is able to prove that the MSE of $\hat{\theta}_T(\lambda)$ is finite, then the theoretical properties of $\hat{\lambda}_{TM}\left(\hat{\theta}^1\right)$ given at (43) would be the same as when the alternative approach described below is used.

5.2. Stochastic expansion plus bootstrap

The current approach is aimed at avoiding the drawback of the naive bootstrap by basing the selection of the regularization parameter on the AMSE deduced from the stochastic expansion. Here, the optimal regularization parameter solves:

$$\lambda_T(\theta_0) = \underset{\lambda \in [0,1]}{\arg\min} \Sigma_T(\lambda, \theta_0), \tag{44}$$

where $\Sigma_T(\lambda, \theta_0)$ is the exact MSE of $\Delta_T(\lambda, \theta_0)$, the leading terms of the expansion of $\hat{\theta}_T(\lambda) - \theta_0$ (see Equation 41).

The expressions of $\Delta_T(\lambda, \theta_0)$ depends on both deterministic and random quantities. The deterministic quantities are the true parameter θ_0, the covariance operator K, the probability limit of the gradient of the moment function $G(\tau, \theta_0)$ and the regularization parameter λ. The random quantities are the moment function $\hat{h}_T(\tau, \theta_0)$ and the empirical covariance operator K_T. We therefore have:

$$\Delta_T(\lambda, \theta_0) = \Delta\left(\lambda, K, G(., \theta_0), K_T(\theta_0), \hat{h}_T(., \theta_0)\right),$$

In the IID case, $G(\tau, \theta_0)$ and $K(\theta_0)$ are known in closed form since $G(\tau, \theta_0) = \frac{\partial \varphi(\tau, \theta_0)}{\partial \theta}$ and

$$k(\tau_1, \tau_2) = \varphi(\tau_1 - \tau_2, \theta_0) - \varphi(\tau_1, \theta_0)\overline{\varphi(\tau_2, \theta_0)}.$$

In the Markov and weakly dependent cases, these quantities can be consistently estimated.

Let $\hat{\theta}_T^1$ be a consistent but inefficient estimator of θ. The steps to estimate the AMSE of $\hat{\theta}_T(\lambda)$ and the optimal regularization parameter $\lambda_T(\theta_0)$ are as follows:

Step 1. Obtain an estimate $\tilde{K}\left(\hat{\theta}_T^1\right)$ of $K(\theta_0)$ and an estimate $\tilde{G}\left(., \hat{\theta}_T^1\right)$ of $G(., \theta_0)$ from a very large sample that is simulated using $\hat{\theta}_T^1$. The simulated sample must be large enough to ensure that the approximation errors of $\tilde{K}$ and $\tilde{G}$ are negligible. Note that this step is not necessary in the IID case as closed form expressions are available for $K(\theta)$ and $\tilde{G}(.,\theta)$.

Step 2. For $j = 1, 2, \ldots, M$:

> *Step 2.1.* Draw independent samples $X_T^{(j)}\left(\hat{\theta}_T^1\right)$ of size T from the data generating process using $\hat{\theta}_T^1$.
>
> *Step 2.2.* Use the sample $X_T^{(j)}\left(\hat{\theta}_T^1\right)$ to compute the moment function $\hat{h}_T^{(j)}\left(\tau,\hat{\theta}_T^1\right)$ and the empirical covariance operator $K_T^{(j)}\left(\hat{\theta}_T^1\right)$.
>
> *Step 2.3.* Compute $\Delta_T^{(j)}\left(\lambda,\hat{\theta}_T^1\right) = \Delta\left(\lambda,\tilde{K}\left(\hat{\theta}_T^1\right),\tilde{G}\left(.,\hat{\theta}_T^1\right),K_T^{(j)}\left(\hat{\theta}_T^1\right),\hat{h}^{T(j)}\left(.,\hat{\theta}_T^1\right)\right)$.

Step 3. Estimate the AMSE of $\hat{\theta}_T(\lambda)$ as:

$$\hat{\Sigma}_{TM}\left(\lambda,\hat{\theta}_T^1\right) = \frac{T}{M}\sum_{j=1}^{M} \parallel \Delta_T^{(j)}(\lambda,\hat{\theta}_T^1) \parallel^2,$$

where T and M denote the sample size and the number of Monte Carlo replications. Step 4: Estimate the optimal regularization parameter as:

$$\hat{\lambda}_{TM}\left(\hat{\theta}_T^1\right) = \underset{\lambda\in[0,1]}{\arg\min}\; \hat{\Sigma}_{TM}(\lambda,\hat{\theta}_T^1). \tag{45}$$

In practice, one will have to loop over λ on a finite grid.

The current approach to estimate $\lambda_T(\theta_0)$ is rather fast as it does not require a numerical optimization at each Monte Carlo replication. However, this procedure rests on the presumptions that the expression of the moment function allows for a doable stochastic expansion and that $\tilde{K}$ is a highly accurate approximation of K. The latter presumption is reasonable given that the simulated sample used to estimate K at Step 1 can be made arbitrarily large.

Carrasco and Kotchoni (2017) establish the consistency of $\hat{\lambda}_{TM}\left(\hat{\theta}^1\right)$ for $\lambda_T(\theta_0)$ by neglecting the estimation errors of $\tilde{K}$ and $\tilde{G}$ and by making the following additional assumption:

Assumption 6: The regularization parameter λ that minimizes $\Sigma_T(\lambda, \theta_0)$ is of the form $\lambda_T(\theta_0) = c(\theta_0)T^{-g(\beta)}$, for some continuous positive function $c(\theta_0)$ that does not depend on T and a positive function $g(\beta)$ that satisfies $\max\left(\frac{1}{6},\frac{1}{2\beta+1}\right) \leq g(\beta) < 1/2$.

This assumption is reasonable given the findings of Theorem 1. The consistency result for $\hat{\lambda}_{TM}\left(\hat{\theta}^1\right)$ is stated in the next theorem.

Theorem 3 *Let $\hat{\theta}^1$ be a $\sqrt{T}-$consistent estimator of θ_0. Then under assumptions 1 to 6,*

$$\frac{\hat{\Sigma}_{TM}(\hat{\lambda}_{TM}(\hat{\theta}^1), \hat{\theta}^1)}{\Sigma_T(\lambda_T(\theta_0), \theta_0)} - 1 = o_p(1)$$

as M goes to infinity first and T goes to infinity second.

Finally, Carrasco and Kotchoni (2017) show that $\sqrt{T}\left(\hat{\theta}\left(\hat{\lambda}_{TM}\right) - \theta_0\right)$ and $\sqrt{T}\left(\hat{\theta}(\lambda_T) - \theta_0\right)$ have the same asymptotic distribution as soon as M goes to infinity first and T goes to infinity second.

Theorem 4 *Let $\hat{\lambda}_{TM} \equiv \hat{\lambda}_{TM}(\hat{\theta}^1)$ and $\hat{\theta}_T(\lambda, \theta_0) \equiv \hat{\theta}_T(\lambda)$. Then under assumptions 1 to 6,*

$$\sqrt{T}\left(\hat{\theta}_T\left(\hat{\lambda}_{TM}\right) - \hat{\theta}_T(\lambda_T(\theta_0))\right) = O_p(T^{1/2}M^{-1/2}),$$

as M goes to infinity first and T goes to infinity second.

Basically, theorem 4 implies that replacing λ_T by $\hat{\lambda}_{TM}$ does not affect the consistency, asymptotic normality and efficiency of the final CGMM estimator $\hat{\theta}\left(\hat{\lambda}_{TM}\right)$.

6. Other implementation issues

This section tackles algorithmic issues related to the implementations of the CGMM estimators. We present methods to evaluate the objective function of the CGMM and explain how to compute the covariance matrix of the CGMM estimator.

6.1. Computing the objective function

The objective function of the CGMM involves a d-dimensional integral against the measure π, where $d = \dim(\tau)$. We have:

$$\hat{Q}_{T,\lambda} = \int_{\mathbb{R}^d} K_{T,\lambda}^{-1/2} \hat{h}_T(\tau, \theta) \overline{K_{T,\lambda}^{-1/2} \hat{h}_T(\tau, \theta)} \pi(\tau) d\tau.$$

When $d \geq 2$, the fast and accurate numerical evaluation of these integrals becomes an important issues. Indeed, the objective function must be evaluated a large number of times until the convergence of a numerical optimization algorithm. Two approaches are proposed here: quadrature methods and Monte Carlo integration.

6.1.1. Quadrature method

Let us first assume that $d = 1$ and consider a $f(\tau, \theta), \tau \in \mathbb{R}$ that is continuously differentiable at any order. Then $f(\tau, \theta)$ can be expanded as:

$$f(\tau, \theta) = \sum_{k=0}^{2n-1} a_k(\theta)\tau^k + R(\tau, \theta) \tag{46}$$

where the remainder $R(\tau, \theta)$ is negligible for n large enough. Our objective is to approximate $\int_{\mathbb{R}} f(\tau, \theta)\pi(\tau)d\tau$ with high accuracy. Assume that the weighting function is Gaussian up to a transformation: $\pi(s) = \exp(-s^2)$. This function puts little weight on extreme values of $\hat{h}_T(s, \theta)$, which is a desirable feature in finite samples where the behavior of the variance of $\hat{h}_t$ is not under control.

Our choice of weighting function allows us to approximate the objective function using Gauss-Hermite quadratures, which amounts to finding n points $(\tau_1, \ldots, \tau_n)$ and weights $(\omega_1, \ldots, \omega_n)$ such that:

$$\int P(\tau) \exp\{-\tau^2\}d\tau = \sum_{k=1}^{n} \omega_k P(\tau_k), \tag{47}$$

for any polynomial function $P(.)$ of order smaller or equal to $2n - 1$. The quadrature points and weights are determined by solving the system of equations:

$$\int s^l \exp\{-s^2\}ds = \sum_{k=1}^{n} \omega_k s_k^l \quad \text{for all } l = 0, \ldots, 2n - 1. \tag{48}$$

This is a nonlinear system of $2n$ equations with $2n$ unknowns. Ultimately, the quadrature points and weights depend on the integration domain, the weighting function and the order of accuracy of the quadrature rule (controlled by n).

For the function $f(\tau, \theta)$ that admits an expansion of the form (46):

$$\int f(\tau) \exp\{-\tau^2\}d\tau - \sum_{k=1}^{n} \omega_k f(\tau_k) = \int R(\tau, \theta) \exp(-\tau^2)d\tau. \tag{49}$$

If $f(\tau)$ is analytic on $\mathbb{R}$, the approximation error $\int R(\tau, \theta)\exp(-\tau)^2)d\tau$ can be made arbitrarily small by increasing n. However, this result has a more general scope as it applies also to functions that are analytic per sub-intervals of $\mathbb{R}$ and bounded functions in particular.

Let us now consider the computation of $K_T \hat{h}_T(\tau, \theta)$. We have:

$$K_T \hat{h}_T(\tau, \theta) = \int \hat{k}_T(\tau, s)\hat{h}_T(s, \theta) \exp(-s^2)ds.$$

$$= \sum_{k=1}^{n} \omega_k \hat{k}_T(\tau, s_k)\hat{h}_T(s_k, \theta)$$

Hence, we have the matrix approximation:

$$K_T \hat{h}_T(\theta) \simeq \hat{W}_T \hat{h}_T(\theta), \tag{50}$$

where $\hat{W}_T$ is the matrix with (j, k) elements

$$W_{jk} = \omega_k \hat{k}_T(s_j, s_k), \tag{51}$$

and $\hat{h}_T(\theta) = \left(\hat{h}_T(s_1, \theta), ..., \hat{h}_T(s_n, \theta) \right)'$.

The matrix $\hat{W}_T$ is the best finite dimensional approximation of the operator K_T. The regularized inverse of K_T is therefore approximated as:

$$K_{T,\lambda}^{-1} \approx \left(\hat{W}_T^2 + \lambda_T I \right)^{-1} \hat{W}_T, \tag{52}$$

so that:

$$K_{T,\lambda}^{-1} \hat{h}_T(\theta) \approx \left(\hat{W}_T^2 + \lambda_T I \right)^{-1} \hat{W}_T \hat{h}_T(\theta). \tag{53}$$

Substituting into the objective function of the CGMM yields:

$$\hat{Q}_{T,\lambda} \approx \sum_{k=1}^{n} \omega_k \left[K_{T,\lambda}^{-1} \hat{h}_T(s_k, \theta) \right] \left[\overline{\hat{h}_T(s_k, \theta)} \right], \tag{54}$$

where $K_{T,\lambda}^{-1} \hat{h}_T(s_k, \theta)$ is the kth element of the vector $K_{T,\lambda}^{-1} \hat{h}_T(\theta)$.

In theory, the extension of the Gauss-Hermite quadrature method to the multivariate case is straightforward. When $\tau \in \mathbb{R}^d$, the d − dimensional set of multivariate quadrature points is given by the Cartesian product:

$$D = \left\{ \tau = (\tau_{(1)}, ..., \tau_{(d)}) : \tau_{(i)} \in \{s_1, ..., s_n\} \text{ for all } i = 1 \text{ to } d \right\},$$

where $\{s_1, \dots, s_n\}$ is the set of quadrature points in a one dimension integration and $\tau_{(i)}$ is the ith coordinate of τ. Associated with each $\tau \in D$ is the weight:

$$\bar{\omega} \left(\tau_{(1)}, ..., \tau_{(d)} \right) = \omega \left(\tau_{(1)} \right) ... \omega \left(\tau_{(d)} \right),$$

where $\omega(\tau_{(i)}) = \omega_k$ if and only if $\tau_{(i)} = s_k$, $i = 1, \dots, d$. Finally:

$$\int_{\mathbb{R}^d} P(\tau) \exp\left\{ -\tau^2 \right\} d\tau = \sum_{k_1=1}^{n} ... \sum_{k_d=1}^{n} \omega_{k_1} ... \omega_{k_d} P(s_{k_1}, ..., s_{k_d}), \tag{55}$$

The multivariate Gauss-Hermite quadrature has the undesirable feature that its complexity increases exponentially with the number of quadrature points in a one dimension. The method is therefore subject to a "curse of dimensionality". Indeed, the size of the matrix $\hat{W}_T$ is n^d in the representation $K_T \hat{h}_T(\theta) \simeq \hat{W}_T \hat{h}_T(\theta)$.

As $\hat{W}_T$ must be inverted at each iteration of the optimization algorithm, the CGMM becomes virtually infeasible by quadrature methods when $d \geq 3$. An alternative approach that circumvents this difficulty is suggested below.

6.1.2. Monte Carlo integration

This approach relies on the alternative formula of the CGMM objective function provided in Carrasco Chernov, Florens, and Ghysels (2007):

$$\hat{Q}_{T,\lambda} = v(\theta)'\left[\lambda_T I_T + \hat{C}_T^2\right]^{-1}\overline{v(\theta)}, \tag{56}$$

where $\hat{C}_T \equiv \hat{C}_T\left(\hat{\theta}^1\right)$ is the square matrix of size T with (t, l) element $c_{t, l}/(T-\dim (\theta))$, I_T is the identity matrix of size T, and $v(\theta) = (v_1, \ldots, v_T)'$ with:

$$v_t = \int \overline{h_t(\tau, \hat{\theta}^1)}h_T(\tau, \theta)\pi(\tau)d\tau \text{ and} \tag{57}$$

$$c_{t,l} = \int \overline{h_t(\tau, \hat{\theta}^1)}h_l(\tau, \hat{\theta}^1)\pi(\tau)d\tau. \tag{58}$$

The main drawback of the above expressions lies in that it involves the inverse of the matrix $\hat{C}_T$ which has size T. However, this must be balanced by the fact that the objective function can be evaluated by Monte Carlo integration whatever the dimensionality of τ as explained below.

Let $\pi(\tau)$ denote the multivariate standard normal density and $(\tau^{(1)}, \ldots, \tau^{(M)})$ be M values of τ simulated according to $\pi(\tau)$. The Monte Carlo approximations of v_t and $c_{t, l}$ are:

$$\tilde{v}_t \approx \frac{1}{M}\sum_{k=1}^{M}\overline{h_t(\tau^{(k)}, \hat{\theta}^1)}h_T(\tau^{(k)}, \theta) \text{ and} \tag{59}$$

$$\tilde{c}_{t,l} \approx \frac{1}{M}\sum_{k=1}^{M}\overline{h_t(\tau^{(k)}, \hat{\theta}^1)}h_l(\tau^{(k)}, \hat{\theta}^1). \tag{60}$$

In order to guarantee the convergence of the optimization algorithm, it is crucial to simulate the set $(\tau^{(1)}, \ldots, \tau^{(M)})$ once and for all at the beginning of the procedure and supply this as a fixed array to the code that evaluates the objective function of the CGMM.

An exercise that compares the performance of the Monte Carlo integration to that of the Hermitian quadrature would not be trivial as it requires to define an objective criteria to balances the computing cost against the statistical efficiency. Focusing on statistical efficiency alone, an intuitive reasoning suggests that Hermitian quadrature should be preferred when the dimensionality of τ is small while Monte Carlo integration is better otherwise.

6.2. Computing the variance of the CGMM estimator

The asymptotic covariance matrix of the second step CGMM estimator is given by:

$$
AVar\left(\hat{\theta}\right) = Var\left[\sqrt{T}\left(\hat{\theta} - \theta_0\right)\right]
$$
$$
= \left\langle K^{-1/2}E\left(\hat{G}_t(.,\theta)\right), K^{-1/2}E\left(\hat{G}_t(.,\theta)\right)\right\rangle^{-1}, \tag{61}
$$

where $\hat{G}_t(\tau,\theta) = \frac{\partial \hat{h}_t(\tau,\theta)}{\partial \theta}$ is a column vector of length q with element $\hat{G}_{t,i}(\tau,\theta) = \frac{\partial \hat{h}_t(\tau,\theta)}{\partial \theta_i}$, and for any vectors f and g, $\langle f, g \rangle$ is a matrix with elements $\langle f, g \rangle_{i,j} = \langle f_i, g_j \rangle$, see Carrasco and Florens (2000). This covariance matrix is consistently estimated by:

$$
\widehat{AVar}\left(\hat{\theta}\right) = \left\langle K_{T,\lambda}^{-1/2}\hat{G}_T(\tau,\hat{\theta}), K_{T,\lambda}^{-1/2}\hat{G}_T(\tau,\hat{\theta})\right\rangle^{-1}, \tag{62}
$$

where $\hat{G}_T(\tau,\hat{\theta}) = \frac{1}{T}\sum_{t=1}^{T}\hat{G}_t(\tau,\hat{\theta})$.

This formula is convenient when the scalar products are evaluated by quadrature methods. Indeed, let us define:

$$
\hat{G}_{T,i}(\theta) = \left(\hat{G}_{T,i}(\tau_1,\theta), ..., \hat{G}_{T,i}(\tau_N,\theta)\right)' \text{ and}
$$
$$
K_{\lambda T}^{-1/2}\hat{G}_{T,i}(\theta) = \left(K_{T,\lambda}^{-1/2}\hat{G}_{T,i}(\tau_1,\theta), ..., K_{T,\lambda}^{-1/2}\hat{G}_{T,i}(\tau_N,\theta)\right)',
$$

where $N = n^d$ and $\hat{G}_{T,i}(\tau,\hat{\theta}) = \frac{1}{T}\sum_{t=1}^{T}\hat{G}_{t,i}(\tau,\hat{\theta})$. Then we have:

$$
K_{T,\lambda}^{-1/2}\hat{G}_{T,i}(\theta) = \left(\hat{W}_T^2 + \lambda_T I\right)^{-1/2}\hat{W}_T^{1/2}\hat{G}_{T,i}(\theta),
$$

where $\hat{W}_T$ is defined in (51). The (i, j) element of $\widehat{AVar}\left(\hat{\theta}\right)^{-1}$ can then be computed as:

$$
\left(\widehat{AVar}\left(\hat{\theta}\right)^{-1}\right)_{ij} = \sum_{k=1}^{N}\omega_k\left(K_{T,\lambda}^{-1/2}\hat{G}_{T,i}(\theta)\right)_k\overline{\left(K_{T,\lambda}^{-1/2}\hat{G}_{T,j}(\theta)\right)}_k, \tag{63}
$$

where $\left(K_{T,\lambda}^{-1/2}\hat{G}_{T,i}(\theta)\right)_k$ is the kth coordinate of $K_{T,\lambda}^{-1/2}\hat{G}_{T,i}(\theta)$.

Alternatively, Carrasco Chernov, Florens, and Ghysels (2007) establish the expression:

$$
\widehat{AVar}\left(\hat{\theta}\right) = \left(\frac{1}{T - \dim(\theta)}V(\hat{\theta})'[\lambda_T I_T + \hat{C}_T^2]^{-1}\overline{V(\hat{\theta})}\right)^{-1}, \tag{64}
$$

where $\hat{C}_T$ is the same as in (56), $V(\hat{\theta})$ is the (T, q) matrix with (t, i) element:

$$
V_{t,i} = \int \overline{h_t(\tau,\hat{\theta})}\hat{G}_{T,i}(\tau,\hat{\theta})\pi(\tau)d\tau,
$$

Formula (64) is best suited when Monte Carlo integration is used to evaluate the objective function. In this case, $V_{t,i}$ is estimated as:

$$\tilde{V}_{t,i} \approx \frac{1}{M} \sum_{k=1}^{M} \overline{h_t(\tau^{(k)}, \hat{\theta})} \, \hat{G}_{T,i}(\tau^{(k)}, \hat{\theta}),$$

where $(\tau^{(1)}, \ldots, \tau^{(M)})$ are M values of τ that are drawn from the multivariate normal density $\pi(\tau)$.

Finally, recall that the set $(\tau^{(1)}, \ldots, \tau^{(M)})$ must be simulated once and for all at the beginning of the estimation procedure and supplied as a fixed array to the code that evaluates the objective function of the CGMM as well as to those that compute post-estimation outputs.

7. Application to the USD/GBP exchange rate

For this application we use the USD/GBP daily exchange rates (1 GBP = x USD) from 1980-01-01 to 2017-05-01, which are publicly available on the website of the Federal Reserve Bank of St. Louis (the FRED database). We obtain the exchange rates at monthly frequency by subsampling the daily data.[8] The descriptive statistics, modeling choices and estimation results are presented in separate subsections below.

7.1. Descriptive analysis

Table 6.1 presents standard descriptive statistics for the time series of daily and monthly increments of the USD/GBP exchange rates. The sample averages are negative as a result of an overall appreciation of the USD vis-à-vis the GBP over the period targeted by our study (see Figure 6.1). The sample means are lower than the medians, which indicates that the empirical distributions are negatively skewed.

Unlike the excess kurtosis, the magnitude of the skewness increases with the level of aggregation. At first glance, the first order autocorrelation suggests that the monthly increments of the USD/GBP exchange rates are more predictable than their daily analogues but significance tests are needed in order to confirm

Table 6.1 Moments of the increments of the USD/GBP exchange rates

	Daily frequency	*Monthly frequency*
Mean	−0.0001	−0.0021
Median	0.0000	−0.0018
Minimum	−0.1161	−0.2620
Maximum	0.0707	0.1567
Standard deviation	0.0103	0.0501
Skewness	−0.3899	−0.6765
Excess kurtosis	4.9847	2.7232
First order autocorrelation	0.0459	0.0833

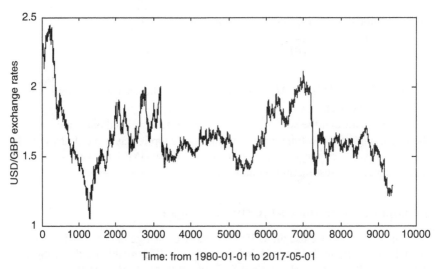

Figure 6.1 Trajectory of the daily USD/GBP exchange rate

this claim. Figure 6.1 suggests that exchange rates obey a mean reverting process.

Figure 6.2 shows the trajectory and distribution of the daily and monthly increments of the USD/GBP exchange rates. It seems that the daily series may be subject to time varying volatility and rare jumps (Figure 6.2a, left). At monthly frequency (Figure 6.2b, left), time varying volatility is still visible but the jumps could probably be ignored at a modest cost. The histograms of the increments of the USD/GBP exchange rates (Figures 6.2a and 6.2b, right) indicate the presence of a modest negative skewness, significant excess kurtosis are rare extreme values. Indeed, a Jarque-Bera test for the null hypothesis that the increments of the USD/GBP exchange rate follow a normal distribution is strongly rejected at both frequencies (see Table 6.2).

Next, we use the daily data to compute the realized variance, skewness, and kurtosis at monthly frequency using the following formulas:

$$\text{Realized Variance: } RV_t = \sum_{j=1}^{m_t}\left(x_{t,j} - x_{t,j-1}\right)^2$$

$$\text{Realized Skewness: } RS_t = \frac{\sqrt{m_t}}{RV_t^{3/2}}\sum_{j=1}^{m_t}\left(x_{t,j} - x_{t,j-1}\right)^3$$

$$\text{Realized Kurtosis: } RK_t = \frac{m_t}{RV_t^2}\sum_{j=1}^{m_t}\left(x_{t,j} - x_{t,j-1}\right)^4$$

where $x_{t,j}$ is the exchange rate that has been observed during day j of month t and m_t is the number of observations during that month.

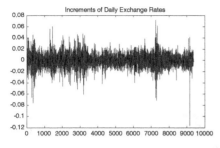
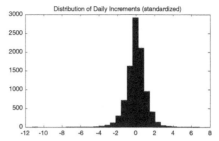

Figure 6.2a Daily frequency

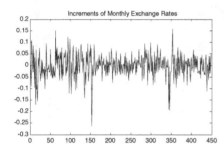
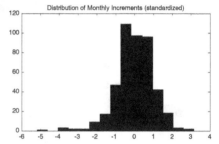

Figure 6.2b Monthly frequency
Figure 6.2 Increments of the USD/GBP exchange rate

Table 6.2 Jarque-Bera normality test for the increments of the USD/GBP exchange rates

	Daily frequency	*Monthly frequency*
Test statistic	9946.7	172.6
Critical value (5%)	5.986	5.842
P-value	< 0.001	< 0.001

As realized measures are computed on intervals of time, the first month ($t = 1$) is January 1980 and the last month ($T = 448$) is April 2017. Figure 6.3 presents the trajectories and distributions of RV_t, RS_t, and RK_t for the period 01/1980—04/2017. It is seen that all three realized moments exhibit substantial time variation. The histogram of the realized variance is reminiscent of a Gamma probability distribution function with a modest shape parameter that is contaminated with a few jumps. The histogram of the realized skewness is rather symmetric on the support [−3,3]. The empirical distribution of the realized kurtosis has a Gamma shape as well, but it is less subject to extreme values than the realized variance.

Many authors have investigated theoretically and empirically whether exchange rates follow a random walk (see Rossi, 2013). Table 6.3 shows the results of Ljung-Box tests for the null hypothesis that the increments of exchange rates has no autocorrelation. We have performed the test at selected lags between

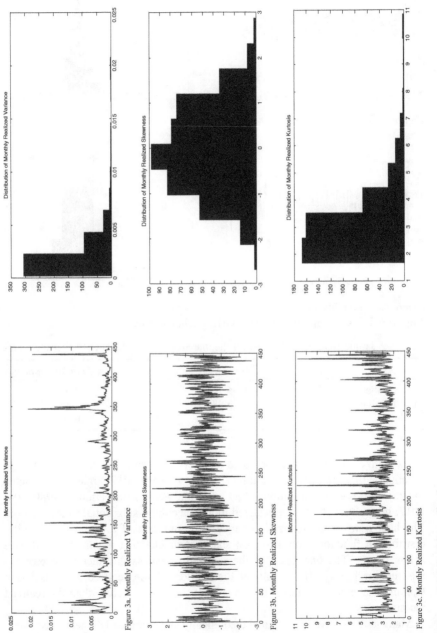

Figure 3a. Monthly Realized Variance

Figure 3b. Monthly Realized Skewness

Figure 3c. Monthly Realized Kurtosis

Figure 6.3 Monthly realized measures

Table 6.3 Ljung-Box tests for the null hypothesis that the increments of exchange rates are uncorrelated over time

Number of lags	Daily frequency			Monthly frequency		
	Test statistic	Critical Value (5%)	P-value	Test statistic	Critical Value (5%)	P-value
2	19.76	5.99	0.0001	3.55	5.99	0.1695
3	23.90	7.81	0.0000	4.00	7.81	0.2605
4	25.82	9.48	0.0000	4.13	9.48	0.3878
5	25.99	11.07	0.0001	4.96	11.07	0.4203
10	36.95	18.30	0.0001	11.81	18.30	0.2976
20	52.74	31.41	0.0001	24.76	31.41	0.2107
30	72.26	43.77	0.0000	35.46	43.77	0.2262
40	87.84	55.75	0.0000	–	–	–
60	122.41	79.08	0.0000	–	–	–
80	144.27	101.87	0.0000	–	–	–
100	172.93	124.34	0.0000	–	–	–
120	202.05	146.56	0.0000	–	–	–

Table 6.4 Variance Ratio tests for the null hypothesis that the increments of exchange rates follow a random walk

Number of lags	Daily frequency			Monthly frequency		
	Test statistic	Critical Value (5%)	P-value	Test statistic	Critical Value (5%)	P-value
2	3.35	1.96	0.0008	4.70	1.96	0.0000
3	3.02	1.96	0.0025	4.65	1.96	0.0000
4	2.29	1.96	0.0216	4.80	1.96	0.0000
5	2.09	1.96	0.0361	4.89	1.96	0.0000
10	1.64	1.96	0.1006	3.42	1.96	0.0006
20	1.34	1.96	0.1801	2.15	1.96	0.0011
30	1.44	1.96	0.1497	2.07	1.96	0.0084
40	1.58	1.96	0.1120	–	–	–
60	1.67	1.96	0.0940	–	–	–
80	1.93	1.96	0.0529	–	–	–
100	2.13	1.96	0.0327	–	–	–
120	2.13	1.96	0.0330	–	–	–

2 and 120 using daily data and between 2 and 30 using monthly data. The null hypothesis is rejected at all lags with daily data and never rejected with monthly data. These results are consistent with the presence of a low order moving average (MA) type noise contaminating the exchange rates.

Table 6.4 shows the results of variance ratio tests for the null hypothesis that the exchange rates obey a random walk.[9] The null hypothesis is rejected at all lags for monthly data. For daily data, the hypothesis is not rejected at lags between 20 and 70 but it is rejected at all other lags. This is quite surprising given that the Ljung-Box tests support that the daily data violate the random walk assumption while the monthly data are uncorrelated. Together, the results of the Ljung-Box and Variance Ratio tests suggest that the monthly increments of exchange rates are uncorrelated and conditionally heteroskedastic.

7.2. *Fitting a variance gamma model to the USD/GBP exchange rate*

We specify a mean reverting dynamics with Gamma variance for the monthly increment of the USD/GBP exchange rates:

$$e_t = x_t - x_{t-1} = \kappa(\mu - x_{t-1}) + \sqrt{y_t}u_t,$$

where x_t is the monthly USD/GBP exchange rate, $y_t \sim Gamma(\delta, \sigma)$ and $u_t \sim N(0, 1)$ is an IID noise. The parameter κ is the strength of mean reversion of the exchange rate process while μ is its unconditional mean. Conditionally on y_t and x_{t-1}, e_t follows a normal distribution with mean $\kappa(\mu - x_{t-1})$ and variance y_t. Therefore:

$$E[\exp(ir_1 e_t)|x_{t-1}, y_t] = \exp\{ir_1\kappa(\mu - x_{t-1}) - r_1^2 y_t/2\}, r_1 \in \mathbb{R}.$$

The variance process (y_t) is allowed to be autocorrelated to the extent that its marginal distribution is a Gamma with the following density:

$$f(y) = \frac{1}{\Gamma(\delta)\sigma^\delta}y^{\delta-1}\exp(-y/\sigma).$$

The dynamic structure of y_t is left unspecified.

The CF of e_t conditional on x_{t-1} is given by:

$$
\begin{aligned}
\varphi(r_1, \theta, x_{t-1}) &= E[\exp(ir_1 e_t)|x_{t-1}] \\
&= \int_0^\infty \frac{1}{\Gamma(\delta)\sigma^\delta}y^{\delta-1}\exp(-y/\sigma)\exp\{ir_1\kappa(\mu - x_{t-1}) - r_1^2 y/2\}dy \\
&= \frac{\exp\{ir_1\kappa(\mu - x_{t-1})\}}{\Gamma(\delta)\sigma^\delta}\int_0^\infty y^{\delta-1}\exp\{-(1/\sigma + r_1^2/2)y\}dy \\
&= (1 + r_1^2\sigma/2)^{-\delta}\exp\{ir_1\kappa(\mu - x_{t-1})\}.
\end{aligned}
$$

where $\theta = (\kappa, \mu, \delta, \sigma)$ collects all the parameters of the model.

The following moment function may be used for the estimation of θ:

$$h_t(\tau, \theta) = \{\exp(ir_1 e_t) - \varphi(r_1, \theta, x_{t-1})\}\exp(ir_2 x_{t-1}), \quad \tau = (r_1, r_2)' \in \mathbb{R}^2.$$

The first step estimator is obtained as:

$$\hat{\theta}^{(1)} = \arg\min_\theta \int h_T(\tau, \theta)\overline{h_T(\tau, \theta)}\,\pi(\tau)d\tau,$$

where $h_T(\tau, \theta) = \frac{1}{T-1}\sum_{t=2}^{T} h_t(\tau, \theta)$ and $\pi(\tau) = \exp\left(-r_1^2 - r_2^2\right)$, $\tau = (r_1, r_2)' \in \mathbb{R}^2$. As explained in Section 6, the objective function above is approximated with high precision by Gauss-Hermite quadrature.

We use this first step estimator to estimate the asymptotic covariance operator K by assuming that $h_t(\tau, \theta)$ is uncorrelated over time. The second step CGMM estimator is given by:

$$\hat{\theta}_T(\lambda) = \arg\min_{\theta} \int h_T(\tau, \theta) \overline{K_{\lambda T}^{-1} h_T(\tau, \theta)} \, \pi(\tau) d\tau,$$

where $K_{\lambda T}^{-1} = \left(K_T^2 + \lambda I\right)^{-1} K_T$, $K_T = K_T\left(\hat{\theta}^{(1)}\right)$ is the estimate of K and $\lambda \in (0, 1)$ is the regularization parameter.[10] It is important to make the parameter space bounded by imposing some restrictions during the numerical optimization. Here we imposed:

$$\theta = (\kappa, \mu, \delta, \sigma) \in (0, 1) \times (0, 2) \times (0, 2) \times (0, 2).$$

These restrictions are useful because the parameters of the Gamma distribution are difficult to identify even when the process is observed.

The ideal value of the regularization parameter is the one that minimizes the MSE of $\hat{\theta}_T(\lambda)$. We estimate this MSE using the two naive bootstrap methods described in Subsection 5.1. In both cases, we use $M = 1,000$ bootstrap samples of size $T - 1 = 447$. In the first approach (parametric bootstrap), $\hat{\theta}^{(1)}$ is used to simulated the bootstrap sample whereas in the second approach (resampling), each bootstrap sample consists of random draws with replacement from $\{h_2(\tau, \theta), \ldots, h_T(\tau, \theta)\}$. We compute the second step CGMM estimator from each sample and for each λ on the following grid:

$$\lambda \in \{10^{-9}; \; 5 \times 10^{-9}; \; 10^{-8}; \; 5 \times 10^{-8}; \; 10^{-7}; \; 5 \times 10^{-7};$$
$$10^{-6}; \; 5 \times 10^{-6}; \; 10^{-5}; \; 5 \times 10^{-5}; \; 10^{-4}\}.$$

Let $\hat{\theta}_T^{(m)}(\lambda_j)$ denote the second step estimator obtained using the mth bootstrap sample and using λ_j as regularization parameter. The MSE of $\hat{\theta}_T^{(m)}(\lambda_j)$ is estimated as:

$$MSE(\lambda_j) = \frac{1}{M} \sum_{m=1}^{M} \| \hat{\theta}_T^{(m)}(\lambda_j) - \hat{\theta}^{(1)} \|^2, j = 1, \ldots, J.$$

The optimal regularization parameter is estimated as the minimizer $\hat{\lambda}^{opt}$ of *MSE* $(\lambda_j), j = 1, \ldots, J$.

Figure 6.4 plots $MSE(\lambda)$ as a function of ln (λ) for the two naive bootstrap approaches. Interestingly, the two MSE curves have similar shapes. The MSE tends to be smaller under the parametric bootstrap than under the naive resampling. Both curves increase slowly and rather erratically between $\lambda = 10^{-9}$ and

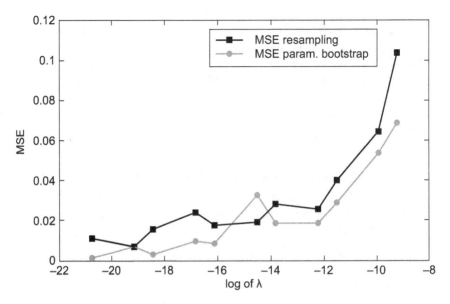

Figure 6.4 MSE of the second step CGMM estimator as a function of ln (λ). Number of
bootstrap replications: M = 1,000.

$\lambda = 5 \times 10^{-6}$, and then increase faster above this range. None of the two curves is
strictly convex, which is possibly due to the fact that $MSE(\lambda)$ is too noisy for the
number of bootstrap replications considered (i.e., M is not large enough), or to
the fact that $MSE(\lambda)$ does not approximate $AMSE(\lambda, \theta_0)$ well enough (i.e., T is
not large enough). Given the shape of the MSE curves, $\hat{\lambda}_{TM} = 10^{-6}$ is a good
choice of regularization parameter for this application. Indeed, the sensitivity
of $MSE(\lambda)$ to λ is low on the range $\lambda \leq 10^{-6}$ while $MSE(\lambda)$ increases fast on
the range $\lambda \geq 10^{-6}$.[11]

The second step CGMM estimator from the *mth* sample is $\hat{\theta}_T^{(m)}\left(\hat{\lambda}_{TM}\right)$. We use
$\hat{\theta}_T^{(m)}\left(\hat{\lambda}_{TM}\right), m = 1, ..., M$ to compute the summary statistics that are presented in
Table 6.5. The rows of the table are respectively the mean, median, standard
deviation, 2.5*th* and 97.5*th* percentiles of the empirical distribution of
$\hat{\theta}_T^{(m)}\left(\hat{\lambda}_{TM}\right)$. The results are rather similar for both estimation methods although
the medians are slightly closer to each other than the means. The standard devi-
ations are often higher under the parametric bootstrap than under the naive
resampling, which is not surprising given that the sampling errors associated
with the latter approach are constrained by the available data. The low value
of $\hat{\kappa}$ suggests that the process in level (x_t) is close to a random walk.

We compute the second step CGMM estimator $\hat{\theta}_T\left(\hat{\lambda}_{TM}\right)$ using the actual data
and use it to filter the latent variance process (y_t). As y_t is assumed to be an IID

Table 6.5 Estimated parameters for the Variance Gamma model. These results are computed using $\hat{\lambda}^{TM} = 10^{-6}$.

		$\hat{\kappa}$	$\hat{\mu}$	$\hat{\delta}$	$\hat{\sigma}$
Naive Resampling	Mean	0.0296	1.5604	0.0763	0.0366
	Median	0.0308	1.5814	0.0754	0.0320
	Standard Dev.	0.0069	0.1265	0.0878	0.0644
	Percentile 2.5%	0.0133	1.2740	0.0404	0.0209
	Percentile 97.5%	0.0440	1.7266	0.1037	0.0586
Parametric Bootstrap	Mean	0.0323	1.5810	0.0786	0.0353
	Median	0.0316	1.5814	0.0732	0.0294
	Standard Dev.	0.0094	0.0649	0.1088	0.0498
	Percentile 2.5%	0.0145	1.4307	0.0224	0.0158
	Percentile 97.5%	0.0567	1.7053	0.1068	0.0899

$Gamma(\delta, \sigma)$ process, the only means to obtain time varying predictions is by conditioning on (e_t, x_{t-1}). The resulting prediction, $E(y_t|e_t, x_{t-1})$ is a backcast rather than a forecast as it updates the constant prior mean $E(y_t) = \delta\sigma$ into the posterior means $E(y_t|e_t, x_{t-1})$, $t = 2, \ldots, T$ upon observing the realizations of e_t and x_{t-1}.

This posterior mean is given by:

$$E(y_t|e_t, x_{t-1}) = \sigma \frac{\int_0^\infty v^{\delta-1/2} \exp\left(\frac{-(e_t - \kappa\theta + \kappa x_{t-1})^2}{2\sigma v} - v\right)}{\int_0^\infty v^{\delta-3/2} \exp\left(\frac{-(e_t - \kappa\theta + \kappa x_{t-1})^2}{2\sigma v} - v\right) dv}.$$

We approximate this expression by Monte Carlo integration as follows:

$$\hat{E}(y_t|e_t, x_{t-1}) \simeq \hat{\sigma} \frac{\frac{1}{1000} \sum_{m=1}^{1000} v_m^{\delta-1/2} \exp\left(\frac{-(e_t - \hat{\kappa}\hat{\theta} + \hat{\kappa} x_{t-1})^2}{2\hat{\sigma} v_m}\right)}{\frac{1}{1000} \sum_{m=1}^{1000} v_m^{\delta-3/2} \exp\left(\frac{-(e_t - \hat{\kappa}\hat{\theta} + \hat{\kappa} x_{t-1})^2}{2\hat{\sigma} v_m}\right)},$$

where v_m, $m = 1, \ldots, 1000$ are independent draws from the exponential distribution $Exp(1)$.

Figure 6.5 shows the time series plot of $\hat{E}(y_t|e_t, x_{t-1})$ superimposed to RV_t. Clearly, the two processes do not capture the same information about the exchange rate variability over time. Indeed, $\hat{E}(y_t|e_t, x_{t-1})$ is much volatile due to the conditioning on e_t. Given that the model only specifies the unconditional distribution for the latent variance process, the conditioning on e_t is the price to pay in order to obtain time varying predictions for y_t. The main lesson learned from this empirical application is that a model that specifies the latent variance of the exchange rate increments as an IID process will in general deliver poor predictions. A model that specifies the autocorrelation structure of the variance

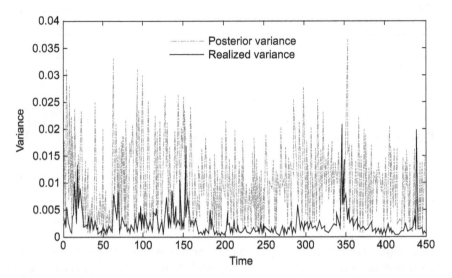

Figure 6.5 Posterior variance vs. realized variance

process (e.g., autoregressive Gamma) does not require the conditioning on e_t and should therefore lead to better variance predictions.

If one chooses to specify the volatility process (y_t) as dependent (e.g., autoregressive Gamma), three empirical strategies are possible from there. The first strategy consists of assuming that the realized volatility (RV_t) is a good proxy for the true volatility (y_t) and fitting the specified model to the proxy. The forecasts obtained for the future values of the proxy, RV_{t+h}, are then taken as good forecasts of y_{t+h}. The second approach consists of assuming that y_t is latent and equal to RV_t plus an IID noise. This assumption and the model specified for y_t jointly provide a state-space representation that can be used for filtering purposes. The third approach consists of ignoring RV_t and specifying a purely *stochastic volatility* model for (x_t, y_t), where x_t denotes the exchange rate process. As y_t is latent, this model will have to be estimated using exchange data only.[12] The estimation of a stochastic volatility model via the characteristic function is beyond the scope of the current paper.

8. Conclusion

This chapter is aimed at popularizing the CGMM to applied researchers. First, we discuss several empirically relevant situations where the CGMM procedure can be successfully used to estimate a finite dimensional parameter. Although most of our examples are based on the characteristic function, we underscore that the CGMM can also be used to deal with conditional moment restrictions. Second, we present the construction of the objective function of the CGMM procedure and review the asymptotic properties of the CGMM estimator. Third, we discuss the selection of the regularization parameter and present numerical algorithms that are useful for the implementation of the CGMM estimator. Finally we present an empirical application where a Variance Gamma model is fitted to the USD/GBP exchange rate.

This model assumes that a monthly increment of exchange rate follows a Gaussian distribution conditional on its variance while the variance itself follows IID Gamma process. The only means to obtain time varying variance predictions within this model is by computing is posterior means, that is, its expectation conditional on the ex-post realizations of the exchange rate increments. We find that the posterior mean of the variance process is a poor predictor of the monthly realized variance inferred from daily data. This suggests that model that specify the variance of the exchange rate increments as IID should be avoided in empirical applications.

By avoiding the discretization of a continuum of moment condition, the CGMM permits its efficient use and therefore permits to achieve the maximum likelihood efficiency when the whole procedure is based on the characteristic function. When the moment restrictions are deduced from a characteristic function, the CGMM has the potential to achieve the maximum likelihood efficiency. In the case where a conditional moment restriction is converted into a continuum of moment condition, the CGMM permits to avoid the arbitrariness of the choice of the instruments and to efficiently exploit the information content of this restriction. However, the efficiency gain of the CGMM over the GMM comes with a slightly higher computation burden.

When the dimensionality of the model is large, quadrature methods are inefficient. In this case, one may resort to the indirect CGMM procedure proposed in Kotchoni (2014), which involves solving a large number of one-dimensional models and optimally combining the solutions into a final estimator.

Notes

1 The density of α-stable distibutions is known in closed form only at isolated points of the parameter space. Nolan (2016) proposes numerical methods to approximate the likelihood of α-stable models.
2 The density of a discretely sampled continuous time process is known for the special case of a square-root diffusion (see Zhou, 1996; Singleton, 2001). Ait-Sahalia and Kimmel (2007) propose closed form approximations to the log-likelihood function of certain continuous-time stochastic volatility models.
3 For all $z > 0$, we have $\Gamma(z) = \int_0^\infty u^{z-1}\exp(-u)du$.
4 Throughout the paper, θ denotes a vector of parameters of interest. The value of θ for a particular dataset of interest is denoted θ_0.
5 Readers who are more interested in the practical aspects than in the theory may jump to the next section.
6 Here, we are using the stochastic version of Landau's notation. If X_T is a random sequence satisfying $X_T = O_p(T^{-1/2})$, then $T^{1/2}X_T$ converges to a non-degenerate random variable. In the deterministic version, we write $X_T = O(T^{-1/2})$ so that $T^{1/2}X_T$ converges to a constant.

7 The expressions of Δ_1, Δ_2, and Δ_3 are not reported here as we want to focus on their convergence rates.
8 The monthly exchange rate data therefore consist of one observation at the beginning of every month, which is distinct from the monthly average of daily exchange rates.
9 For details on the Variance Ratio test used here, see Lo and MacKinlay (1988, 1989).
10 The MATLAB codes used in this chapter are available for sharing.
11 Ultimately, the optimal choice of λ is intended to jointly control two risks, which are the unboundedness of $K_{T,\lambda}^{-1}$ as λ is becomes smaller and smaller, and the inefficiency of the CGMM estimator as λ becomes larger and larger.
12 Knight, Satchell, and Yu (2002) estimate a discrete time stochastic volatility model using the characteristic function. For examples in continuous time, see Jiang and Knight (2002) and Yu (2004).

Bibliography

Andrew, D. W. K. and J. C. Monahan (1992) "An Improved Heteroskedasticity and Auto-correlation Consistent Covariance Matrix Estimator", *Econometrica*, 60, 953–966.

Bierens, H. (1982) "Consistent Model Specification Tests", *Journal of Econometrics*, 20, 105–134.

Buse, A. (1992) "The Bias of Instrumental Variable Estimators", *Econometrica*, 60(1), 173–180.

Carrasco, M., Chernov, M., Florens, J. P. and E. Ghysels (2007) "Efficient Estimation of General Dynamic Models With a Continuum of Moment Conditions", *Journal of Econometrics*, 140, 529–573.

Carrasco, M. and J. P. Florens (2000) "Generalization of GMM to a Continuum of Moment Conditions", *Econometric Theory*, 16, 797–834.

Carrasco, M., Florens, J. P. and E. Renault (2007) "Linear Inverse Problems in Structural Econometrics: Estimation Based on Spectral Decomposition and Regularization", in *The Handbook of Econometrics*, vol. 6, edited by J. J. Heckman and E. E. Leamer.

Carrasco, M. and R. Kotchoni (2017) "Efficient Estimation Using the Characteristic Function", *Econometric Theory*, 33(2), 479–526.

Chacko, G. and L. Viceira (2003) "Spectral GMM Estimation of Continuous-Time Processes", *Journal of Econometrics*, 116, 259–292.

Cochrane, J. H. (2009) *Asset Pricing* (Revised Edition), Princeton University Press.

Cox, J. C., Ingersoll, J. E. and S. A. Ross (1985) "A Theory of the Term Structure of Interest Rates", *Econometrica*, 53, 385–407.

Devroye, L. (1986) *Non-Uniform Random Variate Generation*, Spinger-Verlag.

Dominguez, M. A. and I. N. Lobato (2004) "Consistent Estimation of Models Defined by Conditional Moment Restriction", *Econometrica*, 72(5), 1601–1615.

Donald, S. and W. Newey (2001) "Choosing the Number of Instruments", *Econometrica*, 69, 1161–1191.

Duffie, D. and K. Singleton (1993) "Simulated Moments Estimation of Markov Models of Asset Prices", *Econometrica*, 61, 929–952.

Feuerverger, A. and P. McDunnough (1981a) "On Efficient Inference in Symmetry Stable Laws and Processes", in *Statistics and Related Topics*, edited by M. Csorgo. New York: North Holland, 109–122.

Feuerverger, A. and P. McDunnough (1981b) "On Some Fourier Methods for Inference", *Journal of the Royal Statistical Society*, 76, 379–387.

Feuerverger, A. and P. McDunnough (1981c) "On the Efficiency of Empirical Characteristic Function Procedures", *Journal of the Royal Statistical Society* B, 43, 20–27.

Feuerverger, A. and R. Mureika (1977) "The Empirical Characteristic Function and Its Applications", *The Annals of Statistics*, 5(1), 88–97.

Gourieroux, C. and J. Jasiak (2005) "Autoregressive Gamma Processes", *Journal of Forecasting*, 25, 129–152.

Hansen, L. (1982) "Large Sample Properties of Generalized Method of Moments Estimators", *Econometrica*, 50, 1029–1054.

Jiang, G. and J. Knight (2002) "Estimation of Continuous Time Processes via the Empirical Characteristic Function", *Journal of Business and Economic Statistics*, 20, 198–212.

Knight, J. L., Satchell, S. and J. Yu (2002) "Efficient Estimation of the Stochastic Volatility Model via the Empirical Characteristic Function", *Australian and New Zealand Journal of Statistics*, 44(3), 319–335.

Knight, J. L. and J. Yu (2002) "The Empirical Characteristic Function in Time Series Estimation", *Econometric Theory*, 18, 691–721.

Koenker, R., Machado, J. A. F., Skeels, C. L. and A. H. I. Welsh (1994) "Momentary Lapses: Moment Expansions and the Robustness of Minimum Distance Estimators", *Econometric Theory*, 10, 172–197.

Kotchoni, R. (2012) "Applications of the Characteristic Function Based Continuum GMM in Finance", *Computational Statistics and Data Analysis*, 56(11), 3599–3622.

Kotchoni, R. (2014, August) "The Indirect Continuous-GMM Estimation", *Computational Statistics and Data Analysis*, 76, 464–488.

Lavergne, P. and V. Patilea (2013, November) "Smooth Minimum Distance Estimation and Testing With Conditional Estimating Equations: Uniform in Bandwidth Theory", *Journal of Econometrics*, 177(1), 47–59.

Lo, A. W. and A. C. MacKinlay (1988) "Stock Market Prices Do Not Follow Random Walks: Evidence From a Simple Specification Test", *Review of Financial Studies*, 1, 41–66.

Lo, A. W. and A. C. MacKinlay (1989) "The Size and Power of the Variance Ratio Test", *Journal of Econometrics*, 40, 203–238.

Madan, D. B. and E. Seneta (1990) "The Variance Gamma Model for Share Market Returns", *Journal of Business*, 63(4).

Mandelbrot, B. (1963) "The Variations of Certain Speculative Prices", *Journal of Business*, 36, 394–419.

McCulloch, J. H. (1986) "Simple Consistent Estimators of Stable Distribution Parameters", *Communications in StatisticsSimulation and Computation*, 15, 1109–1136.

McCulloch, J. H. (1998) "Numerical Approximation of the Symmetric Stable Distribution and Density", in *A Practical Guide to Heavy Tails*, edited by R. J. Adler, R. E. Feldman and M. S. Taqqu. Boston: Birkhäuser, 489–500.

Mittnik, S., Rachev, S. T., Doganoglu, T. and D. Chenyao (1999) "Maximum Likelihood Estimation of Stable Paretian Models", *Mathematical and Computer Modelling*, 29, 276–293.

Nagar, A. L. (1959) "The Bias and Moment Matrix of the General k-Class Estimators of the Parameters in Simultaneous Equations", *Econometrica*, 27, 573–595.

Newey, W. K. and D. McFadden (1994) "Large Sample Estimation and Hypotheses Testing", *Handbook of Econometrics*, Vol. IV, edited by R. F. Engle and D. L. McFadden.

Newey, W K. and R. J. Smith (2004) "Higher Order Properties of GMM and Generalized Empirical Likelihood Estimators", *Econometrica*, 72(1), 219–255.

Newey, W. K. and K. West (1987) "A Simple Positive Definite, Heteroskedasticity and Autocorrelation Consistent Covariance Matrix", *Econometrica*, 55, 703–708.

Nolan, J. P. (1997) "Numerical Calculation of Stable Densities and Distribution Functions", *Communication Statistics: Stochastic Models*, 13, 759–774.

Paolella, M. (2007) *Intermediate Probability: A Computational Approach.* Chichester: Wiley.

Paulson, A. S., Holcomb, W. E. and R. A. Leitch (1975) "The Estimation of the Parameters of the Stable Laws", *Biometrika*, 62(1), 163–170.

Phillips, P. C. B. and H. R. Moon (1999) "Linear Regression Limit Theory for Nonstationary Panel Data", *Econometrica*, 67(5), 1057–1112.

Press, S. J. (1972) "Estimation in Univariate and Multivariate Stable Distributions", *Journal of the American Statistical Association*, 67, 842–846.

Rilstone, P., Srivastava, V. K. and A. Ullah (1996) "The Second-Order Bias and Mean-Squared Error of Nonlinear Estimators", *Journal of Econometrics*, 75, 369–395.

Rossi, B. (2013) "Exchange Rate Predictability", *Journal of Economic Literature*, 51(4), 1063–1119. Stable URL: http://www.jstor.org/stable/23644817

Rothenberg, T. J. (1983) "Asymptotic Properties of Some Estimators in Structural Models", in *Studies in Econometrics, Time Series and Multivariate Statistics*, edited by S. Karlin, T. Amemiya and L. A. Goodman. New York: Academic Press.

Rothenberg, T. J. (1984) "Approximating the Distributions of Econometric Estimators and Test Statistics", in *Handbook of Econometrics*, edited by Z. Griliches and M. D. Intriligator. New York: North-Holland.

Singleton, K. J. (2001) "Estimation of Affine Pricing Models Using the Empirical Characteristic Function", *Journal of Econometrics*, 102, 111–141.

Thorton, J. C. and A. S. Paulson (1977) "Asymptotic Distribution of CF-based Estimator for the Stable Laws", *Sankhya*, 39, 341–354.

Weron, R. (1996) "On the Chambers-Mallows-Stuck Method for Simulating Skewed Stable Random Variables", *Statistics & Probability Letters*, 28, 165–171.

Yu, J. (2004) "Empirical Characteristic Function Estimation and Its Applications", *Econometric Reviews*, 23(2), 93–123.

Zolotarev, V. (1986) "One-Dimensional Stable Distributions", in *American Mathematical Society.* Providence, RI: Russian Original, 1983.

Appendix
Prediction of the volatility process

The joint distribution of (e_t, y_t) given x_{t-1} is given by:

$$
\begin{aligned}
f(e_t, y_t | x_{t-1}) &= f(e_t | x_{t-1}, y_t) f(y_t | x_{t-1}) \\
&= f(e_t | x_{t-1}, y_t) f(y_t) \\
&= \frac{y_t^{\delta-3/2}}{\sqrt{2\pi}\Gamma(\delta)\sigma^\delta} \exp\left(\frac{-(e_t - \kappa\theta + \kappa x_{t-1})^2}{2y_t} - \frac{y_t}{\sigma} \right).
\end{aligned}
$$

The distribution of e_t given x_{t-1} is obtained by marginalizing $f(e_t, y_t | x_{t-1})$:

$$
\begin{aligned}
f(e_t | x_{t-1}) &= \int_0^\infty f(e_t, y_t | x_{t-1}) dy_t \\
&= \frac{1}{\sqrt{2\pi}\Gamma(\delta)\sigma^\delta} \int_0^\infty y_t^{\delta-3/2} \exp\left(\frac{-(e_t - \kappa\theta + \kappa x_{t-1})^2}{2y_t} - \frac{y_t}{\sigma} \right) dy_t \\
&= \frac{1}{\sqrt{2\pi\sigma}\Gamma(\delta)} \int_0^\infty v^{\delta-3/2} \exp\left(\frac{-(e_t - \kappa\theta + \kappa x_{t-1})^2}{2\sigma v} - v \right) dv.
\end{aligned}
$$

The distribution of y_t given e_t and x_{t-1} is:

$$
\begin{aligned}
f(y_t | e_t, x_{t-1}) &= \frac{f(e_t, y_t | x_{t-1})}{f(e_t | x_{t-1})} \\
&= \frac{1}{\sigma^{\delta-1/2}} \frac{y_t^{\delta-3/2} \exp\left(\dfrac{-(e_t - \kappa\theta + \kappa x_{t-1})^2}{2y_t} - \dfrac{y_t}{\sigma} \right)}{\int_0^\infty v^{\delta-3/2} \exp\left(\dfrac{-(e_t - \kappa\theta + \kappa x_{t-1})^2}{2\sigma v} - v \right) dv}.
\end{aligned}
$$

Hence, the expectation of y_t given e_t and x_{t-1} is given by:

$$
\begin{aligned}
E(y_t | e_t, x_{t-1}) &= \frac{1}{\sigma^{\delta-1/2}} \frac{\int_0^\infty y_t^{\delta-1/2} \exp\left(\dfrac{-(e_t - \kappa\theta + \kappa x_{t-1})^2}{2y_t} - \dfrac{y_t}{\sigma} \right) dy_t}{\int_0^\infty v^{\delta-3/2} \exp\left(\dfrac{-(e_t - \kappa\theta + \kappa x_{t-1})^2}{2\sigma v} - v \right) dv} \\
&= \frac{\sigma \int_0^\infty v^{\delta-1/2} \exp\left(\dfrac{-(e_t - \kappa\theta + \kappa x_{t-1})^2}{2\sigma v} - v \right) dv}{\int_0^\infty v^{\delta-3/2} \exp\left(\dfrac{-(e_t - \kappa\theta + \kappa x_{t-1})^2}{2\sigma v} - v \right) dv}.
\end{aligned}
$$

7 Seasonal long memory in intra-day volatility and trading volume of Dow Jones stocks

Michelle Voges, Christian Leschinski,
and Philipp Sibbertsen

1. Introduction

The increasing availability of high frequency data poses new challenges for the analysis of seasonality in time series. This is due to the fact that with the increasing frequency of observations, the datasets contain a higher number of meaningful harmonic oscillations. Harmonic oscillations are those whose period lengths are a multiple of the period at which the observations are sampled. For five-minute returns in US stock markets, for example, there are 78 five-minute returns in a trading day and five trading days per week, so that a weekly cycle would have a period of 5×78. Furthermore, a month has about 21 trading days such that the period of a monthly cycle would be 21×78. In contrast to that, for monthly data, we can at most have a yearly cycle with period 12.

This new prevalence of seasonality requires a careful re-assessment of previous assumptions and practices, especially since the explosion in sample sizes that comes with the availability of high frequency data enables us to specify and estimate models that allow for more complex dynamics.

One area where this issue is particularly important is the intra-day dynamics of volatility and trading volume in financial markets. Both volatility and trading volume are usually characterized by long memory and seasonality. For exchange rates, this is documented by Baillie and Bollerslev (1991), Andersen and Bollerslev (1998), Andersen et al. (2001a), and Andersen et al. (2001b), among others. Examples from the literature on stock returns include Andersen and Bollerslev (1997), Andersen et al. (2001c), Giot (2005), and Rossi and Fantazzini (2014). The major part of this literature assumes deterministic seasonality so that it is common practice to remove deterministic seasonality by regressing the data of interest on seasonal dummies or by fitting trigonometric functions. The residuals obtained from this deterministic adjustment are assumed to be free from seasonality.

However, in recent years many parametric seasonal long-memory models for intra-day volatility have been proposed in particular in the GARCH-context but also more general models (details are given in Section 2). These treat the seasonal effects as stochastic. In contrast to deterministic cycles, stochastic seasonal components might change over time. For the example of volatility, this characteristic is illustrated easily because volatility usually depends on market activity which is not deterministic as market participants as well as their behavior change. Therefore, it is sensible to allow for the possibility of stochastic seasonality and to examine the nature of seasonality carefully.

Examples of stochastic seasonal (long-memory) models are seasonal fractionally integrated autoregressive models and generalized autoregressive models which are widely applied in the literature, for example to aggregate output (Gil-Alana (2002)), inflation rates (Arteche (2007), Arteche (2012), Peiris and Asai (2016)), US monthly unemployment, the federal funds interest rate (Gil-Alana (2007)), passenger numbers in public transport (Ferrara and Guegan (2001)), new passenger car registrations and sales of intermediate goods (Ferrara and Guegan (2006)), daily sunspot numbers (Artiach and Arteche (2012)), daily average fine dust pollution (Reisen et al. (2014), Reisen et al. (2018)), or electricity data (Haldrup and Nielsen (2006), Soares and Souza (2006), Diongue et al. (2009), Reisen et al. (2014)). Stochastic seasonality is therefore found in many types of data ranging from physics to economics. In this chapter, we focus on volatility and trading volume data.

As stated above, seasonality is assumed to be deterministic in many cases. If this assumption is incorrect, and the data is actually stochastic, deterministic adjustments could lead to inaccurate conclusions. In the context of seasonally integrated processes, the effect of seasonal demeaning has been studied by Abeysinghe (1991), Abeysinghe (1994), Franses et al. (1995), and da Silva Lopes (1999). They point out that regressing first-differenced time series on seasonal dummies might produce spuriously high R^2 if the seasonality originates from a seasonal unit root and refer to this phenomenon as spurious deterministic seasonality. Hence, it is important to distinguish stochastic and deterministic seasonality. Similar to the seasonal unit root case, ignoring seasonal or periodic long memory results in misspecified models. Correctly specified models, on the other hand, are likely to improve significantly the quality of forecasts that are essential for risk management and option pricing.

In this paper, we analyze intra-day trading volume and realized volatility of the stocks that are components of the Dow Jones Industrial Average (DJIA) index and the index itself and find the typical intra-day features of inverse J-shaped realized volatility and U-shaped trading volume. We obtain non-seasonal long memory estimates at frequency zero in the lower nonstationary region which is in line with the literature. However, our main aim is to investigate the question whether the seasonality in intra-day trading volume and realized volatility is accurately modeled by deterministic dummies or whether it exhibits stochastic seasonality in the shape of seasonal long memory. To do so, we propose a modified version of the *G*-test that was developed by Leschinski and Sibbertsen (2018) in the context of model specification in a GARMA framework. Here, we take a different perspective, since we are interested in testing rather than model specification. We therefore suggest a semi-parametric test for seasonal long memory with a specific periodicity that is robust to the presence of short-memory effects. The test aims to assess the presence of seasonal long memory without specifying a certain model. Hence, we do not assume any parametric structure, for example that the seasonal long memory in the series is generated by a GARMA process. Applying the test to our data, the main finding is that for both trading volume and realized volatility the majority of the components of the DJIA exhibit seasonal long memory, whereas the index does not. Hence, for the index we can only confirm the presence of deterministic seasonality, but for single stock data seasonality appears to be stochastic as well as deterministic. This shows that it is necessary to carefully analyze the nature of seasonality in the series at hand before specifying a parametric model.

The following Section 2 summarizes and discusses the existing models for seasonality considering deterministic as well as stochastic models. The focus is on seasonal long-memory models. Afterwards, in Section 3, we introduce our testing procedure for seasonality at a given frequency. Its finite sample performance is analyzed with help of a Monte Carlo simulation in Section 4. The results of the empirical analysis of Dow Jones stocks are presented in Section 5, and Section 6 concludes.

2. Modeling seasonality

Irrespective of its nature, seasonality can be defined as systematic but not necessarily regular behavior that is characterized by spectral peaks at seasonal frequencies and their harmonics (cf. Hylleberg (1992)). Seasonal data is said to have a period $S \in \mathbb{N}$ that is inferred from the sampling frequency, i.e., it denotes the number of observations per unit of time (e.g., year or day) so that data which are S observations apart are similar (Box et al. (2013)). In a perfectly deterministic setting, this implies $x_t = x_{t-S}$ so that deterministic periodic patterns repeat themselves exactly and can be forecasted perfectly. This characteristic distinguishes seasonal or periodic data from cyclical data because the period length of a cycle (like a business cycle) is unknown in comparison to the known period length S in seasonal data. In the following, we will focus on seasonal data with a known period length S. Regular periodic patterns can be classified as deterministic seasonality that cause bounded peaks in the periodogram. In contrast, stochastic seasonal behavior leads to spectral peaks that can be unbounded in the case of seasonal long memory.

The standard procedure to seasonally adjust data is based on the assumption of deterministic seasonal patterns which are removed by a specific model. One of the simplest and most often applied procedures are seasonal dummies in a linear regression framework

$$X_t = \beta_0 + \sum_{s=1}^{S-1} \beta_s D_{s,t} + Z_t, \tag{1}$$

where $D_{s,t}$ are indicator variables that take the value 1 for $t = s + S(q - 1)$ with $q = 1, \ldots, \lfloor T/S \rfloor$, where $\lfloor \cdot \rfloor$ denotes the greatest integer smaller than the argument and Z_t are the regression residuals. The dummies account for seasonalities like calendar effects, e.g., day of the week, or intra-daily periodicity, e.g., hour of the day, and in a purely deterministic framework the regression residuals Z_t are assumed to be free from seasonality. Further analysis is then based on Z_t. This is considered an appropriate method if the focus is on periodic and regular announcements or other events that repeat themselves periodically, like the US macroeconomic employment report or producer price index announcements (cf. Bollerslev et al. (2000)). If the seasonality is in fact of deterministic nature, Demetrescu and Hassler (2007) show that neglecting the deterministic seasonality distorts the performance of unit root tests, so that the Dickey-Fuller test becomes oversized and loses power at the same time.

The flexible Fourier form – which is a linear combination of sines and cosines – captures slowly varying but still deterministic seasonality (Gallant (1981)). The original data is regressed on sines and cosines that depend on the seasonal frequencies $\omega_s = \frac{2\pi s}{S}$, such that

$$X_t = \sum_{s=1}^{\lfloor S/2 \rfloor} (a_s \cos(\omega_s t) + b_s \sin(\omega_s t)) + Z_t,$$

where a_s and b_s are finite and constant parameters (cf. Andersen and Bollerslev (1997), Andersen and Bollerslev (1998), Martens et al. (2002), Deo et al. (2006)). It is also conceivable to fit a combination of slowly varying seasonality and seasonal dummies. Hereby it is possible to model intra-day cycles with more flexibility and account for announcements through dummies at the same time (Andersen and Bollerslev (1998), Bollerslev et al. (2000)).

When looking at financial data, the volatility of exchange rates or stock returns is often of interest, and seasonality must be taken into account on an intra-day basis. One way of seasonally adjusting this data for intra-day seasonal variance is to calculate the average squared returns, i.e., calculating the variance for each intra-day interval $s = 1, ..., S$ and scale the returns with it. Therefore, let $r_{s,t}$ be the s-th intra-day return on day t and let there be a total of T days. The variance is calculated by

$$\hat{\sigma}_s^2 = \frac{1}{T} \sum_{t=1}^{T} r_{s,t}^2$$

and the deseasonalized returns are given by

$$\tilde{r}_{s,t} = \frac{r_{s,t}}{\hat{\sigma}_s},$$

for $s = 1, ..., S$ and $t = 1, ..., T$. The variance estimation can be altered in order to account for day of the week patterns as well. For example Andersen and Bollerslev (1997), Martens et al. (2002), Andersen et al. (2003), and Bollerslev et al.

(2013) apply this procedure in the context of foreign exchange volatility modeling. This approach can be regarded as deterministic because all returns in an observation interval s are divided by the same variance estimate.

Although deterministic models are still popular, they do not always provide a suitable model fit. Therefore, stochastic time series models are proposed. The typical models for volatility are GARCH models. They offer a lot of flexibility and the potential of specific extensions so that many transformed versions accounting for long-range dependence and seasonality are proposed in the literature. Those GARCH-based methods comprise for example the following models.

The Periodic EGARCH (PE-GARCH) by Bollerslev and Ghysels (1996) is the first example of considering periodic volatility in a GARCH-context allowing for periodically varying parameters. The Periodic Long Memory GARCH (PLM-GARCH) was introduced by Bordignon et al. (2008). In its basic version, it requires the same memory parameter at non-seasonal as well as seasonal frequencies. However, this can be relaxed. The same authors also introduced the log-Gegenbauer-GARCH model which allows for specific memory parameters at each cycle (Bordignon et al. (2007)). This model also nests the PLM-GARCH and its extension, the PLM-EGARCH. Rossi and Fantazzini (2014) extend their model to the Fractionally Integrated Periodic Exponential (FI-PEGARCH) which allows for long-range dependence and nests the PE-GARCH and FIEGARCH (Baillie et al. (1996)) models. They also introduce the Seasonally Fractionally Integrated Periodic Exponential GARCH (SFI-PEGARCH) that allows for long memory within the seasonality. This model nests the PE-GARCH as well as the PLM-GARCH model. Other models are based on the concept of stochastic volatility (cf. Taylor (1986)) and extended to account for long memory (cf. Arteche (2004), Deo et al. (2006)).

These models are only formulated for volatilities. In the following, we focus on two general seasonal long-memory models. The basic model is a seasonal version of the autoregressive integrated moving average (ARIMA) model. Porter-Hudak (1990) introduces the seasonal fractionally differenced (SARFIMA) model, and Ray (1993) generalizes and extends it. A SARFIMA model of order $(p, d_0, q) \times (P, d_S, Q)$ is given by,

$$\phi(L)\Phi(L^S)(1-L)^{d_0}(1-L^S)^{d_S}X_t = \theta(L)\Theta(L^S)\varepsilon_t, \tag{2}$$

where L is the lag-operator defined by $LX_t = X_{t-1}$, $|d_S|, |d_0| < \frac{1}{2}$ are the seasonal and non-seasonal fractional orders of integration and ε_t is defined as white noise with variance σ^2 for the rest of the chapter. As in the deterministic setting, the parameter S determines the period length of the seasonality, and the seasonal frequencies are given by $\omega_s = \frac{2\pi s}{S}$ for $s = 1, \ldots, \lfloor S/2 \rfloor$. The seasonal fractional difference operator is defined in analogy to its non-seasonal counterpart by a binomial expansion such that $(1-L^S)^{d_S} = \sum_{k=0}^{\infty} \binom{d_S}{k}(-L^S)^k$. Furthermore, $\phi(L) = 1 - \phi_1 L - \phi_2 L^2 - \ldots - \phi_p L^p$ and $\theta(L) = 1 - \theta_1 L - \theta_2 L^2 - \ldots - \theta_q L^q$ are polynomials of degree p and q in the lag-operator L. The polynomials $\Phi(L^S)$ of degree P and

$\Theta(L^S)$ of degree Q are defined analogously and they describe the seasonal short-run dynamics. The corresponding spectral density is given by

$$f_X(\lambda) = \frac{\sigma^2}{2\pi} \left| \frac{\theta(e^{-i\lambda})}{\phi(e^{-i\lambda})} \right|^2 \left| \frac{\Theta(e^{-iS\lambda})}{\Phi(e^{-iS\lambda})} \right|^2 |2\sin(\lambda/2)|^{-2d_0} |2\sin(\lambda S/2)|^{-2d_S}, \quad \lambda \in [-\pi, \pi],$$

cf. Bisognin and Lopes (2009). Hence, SARFIMA models offer a certain flexibility like different seasonal and non-seasonal memory parameters, but by construction such series share the same memory parameter d_S at all seasonal frequencies ω_s. This can be relaxed if several periods S_j are allowed.

Gray et al. (1989) introduce the Gegenbauer ARMA (GARMA) process which generates a spectral peak at one specific frequency. Giraitis and Leipus (1995) and Woodward et al. (1998) generalize this model and allow for several spectral peaks of different magnitude by introducing the k-factor GARMA process

$$\phi(L)X_t = \Pi_{j=1}^k \left(1 - 2\cos\omega_j L + L^2\right)^{-d_j} \theta(L)\varepsilon_t, \tag{3}$$

where the filter $\left(1 - 2u_j L + L^2\right)^{-d_j}$ with $u_j = \cos\omega_j$ is the generating function of the Gegenbauer polynomial defined by

$$\left(1 - 2u_j L + L^2\right)^{-d_j} = \sum_{a=0}^{\infty} C_a^{(d_j)}(u_j) L^a$$

$$\text{with } C_a^{(d_j)}(u_j) = \sum_{k=0}^{\lfloor a/2 \rfloor} \frac{(-1)^k (2u_j)^{a-2k} \Gamma(d_j - k + a)}{k!(a-2k)!\Gamma(d_j)},$$

where $\Gamma(\cdot)$ denotes the gamma function and $\omega_j \in [0, \pi], j = 1, \dots, k$ are cyclical frequencies. The corresponding spectral density is given by

$$f_X(\lambda) = \frac{\sigma^2}{2\pi} \left| \frac{\theta(e^{-i\lambda})}{\phi(e^{-i\lambda})} \right|^2 \Pi_{j=1}^k |2(\cos\lambda - \cos\omega_j)|^{-2d_j}, \quad \lambda \in [-\pi, \pi], \omega_j \in [0, \pi].$$

The cyclical frequencies ω_j are not necessarily equal to seasonal frequencies ω_s as in the SARFIMA model and each ω_j has an individual memory parameter d_j so that there may be peaks of different magnitude in the spectrum. For example, this might imply a two-day cycle with memory parameter d_1 and a daily cycle with memory parameter d_2 ($d_1 \neq d_2$). Note that the model is not fractionally integrated in a narrow sense because integration is related to the fractional differencing operator $(1 - L)^d$, but a GARMA model is constructed with a Gegenbauer filter instead. However, the Gegenbauer filter $(1 - 2\cos\omega L + L^2)^d$ is equal to $(1 - L)^{2d}$ for $\omega = 0$ and $(1 + L)^{2d}$ for $\omega = \pi$ so that the squared fractional differencing operator is a special case of the Gegenbauer filter. This is also the reason for frequency-depending stationarity and invertibility requirements. If $0 < \omega_j < \pi$, $|d_j| < \frac{1}{2}$ needs to hold, whereas for $\lambda = \{0, \pi\}, |d_j| < \frac{1}{4}$ is required so that the series is stationary and invertible. Bisaglia et al. (2003) use k-factor GARMA processes to forecast stock market volatility and find that it outperforms the SARFIMA model.

Both the k-factor Gegenbauer model from equation (3) and the rigid SARFIMA model from equation (2) generate spectral poles at one or several frequencies ω that are of the form

$$f(\omega + \lambda) \sim C|\lambda|^{-2d_\omega} \quad \text{as} \quad \lambda \to 0 \tag{4}$$

where $\lambda \in [-\pi, \pi]$, $\omega \in (0, \pi)$, C is a positive and finite constant and $|d_\omega| < \frac{1}{2}$.

Since there is no reason why seasonality should be purely deterministic or purely stochastic, both sources can be considered in one model at the same time. For example Gil-Alana (2005) and Caporale et al. (2012), among others, construct a model with deterministic seasonal means and stochastic seasonal long memory captured with a SARFIMA model, i.e., the regression residuals in equation (1) are replaced with some version of equation (2).

Gil-Alana (2005) suggests a test for seasonality and the seasonal order of integration in a combined setting based on deterministic and SARFIMA components. However, his approach has the drawback that the performance of the test depends on the correct specification of the model. In contrast, our test introduced in Section 3 circumvents this problem with its semiparametric approach.

3. Testing for seasonal long memory

A seasonal long-memory process X_t with period S and seasonal memory parameter d_ω has a pole at frequency $\omega = 2\pi/S$. In its neighborhood, the spectral density is thus given by (4). We are interested in testing the hypothesis that the process does not have seasonal long memory versus the alternative that it has. Thus, our hypotheses are given by

$$H_0 : \; d_\omega = 0 \quad \text{and} \quad H_1 : \; d_\omega > 0.$$

Of course seasonal behavior could also be induced by deterministic patterns. We therefore consider the seasonally demeaned series Z_t from (1). It was shown by Ooms and Hassler (1997) that seasonal de-meaning introduces zeros in the periodogram at all Fourier frequencies that coincide with seasonal frequencies, so that $j'T = jS$, where $j' = 1, \dots, \lfloor S/2 \rfloor$. However, all other periodogram ordinates remain unaffected (cf. also Arteche (2002)).

Define the periodogram of Z_t by

$$I(\lambda) = (2\pi T)^{-1} \left| \sum_{t=1}^{T} Z_t e^{-i\lambda t} \right|^2, \quad \text{with} \quad \lambda \in [-\pi, \pi],$$

which is the square of the discrete Fourier transform. The periodogram is usually computed at the Fourier frequencies $\lambda_j = 2\pi j/T$, for $j = 1, \dots, n$ and $n = \lfloor T/2 \rfloor$.

A semiparametric test for seasonal long memory with period S is obtained by employing a modified version of the G^* test that was suggested by Leschinski and Sibbertsen (2018) in the context of model selection in GARMA models. Their procedure tests for seasonal long memory using the test statistic

$$G_Z^* = \max_j \left\{ \frac{I(\lambda_j)}{\hat{f}_Z(\lambda_j)} \right\} - \log n,$$

where $\hat{f}_Z(\lambda)$ is a consistent estimate of the spectral density under the null hypothesis.

To adapt this to our setting, i.e., a simple test for seasonal long memory with a known period S, we construct a local version of G_Z^*, that only considers m Fourier frequencies to the left and the right of the frequency of interest ω. The bandwidth m has to satisfy the usual condition $(1/m) + (m/T) \to 0$ as $T \to \infty$. Thus, the test statistic is given by

$$G = \max_{j \in [0,m]} \left\{ \frac{I(\omega \pm \lambda_j)}{\hat{f}_Z(\omega \pm \lambda_j)} \right\} - \log(2m). \tag{5}$$

For the implementation of this test statistic we require an estimate $\hat{f}_Z(\lambda)$ of the spectral density that is consistent under the null hypothesis. This is usually done with kernel-smoothed versions of the periodogram. However, this has the disadvantage that a single large periodogram ordinate $I(\lambda_j)$ has a significant impact on the spectral density estimate in the neighborhood of λ_j. To avoid this effect, Leschinski and Sibbertsen (2018) adopt the logspline spectral density estimate originally proposed by Cogburn et al. (1974), who showed that this estimator is asymptotically equivalent to a kernel spectral density estimate. A maximum likelihood version of this estimator based on regression splines was proposed by Kooperberg et al. (1995).

Following their notation, define $A_h = [(h-1)\pi/H_T, h\pi/H_T)$ as a subinterval of $[0, \pi]$, for $1 \leq h < H_T$ and set $A_{H_T} = \pi$, where the number (H_T) of subintervals (A_h) is determined according to $H_T = \lfloor 1 + T^c \rfloor$, with $0 < c < 1/2$. Furthermore, let g denote a cubic spline function defined on $[0, \pi]$. That means it is a polynomial of degree three on each subinterval A_h, it is two times continuously differentiable on $[0, \pi]$, and it can be expressed in terms of Basis-splines as

$$g(\lambda, \beta) = \beta_1 B_1(\lambda) + \cdots + \beta_W B_W(\lambda),$$

where the B_w denote the basis functions, with $1 \leq w \leq 4H_T - 3(H_T - 1) = W$.

The basis for the application of splines in spectral density estimation is the observation that the normalized periodogram ordinates $I(\lambda_j)/f_Z(\lambda_j) = Q_j$ are approximately exponentially distributed with mean one. For the logarithm of $I(\lambda_j)$ follows that $\log I(\lambda_j) = \varphi(\lambda_j) + q_j$, where q_j is the log of the exponential variable Q_j and $\varphi(\lambda_j)$ is the log-spectral density. This linearization allows to apply a spline function $g(\lambda, \beta)$ to estimate $\varphi(\lambda)$. The spectral density estimate $\hat{f}_z(\lambda) = \exp(g(\lambda, \hat{\beta}))$ is then obtained after reversing the log-transformation.

To estimate $\beta = (\beta_1, \ldots, \beta_W)'$, we apply the approach suggested by Leschinski and Sibbertsen (2018) and estimate the spectral density $f_Z(\lambda)$ via the OLS estimator

$$\hat{\beta}_{OLS} = \arg\min_{\beta} \sum_{j=-n}^{n} \left[\log(I(\lambda_j)) + \eta - g(\lambda_j, \beta) \right]^2, \qquad (6)$$

where η denotes the Euler-Mascheroni constant. Since this OLS estimator has a closed form solution, this approach does not require numerical optimization and is much faster to compute than the ML estimator of Kooperberg et al. (1995).

In direct analogy to Leschinski and Sibbertsen (2018), we then have for the test statistic in (5) that for any $\tilde{z} \in \mathbb{R}$

$$\lim_{T \to \infty} P(G > \tilde{z}) = 1 - \exp(-\exp(-\tilde{z}))$$

under the null hypothesis and under the alternative

$$\lim_{T \to \infty} P(G < \tilde{c}) = 0$$

for any $\tilde{c} < \infty$.

Note that our test is constructed such that it detects seasonal long memory while being robust to the potential presence of seasonal short-run dynamics. Thus, non-rejection of the null hypothesis does not imply the absence of stochastic seasonality.

The test is applied at the first seasonal frequency $\omega = 2\pi/S$. In theory one could also consider the harmonics $\omega_s = 2\pi s/S$, for $s = 2, \ldots, \lfloor S/2 \rfloor$. However, the periodogram ordinates are proportional to the fraction of the process variance that can be explained by a sinusoidal cycle of the respective frequency. Since by the nature of the Fourier series, cycles with frequencies that are a multiple of this frequency improve the approximation to a non-sinusoidal seasonality, these will not have an effect if the seasonality is indeed of a sinusoidal form. Without additional knowledge about the seasonal properties of the process at hand, it is therefore not clear whether the inclusion of harmonic frequencies will improve or diminish the performance of the test.

4. Monte Carlo

In order to analyze the finite sample performance of our G-test from equation (5) we conduct a Monte Carlo experiment based on 1,000 replications. We use a 1-factor GARMA model as data generating process

$$X_t = \left(1 - 2\cos\left(\frac{2\pi}{13}\right) + L^2\right)^{-d} u_t, \qquad (7)$$

where $u_t = \phi u_{t-1} + \varepsilon_t$ is an $AR(1)$-process. The sample size is set to $T = \{250, 500, 1,000, 2,500\}$. We consider $\phi = 0$ for the white noise case with zero mean and unit variance and $\phi = 0.4$ in order to examine the influence of short-run dynamics. Based on our empirical application in Section 5, we choose the seasonal frequency $\omega = \frac{2\pi}{13}$, which implies a period length of $S = 13$, and we consider memory parameters in the stationary region, $d = \{0, 0.1, 0.2, 0.3, 0.4\}$. For $d = 0$ the process is non-seasonal so that the corresponding simulation results display empirical sizes. Our G-test requires two bandwidth choices. First, for the periodogram $m = m(\delta) = \lfloor 1 + T^\delta \rfloor$ is the number of Fourier frequencies that are considered, and δ is set to either 0.5, 0.6, or 0.7. Second, a bandwidth that determines the number of knots in the spline-based estimation of the spectral density $H_T = H_T(c) = \lfloor 1 + T^c \rfloor$ is required, and c is set to either 0.1, 0.15, 0.2, or 0.25.

All results are displayed in Table 7.1. Size and power results both improve with increasing sample size T for all parameter constellations. The size results are already satisfying in small samples and very robust to bandwidth choices and short-run dynamics. In small samples and with short-run dynamics we observe slightly liberal results. However, this improves if a smaller bandwidth $H_T(c)$ is selected.

The power results depend on the memory parameter d and improve with higher orders of integration. This is intuitive because low seasonal persistence, e.g., $d = 0.1$, is more difficult to detect than higher persistence. However, in large samples the power is already good for $d = 0.2$, and for $d = 0.4$ results are even satisfying in small samples. As in the size-case, the bandwidth parameter $H_T(c)$ influences the power such that lower values of $H_T(c)$ improve results significantly. For example, for $d = 0.2$ and $T = 2,500$ power is more than twice as high for the lowest value of $H_T(c)$ as for its highest value. For larger samples the choice of $H_T(c)$ becomes less important. We find a similar influence of $m(\delta)$. Smaller values lead to much higher power results for low seasonal persistence (about 20 percentage points), but for higher seasonal persistence the influence of $m(\delta)$ shrinks. Short-run dynamics of medium size cause no systematic distortions in the results. On the contrary, there are only small and random deviations compared to the white noise case. The semiparametric approach of the test therefore successfully mitigates the impact of short-run dynamics.

The bandwidth parameters m and H_T influence the performance of the test in such a way that higher values of m and H_T lead to biased parameter estimates which results in slightly lower power. We therefore recommend choosing low bandwidth parameters. Overall, our G-test statistic has very good finite sample properties independent of short-run dynamics.

5. Empirical analysis of Dow Jones stocks

We analyze the intra-day log-realized volatility and the log-trading volume of the 30 stocks that are components of the Dow Jones Industrial Average (DJIA) and the index itself. To do so, we use five-minute data and aggregate them to half-hourly observations for the time from January 2011 until December 2015, which makes about 16,300 observations for each stock and series. All stocks

Table 7.1 Rejection frequency of the *G*-test statistic for a nominal significance level of α = 0.05 and the DGP given in (7).

ϕ	d	T/δ	0.1			0.15			0.2			0.25		
		c	0.5	0.6	0.7	0.5	0.6	0.7	0.5	0.6	0.7	0.5	0.6	0.7
0	0	250	0.06	0.06	0.05	0.07	0.06	0.06	0.09	0.07	0.07	0.08	0.07	0.06
		500	0.08	0.07	0.06	0.07	0.07	0.05	0.06	0.06	0.07	0.07	0.08	0.06
		1000	0.05	0.04	0.05	0.06	0.06	0.06	0.05	0.06	0.04	0.08	0.07	0.05
		2500	0.05	0.05	0.05	0.05	0.06	0.06	0.04	0.06	0.04	0.06	0.06	0.05
	0.1	250	0.10	0.11	0.08	0.12	0.09	0.09	0.13	0.12	0.09	0.14	0.10	0.08
		500	0.17	0.13	0.09	0.14	0.11	0.09	0.16	0.11	0.10	0.13	0.11	0.09
		1000	0.24	0.16	0.12	0.22	0.16	0.11	0.22	0.16	0.14	0.14	0.10	0.08
		2500	0.35	0.24	0.18	0.35	0.26	0.16	0.31	0.21	0.15	0.15	0.10	0.09
	0.2	250	0.33	0.24	0.23	0.32	0.29	0.23	0.29	0.27	0.23	0.33	0.25	0.22
		500	0.48	0.41	0.30	0.51	0.40	0.35	0.49	0.42	0.36	0.41	0.36	0.27
		1000	0.68	0.56	0.54	0.71	0.60	0.50	0.66	0.59	0.50	0.48	0.38	0.34
		2500	0.92	0.85	0.78	0.91	0.82	0.73	0.84	0.76	0.64	0.43	0.36	0.28
	0.3	250	0.62	0.56	0.47	0.60	0.55	0.50	0.58	0.53	0.51	0.59	0.55	0.51
		500	0.83	0.78	0.71	0.84	0.79	0.73	0.81	0.78	0.70	0.70	0.69	0.63
		1000	0.97	0.93	0.91	0.96	0.94	0.92	0.96	0.94	0.88	0.82	0.76	0.71
		2500	1.00	1.00	0.99	1.00	1.00	0.99	1.00	0.99	0.98	0.83	0.76	0.72
	0.4	250	0.84	0.80	0.76	0.83	0.81	0.75	0.83	0.82	0.76	0.85	0.77	0.76
		500	0.97	0.96	0.94	0.97	0.96	0.94	0.97	0.95	0.93	0.95	0.91	0.89
		1000	1.00	1.00	1.00	1.00	1.00	1.00	1.00	1.00	0.99	0.96	0.95	0.94
		2500	1.00	1.00	1.00	1.00	1.00	1.00	1.00	1.00	1.00	0.98	0.96	0.95
0.4	0	250	0.06	0.07	0.05	0.06	0.07	0.06	0.09	0.07	0.06	0.09	0.08	0.08
		500	0.07	0.07	0.04	0.06	0.06	0.05	0.07	0.06	0.07	0.06	0.08	0.06
		1000	0.05	0.06	0.05	0.04	0.05	0.04	0.06	0.05	0.04	0.06	0.07	0.06
		2500	0.05	0.05	0.05	0.05	0.07	0.07	0.06	0.06	0.06	0.05	0.07	0.06
	0.1	250	0.12	0.09	0.08	0.10	0.11	0.08	0.11	0.12	0.09	0.12	0.08	0.09
		500	0.14	0.11	0.08	0.15	0.12	0.10	0.16	0.12	0.09	0.15	0.11	0.09
		1000	0.20	0.18	0.11	0.22	0.13	0.12	0.21	0.17	0.11	0.14	0.09	0.09
		2500	0.33	0.24	0.17	0.33	0.24	0.15	0.26	0.21	0.15	0.14	0.11	0.08
	0.2	250	0.27	0.26	0.22	0.33	0.26	0.19	0.31	0.25	0.22	0.29	0.25	0.24
		500	0.46	0.38	0.33	0.51	0.42	0.34	0.47	0.39	0.33	0.38	0.32	0.28
		1000	0.66	0.58	0.48	0.67	0.60	0.50	0.65	0.61	0.50	0.43	0.37	0.29
		2500	0.89	0.84	0.75	0.92	0.85	0.74	0.83	0.71	0.66	0.45	0.33	0.29
	0.3	250	0.58	0.53	0.47	0.59	0.53	0.48	0.59	0.53	0.51	0.59	0.52	0.51
		500	0.82	0.78	0.73	0.83	0.78	0.74	0.81	0.75	0.70	0.71	0.67	0.64
		1000	0.96	0.91	0.90	0.97	0.94	0.91	0.95	0.93	0.89	0.81	0.76	0.70
		500	1.00	1.00	1.00	1.00	1.00	0.99	1.00	0.99	0.98	0.83	0.78	0.68
	0.4	240	0.80	0.77	0.75	0.83	0.80	0.75	0.82	0.82	0.77	0.81	0.80	0.78
		500	0.97	0.96	0.94	0.97	0.96	0.93	0.97	0.95	0.94	0.93	0.91	0.87
		1000	1.00	1.00	1.00	1.00	1.00	0.99	1.00	1.00	0.99	0.97	0.96	0.93
		2500	1.00	1.00	1.00	1.00	1.00	1.00	1.00	1.00	1.00	0.98	0.98	0.95

considered are traded on the New York Stock Exchange and on the Nasdaq Stock Market during the trading hours from 09:30 to 16:00 local time. Consequently, we obtain 13 half-hourly observations per day so that our period is $S = 13$ for a daily cycle and the corresponding seasonal frequency of interest is $\omega = \frac{2\pi}{13} = 0.48$. The harmonic seasonal frequencies are disregarded for the reasons given in Section 3.

Note that the index can be interpreted as the average of individual stock data because it is calculated as the sum of single stock prices scaled with the so-called Dow Divisor. The Dow Divisor is adjusted in case of structural changes like stock splits in order to ensure continuity in the index. Originally, the Dow Divisor was 30 so that the index was a simple average but by now the Dow Divisor is smaller than one and the index is a weighted average of its components.

Let $r_{i,t}$ be the i-th return in the t-th 30-minute interval so that realized volatilities (RV) are calculated by $\hat{\sigma}_t^2 = \sum_{i=1}^{6} r_{i,t}^2$ for each half-hour interval $t = 1, \ldots, T$. For trading volume, we proceed analogously by summing up six five-minute observations in order to obtain half-hourly trading volumes. Finally, we take the logarithm of both series. As customary, we add 0.001 to the volatility series before applying the logarithm to avoid infinite values or extremely large negative values in case of constant price and therefore zero volatility (cf. for example Lu and Perron (2010) and Xu and Perron (2014)). The log-transformed series are approximately Gaussian in contrast to the original series that are usually right-skewed (cf. Andersen et al. (2001b), Andersen et al. (2001c), Andersen et al. (2003), among others) and they exhibit less outliers which is desirable from a data analytic point of view.

As expected, the intra-day average return for different times of the day is almost constant for all stocks and slightly positive, see Figure 7.1, and the variance is higher for overnight returns. We also find the typical time of the day phenomena in realized volatility and trading volume. Market opening and closing times are characterized by higher market activity that leads to higher trading volume than at lunch time. This causes a pronounced U-shape in intra-day trading volume. Considering realized volatility, we find higher market activity only in the morning which causes an inverse J-shape instead of a U-shape. Hence, on average volatility does not increase much at the end of trading days. As discussed in the introduction, these observations are well known in the literature, cf. for example Wood et al. (1985) for early evidence of these phenomena, and Bordignon et al. (2008) and Bollerslev et al. (2018) for more recent analyses.

The observation of U- and J-shaped patterns implies intra-day seasonality, but we do not know whether it is deterministic or stochastic. In order to find the source of seasonality, we consider the autocorrelation function (ACF) (Figure 7.2) and the periodogram (Figures 7.3 and 7.4) of individual, non-averaged data as the first step. The left side of all three figures displays the DJIA index, and the right side displays Chevron, a single component of

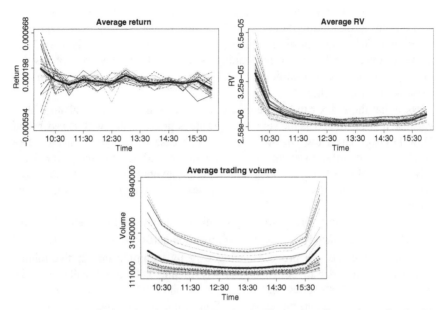

Figure 7.1 Intra-day averaged return, realized volatility and trading volume for the 30 DJIA stocks. The bold lines indicate the overall average.

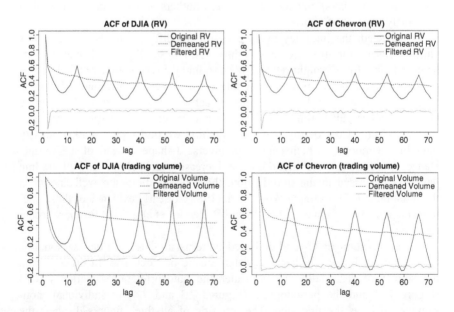

Figure 7.2 Autocorrelation functions for *logarithms of realized volatility* and *logarithms of trading volume* of the index (left panel) and Chevron (right panel).

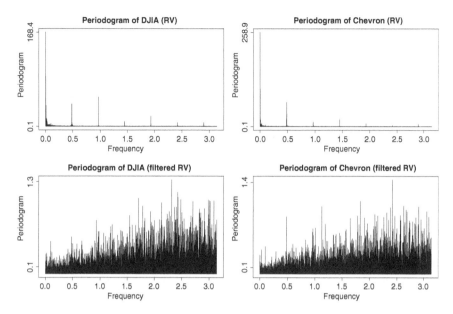

Figure 7.3 Periodogram of original data, and after dummy regression and filtering at zero frequency for *logarithms of realized volatility* of the index (left panel) and of Chevron (right panel).

the index. The solid lines in the four graphs of Figure 7.2 are the ACFs of the data and illustrate clearly seasonal behavior. The same characteristic is also present in the periodograms in the upper panels of Figures 7.3 and 7.4 where we find peaks at seasonal frequencies (and the zero frequency). This observation holds equally for realized volatility and trading volume of both the index and Chevron. In order to assess the influence of seasonal means, we remove them with help of the dummy regression from (1). Again, the ACFs of all four seasonally demeaned series considered in Figure 7.2 show a similar behavior, that is the dashed lines decay slowly at a hyperbolic rate. The corresponding periodograms are omitted for reasons of space, but they all have a clear singularity at zero frequency. Hence, both volatility and trading volume series exhibit long memory. Therefore, we estimate the order of integration at zero frequency with a local Whittle estimator (cf. Kuensch (1987), Robinson (1995)). Here, we apply the exact local Whittle estimator (Shimotsu and Phillips (2005)) that is consistent in stationary and nonstationary data in contrast to the basic local Whittle estimator. The bandwidth is set to $\lfloor T^{0.65} \rfloor$ which implies the inclusion of periodogram ordinates up to $\lambda_m = 0.21$ ($m = 546$). This keeps enough distance to the first seasonal frequency $\omega = 2\pi/13 = 0.48$ so that proper memory estimation is ensured. We obtain memory estimates $d_{RV,DJIA} = 0.52$, $d_{RV,CVX} = 0.52$, $d_{vol,DJIA} = 0.37$, and $d_{vol,CVX} = 0.52$. These results are in line with Wenger et al. (2018), who find memory parameters in volatility data in the lower nonstationary region.

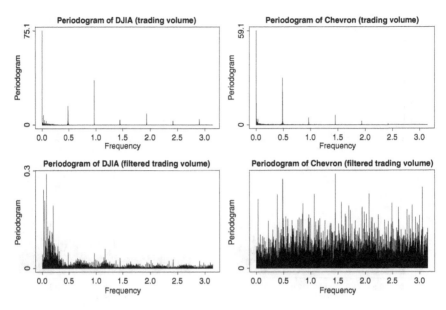

Figure 7.4 Periodogram of original data, and after dummy regression and filtering at zero
frequency for *logarithms of trading volume* of the index (left panel) and of
Chevron (right panel).

Lobato and Velasco (2000) also find a tendency of nonstationary long memory in
volatility and trading volume.

We filter the seasonally-demeaned series with their respective memory estimates in order to get short-memory time series. The dotted lines in Figure 7.2
display the resulting ACFs. Overall, for the index there are only very few significant autocorrelations left. This is similar for Chevron but taking a closer look, we
find a number of borderline significant autocorrelations especially at seasonal
lags. The lower panels of Figures 7.3 and 7.4 show the periodograms of
demeaned and differenced data. These are already close to being constant like
the periodogram of a white noise process. However, small peaks at the seasonal
frequencies, e.g., 0.48, can still be identified. This is more pronounced for
Chevron than for the index – especially for the realized volatilities in Figure 7.3.

In order to examine the question whether the cyclical behavior in the data is
already sufficiently accounted for by removing deterministic seasonality with
seasonal dummies, we apply our test for no seasonal long memory to the
demeaned and fractionally differenced stock data and the index.[1]

Tables 7.3 (realized volatility) and 7.4 (trading volume) show *p*-values of our
G-test from equation (5) applied at frequency $\omega = 2\pi/13$ for all Dow Jones stocks
and the index for the same bandwidth choices as in our Monte Carlo experiment.
We omit the results for $c = 0.25$, since the Monte Carlo results for this bandwidth
are weaker than for smaller bandwidths. Bold numbers indicate a *p*-value lower

Table 7.2 List of RICs and corresponding companies.

.DJI	Dow Jones Index	KO	Coca-Cola
AAPL.O	Apple	MCD	McDonald's
AXP	American Express	MMM	3M
BA	Boeing	MRK	Merck
CAT	Caterpillar	MSFT.O	Microsoft
CSCO.O	Cisco	NKE	Nike
CVX	Chevron	PFE	Pfizer
DD	E.I. du Pont de Nemours & Company	PG	Procter & Gamble
DIS	Disney	TRV	Travelers Companies Inc
GE	General Electric	UNH	UnitedHealth
GS	Goldman Sachs	UTX	United Technologies
HD	Home Depot	V	Visa
IBM	IBM	VZ	Verizon
INTC.O	Intel	WMT	Wal-Mart
JNJ	Johnson & Johnson	XOM	Exxon Mobil
JPM	JPMorgan Chase		

than 0.05 and thus rejection of the null hypothesis of no seasonal long memory at that frequency at the 5% level.

We find no significant seasonal long memory in the volatility of the index at frequency $\omega = 2\pi/13$ at the 5% level, and the results for the index's trading volume data are only significant for large bandwidths. Our Monte Carlo study in Section 4 shows that large bandwidths lead to liberal size results compared to the results of smaller bandwidth parameters. Those slightly liberal sizes suggest the possibility of a false rejection. Therefore, we focus on the results for the smaller bandwidth constellations.

In contrast to the index, we find significant seasonal long memory in a large proportion of our single stock data as we reject the null hypothesis in almost two-thirds of both the volatility and the trading volume series in the small bandwidth case. There are a few stocks where we have significant results in both series but most often we find it in only one of them for the same stock. This suggests that the seasonal components in trading volume and volatility might be driven by different factors. At any rate, the results clearly prove that there is stochastic seasonality in the shape of seasonal long memory in addition to deterministic cycles in individual stock data.

In order to assess the dimension of seasonal long memory, we estimate the seasonal memory parameters at frequency $\omega = 2\pi/13$ with the generalized local Whittle estimator of Arteche and Robinson (2000) for those series where our G-test rejects the null hypothesis of no seasonal long memory for any choice of c. The estimator considers the possibility of asymmetric poles in the spectral density. Therefore, the spectral density from (4) is reformulated to

$$f(\omega + \lambda) \sim C_1 \lambda^{-2d_1}, \qquad f(\omega - \lambda) \sim C_2 \lambda^{-2d_2}, \qquad \text{as } \lambda \to 0^+, \tag{8}$$

Table 7.3 P-values of the G-test at frequency $\omega = 2\pi/13$ for *logarithms of realized volatility*. The data is seasonally demeaned and long memory at frequency zero has been removed.

c	0.1			0.15			0.2		
$RIC\backslash\delta$	0.5	0.6	0.7	0.5	0.6	0.7	0.5	0.6	0.7
.DJI	0.053	0.138	0.354	0.080	0.200	0.462	0.127	0.300	0.605
AAPL.O	**0.031**	0.063	0.066	**0.031**	0.071	0.117	**0.020**	0.055	0.153
AXP	**0.009**	**0.027**	0.074	**0.013**	**0.037**	0.098	**0.025**	0.063	0.156
BA	0.084	0.135	0.421	0.145	0.159	0.456	0.324	0.263	0.591
CAT	**0.002**	**0.009**	**0.027**	**0.005**	**0.018**	**0.050**	**0.008**	**0.019**	**0.048**
CSCO.O	0.310	0.324	0.579	0.339	0.325	0.589	0.400	0.335	0.633
CVX	**0.000**	**0.000**	**0.001**	**0.000**	**0.001**	**0.003**	**0.001**	**0.004**	**0.009**
DD	**0.020**	0.062	0.222	**0.037**	0.070	0.239	0.068	0.087	0.250
DIS	**0.044**	0.143	0.113	0.081	0.224	0.233	0.139	0.314	0.206
GE	**0.047**	0.163	0.417	0.118	0.328	0.676	0.196	0.420	0.755
GS	0.059	0.178	0.395	0.085	0.227	0.481	0.113	0.262	0.493
HD	0.111	0.296	0.160	0.201	0.467	0.339	0.316	0.626	0.362
IBM	**0.008**	**0.034**	0.128	**0.014**	**0.046**	0.139	**0.026**	0.063	0.149
INTC.O	0.490	0.750	0.187	0.623	0.801	0.128	0.607	0.798	0.139
JNJ	**0.036**	0.123	0.094	0.078	0.220	0.147	0.195	0.424	0.150
JPM	0.077	0.206	0.064	0.116	0.287	0.105	0.109	0.259	0.113
KO	**0.000**	**0.001**	**0.005**	**0.001**	**0.003**	**0.008**	**0.001**	**0.003**	**0.009**
MCD	**0.025**	0.092	0.334	0.058	0.171	0.461	0.189	0.410	0.411
MMM	**0.045**	0.077	0.217	0.063	0.084	0.232	0.163	0.155	0.375
MRK	0.119	**0.025**	0.086	0.214	0.062	0.160	0.388	0.115	0.244
MSFT.O	0.104	0.263	0.606	0.116	0.284	0.619	0.162	0.372	0.708
NKE	0.085	0.246	0.548	0.107	0.280	0.592	0.189	0.416	0.756
PFE	**0.006**	**0.025**	0.132	**0.019**	0.063	0.214	**0.050**	0.119	0.261
PG	**0.035**	0.101	0.321	0.061	0.163	0.421	0.108	0.256	0.529
TRV	**0.003**	**0.012**	**0.049**	**0.008**	**0.024**	0.077	**0.017**	**0.043**	0.103
UNH	0.172	0.210	0.517	0.271	0.254	0.593	0.469	0.382	0.619
UTX	**0.021**	0.089	0.245	**0.047**	0.142	0.348	0.063	0.142	0.324
V	0.583	0.653	0.917	0.710	0.705	0.949	0.791	0.734	0.967
VZ	**0.002**	**0.004**	**0.004**	**0.003**	**0.009**	**0.012**	**0.006**	**0.016**	**0.012**
WMT	0.060	0.236	0.224	0.121	0.347	0.228	0.169	0.366	0.234
XOM	**0.000**	**0.001**	**0.005**	**0.001**	**0.003**	**0.010**	**0.002**	**0.004**	**0.010**

allowing for different memory parameters at both sides of the pole. Here, we restrict our estimation to symmetric seasonal long memory and estimate only one seasonal long memory parameter considering two objective functions

$$R_i(d) = \log \tilde{C}_i(d) - \frac{2d}{m-l}\sum_{j=l+1}^{m} \log \lambda_j, \quad i = \{1,2\}$$

$$\tilde{C}_1(d) = \frac{1}{m-l}\sum_{j=l+1}^{m} \lambda_j^{2d} I(\omega + \lambda_j), \quad \tilde{C}_2(d) = \frac{1}{m-l}\sum_{j=l+1}^{m} \lambda_j^{2d} I(\omega - \lambda_j),$$

Table 7.4 P-values of the *G*-test at frequency $\omega = 2\pi/13$ for *logarithms of trading volume*. The data is seasonally demeaned and long memory at frequency zero has been removed.

c	0.1			0.15			0.2		
$RIC\backslash\delta$	0.5	0.6	0.7	0.5	0.6	0.7	0.5	0.6	0.7
.DJI	0.245	0.571	**0.000**	0.092	0.240	**0.000**	**0.016**	**0.040**	**0.000**
AAPL.O	**0.000**	**0.002**	**0.007**	**0.006**	**0.023**	0.068	**0.026**	0.061	0.149
AXP	0.136	0.289	0.402	0.104	0.238	0.417	0.090	0.223	0.513
BA	0.212	0.192	0.190	0.136	0.176	0.161	0.085	0.139	0.163
CAT	0.067	0.180	0.302	0.053	0.140	0.279	**0.036**	0.090	0.230
CSCO.O	0.181	0.460	0.527	0.157	0.387	0.580	0.124	0.288	0.560
CVX	**0.002**	**0.003**	**0.010**	**0.004**	**0.009**	**0.025**	**0.004**	**0.011**	**0.028**
DD	**0.006**	**0.004**	**0.008**	**0.003**	**0.004**	**0.008**	**0.002**	**0.005**	**0.013**
DIS	0.247	0.377	0.674	0.215	0.398	0.719	0.172	0.413	0.760
GE	0.062	0.147	0.256	0.062	0.151	0.304	**0.032**	0.082	0.212
GS	**0.003**	**0.007**	**0.012**	**0.003**	**0.008**	**0.017**	**0.002**	**0.006**	**0.016**
HD	**0.020**	**0.043**	0.077	**0.020**	**0.046**	0.097	**0.026**	0.069	0.177
IBM	0.298	**0.049**	0.073	0.222	**0.047**	0.075	0.186	**0.045**	0.093
INTC.O	**0.015**	**0.034**	**0.050**	**0.014**	**0.033**	0.066	**0.006**	**0.017**	**0.048**
JNJ	0.083	0.127	0.229	0.061	0.117	0.242	**0.049**	0.129	0.313
JPM	**0.005**	**0.009**	**0.021**	**0.005**	**0.010**	**0.025**	**0.003**	**0.007**	**0.019**
KO	0.181	0.081	0.151	0.158	0.077	0.148	0.129	0.062	0.135
MCD	0.080	0.141	0.130	**0.048**	0.096	0.127	**0.018**	**0.045**	0.110
MMM	0.381	0.293	0.473	0.348	0.290	0.476	0.310	0.281	0.511
MRK	**0.004**	**0.008**	**0.007**	**0.002**	**0.004**	**0.006**	**0.001**	**0.002**	**0.007**
MSFT.O	0.573	0.847	0.777	0.552	0.855	0.859	0.415	0.764	0.866
NKE	**0.017**	**0.017**	**0.026**	**0.012**	**0.018**	**0.037**	**0.006**	**0.018**	**0.049**
PFE	**0.006**	**0.011**	**0.030**	**0.009**	**0.020**	0.052	**0.007**	**0.019**	**0.048**
PG	**0.018**	**0.024**	**0.025**	**0.009**	**0.017**	**0.028**	**0.002**	**0.007**	**0.021**
TRV	0.098	0.132	0.300	0.076	0.140	0.321	**0.042**	0.117	0.281
UNH	0.111	0.165	0.253	0.078	0.142	0.236	**0.040**	0.104	0.239
UTX	0.168	0.348	0.495	0.147	0.326	0.553	0.079	0.197	0.460
V	0.113	0.144	0.228	0.113	0.144	0.241	0.094	0.125	0.253
VZ	**0.007**	**0.007**	**0.014**	**0.007**	**0.011**	**0.025**	**0.005**	**0.014**	**0.039**
WMT	0.782	0.911	0.739	0.725	0.909	0.719	0.576	0.866	0.729
XOM	**0.011**	**0.022**	0.083	**0.020**	**0.047**	0.141	**0.029**	0.078	0.184

but optimizing over both at the same time

$$\hat{d}_\omega = \arg \min_\Theta \{R_1(d_\omega) + R_2(d_\omega)\}, \tag{9}$$

where Θ is a closed subset of $(-1/2, 1/2)$. Under certain assumptions (compare Arteche and Robinson (2000)) the estimator is consistent and standard normally distributed.

Tables 7.5 (realized volatility) and 7.6 (trading volume) display the seasonal memory estimates calculated from equation (9) in the cases where we find

Table 7.5 Empty fields indicate no rejection of the G-test applied at frequency $\omega = 2\pi/13$ at the 5%-level for *logarithms of realized volatility*. The numbers give estimates of seasonal long memory at frequency ω and standard errors in brackets.

RIC\δ	0.5	0.6	0.7	RIC\δ	0.5	0.6	0.7
.DJI				KO	0.111 (0.031)	0.072 (0.019)	0.046 (0.012)
AAPL.O	0.147 (0.031)			MCD	0.063 (0.031)		
AXP	0.120 (0.031)	0.058 (0.019)		MMM	0.112 (0.031)		
BA				MRK		0.056 (0.019)	
CAT	0.113 (0.031)	0.059 (0.019)	0.025 (0.012)	MSFT.O			
CSCO.O			0.086 (0.012)	NKE			
CVX	0.179 (0.031)	0.102 (0.019)		PFE	0.002 (0.031)	0.021 (0.019)	
DD	0.038 (0.031)			PG	0.114 (0.031)		
DIS	0.138 (0.031)			TRV	0.163 (0.031)	0.101 (0.019)	0.063 (0.012)
GE	0.101 (0.031)			UNH	0.123 (0.031)		
GS				UTX			
HD				V			
IBM	0.067 (0.031)	0.046 (0.019)		VZ	0.146 (0.031)	0.093 (0.019)	0.058 (0.012)
INTC.O				WMT			
JNJ	0.089 (0.031)			XOM	0.149 (0.031)	0.101 (0.019)	0.066 (0.012)
JPM							

Table 7.6 Empty fields indicate no rejection of the *G*-test applied at frequency $\omega = 2\pi/13$ at the 5%-level for *logarithms of trading volume*. The numbers give estimates of seasonal long memory at frequency ω and standard errors in brackets.

RIC'/δ	0.5	0.6	0.7	RIC'/δ	0.5	0.6	0.7
.DJI	0.113 (0.031)	−0.012 (0.019)	−0.125 (0.012)	KO			
AAPL.O	0.114 (0.031)	0.059 (0.019)	0.063 (0.012)	MCD	0.107 (0.031)	0.063 (0.019)	
AXP				MMM			
BA				MRK	0.160 (0.031)	0.075 (0.019)	0.042 (0.012)
CAT	0.108 (0.031)			MSFT.O			
CSCO.O				NKE	0.194 (0.031)	0.109 (0.019)	0.069 (0.012)
CVX	0.131 (0.031)	0.087 (0.019)	0.063 (0.012)	PFE	0.162 (0.031)	0.084 (0.019)	0.043 (0.012)
DD	0.117 (0.031)	0.065 (0.019)	0.046 (0.012)	PG	0.169 (0.031)	0.080 (0.019)	0.059 (0.012)
DIS				TRV	0.187 (0.031)		
GE	0.099 (0.031)			UNH	0.068 (0.031)		
GS	0.088 (0.031)	0.074 (0.019)		UTX			
HD	0.170 (0.031)	0.071 (0.019)	0.018 (0.012)	V			
IBM		0.107 (0.019)		VZ	0.190 (0.031)	0.076 (0.019)	0.061 (0.012)
INTC.O	0.089 (0.031)	0.064 (0.019)	0.036 (0.012)	WMT		0.087 (0.019)	
JNJ				XOM	0.124 (0.031)		
JPM	0.173 (0.031)	0.078 (0.019)	0.039 (0.012)				

seasonal long memory according to our *G*-test. Standard errors are given in brackets. The estimates are calculated at frequency $\omega = 2\pi/13$ for different bandwidth choices *m*, and $l = 1$. They vary from 0.05 to 0.2 and are significant with only three exceptions. Overall, the trading volume series exhibit slightly higher seasonal persistence than volatility. For trading volume of the index, we find antipersistence ($d = -0.125$) for a large bandwidth which would not be expected. This can be explained by the fact that the larger the bandwidth, the more frequencies are considered in the estimation so that the shifted periodogram ordinates influence the estimation in the large bandwidth case. Therefore, in order to avoid disturbances by other poles, it is sensible to use smaller bandwidth parameters.

Since our test has better power properties for higher seasonal memory parameters, even more seasonal long memory would be found if the series were more persistent. All in all, it seems to be enough to account for deterministic seasonality in averaged data like the DJIA index. Thus, aggregation in an index eliminates the stochastic seasonality present in individual stocks. However, we show that for a large proportion of individual stock data there is seasonal long memory that has to be considered after removing deterministic cycles. This is in line with Bordignon et al. (2007) who show that dummy regression is not sufficient in the context of volatility modeling especially for half-hourly data.

6. Conclusion

In recent years, the availability of larger data sets thanks to intra-day data has become important from an econometric perspective, and by now it is established that this intra-day data exhibits a strong seasonal structure that has to be considered.

In this chapter, we therefore review standard methods in the analysis of seasonality, examine intra-day seasonality and show that it is not always well characterized by deterministic models. To do so, we introduce a semiparametric test for seasonal long memory and prove its good finite sample performance in a Monte Carlo experiment. Due to its semiparametric nature, we do not encounter the problem of a potentially misspecified model and are robust to short-run dynamics.

This testing procedure is applied to intra-day realized volatility and trading volume data of the DJIA index and its constituents. In line with the literature, we observe long memory at frequency zero that has to be accounted for when analyzing such data. In addition to that, we also find that for the index seasonality is deterministic, but the inspection of individual stocks indicates that there is seasonal long memory in both realized volatility and trading volume. Hence, our data is characterized by "normal" long memory, deterministic periodicity and seasonal long memory. In contrast, for the averaged behavior we only find long memory and deterministic seasonality. We therefore conclude that the nature of intra-day seasonality in the index and in individual stock data is not identical so that they should be treated accordingly.

Note

1 We find that using the flexible Fourier form in order to remove slowly varying deterministic seasonality does not have a significant influence because the seasonal dummies already eliminate all deterministic periodicity.

Bibliography

Abeysinghe, T. (1991). Inappropriate use of seasonal dummies in regression. *Economics Letters*, 36(2):175–179.

Abeysinghe, T. (1994). Deterministic seasonal models and spurious regressions. *Journal of Econometrics*, 61(2):259–272.

Andersen, T. G. and Bollerslev, T. (1997). Intraday periodicity and volatility persistence in financial markets. *Journal of Empirical Finance*, 4(2):115–158.

Andersen, T. G. and Bollerslev, T. (1998). Deutsche mark–dollar volatility: Intraday activity patterns, macroeconomic announcements, and longer run dependencies. *The Journal of Finance*, 53(1):219–265.

Andersen, T. G., Bollerslev, T. and Das, A. (2001a). Variance-ratio statistics and high-frequency data: Testing for changes in intraday volatility patterns. *The Journal of Finance*, 56(1):305–327.

Andersen, T. G., Bollerslev, T., Diebold, F. X. and Ebens, H. (2001b). The distribution of realized stock return volatility. *Journal of Financial Economics*, 61(1):43–76.

Andersen, T. G., Bollerslev, T., Diebold, F. X., and Labys, P. (2001c). The distribution of realized exchange rate volatility. *Journal of the American Statistical Association*, 96(453):42–55.

Andersen, T. G., Bollerslev, T., Diebold, F. X., and Labys, P. (2003). Modeling and forecasting realized volatility. *Econometrica*, 71(2):579–625.

Arteche, J. (2002). Semiparametric robust tests on seasonal or cyclical long memory time series. *Journal of Time Series Analysis*, 23(3):251–285.

Arteche, J. (2004). Gaussian semiparametric estimation in long memory in stochastic volatility and signal plus noise models. *Journal of Econometrics*, 119(1):131–154.

Arteche, J. (2007). The analysis of seasonal long memory: The case of Spanish inflation. *Oxford Bulletin of Economics and Statistics*, 69(6):749–772.

Arteche, J. (2012). Standard and seasonal long memory in volatility: An application to Spanish inflation. *Empirical Economics*, 42(3):693–712.

Arteche, J. and Robinson, P. M. (2000). Semiparametric inference in seasonal and cyclical long memory processes. *Journal of Time Series Analysis*, 21(1):1–25.

Artiach, M. and Arteche, J. (2012). Doubly fractional models for dynamic heteroscedastic cycles. *Computational Statistics & Data Analysis*, 56(6):2139–2158.

Baillie, R. T. and Bollerslev, T. (1991). Intra-day and inter-market volatility in foreign exchange rates. *The Review of Economic Studies*, 58(3):565–585.

Baillie, R. T., Bollerslev, T., and Mikkelsen, H. O. (1996). Fractionally integrated generalized autoregressive conditional heteroskedasticity. *Journal of Econometrics*, 74(1):3–30.

Bisaglia, L., Bordignon, S., and Lisi, F. (2003). k-factor GARMA models for intraday volatility forecasting. *Applied Economics Letters*, 10(4):251–254.

Bisognin, C. and Lopes, S. R. C. (2009). Properties of seasonal long memory processes. *Mathematical and Computer Modelling*, 49(9–10):1837–1851.

Bollerslev, T., Cai, J., and Song, F. M. (2000). Intraday periodicity, long memory volatility, and macroeconomic announcement effects in the US treasury bond market. *Journal of Empirical Finance*, 7(1):37–55.

Bollerslev, T. and Ghysels, E. (1996). Periodic autoregressive conditional heteroscedasticity. *Journal of Business & Economic Statistics*, 14(2):139–151.

Bollerslev, T., Li, J., and Xue, Y. (2018). Volume, volatility and public news announcements. *The Review of Economic Studies*, 85(4):2005–2041.

Bollerslev, T., Osterrieder, D., Sizova, N., and Tauchen, G. (2013). Risk and return: Long-run relations, fractional cointegration, and return predictability. *Journal of Financial Economics*, 108(2):409–424.

Bordignon, S., Caporin, M., and Lisi, F. (2007). Generalised long-memory GARCH models for intra-daily volatility. *Computational Statistics & Data Analysis*, 51(12): 5900–5912.

Bordignon, S., Caporin, M., and Lisi, F. (2008). Periodic long-memory GARCH models. *Econometric Reviews*, 28(1–3):60–82.

Box, G. E., Jenkins, G. M., Reinsel, G. C., and Ljung, G. M. (2013). *Time Series Analysis: Forecasting and Control*. John Wiley & Sons.

Caporale, G. M., Cunado, J., and Gil-Alana, L. A. (2012). Deterministic versus stochastic seasonal fractional integration and structural breaks. *Statistics and Computing*, 22(2): 349–358.

Cogburn, R., Davis, H. T., et al. (1974). Periodic splines and spectral estimation. *The Annals of Statistics*, 2(6):1108–1126.

da Silva Lopes, A. C. (1999). Spurious deterministic seasonality and autocorrelation corrections with quarterly data: Further Monte Carlo results. *Empirical Economics*, 24(2): 341–359.

Demetrescu, M. and Hassler, U. (2007). Effect of neglected deterministic seasonality on unit root tests. *Statistical Papers*, 48(3):385–402.

Deo, R., Hurvich, C., and Lu, Y. (2006). Forecasting realized volatility using a long-memory stochastic volatility model: Estimation, prediction and seasonal adjustment. *Journal of Econometrics*, 131(1):29–58.

Diongue, A. K., Guegan, D., and Vignal, B. (2009). Forecasting electricity spot market prices with a k-factor GIGARCH process. *Applied Energy*, 86(4):505–510.

Ferrara, L. and Guegan, D. (2001). Forecasting with k-factor Gegenbauer processes: Theory and applications. *Journal of Forecasting*, 20(8):581–601.

Ferrara, L. and Guegan, D. (2006). Fractional seasonality: Models and application to economic activity in the Euro area. *Eurostat Pulications-Luxembourg*, 137–153.

Franses, P. H., Hylleberg, S., and Lee, H. S. (1995). Spurious deterministic seasonality. *Economics Letters*, 48(3):249–256.

Gallant, A. R. (1981). On the bias in flexible functional forms and an essentially unbiased form: The Fourier flexible form. *Journal of Econometrics*, 15(2):211–245.

Gil-Alana, L. A. (2002). Seasonal long memory in the aggregate output. *Economics Letters*, 74(3):333–337.

Gil-Alana, L. A. (2005). Deterministic seasonality versus seasonal fractional integration. *Journal of Statistical Planning and Inference*, 134(2):445–461.

Gil-Alana, L. A. (2007). Testing the existence of multiple cycles in financial and economic time series. *Annals of Economics & Finance*, 8(1):1–20.

Giot, P. (2005). Market risk models for intraday data. *The European Journal of Finance*, 11(4):309–324.

Giraitis, L. and Leipus, R. (1995). A generalized fractionally differencing approach in long-memory modeling. *Lithuanian Mathematical Journal*, 35(1):53–65.

Gray, H. L., Zhang, N.-F., and Woodward, W. A. (1989). On generalized fractional processes. *Journal of Time Series Analysis*, 10(3):233–257.

Haldrup, N. and Nielsen, M. Ø. (2006). A regime switching long memory model for electricity prices. *Journal of Econometrics*, 135(1):349–376.

Hylleberg, S. (1992). *Modelling seasonality*. Oxford: Oxford University Press.

Kooperberg, C., Stone, C. J., and Truong, Y. K. (1995). Rate of convergence for logspline spectral density estimation. *Journal of Time Series Analysis*, 16(4):389–401.

Kuensch, H. R. (1987). Statistical aspects of self-similar processes. In *Proceedings of the first World Congress of the Bernoulli Society*, volume 1, pp. 67–74. VNU Science Press Utrecht.

Leschinski, C. and Sibbertsen, P. (2019). Model order selection in periodic long memory models. *Econometrics and Statistics*, 9:78–94.

Lobato, I. N. and Velasco, C. (2000). Long memory in stock-market trading volume. *Journal of Business & Economic Statistics*, 18(4):410–427.

Lu, Y. K. and Perron, P. (2010). Modeling and forecasting stock return volatility using a random level shift model. *Journal of Empirical Finance*, 17(1):138–156.

Martens, M., Chang, Y.-C., and Taylor, S. J. (2002). A comparison of seasonal adjustment methods when forecasting intraday volatility. *Journal of Financial Research*, 25(2): 283–299.

Ooms, M. and Hassler, U. (1997). On the effect of seasonal adjustment on the logperiodogram regression. *Economics Letters*, 56(2):135–141.

Peiris, M. S. and Asai, M. (2016). Generalized fractional processes with long memory and time dependent volatility revisited. *Econometrics*, 4(3):37.

Porter-Hudak, S. (1990). An application of the seasonal fractionally differenced model to the monetary aggregates. *Journal of the American Statistical Association*, 85(410): 338–344.

Ray, B. K. (1993). Long-range forecasting of IBM product revenues using a seasonal fractionally differenced ARMA model. *International Journal of Forecasting*, 9(2):255–269.

Reisen, V. A., Monte, E. Z., da Conceição Franco, G., Sgrancio, A. M., Molinares, F. A. F., Bondon, P., Ziegelmann, F. A., and Abraham, B. (2018). Robust estimation of fractional seasonal processes: Modeling and forecasting daily average SO2 concentrations. *Mathematics and Computers in Simulation*, 146:27–43.

Reisen, V. A., Zamprogno, B., Palma, W., and Arteche, J. (2014). A semiparametric approach to estimate two seasonal fractional parameters in the SARFIMA model. *Mathematics and Computers in Simulation*, 98:1–17.

Robinson, P. M. (1995). Gaussian semiparametric estimation of long range dependence. *The Annals of Statistics*, 23(5):1630–1661.

Rossi, E. and Fantazzini, D. (2014). Long memory and periodicity in intraday volatility. *Journal of Financial Econometrics*, 13(4):922–961.

Shimotsu, K. and Phillips, P. C. (2005). Exact local Whittle estimation of fractional integration. *The Annals of Statistics*, 33(4):1890–1933.

Soares, L. J. and Souza, L. R. (2006). Forecasting electricity demand using generalized long memory. *International Journal of Forecasting*, 22(1):17–28.

Taylor, S. (1986). *Modelling financial time series*. John Wiley & Sons.

Wenger, K., Leschinski, C., and Sibbertsen, P. (2018). The memory of volatility. *Quantitative Finance and Economics*, 2(1):137–159.

Wood, R. A., McInish, T. H., and Ord, J. K. (1985). An investigation of transactions data for NYSE stocks. *The Journal of Finance*, 40(3):723–739.

Woodward, W. A., Cheng, Q. C., and Gray, H. L. (1998). A k-factor GARMA long-memory model. *Journal of Time Series Analysis*, 19(4):485–504.

Xu, J. and Perron, P. (2014). Forecasting return volatility: Level shifts with varying jump probability and mean reversion. *International Journal of Forecasting*, 30(3):449–463.

Part 3

Meta-analysis in economics and finance

8 The disinflation effect of central bank independence

A comparative meta-analysis between transition economies and the rest of the world

Ichiro Iwasaki and Akira Uegaki

1. Introduction

In this chapter, we conduct a comparative meta-analysis between studies of transition economies and those of the rest of the world that empirically examined the disinflation effect of central bank independence (CBI). The main point that separates transition economies from other developed and developing economies lies in the fact that the former had to build institutions after the collapse of socialism and stabilize the macro economy needed for simultaneously finding a path of balanced growth. Reforming the banking system in a transition economy is an example of such difficult challenges.

At the initial stage of the transformation process from a planned system to a market economy in Central and Eastern Europe (CEE) and the former Soviet Union (FSU), policy makers and researchers paid little attention to banking sector reforms.[1] Before long, however, people involved in the structural reforms of the former socialist countries came to realize that banking sector reforms, especially central bank reforms, are tasks as important and difficult as economic liberalization and enterprise privatization. In fact, as Table 8.1 shows, even in 2016, not only had the banking sector of none of these countries succeeded in reaching a level that satisfied the standards of a developed market economy, but many of the countries were still stuck in the middle or low stages of development, demonstrating that establishing a banking system appropriate for a market economy is an extremely difficult policy objective.

In the bulk of research work regarding banking reforms in transition economies in the last 27 years, we see that the issue of CBI is one of the main themes of the research. Why is the CBI so important? In socialist economies, the central bank concurrently carried out both the functions of a central bank and those of a commercial bank. However, such a monopoly of the central bank does not necessarily mean that the bank plays a leading role in the national economy. Instead, the important point is that, as money had only a passive role in the planned system, the central bank, therefore, had no means of implementing monetary policies that would actually impact economic activities. From the viewpoint of the banking system, transitioning from a planned economy to a market economy

Table 8.1 Development of the banking sector in transition economies in 2016

Countries[a]	EBRD banking sector transition indicator[b]
Estonia	4-
Poland	4-
Slovak Republic	4-
Croatia	3+
Latvia	3+
Lithuania	3+
Bulgaria	3
Hungary	3
Romania	3
Slovenia	3
Albania	3-
Bosnia and Herzegovina	3-
FYR Macedonia	3-
Georgia	3-
Montenegro	3-
Russia	3-
Serbia	3-
Ukraine	3-
Armenia	2+
Kazakhstan	2+
Kosovo	2+
Azerbaijan	2
Belarus	2
Kyrgyz Republic	2
Moldova	2
Tajikistan	2
Turkmenistan	1
Uzbekistan	1

Notes:
[a]The Czech Republic is not included.
[b]The indicator ranges from 1 to 4+, with 1 representing little or no change relative to a rigid centrally planned economy and 4+ representing the standards of an industrialized market economy.
Source: EBRD (2016, p. 95).

means demolishing such a mono-bank system to create a two-tier system comprised of the central bank as the first tier and commercial banks as the second tier. Along with the establishment of a two-tier banking system, money started to play a more positive role in the economic system; hence, central banks also started to function in newly independent roles. The basic scenario of central bank reform in the former socialist countries was to give the central bank the ability to make independent policy decisions and enable it to carry out monetary policies, even though not necessarily welcomed by the government and/or business circles. Therefore, from a financial perspective, the degree of CBI can be regarded as an important barometer of the system's transformation.

On the other hand, we must pay special attention to an actual policy problem that the leaders of the transition countries faced: inflation. In the earlier years of the 1990s, all transition countries in CEE and the FSU had experienced hyperinflation, where the annual rate of inflation was sometimes higher than 100%, or 1,000% (EBRD, various issues). This had hampered the process of structural reforms there. It is more interesting that since the second half of the 1990s, there appeared a diversification of inflation. In some countries, the inflation was successfully controlled under 10%, while the inflation higher than 50% was still witnessed in other countries. All these promote us to investigate the relation between inflation and institutional settings of each country.

For this reason, and in response to the call from Kydland and Prescott (1977) and Barro and Gordon (1983), many researchers not only have tried to measure the degree of CBI in these countries but have also carried out empirical studies that examined the relationship between CBI and inflation. Since the pioneering research work of Loungani and Sheets (1997), many empirical results have been published, including the recent work of Piplica (2015).

This series of transition studies, however, has never reached a definite conclusion about the disinflation effect of CBI across the literature, probably due to significant differences in study conditions, including target countries, estimation periods, and empirical methodologies. In addition, although Cukierman et al. (2002) pointed out that "[o]n average, aggregate legal independence of new central banks in transition economies (in the 1990s) is substantially higher than CBI in developed economies during the 1980s" (p. 243) and provided an inkling of possible overrating of CBI in transition economies, succeeding studies have not presented any clear answer to the issue they raised.

In this chapter, we will tackle these two crucial issues concerning CBI in transition economies through a meta-analysis of transition studies and comparable studies targeting other developed and developing economies. In a research field where many previous studies are available, a meta-analysis of empirical results reported in the extant literature becomes a more effective means of achieving such an objective than a single study, in many cases. Furthermore, meta-analysis allows us to tackle a question such as whether we can specify the true effect size in the study area in question from the whole of the literature. This is why we will attempt to perform a meta-analysis in this chapter. Klomp and de Haan (2010) offered a pioneering systematic review of this research area and included several works on transition economies in their meta-analysis. However, they did not provide a direct answer to the above question. In addition, due to the timing of publication, this article does not take into account a number of studies on transition economies published in the 2010s. Our paper is unique not only in that it is the first meta-study to focus on transition economies but also in that it carries out a comparative meta-analysis with other world economies.

The meta-synthesis of 125 and 212 estimates collected from the transition and non-transition literature, respectively, indicates that both studies have successfully identified a negative relationship between CBI and inflation. Moreover, our meta-regression analysis (MRA) of the heterogeneity among relevant studies suggested that the choice of estimator, inflation variable type, degree of freedom, and quality level of the study strongly affected the empirical results regarding transition economies, along with the selection of a CBI variable. We also provide evidence that no significant difference exists between the two types of studies, in terms of both effect size and statistical significance, so long as we control for a series of study conditions. This result implies that the socioeconomic setting of a society concerning the CBI-inflation problem has as substantially developed in transition economies as in other developed and developing economies. However, we found that, although transition studies include genuine empirical evidence of the disinflation effect of CBI in their estimates, non-transition studies have prevented us from identifying a true effect. Indeed, the precision-effect test (explained later) cannot reject the null hypothesis of the absence of a genuine effect in the non-transition studies. This is perhaps due to the strong influence of publication selection bias. In this sense, transition studies have made significant contributions to the literature by helping researchers to grasp the real impact of CBI on inflation as a whole.

The remainder of this chapter is organized as follows. Section 2 provides an overall picture of central bank reforms in transition economies. Section 3 theoretically considers the relationship between CBI and inflation and reviews recent empirical studies of transition economies. Section 4 discusses the procedure of the literature search, an outline of the collected estimates, and the meta-analysis methodology. Section 5 conducts a comparative meta-analysis between transition studies and non-transition studies, including an assessment of publication selection bias. Section 6 summarizes the major findings and concludes.

2. Central bank reforms in transition economies

In this section, we describe the value, progress, and diversity of central bank reforms in CEE and FSU countries. To this end, in Subsection 2.1, we argue the significance of establishing a two-tier banking system and central bank reform in the former socialist countries, and in Subsection 2.2, we discuss the process of banking reforms and the promotion of CBI and indicate the divergence of reforms among transition economies.

2.1. Establishment of a two-tier banking system and central bank reform in transition economies

In a socialist planned economy, banking is characterized by a one-tier banking system. In socialist economies, a central bank concurrently carried out both the function of a central bank and that of a commercial bank. In other words, under the socialist system, the central bank not only was an issuing bank but also provided short-term working capital for state enterprises. However, such a monopoly of the central bank does not necessarily mean that the bank plays a leading role in the national economy. Instead, the important point is that, as money had only a passive role in the planned system, the central bank, therefore, had no means of implementing monetary policies that would actually impact economic activities. The "passive" role of money meant that the money in the socialist system was basically functioning as a calculation unit but could not influence the real economy by a system of claims and liabilities of financial resources with the fluctuation of interest rates. In fact, central banks in socialist states have never engaged in any of the traditional operations of central banks, such as open market operations and the discounting of commercial bills (Gregory and Stuart, 1986; Lavigne, 1999). With a rigid price system fixed by the state, the passive role of money led to a non-inflationary society, where inflation was not explicitly evident but had been suppressed or hidden, for example, in the form of long lines of people waiting for consumer goods.

Accordingly, from the viewpoint of a banking system, transitioning from a planned economy to a market economy means demolishing a mono-bank system to create a two-tier system comprised of the central bank as the first tier and commercial banks as the second tier, on one hand, and making money positive on the other. In some countries, the building of a two-tier banking system was formally carried out at a very early stage of transition, even before the collapse of the socialist regime. As a matter of fact, the transition of the Soviet mono-banking system to a two-tier structure occurred in April 1989, when commercial banks were first allowed to operate, and a legal reserve system was introduced (Kokorev and Remizov, 1996). On the other hand, two-tier banking systems were constituted in Hungary, Poland, and Czechoslovakia in 1987, 1989, and 1990, respectively (Barisitz, 2008). Of these, the banking reform in Hungary was particularly advanced. As early as December 1984, the Central Committee of the Hungarian Socialist Workers' Party declared that "the central banking and commercial banking functions have to be separated within the National Bank of Hungary and preparations for the establishment of a two-tier banking system have to begin" (Monetary Policy Department of the National Bank of Hungary, 2000, p. 15); on January 1, 1987, a two-tier banking system actually started to operate (Varhegyi, 1994). In Bulgaria, a two-tier banking system was also built from 1987 to 1989, and in Romania in 1990; almost at the same time, the establishment of private banks was also permitted (Barisitz, 2008).

Along with the establishment of a two-tier banking system, money started to play a more positive role in the economic system; hence, central banks also started to function in new roles. Actually, they began to influence the behaviors of enterprises, commercial banks, households, and the government in an indirect manner through the manipulation of interest rates, the money supply, and the exchange rate. However, this indirect manner did not mean that the influence of the central bank was weak because, in a society where the market economy is fully functioning, a small change in the interest rate, the amount of money in circulation, or the exchange rate could significantly impact the whole national economy. However, in a new society, there was a risk that the central bank would issue money freely with newly obtained tools if it were strongly influenced by the government or business circles.

In this way, the desirable scenario of central bank reform in the former socialist countries was to give the central bank the ability to make independent policy decisions and enable it to carry out monetary policies, even though this would not necessarily be welcomed by the government and/or business circles.

Therefore, from a financial perspective, the degree of CBI can be regarded as an important barometer of systemic transformation.

The important point here is that various European Union (EU) agreements contain provisions concerning the independence of the European Central Bank (ECB) and central banks in member states. For instance, the treaty on the functioning of the EU has the following provision:

> *When exercising the powers and carrying out the tasks and duties conferred upon them by the Treaties and the Statute of the ESCB and of the ECB, neither the European Central Bank, nor a national central bank, nor any member of their decision-making bodies shall seek or take instructions from Union institutions, bodies, offices or agencies, from any government of a Member State or from any other body.*
>
> (Article 130)[2]

This means that the government of a CEE country that intends to join the EU must have a strong awareness that reinforcing CBI is one of its primary policy objectives. With such a mandate, how did CEE and FSU countries try to secure and promote the independence of their central banks?

2.2. *Banking reform progress and the independence of central banks*

As discussed above, central bank reform in transition economies can be viewed as a process of ensuring and strengthening CBI underpinned by the establishment of a two-tier system. However, to answer the question as to under what financial system the policy objectives of the government, including stabilization of the macro-economy and acceleration of economic growth, can be achieved, we should also pay attention to banking reforms in general. In other words, although encompassing central bank reforms, much wider reforms are also important, including the liberalization of interest rates, the abolition of directed credit or interest rate ceilings, the establishment of bank solvency and of a framework for prudential supervision and regulation, the increased presence of private banks in the financial market and their increased lending to private enterprises, well-functioning banking competition, and substantial financial deepening.[3]

In principle, banking reforms and the reinforcement of CBI should keep pace with each other. When we look back on the history of transition economies, however, these two did not necessarily proceed hand in hand. In Figure 8.1, the horizontal axis is the index for banking reform and interest rate liberalization provided by the European Bank for Reconstruction and Development (EBRD). It is a five-grade index ranging from 1 to 4+ and covers most CEE and FSU countries.[4] The vertical axis shows the degree of CBIW (central bank independence weighted) of Dincer and Eichengreen (2014), which is their CBI index based on the legal index of CBI developed by Cukierman et al. (1992) and Cukierman (1992).

Panels (a) and (b) of Figure 8.1 show, respectively, a scatter plot of the EBRD banking reform index and the CBIW indexes in 1998–2002 and 2006–2010.[5] As

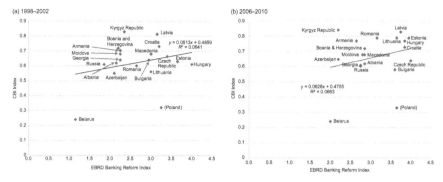

Figure 8.1 Relationship between banking reforms and central bank independence in transition economies.

Note: The vertical axis is the period mean of the CBI index developed by Dincer and Eichengreen (2014), while the horizontal axis is the period mean of the EBRD banking reform index.
Source: Authors' illustration based on Dincer and Eichengreen (2014) and the EBRD Transition Report (various issues).

the approximate line drawn in each graph suggests, there is a weak positive correlation between banking reform progress and the degree of CBI in CEE and FSU countries. At the same time, Figure 8.1 also indicates a significant divergence in the reform paths among these countries, not only at the end of the 20th century and the beginning of 21th century, but even in the second half of the 2000s.

It is easy to understand that the Czech Republic, Estonia (1998–2002), Hungary, Latvia, and Lithuania (2006–2010), which continued its reforms all the way to the introduction of the euro, are ranked high with respect to both indexes,[6] while Russia, Azerbaijan, Albania, and Georgia, which faced weak political influence from the EU, are ranked low in both indexes in Figure 8.1.[7]

On the other hand, the position of the Kyrgyz Republic is interesting. Despite the fact that the CBI index of the country is the highest among the transition countries in 1998–2002 and 2006–10, the banking reform indexes are moderately low in 19 countries. Particularly in 2006–10, the Kyrgyz Republic's CBI was highest among 19 countries, while its banking reform index was second lowest after Belarus. This curious position is a result of interventionist policies of the IMF and other international institutions to formalize CBI through laws under the autocratic system of Askar Akayev with the country's historically underdeveloped financial economy (Sagbansua, 2006; Johnson, 2016; IMF, 2016).

As mentioned above, Hungary seems to be an advanced reformist country, as we can see in Panel (b) of Figure 8.1, where both indicators are considerably high. If we examine Panel (a) of Figure 8.1, however, we find that the CBI index is below the middle level (less than the simple average of index figures), while Hungary's banking reform indexes are the highest among 19 countries. This situation reflects the fact that strict provisions for CBI were not enacted in Hungary until 2001, although general financial and banking reforms had been advancing since even before the dissolution of the previous regime. Furthermore, the situation in Hungary after 2010, which is not shown in the figure, is also worthy of attention because Prime Minister Viktor Orbán, who came back to the administration in 2010, has tried to issue a law that includes clauses that infringe on CBI. In Hungary, intense fluctuations in the political situation had a major influence on the central bank system, showing an interesting example that CBI is impaired despite progress in other domestic reforms (Meagher, 2003; Civelekoğlu, 2013; The Economist, 2013; Djankov, 2015).

In sum, the overall pattern of banking reforms and CBI in the CEE and FSU region is very diverse. On one hand, there is a country such as Estonia, where both elements are highly developed; on the other hand, there are countries such as Russia, where both elements have been at a low level. There are also notable exceptions, such as the Kyrgyz Republic and Hungary. While the question of why such diversity has occurred would be an important research topic from the perspective of historical path dependence, that is not where our interest lies. Rather, we would like to examine in this chapter the relationship between CBI and inflation. For policy makers in CEE and FSU countries, addressing the inflation risk was the most challenging and urgent task in the area of financial policy.

3. Literature review

As mentioned in the introduction, the dynamics of inflation in transition economies had two faces. First, all former socialist countries experienced extremely high inflation with the transformation of their economic systems. However, there was significant diversity from country to country in terms of how inflation proceeded, especially since the mid-1990s.

With respect to why high inflation occurred in all CEE and FSU countries without exception, Rautava (1993) pointed to the serious shortage economy under socialism as well as monetary overhang, which means the excessive accumulation of currency in the hands of citizens and other economic entities. On the other hand, the diversity of inflation dynamics was caused by country-to-country differences in the nature of price liberalization, the scale of subsidiary funding by the issuing of currency to state-owned enterprises, the monopolistic industrial organization under the planned system, and the foreign exchange policies of the central banks.

Because of our interest in this chapter, we cast a spotlight on the diversity observed in the inflation trends. We argue that more fundamental factors should exist behind such diversity, as was observed in the process of price level fluctuations in the transition economies. That is exactly the area in which, under pressure from the government and business circles, central banks are sacrificing their own mission to stabilize the currency value for the sake of other policy objectives. This introduces the issue of the relationship between CBI and inflation.

Many studies, both theoretical and empirical, have examined this issue. From a theoretical point of view, Kydland and Prescott (1977) and Barro and Gordon

(1983), who argued that discretionary financial policies create a "time (or dynamic) inconsistency problem," made notable contributions (Romer, 1996). Of the policy tools developed to deal with this problem, one particularly relevant to our research interest is a delegation strategy advocated by Rogoff (1985), who proposed appointing an individual to head the central bank who is more conscious of inflation than the general public. His model well explains "many of the measures that countries take to insulate their central banks from inflationary pressures" (p. 1180) and, accordingly, implies that there exists a negative correlation between CBI and inflation.

In response to these theoretical arguments, Alesina (1988), Grillini et al. (1991), Cukierman et al. (1992), and Alesina and Summers (1993) developed unique CBI indexes[8] and empirically examined the relationship between inflation and CBI in developed and developing economies. They found that inflation and legal independence were negatively related in industrial economies, while they did not find such a relationship in developing countries. However, when other proxies of independence, such as the actual turnover of central governors, were used, a negative relationship between inflation and independence was also observed in developing countries (Cukierman, 2008; Arnone et al., 2006). Following these pioneering works, studies on former socialist transition economies also started appearing in 1997. They include Loungani and Sheets (1997), Maliszewski (2000), Cukierman et al. (2002), Eijffinger and Stadhouders (2003), Hammermann and Flanagan (2007), Dumiter (2011), Maslowska (2011), Bogoev et al. (2012a, 2012b), Petrevski et al. (2012), Bodea (2014), and Piplica (2015). Hereafter, we will take a closer look at studies after 1997.

As mentioned above, the study by Loungani and Sheets (1997) is a pioneering work that examined 12 CEE and FSU countries. It is a cross-sectional analysis of the relationship between changes in CBI as reflected in statutes adopted between 1989 and 1992, on one hand, and the inflation rate in 1993, on the other. They found that CBI was correlated with lower inflation, even after controlling for the effects of fiscal policy, the overall quality of economic reform efforts, and the average tenure of the central bank's governor (p. 397).

Maliszewski (2000) used panel data of 20 CEE and FSU countries from 1990–1998. He constructed two indexes of legal independence that covered political and economic aspects of independence and found an inverse relationship between inflation and CBI. However, he pointed out that a robust relationship was present only after a high level of economic liberalization. He also noted that CBI is a powerful device for protecting price stability but not for stabilizing the price level (this may mean that CBI is not effective for lowering price levels that had been raised in the past: author) (pp. 749, 773).

As mentioned in the introduction, Cukierman et al. (2002) provided a very important consideration from the perspective of a meta-analysis of the transition literature. Using original indexes of legal independence for new central banks in 26 transition economies during the 1990s, they discovered that the legal independence of central banks in transition economies was much higher than in developed economies observed in the 1980s.[9] Hereafter, we will call their finding "the Cukierman proposition." This fact was pointed out in a preceding study (Wagner, 1999) and has been reemphasized in relatively recent studies as well (Bouyon, 2009; Bogoev et al., 2012b). If there has been a tendency to overemphasize CBI in transition economies as measured by the legal standard, it is possible that, in the transition study, it might become difficult to empirically verify the hypothesis that the higher the CBI, the higher its negative impact on inflation. Actually, Cukierman et al. (2002) reported that "there is no evidence to support conventional wisdom regarding the negative relation between inflation and legal CBI" (p. 249) in former socialist economies.

Eijffinger and Stadhouders (2003) conducted cross-sectional analyses concerning 18 CEE and FSU countries and 44 developed and developing economies for the period from 1990–1996.[10] They invented an original index, "Institutional Quality Indicators" (IQIs), as a proxy for the rule of law (p. 4); they also examined the relationship among legal CBI, IQIs, and the inflation rate (represented as the depreciation rate of the real value of money). They concluded that IQIs are significantly and negatively related to the rate of inflation. They also showed that during the early phases of liberalization, legal CBI is unrelated to inflation; however, when sufficiently high levels of liberalization are reached, with all other things the same, legal CBI and inflation are significantly and negatively related. The important point that they emphasized is that the translation of legal independence into actual independence is primarily determined by the rule of law (p. 20). This is closely connected to the problem of the Cukierman proposition.

A study by Hammermann and Flanagan (2007) did not directly study the relationship between CBI and inflation. Instead, they attempted to investigate why inflation in Russia, Ukraine, Belarus, and Moldova (they called these countries "Western CIS") was higher (about 10%) than that in other transition countries even recently. To answer this question, they used an empirical model, the CB incentive approach, to suggest that a central bank's incentive toward higher short-term inflation is a key reason for the observed outcome (p. 14). They concluded that the central banks in Russia, Ukraine, Belarus, and Moldova appeared to have reasons for choosing higher inflation rates, in some cases due to fiscal pressures but mainly to make up for and to, perhaps, exploit lagging internal and external liberalization in their economies (p. 23).

Dumiter (2011) developed his own comprehensive CBI index and examined the correlation between this original index and macroeconomic indicators, including inflation, output, unemployment rate, fiscal deficits, and the current account balance. His new CBI index was made to eliminate the gap between de jure (legal) independence and de facto (actual) independence. He named it "the new index of central bank independence and inflation targeting" (p. 113). While examining the data of both transition economies and other developed and developing economies, he, interestingly, obtained evidence that, not only in developed countries but also in developing and emerging countries (transition countries), central bank independence (represented by the new index) generates increases in inflation and other macro performance indexes, such as output and unemployment. In this paper, however, there is no explicit explanation concerning the difference between transition economies and non-transition economies.

As Dumiter (2011) did, Maslowska (2011) also covered not only transition economies but also other world economies. Maslowska's aim is unique because, by comparing various scales of CBI, she tried to examine which best empirically verifies a negative correlation between CBI and inflation rates. Thus, her paper provides valuable empirical data for examining heterogeneity among different studies by meta-analysis.

Bogoev et al. (2012a, 2012b) and Petrevski et al. (2012) are heterochromatic empirical studies because they came to different conclusions regarding the disinflation effect of CBI, despite having been published in the same year by the same group of researchers and having dealt with the same subject. In fact, while Bogoev et al. (2012a) reported that "CBI is found to have a statistically significant and economically important negative effect on inflation" (p. 93), Bogoev et al. (2012b) stated that "[t]he role of CBI as a disinflation device in transition economies may have been overstated" (p. 54). Furthermore, Petrevski et al. (2012) concluded that "[t]he results from our empirical models do not provide empirical support for the significant and negative relationship between CBI and inflation in transition economies" (p. 646). We conjecture that the presence of these remarkably different research outcomes is closely related to differences in the study conditions of these papers, including the empirical model, the estimation period, and the target countries. Hence, we will consider these factors in the meta-analysis conducted in this chapter.

Bodea (2014) examined the CBI-inflation nexus using quarterly panel data for 23 post-communist countries from 1991–2007. She investigated whether independent central banks had helped price stability in transition economies and what specific mechanism was involved. The article's contribution lies in the fact that the author distinguished the discipline effects from the credibility effects of an independent central bank. She concluded that an independent central bank, aided by democratic political institutions, had a disciplinary effect on rates of money supply growth; she also asserted that, while controlling for the growth of money, it had a credible effect on lowering inflation. She also investigated the relationship between fixed exchange rates and inflation and drew the same conclusion.

At the time of writing, the latest quantitative analysis of CBI and inflation had been produced by Piplica (2015). Using data from 1994–2012 of 11 transition countries (EU member states), Piplica constructed his own new CBI index, TGMT, based on the GMT index of Grillini et al. (1991) and the index of Cukierman (1992). From empirical analysis based on this new index, the author came to the following conclusion regarding the relationship between CBI and inflation: "Even in early stages of the transition LCBI (Legal CBI) has significantly negative effects on inflation. In later phases all the countries show evidently high levels of the LCBI and low inflation rates, but in this phase increasing the LCBI would not result in decreasing the inflation rate" (p. 167).

What can we deduce from the review of the transition literature mentioned above? First, the empirical results of transition economies regarding the disinflation effect of CBI as a whole are mixed; hence, it is difficult to grasp the whole picture by reviewing the narrative of the previous studies. Second, although Dumiter (2011) and Maslowska (2011) conducted empirical analyses comparing data of developed and developing economies to those of transition economies, these papers do not necessarily work out the differences between the two. This is also true for Eijffinger and Stadhouders (2003). Third, every author is concerned with how to measure CBI or what kind of proxy should be utilized to capture the impact of CBI on inflation. Particularly, one's conclusion would be different depending on how one assesses the Cukierman proposition, which hints at a possible overestimate of CBI in transition economies as compared with developed economies. From our viewpoint, this means that we must assess whether there is a significant difference in empirical results regarding the CBI disinflation effect among legally based CBI indexes such as legal provisions regarding the purpose of the bank, economically based indexes such as power to lend money directly to the private sector, politically based indexes such as the relation between the bank and the state budget, and other actual indexes such as actual average terms of the governor used in previous studies.

On the basis of the above discussions, the task of our meta-analysis becomes clear: we should shed light on the characteristics of transition economies as compared with other developed and developing economies while explicitly incorporating into our meta-analysis the differences in CBI indexes, paying special attention to the Cukierman proposition. To deal with this task, in the following two sections we will conduct a comparative meta-analysis between transition and non-transition studies.

4. Procedure of literature search, outline of collected estimates, and meta-analysis methodology

In this section, as the first step in achieving the task mentioned above, we will discuss our procedure for searching and selecting studies regarding the disinflation effect of CBI and outline the collected estimates as well as the meta-analysis methodology employed in this study.

To identify relevant studies that empirically examined the direct effect of CBI on inflation in CEE and FSU countries as well as those concerning other developed and developing countries that could be targeted for comparison with transition studies, we first searched EconLit, Web of Science, and Google Scholar databases for research works that had been registered from 1989 to 2017.[11] Here, we carried out an AND search using "*central bank*," "*independence*," and "*inflation*" as keywords. As a result, we identified more than 850 references; from these, we obtained 144 papers that actually conducted empirical examinations of the impact of CBI on inflation. After that, we closely examined the content of these 144 works and narrowed the literature list to those containing estimates that could be subjected to meta-analysis for this chapter.

Consequently, as Table 8.2 reports, for transition studies, we selected 12 papers referenced in the preceding section, from Loungani and Sheets (1997)

Table 8.2 List of selected studies of the effect of central bank independence on inflation and the breakdown of collected estimates for meta-analysis

(a) Transition studies

Author (Publication year)	Target country Number of countries	Breakdown by country group CEE EU countries[a]	Other CEE countries	FSU countries[b]	Others[c]	Estimation period[d]	Data type	CBI variable[e] Comprehensive index	Political index	Economic index	Legal index	Governor turnover	Governor term	Number of collected estimates	Average precision (AP)[f]
Loungani and Sheets (1997)	12	7	1	4	0	1993	Cross	✓					✓	7	11.24
Maliszewski (2000)	20	8	2	10	0	1990–1998	Cross, panel	✓	✓	✓				29	113.10
Cukierman et al. (2002)	26	11	2	12	1	1989–1998	Panel				✓			6	25.04
Eijffinger and Stadhouders (2003)	18	10	1	7	0	1990–1996	Cross				✓			20	2.84
Hammermann and Flanagan (2007)	19	10	5	4	0	1995–2004	Panel				✓			2	15.93
Dumiter (2011)	20	8	5	4	3	2006–2008	Panel	✓						2	6.05
Maslowska (2011)	25	11	2	11	1	1990–2007	Panel	✓	✓	✓		✓		11	2.47
Bogoev et al. (2012a)	17	11	4	2	0	1990–2009	Panel	✓			✓			8	87.33
Bogoev et al. (2012b)	28	11	4	12	1	1990–2010	Panel	✓			✓			16	26.46
Petrevski et al. (2012)	17	11	4	2	0	1990–2009	Panel	✓			✓			8	24.96
Bodea (2014)	23	7	3	12	1	1991–2007	Panel				✓			12	2.25
Piplica (2015)	11	11	0	0	0	1994–2012	Cross, panel				✓			4	5.73

(Continued)

Table 8.2 (Continued)

(b) Non-transition studies

Author (Publication year)	Target country Number of countries	Breakdown by country group		Estimation period[d]	Data type	CBI variable[c]				Governor turnover	Governor term	Number of collected estimates	Average precision (AP)[f]
		Developed countries[a]	Developing countries			Comprehensive index	Political index	Economic index	Legal index				
Walsh (1997)	19	19	0	1980–1993	Cross				✓			2	120.69
de Haan and Kooi (2000)	75	0	75	1980–1989	Cross					✓		17	16.62
Sturm and de Haan (2001)	76	0	76	1980–1989	Cross					✓		5	0.09
Eijffinger and Stadhouders (2003)	44	17	27	1980–1989	Cross				✓	✓		31	7.01
Gutiérrez (2004)	25	0	25	1995–2001	Cross		✓		✓			13	108.92
Jácome and Vázquez (2005)	24	0	24	1990–2002	Panel	✓			✓			18	132.09
Crowe and Meade (2008)[g]	56	29	27	1980–2006	Cross		✓	✓	✓	✓		16	8.26
Jácome and Vázquez (2008)	24	0	24	1985–1992	Panel	✓			✓	✓		18	72.61
Krause and Méndez (2008)	12	0	12	1980–1999	Panel				✓	✓		6	24.41
Miles (2009)	1	0	1	1980–2007	Time series				✓			4	6.47
Dumiter (2011)	20	20	0	2006–2008	Panel	✓						2	9.35
Maslowska (2011)	63	0	63	1980–2007	Panel	✓	✓	✓	✓	✓		41	28.44
Perera et al. (2013)	18	6	12	1996–2008	Panel				✓	✓		21	14.10

Posso and Tawadros (2013)[f]	56	29	27	1987–2006	Panel	✓		✓	✓	12	0.04
Alpanda and Honig (2014)	22	22	0	1980–2006	Panel			✓	✓	4	0.13
Fritt et al. (2017)[g]	29	29	0	1990–2014	Panel				✓	2	71.47

Notes:

[a]Including Bulgaria, Croatia, Czech Republic, Estonia, Hungary, Latvia, Lithuania, Poland, Slovak Republic, Slovenia, and Romania.

[b]Excluding Baltic countries.

[c]Denotes Mongolia and other emerging economies.

[d]Estimation period may differ depending on target countries.

[e]The political index reflects the degree of political influence of the government and politicians on the central bank's activities, including monetary policy, the procedure for appointing the board, and the formal goal of the bank. The economic index captures the degree of the central bank's economic freedom to pursue its policy objectives, including control of the quantity of credit to the government and the discount rate. The legal index expresses the organizational independence of the central bank stipulated in relevant laws, including the appointment, dismissal, and term of the governor and other board members as well as policy formations and limitations on lending. The comprehensive index is designed to evaluate the overall level of the central bank's independence, taking into account political, economic, and legal factors. See Cukierman (1992, pp. 373–376), Maliszewski (2000, pp. 756–760), and Maslowka (2011, p. 138) for more detailed arguments.

[f]AP is defined as the mean of the inverse of the standard errors of estimates collected from the study.

[g]Target countries include two or three CEE EU countries.

Source: Compiled by the authors.

to Piplica (2015); for non-transition studies, we chose 16 works, from Walsh (1997) to Ftiti et al. (2017). The latter were selected according to the following three criteria: (1) countries targeted for the study do not include CEE and FSU countries at all or, if they do, only data whose proportion in the observation is less than 10.0% are used; (2) the study was published in or after 1997, the year Loungani and Sheets' paper appeared; (3) with respect to the estimation period, the study reports empirical results after 1980. Non-transition studies that fulfilled the above conditions were comparable to the transition studies in terms of publication timing and the period targeted for study. Furthermore, as mentioned in the preceding section, Eijffinger and Stadhouders (2003), Dumiter (2011), and Maslowska (2011) reported not only estimates for CEE and FSU countries but for other countries of the world individually. Therefore, we included these three studies in both literature categories. As shown in Panel (b) of Table 8.2, these 16 non-transition studies vary widely in the countries targeted and empirical methodologies used and, as reported in the next section, exhibit mixed results regarding the disinflation effect of CBI, as do the 12 selected transition studies.

The total number of country observations in the 12 transition studies listed in Panel (a) of Table 8.2 is 236, of which CEE EU countries account for 49.2% (116 observations); other CEE countries, 14.0% (33 observations); and FSU countries, excluding the Baltic States, 33.9% (80 observations). In addition, five studies also used observations of Mongolia and other emerging economies, although they account for only a very small percentage.

We collected a total of 125 estimates from the transition studies (10.4 per study, on average). Their estimation period covers 24 years, from 1989 to 2012. The average estimation period is 12.3 years (median: 10 years). While 10 out of 12 studies used panel data, only four studies utilized cross-sectional data. CBI variables employed by the transition studies can be categorized into six types: legal index has the largest share and accounts for 63 or 50.4% of total estimates of transition economies. Comprehensive index follows with 54 estimates (43.2% total), while the numbers of estimates of governor term, political index, economic index, and governor turnover are only 3, 2, 2, and 1, respectively.

With respect to the non-transition studies listed in Panel (b) of Table 8.2, their total number of country observations reaches 564, in which the share of developed and developing economies account for 30.3% (171 observations) and 69.7% (393 observations), respectively. From these 16 papers, we collected a total of 212 estimates (13.3 per study, on average). The estimation period of these 212 estimates was 35 years – from 1980 to 2014 – with an average estimation period of 16.4 years (median: 13 years). Nine of 16 works performed panel data analysis, while six papers conducted cross-sectional analyses. Miles (2009) is a time-series study of Colombia. The breakdown of collected estimates of non-transition economies by CBI variable type is as follows: governor turnover accounts for 48.1% (102 estimates); followed by legal index, 33.5% (71); comprehensive index, 8.0% (17); political index, 6.6% (14); and economic index, 3.8% (8). There is no estimate of governor term. As reported above, a notable characteristic of non-transition studies is the frequent use of governor turnover in contrast to transition studies.

Because we adopted estimates of governor turnover, whose theoretically expected sign is positive (i.e., the higher the governor turnover, the lower the CBI), and those of other indexes, for which it is negative (i.e., the higher the value of the index, the higher the CBI), all together for our meta-analysis, we carried out coding by reversing the sign of the coefficient and the t value in the case of governor turnover estimates. Note that the meta-analysis and interpretation of its results in this chapter will be conducted under this condition.

Next, we outline the meta-analysis to be conducted in the next section. In this study, we employed the partial correlation coefficient (PCC) and the t value to synthesize the collected estimates. The PCC is a measure of the association of a dependent variable and the independent variable in question when other variables are held constant. The PCC is calculated in the following equation:

$$r_k = \frac{t_k}{\sqrt{t_k^2 + df_k}}, \quad k = 1, 2, \ldots, K, \tag{1}$$

where t_k and df_k denote the t value and the degree of freedom of the k-th estimate, respectively, while K denotes the total number of collected estimates. As Eq. (1) indicates, the PCC is a unitless measure; hence, empirical results reported in different scales can be compared.

The following method is used to synthesize PCCs. Suppose there are K estimates ($k = 1, 2, \ldots, K$). Here, the PCC of the k-th estimate is labeled r_k, and the corresponding population and standard deviation are labeled θ_k and s_k, respectively. We assume that $\theta_1 = \theta_2 = \ldots = \theta_K = \theta$, implying that each study in a meta-analysis estimates the common underlying population effect, and that the estimates differ only by random sampling errors. An asymptotically efficient estimator of the unknown true population parameter θ is a weighted mean by the inverse variance of each estimate:

$$\bar{R} = \sum_{k=1}^{K} w_k r_k \Big/ \sum_{k=1}^{K} w_k, \tag{2}$$

where $w_k = 1/v_k$ and $v_k = s_k^2$. The variance of the synthesized partial correlation $\bar{R}$ is given by: $1/\sum_{k=1}^{K} w_k$.

This is the meta fixed-effect model. Hereafter, we denote estimates of the meta fixed-effect model using $\overline{R_f}$. In order to utilize this method to synthesize PCCs, we need to confirm that the estimates are homogeneous. A homogeneity test uses the statistic:

$$Q_r = \sum_{k=1}^{K} w_k (r_k - \overline{R_f})^2 \sim \chi^2(K - 1), \tag{3}$$

which has a Chi-square distribution with $N - 1$ degrees of freedom. The null hypothesis is rejected if Q_r exceeds the critical value. In this case, we assume that heterogeneity exists among the studies and adopt a random-effects model that incorporates a sampling variation due to an underlying population of effect sizes as well as a study-level sampling error. If the deviation between estimates is expressed as δ_θ^2, the unconditional variance of the k-th estimate is given as $v_k^u = (v_k + \delta_\theta^2)$. In the meta random-effects model, the population θ is estimated by replacing the weight w_k with the weight $w_k^u = 1/v_k^u$ in Eq. (2).[12] For the between-studies variance component, we use the method of moments estimator computed by the next equation using the value of the homogeneity test value Q_r obtained from Eq. (3):

$$\hat{\delta}_\theta^2 = \frac{Q_r - (K-1)}{\sum_{k-1}^{K} w_k^u - (\sum_{k-1}^{K} w_k^{u^2} / \sum_{k-1}^{K} w_k^u)}. \tag{4}$$

Hereafter, we denote estimates of the meta random-effects model as $\overline{R}_r$.

We combine t values using the next equation:

$$\overline{T}_w = \sum_{k=1}^{K} w_k t_k \bigg/ \sqrt{\sum_{k=1}^{K} w_k^2} \sim N(0,1). \tag{5}$$

Here, w_k is the weight assigned to the t value of the k-th estimate. As the weight w_k in Eq. (5), we utilize a 10-point scale to mirror the quality level of each relevant study $(1 \leq w_k \leq 10)$.[13] Moreover, we report not only the combined t value $\overline{T}_w$ weighted by the quality level of the study, but also the unweighted combined t value $\overline{T}_u$. As a supplemental statistic for evaluating the reliability of the above-mentioned combined t value, we also report Rosenthal's fail-safe N (*fsN*) as computed by the next formula:[14]

$$fsN\,(p = 0.05) = \left(\frac{\sum_{k=1}^{K} t_k}{1.645}\right)^2 - K. \tag{6}$$

Following the synthesis of collected estimates, we conduct MRA to explore the factors causing heterogeneity between selected studies. To this end, we estimate the meta-regression model:

$$y_k = \beta_0 + \sum_{n=1}^{N} \beta_n x_{kn} + e_k, k = 1, 2, \cdots, K, \tag{7}$$

where y_k is either the PCC (i.e., r_k) or the t value of the k-th estimate; x_{kn} denotes a meta-independent variable that captures relevant characteristics of an empirical study and explains its systematic variation from other empirical results in the literature; β_n denotes the meta-regression coefficient to be estimated; and e_k is the meta-regression disturbance term (Stanley and Jarrell, 2005). To check the statistical robustness of coefficient β_n, we perform an MRA using the following seven estimators: (1) the cluster-robust ordinary least squares (OLS) estimator, which clusters the collected estimates by study and computes robust standard errors; the cluster-robust weighted least squares (WLS) estimator, which uses either (2) the above-mentioned quality level of the study, (3) the number of observations, (4) the inverse of the standard error (1/*SE*), or (5) the inverse of the number of estimates reported per study (1/*EST*) as an analytical weight; (6) the cluster-robust unbalanced random-effects panel estimator; and (7) the cluster-robust fixed-effects estimator.[15]

Testing for publication selection bias is an important issue. In this chapter, we examine this problem by using the funnel plot and the Galbraith plot as well as by estimating a meta-regression model that is designed especially for this purpose. If the funnel plot is not bilaterally symmetrical but is deflected to one side, then an arbitrary manipulation of the study area in question is suspected, in the sense that estimates in favor of a specific conclusion (i.e., estimates with an expected sign) are more frequently published (type I publication selection bias). Meanwhile, the Galbraith plot is used for testing another arbitrary manipulation in the sense that estimates with higher statistical significance are more frequently published, irrespective of their sign (type II publication selection bias). In general, the statistic, |(the *k*-th estimate − the true effect) /SE_k|, should not exceed the critical value of ±1.96 by more than 5% of the total estimates. In other words, when a true effect does not exist and there is no publication selection bias, the reported *t* values should vary randomly around zero, and 95% of them should be within a range of ±1.96. The Galbraith plot tests whether the above relationship can be observed in the statistical significance of the collected estimates, and, thereby, identifies the presence of type II publication selection bias.

In addition to the above two scatter plots, we also report estimates of the meta-regression models that have been developed to examine in a more rigorous manner the two types of publication selection bias and the presence of the true effect.

We can test for type I publication selection bias by regressing the *t* value of the *k*-th estimate on the inverse of the standard error (1/*SE*) using the following equation:

$$t_k = \beta_0 + \beta_1(1/SE_k) + v_k, \tag{8}$$

thereby testing the null hypothesis that the intercept term β_0 is equal to zero. In Eq. (8), v_k is the error term. When the intercept term β_0 is statistically significantly different from zero, we can conclude that the distribution of the effect sizes is asymmetric. For this reason, this test is called the funnel asymmetry test (FAT). Meanwhile, type II publication selection bias can be tested by estimating the next equation, where the left side of Eq. (8) is replaced with the absolute *t* value:

$$|t_k| = \beta_0 + \beta_1(1/SE_k) + v_k, \tag{9}$$

thereby testing the null hypothesis of $\beta_0 = 0$ in the same way as the FAT.

Even if there is a publication selection bias, a genuine effect may exist in the available empirical evidence. Stanley and Doucouliagos (2012) proposed examining this possibility by testing the null hypothesis that the coefficient β_1 is equal to zero in Eq. (8). The rejection of the null hypothesis implies the presence of a genuine (i.e., statistically significant non-zero) effect. This is the precision effect test (PET). Moreover, they also state that an estimate of the publication-selection-bias-adjusted effect size can be obtained by estimating the following equation, which has no intercept:

$$t_k = \beta_0 SE_k + \beta_1(1/SE_k) + v_k, \tag{10}$$

thereby obtaining the coefficient β_1. This means that if the null hypothesis of $\beta_1 = 0$ is rejected, then the non-zero effect actually exists in the literature, and the coefficient β_1 can be regarded as its estimate. Stanley and Doucouliagos (2012) call this procedure the precision effect estimate with standard error (PEESE) approach. To test the robustness of the regression coefficient, we estimate Eqs. (8) to (10) above using not only the OLS estimator, but also the cluster-robust OLS estimator and the unbalanced panel estimator,[16] both of which treat possible heterogeneity among the studies.

As mentioned above, we basically follow the FAT-PET-PEESE approach advocated by Stanley and Doucouliagos (2012) as the test procedures for publication selection. However, we also include a test of type II publication selection bias using Eq. (9); this kind of bias is very likely in the literature of transition economies.[17]

5. Meta-analysis

In this section, we will compare the transition and non-transition studies listed in Table 8.2 by meta-analysis, using a total of 337 collected estimates, following the procedure described in the previous section. More specifically, in Subsection 5.1 we will synthesize the collected estimates. In Subsection 5.2, MRA of heterogeneity among studies will be performed. Then in Subsection 5.3, we will test the publication selection bias and the presence of genuine empirical evidence in each study field.

5.1. Synthesis of the collected estimates

Table 8.3 shows descriptive statistics of the PCC and t values of collected estimates, and Figure 8.2 shows their frequency distribution. As shown in Panels (a) of Table 8.3 and Figure 8.2, the PCCs of the transition studies show a skewed distribution in the negative direction with a mode of 0.0. According to Cohen's (1988) criteria for evaluation of correlation coefficients, 36.0% (45 estimates) do not show any practical relationship between CBI and inflation in the transition economies ($|r| < 0.1$), while 32.8% (41 estimates) report a small disinflation effect of CBI ($0.1 \leq |r| < 0.3$); the remaining 31.2% (39 estimates) indicate a medium or large effect ($0.3 \leq |r|$). Since 77 of 125 estimates take a negative PCC, empirical results that support the presence of a disinflation

Table 8.3 Descriptive statistics of the partial correlation coefficients and the *t* values of collected estimates

(a) PCC

	Number of collected estimates (K)	Mean	Median	S.D.	Max.	Min.	Kurtosis	Skewness
Transition studies	125	−0.135	−0.086	0.280	0.477	−0.798	3.007	−0.455
Non-transition studies	212	−0.189	−0.187	0.222	0.445	−0.817	3.983	−0.251

(b) t value

	Number of collected estimates (K)	Mean	Median	S.D.	Max.	Min.	Kurtosis	Skewness
Transition studies	125	−0.963	−0.500	2.424	5.833	−6.000	3.022	0.185
Non-transition studies	212	−1.903	−2.127	2.284	4.510	−9.820	5.748	−0.886

Note: With regard to the estimates of governor turnover, their signs are reversed to use for meta-analysis.
Source: Authors' calculation.

effect of CBI in transition economies account for 61.6% of the total collected estimates.[18]

With respect to the PCC of non-transition studies, although its distribution range is almost the same as in the case of the transition studies, the bias in the negative direction is obviously stronger than that of the transition studies. In fact, the mode of the non-transition studies is −0.4; moreover, 171 PCCs, or 80.7% of their estimates, are negative. As a result, the number of estimates that indicate a practical effect of CBI on inflation ($0.1 \leq |r|$) reaches 148 (69.8%) of 212, which exceeds that of the transition studies.

According to Panels (b) of Table 8.3 and Figure 8.2, although the mode of the *t* values of the estimates obtained from the transition studies is 0.5, they show not only a long, skewed distribution in the negative direction but also that estimates of −2.0 or under account for 34.4% (43 estimates) of the total. On the other hand, with respect to the *t* values of the estimates collected from the non-transition studies, not only is the mode −3.0, but also 110 (51.9%) of 212 estimates have a *t* value equal to or less than −2.0. Judging from the distribution of PCCs and *t* values, it can be said that those studies that target developed and developing economies have detected a negative impact of CBI on inflation that is larger in

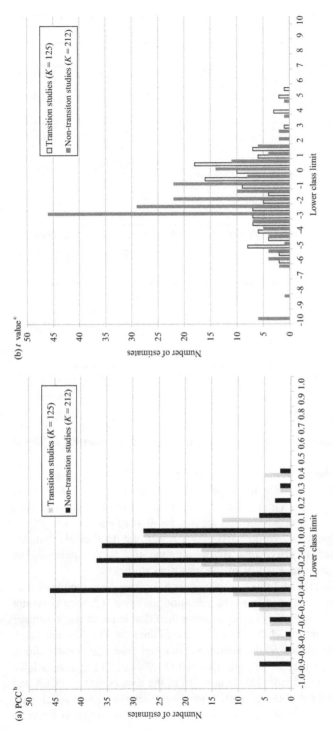

Figure 8.2 Distribution of partial correlation coefficients and *t* values[a]

Notes:
[a] With regard to estimates of governor turnover, their signs are reversed to use for meta-analysis.
[b] Shapiro-Wilk normality test for transition studies: $V = 4.184$, $z = 3.213$, $p = 0.001$; non-transition studies: $V = 4.684$, $z = 3.563$, $p = 0.000$.
[c] Shapiro-Wilk normality test for transition studies: $V = 3.018$, $z = 2.480$, $p = 0.007$; non-transition studies: $V = 13.328$, $z = 5.976$, $p = 0.000$.
Source: Authors' illustration.

effect size and more statistically significant than in those studies that investigated transition economies.

The evaluation above is also supported by the results of meta-synthesis. Columns (1) in Panels (a) and (b) of Table 8.4 report the synthesized PCCs of the transition studies and the non-transition studies, respectively. If we adopt the synthesized effect size $\overline{R_r}$ of the random-effects model as the reference value in accordance with the homogeneity test, the synthesized effect size of the non-transition studies using all collected estimates surpasses that of the transition studies in terms of its absolute value; the former is −0.184, while the latter is −0.109. Hence, the absolute value of the former is 0.075 larger than that of the latter. In other words, as compared to the transition studies, the non-transition studies report an approximately 68.8% greater effect size as a whole of literature. In addition, as Column (2) of Table 8.4 shows, not only in terms of unconditionally combined t value $\overline{T_u}$ but also in terms of the combined t value $\overline{T_w}$ weighted by the quality level of the study, the non-transition studies exceed the transition studies by a large margin. The same applies for Rosenthal's fail-safe N. In this regard, however, we note that, common to both study areas, the value of $\overline{T_w}$ is substantially lower than the value of $\overline{T_u}$, suggesting that there may exist a strong negative correlation between the statistical significance of the estimates and the research quality, irrespective of the target region.

Further, we also conducted meta-synthesis of estimates, focusing on differences in target countries (for the transition studies), estimation periods, data types, and CBI variable types. Based on these results, reported in Table 8.4, we confirmed the following four points: First, transition studies that use observations, of which the share of CEE EU countries is more than 50%, report higher effect sizes than those that use observations, of which the share of CEE EU countries is less than 50%. Second, with respect to transition studies for which the estimation period includes the 2000s and those that used panel data, the effect sizes became smaller than those of studies for which the estimation period was limited to the 1990s or those that used cross-sectional data. The same observations apply to non-transition studies as well. Third, in transition studies, not only did differences in CBI variable types result in a large difference in terms of the synthesized effect sizes, ranging from −0.798 (governor turnover) to −0.056 (legal index), but also estimates that used the economic index could not reject the null hypothesis. On the other hand, in non-transition studies, the synthesized effect sizes had a narrower range from −0.277 (governor turnover) to −0.062 (comprehensive index), and the political index showed an insignificant synthesis. Fourth, in transition studies, although the unconditionally combined t value $\overline{T_u}$ is significant and negative in all 12 cases, the combined t value $\overline{T_w}$ weighted by the quality level of the study dropped below the 10% significance level in six cases, while there is only one similar case in the non-transition studies.

The above results from the meta-synthesis of collected estimates strongly suggest that the empirical results of the transition studies concerning the disinflation effect of CBI are inferior to those of comparable studies in terms of

Table 8.4 Synthesis of collected estimates[a]

(a) Transition studies

	Number of estimates (K)	(1) Synthesis of PCCs			(2) Combination of t values			
		Fixed-effect model (z value)[b]	Random-effects model (z value)[b]	Test of homogeneity[c]	Unweighted combination (p value)	Weighted combination (p value)	Median of t values	Fail-safe N (fsN)
All studies	125	-0.033*** (-5.74)	-0.109*** (-6.26)	809.700***	-10.768*** (0.00)	-1.800** (0.04)	-0.500	5231
Comparison in terms of target country								
Studies that use observations, of which the share of CEE EU countries is more than 50%	49	-0.110*** (-7.72)	-0.138*** (-4.05)	194.418***	-7.357*** (0.00)	-1.615* (0.05)	-0.500	931
Studies that use observations, of which the share of CEE EU countries is less than 50%	76	-0.018** (-2.83)	-0.094*** (-4.70)	580.575***	-7.902*** (0.00)	-1.172 (0.12)	-0.500	1678
Comparison in terms of estimation period								
Studies in which the estimation period range is within the 1990s	62	-0.179*** (-10.44)	-0.165*** (-4.92)	199.579***	-9.020*** (0.00)	-1.288* (0.10)	-0.929	1802
Studies in which the estimation period includes the 2000s	63	-0.014** (-2.35)	-0.067*** (-3.35)	528.483***	-6.219*** (0.00)	-1.305* (0.10)	-0.270	837
Comparison in terms of data type								
Studies that employ cross-sectional data	45	-0.305*** (-9.08)	-0.248*** (-4.45)	115.347***	-7.535*** (0.00)	-1.625** (0.05)	-0.857	899
Studies that employ panel data	80	-0.025*** (-4.23)	-0.072*** (-4.07)	626.923**	-7.809*** (0.00)	-1.180 (0.12)	-0.352	1723
Comparison in terms of CBI variable								
Studies that use the comprehensive index	54	-0.071*** (-6.59)	-0.138*** (-4.47)	384.329***	-9.320*** (0.00)	-1.450* (0.07)	-0.902	1679

	Number of estimates (K)	(1) Synthesis of PCCs		Test of homogeneity	(2) Combination of t values		Median of t values	Fail-safe N (fsN)
		Fixed-effect model (z value)[b]	Random-effects model (z value)[b]		Unweighted combination (p value)	Weighted combination (p value)		
Studies that use the political index	2	−0.395*** (−3.06)	−0.395*** (−3.06)	0.428	−3.069*** (0.00)	−0.538 (0.30)	−2.170	5
Studies that use the economic index	2	−0.476*** (−4.01)	−0.436 (−1.64)	4.829**	−3.781*** (0.00)	−0.663 (0.25)	−2.674	9
Studies that use the legal index	63	−0.013 (−1.88)	−0.056** (−2.73)	346.823***	−4.245*** (0.00)	−0.779 (0.22)	−0.250	356
Studies that use governor turnover	1	−0.798*** (−5.12)	−0.798*** (−5.12)	0.000	−5.120*** (0.00)	−5.120*** (0.00)	−5.120	9
Studies that use governor term	3	−0.392** (−2.31)	−0.376** (−2.02)	2.315	−1.964** (0.02)	−0.218 (0.41)	−0.500	1

(b) Non-transition studies

	Number of estimates (K)	(1) Synthesis of PCCs		Test of homogeneity	(2) Combination of t values		Median of t values	Fail-safe N (fsN)
		Fixed-effect model (z value)[b]	Random-effects model (z value)[b]		Unweighted combination (p value)	Weighted combination (p value)		
All studies	212	−0.135*** (−25.46)	−0.184*** (−13.37)	1220.740***	−27.712*** (0.00)	−4.627*** (0.00)	−2.127	59951
Comparison in terms of estimation period								
Studies in which the estimation period range is within the 1990s	88	−0.172*** (−14.92)	−0.194*** (−11.62)	151.072***	−15.137*** (0.00)	−2.325*** (0.01)	−2.310	7363
Studies in which the estimation period includes the 2000s	124	−0.125*** (−20.95)	−0.175*** (−9.54)	1056.148***	−23.483*** (0.00)	−4.201*** (0.00)	−1.966	25145
Comparison in terms of data type								
Studies that employ cross-sectional data	84	−0.239*** (−14.86)	−0.232*** (−11.03)	136.399***	−13.884*** (0.00)	−2.202** (0.02)	−2.332	5900
Studies that employ panel data	124	−0.118*** (−20.74)	−0.162*** (−9.53)	1012.276***	−23.387*** (0.00)	−4.034*** (0.00)	−1.946	24939

(Continued)

Table 8.4 (Continued)

(b) Non-transition studies

	Number of estimates (K)	(1) Synthesis of PCCs			(2) Combination of t values			
		Fixed-effect model (z value)[b]	Random-effects model (z value)[b]	Test of homogeneity[c]	Unweighted combination (p value)	Weighted combination (p value)	Median of t values	Fail-safe N (fsN)
Studies that employ time-series data	4	-0.268*** (-8.00)	-0.273*** (-5.94)	5.088	-7.906*** (0.00)	-1.581* (0.06)	-4.044	88
Comparison in terms of CBI variable								
Studies that use the comprehensive index	17	-0.059*** (-4.85)	-0.062** (-2.31)	72.911***	-4.825*** (0.00)	-1.495* (0.07)	-1.850	129
Studies that use the political index	14	-0.041** (-2.28)	-0.103 (-1.30)	216.032***	-3.749*** (0.00)	-0.789 (0.22)	-0.021	59
Studies that use the economic index	8	-0.093*** (-4.65)	-0.102*** (-3.23)	15.634**	-4.834*** (0.00)	-1.458* (0.07)	-2.565	61
Studies that use the legal index	71	-0.126*** (-12.64)	-0.120*** (-5.24)	312.309***	-11.030*** (0.00)	-1.938** (0.03)	-0.896	3121
Studies that use governor term	102	-0.207*** (-24.05)	-0.277*** (-13.76)	463.389***	-26.037*** (0.00)	-3.826*** (0.00)	-2.600	25451

Notes:

[a]With regard to the estimates of governor turnover, their signs are reversed to use for meta-analysis.

[b]Null hypothesis: The synthesized effect size is zero.

[c]Null hypothesis: Effect sizes are homogeneous.

***, **, and * denote statistical significance at the 1%, 5%, and 10% levels, respectively.

Source: Authors' estimation

both effect size and statistical significance. From this result, we can argue that, if independence from the government and other economic entities is at the same level, the price control of the central banks in CEE and FSU countries is weaker than that of their counterparts in the rest of the world. However, as hinted in Cukierman et al. (2002), it is likely that, since CBI variables used in transition studies have greater measurement errors than do those employed in non-transition studies, researchers of transition economies were not able to capture the disinflation effect of CBI as effectively as were those who studied other developed and developing economies. At the same time, it is also possible that a strong tendency of publication selection bias exists in studies of developed and developing economies that causes their empirical evidence to tend to over-emphasize the impact of CBI on inflation. We will judge which interpretation is most relevant in Subsection 5.3.

As shown in Table 8.4, studies of transition economies that used the legal index reported unsatisfactory empirical results, particularly in terms of effect size, as compared to those that used other indexes and non-transition studies that employed the legal index. This finding indicates the possibility of the overestimation of CBI in the CEE and FSU countries alluded to in the Cukierman proposition mentioned in Section 3. However, the meta-synthesis in this section has a serious problem, in that it does not consider the differences in study conditions between previous works. Therefore, in the next subsection, we will conduct an MRA to examine whether the results of meta-synthesis can be reproduced while simultaneously controlling for a series of study conditions.

5.2. Meta-regression analysis of heterogeneity among studies

In this subsection, we will estimate the regression equation defined in Eq. (7) to identify factors that may cause heterogeneity among studies of transition economies and between transition and non-transition studies. As explained in Section 4, we will estimate a meta-regression model that takes the PCC or t value as a dependent variable. As meta-independent variables, we will control for the estimator used, the inflation variable type, the lagged structure of the CBI variable, the presence of an interaction term(s) with a CBI variable, and the degree of freedom[19] as well as the quality level of the study, in addition to the composition of target countries, the estimation period, the data type, and the CBI variable type that are mentioned in the previous subsection. Appendix B lists the name, definition, and descriptive statistics of these meta-independent variables.[20]

Table 8.5 shows the estimation results concerning heterogeneity among transition studies.[21] As reported in the table, the Breusch-Pagan test cannot reject the null hypothesis that the variance of the study-level individual effects is zero. Therefore, estimates of the random-effects method are rarely different from those of the OLS model. On the other hand, although WLS models are sensitive to the choice of analytical weights, many variables are uniformly estimated, with statistical significance at the 10% level or less. In other words, the estimates in Table 8.5 are robust beyond the difference estimator.

Table 8.5 Meta-regression analysis of heterogeneity among transition studies[a]

(a) Dependent variable—PCC

Estimator (analytical weight in robust OLS parentheses) / Meta-independent variable (default)/ Model	Cluster-robust OLS	Cluster-robust WLS [Quality level]	Cluster-robust WLS [N]	Cluster-robust WLS [1/SE]	Cluster-robust WLS [1/EST]	Cluster-robust random-effects panel GLS	Cluster-robust fixed-effects panel LSDV
	[1]	[2]	[3]	[4]	[5]	[6][b]	[7][c]
Composition of target countries (CEE EU countries)							
Proportion of other CEEs	1.4242* (0.706)	2.0499* (1.092)	0.5656 (0.841)	0.6783 (0.773)	2.0122** (0.677)	1.4242** (0.706)	10.6743** (4.389)
Proportion of FSUs	2.2703*** (0.653)	1.9181** (0.753)	2.0115*** (0.518)	2.1847** (0.917)	2.9682*** (0.677)	2.2703*** (0.653)	dropped
Proportion of non-CEE/FSU countries	4.9907 (4.518)	−3.7185 (4.640)	11.9408** (4.855)	5.8754 (5.890)	3.7212 (2.346)	4.9907 (4.518)	dropped
Estimation period							
First year of estimation	0.0636** (0.025)	0.0755 (0.043)	0.0879* (0.042)	0.0829** (0.034)	0.0858*** (0.018)	0.0636*** (0.025)	0.1251*** (0.003)
Length of estimation	0.0515*** (0.013)	0.0061 (0.008)	0.0540** (0.019)	0.0418 (0.028)	0.0786*** (0.024)	0.0515*** (0.013)	−0.0719** (0.029)
Data type (cross-sectional data)							
Panel data	−0.9371*** (0.209)	−0.1292 (0.112)	−1.5773** (0.669)	−1.0981* (0.530)	−0.9656*** (0.140)	−0.9371*** (0.209)	−0.7772* (0.413)
Estimator (other than OLS)							
OLS	−1.4334*** (0.271)	−0.3024** (0.131)	−2.0902** (0.762)	−1.4469** (0.610)	−1.4567*** (0.329)	−1.4334*** (0.271)	dropped
Inflation variable type (normal use)							
Transformed variable	0.9467*** (0.271)	0.1384 (0.349)	0.4877 (0.470)	0.5471 (0.717)	1.2516** (0.516)	0.9467*** (0.271)	dropped
Log value	2.2067*** (0.338)	1.0081*** (0.286)	2.0867*** (0.469)	1.9816** (0.794)	2.4233*** (0.554)	2.2067*** (0.338)	0.1298*** (0.025)
Ranking value	2.0197*** (0.310)	0.8461** (0.290)	1.9555*** (0.454)	1.8377** (0.757)	2.2511*** (0.556)	2.0197*** (0.310)	dropped

CBI variable (comprehensive index)

	[8]	[9]	[10]	[11]	[12]	[13]	[14]
Political index	-0.0634 (0.049)	-0.0605* (0.028)	-0.0529 (0.039)	-0.0431*** (0.004)	-0.1940 (0.119)	-0.0634 (0.049)	-0.0005 (0.068)
Economic index	-0.0904 (0.139)	0.0533 (0.081)	-0.0605 (0.127)	0.1061*** (0.007)	-0.1267 (0.203)	-0.0904 (0.139)	-0.0275 (0.116)
Legal index	-0.0189 (0.031)	0.0175 (0.030)	0.0147 (0.012)	0.0324 (0.024)	-0.0309 (0.045)	-0.0189 (0.031)	0.0165 (0.015)
Governor turnover	-0.4294*** (0.033)	-0.3510*** (0.067)	-0.3826*** (0.052)	-0.1741*** (0.049)	-0.6641*** (0.213)	-0.4294*** (0.033)	-0.3804*** (0.020)
Governor term	0.4046*** (0.064)	0.3457*** (0.015)	0.3329** (0.127)	0.4636** (0.192)	0.3914*** (0.050)	0.4046*** (0.064)	0.3466*** (0.005)
Lagged CBI variable (non-lagged variable)	-1.0463*** (0.121)	-0.5589*** (0.152)	-1.2712** (0.433)	-1.1546*** (0.371)	-1.1099*** (0.221)	-1.0463*** (0.121)	dropped
With an interaction variable(s)	-0.0629 (0.051)	-0.0117 (0.019)	-0.0283*** (0.002)	-0.5446 (0.505)	-0.0982 (0.085)	-0.0629 (0.051)	-0.0273*** (0.001)
Degree of freedom and research quality							
√Degree of freedom	-0.0982*** (0.018)	-0.0195 (0.015)	-0.1062*** (0.029)	-0.0703* (0.033)	-0.1182*** (0.035)	-0.0982*** (0.018)	-0.1543 (0.089)
Quality level	0.0754*** (0.012)		0.1324* (0.062)	0.1091* (0.053)	0.0881*** (0.014)	0.0754*** (0.012)	dropped
Intercept	-125.2471** (49.556)	-150.6931 (86.738)	-173.2367* (83.738)	-164.0780** (67.245)	-169.4504*** (36.302)	-125.2471** (49.556)	-248.2229*** (4.796)
K	125	125	125	125	125	125	125
R²	0.5365	0.4863	0.4021	0.2161	0.7609	0.5365	0.0416

(b) Dependent variable—t value

Estimator (analytical weight in robust parentheses)	Cluster-robust OLS	Cluster-robust WLS [Quality level]	Cluster-robust WLS [N]	Cluster-robust WLS [1/SE]	Cluster-robust WLS [1/EST]	Cluster-robust random-effects panel GLS	Cluster-robust fixed-effects panel LSDV
Meta-independent variable (default)/Model	[8]	[9]	[10]	[11]	[12]	[13][d]	[14][e]
Composition of target countries (CEE EU countries)							
Proportion of other CEEs	4.7896 (6.592)	7.7983 (8.600)	-1.9838 (9.786)	-1.3688 (7.165)	7.6928 (7.291)	4.7896 (6.592)	17.0992 (18.312)

(Continued)

Table 8.5 (Continued)

(b) Dependent variable—t value

Estimator (analytical weight in parentheses) / Meta-independent variable (default)/Model	Cluster-robust OLS [8]	Cluster-robust WLS [Quality level] [9]	Cluster-robust WLS [N] [10]	Cluster-robust WLS [1/SE] [11]	Cluster-robust WLS [1/EST] [12]	Cluster-robust random-effects panel GLS [13]^d	Cluster-robust fixed-effects panel LSDV [14]^e
Proportion of FSUs	7.5241** (2.831)	4.8022 (4.066)	16.0649 (9.818)	21.2204** (9.100)	9.9208** (3.308)	7.5241*** (2.831)	dropped
Proportion of non-CEE/FSU countries	65.0070* (30.319)	20.5790 (24.364)	149.2469* (78.650)	69.1624 (68.109)	55.8640*** (17.074)	65.0070** (30.319)	dropped
Estimation period							
First year of estimation	0.2388* (0.121)	0.2612 (0.215)	1.1055 (0.919)	1.0819 (0.719)	0.3292*** (0.092)	0.2388** (0.121)	0.5033*** (0.013)
Length of estimation	0.1304 (0.137)	-0.0982 (0.056)	0.4255 (0.306)	0.4348 (0.296)	0.2363 (0.208)	0.1304 (0.137)	-0.5777*** (0.117)
Data type (cross-sectional data)							
Panel data	-6.1964** (2.452)	-1.9906*** (0.595)	-18.0995 (12.733)	-12.7770 (9.758)	-5.6457** (1.868)	-6.1964** (2.452)	-4.6634** (1.677)
Estimator (other than OLS)							
OLS	-7.3988** (3.315)	-1.6870* (0.797)	-21.1925 (14.914)	-14.5888 (11.346)	-6.5700** (3.275)	-7.3988** (3.315)	dropped
Inflation variable type (normal use)							
Transformed variable	3.2719 (3.055)	0.6324 (2.000)	0.6839 (5.240)	4.1127 (7.481)	4.1979 (4.614)	3.2719 (3.055)	dropped
Log value	9.7662** (3.796)	3.4682 (2.112)	14.4993* (7.206)	16.6067* (8.659)	9.5455 (5.361)	9.7662*** (3.796)	0.7140*** (0.106)
Ranking value	8.5236** (3.727)	2.4337 (2.150)	13.7394 (7.811)	15.4010 (9.271)	8.4527 (5.396)	8.5236** (3.727)	dropped
CBI variable (comprehensive index)							
Political index	-0.4471* (0.226)	-0.2224 (0.257)	-0.1998 (0.381)	-0.0374 (0.033)	-1.0198 (0.792)	-0.4471* (0.226)	0.1851 (0.372)
Economic index	-0.9506 (1.249)	0.3601 (0.684)	-0.5538 (1.033)	0.8113*** (0.072)	-0.7964 (1.496)	-0.9506 (1.249)	-0.3184 (0.803)

Legal index	0.0706 (0.273)	0.2623 (0.331)	0.2784 (0.196)	0.7405 (0.434)	0.0742 (0.440)	0.0706 (0.273)	0.3739* (0.198)
Governor turnover	-3.2621*** (0.211)	-2.8767*** (0.289)	-2.8572*** (0.431)	-1.8584** (0.621)	-4.4606*** (1.232)	-3.2621*** (0.211)	-2.8306*** (0.089)
Governor term	2.0479*** (0.475)	1.6417*** (0.066)	1.5585 (1.235)	3.0388 (1.830)	1.8598*** (0.280)	2.0479*** (0.475)	1.5801*** (0.021)
Lagged CBI variable (non-lagged variable)	-4.6232*** (1.496)	-1.9592* (0.946)	-12.5512 (9.010)	-11.2156 (7.345)	-4.2637* (2.064)	-4.6232*** (1.496)	dropped
With an interaction variable(s)	-1.2289** (0.439)	-0.8665*** (0.054)	-0.9100*** (0.034)	-10.3062 (7.169)	-1.4046** (0.625)	-1.2289*** (0.439)	-0.8872*** (0.004)
Degree of freedom and research quality							
√Degree of freedom	-0.3641 (0.232)	0.0312 (0.105)	-0.8379 (0.549)	-0.5855 (0.404)	-0.4000 (0.328)	-0.3641 (0.232)	-1.0924** (0.370)
Quality level	0.3887* (0.205)		1.5918 (1.229)	1.2734 (1.032)	0.4047* (0.199)	0.3887* (0.205)	dropped
Intercept	-467.7399* (245.422)	-520.8265 (430.919)	-2187.8780 (1823.257)	-2146.3340 (1426.486)	-649.8844*** (187.209)	-467.7399* (245.422)	-987.8587*** (19.062)
K	125	125	125	125	125	125	125
R^2	0.3409	0.1690	0.1451	0.2344	0.5207	0.3409	0.0234

Notes:

[a] With regard to the estimates of governor turnover, their signs are reversed to use for meta-analysis.

[b] Breusch-Pagan test: $\chi^2 = 0.00$, $p = 1.000$.

[c] Hausman test: $\chi^2 = 13.67$, $p = 0.322$.

[d] Breusch-Pagan test: $\chi^2 = 0.00$, $p = 1.000$.

[e] Hausman test: $\chi^2 = 2.20$, $p = 0.999$.

Figures in parentheses beneath the regression coefficients are robust standard errors. ***, **, and * denote statistical significance at the 1%, 5%, and 10% levels, respectively.

Source: Authors' estimation. See Appendix B for definitions and descriptive statistics of independent variables.

On the basis of meta-independent variables that are statistically significant and have the same sign (positive or negative) in more than five of seven models (four of six models in the case of a lack of relevant estimates in fixed-effects models [7] and [14]), we indicate the following six points related to factors that cause significant differences in the empirical results in studies of transition economies.

First, the composition of target countries is a factor that strongly affects empirical findings from transition studies. In fact, in Table 8.5, the proportion of other CEEs and FSUs in Panel (a) and the proportion of FSUs in Panel (b) show a significant and positive estimate in many models. This result implies that studies that are inclined to research EU member states tend to report larger and statistically more significant effects of CBI on inflation, ceteris paribus. It is likely that, in CEE EU countries, a closer nexus between CBI and price fluctuation emerged as compared with non-EU former socialist countries, thanks to their advances in the economic transition, including banking reforms.[22]

Second, the estimation period also strongly impacts the effect size of the estimates. In other words, the closer the first year of the estimation period is to the present and the longer the length of the estimation, the lower the size of the negative impact of CBI on inflation tends to be. The decline of the relative weight of the data regarding the hyperinflation observed in the early 1990s is considered to be closely related to this result.

Third, in contrast to the results of meta-synthesis reported in Table 8.4, if other study conditions are equal, those studies that employed panel data tend to obtain evidence supporting the disinflation effect of CBI, both in terms of the effect size and statistical significance. As compared to using cross-sectional data, using panel data may work favorably for examining the relationship between price fluctuations and CBI by virtue of its larger volume of information. Meanwhile, a similar interpretation can apply to those studies that used the OLS estimator; however, it seems that the main reason for this result is the use of other estimators that take into account country-level fixed effects; the heterogeneity of variance and the endogeneity of dependent and independent variables tend to more strictly assess the effect of CBI.

Fourth, studies that used transformed inflation variables, as compared to those that used price variables without any transformation, tend to more conservatively assess the impact of CBI on inflation. The transformation of variables to smooth price fluctuations might have a mitigating effect on the empirical evaluation of the correlation between the steep price increases observed in the early stage of transition and a low level of CBI.

Fifth, as compared to those studies that used the comprehensive index as a CBI variable, those that used governor turnover tended to obtain estimates that emphasized the negative impact of CBI on inflation more strongly, not only in terms of the effect size but also in terms of the statistical significance.[23] It is also noteworthy that there is no robustly significant difference between those studies that employed political, economic, or legal indexes and those that used a comprehensive index. As argued in Section 2, it is possible that the presence of heterodox countries, such as the Kyrgyz Republic and Hungary, where the promotion of the institutional independence of the central bank and banking reform progress as a whole were not necessarily closely linked, could provide background as to why these pro forma indexes have weaker explanatory power than does governor turnover. Furthermore, the result that the meta-independent variable that captures the use of a lagged CBI variable is estimated to be significant and negative in many models indicates the importance of taking into account the time lag effect of CBI for examining its correlation with inflation.

Sixth, there is a tendency for stricter empirical evaluation of the disinflation effect of CBI in transition economies as the quality of studies increases. This result is consistent with the findings mentioned in the previous subsection.

In sum, the estimation results of Table 8.5 strongly suggest that a series of differences in study conditions and research quality have resulted in significant differences in the empirical results reported in studies concerning transition economies.

Next, we will analyze the relative robustness of the disinflation effect of CBI in transition economies as compared with other developed and developing economies, with the goal of evaluating the substance of the central bank reforms in the CEE and FSU countries in relation to the Cukierman proposition, discussed above. To this end, using all estimates collected from both transition and non-transition studies, we regressed the PCC and *t* values on a dummy variable that specifies the estimates collected from the transition studies by a value of 1, controlling study conditions from the estimation period to the quality level of the study.

Table 8.6 shows the results. In both Panels (a) and (b) of the table, the dummy for the transition studies is not robustly significant. In other words, if a series of study conditions is held constant, no statistically significant differences are found between the empirical results reported in transition studies and those in non-transition studies, irrespective of the difference in the dependent variable.[24] In addition, even when we limited observations to estimates of the legal CBI index, it did not show robust estimates.[25] These results imply that, in terms of the degree of linkage between CBI and inflation, there is not much difference between transition economies and the rest of the world. The concern with central bank reforms in CEE and FSU countries from the viewpoint of the disinflation effect of CBI, triggered by the argument in Cukierman et al. (2002) (namely, the Cukierman proposition), is probably unfounded if policy developments in the 2000s are taken into consideration. In this sense, we can assess that the policy efforts in the former socialist countries actually led to substantial results.[26]

5.3. Assessment of publication selection bias

Last, we will examine publication selection bias and the presence of genuine empirical evidence, following the methodology described in Section 4.

Table 8.6 Meta-regression analysis of the relative robustness of the disinflation effect of central bank independence in transition economies[a]

(a) Dependent variable—PCC

Estimator (analytical weight in parentheses) / Meta-independent variable (default)/ Model	Cluster-robust OLS [1]	Cluster-robust WLS [Quality level] [2]	Cluster-robust WLS [N] [3]	Cluster-robust WLS [1/SE] [4]	Cluster-robust WLS [1/EST] [5]	Cluster-robust random-effects panel GLS [6][b]	Cluster-robust fixed-effects panel LSDV [7][c]
Study type (non-transition studies)							
Transition studies	-0.0814 (0.054)	-0.1147* (0.057)	0.0092 (0.042)	-0.0053 (0.033)	-0.1263* (0.067)	-0.0861 (0.079)	-0.0896 (0.325)
Estimation period							
First year of estimation	0.0067 (0.005)	0.0101** (0.005)	0.0054 (0.004)	-0.0007 (0.003)	0.0181*** (0.006)	0.0110 (0.007)	0.0300 (0.037)
Length of estimation	0.0008 (0.003)	0.0031 (0.004)	0.0019 (0.003)	-0.0021 (0.003)	0.0017 (0.004)	0.0086** (0.004)	0.0351** (0.016)
Data type (cross-sectional data)							
Time-series data	-0.0750 (0.105)	-0.0320 (0.102)	-0.0790 (0.077)	0.0483 (0.086)	-0.0921 (0.130)	-0.1375 (0.122)	dropped
Panel data	0.0064 (0.070)	-0.0076 (0.062)	0.0533 (0.050)	0.0306 (0.056)	-0.1101 (0.130)	0.0785 (0.123)	0.0070 (0.199)
Estimator (other than OLS)							
OLS	0.0902 (0.061)	0.0707 (0.043)	0.1102 (0.066)	0.0459 (0.056)	0.0840 (0.097)	0.0789 (0.058)	0.0571 (0.068)
Inflation variable type (normal use)							
Transformed variable	0.1040 (0.101)	0.1615* (0.089)	-0.0004 (0.090)	0.1612 (0.100)	0.0847 (0.088)	0.0625 (0.099)	-0.1606*** (0.027)
Log value	0.0047 (0.110)	0.0029 (0.099)	-0.0059 (0.100)	0.1340 (0.106)	-0.1261 (0.102)	0.0044 (0.112)	-0.1767*** (0.002)

	(1)	(2)	(3)	(4)	(5)	(6)	(7)
Ranking value	-0.0187 (0.110)	0.0625 (0.099)	-0.1350 (0.089)	0.0529 (0.106)	-0.0775 (0.093)	0.1284 (0.108)	dropped
CBI variable (comprehensive index)							
Political index	0.0513 (0.058)	0.0450 (0.080)	0.1032*** (0.035)	0.0921 (0.055)	0.0095 (0.065)	0.0647* (0.036)	0.0507 (0.036)
Economic index	-0.0136 (0.049)	0.0807 (0.082)	-0.0040 (0.017)	0.0819** (0.032)	0.0918 (0.083)	-0.0222 (0.045)	-0.0462 (0.048)
Legal index	0.0631 (0.055)	0.0837 (0.060)	0.0147 (0.021)	0.0789*** (0.028)	0.0229 (0.052)	0.0478 (0.030)	0.0256 (0.025)
Governor turnover	-0.1084* (0.056)	-0.0127 (0.062)	-0.1051*** (0.032)	-0.0683 (0.041)	-0.0213 (0.073)	-0.1800*** (0.051)	-0.1908*** (0.058)
Governor term	0.0876 (0.091)	0.1972* (0.102)	-0.0513 (0.056)	0.0241 (0.034)	0.1799 (0.124)	0.2850*** (0.023)	0.3560*** (0.000)
Lagged CBI variable (non-lagged variable)	0.0928 (0.069)	0.1528* (0.080)	0.0434 (0.058)	-0.0241 (0.040)	0.1496* (0.078)	0.0822** (0.034)	0.0459*** (0.009)
With an interaction variable(s)	-0.0035 (0.118)	-0.0275 (0.083)	-0.0111 (0.041)	0.2072** (0.078)	-0.2190 (0.154)	-0.0018 (0.060)	-0.0254 (0.000)***
Degree of freedom and research quality							
√Degree of freedom	0.0140** (0.005)	0.0168*** (0.005)	0.0075** (0.003)	0.0099*** (0.003)	0.0253*** (0.008)	0.0111** (0.006)	0.0090 (0.007)
Quality level	-0.0076 (0.005)		-0.0077 (0.005)	-0.0009 (0.003)	-0.0054 (0.007)	-0.0082 (0.010)	dropped
Intercept	-13.7700 (9.249)	-20.6736** (9.560)	-11.0272 (8.394)	0.8836 (6.639)	-36.4170*** (11.506)	-22.3134 (14.523)	-60.2711 (72.748)
K	337	337	337	337	337	337	337
R²	0.2620	0.2529	0.3274	0.1790	0.3590	0.1901	0.0563

(*Continued*)

Table 8.6 (Continued)

(b) Dependent variable—t value

Estimator (analytical weight in parentheses) Meta-independent variable (default)/ Model	Cluster-robust OLS [8]	Cluster-robust WLS [Quality level] [9]	Cluster-robust WLS [N] [10]	Cluster-robust WLS [1/SE] [11]	Cluster-robust WLS [1/EST] [12]	Cluster-robust random-effects panel GLS [13]d	Cluster-robust fixed-effects panel LSDV [14]e
Study type (non-transition studies)							
Transition studies	−0.2221 (0.444)	−0.1282 (0.538)	0.5150 (0.681)	0.1250 (0.590)	−0.3163 (0.503)	−0.4469 (0.539)	0.3620 (1.862)
Estimation period							
First year of estimation	0.0536 (0.044)	0.0406 (0.046)	0.0978* (0.057)	−0.0332 (0.048)	0.1306*** (0.034)	0.0553 (0.043)	0.0037 (0.197)
Length of estimation	0.0049 (0.033)	0.0208 (0.035)	0.0328 (0.047)	−0.0200 (0.053)	0.0050 (0.040)	0.0338 (0.041)	0.0961 (0.082)
Data type (cross-sectional data)							
Time-series data	−1.8843 (1.203)	−1.8401* (1.064)	−3.1202*** (1.044)	−1.7512 (1.131)	−2.1438* (1.245)	−2.7791** (1.256)	dropped
Panel data	−0.2937 (0.597)	−0.5802 (0.534)	−0.5102 (0.682)	−0.0333 (0.641)	−1.0808 (0.829)	0.5366 (0.861)	0.2951 (1.295)
Estimator (other than OLS)							
OLS	1.5965** (0.743)	1.3705*** (0.473)	1.6378* (0.925)	1.0109 (0.706)	2.0501** (0.853)	1.1697** (0.482)	0.8854 (0.548)
Inflation variable type (normal use)							
Transformed variable	0.4405 (1.311)	0.8450 (1.026)	−0.5929 (1.208)	0.7927 (1.277)	−0.2415 (1.076)	−0.2918 (1.331)	−0.5497 (0.394)
Log value	−0.0715 (1.394)	0.4605 (1.122)	−0.3462 (1.313)	1.0943 (1.382)	−1.0923 (1.067)	−0.5062 (1.451)	−1.0251*** (0.020)
Ranking value	0.1667 (1.379)	0.9712 (1.113)	−1.0853 (1.200)	1.0387 (1.406)	−0.7189 (1.082)	0.3977 (1.420)	dropped

CBI variable (comprehensive index)

Political index	0.5278 (0.953)	−0.0743 (0.730)	1.5477* (0.786)	−0.6352 (0.692)	1.1052* (0.596)	1.1310** (0.500)
Economic index	−0.4641 (0.324)	0.0788 (0.706)	−0.0071 (0.234)	0.0936 (0.705)	−0.3051 (0.374)	−0.4057 (0.395)
Legal index	0.1515 (0.460)	0.1529 (0.259)	1.0978** (0.434)	−0.2323 (0.592)	0.2699 (0.241)	0.2737 (0.238)
Governor turnover	−1.3178** (0.480)	−1.3911*** (0.274)	−0.7171 (0.466)	−0.8155 (0.582)	−1.7663*** (0.404)	−1.8061*** (0.419)
Governor term	0.5556 (0.493)	−0.7327 (0.659)	0.5418 (0.363)	0.7024 (0.701)	1.4634*** (0.121)	1.6423*** (0.004)
Lagged CBI variable (non-lagged variable)	0.7414 (0.827)	0.5733 (0.867)	0.0827 (0.693)	1.3206 (0.952)	0.8351*** (0.299)	0.6999*** (0.140)
With an interaction variable(s)	0.5465 (1.509)	−0.2390 (0.794)	2.8654** (1.306)	−1.8143 (1.392)	0.4158 (1.105)	−0.8745*** (0.001)
Degree of freedom and research quality						
√Degree of freedom	0.1215** (0.053)	0.0607 (0.047)	0.0337 (0.048)	0.2091*** (0.074)	0.0443 (0.055)	−0.0092 (0.068)
Quality level	−0.0670 (0.048)	−0.0659 (0.076)	−0.0316 (0.050)	−0.0817 (0.052)	−0.0976 (0.090)	dropped
Intercept	−109.6210 (86.978)	−196.5300* (112.875)	62.6944 (95.477)	−262.7958*** (68.371)	−111.9482 (85.856)	−10.1491 (390.745)
K	337	337	337	337	337	337
R^2	0.2216	0.2005	0.1720	0.3591	0.1488	0.0527

Notes:
[a] With regard to the estimates of governor turnover, their signs are reversed to use for meta-analysis.
[b] Breusch-Pagan test: $\chi^2 = 2.09$, $p = 0.074$.
[c] Hausman test: $\chi^2 = 20.04$, $p = 0.170$.
[d] Breusch-Pagan test: $\chi^2 = 5.54$, $p = 0.009$.
[e] Hausman test: $\chi^2 = 12.89$, $p = 0.611$.
Figures in parentheses beneath the regression coefficients are robust standard errors. ***, **, and * denote statistical significance at the 1%, 5%, and 10% levels, respectively.
Source: Authors' estimation. See Appendix B for definitions and descriptive statistics of independent variables.

Figure 8.3 is a funnel plot using PCCs and the respective inverse of the standard errors. Panel (a) of this figure illustrates the plot for the transition studies. Here, we do not find a bilaterally symmetric and inverted funnel-shaped distribution of the collected estimates in both cases when either zero or the mean value of the top 10% most-precise estimates (-0.356) is used as an approximate value of the true effect.[27] If the true effect exists around zero, then the ratio of the positive versus the negative estimates becomes 48:77, which rejects the null hypothesis that the ratio is 50:50 at the 5% significance level ($z = -2.594$, $p = 0.010$); therefore, type I publication selection bias is suspected. If the true effect is assumed to be close to the mean of the top 10% most-precise estimates, the distribution of collected estimates is greatly skewed to the right, as they are divided into a ratio of 24:101, with a value of -0.356 being the threshold; therefore, the null hypothesis is rejected at the 1% level under this assumption as well ($z = -6.887$, $p = 0.000$). Accordingly, the possibility of type I publication selection bias is considered to be very high among studies of transition economies.

With regard to non-transition studies, the ratio of positive versus negative estimates becomes 41:171, and the ratio of the left and right with the mean value of the top 10% most-precise estimates of -0.153 being the threshold is 119:93; therefore, if the true effect exists around zero, the possibility of the presence of type I publication selection bias is very high ($z = -8.928$, $p = 0.000$); however, if the true value is assumed to be the mean of the top 10% most-precise estimates, the possibility of the presence of type I publication selection bias is considered to be lower because the null hypothesis is rejected at the 10% level ($z = -1.789$, $p = 0.074$). This is represented by the funnel plot in Panel (b) of Figure 8.2, although not in a clear-cut manner, showing a bilaterally symmetric and triangle-shaped distribution, with a value of -0.184 being the threshold.

Figure 8.4 shows a Galbraith plot using t values and the respective inverse of the standard errors. This figure strongly indicates the presence of type II publication selection bias in both study areas. In fact, among the collected estimates of transition studies, only 75 of the 125 estimates show a t value that is within the range of ±1.96 or two-sided critical values at the 5% significance level; therefore, the null hypothesis that the rate as a percentage of total collected estimations is 95% is rejected ($z = -17.955$, $p = 0.000$). With respect to the non-transition studies, only 93 of 212 estimates also show a t value that is within the range of ±1.96; therefore, the null hypothesis that the rate as a percentage of total collected estimations is 95% is also strongly rejected ($z = -34.160$, $p = 0.000$). Furthermore, even on the assumption that the mean of the top 10% most-precise estimates stands for the true effect, the corresponding result also rejects the null hypothesis that estimates in which the statistic $|$(the k-th estimate $-$ the true effect)$/SE_k|$ does not exceed the critical value of 1.96 account for 95% of all estimates in both study areas.[28] Accordingly, we affirm that it is highly likely that type II publication selection bias arises in this research field, regardless of target regions.

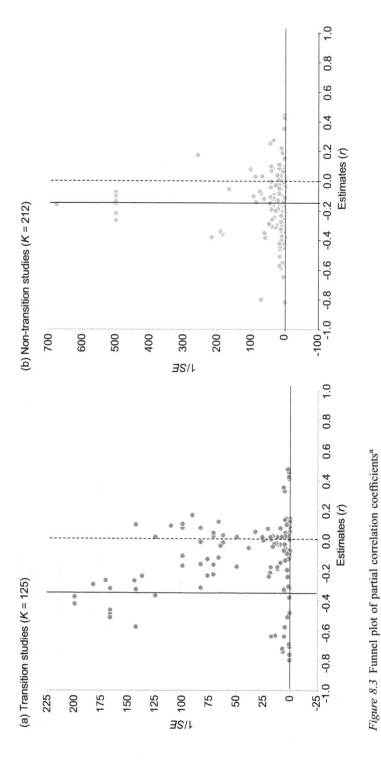

Figure 8.3 Funnel plot of partial correlation coefficients[a]

Notes:
[a]With regard to the estimates of governor turnover, their signs are reversed to use for meta-analysis.
Solid lines indicate the mean of the top 10 percent most-precise estimates: −0.356 for transition studies; −0.153 for non-transition studies.
Source: Authors' illustration.

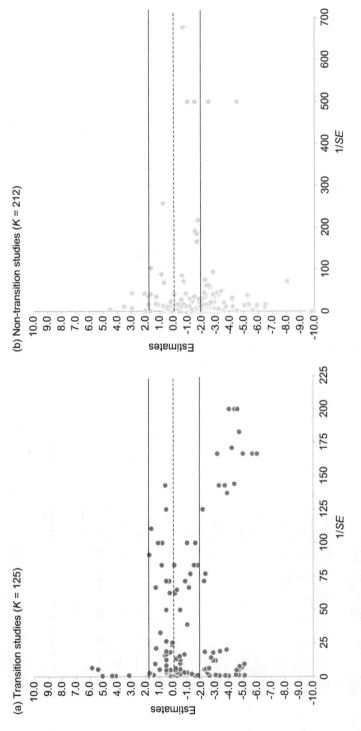

(a) Transition studies (K = 125)

(b) Non-transition studies (K = 212)

Figure 8.4 Galbraith plot of *t* values[a]

Notes:
[a] With regard to the estimates of governor turnover, their signs are reversed to use for meta-analysis.
Solid lines indicate the thresholds of two-sided critical values at the 5% significance level ±1.96.
Source: Authors' illustration.

Table 8.7 Meta-regression analysis of publication selection[a]

(a) FAT-PET test (Equation: $t = \beta_0+\beta_1(1/SE)+v$))

Study type	Transition studies				Non-transition studies			
Estimator	OLS	Cluster-robust OLS	Cluster-robust random-effects panel GLS	Cluster-robust fixed-effects panel LSDV	OLS	Cluster-robust OLS	Cluster-robust random-effects panel GLS	Cluster-robust fixed-effects panel LSDV
Model	[1]	[2]	[3][b]	[4][c]	[5]	[6]	[7][d]	[8][e]
Intercept (FAT: H_0: $\beta_0 = 0$)	−0.3529 (0.271)	−0.3529 (0.442)	0.2824 (0.683)	−0.2653 (0.419)	−1.9209*** (0.171)	−1.9209*** (0.303)	−1.5735*** (0.454)	−1.8293*** (0.027)
1/SE (PET: H_0: $\beta_1 = 0$)	−0.0152*** (0.003)	−0.0152*** (0.004)	−0.0177* (0.009)	−0.0174** (0.008)	−0.0005 (0.001)	−0.0005 (0.001)	−0.0018 (0.002)	−0.0020** (0.001)
K	125	125	125	125	212	212	212	212
R^2	0.1215	0.1215	0.1215	0.1215	0.0004	0.0004	0.0004	0.0004

(b) Test of type II publication selection bias (Equation: $|t| = \beta_0+\beta_1(1/SE)+v$)

Study type	Transition studies				Non-transition studies			
Estimator	OLS	Cluster-robust OLS	Cluster-robust random-effects panel GLS	Cluster-robust fixed-effects panel LSDV	OLS	Cluster-robust OLS	Cluster-robust random-effects panel GLS	Cluster-robust fixed-effects panel LSDV
Model	[9]	[10]	[11][f]	[12][g]	[13]	[14]	[15][h]	[16][i]
Intercept (H_0: $\beta_0 = 0$)	1.6731*** (0.186)	1.6731*** (0.476)	1.8981*** (0.528)	1.3575*** (0.332)	2.3527*** (0.141)	2.3527*** (0.251)	2.3252*** (0.295)	2.2996*** (0.022)
1/SE	0.0079*** (0.003)	0.0079* (0.004)	0.0149** (0.008)	0.0157* (0.008)	−0.0010 (0.001)	−0.0010 (0.001)	0.0001 (0.001)	0.0005 (0.001)
K	125	125	125	125	212	212	212	212
R^2	0.0675	0.0675	0.0675	0.0675	0.0026	0.0026	0.0026	0.0026

(Continued)

Table 8.7 (Continued)

(c) PEESE approach (Equation: $t = \beta_0 SE + \beta_1 (1/SE) + v$)

Study type	Transition studies				Non-transition studies			
Estimator	OLS	Cluster-robust OLS	Random-effects panel ML	Population-averaged panel GEE	OLS	Cluster-robust OLS	Random-effects panel ML	Population-averaged panel GEE
Model	[17]	[18]	[19]	[20]	[21]	[22]	[23]	[24]
SE	-0.1862	-0.1862	2.0266***	0.7233	-0.0441***	-0.0441***	0.0950***	0.0744***
	(0.507)	(0.954)	(0.552)	(1.261)	(0.016)	(0.004)	(0.016)	(0.004)
$1/SE$ (H_0: $\beta_1 = 0$)	-0.0182***	-0.0182***	-0.0159***	-0.0193***	-0.0060***	-0.0060***	-0.0021	-0.0023***
	(0.002)	(0.002)	(0.005)	(0.005)	(0.001)	(0.001)	(0.001)	(0.001)
K	125	125	125	125	212	212	212	212
R^2	0.2318	0.2318	-	-	0.0841	0.0841	-	-

Notes:
[a]With regard to the estimates of governor turnover, their signs are reversed to use for meta-analysis.
[b]Breusch-Pagan test: $\chi^2 = 10.80$, $p = 0.001$.
[c]Hausman test: $\chi^2 = 0.04$, $p = 0.844$.
[d]Breusch-Pagan test: $\chi^2 = 18.92$, $p = 0.000$.
[e]Hausman test: $\chi^2 = 1.01$, $p = 0.314$.
[f]Breusch-Pagan test: $\chi^2 = 84.81$, $p = 0.000$.
[g]Hausman test: $\chi^2 = 1.18$, $p = 0.277$.
[h]Breusch-Pagan test: $\chi^2 = 20.48$, $p = 0.000$.
[i]Hausman test: $\chi^2 = 3.11$, $p = 0.078$.
Figures in parentheses beneath the regression coefficients are standard errors. Except for Models [19] and [23], robust standard errors are estimated. ***, **, and * denote statistical significance at the 1%, 5%, and 10% levels, respectively.
Source: Authors' estimation.

Table 8.7 reports the estimation results of the meta-regression models that are specially designed to examine publication selection bias and the presence of genuine empirical evidence of the disinflation effect of CBI. According to the estimation results of Models [1] to [4], reported in Panel (a) of the table, contrary to the findings from the funnel plot mentioned above, the funnel asymmetry test (FAT) cannot reject the null hypothesis that the intercept term β_0 is zero in all four models and, accordingly, does not prove the presence of type I publication selection bias toward empirical results with an expected sign in the case of transition studies. On the contrary, in Models [5] to [8], the null hypothesis is rejected in all models at the 1% significance level; therefore, type I publication selection bias is strongly suspected in non-transition studies. Meanwhile, Panel (b) of the same table shows that the null hypothesis is rejected at the 1% significance level in all eight models. Thus, the likelihood of type II publication selection bias toward statistically significant results is significantly high in both study areas.[29]

Now, we return to Panel (a) of Table 8.7 and look at the results of a precision-effect test (PET). In all four models, the test results of the transition studies reject the null hypothesis that the coefficient of the inverse of the standard error β_1 is zero, implying that the estimates collected from the transition studies may include genuine evidence concerning the effect of CBI on inflation. In contrast, with regard to the non-transition studies, in three of four models, the null hypothesis is not rejected. Accordingly, it is less likely that there is genuine empirical evidence in the estimates used in this work.[30] In Panel (c) of Table 8.7, in seven of eight models, the precision-effect estimate with standard error (PEESE) rejects the null hypothesis that the coefficient of the inverse of the standard error β_1 is zero, suggesting that the true effect of CBI on inflation is significantly negative irrespective of the study area. However, with respect to the non-transition studies, the publication-bias-adjusted effect size obtained from PEESE cannot be adopted, since the PET cannot reject the null hypothesis as mentioned above.

Judging from these results, we conclude that estimates collected from non-transition studies do not provide genuine empirical evidence, perhaps due to the strong influence of publication selection biases. It is likely that this problem produced the meta-synthesis results reported in Table 8.4, which stress the superiority of developed and developing countries over post-communist transition states in terms of the effect size and statistical significance of the impact of CBI on inflation.

6. Conclusions

It has been more than a quarter century since the collapse of the Communist bloc. During these years, CEE and FSU countries have employed and implemented various structural reforms to establish market economies. Central bank reform is one of the important policy measures to be carried out by these countries; hence, researchers have paid a great deal of attention to every movement in

270 *Ichiro Iwasaki and Akira Uegaki*

this policy area. The large numbers of studies that have been published so far testify to this strong interest.

Central bank reforms have progressed to a certain extent in all transition economies since the collapse of the Berlin Wall to the present. However, reflecting significant differences in policy principles for the transformation to a market-oriented system and other domestic circumstances, the progress of reform differs considerably from country to country. At the same time, price stabilization was an urgent policy concern for every government in the CEE and FSU countries. Although there were several reasons for high inflation and the diversity of price dynamics observed in these economies, in this chapter, we have cast a spotlight on the relationship between CBI and inflation. While a number of empirical studies that focused on this relationship with developed and developing economies as their targets have been published since the early 1990s, researchers of transition economies have also produced a certain number of empirical studies on this issue. By conducting a comparative meta-analysis using the estimates collected from previous studies, we examined whether the disinflation effect of CBI has been actually detected in the transition literature as a whole and whether the empirical results of transition economies are comparable to those of non-transition economies, keeping in mind the Cukierman proposition.

From the results of this meta-analysis using a total of 337 estimates collected from 12 studies of transition economies and 16 studies of non-transition economies, we obtained the following findings.

First, the synthesized PCC and the combined t value of the collected estimates are negative and statistically significant in both study areas, suggesting that, irrespective of the target region, the negative impact of CBI on inflation is verified in the literature as a whole. It was also revealed that the effect size and the statistical significance of the transition studies are inferior to those of non-transition studies. However, the latter results are likely due to the strong presence of publication selection bias in non-transition studies, as detected in Subsection 5.3.

Second, the meta-synthesis of estimates collected from the transition studies indicated that their empirical results may have been strongly affected by a series of study conditions, including the target country, the estimation period, the data type, and the type of index used to measure CBI. This indicates the diversity of transition economies as well as the complexity of investigating their financial sectors.

Third, the MRA also reproduced the close correlation between various study conditions and the estimates reported in the transition studies. More specifically, the heterogeneity among studies of transition economies is caused by the choice of estimator, inflation variable type, CBI variable type, degree of freedom, and research quality, in particular.

Fourth, the MRA using the collected estimates of both transition and non-transition studies revealed that there is no robustly significant difference between the two types of studies so long as we control for a series of study conditions, suggesting that the marked differences in the meta-synthesis results are caused by variations in the methodologies. It is also worth mentioning that we obtained similar results even when we utilized only the estimates of the legal CBI index.

Fifth, according to the assessment of publication selection bias, we found that, while the transition studies contain genuine empirical evidence of the disinflation effect of CBI in their estimates beyond type II publication selection bias, the non-transition studies failed to provide evidence of a non-zero effect of CBI, due to the strong influence of publication selection bias on their empirical results. In this sense, transition studies have made significant contributions to the literature by helping us grasp the real influence of CBI on inflation.

To summarize, the results of our meta-analysis strongly back up the argument that the socioeconomic progress in the post-communist world is substantial, in the sense that there exists a close relationship between CBI and inflation. It is true that there are some statistical differences between transition economies and non-transition economies; however, we must carefully investigate whether the selection of independent variables and publication selection bias might have influenced the results. However, the results never support the contention that the central banks in CEE and FSU countries have reached a desirable level of independence from policy makers and other parties with interests in monetary policies. Rather, in many transition economies, the central bank is still under the strong control of political leaders and the central government. Accordingly, we should pay careful attention to further developments regarding this aspect.

Acknowledgments

This chapter is a fully revised and extended version of Iwasaki and Uegaki (2017). This research work was financially supported by grants-in-aid for scientific research from the Ministry of Education, Culture, Sports, Science and Technology of Japan (Nos. 23243032 and 15H01849) and the Joint Usage and Research Center of the Institute of Economic Research, Kyoto University (FY2016). We thank Josef Brada, Hristos Doucouliagos, David Guerreiro (the editor and referee), Tomáš Havránek, Evžen Kočenda, Tom D. Stanley, Sebastiaan M. Straathof (the referee), and Fumikazu Sugiura for their helpful comments and suggestions. We also would like to thank Eriko Yoshida for her research assistance and Tammy Bicket for her editorial assistance. Needless to say, all remaining errors are solely our responsibility.

Notes

1 In fact, the Washington Consensus stops short of touching on the liberalization of interest as one of its policy packages, mentioning almost nothing about banking reform (Iwasaki and Suzuki, 2016).
2 From the Foundation for EU Democracy (2008, p. 103).
3 These are reform items upon which the EBRD's index for banking reform and interest rate liberalization is based.
4 See the EBRD website (www.ebrd.com/what-we-do/economic-research-and-data/data.html) for more details regarding the index. The EBRD stopped publishing this

272   *Ichiro Iwasaki and Akira Uegaki*

index in 2010; since 2011, a sector-level transition indicator, which is used in Table 8.1, has replaced it.

5 Only 19 countries where the time series data on "EBRD banking reform index" and "independence index (CBIW)" for both periods (a) and (b) are systematically available are depicted in the figure. However, with respect to Belarus, since there is no "independence index" data from 1998–2000, only data from 2001–2 were used in Panel (a). Regarding Latvia, since there is no "independence index" data in 1998, we only used data for 1999–2002 in Panel (a). Regarding the Czech Republic, the "banking reform index" has not been released since 2008, but the country's index had already reached "4" in 2003, and so we regard the average figure for 2006–10 of the Czech Republic to be "4." Judging from the data trends of the previous and next years in all three countries, it is unlikely that these measures will have a major disturbing influence on the results.

6 Regarding Croatia, which was located in the upper middle in 1998–2002 and moved to the upper right in 2006–10, its EU accession was delayed until July 2013 due to the problem of the liberation of war criminals. Therefore, it is necessary to pay attention to the fact that its final efforts for accession were accelerated after 2002 (the formal application for the accession was in February 2003) (Barisitz, 2008).

7 Of course, it is necessary to consider various factors other than EU accession as to what determines the level of CBI and what determines the degree of progress of banking reform. For example, with respect to CBI, Dincer and Eichengreen (2014), who analyzed data of 100 central banks around the world, concluded that countries receiving financial guidance from the IMF and those having a backward financial market have highly independent central banks. They also assert that in more open countries and in those which participate in the IMF program, CBI is improving, while CBI is declining in countries with a tradition of British law (219–32).

8 The first comprehensive attempt to build CBI indexes was made by R. Bade and M. Parkin in 1978. See Parkin (2012).

9 As for the study of non-transition economies, Cukierman proposed combined measurements of CBI that included (I) legal independence, (II) the turnover rate of the CB governor, and (III) the characterization of CBI based on answers to a questionnaire. Cukierman asserted that the turnover rate of the CB governor appears to capture significant variations in independence within less-developed countries (Cukierman, 1992).

10 The period is divided into two or three sub-periods (p. 12).

11 The final literature search using these databases was conducted in January 2018.

12 This means that the meta fixed-effect model is a special case based on the assumption that.

13 For more details $\delta_\theta^2 = 0$ on the method of evaluating the quality level of the study, see Appendix A.

14 Rosenthal's fail-safe N denotes the number of studies with an average effect size equal to zero, which needs to be added in order to bring the combined probability level of all studies to the standard significance level to determine the presence or absence of the effect. The larger value of *fsN* in Eq. (6) means a more reliable estimation of the combined *t* value. For more details, see Stanley and Doucouliagos (2012).

15 In addition to MRA using these orthodox estimators, some meta-analysts employ several types of model-averaging approaches, including frequentist model averaging and Bayesian model averaging to tackle the issue of model uncertainty. For instance, see Ahtiainen and Vanhatalo (2012), Babecky and Havranek (2014), and Havranek and Sokolova (2016).

16 To estimate Eqs. (8) and (9), we use either the cluster-robust random-effects estimator or the cluster-robust fixed-effects estimator according to the results of the Hausman test of the random-effects assumption. With regard to Eq. (10), which does not have an intercept term, we report the random-effects model estimated by the maximum likelihood method.

17 In addition to Babecky and Havranek (2014), meta-studies of the transition literature that employ methodology similar to that of this chapter include Fidrmuc and Korhonen (2006), Babecký and Campos (2011), Hanousek et al. (2011), Kuusk and Paas (2013), Iwasaki and Tokunaga (2014, 2016), Iwasaki and Kočenda (2017), Tokunaga and Iwasaki (2017), Iwasaki and Mizobata (2018), Iwasaki et al. (2018), and Iwasaki and Kumo (2019).

18 Doucouliagos (2011) argued that Cohen's guidelines for zero-order correlations are too restrictive when applied to economics and proposed to use the 25th percentile, 50th percentile (median), and 75th percentile of a total of 22,141 PCCs collected by himself as alternative criteria. According to his new guidelines, for general purposes, 0.070, 0.173, and 0.327 are considered to be the lower thresholds for small, medium, and large effects, respectively. In addition, Doucouliagos (2011) also presented field-specific guidelines, in which 0.103, 0.156, and 0.212 are recommended for use as corresponding criteria for the CBI disinflation effect. His new guidelines give a more positive evaluation of the estimates we have collected than those in accordance with Cohen's guidelines.

19 Sample size has a considerable influence on the statistical significance of estimates. Therefore, many meta-studies, from the perspective of statistics, use the square root of the degree of freedom as a control variable for the meta-regression model.

20 We confirm that, according to the estimates of Model [1] in Table 8.5, all correlation coefficients between the meta-independent variables used for estimation are smaller than a threshold of 0.70, and the variance inflation factor for each of the meta-independent variables is well under a threshold of 10.0 (mean = 4.63).

21 Appendix C provides the results of MRA using estimates extracted from the non-transition literature for comparison. As shown in this appendix, the heterogeneity among non-transition studies is largely explained by the difference in CBI variables employed in the empirical analysis.

22 In this regard, we thank David Guerreiro for his comment that EU membership supports reforms in order to stick with the competition laws implemented by the single market (the end of tariffs and quotas, reduction of subsidies, dismantlement of monopolies); these rules that are operative in new EU members but not systematic in other transition countries are likely to have a real impact on inflation, explaining the difference between these two categories of countries.

23 On the other hand, surprisingly, studies that measured CBI by governor term tended to assess the CBI disinflation effect more conservatively. We surmise that this might happen because the governor term is cut off at the upper limit of the legal term for the sake of data, although the governor of a central bank, in fact, could have served a number of terms or resigned in the middle of the term.

24 This is consistent with the estimation result that a dummy variable for estimates of transition economies is not significant in the meta-regression model of Klomp and de Haan (2010), which takes the t value as a dependent variable (Table 4, p. 606).

25 More precisely, the dummy for the transition studies was insignificant in five of seven models that take the PCC as a dependent variable and in four models using the t value.

26 Cukierman et al. (2002) argued that it is "too extreme" to conclude that the difference in the degree of legal independence of the central banks in transition economies does not have much influence on inflation just because the legal index of central bank independence of transition economies does not reflect the true degree of independence (p. 255).

27 The method for assuming that the mean of the top 10% most-precise estimates is the approximate value of the true effect is in keeping with that reported by Stanley (2005).

28 The z-value and the p-value of the test for equality of proportions are -39.295 and 0.000 for transition studies and -49.286 and 0.000 for non-transition studies, respectively.

29 Estimations of Eqs. (8) and (9) with meta-moderators used in Tables 8.5 and 8.6 showed the same test results in Panels (a) and (b) in Table 8.7. We thank Sebastiaan M. Straathof for his advice on the robustness check.
30 Following Havránek (2015) and Havranek and Sokolova (2016), we also estimated Eq. (8) by the IV method using the inverse of the square root of the number of observations as an instrument and obtained similar estimation results to those in Table 8.7 with slightly lower statistical significance of β_1.

Bibliography

Ahtiainen, Heini and Jarno Vanhatalo (2012) "The Value of Reducing Eutrophication in European Marine Areas: A Bayesian Meta-analysis." *Ecological Economics* 83, 1–10.

Ahtik, Meta, Zrinka Erent Sunko and Ozren Pilipovic (2012) "Legal Aspects of Central Banking in Slovenia and Croatia From Their Beginnings Up to Membership in the Euro Zone." *CYELP* 8, 561–580.

Alesina, Alberto (1988) "Macroeconomics and Politics." *NBER Macroeconomics Annual* 3, 13–52.

Alesina, Alberto and Lawrence Summers (1993) "Central Bank Independence and Macroeconomic Performance: Some Comparative Evidence." *Journal of Money, Credit, and Banking* 25, 151–162.

Alpanda, Sami and Adam Honig (2014) "The Impact of Central Bank Independence on the Performance of Inflation Targeting Regimes." *Journal of International Money and Finance* 44, 118–135.

Arnone, Marco, Bernard J. Laurens and Jean-Francois Segalotto (2006) "The Measurement of Central Bank Autonomy: Survey of Models, Indicators, and Empirical Evidence." *Working Paper No. 06/227*, International Monetary Fund (IMF), Washington, DC.

Babecký, Jan and Nauro F. Campos (2011) "Does Reform Work? An Econometric Survey of the Reform – Growth Puzzle." *Journal of Comparative Economics* 39, 140–158.

Babecky, Jan and Tomas Havranek (2014) "Structural Reforms and Growth in Transition: A Meta-Analysis." *Economics of Transition* 22, 13–42.

Barisitz, Stephan (2008) *Banking in Central and Eastern Europe 1980–2006*. London and New York: Routledge.

Barro, Robert J. and David B. Gordon (1983) "Rules, Discretion and Reputation in a Model of Monetary Policy." *Journal of Monetary Economics* 12, 101–121.

Bodea, Cristina (2014) "Fixed Exchange Rates, Independent Central Banks and Price Stability in Postcommunist Countries: Conservatism and Credibility." *Economics & Politics* 26, 185–211.

Bogoev, Jane, Goran Petrevski and Bruno S. Sergi (2012a) "Investigating the Link Between Central Bank Independence and Inflation in Central and Eastern Europe." *Eastern European Economics* 50, 78–96.

Bogoev, Jane, Goran Petrevski and Bruno S. Sergi (2012b) "Reducing Inflation in Ex-Communist Economies Independent Central Banks Versus Financial Sector Development." *Problems of Post-Communism* 59, 38–55.

Bouyon, Sylvain (2009) "Currency Substitution and Central Bank Independence in the Central and Eastern European Economies." *Journal of Economic Integration* 24, 597–633.

Civelekoğlu, İlke (2013) "It Takes Two to Tango: The Role of the European Union and Domestic Governments in the Making of Central Bank Reform in Hungary." *International Relations/Uluslararasi Iliskiler* 9, 129–148.

Cohen, Jacob (1988) *Statistical Power Analysis in the Behavioral Sciences*. 2nd Edition. Hillsgate: Lawrence Erlbaum Associates.

Crowe, Christopher and Ellen E. Meade (2008) "Central Bank Independence and Transparency: Evolution and Effectiveness." *European Journal of Political Economy* 24, 763–777.

Cukierman, Alex (1992) *Central Bank Strategy, Credibility, and Independence: Theory and Evidence*. Cambridge, MA and London: MIT Press.

Cukierman, Alex (2008) "Central Bank Independence and Monetary Policymaking Institutions: Past, Present, and Future." *European Journal of Political Economy* 24, 722–736.

Cukierman, Alex, Geoffrey P. Miller and Bilin Neyapti (2002) "Central Bank Reform, Liberalization and Inflation in Transition Economies: An International Perspective." *Journal of Monetary Economics* 49, 237–264.

Cukierman, Alex, Steven B. Webb and Bilin Neyapti (1992) "Measuring the Independence of Central Banks and its Effect on Policy Outcomes." *World Bank Economic Review* 6, 353–398.

de Haan, Jakob and Willem J. Kooi (2000) "Does Central Bank Independence Really Matter? New Evidence for Developing Countries Using a New Indicator." *Journal of Banking and Finance* 24, 643–664.

Dincer, Nergiz and Barry Eichengreen (2014) "Central Bank Transparency and Independence: Updates and New Measures." *International Journal of Central Banking* 10, 189–253.

Djankov, Simeon (2015) "Hungary Under Orbán: Can Central Planning Revive Its Economy?" *Peterson Institute for International Economics: Policy Brief*, July 6, 2015.

Doucouliagos, Hristos (2011) "How Large Is Large? Preliminary and Relative Guidelines for Interpreting Partial Correlations in Economics." *Working Paper No. SWP 2011/5*, School of Accounting, Economics and Finance, Faculty of Business and Law, Deakin University, Melbourne.

Dumiter, Florin Cornel (2011) "Estimating the Impact of Central Bank Independence Upon Macroeconomic Performance Using a Panel Data Model." *Romanian Journal of Economic Forecasting* 4, 106–128.

EBRD (2016) Transition Report 2016–17: Transition for All – Equal Opportunities in an Unequal World. EBRD, London.

EBRD (European Bank for Reconstruction and Development) Transition Report. London: EBRD. (various issues).

The Economist (2013) "Hungary's Central Bank, Orban's Soldiers." March 9, 2013.

Eijffinger, Sylvester C. W. and Patrick Stadhouders (2003) "Monetary Policy and the Rule of Law." *Discussion Paper No. 3698*, Centre for Economic Policy Research (CEPR), London.

Fidrmuc, Jarko and Iikka Korhonen (2006) "Meta-Analysis of the Business Cycle Correlation Between the Euro Area and the CEECs." *Journal of Comparative Economics* 34, 518–537.

Foundation for EU Democracy (2008) Consolidated Reader-friendly Edition of the Treaty on European Union (TEU) and the Treaty on the Functioning of the European Union (TFEU) as Amended by the Treaty of Lisbon (2007). (available at: www.eudemocrats.org).

Ftiti, Zied, Abdelkader Aguir and Mounir Smida (2017) "Time-inconsistency and Expansionary Business Cycle Theories: What Does Matter for the Central Bank Independence – inflation Relationship?" *Economic Modelling* 67, 215-227.

Gregory, Paul R. and Robert Stuart (1986) *Soviet Economic Structure and Performance*. 3rd Edition. New York: Harper and Row.

Grillini, Vittorio, Danato Masciandaro and Guido Tabellini (1991) "Political and Monetary Institutions and Public Financial Policies in the Industrial Countries." *Economic Policy* 6, 342–392.

Gutiérrez, Eva (2004) "Inflation Performance and Constitutional Central Bank Independence: Evidence From Latin America and the Caribbean." *Economía Mexicana – NUEVA ÉPOCA* 13, 255–287.

Hammermann, Felix and Mark Flanagan (2007) "What Explains Persistent Inflation Differentials Across Transition Economies?" *Working Paper No. 07/189*, IMF, Washington, DC.

Hanousek, Jan, Evžen Kočenda and Mathilde Maurel (2011) "Direct and Indirect Effects of FDI in Emerging European Markets: A Survey and Meta-Analysis." *Economic Systems* 35, 301–322.

Havránek, Tomáš (2015) "Measuring Intertemporal Substitution: The Importance of Method Choices and Selective Reporting." *Journal of the European Economic Association* 13, 1180–1204.

Havranek, Tomas and Anna Sokolova (2016) "Do Consumers Really Follow a Rule of Thumb? Three Thousand Estimates from 130 Studies Say 'Probably Not'." *Working Paper No. 15/2016*, Institute of Economic Studies, Faculty of Social Sciences, Charles University in Prague, Prague.

IMF (International Monetary Fund) (2016) "Kyrgyz Republic Selected Issues." *Country Report No.16/56*, IMF, Washington, D.C.

Iskrov, Ivan (2009) "Bulgarian National Bank – Independence, Predictability and Transparency. Speech by Mr. Ivan Iskrov, Governor of the Bulgarian National Bank, Before the 41st National Assembly of the Republic of Bulgaria on the Occasion of His Election to a Second Term of Office, Sofia, 26 August 2009." *BIS Review* 104, 1–2.

Iwasaki, Ichiro and Evžen Kočenda (2017) "Are Some Owners Better Than Others in Czech Privatized Firms? Even Meta-Analysis Can't Make Us Perfectly Sure." *Economic Systems* 41, 537–568.

Iwasaki, Ichiro and Kazuhiro Kumo (2019) "J-Curve in Transition Economies: A Large Meta-Analysis of the Determinants of Output Changes." *Comparative Economic Studies* 61, 149-191.

Iwasaki, Ichiro and Satoshi Mizobata (2018) "Post-Privatization Ownership and Firm Performance: A Large Meta-Analysis of the Transition Literature." *Annals of Public and Cooperative Economics* 89, 263-322.

Iwasaki, Ichiro, Satoshi Mizobata and Alexander A. Muravyev (2018) "Ownership Dynamics and Firm Performance in an Emerging Economy: A Meta-Analysis of the Russian Literature." *Post-Communist Economies* 30, 290-333.

Iwasaki, Ichiro and Masahiro Tokunaga (2014) "Macroeconomic Impacts of FDI in Transition Economies: A Meta-Analysis." *World Development* 61, 53–69.

Iwasaki, Ichiro and Masahiro Tokunaga (2016) "Technology Transfer and Spillovers From FDI in Transition Economies: A Meta-Analysis." *Journal of Comparative Economics* 44, 1086–1114.

Iwasaki, Ichiro and Akira Uegaki (2017) "Central Bank Independence and Inflation in Transition Economies: A Comparative Meta-Analysis with Developed and Developing Economies." *Eastern European Economics* 55, 197–235.

Iwasaki, Ichiro and Taku Suzuki (2016) "Radicalism Versus Gradualism: An Analytical Survey of the Transition Strategy Debate." *Journal of Economic Surveys* 30, 807–834.

Jácome, Luis I. and Francisco Vázquez (2005) "Any Link Between Legal Central Bank Independence and Inflation? Evidence From Latin America and the Caribbean." *Working Paper No. 05/75*, International Monetary Fund (IMF), Washington, DC.

Jácome, Luis I. and Francisco Vázquez (2008) "Is There Any Link Between Legal Central Bank Independence and Inflation? Evidence From Latin America and the Caribbean." *European Journal of Political Economy* 24, 788–801.

Johnson, Juliet (2016) *Priests of Prosperity: How Central Bankers Transformed the Post-communist World*. Ithaca: Cornell University Press.

Klomp, Jeroen and Jakob de Haan (2010) "Inflation and Central Bank Independence: A Meta-Regression Analysis." *Journal of Economic Surveys* 24, 593–621.

Kokorev, V. and A. Remizov (1996) "Modernization of Russia's Credit System under Conditions of a Liquidity Crisis: Is It Possible to Devalue Money without a Rise of Inflation?" *Problems of Economic Transition* 39, 41–65.

Krause, Stefan and Fabio Méndez (2008) "Institutions, Arrangements and Preferences for Inflation Stability: Evidence and Lessons from a Panel Data Analysis." *Journal of Macroeconomics* 30, 282–307.

Kuusk, Andres and Tiiu Paas (2013) "A Meta-Analysis-Based Approach for Examining Financial Contagion with Special Emphasis on CEE Economies." *Eastern European Economics* 51, 71–90.

Kydland, Finn E. and Edward C. Prescott (1977) "Rules Rather Than Discretion: The Inconsistency of Optimal Plans." *Journal of Political Economy* 85, 473–492.

Lavigne, Marie (1999) *The Economics of Transition From Socialist Economy to Market Economy*. New York: Macmillan.

Loungani, Prakashl and Nathan Sheets (1997) "Central Bank Independence, Inflation, and Growth in Transition Economies." *Journal of Money, Credit, and Banking* 29, 381–399.

Maliszewski, Wociech S. (2000) "Central Bank Independence in Transition Economies." *Economics of Transition* 8, 749–789.

Maslowska, Aleksandra A. (2011) "Quest for the Best: How to Measure Central Bank Independence and Show Its Relationship With Inflation." *AUCO Czech Economic Review* 5, 132–161.

Meagher, Patrick (2003) "Changing Hands: Governance and Transformation in Hungary's Financial Sector." *Review of Central and East European Law* 28, 1–76.

Miles, William (2009) "Central Bank Independence, Inflation and Uncertainty: The Case of Colombia." *International Economic Journal* 23, 65–79.

Monetary Policy Department of the National Bank of Hungary (2000) *Monetary Policy in Hungary*, edited by Ilona Bozo. Budapest: National Bank of Hungary.

National Bank of Slovakia (2011) *The National Bank of Slovakia: Its Tasks and Activities*. Bratislava: National Bank of Slovenia.

Parkin, Michael (2012) "Central Bank Laws and Monetary Policy Outcomes: A Three Decade Perspective." *Working Paper No. 2013–1*, Economic Policy Research Institute, University of Western Ontario, Ontario.

Perera, Anli, Deborah Ralston and Jayasinghe Wickramanayake (2013) "Central Bank Financial Strength and Inflation: Is There a Robust Link?" *Journal of Financial Stability* 9, 399–414.

Petrevski, Goran, Jane Bogoev and Bruno S. Sergi (2012) "The Link Between Central Bank Independence and Inflation in Central and Eastern Europe: Are the Results Sensitive to Endogeneity Issue Omitted Dynamics and Subjectivity Bias?" *Journal of Post Keynesian Economics* 34, 611–652.

Piplica, Damir (2015) "Legal Central Bank Independence and Inflation in Various Phases of Transition." *Economic Research-Ekonomska Istraživanja* 28, 167–186.

Posso, Alberto and George B. Tawadros (2013) "Does Greater Central Bank Independence Really Lead to Lower Inflation? Evidence From Panel Data." *Economic Modelling* 33, 244–247.

Rautava, Jouko (1993) "Monetary Overhang, Inflation and Stabilization in the Economies in Transition." In *Review of Economies in Transition 4*, Helsinki: Bank of Finland, Institute for Economies in Transition.

Rogoff, Kenneth (1985) "The Optimal Degree of Commitment to an Intermediate Monetary Target." *Quarterly Journal of Economics* 100, 1169–1189.

Romer, David (1996) *Advanced Macroeconomics*. Columbus, OH: McGraw-Hill.

Sagbansua, Lutfu (2006) "Banking System in Kyrgyz Republic." *IBSU Scientific Journal* 1, 39–53.

Stanley, T. D. (2005) "Beyond Publication Bias." *Journal of Economic Surveys* 19, 309–345.

Stanley, T. D. and Hristos Doucouliagos (2012) *Meta-Regression Analysis in Economics and Business*. London and New York: Routledge.

Stanley, T. D. and Stephen B. Jarrell (2005) "Meta-Regression Analysis: A Quantitative Method of Literature Surveys." *Journal of Economic Surveys* 19, 299–308.

Sturm, Jan-Egbert and Jakob de Haan (2001) "Inflation in Developing Countries: Does Central Bank Independence Matter? New Evidence Based On a New Data Set." *Working Paper No. 511*, CESifo, Munich.

Tokunaga, Masahiro and Ichiro Iwasaki (2017) "The Determinants of Foreign Direct Investment in Transition Economies: A Meta-Analysis." *The World Economy* 40, 2771–2831.

Varhegyi, Eva (1994) "The Second' Reform of the Hungarian Banking System." In Bonin, John P. and Istvan P. Szekely (eds.). *The Development and Reform of Financial Systems in Central and Eastern Europe* (pp. 293–308). Aldershot: Edward Elgar.

Wagner, Helmut (1999) "Central Bank Independence and the Lessons for Transition Economies From Industrial Countries and Developing Countries." *Comparative Economic Studies* 41, 1–22.

Walsh, Carl E. (1997) "Inflation and Central Bank Independence: Is Japan Really an Outlier?" *Monetary and Economic Studies* 15, 89–117.

Appendix A
Method for evaluating the quality level of a study

This appendix describes the evaluation method used to determine the quality level of the studies subjected to our meta-analysis.

For journal articles, we used the rankings of economics journals published as of November 1, 2012, by IDEAS – the largest bibliographical database dedicated to economics and available freely on the Internet (http://ideas.repec.org/) – as the most basic information source for our evaluation of quality level. IDEAS provides the world's most comprehensive ranking of economics journals, and, as of November 2012, 1,173 academic journals were ranked.

We divided these 1,173 journals into 10 clusters, using a cluster analysis based on overall evaluation scores (for more details regarding the scores, see the following website: https://ideas.repec.org/t/ranking.html), and assigned each of these journal clusters a score (weight) from 1 (the lowest journal cluster) to 10 (the highest).

For academic journals not ranked by IDEAS, we referred to the Thomson Reuters Impact Factor and other journal rankings and identified the same level of IDEAS ranking-listed journals that correspond to these non-listed journals; we assigned each of them the same score as its counterparts.

Meanwhile, for academic books and book chapters, we assigned a score of 1, in principle; however, if at least one of the following conditions was met, each of the relevant books or chapters uniformly received a score of 4, which is the median value of the scores assigned to the above-mentioned IDEAS ranking-listed economics journals: (1) The academic book or book chapter clearly states that it has gone through the peer review process; (2) its publisher is a leading academic publisher that has external evaluations carried out by experts; or (3) the research level of the study was evaluated by the authors as being obviously high.

Appendix B. Name, definition, and descriptive statistics of meta-independent variables

Variable name	Definition	Descriptive statistics								
		Transition studies			Non-transition studies			All selected studies		
		Mean	Median	S.D.	Mean	Median	S.D.	Mean	Median	S.D.
Proportion of other CEEs	Proportion of non-EU CEE countries in observations	0.1154	0.1000	0.0622	-	-	-	-	-	-
Proportion of FSUs	Proportion of FSU countries in observations	0.3772	0.4286	0.1402	-	-	-	-	-	-
Proportion of non-CEE/FSU countries	Proportion of Mongolia and other emerging countries in observations	0.0160	0.0000	0.0250	-	-	-	-	-	-
Transition studies	1 = transition studies, 0 = non-transition studies	-	-	-	-	-	-	0.3709	0	0.4838
First year of estimation	First year of the estimation period	1991.1920	1990	2.7787	1984.5900	1980	6.4468	1987.0390	1990	6.2570
Length of estimation	Years of the estimation period	12.2560	10	6.0481	16.4245	13	8.3846	14.8783	13	7.8558
Time-series data	1 = if time-series data is employed for the estimation, 0 = otherwise	-	-	-	0.0189	0	0.1364	0.0119	0	0.1085
Panel data	1 = if panel data is employed for the estimation, 0 = otherwise	0.6400	1	0.4819	0.5849	1	0.4939	0.6053	1	0.4895
OLS	1 = if ordinary least squares estimator is used for the estimation, 0 = otherwise	0.4400	0	0.4984	0.5519	1	0.4985	0.5104	1	0.5006
Transformed variable	1 = if the inflation variable is the transformed value, 0 = otherwise	0.7440	1	0.4382	0.6509	1	0.4778	0.6855	1	0.4650
Log value	1 = if the inflation variable is the log value, 0 = otherwise	0.1280	0	0.3354	0.2358	0	0.4255	0.1958	0	0.3974
Ranking value	1 = if the inflation variable is the ranking value, 0 = otherwise	0.0160	0	0.1260	-	-	-	0.0059	0	0.0769

(Continued)

Variable	Description									
Political index	1 = if CBI is measured by the political index, 0 = otherwise	0.0160	0	0.1260	0.0660	0	0.2489	0.0475	0	0.2130
Economic index	1 = if CBI is measured by the economic index, 0 = otherwise	0.0160	0	0.1260	0.0377	0	0.1910	0.0297	0	0.1699
Legal index	1 = if CBI is measured by the legal index, 0 = otherwise	0.5040	1	0.5020	0.3349	0	0.4731	0.3976	0	0.4901
Governor turnover[a]	1 = if CBI is measured by governor turnover, 0 = otherwise	0.0080	0	0.0894	0.4811	0	0.5008	0.3056	0	0.4614
Governor term	1 = if CBI is measured by the governor term, 0 = otherwise	0.0240	0	0.1537	-	-	-	0.0089	0	0.0941
Lagged CBI variable	1 = if a lagged variable of index for central bank independence is used for the estimation, 0 = otherwise	0.2320	0	0.4238	0.0236	0	0.1521	0.1009	0	0.3016
With an interaction term(s)	1= if estimation is carried out with an interaction term(s) of CBI variable, 0 = otherwise	0.0800	0	0.2724	0.0094	0	0.0969	0.0356	0	0.1856
√Degree of freedom	Root of the degree of freedom of the estimated model	12.0655	9.5394	9.3550	11.0708	8.5438	6.1346	11.4398	9.3808	7.4941
Quality level[b]	Ten-point scale of the quality level of the study	4.8480	5	3.5197	4.7311	4	3.6814	4.7745	4	3.6174

Notes:
[a]With regard to the estimates of governor turnover, their signs are reversed to use for meta-analysis.
[b]See Appendix A for more details.
Source: Authors' calculation.

Appendix C. Meta-regression analysis of heterogeneity among non-transition studies[a]

(a) Dependent variable—PCC

Estimator (analytical weight in parentheses) Meta-independent variable (default)/ Model	Cluster-robust OLS	Cluster-robust WLS [Quality level]	Cluster-robust WLS [N]	Cluster-robust WLS [1/SE]	Cluster-robust WLS [1/EST]	Cluster-robust random-effects panel GLS	Cluster-robust fixed-effects panel LSDV
	[1]	[2]	[3]	[4]	[5]	[6][b]	[7][c]
Estimation period							
First year of estimation	0.0034 (0.002)	0.0028 (0.003)	0.0007 (0.003)	−0.0014 (0.003)	0.0059** (0.003)	0.0034 (0.002)	−0.0553*** (0.004)
Length of estimation	−0.0015 (0.002)	−0.0023 (0.002)	−0.0020 (0.001)	−0.0014 (0.002)	−0.0021 (0.002)	−0.0015 (0.002)	dropped
Data type (cross-sectional data)							
Time-series data	−0.0623 (0.098)	−0.0355 (0.114)	−0.1907 (0.121)	0.0394 (0.098)	−0.0726 (0.085)	−0.0623 (0.098)	dropped
Panel data	−0.0334 (0.041)	−0.0516 (0.056)	−0.0185 (0.041)	−0.0159 (0.063)	−0.0640 (0.047)	−0.0334 (0.041)	dropped
Estimator (other than OLS)							
OLS	0.1287*** (0.040)	0.1283*** (0.025)	0.0738 (0.053)	0.0366 (0.055)	0.1684*** (0.024)	0.1287*** (0.040)	0.1099** (0.039)
Inflation variable type (normal use)							
Transformed variable	0.0752 (0.090)	0.0643 (0.079)	−0.0573 (0.122)	0.1891** (0.090)	0.0241 (0.063)	0.0752 (0.090)	0.0138 (0.024)
Log value	0.1285 (0.093)	0.1033 (0.090)	−0.0303 (0.127)	0.1896** (0.094)	0.0765 (0.066)	0.1285 (0.093)	dropped
CBI variable (comprehensive index)							
Political index	0.0733	0.0098	0.1314***	0.1214***	−0.0473	0.0733	0.0996**

	(0.073)	(0.065)	(0.024)	(0.033)	(0.059)	(0.073)	(0.056)
Economic index	0.0092	0.0609	0.0247**	0.0590**	0.0289	0.0092	0.0065
	(0.033)	(0.055)	(0.009)	(0.029)	(0.065)	(0.033)	(0.031)
Legal index	0.0391	−0.0083	0.0406**	0.0560**	−0.0184	0.0391	0.0720**
	(0.041)	(0.042)	(0.017)	(0.026)	(0.051)	(0.041)	(0.036)
Governor turnover	−0.1649***	−0.1465**	−0.1043***	−0.0969**	−0.1922***	−0.1649***	−0.1462**
	(0.053)	(0.060)	(0.027)	(0.045)	(0.062)	(0.053)	(0.054)
Lagged CBI variable (non-lagged variable)	0.2071**	0.3641***	0.1417**	0.0008	0.2244**	0.2071**	0.0530***
	(0.113)	(0.074)	(0.076)	(0.015)	(0.116)	(0.113)	(0.011)
With an interaction variable(s)	0.1251**	0.1238	0.1938***	0.2548***	0.0789	0.1251**	dropped
	(0.052)	(0.085)	(0.049)	(0.042)	(0.083)	(0.052)	
Degree of freedom and research quality							
√Degree of freedom	0.0140***	0.0150**	0.0112***	0.0095**	0.0169**	0.0140***	0.0063
	(0.004)	(0.007)	(0.003)	(0.004)	(0.006)	(0.004)	(0.005)
Quality level	−0.0008		−0.0040	0.0006	−0.0015	−0.0008	dropped
	(0.004)		(0.003)	(0.003)	(0.003)	(0.004)	
Intercept	−7.1935	−5.9820	−1.6659	2.2969	−12.1161**	−7.1935	109.5471***
	(4.958)	(6.611)	(6.461)	(6.475)	(5.135)	(4.958)	(7.655)
K	212	212	212	212	212	212	212
R^2	0.3471	0.2741	0.4067	0.2770	0.3756	0.3471	0.0044

(b) Dependent variable—t value

Estimator (analytical weight in parentheses)	*Cluster-robust OLS*	*Cluster-robust WLS [Quality level]*	*Cluster-robust WLS [N]*	*Cluster-robust WLS [1/SE]*	*Cluster-robust WLS [1/EST]*	*Cluster-robust random-effects panel GLS*	*Cluster-robust fixed-effects panel LSDV*
Meta-independent variable (default)/Model	*[8]*	*[9]*	*[10]*	*[11]*	*[12]*	*[13]*[d]	*[14]*[e]
Estimation period							
First year of estimation	0.0105	−0.0324	0.0142	−0.0384	0.0441	0.0105	−0.2066***
	(0.032)	(0.036)	(0.038)	(0.040)	(0.032)	(0.032)	(0.044)

(*Continued*)

Appendix C (Continued)

(b) Dependent variable—t value

Estimator (analytical weight in parentheses)	Cluster-robust OLS	Cluster-robust WLS [Quality level]	Cluster-robust WLS [N]	Cluster-robust WLS [1/SE]	Cluster-robust WLS [1/EST]	Cluster-robust random-effects panel GLS	Cluster-robust fixed-effects panel LSDV
Meta-independent variable (default)/Model	[8]	[9]	[10]	[11]	[12]	[13][d]	[14][e]
Length of estimation	-0.0123	-0.0285	-0.0235	-0.0064	-0.0125	-0.0123	dropped
	(0.021)	(0.022)	(0.018)	(0.029)	(0.018)	(0.021)	
Time-series data	-1.1191	-0.6484	-4.0157**	-1.9172	-1.0715	-1.1191	dropped
	(1.147)	(1.168)	(1.709)	(1.382)	(1.070)	(1.147)	
Panel data	-0.3846	-0.3773	-1.1245	-0.5165	-0.5243	-0.3846	dropped
	(0.503)	(0.600)	(0.697)	(0.815)	(0.667)	(0.503)	
OLS	1.7832***	1.6813***	1.0473	0.8687	2.4886***	1.7832***	1.2371***
	(0.541)	(0.315)	(0.793)	(0.710)	(0.402)	(0.541)	(0.418)
Transformed variable	0.8136	0.8810	-0.9852	1.0046	0.0952	0.8136	0.4670
	(1.193)	(0.843)	(1.632)	(1.122)	(0.844)	(1.193)	(0.373)
Log value	1.3620	1.7364	-0.5152	1.3496	0.7678	1.3620	dropped
	(1.247)	(1.052)	(1.684)	(1.185)	(0.908)	(1.247)	
Political index	0.7025	-0.5190	2.1613***	1.8947**	-1.6479	0.7025	1.4938**
	(1.256)	(0.875)	(0.539)	(0.693)	(1.051)	(1.256)	(0.717)
Economic index	-0.3420	-0.1908	0.1688**	0.6670**	-0.7725	-0.3420	-0.1542
	(0.391)	(0.538)	(0.083)	(0.365)	(0.867)	(0.391)	(0.265)
Legal index	-0.1934	-0.5700	0.2402	0.7140**	-1.2921	-0.1934	0.4352
	(0.600)	(0.569)	(0.222)	(0.318)	(0.993)	(0.600)	(0.295)
Governor turnover	-1.9900***	-2.0016***	-1.5298***	-1.0821**	-2.8239**	-1.9900***	-1.6247***
	(0.567)	(0.676)	(0.199)	(0.504)	(0.980)	(0.567)	(0.383)
Lagged CBI variable (non-lagged variable)	2.3768**	3.9249***	1.8284**	0.2672**	2.5130**	2.3768**	0.7257***
	(1.197)	(0.878)	(0.857)	(0.127)	(1.231)	(1.197)	(0.171)
With an interaction variable(s)	2.9970***	3.4133***	3.6548***	3.9646***	2.3789***	2.9970***	dropped
	(0.755)	(0.998)	(0.646)	(0.504)	(1.185)	(0.755)	

√Degree of freedom	0.0529	0.0207	0.0759**	0.0173	0.0680	0.0529	-0.0310
	(0.047)	(0.076)	(0.033)	(0.052)	(0.084)	(0.047)	(0.079)
Quality level	-0.0245	61.8677	-0.0377	-0.0002	-0.0387	-0.0245	dropped
	(0.040)	(71.165)	(0.039)	(0.039)	(0.039)	(0.040)	
Intercept	-23.7476	-23.7476	-28.9483	73.2297	-89.3887	-23.7476	408.0217***
	(62.982)	(62.982)	(74.814)	(79.031)	(64.703)	(62.982)	(86.847)
K	212	212	212	212	212	212	212
R^2	0.2976	0.2937	0.3502	0.3194	0.4059	0.2976	0.0605

Notes:
[a]With regard to the estimates of governor turnover, their signs are reversed to use for meta-analysis.
[b]Breusch-Pagan test: χ^2=0.00, p=1.000.
[c]Hausman test: χ^2 = 45.61, p = 0.000.
[d]Breusch-Pagan test: χ^2 = 0.00, p = 1.000.
[e]Hausman test: χ^2 = 92.96, p = 0.000.
Figures in parentheses beneath the regression coefficients are robust standard errors.***, **, and * denote statistical significance at the 1%, 5%, and 10% levels, respectively.

Source: Authors' estimation. See Appendix B for definitions and descriptive statistics of independent variables.

9 Is there really causality between inflation and inflation uncertainty?

Jamal Bouoiyour and Refk Selmi

1. Introduction

The inflation, its uncertainty and the challenges ahead have been and continue to be a topic of considerable dispute. Even though policy discussions are likely to be guided by a belief that inflation rate serves as the nominal anchor on which the central banks rely to appropriately fulfill price stability, the research literature –both theoretical and empirical– fails to reach firm conclusions in this respect. Having precise information on the causal relationship between inflation and inflation uncertainty is pivotal for monetary authorities, because great uncertainty about future inflation necessitates more active policies (see, for instance, Soderstrom, 2002; Elder, 2004; Fountas et al. 2006; Chowdhury, 2014).

Some economists argued that inflation leads to an increase in the opportunity cost of holding money and a heightened inflation uncertainty which may be very harmful for investments and savings, leading to a misallocation of resources and sharp distortions in the economy (for example, Friedman, 1977; Ball, 1992; Dotsey and Ireland, 1996; Lucas, 2003). Friedman (1977) indicated that a rise in average inflation may prompt an erratic policy response by the monetary authorities, leading to a higher uncertainty about the future rate of inflation and then to a detrimental effect on the output growth. Such a negative effect runs via the ineffectiveness of price system in allocating resources. Consistently with Friedman's hypothesis, Ball (1992) suggested, using game asymmetric information, that higher inflation causes more inflation uncertainty since the public is uncertain about the type of future policy making.

Others, however, claimed that even though inflation may sound like a "terrifying" concept, a small amount isn't necessarily a bad thing. The possible benefits of inflation include lightening the real burden of public and private debt, retaining nominal interest rates above zero so that central banks can avoid tax distortion and in turn generate a stable investment environment, and reducing unemployment due to nominal wage rigidity. According to Cukierman and Meltzer (1986), inflation uncertainty creates higher average inflation owing to the opportunistic behavior of central banks. More accurately, they deduced that when there is uncertainty about increased inflation, central banks tend to create inflation surprises to establish real economic gain, yielding to high inflation rates. Furthermore, Ungar and Zilberfarb (1993) found evidence that high inflation lowers the uncertainty about inflation since people invest resources to foresee the future inflation rate. Holland (1995) showed that stronger inflation uncertainty decreases the average inflation rate mainly due to the stabilization motive of the monetary authority, also dubbed "the stabilizing Fed hypothesis".

Recently, Balima et al. (2017) conducted a meta-regression analysis of the empirical literature on the macroeconomic consequences of inflation targeting adoption. They documented that referees and editors favor findings underscoring the positive outcomes of the conduct of inflation targeting on inflation volatility, real GDP growth, and fiscal performances. After correcting for publication biases, no significant genuine effects on inflation volatility and the real GDP growth were found. The authors also deduced that the effects of inflation targeting change sharply conditional on time spans, econometric strategies, and country-specific characteristics. To our best knowledge, this paper is the first to conduct a meta-regression analysis (MRA) of the literature on testing for causality between inflation and inflation uncertainty to (a) determine if there is a genuine effect in this literature and (b) identify the main factors behind the mixed results.

The MRA helps to enhance the estimation of the parameter of interest by filtering out any publication bias, and by accurately explaining heterogeneity in the findings of prior studies (Ćorić and Pugh 2010; Rose and Stanley 2005). The standard approach to test for a genuine effect is to regress the ratio of the estimated coefficient and its standard error on a constant, the inverse of the standard error, and control variables. Based on Bruns et al.'s (2014) study, we modify the standard meta-regression model to meta-analyze Granger causality test statistics. The use of this meta-regression model-based causality testing is dominantly motivated by the wide and inconclusive literature that tests the causality between inflation and its related uncertainty. Potentially larger biases may exist in the published literature on the focal issue. One can cite the publication bias owing to the usual tendency for statistically significant findings to be approvingly published. In addition, the results may suffer from omitted variables bias. This problem arises when a potential factor that may exert a strong influence on the relationship between the variables of interest is omitted from the regression. We can also add the overfitting bias. Statistically, in moderate samples, there is a tendency for vector autoregression model fitting procedures to choose more lags of the time series than the "true" underlying data generation process has. Besides, there is a tendency to over-reject the null hypothesis of no causality in these overfitted models. This deeply suggests that several Granger causality findings from small sample researches might be misleading. In this context, Zapata and Rambaldi (1997) claimed that overfitting yields to losing trust in research outcomes. In the current study, we follow Bruns et al. (2014) and control for these effects by incorporating the number of degrees of freedom lost in fitting the underlying models as a relevant control variable.

Our results reveal that the presence of excess significance in the inflation-inflation uncertainty literature can be attributed to overfitting bias rather than the presence of genuine Granger causality. In other words, due to overfitting bias, a literature can support evidence for a significant causality between inflation and inflation uncertainty, whereas in reality the Granger causality is seemingly absent. Therefore, revisiting the causal relationship between inflation and inflation uncertainty using more adequate techniques appear very prominent for formulating effective evidence-based policy.

The rest of the paper is organized as follows: Section 2 presents a review of empirical studies on the causality between inflation and inflation uncertainty. Section 3 describes how we proceeded in order to construct the meta-sample, which, in turn, served as a basis for our meta-regression assessment. Section 4 reports and discusses the empirical results. Section 5 concludes.

2. Literature review

The unfavorable economic consequences of inflation and its related uncertainty have inspired a growing literature to assess the relationship between the two. Nevertheless, no firm conclusions have been reached. Clearly, the macroeconomic literature on this issue encompasses different countries and various econometric methods, making it difficult to draw robust conclusions.

Friedman (1977) was the first to deduce that an upward pressure in inflation could lead to greater inflation uncertainty. Several theories formulated to spell out this outcome indicated that the impact of inflation on inflation uncertainty can be either positive or negative. Following Friedman (1977), Ball (1992) found that higher inflation generates heightened inflation uncertainty due to the difficulty of modeling decision-making under uncertain and risky situations. Further views pointing to similar causality were advanced by Brunner and Hess (1993), Golob (1994), Joyce (1995), Ricketts and Rose (1995), Grier and Perry (1998, 2000), Nas and Perry (2000), Neyapti and Kaya (2001), Zeynel and Mahir (2008), Heidari and Bashiri (2010), and Chowdhury (2014). However, the possibility of an adverse effect of inflation on its uncertainty was then taken into account by Pourgerami and Maskus (1987) and Ungar and Zilberfarb (1993), who argued that in an environment of growing inflation, economic agents may invest more resources in inflation forecasting, thus mitigating uncertainty about future inflation and its adverse consequences.

By contrast, there are hypotheses suggesting a significant causality in the opposite direction (i.e., from inflation uncertainty to inflation). Also, there are views which indicate that the impact of inflation uncertainty on inflation can be either positive or negative. Cukierman and Meltzer (1986), for instance, showed that an increase in inflation uncertainty prompts a rise in inflation as it brings an incentive to policymakers to respond opportunistically to spur output growth by making monetary expansions, which may create inflation pressures. The Cukierman and Meltzer hypothesis was supported by Holland (1993), Baillie et al. (1996), Grier and Perry (1998), Kontanikas (2004), and Hachicha and Lean (2013). Conversely, Holland (1995) claimed that more inflation uncertainty generates lower average inflation rate due to the fact that the central bank attempts to lighten the welfare losses emanating from inflation uncertainty, taking an anti-inflation stance by contracting the money supply, thereby lessening inflationary pressures. This is well known in the literature as the "Stabilizing Fed hypothesis". By delving into the experience of Thailand, Payne (2009 a) found that an increase in inflation uncertainty causes a decrease in inflation, consistently with the Holland's stabilization hypothesis.

More recently, a number of empirical studies explored the relationship between inflation and inflation uncertainty, from a fresh perspective, by carrying out newly econometric techniques. Most of these works rely on the Generalized Autoregressive Conditional Heteroskedasticity (GARCH) extensions to measure inflation volatility. These studies have examined the causality between inflation and inflation uncertainty by carrying out multiple dynamic methods including a system of simultaneous equations, nonlinear Granger causality tests, Granger causality tests-based wavelets, Granger causality testing in quantiles, and so forth.

Using different GARCH extensions as proxies of inflation uncertainty, Kontonikas (2004) showed a positive link between inflation and inflation uncertainty for the case of United Kingdom during the period 1972–2002, which is in line with the Friedman-Ball hypothesis. The author added that the conduct of inflation targeting in UK since 1992 has allowed reducing inflation rate and its associated uncertainty. Besides, Keskek and Orhan (2010) applied a GARCH-in-mean model as an inflation volatility measure to analyze the relationship between inflation and inflation uncertainty in Turkey for the period from 1984 to 2005. They argued that high inflation leads to excessive inflation volatility, while the impact of inflation uncertainty on inflation is found to be negative owing to the opportunistic incentives of policymakers.

Moreover, Karahan (2012) used a two-step procedure to test whether a causal link between inflation and inflation uncertainty exists in Turkey over the period 2002–2011, and found that higher inflation rises uncertainty about future inflation. Using quarterly data from Australian case over a large period from 1949 to 2013, Hossain (2014) showed that inflation uncertainty responds more substantially to positive rather than negative inflation shocks. By conducting a nonlinear Granger causality test-based wavelet approach, Bouoiyour and Selmi (2014) investigated the causal relationship between inflation and inflation uncertainty in Egypt from 1960 to 2013. They deduced that the relationship between inflation and inflation uncertainty is time-varying. There is no evidence of significant causality in the short-term. In the medium term, an increase in the inflation rate leads to an increase in its uncertainty, whereas over the long-term horizons, bidirectional causality was shown. They attributed the mixed results to demand pull and cost push factors as well as conflicting objectives required to mitigate the damageable effects of the political uncertainty surrounding the Arab Spring. In a cross country study of 12 emerging market economies and by performing linear vs. nonlinear Granger causality tests, Thornton (2007) showed that great inflation uncertainty yields to a drop of inflation rate in Colombia, Mexico, and Turkey, consistently with Holland's (1995) hypothesis, whereas in Hungary, Indonesia, and Korea, the Cukierman and Meltzer hypothesis was supported.

Moreover, in a panel of 105 countries for the period 1960–2007, Kim and Lin (2012) applied a system of simultaneous equations and demonstrated a two-way interaction between inflation and its related uncertainty. Furthermore, Živkov et al. (2014) tested for Granger-causality between inflation and inflation uncertainty in quantiles for 11 Eastern European countries. They provided multisided evidence regarding the direction of causality between the two variables. Both Friedman-Ball and Cukierman-Meltzer hypotheses were supported for larger Eastern European economies with flexible exchange rate, whereas these hypotheses do not hold true when focusing on smaller economies with fixed exchange rate regime.

3. A meta-Granger causality testing

The meta-regression analysis (MRA) consists of reviewing empirical studies each reporting several regressions and providing conflicting results. This study carries out an improved meta-regression analysis, dubbed a meta-Granger causality testing, to help explain the wide variation of findings – ranging from insignificantly to significantly negative/positive effects of inflation on inflation uncertainty and vice versa – in the empirical literature. We also try to test whether there is evidence of genuine effect between inflation and inflation uncertainty. Another objective is to suggest new lines of enquiry by controlling for possible overfitting bias. More specifically, we evaluate if the excess significance in the inflation-inflation uncertainty literature is due to overfitting bias.

3.1. Meta-sample

We first focus on the strategy conducted to build the meta-dataset utilized in the MRA. There are a very large number of papers dealing with the causality between inflation and inflation uncertainty. These studies vary noticeably in terms of country coverage, methodology, data, and econometric quality. This section depicts the methods and criteria we used in order to effectively select our sample of studies, which are reported in Table A.1 (Appendices). We searched Scopus, EconLit, and Google Scholar for combinations of the keywords "inflation", "consumer prices", "inflation uncertainty", "inflation volatility", "causality", "nexus", and "relationship" to find more studies on the field. We incorporated some unpublished studies while trying to reduce the possible publication selection bias. Although we collected more than 100 papers on focal subject, only 32 studies with 812 estimates were accounted for in our MRA. We filtered empirical works for econometric quality and we excluded those that did not offer the required information for our MRA. More accurately, we incorporated researches that have applied causality tests developed by Granger (1969), Sims (1972), Hsiao (1979), Toda and Yamamoto (1995), or cointegration tests developed by Engle and Granger (1987) or Johansen (1988; 1991). Studies performing nonparametric causality tests were also considered. We excluded, however, the autoregressive distributed lags (ARDL) bounds test developed by

Pesaran and Shin (1999) and Pesaran et al. (2001) since it presumes the direction of Granger causality a priori.

3.2. Publication selection bias and genuine effect

Since the findings in several issues were inconclusive, meta-regression analysis is a helpful tool aimed at reconciling the inconsistencies (Stanley, 2005). MRA is a statistical technique for combining different results from independent researches. To combine the different results, we start by a standard model of simple meta-regression. To detect the between study heterogeneity, a model that enables for heterogeneity at the study and the estimate levels is most effective (Doucouliagos and Stanley, 2009). In particular, we consider the following equations (1) and (2):

$$\theta_{ij} = \beta_1 + \beta_0 SE_{ij} + \varepsilon_{ij} \tag{1}$$

$$\theta_{ij}' = \beta_1' + \beta_0' SE_{ij} + \varepsilon_{ij}' \tag{2}$$

where θ_{ij} is the i-th estimated effect-size of inflation on inflation uncertainty of study j, and θ_{ij}' is the i-th estimated effect-size of inflation uncertainty on inflation of study j, $\beta_1(\beta'_1)$ is the true value of inflation (inflation uncertainty) coefficient, $\beta_0 SE_{ij}(\beta_0' SE_{ij})$ detect the tendency from the authors and reviewers to favor findings that are statistically significant, SE_{ij} is the i-th standard error of the coefficient of study j and ε_{ij} and ε'_{ij} are the meta-regression disturbance terms.

To control then for heteroskedasticity due to dissimilarities across studies on the sample size and model specifications performed, we thereafter estimate this model with weighted least squares (WLS) by dividing equations (1) and (2) by SE_{ij}, which become:

$$t_{ij} = \beta_0 + \beta_1 \left(1 \Big/ SE_{ij} \right) + \xi_{ij} \tag{3}$$

$$t_{ij}' = \beta_0' + \beta_1' \left(1 \Big/ SE_{ij} \right) + \xi_{ij}' \tag{4}$$

Where t_{ij} is the t-stat associated to θ_{ij} and t_{ij}' is the t-stat associated to θ_{ij}', respectively, ξ_{ij} and ξ_{ij}' are the weighted error terms.

Afterwards, we examine whether there exists a publication bias by testing the null hypothesis that the intercept terms in the equations (3) and (4) are equal to zero ($\beta_0 = 0$ and $\beta_0' = 0$). It is commonly recognized that publication bias threats the distribution of estimated effects since for example insignificant results may not be considered by editors for publication. This is seemingly a great problem in meta-analysis. In the presence of publication selection, authors of studies with smaller sample sizes tend to select large and significant effects to mitigate less accurate estimates. Thus, the statistical significance of β_0 ($\beta_0{}'$) can be an indicator for publication selection bias (Stanley, 2005). This is known as the funnel asymmetry test (FAT). If we find that β_0 and $\beta_0{}'$ are different from zero, this would imply a tendency to favor estimates with a well specific t-statistic, which may surpass the threshold of statistical significance. In other words, the causal relationship between inflation and inflation uncertainty would be overestimated.

Then, to verify the existence of a genuine effect after filtering out the publication bias (if any), we pursue Stanley and Doucouliagos's (2012) study and perform the so-called precision-effect test (PET). Concretely, we evalute the null hypothesis that the parameter associated with the inverse standard error in the equations (3) and (4) are equal to zero ($\beta_1{=}0$ and $\beta_1{}'{=}0$). Dismissing the null hypothesis would underscore that a genuine effect is present after filtering the publication selection bias.

Because the publication selection is a complex phenomenon, we next turn to multiple meta-regressions by extending equations (3) and (4) while including a vector Z of k covariates. More specifically, Equations (3) and (4) become:

$$t_{ij} = \beta_0 + \beta_1 \left(1 \Big/ SE_{ij} \right) + \beta_k \left(Z_{ik} \Big/ SE_{ij} \right) + \upsilon_{ij} \tag{5}$$

$$t_{ij}{}' = \beta_0{}' + \beta_1{}' \left(1 \Big/ SE_{ij} \right) + \beta_k{}' \left(Z_{ik} \Big/ SE_{ij} \right) + \upsilon_{ij}{}' \tag{6}$$

The results derived from the existing literature reported in Tables A.1 and A.2 (Appendices) indicate a sharp variation in findings among the empirical studies surveyed. Additional covariates allow detecting study characteristics from the meta-sample that explain the heterogeneous estimates between studies. We list in Table A.3 (Appendices) the moderator variables expected to have a systematic influence on the causal relationship between inflation and inflation uncertainty. From our sample, we extracted information about the design of studies including the countries features, the volatility proxies used (standard or new volatility measures, i.e., *SVM* and *NVM*, respectively) and the econometric strategies conducted to analyze the causal relationship between inflation and its related uncertainty such as the Vector Autoregressive model (*VAR*), the Markov-Switching Vector Autoregression (*MS-VAR*), the game-theoretic model of monetary policy (*GTM*), the parametric (*PCT*) vs. nonparametric (*NPCT*) causality tests, and the asymmetric (*ASCT*) vs. nonlinear (*NLCT*) causality tests. Another potential factor that was accounted for is whether the study controls for the independence of central banks (*CBI*). Moreover, we controlled for the earliest and latest year of the sample in the investigated studies (*PUBY*) to see whether the estimated coefficient can be significantly impacted by the sample period. The strength of findings may change substantially with the year of publication. Accordingly, Simmons et al. (1999) documented that, during the initial stages of research in a particular area, it might be easier to publish confirmatory findings than later (in particular, when fresh insights on the central issue are shown). Some recent MRA studies included dummies that consider the earliest and the latest year of publication in order to explore whether the sample period influences the estimated coefficients (see, for example, Benos and Zotou, 2014; Bouoiyour and Selmi, 2016).

3.3. Control for overfitting

The selection of significant or theory-confirming findings may distort the conclusions of published studies (Ioannidis, 2005). According to Rosenthal (1979), the published literature on testing for Granger causality consists of 5% of findings where the null hypothesis was absolutely disproved, while 95% of results where the null hypothesis was rejected are generally unpublished. In the case of Granger causality tests, potentially misleading findings can be drawn if the Vector Autoregression (VAR) model is overfitted. It must be pointed out here that the VAR model behaves very poorly in small sized samples. The limited sample is usual in the macroeconomic empirical literature which employs annual data. The meta-regression models allow summarizing the Granger causality tests from various primary studies while attempting to identify the existence/inexistence of genuine Granger causality while accounting for potential biases. More specifically, the current research performs a newly meta-Granger causality testing that assesses the presence of genuine Granger causality in the presence of publication bias due to sampling variability and overfitting bias.

The Granger causality is a frequently used concept in several economic issues including monetary policy (Lee and Yang 2012), economic development (Ang 2008), energy economics (Ozturk et al. 2010; Bouoiyour and Selmi 2013), and environmental issues (Stern and Kaufmann 1997; Bouoiyour and Selmi 2017), among others. Nevertheless, Granger causality test statistics are highly sensitive to the selected lag length for the VAR model (Zapata and Rambaldi 1997). In the same context, Hafer and Sheehan (1989) indicated that the precision of forecasts from VAR models varies hugely depending to lag lengths. Because the true lag length is rarely known, the identification of the ideal or the optimal lag length prompts higher uncertainty with respect the appropriateness of Granger causality tests.[1] To properly determine the optimal lag structure one must choose across a large variety of model selection criteria. The performance of several information criteria, namely Akaike (AIC), Schwarz-Bayesian (SBC), and Hannan-Quinn (HQ), was largely evaluated in order to identify the optimal lag length. Hacker and Hatemi (2008) tried to choose the ideal lag length by covering large and limited sample sizes and either in stable and unstable VAR models. Using Monte Carlo simulation, the authors demonstrated that SBC performs much better than AIC and HQ in lag-choice accuracy under various conditions, in particular in the case of financial data, which are often highly volatile. Regardless of the performance of SBC, all the information criteria have been widely criticized because of their tendency to overestimate and underestimate the true lag length (Lütkepohl, 1985). Indeed, the overfitted VAR models tend to overreject the null hypotheses of Granger non-causality compared to the rejection rate of a VAR model estimated with the "true" lag length (Zapata and Rambaldi, 1997). An overfitted VAR model leads to increased false-positive Granger causality outcomes in the absence of genuine Granger causality. Given the tendency to publish significant findings, the outcomes that are statistically significant owing to overfitting bias will be more likely to be published than insignificant results as authors may select the information criteria that permit to provide significant evidence.

In the absence of genuine Granger causality even if when using the "true" lag length, false-positive Granger causality results may also occur. If authors, for instance, choose the significant results based on estimates for a broad range of countries, distinct time spans, different econometric strategies, the empirical literature will be misleading. Following Bruns et al. (2014), we first test whether there is a genuine Granger causality in the presence of publication selection bias due to sampling variability but not to overfitting bias:

$$z_j^{gc} = \alpha_B^{gc} + \beta_B^{gc} \sqrt{df_j} + \varepsilon_j^{gc} \tag{7}$$

where df_j is the number of degrees of freedom of the equation of the VAR employed in the primary study j and $z_j^{gc} = \phi^{-1}(1 - \pi_j^{gc})$, where ϕ^{-1} is the inverse cumulative distribution function of the standard normal distribution and π_j^{gc} is the p-value of the study j. The direction of Granger causality is expressed as $g = 1,..., (1 - g)$ designating the independent variable in equation $c = 1, \ldots, q$ of the VAR. The strong values of z_j^{gc} mean weak p-values and then high levels of statistical significance.

If there exists genuine Granger causality effect, the level of significance should surge as df_j rises. Nevertheless, if there is no genuine Granger causality df_j shouldn't be associated to the significance levels. In the presence of publication selection bias based on estimates for different countries and using various econometric models and data sources, wider estimates of the VAR coefficients are needed to fulfill statistical significance for lower degrees of freedom, while modest estimates of the VAR coefficients appear enough when there are strong degrees of freedom. For such a case, the p-values will be not significantly linked to the degrees of freedom albeit the existing literature on the central issue reports significant findings derived from sampling variability. Based on Bruns and Stern's (2015) study, we can address whether there exists genuine Granger causality in the presence of this publication selection bias by testing the following null hypothesis:

$$H_0 : \beta_B^{gc} \leq 0 \tag{8}$$

Bruns and Stern (2015) claimed that an overfitting bias may yield to larger z^{gc} values compared to those shown when employing the optimal lag length. This highlights that β_B^{gc} does not completely reflect to the true link between z^{gc} and $\sqrt{df}$. Such a bias in β_B^{gc} minimizes the power of the basic meta-regression model in the presence of overfitting bias. To avoid methodological pitfall and to control for possible potential bias, we include the underlying lag length (p) of the VAR model in the meta-regression specification, denoted as:

$$z_j^{gc} = \alpha_L^{gc} + \beta_L^{gc} \sqrt{df_j} + \gamma^{gc} p_j + v_j^{gc} \tag{9}$$

Next, we examine the existence of genuine Granger causality in the presence of publication selection bias by evaluating the following null hypothesis:

$$H_0 : \beta_L^{gc} \leq 0 \tag{10}$$

4. Meta-regression results

4.1. Testing for publication bias and genuine empirical effect

To establish that the results are not plagued with publication bias, we conduct the FAT-PET-PEESE (FPP) procedure, a commonly applied approach for controlling for publication bias in the economics meta-analysis literature (Stanley and Doucouliagos, 2012). As mentioned above, the first step consists of a Funnel Asymmetry Testing (FAT) to test if the sample of estimates is significantly affected by publication selection bias. If β_0 and $\beta_0{}'$ in equations (3) and (4) are different from zero, then the estimates suffer from publication bias. The second step consists of conducting a Precision Effect Test (PET) to test if there is a genuine, non-zero, true effect of estimates once publication bias is corrected. We employ the same equations as the FAT, but we test the null hypothesis that the parameter associated with the inverse standard error in equations (3) and (4) are equal to zero ($\beta_1 = 0$ and $\beta_1{}' = 0$). If the PET rejects the null hypothesis, then one can deduce that there is a genuine non-zero true effect after addressing the publication selection bias. In that case, we estimate a novel specification dubbed the Precision Effect Estimate with Standard Error (PEESE) to find an improved estimate of the overall mean effect. Our FPP procedure results reported in Table 9.1 clearly reveal that a publication selection bias exists for both the causality running from inflation to inflation uncertainty and the reverse causality, because the constant term ($\beta_0/\beta_0{}'$) is statistically significant among all the estimators used. The FPP procedure allows going beyond the publication selection bias by assessing whether there is a genuine causality between inflation and its related uncertainty. The genuine causal effects after correcting the publication

Table 9.1 The FAT-PET-PEESE (FPP) results

	(1): Inflation causes Inflation Uncertainty				(2): Inflation Uncertainty causes Inflation			
	FAT-PET		PEESE		FAT-PET		PEESE	
	Coef.	p-value	Coef.	p-value	Coef.	p-value	Coef.	p-value
β_0/β_0'	-1.23851	0.0023**	-2.1568	0.0110*	1.8615	0.0305*	1.9587	0.0002***
β_1/β_1'	0.001317	0.0513*	0.006152	0.9124	0.001439	0.0312*	0.000318	0.4486
R2	0.23451		0.41065		0.40123		0.43567	
Ramsey Reset test	F(3,812)= 6.023451 Prob>F= 0.000000		F(3,812)= 6.15432 Prob>F= 0.000000		F(3,812)= 6.189324 Prob>F= 0.000000		F(3,812)= 6.752708 Prob>F= 0.000000	

Notes: *, **, *** denote statistical significance at 10%, 5%, and 1% levels, respectively.

bias (β_1/β_1') suggest a positive causal effect of inflation on inflation uncertainty and vice versa. But such genuine causal effects seem moderate.

4.2. Drivers of heterogeneity

A meta-regression analysis helps to explain potential reasons for the heterogeneity among estimates. After testing for publication selection bias and genuine empirical effect, we try in the following to address what are the main factors that explain the sharp heterogeneity in the results. To do so, we estimate equations (5) and (6).

Although the meta-independent variables for researches examining the causality between inflation and inflation uncertainty across developed and developing countries is statistically significant and positive, the correlation appears much more pronounced for developed than developing economies when focusing on the causality from inflation to inflation uncertainty. Insignificant effect is displayed for developed economies when taking into account the inverse causal link. Expectedly, developed countries pursued appropriate financial reforms and use effective hedging tools that may help to mitigate the possible costs of

Table 9.2 Meta-regression analysis

Moderator variables	(1)Inflation causes Inflation Uncertainty		(2): Inflation Uncertainty causes Inflation	
	Estimate	p-value	Estimate	p-value
RSE = 1/SE	1.281454	0.0067***	0.182496	0.0683*
Intercept	0.634267	0.2175	−1.147232	0.0744*
SZ	0.592746	0.0148**	0.160279	0.0400**
DC/SE	1.048674	0.0000***	0.107417	0.1992
DEC/SE	0.180590	0.0000***	0.124664	0.0991*
CM/SE	0.478192	0.0517*	−0.171058	0.0867*
SM/SE	0.682035	0.0743*	0.139499	0.0364**
VAR/SE	−0.223253	0.0550*	−0.066638	0.0607*
MS-VAR/SE	0.812829	0.0145**	0.064527	0.0039***
GTM/SE	0.205526	0.0063***	0.037726	0.1516
PCT/SE	−0.960644	0.0282**	0.042411	0.2952
NPCT/SE	−0.488498	0.0480**	0.042117	0.0065***
ASCT/SE	0.148170	0.0007***	−0.045793	0.0001***
NLCT/SE	0.266116	0.0039***	0.144196	0.0132**
CBI/SE	0.607723	0.0008***	0.206078	0.0052***
AJ/SE	0.290312	0.0073***	0.134421	0.0081***
PUBY/SE	0.150320	0.0046***	0.041077	0.0077***
R-squared	0.81		0.67	
Ramsey Reset test	F(3,803) = 1.09; Prob>F = 0.026		F(3,803) = 1.01; Prob>F = 0.019	

Notes: *, **, *** denote statistical significance at 10%, 5%, and 1% levels respectively; dependent variable: t-statistic. The data analysis presents the MRA results with cluster-robust standard errors. The Ramsey reset test rejects the null at all levels of statistical significance, indicating an incorrect specification of the model.

inflation uncertainty. Nevertheless, non-existent forward markets coupled with the inefficiency of the financial system in developing economies may aggravate the effect of sizable inflation volatility on inflation outcomes (positive effect for developing countries). Furthermore, the wide range of econometric method-ologies may highly explain the mixed findings in the existing literature. Indeed, the coefficients measuring the effect of new volatility models (*NVM*) as proxies of inflation volatility are statistically positive and significant for both directions (from inflation to inflation uncertainty and vice versa). On the contrary, studies carrying out standard volatility models (*SVM*) are more likely to reach controver-sial effects. Although the broad range of inflation uncertainty measures have been largely documented in the existing literature, there is still no consensus on which measure is the most appropriate. The standard deviation and the moving average deviation applied in several studies may overlook the informa-tion on stochastic inflation processes. In this background, the different GARCH extensions (symmetric vs. asymmetric, and linear vs. nonlinear)[2] may be more useful because inflation is a complex economic phenomenon and then may show periods of low and high volatility, instead of periods of constant volatility (i.e., volatility clustering). In addition, the Markov-switching vector autoregres-sive model (*MS-VAR*),[3] the parametric causality test (*PCT*) and the game-theoretic model of monetary policy (*GTM*) are more likely to display positive inflation effect on inflation uncertainty, while a negative connection between the two time series of interest is discovered when using VAR approach and non-parametric causality tests (*NPCT*). For the inverse relationship running from inflation uncertainty to inflation, all the models (*MS-VAR, GTM, NPCT*) display positive coefficient with the exception of VAR approach showing a neg-ative relationship. Interestingly, the fact that the majority of researches have excluded models that account for asymmetry and nonlinearity may be also con-sidered as main contributors of the conflicting outcomes previously obtained. The historical data of time series are generally the result of complex economic processes which include policy shifts, structural changes, sudden shocks, and so forth. The combined influence of these various events are the root of distribu-tional characteristics of macroeconomic time series such as asymmetry, nonlin-earity, heavy-tailness, and extreme values. So, without considering nonlinearity (*NLCT*) and asymmetry (*ASCT*), it is not surprising to discover an ambiguous relationship between inflation and its associated uncertainty. Also, the central bank independence (*CBI*) is likely to play a potential role in explaining this debated topic. In general, countries with more independent central banks have lower inflation (Loungani and Sheets 1997). This underscores that the specific-ities of each country may explain the study-to-study variation on the focal issue. Ultimately, we include the earliest and latest year of the sample in the considered studies (*PUBY*) to view whether the sample period significantly affects the inflation-inflation uncertainty causal link. Also, we incorporate another test-dummy variable to test if a publication in an academic journal (*AJ*) may influence the inflation-inflation literature. We deduce that the publication outlet and the pub-lication year exert a significant impact on this issue's outcomes, consistently with

Alatalo et al. (1997), Gontard-Danek and Moller (1999), Simmons et al. (1999), and Poulin (2000).

3.1. Controlling for overfitting bias

We summarize in Table 9.3 the findings drawn from the MRA for the causality running from inflation to inflation uncertainty and vice versa. The first columns (Equation (3) for the causality from inflation to inflation uncertainty, and Equation (6) for the inverse causality) present the basic models before incorporating the lags. We clearly note that the estimate of β_B^{gc} is negative and significant at the 10% level for inflation causes inflation uncertainty in a two-sided test.[4] This highlights that the significance of the causal relationship from inflation to inflation uncertainty can be attributed to an overfitting bias.

The second columns show the extended models (Equations (4) and (7) for the causality from inflation to inflation uncertainty and vice versa, respectively). Incorporating the lag length as a potential control variable leads to an estimate of β_L^{gc} that is statistically insignificant (Equation (2)). Unlike the Equation (7), we find that we cannot reject the null hypothesis $H_0 : \beta_L^{gc} \leq 0$ for the causality from inflation uncertainty to inflation. This implies that the significance of this direction of causation is more generated by overfitting bias than by the presence of genuine Granger causality. In addition, we show a positive and strong correlation between γ^{gc} and z^{gc} values, suggesting that even causality tests with one lag may lead to strong z^{gc} values. The greater values of z^{gc} imply smaller

Table 9.3 Control for overfitting bias: A before-after analysis

	Inflation rate causes inflation uncertainty			Inflation uncertainty causes inflation rate		
	(3)	(4)	(5)	(6)	(7)	(8)
Constant	3.1472***	2.7186**	3.1523	2.7923	1.2455	1.7655
	(0.0003)	(0.0045)	(0.2341)	(0.0045)	(0.1419)	(0.6132)
$\sqrt{df}$	−0.1137*	−0.1109	0.1329	−0.1852	−0.0973*	0.1018
	(0.0692)	(0.1683)	(0.2875)	(0.2347)	(0.0164)	(0.2346)
γ^{gc}	0.1562	0.7125*	0.5610	0.1651*	0.5943**	0.0145**
	(0.2184)	(0.0641)	(0.1732)	(0.0589)	(0.0011)	(0.0098)
CBI	-	-	−0.0954*	-	-	−0.0358*
			(0.0461)			(0.0376)
$CBI * \sqrt{df}$	-	-	0.1428	-	-	0.1123
			(0.5010)			(0.4271)
R2	0.42	0.53	0.28	0.44	0.61	0.32

Notes: *, **, *** denote statistical significance at 10%, 5%, and 1% levels, respectively. We bootstrap primary studies rather than single Granger causality testing in order to take into account the multiple Granger causality tests carried out per primary study, columns (3) and (6) present the basic models, columns (4) and (7) correspond to the extended models after accounting for the underlying lag length of the VAR model, and columns (5) and (8) refer to the prolonged specifications after accounting for the central bank independence as relevant control variable (this task was conducted for robustness check). Significance codes represent a two-sided *t*-test. The level of significance should be splitted in half to account for the two sides.

p-values and therefore higher significance levels. This can be probably due to publication selection from sampling variability. In fact, the frequent tendency for significant findings to be favorably published, either since reviewers and associate editors generally reject papers that don't reveal statistically significant results or because authors don't submit papers containing insignificant outcomes. Overall, the published studies may over-represent the frequency of significant tests.

Interestingly, our MRA also indicate that there is no genuine relation between inflation and inflation uncertainty in specifications that account for the central bank independence (*CBI*) as a relevant control variable (Equations (5) and (8)). This highlights that the regression of the links between inflation and its related uncertainty may suffer from omitted-variable biases that obscure the genuine causal effects. Granger causality tests are very susceptible to omitted variables bias. This is a very serious problem in the actual empirical Granger causality literature. For instance, inflation might appear to cause inflation uncertainty (or vice versa) in a bivariate Granger causality test as both inflation and its uncertainty are strongly correlated with *CBI*. The paramount importance of *CBI* in ensuring low and stable inflation rates has been largely studied. Further, the existing measures of *CBI* have been found to effectively predict both the level and the volatility of inflation across countries (see, for example, Cukierman 1992; Loungani and Sheets 1997; Bouoiyour and Selmi 2013).

In sum, we deduce that in addition to the publication selection bias due to sampling variability, the overfiting bias and the omitted variables bias, are also very serious problems in the empirical literature on the Granger causality between inflation and inflation uncertainty. Each graph in Figure 9.2 reports the normalized test statistics for causality in one of the two directions. We observe that fewer degrees of freedoms are more associated to studies with two and three lags rather than with one. This highlights that researchers tend to deplete the degrees of freedom by using more lags. Besides, we show that the average significance level increases as the lags rise (i.e., for two and three lags rather than for one) and the degrees of freedom drop. This means that there is a tendency, for the case of limited sized samples, to select more lags of the time series than the true data generation process may have. This implies that a lot of Granger causality outcomes derived from researches based on small samples are erroneous.

4.3. Simulation and performance analysis

The recent empirical studies have attempted to address the critical issue of sample size. Even though various design factors have been assessed in these researches, accurate information about the potential problems of small sample sizes is not yet available. To help fill this gap in the empirical literature, we apply a Monte Carlo simulation (MCS) that varies in terms of sample size (small vs. large). MCS aimed at modeling the probability of various outcomes in a process that might seem very difficult to be estimated or predicted. Crucially,

(1) Inflation rate causes inflation uncertainty

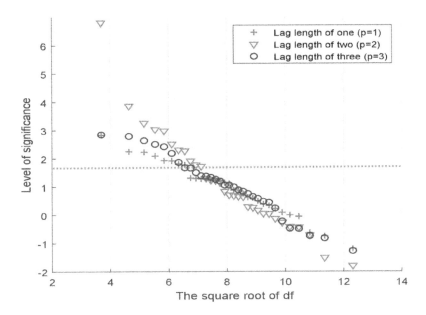

(2) Inflation uncertainty causes inflation rate

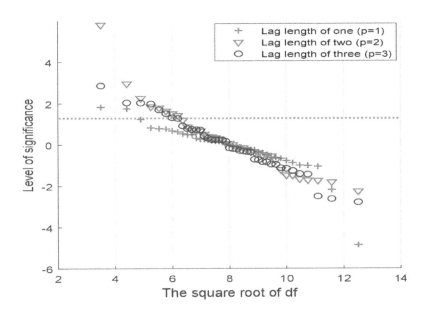

Figure 9.1 The link between the lag length, degrees of freedom, and the level of significance

Notes: The dashed line is at 1.64 separating the graph into statistically significant Granger causality tests (above) and insignificant Granger causality tests (below).

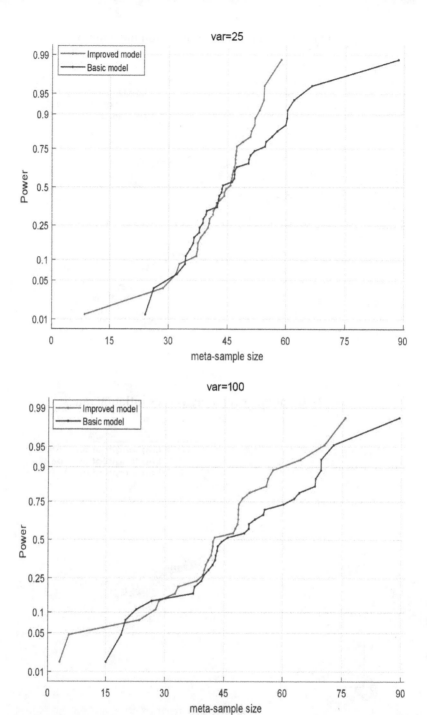

Figure 9.2 Basic vs. improved meta-regression models

Notes: The meta sample size (X-axis) is the number of studies that are brought together in the meta-regression analysis; Power (Y-axis) is the probability of reject the null hypothesis of no causality when it is incorrect; var is the variance of the sample size of the primary studies included in our simulation.

when faced with greatest uncertainty in the process of making an estimation, MCS might be perceived as an effective solution. The simulation procedure will be applied multiple times by altering parameters in the considered models. The comparison of the estimated coefficients from all iterations allows identifying the performance of each model.[5]

The left-hand graph in Figure 9.2 is a simulation of small sample studies (with small variance "var = 25"), whereas the right-hand graph focuses on larger sample studies (with large variance "var = 100"). The graphs indicate that when the samples in primary studies are small and we only have a meta sample of 15 studies, it is hard (even impossible) to detect a genuine effect. By performing a standard meta-regression analysis (or basic model) with a modest effect size, it remains difficult to capture an effect even when we have 30 primary studies. However, the use of an improved meta-regression model which takes into account the number of lags deals with this problem. Our results reported in the right-hand graph reveal that with large primary study sample sizes, it seems easier to capture a true effect with 20 studies in the meta-analysis (basic model) but the improved model performs better in this matter.

5. Conclusions

Understanding the costs of inflation entails to comprehend the causality between inflation and inflation uncertainty. This is very prominent for policymakers since if systematic inflation has any real impacts, governments can exert an effect on economic performance through monetary policy. Even though policy discussions appear to be guided by a belief that inflation raises inflation uncertainty, following the Friedman-Ball Hypothesis, the plethora of studies on this issue fail to reach "one-sided" conclusions in this respect. The findings are heterogeneous due to the variety of countries studied, the different data sources, the diverse inflation uncertainty indicators used and the various conducted econometric strategies.

The primary purpose of the present research is to use a meta-regression analysis to summarize and explain the heterogeneity of the results. The findings drawn from the basic model (WLS and FPP procedure) seem quite interesting. We find that there is a significant publication selection bias for the two-way causality between inflation to inflation uncertainty. After filtering out the publication bias, the genuine causal effects are still present, but such effects are likely to be small. In addition, we show that a broad set of factors explains the variation in the causal relationship between inflation and inflation uncertainty observed from this literature. These factors include the way in which inflation uncertainty was measured, the countries under study, and the econometric tools carried out for testing the causal relations between inflation and its associated uncertainty. The study also offers findings that may have implications for policymakers, especially insofar as some policy factors (including the central bank independence) appear to significantly affect the inflation-inflation uncertainty nexus.

Instead, we introduce a meta-regression model that accounts for overfitting bias to help identify the source of statistically significant Granger causality tests that can be either resulted from genuine Granger causality or biases. In doing so, we find no genuine causal effect in the literature supporting a significant causality from inflation to inflation uncertainty. However, there is a genuine causal effect when we account for the inverse causality running from inflation uncertainty to inflation. We attribute the excess of significance to overfitting bias rather than to the presence of genuine Granger causality. Also interestingly, it is noted that the causality between inflation and inflation uncertainty suffers from omitted-variable biases that obscure the genuine linkages, highlighting flawed policy implications.

Last but not least, we perform a Monte Carlo simulation aimed at comparing the statistical properties of the standard meta-regression and the improved meta-regression that accounts for potential overfitting bias in addition to the sampling variability. We show that the improved model outperforms the standard model. At this stage, we need to figure out that the overfitting bias leaves researchers with great uncertainty surrounding the reliability of inferences. This underscores that if authors adjust to the incentives of publishing statistically significant and theory-consisting results, the reliability and validity of published findings is even more uncertain and an abundance of statistically significant findings may not necessarily mean a genuine effect. In short, we may fail to capture the genuine effects in the literature due to shortcomings in existing research that cannot be effectively and fully controlled by conducting a standard meta-regression analysis. These shortcomings include, for instance, the insufficiently frequent observations (Granger, 1988) or errors in measurement.

Acknowledgment

The authors would like to thank David Guerreiro and an anonymous reviewer for helpful and insightful comments and suggestions on earlier versions of this article.

Notes

1 The high lag length, for example, may spuriously yield to the reject of the estimated coefficients owing to the low precision of estimates (Seddigui 2012).
2 Even though the ARCH and GARCH models effectively capture volatility clustering and leptokurtosis, their distributions do not account for possible asymmetry and nonlinearity in the volatility dynamics. To address these issues, recent studies use generally GARCH models that may detect more adequately the inflation volatility including the Exponential GARCH (EGARCH) model, the Asymmetric Power ARCH (APARCH), and the threshold GARCH, among others.
3 The MS-VAR model is able of detecting the nonlinear, long memory and seasonal features of the inflation series.
4 The two-sided test allows examining the possibility of a statistically significant linkage in both directions. The significance level is divided in half to account for the two sides. If the level of significance is 0.05, a two-tailed test enables half of this level to assess the statistical significance in one direction, and half of the same level to examine the

significance in the other direction. This implies 0.025 is in each tail of the distribution of the test statistic.

5 For more details about Monte Carlo simulation, you can refer to the following link: www.mathworks.com/discovery/monte-carlo-simulation.html.

Bibliography

Achour, M., and Trabelsi, A. (2011): Markov Switching and State-Space Approaches for Investigating the Link between Egyptian Inflation Level and Uncertainty. *Review of Middle East Economics and Finance*, 6(3), pp. 46–62.

Akaike, H. (1974): A New Look at the Statistical Model Identication. *IEEE Transactions on Automatic Control*, 19(6), pp. 716–723.

Alatalo, R. V., Mappes, J., and Elgar, M. (1997): Heritabilities and Paradigm Shifts. *Nature*, 385, pp. 402–403.

Alinaghi, N., and Reed, W. (2016): *Meta-Analysis and Publication Bias: How Well Does the FAT-PET-PEESE Procedure Works?* Working Paper, University of Canterbury. Avaliable at: www.econ.canterbury.ac.nz/RePEc/cbt/econwp/1626.pdf

Ang, J. B. (2008): Economic Development, Pollutant Emissions and Energy Consumption in Malaysia. *Journal of Policy Modeling*, 30, pp. 271–278.

Baillie, R., Chung, C., and Tieslau, M. (1996): Analyzing Inflation by the Fractionally Integrated ARFIMA-GARCH Model. *Journal of Applied Econometrics*, 11, pp. 23–40.

Balcilar, M., Özdemir, Z. A., and Cakan, E. (2011): On the Nonlinear Causality Between Inflation and Inflation Uncertainty in the G3 Countries. *Journal of Applied Economics*, XIV, pp. 269–296.

Balima, H. W., Kilama, E. G., and Tapsoba, R. (2017): *Settling the Inflation Targeting Debate: Lights From a Meta-Regression Analysis IMF Working Papers WP17/213*, International Monetary Fund.

Benos, N., and Zotou, S. (2014): Education and Economic Growth: A Meta-Regression Analysis. *World Development*, 64(C), pp. 669–689.

Bhar, R., and Hamori, S. (2004): The Link Between Inflation and Inflation Uncertainty: Evidence From G7 Countries. *Empirical Economics*, 29, pp. 825–853.

Bollerslev, T. (1986): Generalized Autoregressive Conditional Heteroscedasticity. *Journal of Econometrics*, 31, pp. 307–327.

Bouoiyour, J., and Selmi, R. (2013): The Effects of Central Banks' Independence on Inflation Outcomes in Emerging Countries: Does the Choice of Exchange Regime Matter? In *Exchange Rates in Developed and Emerging Markets: Practices, Challenges and Economic Implications*, Edited by Mohsen Bahmani-Oskooee: Chapter 9: pp. 155–180. Nova Science Publisher. New-York.

Bouoiyour, J., and Selmi, R. (2014): The Nexus Between Inflation and Inflation Uncertainty via Wavelet Approach: Some Lessons From Egyptian Case. *Economics Bulletin*, 34(4), pp. 2093–2106.

Bouoiyour, J., and Selmi, R. (2016): A Synthesis of the Effects of Exchange Rate Volatility on International Trade: A Meta-Regression Analysis. *International Trade Journal*, 30(4), pp. 263–294.

Bouoiyour, J., and Selmi, R. (2017): *Electricity Consumption, Economic Growth and Environment in Algeria: New Insights From a Multi-scale Analysis*. Working paper, University of Pau, France.

Brunner, A. D., and Hess, G. D. (1993): Are Higher Levels of Inflation Less Predictable? A State-dependent Conditional Heteroskedasticity Approach. *Journal of Business and Economic Statistics*, 11, pp. 187–197.

Bruns, S. B., Gross, C., and Stern, D. I. (2014): Is There Really Granger Causality Between Energy Use and Output? *Energy Journal*, 35(4), pp. 101–134.

Bruns, S. B., and Stern, D. I. (2015): *Meta Granger Causality Testing*. CAMA Working Paper 22/2015.

Caporale, G.M., Onorante, L., and Paesani, P. (2012): Inflation and Inflation Uncertainty in the Euro Area. *Empirical Economics*, 43, pp. 597–615.

Chowdhury, A. (2014): Inflation and Inflation-uncertainty in India: The Policy Implications of the Relationship. *Journal of Economic Studies*, 41, pp. 71–86.

Ćorić, B., and Pugh, G. (2010): The Effects of Exchange Rate Variability on International Trade: A Meta-Regression Analysis.*Applied Economics*, 42, pp. 2631–2644.

Cukierman, A., and Meltzer, A. (1986): A Theory of Ambiguity, Credibility and Inflation Under Discretion and Asymmetric Information. *Econometrica*, 54, pp. 1099–1128.

Devereux, M. (1989): A Positive Theory of Inflation and Inflation Variance. *Economic Inquiry*, 27, pp. 105–116.

Dotsey, M., and Ireland, P. (1996): The Welfare Cost of Inflation in General Equilibrium. *Jounal of Monetary Economics*, 37, pp. 29–47.

Doucouliagos, C., and Stanley, T. D. (2009): Publication Selection Bias in Minimum-Wage Research? A Meta-Regression Analysis. *British Journal of Industrial Relations*, 47(2), pp. 406–428.

Duval, S., and Tweedie, R. (2000): Trim and Fill: A Simple Funnel-Plot-Based Method of Testing and Adjusting for Publication Bias in Meta-Analysis. *Biometrics*, 56(2), pp. 455–463.

Effendic, A., Pugh, G., and Adnett, N. (2011): Institutions and Economic Performance: A Meta Regression Analysis. *European Journal of Political Economy*, 27(3), pp. 586–599.

Fountas, S. (2001): The Relationship Between Inflation and Inflation Uncertainty in the UK: 1885–1998. *Economics Letters*, 74, pp. 77–83.

Fountas, S., Karanasos, M., and Kim, J. (2006): Inflation Uncertainty, Output Growth Uncertainty and Macroeconomic Performance. *Oxford Bulletin of Economics and Statistics*, 68, pp. 319–343.

Friedman, M. (1977): Nobel Lecture: Inflation and Unemployment. *Journal of Political Economy*, 85, pp. 451–472.

Golob, J. E. (1994): Does inflation uncertainty increase with inflation? *Federal Reserve Bank of Kansas City, Economic Review*, Third Quarter.

Gontard-Danek, M. C., and Moller, A. P. (1999): The Strength of Sexual Selection: A MetaAnalysis of Bird Studies. *Behavioral Ecology*, 10, pp. 476–486.

Granger, C. W. J. (1969): Investigating Causal Relations by Econometric Models and Crossspectral Methods. *Econometrica*, 37(3), pp. 424–438.

Granger, C. W. J. (1988): Some Recent Developments in a Concept of Causality. *Journal of Econometrics*, 39, pp. 199–211.

Grier, K., Henry, O. T., and Shields, K. (2004): The Asymmetric Effects of Uncertainty on Inflation and Output Growth. *Journal of Applied Econometrics*, 19, pp. 551–565.

Grier, K., and Perry, M. (1998): On Inflation and Inflation Uncertainty in the G7 Countries. *Journal of International Money and Finance*, 17, pp. 671–689.

Hachicha, A., and Lean, H.-H. (2013): *Inflation, Inflation Uncertainty and Output in Tunisia*. Economics Discussion Papers, No 2013–1, Kiel Institute for the World Economy.

Hacker, R. S., and Hatemi, J. A. (2008): Optimal Lag-length Choice in Stable and Unstable VAR Models Under Situations of Homoscedasticity and ARCH. *Journal of Applied Statistics*, 35(6), pp. 601–615.

Hafer, R. W., and Sheehan, R. G. (1989): The Sensitivity of VAR Forecasts to Alternative Lag Structures. *International Journal of Forecasting, Elsevier*, 5(3), pp. 399–408.

Haile, G. M̦., and Pugh, G. (2011): Does Exchange Rate Volatility Discourage International Trade? A Meta-regression Analysis. *The Journal of International Trade and Economic Development* 22, pp. 321–350. doi:10.1080/09638199.2011.565421

Harmon, C., Oosterbeek, H., and Walker, I. (2003): The Returns to Education: Microeconomics. *Journal of Economic Surveys*, 17(2), pp. 115–155.

Hartmann, M., and Herwartz, M. (2012): Causal Relations Between Inflation and Inflation Uncertainty- Cross Sectional Evidence in Favour of the Friedman-Ball Hypothesis. *Economics Letters*, 115, pp. 144–147.

Hermann, S.-A., Chanana, C., and Serapio, B. (2012): Uncertainty of Inflation and Inflation Rate: Does Credibility of Inflation Policy Matter? *Economic Issues*, 17(2), pp. 95–110.

Holland, S. A. (1993): Comments on Inflation Regimes and the Sources of Inflation Uncertainty. *Journal of Money, Credit, and Banking*, 25, pp. 514–520.

Hsiao, C. (1979): Autoregressive Modeling of Canadian Money and Income Data. *Journal of the American Statistical Association*, 74, pp. 553–560.

Ibrahim, M., and Alagidede, P. (2016): *Financial Sector Development, Economic Volatility and Shocks in Sub-Saharan Africa*. ERSA Working Paper n° 648, November.

Ioannidis, J. P. A. (2005): Why Most Published Research Findings Are False. *PLoS Medicine*, 2(8), p. e124.

Johansen, S. (1988): Statistical Analysis of Cointegration Vectors. *Journal of Economic Dynamics and Control*, 12(2–3), pp. 231–254.

Johansen, S. (1991): Estimation and Hypothesis Testing of Cointegration Vectors in Gaussian Vector Autoregressive Models. *Econometrica*, 59(6), pp. 1551–1580.

Joyce, M. (1995): *Modeling U.K. Inflation Uncertainty: The Impact of News and the Relationship with Inflation*. Bank of England Working Paper, April.

Karahan, Ö. (2012): The Relationship Between Inflation and Inflation Uncertainty: Evidence From the Turkish Economy. *Procedia Economics and Finance*, 1, pp. 219–228.

Karanasos, M., Karanassou, M., and Fountas, S. (2004): Analyzing US Inflation by a GARCH Model With Simultaneous Feedback. *WSEAS Transactions on Information Science and Applications*, 1, pp. 767–772.

Karanasos, M., and Stefanie, S. (2008): Is the Relationship Between Inflation and Its Uncertainty Linear? *German Economic Review*, 9(3), pp. 265–286.

Kaufmann, R. K., and Stern, D. I. (1997): Evidence for Human Influence on Climate From Hemispheric Temperature Relations. *Nature*, 388, pp. 39–44.

Keskek, S., and Orhan, M. (2010): Inflation and Inflation Uncertainty in Turkey. *Applied Economics*, 42, pp. 1281–1291.

Lee, T.-H., and Yang, W. (2012): Money-Income Granger-Causality in Quantiles. *Advances in Econometrics*, 30, pp. 385–409.

Loungani, P., and Sheets, N. (1997): Central Bank Independence, Inflation, and Growth in Transition Economies. *Journal of Money, Credit and Banking*, 29(3), pp. 381–399.

Lucas, R. E. (2003): Inflation and Welfare. *Econometrica*, 68, pp. 247–274.

Lütkepohl, H. (1982): Non-causality Due to Omitted Variables. *Journal of Econometrics*, 19, pp. 367–378.

Lütkepohl, H. (1985): Comparison of Criteria for Estimating the Order of a Vector Autoregressive Process. *Journal of Time Series Analysis*, 6(1), pp. 35–52.

Nas, T. F., and Perry, M. J. (2000): Inflation, Inflation Uncertainty, and Monetary Policy in Turkey: 1960–1998. *Contemporary Economic Policy*, 18, pp. 170–180.

Okun, A. (1971): The Mirage of Steady Inflation. *Brookings Papers on Economic Activity*, 1971, pp. 485–498.

Ozturk, I., Aslan, A., and Kalyoncu, H. (2010): Energy Consumption and Economic Growth Relationship: Evidence From Panel Data for Low and Middle Income Countries. *Energy Policy*, 38(8), pp. 4422–4428.

Payne, J. E. (2009a): Inflation and Inflation Uncertainty: Evidence From the Caribbean Region. *Journal of Economic Studies*, 35, pp. 501–511.

Payne, J. E. (2009b): Inflation Targeting and the Inflation-Inflation Uncertainty Relationship: Evidence From Thailand. *Applied Economics Letters*, 16(3), pp. 233–238.

Pesaran, M. H., and Shin, Y. (1999): An Autoregressive Distributed Lag Modelling Approach to Cointegrated Analysis. In S. Strom, ed., *Econometrics and Economic Theory in the 20th Century: The Ragnar Frisch Centennial Symposium*. Cambridge: Cambridge University Press.

Pesaran, M. H., Shin, Y., and Smith, R. J. (2001): Bounds Testing Approaches to the Analysis of Level Relationships. *Journal of Applied Econometrics*, 16(3), pp. 289–326.

Poulin, R. (2000): Manipulation of Host Behaviour by Parasites: A Weakening Paradigm? *Proceedings of the Royal Society of London*, 267, pp. 787–792.

Pourgerami, A., and Maskus, K. (1987): The Effects of Inflation on the Predictability of Price Changes in Latin America: Some Estimates and Policy Implications. *World Development*, 15(2), pp. 287–290.

Pugh, G., Ćorić, B., and Haile, M.-G. (2012): *An Introduction to Meta-Regression Analysis (MRA): Using the Example of Trade Effects of Exchange Rate Variability*. Chapter 20 of the edited Book: Macroeconomics and Beyond in Honour of WimMeeusen.

Ricketts, N., and Rose, D. (1995): *Inflation, Learning and Monetary Policy Regimes in the G7 Economies*. Bank of Canada Working Paper 95–96.

Rosenthal, R. (1979): The File Drawer Problem and Tolerance for Null Results. *Psychological Bulletin*, 86(3), pp. 638–641.

Schwarz, G. (1978): Estimating the Dimension of a Model. *The Annals of Statistics*, 6(2), pp. 461–464.

Simmons, L. W., Tomkins, J. L., Kotiaho, J. S., and Hunt, J. (1999): Fluctuating Paradigm. *Proceedings of the Royal Society of London*, 266, pp. 593–595.

Sims, C. (1972): Money, Income, and Causality. *American Economic Review*, 62(4), pp. 540–552.

Soderstrom, U. (2002): Monetary Policy With Uncertain Parameters. *The Scandinavian Journal of Economics*, 104(1), pp. 125–145.

Stanley, T. D. (2005): Beyond Publication Bias. *Journal of Economic Survey*, 19(3), pp. 309–345.

Stanley, T. D. (2008): Meta-regression Methods for Detecting and Estimating Empirical Effects in the Presence of Publication Selection. *Oxford Bulletin of Economics and Statistics*, 70(1), pp. 103–127.

Stanley, T. D., and Doucouliagos, C. (2012): *Meta-Regression Analysis in Economics and Business. Routledge Advances in Research Methods*. London: Routledge.

Stern, D. I., and Kaufmann, R. K. (1997): *Time Series Properties of Global Climate Variables: Detection and Attribution of Climate Change*. Working Papers in Ecological Economics 9702, Australian National University.

Sutton, A. J., Abrams, K. R., Jones, D. R. et al. (2000): *Methods for Meta-Analysis in Medical Research*. London: John Wiley.

Thornton, J. (2007): *The Relationship Between Inflation and Inflation Uncertainty in Emerging Market Economies. Southern Economic Journal*, 73(4), pp. 858–870.

Thornton, J. (2008): Inflation and Inflation Uncertainty in Argentina, 1810–2005. *Economics Letters*, 98, pp. 247–252.

Toda, H. Y., and Yamamoto, T. (1995): Statistical Inference in Vector Autoregressions With Possibly Integrated Processes. *Journal of Econometrics*, 66(1), pp. 225–250.

Ungar, M., and Zilberfarb, B. (1993): Inflation and Its Unpredictability, Theory and Empirical Evidence. *Journal of Money, Credit, and Banking*, 25(4), pp. 709–720.

Zeynel, A., zdemir, O., and Mahir, F.-L. (2008): On the Inflation-uncertainty Hypothesis in Jordan, Philippines and Turkey: A Long Memory Approach. *International Review of Economics and Finance*, 17, pp. 1–12.

Živkov, D., Njegić, J., and Pećanac, M. (2014): Bidirectional Linkage Between Inflation and Inflation Uncertainty – The Case of Eastern European Countries. *Baltic Journal of Economics*, 14, pp. 124–139.

Appendix

Table A.1 A macroeconomic literature review on the causality between inflation and inflation uncertainty

Studies	Studied countries	Model	Hypothesis
Okun (1971)	Panel of 17 OECD countries	Standard deviation and parametric causality test	Countries with high average inflation display inflation uncertainty.
Friedman (1977)	G7 countries	Standard average deviation and Granger causality test	A rise in the average rate of inflation prompts more uncertainty about inflation.
Cukierman and Meltzer (1986)	France, Italy, Japan, Spain	Game-theoretic model	Central banks create inflation surprises when there is a great uncertainty about inflation.
Bollerslev (1986)	United States	GARCH model	The conditional variance of inflation is lower when inflation level is highest.
Pourgerami and Maskus (1987)	Seven Latin American countries	Standard deviation and Granger causality test	A rise in inflation increases resources' investment in forecasting inflation leading then to a drop of inflation uncertainty.
Devereux (1989)	Germany, Hungray, Indonesia, Korea, Netherlands, Sweden	Barro-Gorden model	The inflation uncertainty can have an adverse effect on inflation.
Ball (1992)	G7 countries	Asymmetric information game model	Formal derivation of Friedman hypothesis
Cukierman (1992)	France, Japan, Germany, United States	OLS with interactive terms	Central bank independence plays an important role in how

			interacts inflation level to its uncertainty.
Holland (1993)	Colombia, Germany, Hungary, Indonesia, Israel, Korea, Mexico, the Netherlands, Sweden, and Turkey	Barro-Gorden model	The inflation uncertainty can have a positive impact on inflation via real uncertainty canal.
Golob (1994)	United States	Parametric causality test	Positive effect of inflation on inflation uncertainty.
Joyce (1995)	United Kingdom	GARCH model	Inflation uncertainty is more sensitive to positive inflation shocks than negative ones.
Ricketts and Rose (1995)	Canada	Markov-switching model	Inflation uncertainty increases widely during high inflation periods.
Baillie et al. (1996)	United Kingdom	ARCH model and linear causality test	Evidence in favor of Cukierman and Meltzer hypothesis above mentioned.
Grier and Perry (1998)	G7 countries	GARCH model and parametric causality test	Unidirectional link that runs from inflation uncertainty to the level of inflation rate.
Nas and Perry (2000a)	G7 countries	GARCH model	The changing in policy makers behavior toward inflation can precipate the time-varying in the structure of inflation.
Nas and Perry (2000b)	Turkey	Standard deviation and linear causality test	Inflation rate increases inflation uncertainty.
Grier and Perry (2000)	France, Germany, Japan, United Kingdom, and United States	GARCH model and parametric causality test	Significant bidirectional link between inflation and inflation uncertainty.
Neyapti and Kaya (2001)	Turkey	ARCH model and parametric causality tests	Unidirectional link that runs from inflation level to its uncertainty.
Foutnas et al. (2003)	France, Germany, Italy, the Netherlands, and Spain	GARCH model	A joint feedback between the mean and the conditional variance of inflation.
Foutnas and Karanasos (2004)	France, Germany, Japan, United Kingdom, and United States	GARCH model and parametric causality test	Support of feedback hypothesis.

(*Continued*)

Table A.1 (Continued)

Studies	Studied countries	Model	Hypothesis
Kontanikas (2004)	United Kingdom	GARCH model	The adoption of inflation targeting reduces the long-run effect of inflation uncertainty on the level of inflation rate.
Elder (2004)	Euro area	GARCH model and VAR specification	The linkage between inflation and inflation uncertainty depends intensely to studied time periods.
Bhar and Hamori (2004)	G7 countries	Markov switching vector autoregressive model	The relationship between inflation and its uncertainty depends considerably on whether the shock is transitory or permanent and differs depending to countries' characteristics.
Thornton (2008)	Argentina	GARCH model	Evidence in accordance with that of Friedman-Ball hypothesis.
Zeynel and Mahir (2008)	Jordan, Philippines, Turkey	GARCH model	Strong evidence in favor of Friedman-Ball hypothesis and weak evidence in accordance with Cukierman and Meltzer (1986).
Corporale et al. (2010)	Panel of European countries	GARCH model and VAR framework	In the euro period, the European Central Bank can achieve lower inflation uncertainty by lowering inflation rate.
Achour and Trabelsi (2011)	Egypt	The state-space model with Markov switching heteroskedasticity	Inflation uncertainty has a positive effect on inflation level in the short run but this effect dies out in the long run.
Balcilar et al. (2011)	Japan, United Kingdom, and United States	GARCH model and nonparametric causality test	Inflation and inflation uncertainty have a positive predictive content for each other, which is in accordance therefore to the Friedman and Cukierman-Meltzer hypotheses, respectively.

Hermann et al. (2012)	Panel of 22 emerging countries	GARCH model and cointegration framework	The nexus between inflation and its uncertainty is highly conditional to the degree of central bank independence.
Hachicha and Lean (2013)	Tunisia	GARCH-in-mean and linear Granger causality test	Inflation uncertainty has a positive and significant effect on inflation rate.
Bouoiyour and Selmi (2013)	Panel of 12 emerging countries	GMM model with interactive terms	Countries with high level of central bank independence and chosen pegged exchange regime as exchange policy tend to exhibit low and stable inflation.
Bouoiyour and Selmi (2014)	Egypt	GARCH model and nonlinear causality test-based on wavelet approach	The nexus between inflation and inflation uncertainty changes substantially in sign among the frequencies involved.

Source: Authors' compilation.

Table A.2 Descriptive statistics

Studies	Mean	Maximum	Minimum	Std. Dev.
Okun (1971)	0.108750	0.740000	0.000000	0.256762
Friedman (1977)	0.186000	0.239000	0.135000	0.052029
Cukierman and Meltzer (1986)	−0.657500	1.190000	−5.700000	3.064058
Bollerslev (1986)	0.003500	0.110000	−0.073000	0.050687
Pourgerami and Maskus (1987)	0.057333	0.156000	0.000000	0.085822
Devereux (1989)	0.014375	0.321000	−0.128000	0.133018
Ball (1992)	0.010000	0.080000	0.000000	0.028284
Cukierman (1992)	0.003500	0.005300	0.000000	0.003032
Holland (1993)	0.014625	0.303000	−0.206000	0.140272
Golob (1994)	0.020375	0.344000	−0.276000	0.167282
Joyce (1995)	0.010750	0.603000	−0.517000	0.299994
Ricketts and Rose (1995)	−0.023750	0.000000	−0.080000	0.031139
Baillie et al. (1996)	−0.111250	0.000000	−0.404000	0.167798
Grier and Perry (1998)	−1.280875	6.330000	−8.873000	4.855417
Nas and Perry (2000a)	−0.057625	1.968000	−1.501000	1.099717
Nas and Perry (2000b)	0.864333	0.941000	0.754000	0.097940
Grier and Perry (2000)	0.636250	3.950000	−1.590000	1.952675
Neyapti and Kaya (2001)	0.006333	0.288000	−0.498000	0.437761
Foutnas et al. (2003)	0.303333	0.570000	−0.020000	0.299054
Foutnas and Karanasos (2004)	−0.020763	0.000000	−0.155000	0.054294
Kontanikas (2004)	0.294000	0.541000	0.014000	0.265045

(*Continued*)

Table A.2 (Continued)

Studies	Mean	Maximum	Minimum	Std. Dev.
Elder (2004)	−0.179125	0.025000	−1.358000	0.477900
Bhar and Hamori (2004)	−0.171750	0.289000	−1.540000	0.564065
Thornton (2008)	0.127763	2.098000	−1.075000	0.880474
Zeynel and Mahir (2008)	0.012625	0.081000	0.000000	0.027989
Corporale et al. (2010)	−0.008000	0.123000	−0.098000	0.065380
Achour and Trabelsi (2011)	0.011125	0.203000	−0.114000	0.087190
Balcilar et al. (2011)	0.067800	0.437000	0.000000	0.153671
Hermann et al. (2012)	0.014667	0.283000	−0.239000	0.261309
Hachicha and Lean (2013)	−0.050000	0.040000	−0.130000	0.085440
Bouoiyour and Selmi (2013)	0.033500	0.160000	0.000000	0.057857
Bouoiyour and Selmi (2014)	0.001938	0.006100	0.000000	0.002381

Table A.3 The moderator variables for the MRA

	Description of the variables
Variables[a]	
t-statistic	The t-statistic of the coefficient of interest of the study.
K-variables[b]	
Sample size (SZ)	The sample size used in this study.
Z-variables[c]	
RSE (=1/SE)	=1/the standard error of the coefficient of interest of the study.
Developed countries (DC)	=1, if the study focuses on the case of developed countries.
Developing countries (DEC)	=1, if the study focuses on the case of developing countries.
Standard volatility measures (SVM)	=1, if the study uses "standard volatility models" (for example, standard deviation) as proxies of volatility.
New volatility measures (NVM)	=1, if the study uses "new volatility measures" (i.e., GARCH extensions) as proxies of volatility.
Vector Autoregressive model (VAR)	=1, if the study uses VAR model to analyze the inflation-inflation uncertainty nexus.
Markov-Switching Vector Autoregression (MS-VAR)	=1, if the study uses MS-VAR model to analyze the inflation-inflation uncertainty nexus.
A game-theoretic model of monetary policy(GTM)	=1, if the study uses a game-theoretic model to analyze the inflation-inflation uncertainty nexus.
Parametric causality tests (PCT)	=1, if the study uses parametric causality test to analyze the inflation-inflation uncertainty nexus.
Nonparametric causality tests (NPCT)	=1, if the study uses nonparametric causality test to analyze the inflation-inflation uncertainty nexus.
Asymmetric causality tests (ASCT)	=1, if the study accounts for asymmetry in the causality testing by using the cumulative sums of positive and negative shocks.

Nonlinear causality tests (*NLCT*)	=1, if the study uses a nonlinear Granger causality test in to investigate the nonlinear causal relationship between inflation and inflation uncertainty.
Central Bank Independence (*CBI*)	=1, if the study controls for the independence of the Central Bank.
Academic journal (*AJ*)	=1, if the study has been published by an academic journal.
Publication year (*PUBY*)	The year the study was published.

Notes: [a]All variables are included in a general-to-specific modeling approach; [b]*K* variables may affect the likelihood of being selected for publication; [c]*Z* variables may affect the magnitude of the inflation coefficient.

10   More R&D with tax incentives?*

A meta-analysis

Elīna Gaillard-Ladinska, Mariëlle Non,
and Bas Straathof

1. Introduction

In the past 20 years, tax incentives for research and development (R&D) have become a popular policy instrument in advanced economies. By the end of 2014, 26 out of 28 EU member states used R&D tax incentives (CPB et al., 2015). The aim of this policy instrument is to stimulate firms to invest more in research and development, which should result in more innovation, productivity, and economic growth. In this paper, we perform a meta-regression analysis (MRA)[1], in order to obtain more insight into the effectiveness of R&D tax incentives in stimulating private R&D expenditures.[2] We find robust evidence for the hypothesis that R&D tax incentives are effective.

The generic nature of R&D tax incentives distinguishes them from R&D subsidies and other innovation policies. Tax incentives leave firms free to choose their R&D projects, allowing markets to select the most promising research projects. Tax incentives also have lower administrative costs for both governments and firms than other innovation policies. A drawback of R&D tax incentives is that they amplify the private returns to R&D regardless of the social returns, while the gap between private and social return can be substantial (Hall and Van Reenen, 2000).

The empirical methods researchers have applied to measure the effectiveness of R&D tax incentives can be grouped in two categories. In the first category, researchers estimate a structural relation between the user cost of R&D (which includes R&D tax incentives) and R&D expenditure. We refer to this as the 'structural approach'. The second category of studies estimates the impact of R&D tax incentives on R&D expenditure directly, mostly using an indicator variable for the presence of R&D tax incentives.

We limit our MRA to studies that have adopted the structural approach. The reason for this is twofold. First, studies that follow the structural approach report an elasticity while studies following the direct approach often express the effect of tax incentives in terms of euros (or dollars) of additional expenditure on R&D. Therefore, the estimates from the two approaches cannot be directly compared in a single MRA. Second, within the group of studies that use the direct approach there is a large heterogeneity in identification strategies. For example, Yang et al. (2012) estimates the effect of a tax incentive compared to no incentive, while Paff (2005) investigates the effect of a change in an existing tax incentive. This makes it impossible to compare those studies in a meaningful way in an MRA.

Focusing on the structural approach and after correcting for publication bias, we find that a decrease in the user cost of R&D of ten percent increases the R&D expenditures by 1.5 percent. This elasticity of R&D expenditure with respect to user cost of R&D cannot be interpreted as a direct measure of the effectiveness of R&D tax incentives, but can be used to compute the effect of a change in a tax incentive on R&D expenditure (Lokshin and Mohnen, 2012). The user cost elasticity, however, can be considered to be an upper bound on the elasticity of R&D expenditure with respect to one minus the subsidy rate of the tax incentive.[3]

Publication bias occurs when researchers only present results that are considered plausible a priori or select results on their statistical significance (Stanley, 2008). The vast majority of meta-studies on economic papers have found evidence of publication bias. Also in the literature on the effectiveness of R&D tax incentives, we find considerable publication bias: the uncorrected effect is 7.9 percent.

Despite our focus on studies that report a user-cost elasticity, we still find substantial heterogeneity in the reported estimates. The MRA indicates several sources of this heterogeneity. Studies that focus on manufacturing firms report smaller elasticities than studies that consider a general sample of firms. Also, we find that studies estimating an average effect report stronger elasticities than studies that estimate either a short-run or a long-run effect.

Apart from the above mentioned sources of heterogeneity, we find a large effect of the publication status of the study. Recent published work provides smaller elasticities than both unpublished papers and older published articles. And studies published in more highly ranked working paper series or journals report larger elasticities. Those results give some insight in the way the publication process functions, but they do not refer to a source of heterogeneity that is rooted in economic theory. After all, the fact that a recent article with small elasticities is more likely to get published than a recent article with large elasticities does not explain where the difference in elasticity estimates comes from in the first place.

Given the limited number of studies and the large number of ways in which studies might differ, our results might be sensitive to omitted-variable bias. However, tentative regressions with fixed and random study effects did not suggest bias.

Our analysis relates to two other meta-studies on the effects of R&D tax incentives. First, Ientile and Mairesse (2009) provide a tentative meta-analysis summarizing the estimates of the bang for the buck (BFTB) from a sample of studies in the United States and Canada over 30 years. BFTB is a measure that shows how many euros of R&D are generated by one euro of forgone R&D tax revenue. They report that the number of estimates of a BFTB below one is approximately the same as the number of estimates above one; yet the BFTB has a tendency to increase over time with an annual rate of about 2.5 percent. Ientile and Mairesse also find indications of publication bias, which suggests inflated estimates. In our analysis we focus on estimates of elasticity with respect to user costs. Given the fact that only few studies report BFTB estimates, our alternate focus allows us to study a larger number of estimates.

Second, Castellacci and Lie (2015) perform MRA's on R&D tax incentives for both the structural and the direct approach, focussing on the difference in effectivity between industries. They show that high-tech companies respond less strongly to R&D tax incentives, while tax incentives have a higher than average impact on manufacturing firms. However, the estimated impact on high-tech companies hinges on a small number of estimates. The difference with our results for manufacturing firms stems from different sets of studies being analyzed.[4] Moreover, we use different variables in the MRA by including a dummy that indicates whether the result is obtained for a stock or a flow of R&D expenditures. Also, we add a different set of variables on the methodology of the study and include the publication status of the study. In line with our results, Castellacci and Lie find strong evidence for publication bias.

The remainder of the paper is structured as follows. Section 2 provides an overview of the research on the impact of R&D tax incentives. The methodology of meta-analysis is presented in Section 3. Section 4 describes the data collection process and the final dataset. Section 5 presents the results of the meta-regression analysis. Robustness checks are presented in Section 6 and Section 7 concludes.

2. Evaluations of R&D tax incentives

The structural approach is founded on an R&D investment model, in which R&D expenditure is explained through various company characteristics and a firm-specific R&D user cost. The general model is

$$RD_{jt} = \delta + \gamma * UC_{jt} + \theta * X_{jt} + \varepsilon_{jt} \tag{1}$$

where RD_{jt} is the R&D expenditure for firm j at time t, UC_{jt} is the R&D user-cost measure and X_{jt} summarizes firm-specific covariates. R&D expenditure can refer to the current expenditure on R&D (flow) or to the stock of R&D capital. The user cost of R&D capital services is normally defined as the costs of using a given stock of R&D investments and includes the depreciation of the R&D stock, financing costs, as well as the statutory tax obligations and, if data is available, the tax incentive (Hall and Van Reenen, 2000). The main coefficient of interest is γ, which measures the response of R&D expenditure to changes in the user cost. If the information about the R&D tax incentives has already been included in the user-cost variable, then the impact of R&D tax incentives is directly estimated. If the user costs do not contain data on tax incentives, then the estimated effect can be used to infer what the effect would be if the user cost would decrease by the amount of the tax subsidy.

The structural estimation approach has several advantages over direct approaches. First, specific information about the R&D tax incentives can be included in the analysis. Second, if panel data is available, then unobserved firm-specific characteristics can be accounted for by including firm fixed effects. Third, in case a dynamic specification has been estimated, short- and long-term effects can be measured, which is important given that the impact might take a longer period to materialize (Chirinko et al., 1999; Hall and Van Reenen, 2000; Mairesse and Mulkay, 2004).

The main identification problem for the structural approach arises from reverse causality between the amount of R&D expenditure and the user cost of R&D. In many countries the tax benefit that a firm receives depends directly on the amount of R&D in this firm. In the absence of a social experiment or suitable instrumental variable, some studies try to reduce this problem by controlling for lagged R&D expenditure and fixed firm effects using a dynamic panel data estimator (examples are Baghana and Mohnen, 2009, and Harris et al., 2009).[5]

3. Empirical strategy

The two main concerns in meta-analysis are excess heterogeneity and publication bias. Excess heterogeneity occurs when the variation in observed estimates is higher than expected based on the standard errors of the estimates.[6] Excess heterogeneity might partly be explained by differences in study characteristics, e.g., methodology and sample characteristics. Publication bias is defined as bias that originates from results being suppressed in the literature. This occurs for instance if only significant and/or expected results are included in a paper, or if, due to unexpected results, the researchers decide not to write a paper at all.[7] There are several tools to detect and correct for heterogeneity and publication bias. Overviews are given in e.g., Stanley (2005), Nelson and Kennedy (2009) and Kepes et al. (2012).

A formal test for heterogeneity is provided by Cochran's Q-test, which is commonly used in meta-analysis (e.g., Stanley and Doucouliagos, 2012).[8] To derive the test, assume that each estimate in the meta-analysis sample is an estimate of the same 'true effect' α plus some random error term ε, which has expectation 0 and a standard deviation equal to the standard deviation of the estimate. Dividing both sides by this standard error gives

$$t_{is} = \alpha \frac{1}{SE_{is}} + v_{is}$$

where t_{is} is the t-value of estimate i from study s in the meta-analysis sample, that is, t_{is} equals the *ith* estimate of study s divided by SE_{is}, the standard error of estimate i from study s. The term v_{is} is the random error term ε divided by the standard error. If the assumption of a single main effect α is correct, that is, if there is no excess heterogeneity in the estimates, the error term v_{is} has a variance equal to 1. The test statistic of the Q-test is the sum of squared errors from regressing t_{is} on $1/SE_{is}$ and has (under the null hypothesis) a chi-square distribution with L-1 degrees of freedom, with L the number of estimates in the sample.

The Q-test has low power when the number of included studies is small. For that reason, Higgins et al. (2003) propose the I^2 measure, which is computed as $100\% \times (Q - df)/Q$, where Q is Cochran's Q and df the degrees of freedom of Cochran's Q ($L - 1$ in the case of the regression above). If there is no excess heterogeneity in the estimates, the expected value of the Q-statistic is df. Therefore, the I^2 measure compares the Q-statistic with its expected value under the assumption of no excess heterogeneity. Negative values of I^2 indicate there is no excess heterogeneity, while larger positive values show increasing heterogeneity.

Publication bias is a second concern in meta-analysis. A starting point to get some insight in the presence of publication bias is a visual inspection of a funnel plot. The funnel plot is a scatter plot of the estimates in the sample against the precision of the estimates as measured by $1/SE_{is}$. In the absence of publication bias the funnel plot should be symmetric, with a peak at the 'true effect'. Publication bias, for instance a bias towards negative results, will show as asymmetry in the funnel plot. A visual inspection of the funnel plot is simple and intuitively appealing, but a weakness of this method is its subjectivity.

A formal test for the presence of publication bias is the FAT-PET method, first proposed by Egger et al. (1997). The basis of this method is the regression

$$estimate_{is} = \beta_0 + \beta_1 SE_{is} + \varepsilon_{is} \tag{2}$$

When publication bias is absent, the estimate does not depend on SE_{is} and β_1 is not significant. However, when there is publication bias the estimate does depend on SE_{is}. For higher SE_{is} the probability increases that the estimate is non-significant or of the 'wrong' sign and therefore not reported in the research results. When the expected effect is positive, publication bias will lead to a positive and significant β_1 while a negative expected effect leads to a negative and significant β_1.

Regression (2) suffers from heteroskedasticity, since the variance of ε_{is} increases in SE_{is}. To correct for this, WLS is used with a diagonal weight matrix with elements $1/VAR_{is}$. This gives the regression

$$t_{is} = \beta_0 \frac{1}{SE_{is}} + \beta_1 + v_{is}. \tag{3}$$

The Funnel Asymmetry Test (FAT) detects the presence of publication bias by testing the significance of β_1 in regression (3). The Precision Estimate Test (PET) determines whether or not there is a significant 'true' effect by testing the significance of β_0. The value of β_0 is in general considered as the value of the 'true' effect, as β_0 gives the size of an effect estimated with infinite precision (SE_{is} equal to zero in equation (2)).

The main weakness of all methods mentioned above is that they either only consider excess heterogeneity or only consider publication bias. However, it is known that the FAT-PET regression can give false significant results when there are very high levels of excess heterogeneity (see e.g., Stanley, 2008 and Stanley, 2017). Excess heterogeneity can also affect the symmetry of the funnel plot, suggesting asymmetry even when publication bias is absent (see e.g., Terrin et al., 2003). Therefore, the preferred method is an extension of the FAT-PET regression that corrects for heterogeneity by adding explanatory variables that are a likely source of heterogeneity. We will refer to this method as Meta Regression Analysis, or MRA.

In Section 5 we use the regression

$$estimate_{is} = \beta_0 + \beta_1 VAR_{is} + \sum_{k=2}^{K} \beta_k X_{isk} + \varepsilon_{is} \tag{4}$$

as our main specification. In this regression, $K - 1$ explanatory variables, X_{is2} to X_{isK}, are added. VAR_{is} is the variance of estimate i from study s. We use VAR_{is} to control for publication bias instead of SE_{is}. Research has shown that when using SE_{is} the estimated 'true' effect β_0 is biased towards zero (Stanley and Doucouliagos, 2014). The bias is much smaller when the variance is used instead. As robustness check we also present the results when using SE_{is} (see Section 6).

The extent of publication bias might depend on the regressors X_{isk}. For instance, if the effect of tax incentives is weaker for manufacturing firms, it is likely that there is more publication bias in results based on manufacturing firms. Those results in general would be less significant and more likely to have the 'wrong' sign. To correct for this, interaction terms between the regressors and VAR_{is} should be added to equation (4). This, however, almost doubles the number of regressors, putting additional strain on a relatively small sample. We will therefore present the results of the regression without interaction terms. The full specification with all interaction terms included is presented in Section 6 as a robustness check.

We use WLS to estimate equation (4). As before, we weigh by $1/VAR_{is}$ to correct for the obvious heteroskedasticity in the data. Note that weighting by $1/VAR_{is}$ not only corrects for heteroskedasticity, but also provides a correction for publication bias. For higher VAR_{is} more estimates are missing, so the average estimate is more biased. In the WLS regression those biased estimates get less weight.

A last concern in our analysis is the fact that a single study can report multiple estimates. Estimates from the same study usually are based on the same dataset and are likely to be correlated. Nelson and Kennedy (2009), amongst others, suggest to correct for the number of estimates per study by using a panel data model with study-level fixed effects. Alternatively, one might use cluster-robust error terms with clusters at the study level. These methods explicitly take into account the correlation between estimates from the same study and theoretically are to be preferred over the specification in equation (4). However, a downside of those methods is that they need to estimate many more parameters. In the case of a small sample, like we have, this might lead to estimation problems.

In our main analysis, we decided to use the more simple specification in equation (4). To prevent a disproportional effect from studies with many correlated estimates, we multiply the weights $1/VAR_{is}$ with $1/n_s$, where n_s is the number of estimates from study s. This number ranges from one to ten estimates. Theoretically, this addition to the model might (re)introduce heteroskedasticity as the error terms from studies with more estimates are divided by a larger number. However, we will show that in our study this is not a major concern. Also, we report Huber-White robust standard errors that correct for any remaining heteroskedasticity.

As a robustness check we also present the results of regressions with a correction factor $(1/n_s)^2$ and with no correction for the number of estimates per study. Furthermore, in the section on robustness checks we explore the results from a fixed effects panel model and a model with cluster robust standard errors. There, we will also discuss the estimation issues we encountered in more detail.

4. Data

To construct the dataset we electronically searched for both published and unpublished studies that assess the impact of R&D tax incentives on R&D expenditure. The key-words used were: "R&D tax incentives", "R&D fiscal incentives", "R&D tax credits", "R&D tax subsidies". We covered the standard databases and search engines, such as EBSCO Host; JSTOR; IDEAS; Science Direct; SAGE Journals Online; Emerald; Google Scholar and Google. We also examined the reference lists of the encountered evaluation studies and previously published literature reviews.[9]

We restricted our sample to more recent studies, using 1990 as cut-off year. These studies are more relevant with respect to the policies assessed and estimation techniques applied. Also, only those studies presenting sufficient information on standard errors or t-statistics were included. We chose to include all estimates reported, as far as they differ in terms of model specification, sample or methodology applied.

To ensure comparability, meta-analysis can be applied only on those estimates that have identical interpretations. We consider only estimates of elasticities of R&D expenditure with respect to the costs of R&D. In some studies the elasticities are estimated directly, while in other studies additional computations are performed to obtain elasticities.

Our final samples consist of 86 estimates (16 studies). Table 10.1 lists the studies used in the meta-analysis and provides an overview of their results. As expected, the studies show a negative mean estimate.

Table 10.1 Summary of studies

Reference	Number of estimates (n_s)	Mean estimate	Standard deviation of estimates	Mean of standard errors ($1/n_s \sum_i SE_{is}$)
Agrawal et al. (2014)	10	−1.52	0.51	0.16
Baghana and Mohnen (2009)	8	−0.10	0.06	0.05
Corchuelo Martínez-Azúa (2006)	7	−1.57	1.34	0.99
Corchuelo and Martínez-Ros (2009)	6	−0.47	0.33	0.28
Dagenais et al. (1997)	1	−0.07	–	0.04
Hall (1993)	4	−1.76	0.79	0.53
Harris et al. (2009)	2	−0.95	0.59	0.26
Hines et al. (1993)	8	−1.13	0.45	0.41
Koga (2003)	6	−0.61	0.38	0.27
Lokshin and Mohnen (2007)	10	−0.55	0.34	0.22
Lokshin and Mohnen (2012)	6	−0.50	0.19	0.18
Mulkay and Mairesse (2003)	6	−0.48	0.90	0.21
Mulkay and Mairesse (2008)	4	−0.17	0.07	0.04
Mulkay and Mairesse (2013)	5	−0.16	0.19	0.16
Poot et al. (2003)	1	−0.11	–	0.02
Wilson (2009)	2	−1.70	0.69	0.63

The estimated effects of R&D tax incentives vary considerably across studies and within studies. The last column of Table 10.1 gives the means of the reported standard errors SE_{is}. For comparison, the fourth column gives the variation in observed estimates, calculated as the standard deviation of the estimates that are reported in study s.[10] If there would be no excess heterogeneity, the mean of the reported standard errors SE_{is} should have the same magnitude as the within-study standard deviation of the estimates. However, for most studies the spread in estimates within a study (column 4) is higher than the standard error of those estimates (column 5). This indicates that also within a study the variation in estimates is considerable.

To account for the heterogeneity in estimates, we add a dummy in equation (4) indicating whether the dependent variable refers to R&D stocks or R&D flows. We expect that estimates of elasticities based on R&D stocks are smaller than estimates based on R&D flows as stocks take longer to adjust to changes in the user costs of R&D than flows. We also include a dummy for the estimates based on a (sub-)sample of small and medium-sized enterprises (SMEs). The effectiveness of tax credits might vary with firm size, for example because the credit might have a different (e.g., simpler) design for SMEs, administrative costs might be relatively high for SMEs or capital market imperfections might hit SMEs harder. Another indicator is included for estimates relating to a sample of manufacturing firms. The manufacturing sector is more R&D-intensive than other sectors of the economy, which might affect the impact of the incentive. Studies also differ with respect to the time horizon of the estimate.

We distinguish between estimates that refer to a short term effect (default), a long term effect, and studies that only report an average effect over time ("static effect"). Finally a dummy is included for estimates obtained using a dynamic panel regression model (GMM). GMM estimates can be influenced by the choice of instruments, giving the researcher the opportunity to select a set of instruments that gives a high estimate with relatively low standard error. Note that all these dummies might vary within a study.

We further include a dummy that indicates whether the study has been published in an academic journal. It might be expected that over time the refereeing process has shifted focus from the effect size to the quality of the econometric model. This would imply that older publications show larger and more significant elasticities than older working papers, while recent publications show smaller effects. To allow for this pattern, we include the age of published studies and the age of working papers (both ages normalized to between 0 and 1) as separate covariates. Finally, we include a normalized ranking of the journal or discussion paper series where the study has been published, using the RePec Simple Impact Factor for Working Paper Series and Journals.

Table 10.2 illustrates how much heterogeneity is related to the variables mentioned above. In the table, the last column provides a weighted mean of the estimate of the user-cost elasticity, weighted by $1/(VAR_{is}*n_s)$. Based on the weighted mean, it appears that the estimates for stock elasticities are slightly smaller (in absolute values). Also, effects from a static model are larger than long-run effects and short-run effects. Estimates based on dynamic panel regression models are stronger than estimates based on other techniques. Finally, published studies show smaller effects. The first row of Table 10.2 indicates that the unweighted average of the estimated user cost elasticity is −0.79 and the

Table 10.2 Descriptive statistics

Variable	Value	# estimates	Unweighted mean of the estimates	Weighted mean of the estimates
All studies		86	−0.79	−0.15
Stock	0	39	−1.18	−0.20
	1	47	−0.46	−0.13
SME	0	81	−0.81	−0.15
	1	5	−0.39	−0.15
Manufacturing	0	58	−0.78	−0.15
	1	28	−0.80	−0.13
Time horizon	Short-run	25	−0.52	−0.13
	Long-run	24	−0.55	−0.10
	Static model	37	−1.13	−1.33
GMM	0	66	−0.75	−0.15
	1	20	−0.92	−0.25
Published	0	46	−0.79	−0.16
	1	40	−0.79	−0.11

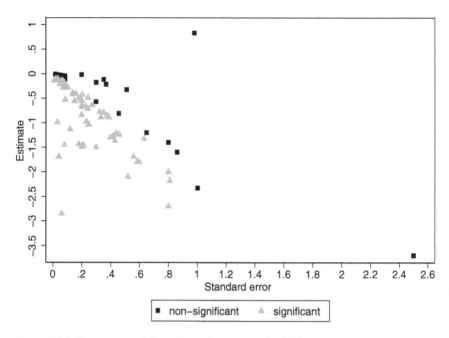

Figure 10.1 Scatter plot of the estimated user-cost elasticities

average weighted by $1/(VAR_{is} * n_s)$ is −0.15. The sizable difference between the two weighted averages suggests the presence of publication bias.

The Q-test for heterogeneity has a test statistic of 5,109.43 (df = 85, p = 0.00), indicating the presence of strong heterogeneity. The I^2 measure confirms this; its value is 98%. The scatter plot in Figure 10.1 illustrates this as well. For standard errors between 0 and 0.2, the observed estimates range broadly between 0 and −2.8 and therefore show a much higher variation as would be expected based on the standard error alone. In our MRA in section 5 we will gain more insight in the determinants of this heterogeneity by adding several variables to the regression that might explain the heterogeneity in estimates.

The scatter plot in Figure 10.1 also suggests the presence of publication bias. First, many estimates are only just significant at the five percent significance level. Second, from the plot it seems that most estimates are clustered between 0 and −1, with a substantial number of estimates even below −1. Estimates above 0 are almost absent.[11] The same pattern is shown in the funnel plot in Figure 10.2. The most precise estimates are clustered between −0.5 and 0, with a long tail to the left and a missing tail on the right.

5. Meta-regression results

Table 10.3 presents the results of the meta-regression. Column (I) shows the mean elasticity controlling for publication bias through the inclusion of the

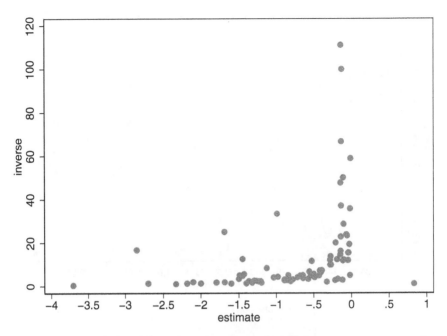

Figure 10.2 Funnel plot of the estimated user-cost elasticities

variance of the estimate as a regressor. The 'corrected elasticity' (which is identical to the constant in this specification) equals −0.15. This is the same value as the weighted mean reported in Table 10.2, but is substantially smaller than the unweighted mean of −0.79. There is significant publication bias as the variance has a negative and significant coefficient. This is a strong result as the weighting with $1/(n_s*VAR_i)$ also corrects for publication bias by giving estimates with a high variance, which are more prone to bias, a lower weight.

As mentioned in section 3, the weighting by n_s might lead to heteroskedasticity. We performed a Breusch-Pagan test for heteroskedasticity, testing whether the residuals of the model in column (I) are related to n_s. This test indeed indicates strong heteroskedasticity (p-value 0.0000). However, when we perform the same test relating the error terms to SE_{is} we also find strong heteroskedasticity (p = 0.0000), even though theoretically the weighting should solve this part of the heteroskedasticity problem.[12] For this reason, we think that the benefit of weighting with n_s is more important than the added heteroskedasticity. Note that in Table 10.3 we report Huber-White robust standard errors that correct for general heteroskedasticity. Hence, the standard errors and confidence intervals are reliably estimated.

Column (II) ads indicators related to the characteristics of estimates.[13] The adjusted R^2 of 0.71 suggests that those indicators can explain a considerable part of the variation in the estimates. The I^2 measure however gives a different view; adding the explanatory variables of model (II) decreases the I^2 from 98%

Table 10.3 Meta-regression results

	(I)	(II)	(III)	(IV)
Constant	−0.15***	−0.10***	−0.17***	−0.16***
	(0.02)	(0.01)	(0.03)	(0.03)
Variance	−3.18***	−1.38**	−1.44***	
	(0.86)	(0.66)	(0.54)	
Stock		−0.03***	0.04	0.03
		(0.01)	(0.02)	(0.02)
SME		0.14	0.05	0.05
		(0.12)	(0.08)	(0.09)
Manufacturing		0.12***	0.26***	0.30***
		(0.02)	(0.10)	(0.10)
Static specification		−1.20***	−0.45***	−0.52***
		(0.24)	(0.12)	(0.12)
Long-run time horizon		0.06	0.04	0.03
		(0.04)	(0.05)	(0.05)
GMM		−0.19**	−0.13	−0.14
		(0.08)	(0.08)	(0.08)
Published			0.39***	0.40***
			(0.11)	(0.12)
Age of working paper			0.11**	0.09*
			(0.05)	(0.05)
Age of publication			−1.29***	−1.54***
			(0.37)	(0.44)
Impact ranking			−0.80***	−0.75***
			(0.25)	(0.26)
N	86	86	86	86
Adjusted R^2	0.04	0.71	0.75	0.75

Notes: Robust standard errors in parentheses; *p < 0.1;** p < 0.05; ***p < 0.01.

to 93%, still indicating significant remaining heterogeneity.[14] This difference between the R^2 and I^2 measure is caused by the fact that the I^2 is increasing but concave in the sum of squared errors (SSE). When the SSE is very large to begin with, a large decrease in SSE only leads to a small decrease in I^2. The R^2 value instead is linear in SSE. Apparently, as indicated by the increase in R^2, the explanatory variables do explain a considerable part of the variation, but as the variation was very large to begin with (recall that without the explanatory variables the I^2 value was 98%), I^2 does not respond strongly.

Whether R&D expenditures are measured as a stock or a flow has a relatively small but significant effect on the user-cost elasticity. The effect is unexpected as it implies that estimates that are based on a stock of R&D show stronger elasticities than estimates that are based on R&D flows. However, in subsequent models the effect disappears. Studies that focus on SMEs do not differ significantly from other studies. The coefficient on the manufacturing dummy is positive and significant, contradicting the finding by Castellacci and Lie (2015). There is no significant difference between short- and long-term estimates, but static estimates are much larger in absolute terms. This result is not driven by a single study or estimate; most of the estimates from static specifications are relatively large. In general, the static model is quite simple, while the model used to disentangle long- and short-run effects uses more economic theory to derive a more complex econometric specification. It is not unlikely that the static estimates are biased as the model to estimate long- and short-run effects is economically and econometrically superior. The coefficient for GMM-estimates is weakly significant here (but not in subsequent specifications). The variables that measure the status of a publication are included in model (III).[15] The variables 'Published', 'Age of working paper', 'Age of publication', and 'Impact ranking' are measured at the study level. Recall that the age variables and the impact ranking are all normalized between 0 and 1, with the oldest study in the set having normalized age 1 and the highest ranked study having a normalized impact ranking of 1. Since the sample consists of 16 studies, the size of the coefficients is quite sensitive to outliers. Nevertheless, the coefficients on 'Published', 'Age of publication', and 'Impact ranking' are highly significant. Also, the adjusted R^2 value increases after adding those variables, and the I^2 value decreases from 93% to 92%.

The impact ranking has a negative effect, indicating that studies with large elasticities are more likely to get published in higher ranked outlets. The variable 'Age of publication' is an interaction term, which is zero for working papers, and is the (normalized) age of published studies. The total effect of a study being published therefore is a combination of the coefficients for 'Published' and 'Age of publication'. The coefficient of 'Published' suggests that recent publications provide smaller elasticities than recent working papers. For older publications this effect reverses: older publications provide larger elasticities than older working papers, and also provide larger elasticities than recent publications. This might reflect that over time the size of the coefficient has become less relevant in the referee process and correction for endogeneity has gained importance.[16]

When controlling for publication status, the constant changes from −0.10 to −0.17. This does not imply that the effect of R&D tax incentives has doubled: the added controls have a non-zero mean, such that the interpretation of the constant in (II) differs from that in (III). For several other variables the coefficients also change after controlling for publication status. As the publication status appears to be highly relevant, we prefer specification (III) over specification (II). However, we acknowledge that the publication status in itself is not a cause of the variation in estimates. Only the variables that were added in equation (II) can be interpreted as such.

Specification (IV) shows that the exclusion of the variance as explanatory variable has only a minor impact on the other variables in the regression. Because of the weighting with $1/(n_s * VAR_i)$, the influence of the correction for publication bias is likely to be limited.

We checked specifications (II), (III) and (IV) for multicollinearity by computing the VIF value. The Variance Inflation Factor (VIF) indicates the severity of multicollinearity on a scale from 1 to infinity. If all variables are orthogonal the VIF equals one. A common rule of thumb is that multicollinearity is problematic if the VIF is larger than ten, although for small samples (like we have) the maximum VIF value might be higher (see O'Brien, 2007). For specification (II), the highest VIF value is 1.75, for specification (III) this is 12.51 and for specification (IV) the highest VIF value is 11.56. Given our modest sample size, this does not indicate major multicollinearity problems.

6. Robustness analysis

This section analyzes the robustness of the results. Our first robustness check, presented in specification (I) in Table 10.4, is to include a dummy that indicates for each study which estimates are preferred by the authors of that study. The coefficient of the dummy shows that the preferred estimates are not significantly different from the non-preferred estimates. Also, the coefficients on the other covariates do not change qualitatively.

As a second robustness check, we include interaction terms between the explanatory variables and the variance. As the interaction terms are most relevant for those regressors that are significant, in model (II) we only include the interaction terms between the variance and the variables 'manufacturing', 'static specification', 'published', 'age of working paper', 'age of publication', and 'ranking'. The highest VIF value of this regression is 36, indicating that multicollinearity might be an issue in this specification. The main results are robust to the inclusion of the interaction terms. When all interaction terms are included (model (III)) the highest VIF value increases to 133. Despite this, the main results still hold in this regression. The last two columns in Table 10.4 show the results of the meta-regression when the standard error instead of the variance is used to correct for publication bias. Note that specification (IV) gives the FAT test as originally proposed by Egger et al. (1997). Except for the results on the static specification and long-run time horizon dummies, the results on the covariates are robust to the change in the correction for publication bias. The estimated 'corrected' elasticity (the constant in specification (IV)) is smaller. This can be explained by the fact that a regression with the standard error instead of the variance has a constant that is biased towards zero (Stanley and Doucouliagos, 2014).

The meta-regression in Section 5 uses $1/(VAR_{is}\ n_s)$ as weight. Table 10.5, columns one and two, shows the results when instead weights $1/VAR_{is}$ or $1/(VAR_{is}\ (n_s)^2)$ are used. The results are largely robust to this change in weights.

The third column of Table 10.5 presents the results of a weighted regression with cluster-robust standard errors. The clusters here are the different studies s. Because now the cluster-robust standard errors correct for the correlation between estimates from the same study, we do not use the correction of $1/n_s$, but instead weigh with $1/VAR$.

Table 10.4 Alternative specifications

	(I)	(II)	(III)	(IV)	(V)
Constant	−0.24***	−0.16***	−0.16***	−0.10***	−0.20***
	(0.05)	(0.03)	(0.03)	(0.02)	(0.04)
Variance	−1.49***	−4.50**	−4.67		
	(0.55)	(1.97)	(5.31)		
Standard error				−2.67***	−1.91***
				(0.43)	(0.42)
Stock	0.05**	0.03	0.03		0.06**
	(0.03)	(0.02)	(0.03)		(0.03)
SME	0.04	0.04	0.03		0.04
	(0.09)	(0.08)	(0.08)		(0.08)
Manufacturing	0.25***	0.24**	0.21**		0.20**
	(0.09)	(0.10)	(0.10)		(0.09)
Static specification	−0.43***	−0.50***	−0.61**		−0.15
	(0.12)	(0.16)	(0.23)		(0.15)
Long-run time horizon	0.04	0.06	0.04		0.13**
	(0.05)	(0.05)	(0.05)		(0.05)
GMM	−0.16*	−0.12	−0.11		−0.07
	(0.08)	(0.08)	(0.08)		(0.06)
Published	0.44***	0.37***	0.36***		0.43***
	(0.12)	(0.12)	(0.13)		(0.10)
Age of working paper	0.17***	0.10*	0.11*		0.24***
	(0.06)	(0.05)	(0.06)		(0.08)
Age of publication	−1.28***	−1.17***	−1.07**		−0.85**
	(0.37)	(0.38)	(0.42)		(0.37)
Impact ranking	−0.75***	−0.77***	−0.65*		−0.98***
	(0.25)	(0.27)	(0.35)		(0.23)
Preferred estimate	0.03				
	(0.02)				
Manufacturing*VAR		−2.81**	−0.61		
		(1.30)	(4.27)		
Static*VAR		3.66**	5.68*		
		(1.37)	(3.18)		
Published*VAR		−2.75	−5.49		
		(2.96)	(5.51)		
Age working paper*VAR		1.98	−1.05		
		(4.32)	(10.05)		
Age of publication*VAR		7.71***	9.85*		
		(2.65)	(5.15)		
Ranking*VAR		1.78	1.10		
		(2.19)	(3.47)		
Stock*VAR			−0.99		
			(2.62)		
SME*VAR			1.19		
			(1.94)		
Long run*VAR			3.15		
			(2.49)		
GMM*VAR			−1.56		
			(4.30)		
N	86	86	86	86	86
Adjusted R^2	0.75	0.75	0.74	0.12	0.78

Notes: Robust standard errors in parentheses; *p < 0.1; **p < 0.05; ***p < 0.01.

Table 10.5 Alternative regression techniques

	Weight 1/VAR	Weight 1/(VAR*n²)	Cluster-robust	FE	RE
Constant	-0.16***	-0.19***	-0.16***		-0.17
	(0.04)	(0.02)	(0.04)		(0.20)
Variance	-1.17**	-1.98***	-1.17**	-1.08	-1.18
	(0.50)	(0.60)	(0.55)	(1.16)	(1.05)
Stock	0.04	0.05**	0.04	0.27	0.04
	(0.03)	(0.02)	(0.02)	(0.93)	(0.11)
SME	-0.02	0.17	-0.02	-0.05	-0.04
	(0.05)	(0.11)	(0.06)	(0.15)	(0.15)
Manufacturing	0.31***	0.16	0.31**		0.25
	(0.10)	(0.11)	(0.13)		(0.27)
Static specification	-0.44***	-0.43***	-0.44**		-0.45
	(0.12)	(0.12)	(0.17)		(0.47)
Long-run time horizon	0.02	0.05	0.02	-0.05	-0.02
	(0.04)	(0.06)	(0.06)	(0.09)	(0.09)
GMM	-0.08	-0.23*	-0.08*	-0.05	-0.06
	(0.05)	(0.12)	(0.04)	(0.09)	(0.09)
Published	0.42***	0.39***	0.42**		0.45*
	(0.13)	(0.11)	(0.15)		(0.27)
Age of working paper	0.09	0.15***	0.09		0.10
	(0.07)	(0.03)	(0.07)		(0.32)
Age of publication	-1.52***	-0.98***	-1.52***		-1.46
	(0.43)	(0.35)	(0.40)		(1.21)
Impact ranking	-0.82***	-0.76***	-0.82***		-0.80*
	(0.27)	(0.24)	(0.17)		(0.48)
N	86	86	86	84	86
Adjusted R^2	0.77	0.73	0.77		

Notes: Standard errors in parentheses; robust standard errors for first two models; *p < 0.1; **p < 0.05; ***p < 0.01.

As mentioned before, this model theoretically is to be preferred over the model we presented in the previous section. However, the estimation of cluster-robust error terms does put quite some strain on the sample. When there is a small number of clusters, like in our sample, the estimated standard errors could be biased. Despite those problems, the estimates are similar to the estimates of the main model in Section 5.

Another option to correct for the correlation between estimates from the same study is to use a panel data model. The fourth column in Table 10.5 shows the results of a fixed effects model (with weights $1/VAR_{is}$). Two studies with a single observation per study are removed from the dataset. Study-level constants are not reported.

A first observation is that several variables, like the impact ranking and age, are missing from the model. Those variables are constant at study level. Logically, estimates from the same study have the same impact ranking, publication status, and age. Also, studies either use only manufacturing firms or use a general sample. And studies either use a static model or a dynamic model; there are no studies combining both. The study-specific constant in the fixed effects panel model therefore absorbs the effects from all those variables. This is one major disadvantage of the fixed effects panel model.

Another major disadvantage in our context is that the standard errors of the estimated coefficients in the panel model are much higher than in the main specification in Section 5. Since the fixed effects model uses 13 study-specific constants, and exploits only within-study variance, higher standard errors are conform expectations. Most of the estimates have the same order of magnitude as in the main specification, but the higher standard errors cause a decrease in significance. Also note that most of the included variables were not significant in the main model either, and that two important explanatory variables (manufacturing and static specification) had to be dropped from the model and are now included in the study-level constant.

The last column in Table 10.5 presents the results of a random effects panel model with weights $1/VAR_{is}$. The advantage of a random effects panel model is that variables which are constant at study level can still be included. However, a major drawback is that the random effects panel model requires the estimation of additional parameters, and that the estimates are only consistent when either the number of studies or the number of estimates per study is large enough. With our limited sample, consistency of the estimates is not guaranteed.

The estimates of the random effects panel model have the same order of magnitude as the estimates in the main specification. However, the standard errors are considerably higher, leading to less significant coefficients.

7. Conclusions

After correcting for publication bias, we find a significant elasticity for the user cost of R&D capital of -0.15. The publication bias is substantial: the uncorrected average elasticity is -0.79. Also, the estimates of the user cost elasticity are quite heterogeneous. Part of this heterogeneity is caused by the significant lower elasticity for the manufacturing sector, while for SMEs we do not find significant differences. Another significant cause of heterogeneity is the specification that the underlying studies use: a static specification leads to significantly higher elasticities than either a short-run or a long-run specification. Whether the study uses GMM and whether the study considers the flow of R&D expenditures or the stock of R&D capital, does not significantly influence the estimates. We did find publication effects. Recently published studies provide smaller elasticities compared to either older published studies or unpublished work. In addition, outlets with a higher impact factor tend to publish higher elasticities. All the results we found are robust to different model specifications.

Despite our focus on a relatively homogeneous set of studies, the heterogeneity among estimates is large. Our MRA identifies several variables that explain part of this variation. However, some of those variables relate to the academic publishing process and do not clarify why those estimates differ in the first place. Studies that use identical methodologies for different countries are required for reliably assessing the impact of differences across R&D tax incentives and target firms.

All in all, after correction for publication bias we found a robust but modest effect of user cost of R&D capital on private R&D expenditure. This suggests that R&D tax incentives help to increase the level of private R&D, but are probably not a major determinant of a country's innovativeness.

Notes

* We would like to thank Piet Donselaar, Bronwyn Hall, Carl Koopmans, Jacques Mairesse, and Pierre Mohnen and seminar participants for their helpful comments. All errors are ours.

1 Meta-analysis is becoming more popular in economic sciences across many fields, see for example the special issues of the Journal of Economic Surveys, vol. 19, issue 3, 2005 and vol. 25, issue 2, 2011.

2 Most of the literature focuses on the first-order effect, i.e., the effect of R&D tax incentives on R&D expenditure, since higher-order effects, like innovation and productivity growth, are hard to estimate. In the remainder of this paper, the 'effectiveness of R&D tax incentives' refers to the first-order effect.

3 Not all R&D costs are considered eligible for the tax incentive. For this reason, any change in one minus the subsidy rate of the tax incentive will lead to smaller change the user cost of R&D. Which costs are eligible differs across countries or even across schemes within a country.

4 We found several (recent) studies that were not included by Castellacci and Lie. Also, some of the studies included by Castellacci and Lie did not exactly follow the structural approach and were not included in our analysis.

5 Dynamic panel data estimators apply the generalized method of moments estimator (GMM) in order to prevent correlation between fixed effects and lagged dependent variables (Arellano and Bond, 1991).

6 For a given standard error, one would expect that roughly 95 percent of the estimates deviate at most two standard errors from the mean estimate.

7 Note that the fact that some working papers get better or more quickly published than others in itself does not lead to a bias in the meta-analysis, as long as all available working papers are included in the sample.

8 Hoaglin (2015) provides a discussion of the limitations of the Q-test and alternative heterogeneity tests.

9 Castellacci and Lie (2015), Parsons and Phillips (2007), Ientile and Mairesse (2009), Hall and Van Reenen (2000).

10 Note that for studies which provide only one estimate, we cannot calculate a standard deviation of the reported estimates.

11 Note that one of the estimates seems to be an outlier as it is very large (-3.6) and has a standard error of 2.5. Because we weigh with the standard error in our MRA, this estimate gets a very low weight and hence has almost no influence on our estimates.

12 Interestingly, when we estimate a model with weights $1/VAR_{is}$, we also find heteroskedasticity in both n_s and SE_{is}.

13 The Breusch-Pagan test for heteroskedasticity again indicates a significant ($p = 0.0000$) relation between the residuals of model (II) and both n_s and SE_{is}.

14 Note that the models in Table 3 are weighted by $1/(VAR_{is} * n_s)$. To calculate the I^2 value we re-estimated model (II) using weights $1/VAR_{is}$ or, equivalently, dividing both the dependent and independent variables by $1/SE_{is}$.

15 Again, the Breusch-Pagan test for heteroskedasticity indicates a significant ($p = 0.0000$) relation between the residuals of model (III) and both n_s and SE_{is}.

16 Note that one of the working papers dates from 2014 (Agrawal et al., 2014). This paper most likely has not yet been through a referee process. As robustness check we estimated model (III) with Agrawal et al. (2014) coded as 'published in 2014'. This did not lead to major changes in the results.

Bibliography

Agrawal, A., C. Rosell and T.S. Simcoe, 2014, *Do Tax Credits Affect R&D Expenditures by Small Firms? Evidence from Canada*, NBER Working Paper 20615.

Arellano, M. and S. Bond, 1991, Some tests of specification for panel data: Monte Carlo evidence and an application to employment equations, *The Review of Economic Studies*, vol. 58, no. 2, pp. 277–297.

Baghana, R. and P. Mohnen, 2009, Effectiveness of R&D tax incentives in small and large enterprises in Quebec, *Small Business Economics*, vol. 33, no. 1, pp. 91–107.

Castellacci, F. and C.M. Lie, 2015, Do the effects of R&D tax credits vary across industries? A meta-regression analysis, *Research Policy*, vol. 44, no. 4, pp. 819–832.

Chirinko, R.S., S.M. Fazzari and A.P. Meyer, 1999, How responsive is business capital formation to its user cost?: An exploration with micro data, *Journal of Public Economics*, vol. 74, no. 1, pp. 53–80.

Corchuelo Martínez-Azúa, M.B., 2006, Incentivos Fiscales en I+D y Decisiones de innovación, *Revista de Economía Aplicada*, vol. 14, no. 40, pp. 5–34.

Corchuelo Martínez-Azúa, M.B. and E. Martínez-Ros, 2009, *The Effects of Fiscal Incentives for R&D in Spain*, Universidad Carlos III de Madrid Working Paper 09–23.

CPB, CASE, ETLA and IHS, 2015, *A Study on R&D Tax Incentives: Final Report*, DG TAXUD Taxation Paper 52.

Dagenais, M.G., P. Mohnen and P. Therrien, 1997, *Do Canadian Firms Respond to Fiscal Incentives to Research and Development?*, CIRANO Working Paper 97s–34.

Egger, M., G.D. Smith, M. Schneider and C. Minder, 1997, Bias in meta-analysis detected by a simple, graphical test, *British Medical Journal*, vol. 315, no. 7109, pp. 629–634.

Hall, B.H., 1993, R&D tax policy during the 1980s: Success or failure?, *Tax Policy and the Economy, Volume 7*, MIT Press.

Hall, B.H. and J. Van Reenen, 2000, How effective are fiscal incentives for R&D? A review of the evidence, *Research Policy*, vol. 29, no. 4, pp. 449–469.

Harris, R., Q.C. Li and M. Trainor, 2009, Is a Higher Rate of R&D Tax Credit a Panacea for Low Levels of R&D in Disadvantaged Regions?, *Research Policy*, vol. 38, no. 1, pp. 192–205.

Higgins, J.P., S.G. Thompson, J.J Deeks and D.G. Altman, 2003, Measuring inconsistency in meta-analyses, *British Medical Journal*, vol. 327, no. 7414, pp. 557–560.

Hines Jr, J.R., R.G. Hubbard and J. Slemrod, 1993, On the sensitivity of R&D to delicate tax changes: The behavior of US multinationals in the 1980s, *Studies in International Taxation*, Chicago: University of Chicago Press.

Hoaglin, D.C., 2015, Misunderstandings about Q and Cochran's Q test' in meta-analysis, *Statistics in Medicine*, vol. 35, no. 4, pp. 485–495.

Ientile, D. and J. Mairesse, 2009, *A Policy to Boost R&D: Does the R&D Tax Credit Work?*, EIB Papers 6/2009.

Kepes, S., G.C. Banks, M. McDaniel and D.L. Whetzel, 2012, Publication bias in the organizational sciences, *Organizational Research Methods*, vol. 15, no. 4, pp. 624–662.

Koga, T., 2003, Firm size and R&D tax incentives, *Technovation*, vol. 23, no. 7, pp. 643–648.

Lokshin, B. and P. Mohnen, 2007, *Measuring the Effectiveness of R&D Tax Credits in the Netherlands*, UNU-MERIT Working Paper 2007–025.

Lokshin, B. and P. Mohnen, 2012, How effective are level-based R&D tax credits? Evidence from the Netherlands, *Applied Economics*, vol. 44, no. 12, pp. 1527–1538.

Mairesse, J. and B. Mulkay, 2004, Une évaluation du crédit d'impot recherche en France, 1980–1997, *Revue d'Economie Politique*, vol. 114, pp. 747–778.

Mulkay, B. and J. Mairesse, 2003, *The Effect of the R&D Tax Credit in France*, EEA-ESEM Conference.

Mulkay, B. and J. Mairesse, 2008, *Financing R&D Through Tax Credit in France*, LEREPS and UNU-MERIT Preliminary Draft.

Mulkay, B. and J. Mairesse, 2013, The R&D tax credit in France: Assessment and ex ante evaluation of the 2008 reform, *Oxford Economic Papers*, vol. 65, no. 3, pp. 746–766.

Nelson, J.P. and P.E. Kennedy, 2009, The use (and abuse) of meta-analysis in environmental and natural resource economics: An assessment, *Environmental and Resource Economics*, vol. 42, no. 3, pp. 345–377.

O'Brien, R.M., 2007, A caution regarding rules of thumb for variance inflation factors, *Quality & Quantity*, vol. 41, pp. 673–690.

Paff, L.A., 2005, State-level R&D tax credits: A firm-level analysis, *The B.E. Journal of Economic Analysis & Policy*, vol. 5, no. 1.

Parsons, M. and N. Phillips, 2007, *An evaluation of the federal tax credit for scientific research and experimental development, Department of Finance, Canada*, Working Paper 2007–08.

Poot, T., P. den Hertog, T. Grosfeld and E. Brouwer, 2003, *Evaluation of a major Dutch Tax Credit Scheme (WBSO) aimed at promoting R&D*, FTEVAL Conference on the Evaluation of Government Funded R&D, Vienna.

Stanley, T.D., 2005, Beyond publication bias, *Journal of Economic Surveys*, vol. 19, no. 3, pp. 309–345.

Stanley, T.D., 2008, Meta regression methods for detecting and estimating empirical effects in the presence of publication selection, *Oxford Bulletin of Economics and Statistics*, vol. 70, no. 1, pp. 103–127.

Stanley, T.D., 2017, Limitations of PET-PEESE and other meta-analysis methods, *Social Psychology and Personality Science*, vol. 8, no. 5, pp. 581–591.

Stanley, T.D. and H. Doucouliagos, 2012, *Meta-regression Analysis in Economics and Business*, Routledge.

Stanley, T.D. and H. Doucouliagos, 2014, Meta-regression approximations to reduce publication selection bias, *Research Synthesis Methods*, vol. 5, no. 1, pp. 60–78.

Terrin, N., C.H. Schmid, J. Lau and I. Olkin, 2003, Adjusting for publication bias in the presence of heterogeneity, *Statistics in Medicine*, vol. 22, no. 13, pp. 2113–2126.

Wilson, D.J., 2009, Beggar thy neighbor? The in-state, out-of-state, and aggregate effects of R&D tax credits, *The Review of Economics and Statistics*, vol. 91, no. 2, pp. 431–436.

Yang, C.H., C.H. Huang and T.C.-T. Hou, 2012, Tax incentives and R&D activity: Firm-level evidence from Taiwan, *Research Policy*, vol. 41, no. 9, pp. 1578–1588.

11 Political cycles

What does a meta-analysis reveal about?

Antoine Cazals and Pierre Mandon

1. Introduction

Since the pioneering work of Nordhaus (1975), researchers have scrutinized whether elected officials adopt strategic behavior in order to hold office. More specifically, under the assumption of shortsighted voters, political leaders may be tempted to distort policy-making so that they increase their popularity as much as possible before elections. According to Paldam (1979), a rational incumbent will try to please voters the year before elections by manipulating economic instruments.

During four decades, researchers have extensively studied one specific instrument that is budget policy on a theoretical and an empirical ground. Empirically scientists have assessed any association between pre-electoral years and the level of public revenue, public expenditure, and fiscal balance. Such a systematic association would support the hypothesis of political budget cycles (PBC). However, empirical studies differ in their results. Most studies reveal insights of PBC, but some of them report statistically not significant results. A second generation of studies rather discusses the conditions and contexts under which PBC emerge. In other words, beyond the question of existence itself, the literature has then focused on which economic and political factors affect the magnitude of PBC the most. This has spread the literature in multiple directions, so that conclusions are not only heterogeneous but also difficult to compare and to put in perspective.

In order to provide some insights and answers to this debate, we realize a meta-regression analysis (MRA) of the empirical literature on political budget cycles. Recent literature reviews on PBC have been produced by Shi and Svensson (2003), Eslava (2011), de Haan and Klomp (2013), and Dubois (2016), for instance. They provide updated overviews of the research and deliver informative and qualitative conclusions. Due to the very nature of narrative reviews and space constraints, such overviews provide partial panoramas of the whole literature, that may incline towards their authors' ideological positions (Stanley, 2001). MRA does not substitute to narrative reviews but offer a good quantitative complement. Unlike literature reviews, MRA rely on an exhaustive collection of empirical evidence provided in the literature, where the same weight is given to any study. In the present case, we collected 1,037 exploitable estimates of national PBC from 46 distinct studies. After having coded the characteristics of the estimates collected, we exploit the resulting dataset to perform the statistical analysis with the MRA approach.

The results indicate the statistical existence of some forms of pre-electoral manipulation of public accounts by political leaders. However, the magnitude of the effect is limited and may be considered as practically negligible. We also detect some evidence of publication-selection bias. Common to most bodies of literature, this bias emerges form an over-reporting of results in line with the theory. More precisely, we identify an asymmetry in the distribution of estimates. At the end, empirical estimates of PBC in the literature are somewhat exaggerated. To investigate further the sources of heterogeneities and factors affecting the magnitude of PBC, we run a Bayesian model averaging (BMA) analysis. It allows us to identify the covariates with the greatest impact on PBC, that we subsequently include in a multiple MRA equation. This multiple analysis suggests heterogeneous results according to the fiscal output considered. Moreover, methodological choices made by researchers appear to modulate the magnitude of effects they report.

Section 2 presents a brief overview of the literature on PBC and some of its major empirical insights. Section 3 describes the data used to conduct the MRA. In particular, we develop how we collected primary estimates from the empirical literature, which criteria of inclusion we adopt and how we coded, with a focus on the dependent variable of primary studies (fiscal output variables) and the interest variable (capturing the electoral period). The methodology and MRA models estimated are presented in Section 4, and the results in Section 5. Finally, Section 6 concludes.

2. Literature insights

Since Nordhaus (1975), a large and increasing number of studies have scrutinized whether elected officials adopt strategic behavior in order to hold office. On the theoretical ground, the predictions are rather unequivocal: a rational incumbent will *"try to make the year before an election a 'happy one' in order to be re-elected"* (Paldam, 1979, p. 324). According to this statement, incumbents have an incentive to distort policy-making before elections in order to please and incite voters to vote for them again, whatever the underlying mechanism of electoral manipulation such as (i) competency signaling, (ii) fooling of short-sighted voters, or (iii) targeting of swing voter groups (Rogoff, 1990). As leaders have a greater and more direct power over policy instruments, such as fiscal policy, rather than economic outcomes, such as employment, growth or inflation, the literature has progressively redirected its main focus from political business cycles to political budget cycles where findings remain heterogeneous and even conflicting.

Indeed, as the empirical evidence grows, its heterogeneity increases. Actually there are three sources of increasing heterogeneity (Philips, 2016). The first consists in an expansion of the unit of analysis through the scrutiny of PBC from more countries – especially developing countries – and not only at the national level but also at the local level. The second lies in the wider and deeper exploration of conditions affecting political cycles (de Haan and Klomp, 2013). The third comes from the analysis of disaggregated fiscal data. As a result the conclusions highlighted by the empirical research becomes more diverse regarding PBC. In particular, the debate is still open regarding the existence, the magnitude and the factors determining the occurrence of PBC (Wittman et al., 2006).

In addition, some scholars question the effectiveness of these strategic manipulations. Several country-specific studies show that incumbents that resort to PBC have a lower probability of being re-elected. This phenomenon is evidenced by Peltzman (1992) for the United States, Brender (2003) for Israel, Drazen and Eslava (2010) for Colombian mayors, and Brender and Drazen (2007) in a worldwide cross-country study.[1] If voters punish incumbents who create fiscal expansions before elections, then there should be no incentive to adopt such strategies.

Arvate, Avelino, and Tavares (2009) investigate this paradox and explain that strategic manipulation of fiscal tools is more rewarding when voters are less sophisticated and less informed. Unsurprisingly, PBC appear to be more pronounced in developing countries (Shi and Svensson, 2006), low-level democratic regimes (Gonzalez, 2002),[2] and new democracies (Brender and Drazen, 2005), where voters are usually less informed and experienced, and thus, where manipulation can be expected to be more effective.

Some recent literature reviews depict the main trends of the academic findings (Eslava, 2011; de Haan and Klomp, 2013; Dubois, 2016).[3] Despite their usefulness, due to their very nature, they are not able to definitely resolve the empirical conflicts in the literature. Recently, Philips (2016) and Mandon and Cazals (2019) have undertaken to apply the tools of meta-regression analysis on the literature of PBC. Philips (2016) finds a statistically significant manipulation of leaders before elections, yet substantively small. So small that PBC may be considered as economically insignificant since their practical significance is negligible (Mandon and Cazals, 2019). Conversely, they emphasize a publication selection that may be considered as moderate to substantial according to the classification of Doucouliagos and Stanley (2013). This suggests that researchers selectively report that leaders manipulate fiscal tools before elections, more than they actually do. Additionally they evidence a reduction in size of PBC over time explained by a decrease of this publication bias rather than more virtuous practice from incumbents.

3. Data

The realization of the MRA relies on three stages, successively: collection, coding, and statistical analysis. Collection consists in gathering all the econometric estimates of PBC in the literature. The collected estimates are then coded in order to produce a dataset from which the statistical analysis is run. This section portrays the process of collection and some coding patterns of the data, whereas Section 4 discusses the statistical analysis.[4]

A conventional narrative review displays panoramas of the literature, emphasizing the most rigorous, the newest or the most convincing results according to the academia or its author. This approach especially produces qualitative insights. Conversely and in a complementary manner, a meta-analysis relies on a quantitative approach, and thus requires exhaustiveness as a condition of validity. In order to be objective, a meta-analysis must contain and give the same emphasis to each piece of evidence of the literature whatever its presupposed quality. To fulfill this requirement, we screen the literature by successively entering the keywords "*political budget cycle*", "*political business cycle*", and "*electoral cycle*" in the most comprehensive electronic search engines in economics: EconLit, Google Scholar, Ideas Repec, Science Direct, Springer, and Wiley. This step results in the identification of over 7,000 sources.[5] Most of them are not suitable since they do not produce any statistical estimates of PBC and/or are not written in English. To ensure the rigor of the collection, we screen the references listed in the remaining papers identified from the electronic search and check the publication record of their authors.

Lastly the reading of relevant studies allow to discard those not respecting a list of objective criteria set in order to make the statistical analysis both possible and consistent. To be eligible studies may be peer-review articles or working papers whose the publication/release date is strictly before 1 January 2015. When multiple versions of a same paper appear (e.g., a working paper and its published version), we retain the most recent, in order to avoid multiple counting related bias. We consider only cross-country estimates of national PBC. We exclude post-electoral cycles estimates. The theory essentially focuses on the behavior of leaders before elections. As a result empirical research on post-electoral effects is limited (de Haan and Klomp, 2013) and we restrict our attention to manipulation during the run-up period. We select only estimates of PBC whose the dependent variable is either fiscal balance, revenue, expenditure, or a subdivision of one of these three broad budget variables. Econometric regressions estimating how elections affect an index of budget composition change are thus not taken into consideration since they are not comparable to budget level changes, making impossible to merge them for a consistent analysis.[6] Additionally, for being exploitable in the MRA, estimates must provide the minimum statistical information, that is (i) a correlation coefficient and (ii) its associated standard error or t-statistics. Estimates not offering these two requirements are removed. Finally, we discard estimates from interactive models since their coefficients are not directly comparable with those from linear models. Applying all those criteria, we collect 1,037 eligible estimates from 46 papers, listed in Table B.1 in the Appendix.

The literature investigates the effects of electoral agenda on the level of the three broad budget variables: fiscal balance, expenditure, and revenue. Among the 1,037 estimates collected, 309 assess pre-electoral changes of the national fiscal balance,[7] 205 the overall expenditure, and 165 the overall revenue (all of them are computed over GDP). Additionally, some studies examine electoral effects on sub-components of expenditure (218 estimates) and revenue (140 estimates). This is especially the case for specific expenditure and taxes that are likely to be more easily and/or usefully manipulate by leaders before elections. We census eight sub-components of overall expenditure and 13 of overall revenue. Tables B.1 and B.2 in the Appendix display additional information and show that most studies focus on several fiscal variables. Overall, 679 estimates use one of the three main variables, that is the ratio of either revenue, expenditure or fiscal balance to GDP, whereas the 358 remaining estimates consider one of their specific components.

The interest variable of the estimates, that is the pre-election period variable, is also captured in several ways. The most common consists in computing a dummy variable that equals one during election years. Consequently, when an election occurs early in the civil year (e.g., January), the dummy built in this manner takes mostly account of the post-electoral period rather than pre-electoral period. To tackle this issue, some authors use instead a dummy coded one for the year preceding the actual civil year of an election. But this raises a symmetrical problem, that is, when an election occurs lately in the year (e.g., December), the dummy mostly fail to capture the actual year preceding the election. This leads to potential identification troubles, that may be even more sensitive for shorter terms. These issues of identification are highlighted in Cazals and Sauquet (2015) and considered by Akhmedov and Zhuravskaya (2004) as the main technical challenge for the study of PBC. In order to better capture leaders' behavior during the year preceding elections, scholars have used various adjustments for this "electoral year dummy," such as coding the pre-electoral year rather than actual electoral year when the ballot occurs in the first months of the calendar year (Shi and Svensson, 2006), or by differentiating between elections according to the period of the year during which they occur (Brender and Drazen, 2005; Mink and de Haan, 2006). Alternatively, Franzese (2000) proposes an index measuring which part of a year of the year occurs during the 12 months preceding the actual date of an election.

Another concern is the nature of elections. Most countries have (general) parliamentary and presidential elections. Fatás and Mihov (2003) for instance, take into account of these both types of elections without distinction. However, most authors consider that a given type of elections is more likely to generate PBC (Hagen, 2007) according to the countries of their samples (Block, 2002; Hanusch and Vaaler, 2013; Bayar and Smeets, 2009), or rely on the most important election for each given country (Shi and Svensson, 2006, for instance). In such cases, parliamentary (resp. presidential) elections are considered for parliamentary (resp. presidential) systems. Finally, like Klomp and de Haan (2013a, b, d), some studies remove unanticipated elections and focus explicitly on predetermined ones in order to avoid endogeneity issues related to the timing of elections.

4. Methodology

Once extracted all the primary regression coefficients estimating PBC from the studies collected, we convert them into partial correlation coefficients. Since authors use various measures and scales of electoral and fiscal variables (see Section 3), primary regression coefficients are not directly comparable. On the contrary, partial correlation coefficients are a unitless measure. As a consequence, they have no formal economic meaning, but are still informative on the magnitude and sign of PBC and are quantitatively comparable. To calculate them, we proceed as follows:

$$r = \frac{t}{\sqrt{t^2 + df}} \tag{1}$$

where t is the t-statistic and df the degrees of freedom of this t-statistic. Partial correlations are weakly sensitive to imprecise degrees of freedom calculations (Stanley and Doucouliagos, 2012). As the statistics on the degrees of freedom are rarely reported by authors, and since the regressions in the literature on PBC are based on hundreds of observations, we use the number of observations to compute the partial correlation coefficients.

Funnel graphs in Figure 11.1 consist of plotting the estimates of the effect of the election on fiscal aggregates (horizontal axis) against their precision (vertical axis), where the precision is measured by the inverse of the standard error of the estimates ($\frac{1}{SE}$). They reveal two patterns. First, the pre-electoral manipulation of budget by political leaders is at best small. Second, their asymmetric distributions suggest some publication-selection issues within empirical results. In the upper-left quadrant, the top of the distribution, where the most precise estimates are displayed indicate that the variations in revenue during pre-electoral years is close to zero. Similarly the upper-right quadrant exhibits an increase of expenditure but of a very small magnitude along with a right-skewed distribution still reflecting some publication-selection bias. As the combination (difference) of revenue and expenditure, unsurprisingly same patterns emerge for fiscal balance (lower-left quadrant). Pre-electoral years are associated with a fiscal balance deterioration of a limited magnitude. This result is disproportionately reported by researchers as suggested by the clear inclination of the distribution towards the left. In order to get an overall picture of the pre-electoral budget manipulation by leaders we gather all the estimates by multiplying by −1 those on revenue and fiscal balance so that they are all coded in the same direction and can be combined. A limited manipulation by leaders associated with some over-reporting of PBC by researchers may thus be observed in the lower-right panel.

In order to produce more rigorous insights into the patterns highlighted by the previous graphs, we use a standard model of simple meta-regression:

$$r_{ij} = \beta_0 + \beta_1 SE_{ij} + v_j + \varepsilon_{ij}, \tag{2}$$

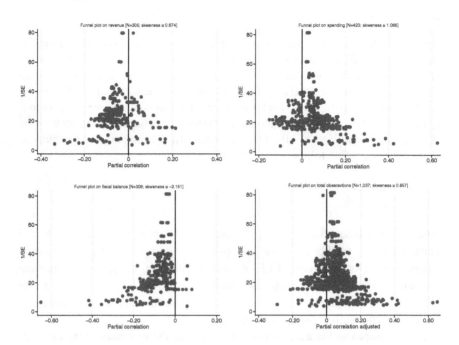

Figure 11.1 Funnel graphs of election-on-fiscal outputs partial correlations

Notes: Partial correlation relative to the precision (i.e., inverse of standard errors). Upper-left quadrant: funnel plot on revenue. Upper-right quadrant: funnel plot on spending. Lower-left quadrant: funnel plot on fiscal balance. Lower-right quadrant: funnel plot on all fiscal outputs (we inverse the sign of partial correlation for revenue and fiscal balance)

Source: Mandon and Cazals (2019).

where r and SE denote the *ith* computed partial correlation and standard error from study j. v_j is a paper fixed effect and ε_{ij} is the idiosyncratic error term. It consists of regressing the partial correlations between elections and fiscal outputs on an intercept and its standard errors, while controlling for unobserved paper effects. Then, this model is estimated with a LSDV estimator (to absorb paper fixed effects) using precision squared ($\frac{1}{SE^2}$) as weight, so that more weight is attributed to more precise estimates, and study fixed-effects, to tackle estimates dependence within studies. Through the estimation of β_0 and β_1, the model allows testing respectively for funnel asymmetry (publication-selection bias) and precision effect (magnitude of PBC).

Nonetheless, as reviewed by de Haan and Klomp (2013), scholars' disagreement does not mainly lie in the existence of PBC but rather in the conditions of their existence and factors affecting their magnitude. The present paper turns to a multiple meta-regressions analysis in order to examine the conditional nature of PBC inherent to all socio-economic phenomenon. We then augment Equation 2 by adding a vector Z of k covariates:

$$r_{ij} = \beta_0 + \beta_1 SE_{ij} + \sum_{k=1}^{K} \beta_k \mathbf{Z}_{ki} + v_j + \varepsilon_{ij}, \tag{3}$$

Additional covariates allow assessing how PBC differ across countries and over time, and how authors' methodological choices affect them. However, conditional factors explored in the literature and methodological differences among the studies of researchers are numerous. These sources of heterogeneities lead to consider a vast list of potential explanatory variables to include in the model. In order to reduce the arbitrariness of our selection and run more parsimonious multiple-MRA models, we first implement a BMA encompassing a comprehensive list of explanatory variables. Then we run Equation 3 by including only significant covariates identified through the BMA.

5. Results

5.1. Baseline results

We estimate a standard MRA regression from Equation 2 or an LSDV FAT-PET, which stands for funnel asymmetry ($\hat{\beta}_1$) and precision-effect test ($\hat{\beta}_0$). Results are presented in Table 11.1, where each line displays a different estimate of any kind of PBC (panel (i)) or specific PBC, regarding revenue (panels (ii) and (iii)), spending (panels (iv) and (v)), or fiscal surplus (panel (vi)). Each regression is replicated by: (i) employing robust standard errors; (ii) clustering on studies; and (iii) double clustering on studies and types of fiscal output (when we account for several fiscal outputs simultaneously).

Overall results in panel (i) exhibit a strongly significant coefficient associated to all types of pre-electoral fiscal distortions, suggesting that PBC do exist.[8] However, the magnitude of the effect is so small ($\hat{\beta}_0 = 0.034$) that it may be considered as practically negligible according to Cohen's (1988) guidelines ($\hat{\beta}_0 < 0.10$).[9] In addition, we do not find robust evidence of publication-selection bias when accounting for unobserved paper effects. The disaggregation of results by output reveal mixed patterns.

First, there is a negative and statistically significant association between elections and the level of revenue. Yet, once again, the economic strength of this association is limited and no publication-selection bias is detected (panel (ii)). Results hold when we exclude observations dealing with subcomponents of revenue and rely only on observations estimating PBC on overall revenue (panel (iii)).[10]

Second, results for spending appear quite opposite. The coefficient associated to the FAT is significant and may be considered as modest (0.917 in panel (iv)) to substantial (1.329 in panel (v)) when excluding estimates of PBC on subcomponents of spending according to Doucouliagos and Stanley's (2013) guidelines.[11]

Table 11.1 MRA [Baseline Results]

Regression	LSDV estimator						
	(1) FAT ($\hat{\beta}_1$)		(2) PET ($\hat{\beta}_0$)				
	Funnel asymmetry		Meta-average		RMSE	n (# studies)	N
(i) All Observations (Adjusted Partial Correlation)							
White correction	**0.432****	**(0.188)**	**0.034*****	**(0.006)**	0.048	46	1,037
Cluster	0.432	(0.334)	**0.034*****	**(0.011)**	0.048	46	1,037
Double cluster	0.432	(0.264)	**0.034*****	**(0.009)**	0.048	46	1,037
(ii) Revenue							
White correction	0.179	(0.277)	**−0.050*****	**(0.009)**	0.040	20	305
Cluster	0.179	(0.246)	**−0.050*****	**(0.008)**	0.040	20	305
Double cluster	0.179	(0.338)	**−0.050*****	**(0.011)**	0.040	20	305
(iii) Restrictive measure of revenue							
White correction	0.216	(0.359)	**−0.046*****	**(0.011)**	0.0275	13	165
Cluster	0.216	(0.265)	**−0.046*****	**(0.008)**	0.0275	13	165
(iv) Spending							
White correction	**0.917*****	**(0.346)**	0.005	(0.013)	0.051	28	423
Cluster	**0.917***	**(0.498)**	0.005	(0.018)	0.051	28	423
Double cluster	**0.917****	**(0.428)**	0.005	(0.020)	0.051	28	423
(v) Restrictive measure of spending							
White correction	**1.329*****	**(0.351)**	−0.011	(0.011)	0.036	20	205
Cluster	**1.329****	**(0.524)**	−0.011	(0.017)	0.036	20	205
(vi) Fiscal surplus							
White correction	**−1.092*****	**(0.246)**	**−0.029*****	**(0.007)**	0.030	39	309
Cluster	**−1.092*****	**(0.376)**	**−0.029****	**(0.011)**	0.030	39	309

Notes: Each line represents a different estimated model, where the dependent variable is the adjusted partial correlation between election and fiscal outputs in panel (i) (we reverse the sign of partial correlation for revenue and fiscal balance), and the (non-adjusted) partial correlation between election and fiscal outputs in panels (ii)-(vi). Regressions' standard errors in parentheses. Panel (i) reports all observations. Panel (ii) reports observations on revenue. Panel (iii) excludes subcomponents of revenue. Panel (iv) reports observations on spending. Panel (v) excludes subcomponents of spending. Panel (vi) reports observations on fiscal balance. Estimates are obtained by employing successively: robust standard errors, cluster on studies, and double-cluster on studies and fiscal output (when several fiscal outputs are accounted simultaneously). All models are estimated from Equation 2 and the LSDV estimator to absorb paper fixed effects (precision squared weights). Results with the 294 interactive models are available upon request. A detailed description of all variables is available in Table C.1 in Appendix. Cohen1988's (1988) guidelines for the genuine effect (PET, $\hat{\beta}_0$): negligible if $| \hat{\beta}_0 | \leq 0.10$; small if $| \hat{\beta}_0 | > 0.10$; medium if $| \hat{\beta}_0 | > 0.30$; large if $| \hat{\beta}_0 | > 0.50$. Doucouliagos and Stanley's (2013) guidelines for the publication bias (FAT, $\hat{\beta}_1$): modest if $| \hat{\beta}_1 | < 1$, substantial if $1 \leq | \hat{\beta}_1 | \leq 2$, and severe if $| \hat{\beta}_1 | > 2$. *$p < 0.10$,**$p < 0.05$,***$p < 0.01$.

Once controlled for publication-selection bias, no pre-electoral manipulation of spending remain.

Finally, last panel exhibits estimates on fiscal surplus, that is the difference of revenue and spending. We observe both significant evidence of PBC yet practically negligible in magnitude, and a selective over-reporting of results conform to the theory in which a rational incumbent will deteriorate fiscal surplus before an election in order to hold office.

In conclusion, once controlled for publication selection, PBC still have a statistical existence when the fiscal output studied is either revenue or fiscal surplus, but their magnitude are close to zero. Additionally, some modest to substantial evidence of publication-selection bias is found for spending and fiscal surplus.[12] This simple analysis shows that PBC patterns differ according with the fiscal output considered. To dig deeper into the sources of heterogeneity regarding PBC, we implement a multiple MRA specific for each output.

5.2. Sources of heterogeneity

The BMA analysis offers a rigorous and agnostic approach to determine which factors affect the heterogeneity of the results found in the literature and quantify these effects. Among other appealing features, the BMA approach allows to determine the model maximizing the explained variation of the dependent variable by successively including and excluding covariates without imposing them any restriction. By assessing all the possible models from the most comprehensive to the most parsimonious, this approach limits the issue of over-specification and respectively under-specification. In line with Havránek (2015) – in which the interested reader can find more technical developments – we run the BMA analysis to build an agnostic multiple MRA, by considering an ordinary least squares estimator (OLS) and use a uniform model prior. For each categories of output we consider a chain of 200 million recorded draws with 100 million burn-ins, by applying the birth-death sampler.[13]

Appendix D provides additional evidence about a geography of PBC and that country characteristics such as political insitutions seem to affect heterogeneously the magnitude of electoral manipulation of fiscal outputs. Accordingly, Table D.1 and Figures D.1 to D.5 highlight that PBC are generally higher (lower) in new and low-level (established and high-levels) democracies.

5.2.1. Revenue

Mixed patterns identified in Section 5.1 lead us to conduct a specific analysis of factors affecting PBC for each fiscal output. Figure 11.2 displays a graphical analysis of BMA applied to revenue. All covariates included in the model appear in column and are sorted by posterior inclusion probability (PIP) in descending order. The horizontal axis represents the cumulative posterior model probabilities. The models are sorted in descending order, best models are thus on the left. Blue (red) color (lighter in grayscale) indicates the variable

Model Inclusion Based on Best 5000 Models

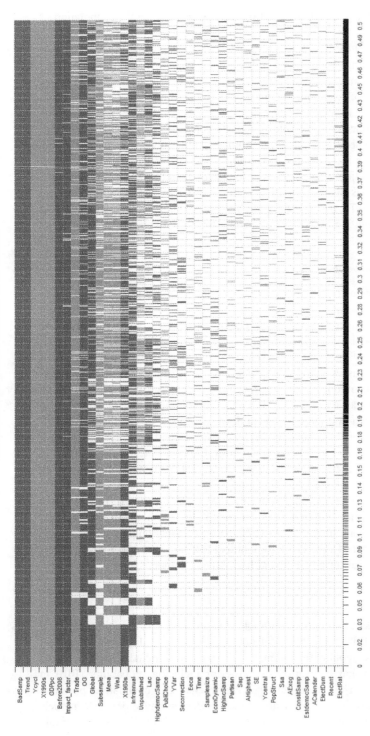

Cumulative Model Probabilities

Figure 11.2 BMA: Model inclusion on revenue [UIP g-prior; uniform model prior]

Notes: The dependent variable is the adjusted partial correlation between election and measures of revenue. Birth-death sampler used. Columns denote individual models; the variables are sorted by posterior inclusion probability (PIP) in descending order. Blue color (darker in grayscale): the variable is included and the estimated sign is positive. Red color (lighter in grayscale): the variable is included and the estimated sign is negative. No color: the variable is not included in the model. The horizontal axis measures the cumulative probabilities of the best 5,000 models. Numerical results of the BMA estimation are reported in Table 11.2. A detailed description of all variables is available in Table C.1.

Table 11.2 BMA on revenue [UIP g-prior; uniform model prior]

	BMA, Model Prior: Uniform			
	PIP	*Post. mean*	*Post.s.d.*	*Cond.pos.sign*
Publication bias				
SE	0.039	−0.004	0.049	0.326
Model structure				
Subsample	**0.719**	**−0.019**	**0.014**	**0.000**
ConstitSamp	0.033	0.000	0.002	0.082
HighincSamp	0.061	0.001	0.008	0.971
EstdemocSamp	0.031	0.000	0.002	0.855
HighdemocSamp	0.218	0.011	0.024	0.996
BadSamp	**1.000**	**0.151**	**0.027**	**1.000**
Time and Regions				
1980s	**0.641**	**0.044**	**0.037**	**1.000**
1990s	**1.000**	**−0.110**	**0.026**	**0.000**
Recent	0.029	0.000	0.003	0.627
Eeca	0.092	−0.002	0.006	0.000
Lac	0.339	0.015	0.023	0.999
Mena	**0.681**	**−0.060**	**0.046**	**0.003**
Sap	0.045	0.000	0.006	0.266
Ssa	0.036	0.000	0.005	0.686
WeJ	**0.645**	**−0.030**	**0.025**	**0.008**
Global	**0.759**	**0.064**	**0.043**	**1.000**
Paper				
Public Choice	0.162	−0.007	0.018	0.015
Unpublished	0.359	−0.015	0.023	0.007
Impact factor	**0.984**	**0.001**	**0.000**	**1.000**
Trend	**1.000**	**0.027**	**0.004**	**1.000**
Before 2008	**0.997**	**0.211**	**0.052**	**1.000**
Methodology				
Samplesize	0.062	0.000	0.000	0.145
Infrannual	**0.557**	**0.037**	**0.039**	**1.000**
YVar	0.118	0.003	0.011	0.998
YCycl	**1.000**	**−0.097**	**0.019**	**0.000**
YCentral	0.038	0.000	0.005	0.730
ElectDum	0.029	0.000	0.002	0.882
ElectRat	0.028	0.000	0.002	0.061
ACalendar	0.030	0.000	0.002	0.575
AHighest	0.042	−0.001	0.005	0.046
AExog	0.035	0.000	0.002	0.893

(Continued)

Table 11.2   (Continued)

| | BMA, Model Prior: Uniform | | | |
	PIP	Post. mean	Post.s.d.	Cond.pos.sign
EconDynamic	0.062	0.001	0.003	0.994
Se Correction	0.095	0.001	0.005	1.000
Covariates				
GDPpc.	**1.000**	**−0.151**	**0.029**	**0.000**
Trade	**0.922**	**−0.058**	**0.025**	**0.000**
PopStruct	0.037	0.000	0.004	0.270
OG	**0.873**	**0.060**	**0.031**	**1.000**
Partisan	0.050	−0.001	0.009	0.020
Time	0.083	−0.002	0.008	0.035
Constant	**1.000**	**−0.441**	NA	NA
n (# studies)	20			
N	305			

Notes: The dependent variable is the partial correlation between election and measures of revenue. Post.s.d.: posterior standard deviation conditional on inclusion. Cond.pos.sign: probability of positive sign conditional on inclusion. We highlight explanatory variables with PIP >0.500. A detailed description of all variables is available in Table C.1.

is included in the regression and its coefficient is positive (negative). The figure shows the best 5,000 models (which have a cumulative probability of 50 percent), among 50,293,243 models visited.

Table 11.2 displays the associated results of the BMA analysis on revenue. It displays the weighted average over all models with weights equal to posterior model probabilities. These results help us to select the covariates that will enter Equation 3. To do so, we retain variables having a PIP exceeding the threshold of 0.50. This is the case for 16 variables (including the intercept).

We then run Equation 3 with these 16 variables along with the variable SE, that has a PIP under 0.50 but that is necessary to include in order to estimate a proper meta-analysis regression. Results are presented in Table 11.3. Basically, we see that both characteristics of countries and researchers' methodological choices affect the magnitude of PBC estimates. In particular, we note estimates of PBC based on data including Western countries (variable *WeJ*) exhibit a greater reduction in revenue before elections. This is surprising since the theory suggests that countries having more developed political institutions and widespread media, experience less strong cycles. In particular leaders behavior should be more constrained and more exposed. One first assumption is that these countries are studied since a long time in PBC literature (see Tables B.1 and B.2), and earlier studies may be more prone to find such a manipulation due to, for instance, the late democratization process in some countries (e.g.,

Table 11.3 Multiple MRA on revenue [Only variables with PIP > 0.500]

| | Frequentist check (LSDV) | | | |
| | (1) Cluster: study | | (2) Double cluster | |
	Coefficient	Standard Error	Coefficient	Standard Error
Publication bias				
SE	0.325	(0.285)	0.325	(0.366)
Model structure				
Subsample	−0.007	(0.004)	−0.007	(0.004)
BadSamp	**0.118*****	**(0.004)**	**0.118*****	**(0.007)**
Time and Regions				
1980s	**0.050*****	**(0.004)**	**0.050*****	**(0.012)**
1990s	**−0.097*****	**(0.006)**	**−0.097*****	**(0.010)**
Mena	**−0.006****	**(0.003)**	−0.006	(0.004)
WeJ	**−0.018*****	**(0.005)**	**−0.018*****	**(0.006)**
Global	**0.039*****	**(0.004)**	**0.039*****	**(0.004)**
Paper				
Impact factor	–	–	–	–
Trend	–	–	–	–
Before 2008	–	–	–	–
Methodology				
Infrannual	**0.074*****	**(0.007)**	**0.074*****	**(0.009)**
YCycl	**−0.076*****	**(0.004)**	**−0.076*****	**(0.006)**
Covariates				
GDPpc.	−0.002	(0.003)	−0.002	(0.003)
Trade	**−0.094*****	**(0.003)**	**−0.094*****	**(0.002)**
OG	**0.092*****	**(0.003)**	**0.092*****	**(0.003)**
Constant	−0.022	(0.019)	−0.022	(0.025)
RMSE		0.034		0.034
Adjusted R^2		0.543		0.543
Paper FE		Yes		Yes
# cluster		20		31
n (# studies)		20		20
N		305		305

Notes: The dependent variable is the partial correlation between election and measures of revenue. Estimates are obtained by employing successively: cluster on studies, and double-cluster on studies and fiscal output. All models are estimated from Equation 3 and the LSDV estimator to absorb paper fixed effects (precision squared weights). Results with the 294 interactive models are available upon request. We only include explanatory variables with PIP > 0.500. A detailed description of all variables is available in Table C.1.

Portugal, Spain, Greece). As an alternative assumption we may imagine that voters in these countries are *relatively* more able to detect a reduction of the tax burden (and also the benefits of new tax expenditures – one U.S. fiscal "specialty"), due to a generally satisfying furniture of public services, which may encourage leaders to try to please voters in this way, expecting a greater payoff of such a policy. These assumptions would explain this primarily surprising result, but the last one as few echoes from Table D.1. Less surprisingly, a similar effect, yet smaller, emerges when using samples containing Northern Africa and Middle East countries (variable *Mena*). We note that regressions based on countries from several parts of the world report cycles of lower magnitude, since the positive coefficient associated to the variable *Global* translates a fewer reduction in revenue. Variables *1980s* and *1990s* suggest that the strength of cycles in revenue is not constant over time. Finally, we see that the choice of covariates and how authors model their estimates affect results.[14] Interestingly, among these effects the magnitude of cycles appears significantly reduced when researchers estimate PBC through infra-annual data. This result does not corroborate here Labonne (2016) arguing that PBC are more likely to be detected with more disaggregated data.

5.2.2. Expenditure

We replicate the same approach for analyzing conditional cycles in expenditure. First, we run the BMA analysis in order to determine a parsimonious model which contains the covariates with the best predictive power. In total, 58,858,028 models are visited, and Figure 11.3 and Table 11.4 present the graphical and statistical analyses. The best 5,000 models have have a cumulative probability of 42 percent.

The statistical analysis identifies eight covariates with a PIP above 0.50 (including the intercept). We run Equation 3 on these variables and display results in Table 11.5. Unlike revenue, we do not find any geographical or time effects for expenditure. However, estimates relying on subsamples containing only established democracies exhibit lower cycles in revenue. This may translate a lower ability of leaders to manipulate revenue where democratic systems are well-established. Another and non-rival explanation would be that experienced voters are less likely to reward pre-electoral increases in expenditure compared to pre-electoral reductions of tax. Incumbents would then be more reluctant to create cycles in revenue. Once again, using a cyclically-adjusted dependent variable seem to be non-neutral in estimating the magnitude of cycles (variable *Ycycl*). The way researchers capture electoral periods and build the associated variables also has an impact. Specifically, using a ratio à la Franzese, which is considered as a more precise way of capturing electoral periods than standard dummies, leads to lower cycles. Finally, correcting for heteroskedasticity also reduces their magnitude. More precise and robust methods of estimates seem to deliver lower cycles.

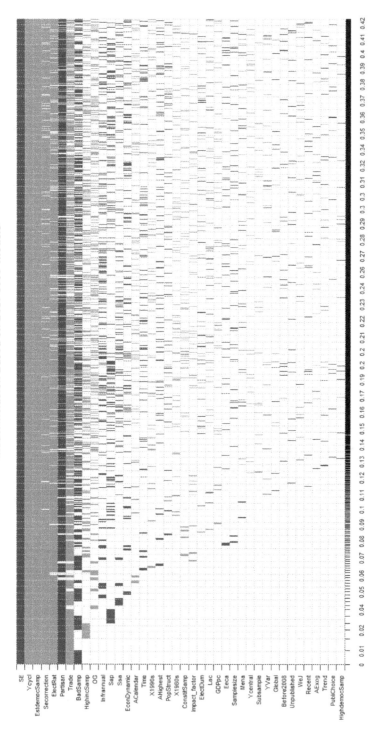

Figure 11.3 BMA: Model inclusion on spending [UIP g-prior; uniform model prior]

Notes: See Figure 11.2. The dependent variable is the adjusted partial correlation between election and measures of spending.

Table 11.4 BMA on spending [UIP g-prior; uniform model prior]

	BMA, Model prior: Uniform			
	PIP	*Post. mean*	*Post.s.d.*	*Cond.pos.sign*
Publication bias				
SE	**1.000**	**1.726**	**0.169**	**1.000**
Model structure				
Subsample	0.027	0.000	0.002	0.915
ConstitSamp	0.058	−0.001	0.004	0.000
HighincSamp	0.249	−0.006	0.012	0.000
EstdemocSamp	**1.000**	**−0.047**	**0.011**	**0.000**
HighdemocSamp	0.017	0.000	0.003	0.483
BadSamp	0.487	0.027	0.032	0.000
Time and Regions				
1980s	0.059	−0.001	0.005	0.317
1990s	0.065	−0.002	0.011	0.000
Recent	0.021	0.000	0.002	0.993
Eeca	0.039	0.000	0.003	1.000
Lac	0.046	−0.001	0.006	0.372
Mena	0.034	0.000	0.004	0.052
Sap	0.148	0.003	0.009	0.995
Ssa	0.104	0.002	0.007	0.120
WeJ	0.021	0.000	0.002	1.000
Global	0.024	0.000	0.002	0.000
Paper				
Public Choice	0.018	0.000	0.002	1.000
Unpublished	0.022	0.000	0.002	0.572
Impact factor	0.058	0.000	0.000	0.000
Trend	0.020	0.000	0.000	0.012
Before 2008	0.022	0.000	0.002	0.842
Methodology				
Samplesize	0.037	0.000	0.000	0.906
Infrannual	0.169	0.006	0.015	0.671
YVar	0.025	0.000	0.002	0.000
YCycl	**1.000**	**−0.204**	**0.024**	**0.000**
YCentral	0.029	0.000	0.003	0.024
ElectDum	0.053	0.000	0.005	0.548
ElectRat	**0.925**	**−0.030**	**0.013**	**0.000**
ACalendar	0.079	−0.001	0.006	0.000
AHighest	0.064	0.001	0.004	1.000
AExog	0.020	0.000	0.002	0.289
EconDynamic	0.101	0.002	0.005	1.000
Se Correction	**0.963**	**−0.025**	**0.009**	**0.000**
Covariates				
GDPpc.	0.041	0.000	0.003	0.617
Trade	**0.725**	**−0.022**	**0.016**	**0.001**
PopStruct	0.064	0.000	0.006	0.208
OG	0.246	−0.008	0.015	0.391

(Continued)

Partisan	**0.878**	**0.045**	**0.022**	**1.000**
Time	0.077	0.001	0.004	1.000
Constant	**1.000**	**0.004**	NA	NA
n (# studies)	28			
N	423			

Notes: See Table 11.2. The dependent variable is the adjusted partial correlation between election and measures of spending.

Table 11.5 Multiple MRA on spending [Only variables with PIP>0.500]

	Frequentist check (LSDV)			
	(1) Cluster: study		*(2) Double cluster*	
	Coefficient	*Standard Error*	*Coefficient*	*Standard Error*
Publication bias				
SE	**1.358***	**(0.424)**	**1.358***	**(0.406)**
Model structure				
EstdemocSamp	**−0.040***	**(0.010)**	**−0.040***	**(0.014)**
Methodology				
YCycl	**−0.207***	**(0.008)**	**−0.207***	**(0.008)**
ElectRat	**−0.023***	**(0.004)**	**−0.023***	**(0.005)**
Se Correction	**−0.018***	**(0.004)**	**−0.018***	**(0.003)**
Covariates				
Trade	−0.002	(0.003)	−0.002	(0.004)
Partisan	0.002	(0.001)	0.002	(0.007)
Constant	0.009	(0.014)	0.009	(0.0118)
RMSE	0.049		0.049	
Adjusted R^2	0.338		0.338	
Paper FE		Yes		Yes
# cluster		28		52
n (# studies)		28		28
N		423		423

Notes: See Table 11.3. The dependent variable is the adjusted partial correlation between election and measures of spending.

5.2.3. Fiscal balance

We proceed similarly for the last output, that is, fiscal balance. Figure 11.4 and Table 11.6 provide the graphical and statistical analyses of the BMA applied to regressions with fiscal balance as dependent variable. The best 5,000 models have have a cumulative probability of 31 percent. Unlike revenue and

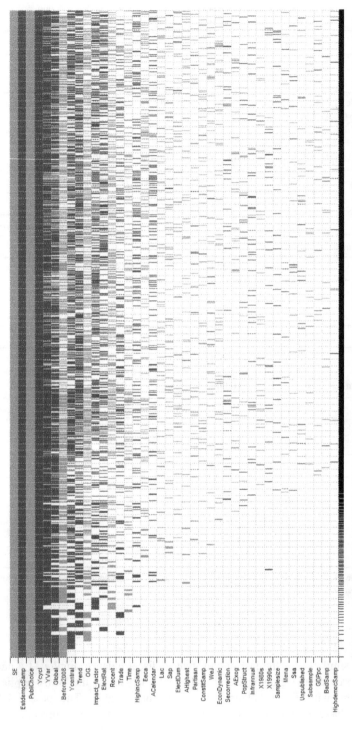

Figure 11.4 BMA: Model inclusion on fiscal balance [UIP g-prior; uniform model prior]

Notes: See Figure 11.2. The dependent variable is the adjusted partial correlation between election and measures of fiscal balance.

Table 11.6 BMA on fiscal balance [UIP g-prior; uniform model prior]

	BMA, Model prior: Uniform			
	PIP	*Post. mean*	*Post.s.d.*	*Cond.pos.sign*
Publication bias				
SE	**1,000**	**−1,288**	**0,146**	**0,000**
Model structure				
Subsample	0,019	0,000	0,001	0,027
ConstitSamp	0,040	−0,001	0,004	0,020
HighincSamp	0,140	0,003	0,008	1,000
EstdemocSamp	**1,000**	**0,059**	**0,011**	**1,000**
HighdemocSamp	0,014	0,000	0,003	0,457
BadSamp	0,015	0,000	0,002	0,381
Time and Regions				
1980s	0,029	0,000	0,003	0,147
1990s	0,028	0,000	0,005	0,956
Recent	0,246	−0,008	0,016	0,000
Eeca	0,112	−0,002	0,007	0,004
Lac	0,070	−0,001	0,005	0,019
Mena	0,024	0,000	0,002	0,468
Sap	0,067	−0,001	0,005	0,038
Ssa	0,022	0,000	0,002	0,353
WeJ	0,040	0,000	0,004	0,155
Global	**0,702**	**0,021**	**0,017**	**1,000**
Paper				
Public Choice	**1,000**	**−0,074**	**0,015**	**0,000**
Unpublished	0,021	0,000	0,002	0,536
Impact factor	0,336	0,000	0,000	1,000
Trend	0,491	0,002	0,003	0,999
Before 2008	**0,539**	**−0,024**	**0,024**	**0,002**
Methodology				
Samplesize	0,028	0,000	0,000	0,991
Infrannual	0,031	0,000	0,003	0,981
YVar	**0,892**	**0,051**	**0,024**	**1,000**
YCycl	**1,000**	**0,115**	**0,019**	**1,000**
YCentral	**0,512**	**0,013**	**0,015**	**1,000**
ElectDum	0,046	−0,001	0,004	0,125
ElectRat	0,266	0,007	0,013	1,000
ACalendar	0,096	0,002	0,006	1,000
AHighest	0,045	−0,001	0,003	0,052
AExog	0,033	0,000	0,004	0,162
EconDynamic	0,040	0,000	0,003	0,005
Se Correction	0,037	0,000	0,003	0,965
Covariates				
GDPpc.	0,018	0,000	0,002	0,269

(*Continued*)

Table 11.6   (Continued)

| | BMA, Model prior: Uniform | | | |
	PIP	Post. mean	Post.s.d.	Cond.pos.sign
Trade	0,171	0,004	0,011	0,986
PopStruct	0,033	0,000	0,003	0,577
OG	0,369	−0,011	0,016	0,001
Partisan	0,045	−0,001	0,005	0,156
Time	0,145	−0,002	0,007	0,000
Constant	**1,000**	**−0,083**	NA	NA
n (# studies)		39		
N		309		

Notes: See Table 11.2. The dependent variable is the adjusted partial correlation between election and measures of fiscal balance.

expenditure, the measure of fiscal surplus in the literature is unique, so that there is no need to cluster in this respect.

63,955,951 models are visited and the 9 variables (including the intercept) with a PIP above 0.50 in the BMA analysis are incorporated in Equation 3. The results are presented in Table 11.7. Consistently with expenditure cycles, the binary variable associated with subsamples of established democracies is here positive and significant. This suggests that older democracies experience lower deterioration of the fiscal balance before elections than their counterparts. Authors' choices over the way of modeling the dependent variable also exert significant effects on the strength of cycles they obtain.

6. Conclusion

Strategic behavior of political leaders has been long studied in social sciences, and the pre-electoral period has received particular attention. An important subset of this literature has investigated the question of political budget cycles by scrutinizing whether incumbents modify national accounts before elections in a way to please voters and maximize their reelection prospects. Despite substantial empirical research, the existence, magnitude and factors affecting such cycles are still not well-established. To provide some insights and answers to this debate we realize a meta-regression analysis of PBC. Through an exhaustive search of empirical papers assessing national PBC, we perform our analysis on the 1,037 estimates collected.

A simple MRA reveal that in average manipulation of budget by national leaders before elections is in average limited at best. We find statistically significant evidence of cycles in revenue and fiscal balance in particular, however the magnitude of these effects is practically negligible. Additionally, we detect some evidence of publication-selection for estimates of cycles in expenditure and fiscal

Table 11.7 Multiple MRA on fiscal balance [Only variables with PIP > 0.500]

| | Frequentist check (LSDV) | |
| | Cluster: study | |
	Coefficient	Standard Error
Publication bias		
SE	**−1.206*****	**(0.321)**
Model structure		
EstdemocSamp	**0.059*****	**(0.003)**
Time and Regions		
Global	**0.010*****	**(0.001)**
Paper		
Public Choice	–	–
Before 2008	–	–
Methodology		
YVar	**−0.011*****	**(0.000)**
YCycl	**0.155*****	**(0.006)**
YCentral	**−0.067*****	**(0.005)**
Constant	**−0.016***	**(0.008)**
RMSE	0.026	
Adjusted R^2	0.602	
Paper FE	Yes	
# cluster	39	
n # studies	39	
N	309	

Notes: See Table 11.3. The dependent variable is the adjusted partial correlation between election and measures of fiscal balance.

balance. These biases are due to an over-reporting of results in line with the theory, that is, predicting an increase of expenditure and a deterioration of fiscal balance before elections.

Extending these results we perform a multiple analysis. In order to select the most relevant variables explaining our dependent variable, we first run a BMA analysis. This first step allows us to build multiple-MRA models that are not over-specified by including only the most significant variables identified during the BMA analysis. We then realize a standard multiple MRA. Few characteristics of sample appear to affect the magnitude of effects such as geography, time, or the length of democracy experience. Finally, methodological choices operated by researchers lead to results of different magnitude. Although PBC appear as limited at an aggregate level, more research may be undertaken on political cycles at local level, with finer data, and beyond the manipulation on national accounts on a wide range of public policies.

Notes

1 The literature is ambiguous regarding the detrimental effects of PBC on incumbent chances of reelection. Indeed, Sakurai and Menezes-Filho (2008) and Jones, Meloni, and Tommasi (2012), among others, find beneficial effects for Brazilian mayors and Argentinean governors, respectively.
2 Gonzalez (2002) finds higher PBC during the democratization process of Mexico, i.e., when Mexico had a low-level democratic framework.
3 Other reviews such as Drazen (2001) are specifically focused on political business cycles.
4 The interested reader may find additional details related to the collection and coding of the meta-data in Mandon and Cazals (2019).
5 See Table A.1 in Appendix for supplementary details.
6 We exclude estimates whose the dependent variable is not expressed as a nominal value, as a fraction (e.g., of GDP), as a variation or as a growth rate. For instance, in some regressions, Katsimi and Sarantides (2012) use the ratio of current (or capital) spending over total spending. In these cases, we can measure the variation in the ratio but we are not able to identify if this variation results from an electoral manipulation on the numerator, the denominator, or both. As a consequence, we cannot know how the level of current (or capital) expenditure is affected by the closeness of elections. Similar cases of composition-related regressions can be found in Chang (2008), Vergne (2009), or Klomp and de Haan (2013a), among others.
7 Numerous estimates focus on deficits rather than surpluses. In such cases, we multiply the estimate values by -1 so that all estimates dealing with fiscal balance are coded in the same direction.
8 As explained in Section 4, we combine in this panel all fiscal outputs to observe any pre-electoral use of budget. So, we employ the adjusted t-statistics of partial correlations between election and fiscal outputs as the dependent variable, by multiplying by -1 the inverse partial correlation for revenue and fiscal balance.
9 In Cohen's classification, an effect is negligible when the coefficient $|\hat{\beta}_0|$ is under ($\leq$) 0.10, small between 0.10 and 0.30, medium above (>) 0.30 and large above (>) 0.50 (Cohen, 1988).
10 Strategic manipulation of subcomponents of budget are acknowledged as "pork barrel" (Drazen and Eslava, 2006).
11 Doucouliagos and Stanley (2013) consider the selective reporting is modest if $|\hat{\beta}_1|<1$, substantial if $1\leq|\hat{\beta}_1|\leq 2$, and severe if $|\hat{\beta}_1|>2$. Evidence of such a bias is found in most research areas in economics (Doucouliagos and Stanley, 2013; Paldam, 2017).
12 Evidence of such a bias is found in most research areas in Economics (Doucouliagos and Stanley 2013; Paldam, 2017). We note that results obtained by estimating the model with weighted least squares in Mandon and Cazals (2019) differ. In particular they suggest the existence of a moderate selection bias for all types of output. Evidence of such a bias is here only revealed for PBC on spending and fiscal balance. Qualitative differences in publication selection bias for revenue outputs emerge from the use of the LSDV estimator and the introduction of unobserved paper effects, and the results hold regarding the negligible magnitude of genuine electoral manipulation.
13 We use the BMS package of Martin Feldkircher and Stefan Zeugner. Additional details on BMA computation are available upon request.

14 Due to the inclusion of study fixed effects in the unrestricted weighted least squares, we are unable to estimate paper specific characteristics.

Bibliography

Afonso, Antonio. 2008. "Ricardian Fiscal Regimes in the European Union." *Empirica* 35(3):313–334.

Akhmedov, Akhmed and Ekaterina Zhuravskaya. 2004. "Opportunistic Political Cycles: Test in a Young Democracy Setting." *The Quarterly Journal of Economics* 119(4): 1301–1338.

Alesina, Alberto, Silvia Ardagna and Francesco Trebbi. 2006. *Who Adjusts and When? On the Political Economy of Reforms*. NBER Working Papers 12049 National Bureau of Economic Research, Inc. URL: https://ideas.repec.org/p/nbr/nberwo/12049.html

Alesina, Alberto, Gerald D. Cohen and Nouriel Roubini. 1992. "Macroeconomic Policy and Elections in OECD Democracies." *Economics & Politics* 4(1):1–31.

Alesina, Alberto, Gerald D. Cohen and Nouriel Roubini. 1993. "Electoral Business Cycle in Industrial Democracies." *European Journal of Political Economy* 9(1):1–23.

Alt, James E. and David D. Lassen. 2006. "Transparency, Political Polarization, and Political Budget Cycles in OECD Countries." *American Journal of Political Science* 50(3):530–550.

Arvate, Paulo Roberto, George Avelino and Jose Tavares. 2009. "Fiscal Conservatism in a New Democracy: Sophisticated Versus Naïve Voters." *Economics Letters* 102(2): 125–127.

Ashworth, John and Bruno Heyndels. 2002. "Tax Structure Turbulence in OECD Countries." *Public Choice* 111(3–4):347–376.

Barberia, Lorena and George Avelino. 2011. "Do Political Budget Cycles Di er in Latin American Democracies?" *Journal of Lacea EconomÂa* 11(2):101–134.

Bayar, Ali and Bram Smeets. 2009. *Economic, Political and Institutional Determinants of Budget Deficits in the European Union*. CESifo Working Paper Series 2611 CESifo Group Munich. URL: https://ideas.repec.org/p/ces/ceswps/_2611.html

Block, Steven A. 2002. "Political Business Cycles, Democratization, and Economic Reform: The Case of Africa." *Journal of Development Economics* 67(1):205–228.

Block, Steven A., Karen E. Ferree and Smita Singh. 2003. "Multiparty Competition, Founding Elections and Political Business Cycles in Africa." *Journal of African Economies* 12(3):444–468.

Boix, Carles, Michael K. Miller and Sebastian Rosato. 2013. "A Complete Data Set of Political Regimes, 1800–2007." *Comparative Political Studies* 46(12):1523–1554.

Bove, Vicenzo, Georgios Efthyvoulou and Antonio Navas. 2014. *Political Cycles in Public Expenditure: Butter vs Guns*. Working Papers 2013016 The University of Sheffield, Department of Economics. URL: https://ideas.repec.org/p/ris/nepswp/2013_007. html

Brender, Adi. 2003. "The Effect of Fiscal Performance on Local Government Election Results in Israel: 1989–1998." *Journal of Public Economics* 87(9–10):2187–2205.

Brender, Adi and Allan Drazen. 2003. *Where Does the Political Budget Cycle Really Come From?* CEPR Discussion Papers 4049 C.E.P.R. URL: https://ideas.repec.org/p/cpr/ceprdp/4049.html

Brender, Adi and Allan Drazen. 2005. "Political Budget Cycles in New Versus Established Democracies." *Journal of Monetary Economics* 52(7):1271–1295.

Brender, Adi and Allan Drazen. 2007. *Why Is Economic Policy Different in New Democracies? Affecting Attitudes About Democracy.* NBER Working Papers 13457 National Bureau of Economic Research, Inc. URL: https://ideas.repec.org/p/nbr/nberwo/13457.html

Buti, Marco and Paul Van Den Noord. 2004. "Fiscal Discretion and Elections in the Early Years of EMU." *JCMS: Journal of Common Market Studies* 42(4):737–756.

Cazals, Antoine and Alexandre Sauquet. 2015. "How Do Elections Affect International Cooperation? Evidence From Environmental Treaty Participation." *Public Choice* 162(3):263–285.

Chang, Eric. 2008. "Electoral Incentives and Budgetary Spending: Rethinking The Role of Political Institutions." *Journal of Politics* 70(4):1086–1097.

Cheibub, José A., Jennifer Gandhi and James R. Vreeland. 2010. "Democracy and Dictatorship Revisited." *Public Choice* 143(1):67–101.

Cohen, Jacob. 1988. *Statistical Power Analysis in the Behavorial Sciences* (2nd ed.). Hillsdale: Erlbaum.

Combes, Jean-Louis, Mathilde Maurel and Christian Ebeke. 2013. *The Effect of Remittances Prior to an Election.* Working Papers 201307 CERDI. URL: https://ideas.repec.org/p/cdi/wpaper/1430.html

Combes, Jean-Louis, Mathilde Maurel and Christian Ebeke. 2015. "The Effect of Remittances Prior to an Election." *Applied Economics* 47(28):1–16.

Costa-Fernandes, Abel L. and Paulo R. Mota. 2013. "The Present Sovereign Debt Crisis of the Euro Zone Peripheral Countries: A Case of Non-Mature Democracies and Less Developed Economies." *Panaoeconomicus* 3(Special Issue):291–310.

de Haan, Jakob and Jeroen Klomp. 2013. "Conditional Political Budget Cycles: A Review of Recent Evidence." *Public Choice* 157(3):387–410.

Doucouliagos, Hristos and Tom D. Stanley. 2013. "Are All Economic Facts Greatly Exaggerated? Theory Competition and Selectivity." *Journal of Economic Surveys* 27(2): 316–339.

Drazen, Allan. 2001. "The Political Business Cycle After 25 Years." In *NBER Macroeconomics Annual 2000, Volume 15*, ed. B. S. Bernanke and K. Rogoff. NBER Chapters. Cambridge, MA: National Bureau of Economic Research, Inc, pp. 75–138.

Drazen, Allan and Marcela Eslava. 2006. *Pork Barrel Cycles.* NBER Working Papers 12190 National Bureau of Economic Research, Inc. URL: https://ideas.repec.org/p/nbr/nberwo/12190.html

Drazen, Allan and Marcela Eslava. 2010. "Electoral Manipulation via Voter-Friendly Spending: Theory and Evidence." *Journal of Development Economics* 92(1):39–52.

Dreher, Axel and Roland Vaubel. 2004. "Do IMF and IBRD Cause Moral Hazard and Political Business Cycles? Evidence From Panel Data." *Open Economies Review* 15(1):5–22.

Dubois, Eric. 2016. "Political Business Cycles 40 Years After Nordhaus." *Public Choice* 166(1):235–259.

Ebeke, Christian and Dilan Ölçer. 2013. *Fiscal Policy over the Election Cycle in Low-Income Countries.* IMF Working Papers 13/153 International Monetary Fund. URL: https://ideas.repec.org/p/imf/imfwpa/13-153.html

Efthyvoulou, Georgios. 2012. "Political Budget Cycles in the European Union and the Impact of Political Pressures." *Public Choice* 153(3):295–327.

Ehrhart, Helene. 2013. "Elections and the Structure of Taxation in Developing Countries." *Public Choice* 156(1):195–211.

Eslava, Marcela. 2011. "The Political Economy of Fiscal Deficits: A Survey." *Journal of Economic Surveys* 25(4):645–673.

Fatás, Antonio and Ilian Mihov. 2003. "The Case for Restricting Fiscal Policy Discretion." *The Quarterly Journal of Economics* 118(4):1419–1447.

Franzese, Jr., Robert J. 2000. "Electoral and Partisan Manipulation of Public Debt in Developed Democracies, 1956–90." In *Institutions, Politics and Fiscal Policy*, ed. R. R. Strauch and J. von Hagen. Vol. 2 of *ZEI Studies in European Economics and Law*. New York City: Springer, pp. 61–83.

Galeotti, Andrea and Gianluca Salford. 2001. *Electoral Cycles: Do they really fit the Data?* Tinbergen Institute Discussion Paper 2001/76 Tinbergen Institute. URL: https://ideas.repec.org/p/tin/wpaper/20010076.html

Golinelli, Roberto and Sandro Momigliano. 2006. "Real-Time Determinants of Fiscal Policies in the Euro Area." *Journal of Policy Modeling* 28(9):943–964.

Gonzalez, Maria de los Angeles. 2002. "Do Changes in Democracy Affect the Political Budget Cycle? Evidence From Mexico." *Review of Development Economics* 6(2): 204–224.

Gründler, Klaus and Tommy Krieger. 2016. "Democracy and Growth: Evidence From a Machine Learning Indicator." *European Journal of Political Economy* 45(S):85–107.

Hagen, Tobias. 2007. "Estimating the Effect of Parliamentary Elections on Primary Budget Deficits in OECD Countries." *Economics Bulletin* 8(8):1–5.

Hallerberg, Mark, Lucio Vinhas de Souza and William Roberts Clark. 2002. "Political Business Cycles in EU Accession Countries." *European Union Politics* 3(2):231–250.

Hanusch, Marek. 2012. "Mooted Signals: Economic Disturbances and Political Budget Cycles." *Journal of Applied Economics* 15(2):189–212.

Hanusch, Marek and Philip Keefer. 2014. "Younger Parties, Bigger Spenders? Party Age and Political Budget Cycles." *European Economic Review* 72(C):1–18.

Hanusch, Marek and Paul M. Vaaler. 2013. "Credit Rating Agencies and Elections in Emerging Democracies: Guardians of Fiscal Discipline?" *Economics Letters* 119(3): 251–254.

Havránek, Tomas. 2015. "Measuring Intertemporal Substitution: The Importance of Method Choices and Selective Reporting." *Journal of the European Economic Association* 13(6):1180–1204.

Jones, Mark P., Osvaldo Meloni and Mariano Tommasi. 2012. "Voters as Fiscal Liberals: Incentives and Accountability in Federal Systems." *Economics & Politics* 24(2):135–156.

Jong-A-Pin, Richard, Jan-Egbert Sturm and Jakob de Haan. 2012. *Using Real-Time Data to Test for Political Budget Cycles.* CESifo Working Paper Series 3939 CESifo Group Munich. URL: https://ideas.repec.org/p/ces/ceswps/_3939.html

Kaplan, Stephen B. and Kaj Thomsson. 2014. *The Political Economy of Sovereign Borrowing: Explaining the Policy Choices of Highly Indebted Governments.* Working Papers 2014–10 The George Washington University, Institute for International Economic Policy. URL: https://ideas.repec.org/p/gwi/wpaper/2014-10.html

Katsimi, Margarita and Vassilis Sarantides. 2012. "Do Elections Affect the Composition of Fiscal Policy in Developed, Established Democracies?" *Public Choice* 151(1): 325–362.

Klašnja, Marko. 2008. "Electoral Rules, Forms of Government, and Political Budget Cycles in Transition Countries." *Panoeconomicus* 55(2):185–218.

Klomp, Jeroen and Jakob de Haan. 2013a. "Conditional Election and Partisan Cycles in Government Support to the Agricultural Sector: An Empirical Analysis." *American Journal of Agricultural Economics* 95(4):793–818.

Klomp, Jeroen and Jakob de Haan. 2013b. "Do Political Budget Cycles Really Exist?" *Applied Economics* 45(3):329–341.

Klomp, Jeroen and Jakob de Haan. 2013c. "Political Budget Cycles and Election Outcomes." *Public Choice* 157(1–2):245–267.

Klomp, Jeroen and Jakob de Haan. 2013d. "Popular Protest and Political Budget Cycles: A Panel Data Analysis." *Economics Letters* 120(3):516–520.

Kouvavas, Omiros. 2013. *Political Budget Cycles Revisited, the Case for Social Capital.* MPRA Paper 57504 University Library of Munich. URL: https://ideas.repec.org/p/pra/mprapa/57504.html

Kraemer, Moritz. 1997. *Electoral Budget Cycles in Latin America and the Caribbean: Incidence, Causes, and Political Futility.* Research Department Publications 4084 Inter-American Development Bank, Research Department. URL: https://ideas.repec.org/p/idb/wpaper/4084.html

Labonne, Julien. 2016. "Local Political Business Cycles: Evidence From Philippine Municipalities." *Journal of Development Economics* 121(1):56–62.

Mandon, Pierre and Antoine Cazals. 2019. "Political Budget Cycles: Manipulation by Leaders Versus Manipulation by Researchers? Evidence From a Meta-Regression Analysis." *Journal of Economic Surveys* 33(1):274–308.

Maurel, Mathilde. 2006. *The Political Business Cycles in the EU Enlarged. UniversitÃ© Paris1 PanthÃ©on-Sorbonne.* Post-Print and Working Papers halshs-00267475 HAL. URL: https://ideas.repec.org/p/hal/cesptp/halshs-00267475.html

Mink, Mark and Jakob de Haan. 2006. "Are There Political Budget Cycles in the Euro Area?" *European Union Politics* 7(2):191–211.

Morozumi, Atsuyoshi, Francisco Jose Veiga and Linda Goncalves Veiga. 2014. *Electoral Effects on the Composition of Public Spending and Revenue: Evidence From a Large Panel of Countries.* Discussion Papers 2014/16 University of Nottingham, Centre for Finance, Credit and Macroeconomics (CFCM). URL: https://ideas.repec.org/p/not/notcfc/14-16.html

Mosley, Paul and Blessing Chiripanhura. 2012. *The African Political Business Cycle: Varieties of Experience.* Working Papers 2012002 The University of Sheffield, Department of Economics. URL: https://ideas.repec.org/p/shf/wpaper/2012002.html

Mourão, Paulo Reis. 2011. "Has Trade Openness Already Voted? A Panel Data Study." *Emerging Markets Finance and Trade* 47(5):53–71.

Nieto-Parra, Sebastian and Javier Santiso. 2009. *Revisiting Political Budget Cycles in Latin America.* OECD Development Centre Working Paper 281 281 OECD. URL: https://ideas.repec.org/p/oec/devaaa/281-en.html

Nordhaus, William D. 1975. "The Political Business Cycle." *Review of Economic Studies* 42(2):169–190.

Nyblade, Benjamin and Angela O'Mahony. 2014. "Playing With Fire: Pre-Electoral Fiscal Manipulation and the Risk of a Speculative Attack." *International Studies Quarterly* 58(4):828–838.

Paldam, Martin. 1979. "Is There an Election Cycle? A Comparative Study of National Accounts." *Scandinavian Journal of Economics* 81(2):323–342.

Paldam, Martin. 2017. *A Model of the Rational Economist.* Mimeo. URL: https://www.martin.paldam.dk/Papers/Meta-method/9-Econ-model.pdf

Peltzman, Sam. 1992. "Voters as Fiscal Conservatives." *The Quarterly Journal of Economics* 107(2):327–361.

Persson, Torsten and Guido Tabellini. 2003. *Do Electoral Cycles Differ Across Political Systems?* Working Papers 232 IGIER (Innocenzo Gasparini Institute for Economic Research), Bocconi University. URL: https://ideas.repec.org/p/igi/igierp/232.html

Philips, Andrew Q. 2016. "Seeing the Forest Through the Trees: A Meta-Analysis of Political Budget Cycles." *Public Choice* 168(3):313–341.

Potrafke, Niklas. 2007. *Social Expenditures as a Political Cue Ball? OECD Countries Under Examination*. Discussion Papers of DIW Berlin 676 DIW Berlin, German Institute for Economic Research. URL: https://ideas.repec.org/p/diw/diwwpp/dp676.html

Potrafke, Niklas. 2010. "The Growth of Public Health Expenditures in OECD Countries: Do Government Ideology and Electoral Motives Matter?" *Journal of Health Economics* 29(6):797–810.

Rogoff, Kenneth. 1990. "Equilibrium Political Budget Cycles." *American Economic Review* 80(1):21–36.

Sakurai, Sergio Naruhiko and Naercio Aquino Menezes-Filho. 2008. "Fiscal Policy and Reelection in Brazilian Municipalities." *Public Choice* 137(1–2):301–314.

Schuknecht, Ludger. 1996. "Political Business Cycles and Fiscal Policies in Developing Countries." *Kyklos* 49(2):155–170.

Schuknecht, Ludger. 2000. "Fiscal Policy Cycles and Public Expenditure in Developing Countries." *Public Choice* 102(1–2):115–130.

Shelton, Cameron. 2014. "Legislative Budget Cycles." *Public Choice* 159(1):251–275.

Shi, Min and Jakob Svensson. 2003. "Political Budget Cycles: A Review of Recent Developments." *Nordic Journal of Political Economy* 29:67–76.

Shi, Min and Jakob Svensson. 2006. "Political Budget Cycles: Do They Differ Across Countries and Why?" *Journal of Public Economics* 90(8–9):1367–1389.

Stanley, Tom D. 2001. "Wheat From Chaff: Meta-analysis as Quantitative Literature Review." *Journal of Economic Perspectives* 15(3):131–150.

Stanley, Tom D. and Hristos Doucouliagos. 2012. *Meta-Regression Analysis in Economics and Business*. London: Routledge.

Stanova, Nadja. 2009. *Are There Political Fiscal Cycles in NMS?* Working Papers 2009013 University of Antwerp, Faculty of Applied Economics. URL: https://EconPapers.repec.org/RePEc:ant:wpaper:2009013

Streb, Jorge M., Daniel Lema and Pablo Garofalo. 2012. "Temporal Aggregation in Political Budget Cycles." *Journal of Lacea Economia* 11(1):39–78.

Streb, Jorge M., Daniel Lema and Gustavo Torrens. 2009. "Checks and Balances on Political Budget Cycles: Cross-Country Evidence." *Kyklos* 62(3):426–447.

Troeger, Vera and Christina J. Schneider. 2012. *Strategic Budgeteering and Debt Allocation*. CAGE Online Working Paper Series 85 Competitive Advantage in the Global Economy (CAGE). URL: https://ideas.repec.org/p/cge/wacage/85.html

Tujula, Mika and Guido Wolswijk. 2007. "Budget Balances in OECD Countries: What Makes Them Change?" *Empirica* 34(1):1–14.

Vergne, Clemence. 2009. "Democracy, Elections and Allocation of Public Expenditures in Developing Countries." *European Journal of Political Economy* 25(1):63–77.

Wittman, Donald A., Barry R. Weingast, Robert J. Franzese, Jr. and Karen Long Jusko. 2006. *Political Economic Cycles*. Oxford: Oxford University Press.

Wright, Joseph. 2011. *Electoral Spending Cycles in Dictatorships*. Manuscript, Pennsylvania State University. URL: https://www.personal.psu.edu/jgw12/blogs/josephwright/ESC1.pdf

Appendix A

Selection of studies

Table A.1 Process of data building

Steps	Process	n # studies	
	Identification & screening		
Step 1:	Keywords "political budget cycles", "political business cycle" and "electoral cycle" on EconLit, Science Direct, Ideas Repec, Springer, Wiley and Google Scholar.	7,319	
Step 2:	Manual complementary research: (i) additional studies in the references listed in the papers already selected; (ii) publications and working papers of the authors identified in the first round; and (iii) use of alternative web engines.	7,387	
Step 3:	Screening based on title and abstract.	6,184	
Eligibility criteria			
Step 1:	Criteria on full text: keeping (i) working papers and peer-review articles written in English; (ii) panel cross-sectional studies at the macro level on fiscal variables; and (iii) publication or relase strictly before 1 January 2015.	69 (2,121 estimates)	
Step 2:	Excluding regressions without coefficients, standard errors or t-statistics available.	66 (1,627 estimates)	Data available upon request
Step3:	Excluding multiple-counting papers.	60 (1,432 estimates)	
Step 4:	Excluding estimates on fiscal composition change index/ratios.	57 (1,331 estimates)	
Step 5:	Excluding interactive models.	46 (1,037 estimates)	Our MRA

Notes: Additional details are available upon request.

Appendix B

List of studies and descriptive statistics

Table B.1 List of studies

Author(s)		Author(s)		Author(s)	
1	Alesina, Cohen, and Roubini (1992)	21	Hanusch (2012)	41	Shi and Svensson (2006)
2	Alesina, Cohen, and Roubini (1993)	22	Jong-A-Pin, Sturm, and de Haan (2012)	42	Stanova (2009)
3	Alesina, Ardagna, and Trebbi (2006)	23	Kaplan and Thomsson (2014)	43	Streb, Lema, and Torrens (2009)
4	Alt and Lassen (2006)	24	Katsimi and Sarantides (2012)	44	Streb, Lema, and Garofalo (2012)
5	Barberia and Avelino (2011)	25	Klašnja (2008)	45	Tujula and Wolswijk (2007)
6	Bayar and Smeets (2009)	26	Klomp and de Haan (2013a)	46	Wright (2011)
7	Block (2002)	27	Klomp and de Haan (2013b)		
8	Bove, Efthyvoulou, and Navas (2014)	28	Klomp and de Haan (2013d)		
9	Brender and Drazen (2003)	29	Kouvavas (2013)		
10	Brender and Drazen (2005)	30	Kraemer (1997)		
11	Combes, Maurel, and Ebeke (2015)[a]	31	Maurel (2006)		
12	Costa-Fernandes and Mota (2013)	32	Mosley and Chiripanhura (2012)		
13	Dreher and Vaubel (2004)	33	Morozumi, Veiga, and Veiga (2014)[b]		
14	Ebeke and Ölçer (2013)	34	Nieto-Parra and Santiso (2009)		
15	Efthyvoulou (2012)	35	Persson and Tabellini (2003)		
16	Ehrhart (2013)	36	Potrafke (2007)		
17	Franzese (2000)	37	Potrafke (2010)		
18	Galeotti and Salford (2001)	38	Schuknecht (1996)		
19	Golinelli and Momigliano (2006)	39	Schuknecht (2000)		
20	Hagen (2007)	40	Shelton (2014)		

Notes: [a]: As the publication date is after 1 January 2015 we take into account the working paper version (Combes, Maurel, and Ebeke, 2013). [b]: We do not consider regressions from Table 2 to Table 5 in Morozumi, Veiga, and Veiga (2014) due to lack of information on effective reference category for elections.

Table B.2 Summary of studies [Including the number of interactive models per study]

#	Paper	Sample[a]	Time period	Estimator	Fiscal output[b]	Election	Mean (adjust) partial	Median (adjust) partial	# estimates	# interactive terms
1	Afonso (2008)	15 European Union countries	1970–2003[c]	OLS pooling & Fixed effects	Fiscal balance	Binary variable	-0.11	-0.09	15	15
2	Alesina, Cohen and Roubini (1992)	18 OECD countries	1960–1987	Fixed effects	Fiscal balance	Binary variable	0.13	0.13	3	1
3	Alesina, Cohen and Roubini (1993)	14 OECD countries	1960–1987	Fixed effects	Fiscal balance	Binary variable	0.11	0.12	8	1
4	Alesina, Ardagna and Trebbi (2006)	Developed and developing countries	1960–2003	Fixed effects	Fiscal balance	Binary variable	0.03	0.03	3	1
5	Alt and Lassen (2006)	19 OECD countries[c]	1989–1998	AB GMM	Fiscal balance	Binary variable	0.15	0.15	7	6
6	Ashworth and Heyndels (2002)	18 OECD countries	1965–1995	Fixed effects & Random effects	Direct taxes & Nonfiscal revenue	Binary variable	0.03	0.04	12	12
7	Barberia and Avelino (2011)	18 LAC countries	1973–2008	OLS pooling & Fixed effects & AB GMM & System GMM	Fiscal balance & Total spending & Total revenue	Binary variable	0.04	0.05	120	60
8	Bayar and Smeets (2009)	15 European Union countries	1971–2006	Fixed effects	Fiscal balance	Binary variable	0.08	0.13	3	0
9	Block (2002)	44 SSA countries	1980–1995	OLS pooling & Fixed effects & AB GMM & System GMM	Fiscal balance & Current spending & Nonfiscal revenue	Binary variable	0.07	0.09	12	0

No.	Study	Sample	Period	Method	Fiscal variables	Measure				
10	Block, Ferree and Singh (2003)	44 SSA countries[c]	1980–1995	OLS pooling & Fixed effects & AB GMM	Current spending	Binary variable	0.01	−0.01	3	3
11	Bove, Efthyvoulou and Navas (2014)	22 OECD countries[c]	1981–2009[c]	Random effects & Panel corrected SE & LSDV	Broad public goods & Local public goods	Binary variable	0.12	0.12	19	0
12	Brender and Drazen (2003)	80 Developed and developing countries[c]	1960–2001[c]	Fixed effects	Fiscal balance & Total spending & Total revenue	Binary variable	0.04	0.05	87	0
13	Brender and Drazen (2005)	68 Developed and developing countries[c]	1960–2001	Fixed effects	Fiscal balance & Total spending & Total revenue	Binary variable	0.06	0.04	45	0
14	Buti and Van Den Noord (2004)	11 European & Monetary Union countries	1999–2002	OLS pooling	Fiscal balance & Total spending & Total revenue	Binary variable	−0.09	0.04	5	5
15	Combes, Maurel and Ebeke (2015)[d]	70 Developing countries[c]	1990–2010	AB GMM & System GMM	Current spending & Capital spending	Binary variable	0.07	0.06	10	8
16	Costa-Fernandes and Mota (2013)	12 European Union countries	1976–2008	AB GMM & System GMM	Fiscal balance & Total spending & Total taxes & Broad public goods	Franzese's full ratio	0.00	0.01	16	12
17	Dreher and Vaubel (2004)	77 Developed and developing countries[c]	1975–1997	OLS pooling & 2SLS estimator & System GMM	Fiscal balance	Other	0.07	0.06	3	0
18	Ebeke and İlçer (2013)	61 Developing countries[c]	1990–2010	OLS pooling & 2SLS estimator & System GMM	Fiscal balance & Current spending & Capital spending & Direct taxes & Indirect taxes & External taxes	Binary variable	0.01	0.01	16	2

(Continued)

Table B.2 (Continued)

#	Paper	Sample[a]	Time period	Estimator	Fiscal output[b]	Election	Mean (adjust) partial	Median (adjust) partial	# estimates	# interactive terms
19	Efthyvoulou (2012)	27 European Union countries[c]	1997–2008[c]	Fixed effects & System GMM	Fiscal balance & Total spending & Current revenue & Capital spending & Current revenue & Total taxes	Binary variable	0.21	0.21	35	12
20	Ehrhart (2013)	56 Developing countries[c]	1980–2006	Fixed effects & System GMM	Direct taxes & Indirect taxes	Binary variable	0.03	0.04	28	0
21	Franzese (2000)	21 OECD countries	1956–1990	Panel corrected SE	Fiscal balance	Other	0.12	0.12	1	0
22	Galeotti and Salford (2001)	18 OECD countries	1961–1995[c]	GLS estimator	Fiscal balance & Total spending & Total taxes	Binary variable	0.09	0.08	4	0
23	Golinelli and Momigliano (2006)	11 European Union countries	1988–2006	GUM estimator	Fiscal balance	Binary variable	0.23	0.23	1	0
24	Hagen (2007)	24 OECD countries	1989–2005	System GMM	Fiscal balance	Binary variable	0.13	0.13	5	0
25	Hallerberg, de Souza and Clark (2002)	10 EU accession countries	1990–1999	OLS pooling	Fiscal balance	Franzese's full ratio	0.2	0.20	2	2
26	Hanusch (2012)	28 Developed countries[c]	1980–2008	OLS pooling & Fixed effects & System GMM	Fiscal balance	Binary variable	0.08	0.09	18	9
27	Hanusch and Vaaler (2013)	18 Emerging countries[c]	1989–2004	Fixed effects & System GMM	Fiscal balance	Binary variable	0.17	0.17	8	8

#	Study	Countries	Period	Method	Dependent variables	Measure				
28	Hanusch and Keefer (2014)	67 Developed and developing countries[c]	1975–2008	Fixed effects & AB GMM & System GMM	Total spending & Current spending	Binary variable	0.06	0.06	26	26
29	Jong-A-Pin, Sturm and de Haan (2012)	25 OECD countries	1996–2011	Fixed effects & SUR estimates	Fiscal balance & Current spending & Capital spending & Current revenue	Binary variable	0.00	−0.02	27	0
30	Kaplan and Thomsson (2014)	16 LAC countries	1961–2011	Fixed effects & AB GMM	Fiscal balance	Binary variable	0.22	0.23	7	5
31	Katsimi and Sarantides (2012)	19 OECD countries	1972–2008[c]	Fixed effects & AB GMM	Fiscal balance & Total spending & Current revenue & Current spending & Capital spending & Direct taxes & Indirect taxes	Binary variable & Other	0.03	0.02	73	0
32	Klašnja (2008)	25 EECA countries[c]	1990–2006	Fixed effects	Fiscal balance & Total spending & Total revenue & Broad public goods & Local public goods	Binary variable	0.13	0.15	5	0
33	Klomp and de Haan (2013a)	70 Developed and developing countries[c]	1970–2007[c]	PMG & MG & DFE estimator	Fiscal balance & Total spending	Franzese's full ratio	0.04	0.05	38	0
34	Klomp and de Haan (2013b)	65 Developed and developing countries	1975–2005	Semi-pooled model	Fiscal balance & Total spending	Franzese's full ratio	0.04	0.04	2	0
35	Klomp and de Haan (2013c)	65 Developed and developing countries[c]	1975–2005	(IV) Fixed effects	Fiscal balance & Total spending	Franzese's full ratio	0.08	0.06	14	14
36	Klomp and de Haan (2013d)	67 Developed and developing countries[c]	1975–2005	System GMM	Broad public goods & Local public goods	Binary variable & Franzese's full ratio	0.09	0.08	13	7

(Continued)

Table B.2 (Continued)

#	Paper	Sample[a]	Time period	Estimator	Fiscal output[b]	Election	Mean (adjust) partial	Median (adjust) partial	# estimates	# interactive terms
37	Kouvavas (2013)	63 Developed and developing countries[c]	1960–2001	Fixed effects & ABO GMM	Fiscal balance	Binary variable	0.07	0.06	15	10
38	Kraemer (1997)	20 LAC countries	1983–1996	Fixed effects & ABO GMM	Fiscal balance & Total spending & Current revenue & Capital spending	Other	0.09	0.09	5	0
39	Maurel (2006)	26 European countries	1990–2005[c]	Fixed effects & ABO GMM	Fiscal balance & Total spending & Total revenue	Binary variable	0.03	0.04	12	0
40	Mosley and Chiripanhura (2012)	21 SSA countries[c]	1980–2008	OLS pooling & Fixed effects & ABO GMM	Fiscal balance	Binary variable	0.10	0.08	5	0
41	Morozumi, Veiga and Veiga (2014)	107 Developed and developing countries[c]	1975–2010	OLS pooling & Fixed effects & ABO GMM	Fiscal balance & Total spending & revenue & Current spending & Capital spending & Direct taxes & Indirect taxes & External taxes	Binary variable & Franzese's full ratio	0.05	0.07	232	0
42	Mourâ£o	60 Developed and developing countries[c]	1960–2006	AB GMM	Fiscal balance & Total spending & Total revenue	Binary variable	0.02	0.02	30	30
43	Nieto-Parra and Santiso (2009)	46 OECD & LAC countries[c]	1990–2006	Fixed effects & AB GMM	Fiscal balance & Total spending & Current spending & Capital spending	Binary variable	0.09	0.08	48	0

#	Study	Countries	Period	Method	Dependent variable	Type				
44	Nyblade and O'Mahony (2014)	97 Developing countries	1975–2005	Fixed effects	Fiscal balance	Binary variable	0.06	0.06	1	1
45	Persson and Tabellini (2003)	60 Developed and developing countries[c]	1960–1998	Fixed effects	Fiscal balance & Total spending & Total revenue & Broad public goods	Binary variable	0.03	0.03	12	0
46	Potrafke (2007)	20 OECD countries	1980–2003	OLS pooling & Panel corrected SE & LSDV	Broad public goods	Other	0.03	0.03	6	0
47	Potrafke (2010)	18 OECD countries	1971–2004	Random effects & LSDV	Broad public goods	Other	0.09	0.09	24	12
48	Schuknecht (1996)	35 Developing countries[c]	1970–1992	OLS pooling	Fiscal balance	Other	0.15	0.15	3	0
49	?	24 Developing countries	1973–1992	Fixed effects	Fiscal balance & Total spending & Current spending & Capital spending & Local public goods	Other	0.10	0.09	6	0
50	Shelton (2014)	108 Developed and developing countries[c]	1980–2007	Fixed effects & AB GMM	Fiscal balance	Binary variable	0.10	0.10	16	12
51	Shi and Svensson (2006)	85 Developed and developing countries[c]	1975–1995	Fixed effects & System GMM	Fiscal balance	Binary variable	0.07	0.08	24	14
52	Stanova (2009)	10 NMS countries[c]	1998–2008[c]	OLS pooling	Fiscal balance & Total spending & Total revenue	Binary variable	0.15	0.14	102	0
53	Streb, Lema and Torrens (2009)	67 Developed and developing countries[c]	1960–2001	OLS pooling & Fixed effects	Fiscal balance & Total spending & Total revenue	Binary variable & Other	0.09	0.10	6	2

(Continued)

Table B.2 (Continued)

#	Paper	Sample[a]	Time period	Estimator	Fiscal output[b]	Election	Mean (adjust) partial	Median (adjust) partial	# estimates	# interactive terms
54	Streb, Lema and Garofalo (2012)	30 OECD & LAC countries[c]	1980–2005	Fixed effects	Fiscal balance & Total spending & Total revenue	Binary variable & Other	0.04	0.04	72	0
55	Troeger and Schneider (2012)	17 OECD countries	1975–2009	FEVD estimator	Total spending & Direct taxes & Indirect taxes	Binary variable	0.03	0.03	4	4
56	Tujula and Wolswijk (2007)	22 OECD countries[c]	1970–2002	Fixed effects	Fiscal balance	Binary variable	0.11	0.11	6	0
57	Wright (2011)	116 Dictatorships[c]	1961–2006	Fixed effects	Total expenditure	Binary variable	0.04	0.03	8	0
	Total/Average/ Median						0.07	0.06	1,331	294

Notes: For a matter of information, we count the number of interactive models in collected studies though they are discarded in our econometric analysis. The adjusted partial correlation in blue (darker in grayscale) are below the global average/median, in the sample. The adjusted partial correlations below (resp. above) the global average/median (0.07/0.06) are displayed in blue (resp. red). [a]: Subsamples among countries and/or time period, within considered studies.[c]: As the publication date is after December 31, 2014 we take into account the working paper version (Combes, Maurel and Ebeke, 2013). [b]: Fiscal balance refers to fiscal surplus or fiscal deficit.

Appendix C
Variable definitions

Table C.1 Variable definitions

#	Variables	Variable Description (BD for binary dummy)	N	Mean	Median	S.D.	Min	Max
1	Adjustedpartial	Partial correlation (adjusted for revenue and fiscal surplus).	1,331	0.07	0.06	0.09	−0.29	0.65
2	Partial	Partial correlation (non adjusted for revenue and fiscal surplus).	1,331	−0.02	−0.04	0.11	−0.65	0.63
3	SE	Standard error of the correlation.	1,331	0.05	0.05	0.03	0.01	0.26
4	Adjustedpartial no iterms	Partial correlation (adjusted) after excluding interactive models.	1,037	0.07	0.07	0.09	−0.29	0.65
5	Partial no iterms	Partial correlation (non adjusted) adjusted) after excluding interactive models.	1,037	−0.02	−0.04	0.11	−0.65	0.63
6	SE no iterms	Standard error of the correlation after excluding interactive models.	1,037	0.05	0.05	0.04	0.01	0.26
	Group 1: Measures of cycle							
7	YSur	BD if used fiscal balance (with deficit normalized at a reverse surplus) over GDP.	1,037	0.30	0.00	0.46	0.00	1.00
8	YSpen	BD if used total expenditure over GDP.	1,037	0.20	0.00	0.40	0.00	1.00

(*Continued*)

Table C.1 (Continued)

#	Variables	Variable Description (BD for binary dummy)	N	Mean	Median	S.D.	Min	Max
9	YRev	BD if used total revenue over GDP.	1,037	0.16	0.00	0.37	0.00	1.00
10	YSpen bis	BD if used total (or subcomponents) expenditure over GDP, in level, or per capita.	1,037	0.41	0.00	0.49	0.00	1.00
11	YRev bis	BD if used total (or subcomponents) revenue over GDP.	1,037	0.29	0.00	0.46	0.00	1.00
12	YVar	BD if dependent variable is in first difference or growth rate.	1,037	0.14	0.00	0.35	0.00	1.00
13	Ycycl[a]	BD if dependent variable is cyclically adjusted.	1,037	0.05	0.00	0.22	0.00	1.00
14	YCentral	BD if dependent variable explicitly refers to central government.	1,037	0.57	1.00	0.50	0.00	1.00
	Group 2: Measure of elections[b]							
15	ElectDum	BD if elections are captured by electoral dummies.	1,037	0.80	1.00	0.40	0.00	1.00
16	ElectRat	BD if elections are captured by ratio *a la Franzese*.	1,037	0.20	0.00	0.40	0.00	1.00
17	ElectOth	BD if elections are captured by other methods (used as the base).	1,037	0.03	0.00	0.17	0.00	1.00
	Group 3: Adjustment on elections							
18	ACalendar	BD if adjustment for electoral or fiscal calendar.	1,037	0.16	0.00	0.37	0.00	1.00
19	AHighest	BD if adjustment on election for the executive.	1,037	0.66	1.00	0.48	0.00	1.00
20	AExog	BD if adjustment on predetermined election.	1,037	0.32	0.00	0.47	0.00	1.00
	Group 4: Other methodologies							
21	Samplesize		1,037	730.68	453.00	923.88	15.00	6,631.00

(*Continued*)

Table C.1 (Continued)

#	Variables	Variable Description (BD for binary dummy)	N	Mean	Median	S.D.	Min	Max
		Number of observations included in the sample.						
22	Infra	BD if infra annual data used.	1,037	0.08	0.00	0.27	0.00	1.00
23	EconDynamic	BD if used dynamic panel estimator.	1,037	0.25	0.00	0.44	0.00	1.00
24	EconOther	BD if used other estimator (used as the base).	1,037	0.75	1.00	0.44	0.00	1.00
25	SE correction	BD if used SE correction for heteroskedasticity or autocorrelation.	1,037	0.46	0.00	0.50	0.00	1.00

Group 5: Model structure								
26	Subsample	BD if author(s) use subsample technique.	1,037	0.60	1.00	0.49	0.00	1.00
27	ConstitSamp	BD if subsample on specific constitutional forms.	1,037	0.27	0.00	0.44	0.00	1.00
28	HighincSamp	BD if subsample on high-income countries.	1,037	0.23	0.00	0.42	0.00	1.00
29	EstdemocSamp	BD if subsample on established democracies.	1,037	0.18	0.00	0.38	0.00	1.00
30	HighdemocSamp	BD if subsample on high level democracies.	1,037	0.03	0.00	0.16	0.00	1.00
31	BadSamp	BD if subsample on other bad-case senarii for PBC.	1,037	0.04	0.00	0.19	0.00	1.00

Group 6: Decades								
32	Elder	BD if data for the 50's, 60's or 70's (used as the base).	1,037	0.61	1.00	0.49	0.00	1.00
33	1980s	BD if data for the 80's.	1,037	0.78	1.00	0.41	0.00	1.00
34	1990s	BD if data for the 90's.	1,037	0.97	1.00	0.18	0.00	1.00

(*Continued*)

Table C.1 (Continued)

#	Variables	Variable Description (BD for binary dummy)	N	Mean	Median	S.D.	Min	Max
35	Recent	BD if data for the 00's and 10's.	1,037	0.87	1.00	0.34	0.00	1.00
	Group 7: Region[c]							
36	WeJ[d]	BD if Western Europe, neo Europes & (or) Japan were included in samples.	1,037	0.70	1.00	0.46	0.00	1.00
37	Eeca[e]	BD if countries from Eastern Europe & Central Asia were included in samples.	1,037	0.56	1.00	0.50	0.00	1.00
38	Lac	BD if countries from Latin America & Caribbean were included in samples.	1,037	0.62	1.00	0.49	0.00	1.00
39	Mena	BD if countries from Middle-east & North Africa were included in samples.	1,037	0.47	0.00	0.50	0.00	1.00
40	Sap[f]	BD if countries from South/East Asia & Pacific were included in samples (except Japan).	1,037	0.51	1.00	0.50	0.00	1.00
41	Ssa	BD if countries from Sub-Saharan Africa were included in samples.	1,037	0.48	0.00	0.50	0.00	1.00
42	Global	BD if at least two regions were included in samples.	1,037	0.63	1.00	0.48	0.00	1.00
	Group 8: Publications outlet							
43	Public Choice	BD if article is published on Public Choice.	1,037	0.13	0.00	0.34	0.00	1.00

(*Continued*)

Table C.1 (Continued)

#	Variables	Variable Description (BD for binary dummy)	N	Mean	Median	S.D.	Min	Max
44	Unpublished	BD for unpublished paper.	1,037	0.56	1.00	0.49	0.00	1.00
45	Impact Factor	2015 Google Scholar 5 years index of journal.	1,037	27.11	11.00	29.99	0.00	168.00
46	Trend	Publication's year trend.	1,037	19.09	21.00	4.24	1.00	23.00
47	Before2008	BD if paper is released $\leq$ 2008.	1,037	0.23	0.00	0.42	0.00	1.00
48	After2008	BD if paper is released > 2008 (used as the base).	1,037	0.77	1.00	0.42	0.00	1.00
	Group 9: Covariates							
49	GDPpc.	BD for per capita GDP as control.	1,037	0.76	1.00	0.43	0.00	1.00
50	Trade	BD for trade as control.	1,037	0.53	1.00	0.50	0.00	1.00
51	PopStruct	BD for population structure as control.	1,037	0.55	1.00	0.50	0.00	1.00
52	OG	BD for output gap as control.	1,037	0.43	1.00	0.50	0.00	1.00
53	Partisan	BD for partisan measure (such as political ideology) as control.	1,037	0.11	0.00	0.31	0.00	1.00
54	Time	BD for time dummies or time trend as control.	1,037	0.52	1.00	0.50	0.00	1.00

Notes: We keep two digits after decimal point for convenience. Descriptive statistics with the 294 interactive models are available upon request. [a]: We include the discretionary measures of Buti and Van Den Noord (2004) in this category. [b]: Authors can use several measures of elections in the same regression. [c]: We readapt the geographical classification from the World Bank Group. [d]: All OECD member countries before the fall of the USSR (except Turkey, but including Cyprus) are included to the definition. [e]: All former European USSR satellites or independent European communist countries are included to the definition. [f]: South Asia and East Asia and Pacific are considered together as one region.

Appendix D
Mapping PBC

Table D.1 Geopolitics of PBC

Geography of PBC	# estimates	Mean (adjust) partial	Median (adjust) partial	Lower bound	Upper bound
WeJ	151	0.063	0.067	−0.119	0.233
Eeca	110	0.145	0.138	−0.291	0.652
Lac	101	0.066	0.075	−0.094	0.214
Ssa	17	0.079	0.092	−0.213	0.386
Low-level democracies	43	0.038	0.039	−0.071	0.211
High-level democracies	26	0.060	0.034	−0.167	0.330
Including authoritarian (all regressions including authoritarian obs.)	175	0.073	0.074	−0.213	0.386
Young democracies	126	0.088	0.080	−0.167	0.652
Established democracies	187	0.041	0.039	−0.165	0.411

Notes: The variable of interest is the adjusted partial correlation between elections and fiscal output. We focus on the following geographic regions: Western Europe & Japan (WeJ), Eastern Europe & Central Asia (Eeca), Latin America & Caribbean (Lac), and Sub-Saharan Africa (Ssa). Not any one of the 46 studies focus exclusively on other regions. Descriptive statistics regarding the age and quality of democracy also include countries from other regions. To capture the age and quality of democracy we follow Brender and Drazen (2005), and we consider Cheibub, Gandhi, and Vreeland (2010) and Boix, Miller, and Rosato (2013) for uncovered countries. Descriptive statistics with the 294 interactive models are available upon request.

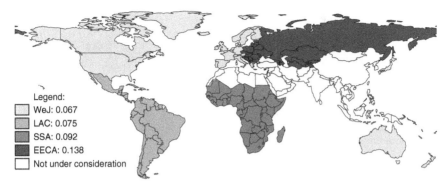

Legend:
WeJ: 0.067
LAC: 0.075
SSA: 0.092
EECA: 0.138
Not under consideration

Scale 1:110,000,000.

Figure D.1 PBC across the world

Notes: ISO codes available upon request. We compute the median partial correlation for each geographic region defined in Table D.1. This repartition of PBC is not relevant in failed states, due to the absence of state apparatus, or in countries without electoral races. For more details, see the Center for Systemic Peace website; the Fund for Peace website; V-Dem website; Cheibub, Gandhi, and Vreeland (2010); Boix, Miller, and Rosato (2013), and Gründler and Krieger (2016), among others.

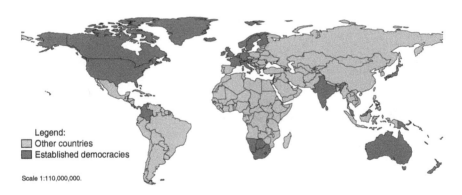

Legend:
Other countries
Established democracies

Scale 1:110,000,000.

Figure D.2 Established democracies as of 1 January 2015

Notes: ISO codes available upon request. Age of democracy, regarding the methodology of Brender and Drazen (2005). Despite overlapping in spmap code, Lesotho should be considered in "Other countries".

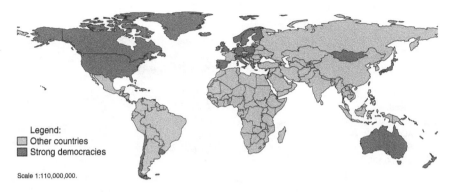

Figure D.3 High-level democracies as of 1 January 2015

Notes: ISO codes available upon request. Level of democracy, regarding the methodology of Brender and Drazen (2005).

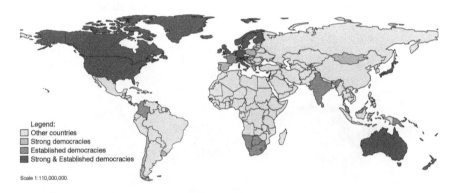

Figure D.4 Quality of democracy as of 1 January 2015

Notes: ISO codes available upon request. Age and level of democracy regarding the methodology of Brender and Drazen (2005). Despite overlapping in spmap code, Lesotho should be considered in "Other countries".

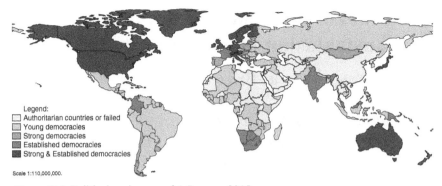

Figure D.5 Political regime as of 1 January 2015

Notes: ISO codes available upon request. Age and level of democracy regarding the methodology of Brender and Drazen (2005). To split between authoritarian countries, and democratic states, we consider a positive polity2 score, but also Cheibub, Gandhi, and Vreeland (2010), and Boix, Miller, and Rosato (2013), for uncovered countries. Despite overlapping in spmap code, Lesotho should be considered in "Young democracies".

12 Market efficiency in Asian and Australasian stock markets

A fresh look at the evidence

Jae Kim, Hristos Doucouliagos, and T.D. Stanley

1. Introduction

The Efficient Market Hypothesis (EMH) is one of the major theoretical predictions of finance theory. When a stock market is informationally efficient, stock prices fully reflect all available information (Fama, 1970). All freely traded stocks are then correctly priced, given expected risk and returns, as new information is instantly and fully reflected in stock prices. As a result, no arbitrage opportunities exist since excess profits cannot be made from mispriced assets. There has been considerable debate concerning the degree to which stock markets are actually efficient.[1] In light of Lo's (2005) adaptive markets hypothesis, recent studies provide empirical evidence that market efficiency is highly context dependent and dynamic and that abnormal returns can arise from time to time in response to changing market conditions (see Neely et al., 2009; Lim and Brooks, 2011; Kim et al., 2011). Stock market inefficiency can arise from several sources, including structural impediments such as market manipulation (Comerton-Forde and Putniņš, 2014); poor information disclosure and communication (e.g., Shamsuddin and Kim, 2010; Defusco et al., 2010); and market frictions such as transaction and agency costs (Shleifer and Vishny, 1997). There may be behavioral factors that limit efficiency. For example, many investors' decisions may be dominated by fear and greed and not all investors may rationally process available information (e.g., Kahneman and Tversky, 2002). In addition, underdeveloped markets, particularly those in emerging markets and transitional economies, may hinder the efficient communication of new information so that prices do not fully reflect all publicly available information.

Testing for market efficiency has attracted a great deal of attention in the literature (see, for example, Ferson et al., 2005). A number of statistical tests have been developed and conducted. The EMH has been tested for a large number of stock markets over different time periods. However, as the qualitative reviews by Park and Irwin (2007), Yen and Lee (2008), and Lim and Brooks (2009) document, the evidence is rather mixed and often conflicting. In this paper, we conduct a *quantitative* review of empirical results on stock market efficiency by employing the meta-analysis methodology.[2] Meta-analysis is an effective way of drawing valid inferences from a diverse evidence base that reports conflicting findings (Stanley and Doucouliagos, 2012). It is capable of systematically exploring the differences in empirical findings, by identifying the degree to which they are driven by factors such as cross-country variations or time variations. Meta-analysis can also reveal how the systematic component of market efficiency changes as a function of economic fundamentals, such as the degree of market development and market liberalization. It can also isolate, from the systematic component, data snooping bias, sample selection bias, and measurement errors, which may be associated with individual empirical studies.

Our meta-analysis focuses on the empirical studies which use the variance ratio (VR) test of Lo and MacKinlay (1988), since it is the most popular test for market efficiency or return predictability, with highly desirable statistical properties (see Charles and Darné, 2009). The VR test also provides an appealing and natural measure for the degree of market efficiency or return predictability (Griffin et al., 2010). We focus on Asian and Australasian stock markets, including those of Australia, Bangladesh, China, Hong Kong, India, Indonesia, Japan, Korea, Malaysia, New Zealand, Pakistan, Singapore, Sri Lanka, Taiwan, and Thailand.[3] This group of stock markets has diverse characteristics, showing varying degrees of development and maturity over time. Our analysis does not cover the U.S. market, since its evolution of market efficiency for the past 100 years is well-documented in the literature (e.g., Gu and Finnerty, 2002; Kim et al., 2011). This chapter is the first meta-analytic study of market efficiency based on empirical results from a cross-section of emerging and developed stock markets.

The main findings from our meta-analysis are summarized as follows. We find violation of the EMH for Asian and Australasian stock markets, with stock market inefficiency being higher, in general, for the countries with the least developed and more regulated stock markets and that stock market efficiency has improved over time and that data frequency matters. Specifically, there are small to medium sized inefficiencies among daily and weekly returns and negative autocorrelation among monthly returns.

The paper is set out as follows. Section 2 provides a brief review of market efficiency and presents the details of the VR test. In section 3 we discuss the meta-regression methodology and its attractive features, especially in the context of testing for market efficiency. Section 4 discusses the details of the data used in the meta-analysis, and Section 5 presents the results of the meta-regression analysis. Section 6 concludes the paper.

2. Stock market efficiency and the variance ratio test statistic

In this section, we provide a brief review of the recent literature on stock market efficiency and present the variance ratio test statistic as a measure of the degree of market efficiency. We also discuss its usefulness and limitations as a measure of market efficiency.

2.1. Brief review of stock market efficiency

When a stock market is efficient, prices adjust instantaneously and accurately in response to new information. According to the EMH, all publicly available information is fully reflected in stock prices, and no market participant can systematically make abnormal profits (Fama, 1970). When the information set is limited to past prices and returns, the market is said to be weak-form efficient, where the current price reflects all available information from past price history. Whether a stock market is efficient in the weak-form has been a highly contentious issue in finance. While most finance academics believe in weak-form efficiency (Doran et al., 2010), predictable patterns of stock returns have been widely observed. For example, Jegadeesh and Titman (1993) document strong momentum effects; and behavioral finance researchers recognize that investor behavior such as overreaction and overconfidence can cause systematic departure from efficiency (e.g., De Bondt and Thaler, 1985; Barber and Odean, 2001).

The accumulated empirical evidence is rather mixed and conflicting. In their historical survey, Yen and Lee (2008) report empirical findings in support of market efficiency in the 1960s, "mixed evidence" in the 1970s and 1980s, and "refuting evidence" in the 1990s. Park and Irwin (2007) present a survey with similar findings in the context of the profitability of technical trading rules. Harvey (1995) observes that stock returns of emerging markets are generally more predictable than those of developed markets, possibly due to their segmentation from global capital markets. In contrast, Griffin et al. (2010) provide evidence that stock returns in emerging markets are as unpredictable as those of advanced markets. With these highly mixed empirical results, stock market efficiency remains one of the most controversial and contested hypothesis in finance.

The EMH also has strong implications to practitioners, investors, and regulators. There is an enormous industry based on the technical analysis of stocks and commodities, with numerous trading strategies employed by traders.[4] Moreover, many mutual fund managers try to outperform the market and claim that they have done so. The EMH has also found its way into securities litigation (e.g., Fischel, 1989; Cornell and Rutten, 2006). These are all in large part inconsistent with the EMH. On the other hand, there are arguments that these observations against the EMH are in fact spurious. For example, Bender et al. (2013) argue that technical analysis rules might reflect imperfectly rational noise trading and stock chart patterns might just be "illusory correlations". Zhang and Jacobsen (2013), find that monthly seasonal effects may not be real, as they could be subject to data snooping bias, noise, and sample selection bias.

As a compromise between the efficient market hypothesis and its behavioral critics, Lo (2004) proposes the *adaptive markets hypothesis*. One of its implications is that market efficiency is highly context dependent and dynamic; and that abnormal returns can predictably arise from time to time due to changing market conditions. Lim and Brooks (2011) provide a comprehensive review of recent empirical studies in the weak-form efficiency of stock market, which strongly support the time-varying nature of return predictability. Kim et al. (2011)

examine the case of the US stock market over 100 years and provide empirical evidence that return predictability changes over time depending on prevailing market and economic conditions. Based on a cross-sectional study of more than 50 stock markets, Shamsuddin and Kim (2010) find that return predictability depends on a number of measures for equity market development. Hence, the extant literature on the empirical testing of the weak-form market efficiency of stock market holds the view that the degree of market efficiency changes over time depending on economic and market conditions surrounding the market. The latter includes a range of factors such as market fundamentals, regulations, trading technologies, psychology of market participants, political landscape, and the state of the economy.

2.2. Variance ratio as a measure of stock market efficiency

As Grossman and Stiglitz (1980) theoretically demonstrate, a perfectly efficient market is not possible. Since Campbell et al. (1997) proposed the notion of relative efficiency, the research focus has moved to measuring the degree of relative efficiency from testing absolute market efficiency. While there are alternative measures of relative efficiency (Griffin et al., 2010), the variance ratio (VR) test of Lo and MacKinlay (1988) is the most popular and appealing, based on autocorrelations of returns.[5] While there have been a number of improvements and extensions (see Charles and Darné, 2009), the test is essentially based on the statistic as a ratio of the variance of k-period stock returns to one-period returns, which can be re-written as a function of return autocorrelation as follows:

$$V(k) = 1 + 2 \sum_{j=1}^{k-1} \left(1 - \frac{j}{k}\right) \rho_j, \tag{1}$$

where ρ_j is the autocorrelation of asset returns of order j. By construction, $V(k)$ is one plus the weighted average of autocorrelations up to order $k - 1$, with positive and declining weights. The main attraction of the VR statistic over its alternatives is that it provides an estimate of the size of return autocorrelations, as well as its overall sign. A value of $V(k)$ greater (less) than 1 indicates the presence of overall positive (negative) autocorrelations up to the order $k - 1$. Due to this property, $V(k)$ is widely used as a measure for the degree of market efficiency or return predictability (e.g., Griffin et al., 2010; Kim et al., 2011).

To evaluate market efficiency or the presence of return predictability, researchers test for H$_0$: $V(k) = 1$, implying that all autocorrelations (ρ_js) to order $k - 1$ are zero. When $V(k) = 1$, stock returns are not predictable from their own past. To test H$_0$: $V(k) = 1$, Lo and MacKinlay (1988) propose the test statistic:

$$M(k) = \frac{\hat{V}(k) - 1}{se(\hat{V}(k))}, \tag{2}$$

where $\hat{V}(k)$ is the sample estimator for $V(k)$ and $se(\hat{V}(k))$ represents the standard error of $\hat{V}(k)$. Note that Lo and MacKinlay (1988) propose two versions of the above test statistic. The first version (denoted $M_1(k)$) is valid when the asset returns are generated from an identical and independent distribution (i.i.d.); and the second version (denoted $M_2(k)$) is valid when the asset returns follow a martingale difference sequence (MDS). This test allows for asset returns with a general form of conditional or unconditional heteroskedasticity, widely observed in asset returns. Note that the two statistics are different only in the form of standard error estimators. Lo and MacKinlay (1988) show that $M_1(k)$ asymptotically follows the standard normal distribution under i.i.d. asset returns, and so does $M_2(k)$ under the MDS.

As mentioned earlier, our meta-analysis exploits sample estimates of $\hat{V}(k)$ reported in the past empirical studies. However, we note that the VR statistic has some limitations as a measure for the degree of market inefficiency. First, it does not capture the effects of the costs associated with transactions and gathering information (Griffin et al., 2010; Section 6), which can be high in emerging markets and dissimilar across different international markets. Second, the measure may contain noise from market microstructure and nonsynchronous trading (Boudoukh et al., 1994). Griffin et al. (2010) warn that caution should be exercised when VR values are directly compared across different international markets. On these points, we argue that meta-analysis is an effective way of isolating noise and various biases from the fundamental component of the VR estimates and it facilitates their comparison in a systematic way. That is, it controls the systematic component of VR estimates over time and across different international markets, isolating the noise and non-fundamental components of VR estimates, including the effects of potential publication bias. For example, the effect of declining transaction and information costs that stock markets have experienced since the 1990s may not be captured in the VR estimates reported in individual studies: however, it can be revealed in a meta-regression with the VR estimates showing a downward trend over time. The VR estimates from two dissimilar markets during different time periods may not be directly comparable, but their responses to the market fundamentals such as the market capitalization can be analyzed in the framework of meta-analysis.

Various market microstructure factors, such as the level of liquidity, cost of trading, and speed of information incorporation, are important for the degree of market efficiency. While there are methods indirectly measuring the degree of liquidity (see Lesmond et al., 1999; Amihud, 2002), we are limited by data availability since these measures require the use of daily volume or transaction costs. However, as Lagoarde-Segot (2009) reports from an extensive empirical analysis of emerging markets, higher market capitalization decreases both transaction costs and illiquidity levels. In addition, Lagoarde-Segot (2009) finds that the degrees of market microstructure in emerging markets are time-varying, strongly related to one another depending on economic and political contexts such as financial industry development and institutional reforms. On this basis, we use market capitalization and economic freedom as proxies for the economic fundamentals which control the degree of market microstructure factors, also paying attention to the variation of the VR estimates over time.

Conrad and Kaul (1988) argue that autocorrelation in stock returns represents time variation of expected returns. However, their model depends heavily on its parametric structure and their result may not be robust to different model specifications. For example, if their model is specified with a constant expected returns allowing for time-varying return predictability, the observed autocorrelation can be regarded as a reflection of market inefficiency. In addition, according to Fama and French (1988a), time-varying equilibrium of expected returns occurs over long horizons, such as three to five years. We note that the VR test is widely used as a test for short-horizon return predictability, with the value of holding period k typically set to far less than one year. It is well-known that the test is not suitable for long-horizon analysis, because the VR statistic can be severely biased with undesirable small sample properties when the value of holding period k is high (see, for example, Chen and Deo, 2006).

Needless to say, advocates of stock market efficiency, such as Fama (1991) and Malkiel (2003) have expressed some skepticism. In particular, Malkiel (2003) stresses the importance of the economic, rather than the statistical, significance of a predictable pattern of returns, arguing that it is unclear if merely statistically predictable patterns are useful for investors in fashioning a profitable investment strategy. While reminders of practical significance are always relevant, the variance ratio, $V(k)$, provides a measure of the degree of departure from perfect market efficiency. That is, $V(k)$ is an effective measure of relative efficiency (Campbell et al., 1997), even after one considers the impossibility of perfect efficiency (Grossman and Stiglitz, 1980) and the adaptive nature of financial markets (Lo, 2004).

3. Meta-regression methodology

The key challenge behind all empirical analyses is making valid inference. Meta-regression analysis (MRA) has been developed to meet this fundamental challenge (Stanley and Doucouliagos, 2012). We employ meta-regression to achieve three tasks: (1) to formally test the EMH, (2) to analyze the distribution of the reported estimates and identify the factors that drive heterogeneity in this literature, and (3) to identify and correct potential publication selection bias. MRA can concurrently inform on each of these dimensions.

3.1. Publication selection

There is much evidence to suggest that researchers often have a preference for reporting empirical results that conform to researcher beliefs and suppress evidence that is at odds with these preferences (Roberts and Stanley, 2005; Stanley and Doucouliagos, 2012; Havranek, 2015; Ioannidis et al., 2017). Reported estimates may then be a biased sample of all estimates, potentially resulting in erroneous statistical inferences. A recent survey of over 64,000 economic estimates from 6,700 empirical economic studies finds that reported economic effects are typically inflated by 100% with one-third inflated by a factor of four or more (Ioannidis et al., 2017). Thus, potential selective reporting bias should be a concern of any meta-analysis, and all meta-analyses should accommodate potential selective reporting (or publication bias). Following Stanley and Doucouliagos (2012), we apply the so-called Funnel-Asymmetry Test Precision-Effect Test (FAT-PET) meta-regression model:

$$VR1_{ij} = \beta_0 + \beta_1 se_{ij} + \varepsilon_{ij}, \tag{3}$$

where $VR1_{ij} = \hat{V}(k) - 1$ ($VR1_{ij}$ is the ith variance ratio minus one reported in the jth study), se_{ij} is its standard error, and ε_{ij} denotes the usual regression error term.[6] See Stanley (2008) and Stanley and Doucouliagos (2012; 2014) for further details on this model.

Stanley and Doucouliagos (2012; 2014) suggest that a more accurate estimate of the underlying effect corrected for publication selection bias can sometimes be derived by replacing se_{ij} by se_{ij}^2. Doing so gives the precision-effect estimate with standard error (PEESE) model:

$$VR1_{ij} = \alpha_0 + \alpha_1 se_{ij}^2 + v_{ij}. \tag{4}$$

The logic behind the FAT-PET is as follows. When an empirical literature is free of publication selection bias, then the estimated effect sizes (say VR estimates) will not be correlated with their standard errors (Egger et al., 1997; Stanley and Doucouliagos, 2012). In fact, the validity of regression's conventional t-test requires this independence. In contrast, if researchers search for estimates that are statistically significant (e.g., a rejection of the EMH), they will re-estimate their models until they achieve some 'acceptable' level of statistical significance (e.g., statistical significance at the 5% or 10% level).[7] This selection will generate a correlation between an estimated effect and its standard error and will result in a truncated or asymmetric distribution of reported VR estimates (Stanley, 2008). Hence, a test of $\beta_1 = 0$ (known as the FAT or Funnel Asymmetry Test) provides a test of the existence of asymmetry in the estimates and publication selection and the $\beta_1 se_{ij}$ term reflects the impact of publication selection bias. A test of $\beta_0 = 0$, known as the PET or Precision Effect Test, provides a test of the overall existence of market inefficiency in the research record, corrected for publication selection. Also, the estimate of α_0 provides an estimate of the degree to which markets are inefficient.[8]

Although the FAT-PET-MRA model remains the foundation of the tests investigated here, application to variance ratios introduces new challenges. In particular, the variance ratio is known to have small-sample bias (Lo and MacKinlay, 1988), and publication selection may 'go both ways.' Typically, selection bias in empirical economics is in favor of rejecting the null hypothesis of a zero effect

(Card and Krueger, 1995; Doucouliagos and Stanley, 2014). In such cases, authors do not report all of the results they uncover. Rather, they select results that are consistent with their prior expectations, conventional theory, or results which they believe have a stronger chance of being published. The effect of this process is that certain findings may be suppressed while others are over-represented. Consequently, publication selection bias may tend to overstate the evidence against the EMH. This could happen if *some* researchers have a prior that the market is inefficient and experiment with their models, data, and methods to find a variance ratio that differs from 1 (either greater than 1 or less than 1). However, other researchers may believe that investors are rational and markets are efficient and dismiss some large variance ratios as faulty. In this case, evidence that rejects the null may go unreported. That is, there may be selection in this research literature in both directions: for statistical significance (rejection of EMH) and for statistical insignificance (acceptance of market efficiency). A priori, it is not possible to predict the net direction of this bias or whether any net bias is likely to remain. This is an empirical matter about which meta-regression analysis can inform.[9]

An additional complication arises because even in the absence of reporting or publication selection, small-sample bias will cause the effect size, $VR1$ (=VR-1), to be correlated with its sample size and thereby inversely with its own standard error. The conventional FAT-PET-MRA (equation (3)) may therefore be affected by this small-sample bias.

Given the above concerns with conventional meta-analysis, we conducted simulations for meta-regression models of the variance ratio tests to accommodate possible publication selection bias. Appendix A provides details of the simulation design and results. The central purpose of these simulations is to investigate the statistical properties of PET for the application to the EMH and thereby insure the validity of our MRA methods in assessing this literature's evidence of market efficiency. Past simulations (e.g., Stanley, 2008) have only reported the performance of these MRA models of publication bias when there are various incidences of selection for statistical significance – not when selection is for statistical *insignificance*. This too may potentially invalidate the FAT-PET-MRA by adding a yet another correlation of the reported effect to its standard error. Our simulations suggest that using a larger critical value, 3.5, instead of the normal critical value of 1.96 will accommodate both small-sample bias as well as potential selection for insignificance – see Appendix A for details.

3.2. Heterogeneity

Eq. (3) can be extended to explain observed variation in the variance ratio test.

$$VR1_{ij} = \beta_0 + \beta_1 se_{ij} + \sum \beta_k Z_{kij} + \varepsilon_{ij}, \qquad (5)$$

where Z_k represents variables coded from the studies themselves and exogenous variables on market capitalization and economic freedom coded by us from public information. Other examples of **Z**-variables include: country, level of development, holding period, and data frequency. See Table 12.3 below for a full list and description.

3.3. Estimation

Equations (3) to (5) are estimated by weighted least squares (WLS) in order to accommodate differences in the variances of the VR estimates across studies. Optimal weights for WLS are given by the inverse variance (Hedges and Olkin, 1985). For most of the analysis we use $w = 1/se_{ij}^2$. However, for robustness, we also use *random* effects weights, $w = 1/(se_{ij}^2 + \tau^2)$, where τ^2 is the between-study or heterogeneity variance. Stanley and Doucouliagos (2017) demonstrate that WLS MRA is superior to both conventional fixed- and random-effects multiple MRA because WLS MRA has lower bias and mean squared error if there is publication bias and is practically equivalent to random-effects when there is no publication bias.

As can be seen from Table 12.1 below, we employ multiple estimates from the same study. Dependence within studies is often an issue in meta-regression analysis and can result in downward bias in meta-regression analysis standard errors (Moulton, 1990; Cameron et al., 2008; MacKinnon and Webb, 2013). However, it is worth noting that tests of the EMH are different to most empirical research in economics. A common feature of empirical economics is that authors typically estimate numerous versions of a given econometric model: this typically involves alternate specifications, estimators and data samples. This dimension for experimentation and selection is not available to VR tests of the EMH. For example, there can be no specification searching for alternate control variables, which ordinarily generates much excess variation in reported empirical estimates in other areas of economics research. Here, we have multiple estimates but these should be largely statistically independent. For example, authors often report VR tests for several countries, and estimates for different countries can be considered to be statistically independent (Hunter and Schmidt, 2004). Variance ratio testing involves application of a specific formula, and there is little scope for experimentation with alternate specifications, functional forms and estimators. Nevertheless, there are still design choices made by authors, including the choice of countries to analyze, the time period studied, and the holding period for the VRT. Among the VR tests that we find, the intraclass correlation is 0.251, suggesting that there is actually a significant degree of dependence. Hence, we take the potential for data dependence into account by estimating hierarchical models and panel data models that accommodate data dependence.

4. Quantifying the research record on market efficiency

The search for studies and data coding followed the MAER-NET guidelines for meta-regression analysis (Stanley et al., 2013). Specifically, we conducted a comprehensive search for studies that tested the EMH for Asian and Australasian stock markets. Numerous search engines were used: Econlit, Google Scholar, Academic Search Complete, Business Source Complete, Science Direct, Scopus, Web of Science, and Wiley Online Library. Keywords used included 'variance ratio', 'efficient market hypothesis', 'random walk', 'predictability', 'stock markets', 'market efficiency', and 'market inefficiency'. In addition, we pursued cited references from studies, and we also physically checked numerous economics, finance and accounting journals. The database searches were terminated June 2014.

The empirical literature on the EMH is enormous. In order to make sense from a diverse literature with diverse findings, it is essential to construct a set of comparable estimates. Our criteria for inclusion were as follows. First, the study had to report an estimate of the variance ratio. There are other tests that explore the EMH. However, in order to ensure comparability, only those that report estimates of VR are included in our dataset. For example, we do not consider studies on the predictability of stock returns using macro variables. Second, the study had to report an estimate using Asian or Australasian data. Some studies report estimates also for other countries. These estimates are excluded from the meta-analysis. Third, the study had to be published. Some researchers prefer to include the so-called gray literature, such as working papers and doctoral thesis. Others prefer to stick to the published literature.[10] Fourth, for practical reasons, we exclude any study that was not written in English. Fifth, we focus on overall market efficiency and thereby exclude any estimates for individual stocks to avoid potentially overwhelming volatility and unreliability, particularly if individual stocks in emerging countries experience thin trading; aggregate indices are less vulnerable to thin trading. Also, testing efficiency of individual stocks is likely to be statistically less powerful, since no account is taken of cross stock correlations. Finally, we exclude estimates from multiple variance ratio tests (MV) as we cannot normally recover VR values from the MV statistic and the MV test statistic does not have a standard error estimator. In addition, it is difficult to justify an MV statistic as an appealing measure of predictability.

This search process identified 38 studies that report a variance ratio for Asian or Australasian stock markets. Although other tests statistics are reported in the research literature, the variance ratio test is by far the most prevalent. However, only 29 report sufficient information from which we could calculate the standard error of the VR.[11] The standard error is necessary in order to explore whether the EMH literature is afflicted by publication selection bias and it is also needed to properly weight the reported findings. Many studies report only the statistical significance of the VR without reporting the associate standard errors. The 29 studies report a total of 1,560 VR estimates. We make only one further adjustment to the quantifiable relevant empirical record – outliers. 14 estimates have an absolute value of the standardized residual greater than 3.5 from the FAT-PET, Eq. (3), and these outliers are removed from further statistical investigation.[12] The 1,560 estimates used in our study are the population of comparable VR estimates for Asia and Australasia. While these come from 29 studies, the sample size is large. Moreover, our analysis makes use of 92 statistically independent samples. Hunter and Schmidt (2004) show that samples from different countries can be treated as being statistically independent, even if analysis of such samples is reported in the same study. In other words, the 29 studies can effectively be treated as 92 distinct cases that report 1,560 estimates of the EMH. Consequently, we have a high degree of confidence in the quality of the sample for inference purposes.

In addition to collecting data on the VR and its standard error, we also coded several other study characteristics (see Table 12.3). Two of the authors coded the studies and then checked each other's coding. All included studies are referenced in Appendix B.

Table 12.1 lists the studies that form our meta-analysis dataset, including the countries studied and the number of estimates from each study. The first study was published in 1992 (Lee) and the two most recent studies in 2013 (Guidi and Gupta and Youssef and Galloppo). Table 12.2 presents the country distribution of the estimates and the average value of the VR for each country.

Figure 12.1 presents the *VR1* estimates in the form of a funnel plot, illustrating the association between *VR1* and its precision, where precision is measured as the inverse of *VR1's* standard error. The funnel plot is a convenient way of illustrating the distribution of the reported findings. It can highlight outliers and influential observations and it can also, potentially, highlight publication selection bias (see Stanley and Doucouliagos, 2010, 2012). Estimates that stand out are potentially leverage points or outliers. Severe selection bias would cause a noticeably asymmetric distribution of results.

The funnel graph reveals a long tail of relatively high *VR1* values, even after the very large positives VR values are removed. Asymmetry in effect sizes is typical of meta-data sets, and it is often an outcome of publication selection bias and/or heterogeneity inherent in different samples (Roberts and Stanley, 2005; Stanley and Doucouliagos, 2012). Figure 12.1 suggests that publication bias might be an issue in this literature, with the long tail suggesting preference for reporting violation of the EMH.

About 21 percent of the estimates report a VR1 less than 0 and the remainder (about 79 percent) report a VR1 that is greater than 0. The weighted-average VR1 is 0.13; this value is shown as the vertical line in the figure.

Table 12.3 lists the variables used in the multiple MRA. Some are dummy (0/1) variables (*Weekly*, *Monthly*, and the various country dummy variables), while others are continuous (*Standard error*, *Average year*,[13] *Holdingperiod*, *MarketCap*, and *EcoFreedom*). The binary variables *Weekly* and *Monthly*[14] reflect the data frequency used (with daily as the base). We also include the length of the holding period k used to construct the VR; recall Eq. (1). The time horizon can potentially inform on the degree of predictability.[15] These three variables, *Weekly, Monthly,* and *Holdingperiod*, are included in the MRA to capture potential differences in predictability of investment horizons. Stock price predictability may increase with the investment horizon as has been reported in some prior studies (e.g., Fama and French, 1988b). In particular, by applying the *VR* test to

Table 12.1 Studies included in the meta-regression analysis

Authors	Countries	Number of estimates	Average VR (range)
Alam, Hasan & Kadapakkam (1999)	Bangladesh, Hong Kong, Malaysia, Sri Lanka, Taiwan	40	1.23 (0.45–2.32)
Ayadi & Pyun (1994)	Korea	42	0.96 (0.10–4.71)
Chakraborty (2006)	Pakistan	42	1.39 (1.07–1.62)
Chang & Ting (2000)	Taiwan	87	1.55 (0.57–3.40)
Chen & Jarrett (2011)	China	32	1.25 (1.07–1.60)
Cheung & Coutts (2001)	Hong Kong	14	1.07 (0.84–1.21)
Claessens, Dasgupta & Glen (1995)	India, Indonesia, Korea, Malaysia, Pakistan, Philippines, Taiwan, Thailand	16	1.24 (0.99–1.74)
Cohen (1999)	Japan	12	1.04 (0.90–1.23)
Darrat & Zhong (2000)	China	20	1.26 (0.87–1.52)
Fuss (2005)	Indonesia, Korea, Malaysia, Philippines, Taiwan, Thailand	112	1.61 (0.92–4.06)
Groenewold & Ariff (1998)	Australia, Hong Kong, Indonesia, Japan, Korea, Malaysia, New Zealand, Singapore, Taiwan	36	1.79 (0.88–3.34)
Guidi & Gupta (2013)	Indonesia, Malaysia, Philippines, Singapore, Thailand	40	1.15 (0.98–1.38)
Hassan & Chowdhury (2008)	Bangladesh	4	1.34 (1.26–1.40)
Hiremath & Kamaiah (2010)	India	8	1.06 (1.04–1.09)
Huang (1995)	Hong Kong, Indonesia, Japan, Korea, Malaysia, Philippines, Singapore, Thailand, Taiwan	105	1.27 (0.6–2.81)
Hung (2009)	China	48	1.15 (0.97–1.68)
Islam & Khaled (2005)	Bangladesh	18	1.30 (0.99–1.92)
Karemera, Ojah & Cole (1999)	Hong Kong, Indonesia, Korea, Malaysia, Philippines, Singapore, Taiwan, Thailand	128	0.98 (0.17–2.13)
Kawakatsu & Morey (1999)	India, Korea, Thailand, Malaysia, Philippines	59	1.44 (0.74–9.26)
Lai, Balachandher & Nor (2003)	Malaysia	56	1.36 (1.09–1.89)

(Continued)

Table 12.1 (Continued)

Authors	Countries	Number of estimates	Average VR (range)
Lee (1992)	Australia, Japan	32	1.23 (0.98–1.77)
Lee, Chen & Rui (2001)	China	16	1.21 (1.06–1.46)
Lock (2007)	Taiwan	16	1.25 (0.97–1.78)
Long, Payne & Feng (1999)	China	4	1.21 (1.10–1.30)
Lu & Wang (2007)	China	47	1.06 (0.46–2.01)
Rashid (2006)	Pakistan	24	0.85 (0.60–1.17)
Patro & Wu (2004)	Australia, Hong Kong, Japan, Singapore,	360	1.12 (0.75–1.42)
Youssef & Galloppo (2013)	China, India, Indonesia	48	1.17 (0.91–1.39)
Worthington & Higgs (2006)	Australia, China, Hong Kong, Indonesia, Japan, Korea, Malaysia, New Zealand, Pakistan, Philippines, Singapore, Sri Lanka, Taiwan, Thailand	120	1.18 (0.17–2.06)

Notes: See Appendix B for the full references to these papers.

Table 12.2 Individual Country Estimates, Variance Ratio Tests

Country	Number of studies (estimates)	Average VR1	Average market capitalization	Average economic freedom
Australia	4 (118)	0.096	50.26	7.19
Bangladesh	3 (30)	0.309	2.54	5.21
China	8 (191)	0.188	23.84	5.56
Hong Kong	7 (154)	0.029	187.82	8.52
India	6 (60)	0.204	34.87	5.81
Indonesia	8 (84)	0.585	16.35	6.27
Japan	6 (136)	0.085	82.98	7.11
Korea	8 (105)	0.131	44.67	6.13
Malaysia	10 (138)	0.272	160.65	6.99
New Zealand	2 (12)	0.732	38.64	7.63
Pakistan	4 (76)	0.203	15.73	5.58
Philippines	7 (74)	0.419	36.62	6.04
Singapore	6 (139)	0.170	133.53	8.01
Sri Lanka	2 (16)	0.794	14.10	5.61
Taiwan	9 (166)	0.351	65.62	6.95
Thailand	7 (76)	0.378	44.34	6.68

Notes: Average VR1 calculated by the authors from the included studies. VR1 = VR − 1.

Table 12.3 Multiple MRA variables, descriptions and mean and standard deviation

Variable	Description	Mean (standard deviation)
VR1	Variance-ratio, the dependent variable	0.224 (0.42)
Standard error	Standard error of the VR1	0.243 (0.51)
Average year	Mean year of the data used normalized to 1992	0.000 (6.28)
Weekly	Data frequency is weekly (daily is the base). Binary variable.	0.331 (0.47)
Monthly	Data frequency is monthly (daily is the base). Binary variable.	0.280 (0.45)
Holdingperiod	The length of the holding period.	18.098 (59.11)
HoldingperiodA	The length of the holding period minus the mean for Australasia, 29.850	2.030 (59.11)
Marketcap	Average degree of market capitalization	74.864 (59.49)
MarketcapA	Average degree of market capitalization minus the mean for Australasia, 48.12	25.692 (59.49)
EcoFreedom	Average economic freedom	6.783 (0.96)
EcoFreedomA	Average economic freedom minus the mean for Australasia, 7.236	−0.444 (0.96)
LesserIncome	Binary variable for middle and low income countries	0.477 (0.50)
China	Dummy variable with a value of 1 if the data relate to China.	0.122 (0.33)
Korea	Dummy variable with a value of 1 if the data relate to Korea.	0.064 (0.19)
Hong Kong	Dummy variable with a value of 1 if the data relate to Hong Kong.	0.098 (0.30)
India	Dummy variable with a value of 1 if the data relate to India.	0.040 (0.19)
Indonesia	Dummy variable with a value of 1 if the data relate to Indonesia.	0.054 (0.23)
Japan	Dummy variable with a value of 1 if the data relate to Japan.	0.085 (0.28)
Malaysia	Dummy variable with a value of 1 if the data relate to Malaysia.	0.088 (0.28)
Pakistan	Dummy variable with a value of 1 if the data relate to Pakistan.	0.048 (0.21)
Philippines	Dummy variable with a value of 1 if the data relate to Philippines.	0.048 (0.21)
Singapore	Dummy variable with a value of 1 if the data relate to Singapore.	0.092 (0.29)
Sri Lanka	Dummy variable with a value of 1 if the data relate to Sri Lanka.	0.010 (0.10)
Taiwan	Dummy variable with a value of 1 if the data relate to Taiwan.	0.102 (0.30)
Thailand	Dummy variable with a value of 1 if the data relate to Thailand.	0.048 (0.21)
Australasia	Dummy variable with a value of 1 if the data relate to Australia or New Zealand.	0.081 (0.27)

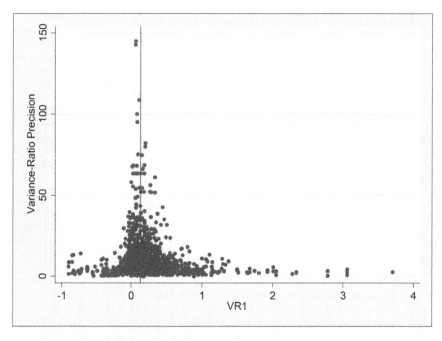

Figure 12.1 Funnel graph, variance ratio estimates

Note: The vertical line illustrates the value of the weighted-average variance-ratio minus one (*VR1*) (0.13), using the inverse variance as weights. Outliers removed.

U.S. stock return, Poterba and Summers (1988) report negative serial correlation in the long horizon and positive serial correlation in the short horizon.

As noted earlier, the VR can be estimated assuming either homoscedasticity or heteroskedasticity. The difference affects only the calculation of the standard error and not the value of the VR or *VR1*. Hence, we do not include this research design choice in the MRA as a moderator variable.[16] *Average year* is included to investigate whether the reported VR estimates have been changing over time. Generally, if stock markets are becoming more (less) efficient over time, then the expected or fundamental component of VR should be falling (rising).[17]

Finally, we explore the effects of the degree of market capitalization and the degree of economic freedom prevalent in the countries and time periods sampled.[18] As discussed earlier, we use market capitalization as a proxy for the level of market microstructure factors. We use economic freedom as a proxy for economic and political factors which drive financial industry development and institutional reforms. Market capitalization data was collected from the World Bank Development Indicators and from individual stock exchanges. Data on economic freedom was collected from the Fraser Institute (Economic Freedom of the World).[19] Economic freedom is a measure of the degree to which market forces are allowed to allocate resources and the degree to which regulations hinder this operation. The series ranges from 1 to 10, with higher values denoting higher levels of economic freedom. This is an aggregate measure of several factors, including legal structure and protection of property rights, freedom to trade, and regulation of markets.

Both the market capitalization and the economic freedom series were matched with the countries and time periods used by the primary studies. Table 2 reports the average market capitalization and economic freedom for the samples used by authors for each of the countries included in our data. In light of empirical evidence of Lagoarde-Segot (2009), market capitalization is expected to be inversely related to market inefficiency; the more capitalized is a market the more efficient it should be, ceteris paribus. Market capitalization is a measure of equity market development. Underdeveloped stock markets are more likely to contain opportunities for stock market predictability. Underdeveloped markets will contain a larger proportion of small and illiquid stocks, they are more likely to be characterized by thin trading and there is a greater likelihood of market manipulation.

Similarly, the greater the degree of economic freedom (market liberalization), the more efficient should be stock markets. That is, if regulations restrict the operation of markets in terms of their role in price revelation and market clearing function, then restrictions on economic freedom should, ceteris paribus, reduce market efficiency. Regulations impose frictions on markets and hence restrict traders from profiting from mispriced assets. Hence, we expect a negative coefficient on the MRA variables, market capitalization, and economic freedom.

5. Results

We commence the analysis by calculating basic averages of all *VR1* estimates; these are presented in Table 12.4. Columns (1) report the simple unadjusted average, while Columns (2) and (3) offer weighted averages that have been shown to be less biased when there is selective reporting but as good as conventional meta-analysis when there is no selective reporting (Stanley and Doucouliagos, 2015; Stanley et al., 2017). WLS is an unrestricted WLS weighted average, while WAAP is the WLS weighted average of the only the adequately powered estimates (Stanley and Doucouliagos, 2015; Stanley and Doucouliagos, 2017; Ioannidis et al., 2017; Stanley et al., 2017).

The unrestricted weighted least squares weighted average, WLS, has recently been proposed and evaluated in Stanley and Doucouliagos (2015) and Stanley and Doucouliagos (2017). This unrestricted WLS is neither 'fixed' nor 'random effects,' as meta-analysts use these terms. Its point estimate is identical to the fixed-effect weighted average, but WLS takes passive advantage of the multiplicative invariance property implicit in all WLS and GLS regression to adjust for any excess heterogeneity should it be present in the research record (Stanley and Doucouliagos, 2015). It is calculated by running a simple meta-regression, with no intercept, of t-statistics versus precision ($1/SE$). Ordinary least squares of this simple regression using any standard statistical software will calculate this unrestricted WLS weighted average, its standard error, and

Table 12.4 Average and meta-average variance ratio and publication selection bias tests (dependent variable is the *VR1*)

	Simple average (1)	Weighted averages		Publication bias corrected	
		WLS (2)	WAAP (3)	FAT-PET (4)	PEESE (5)
Average VR1	0.224*	0.130*	0.115*	0.102*	0.129*
	(21.22)	(17.81)	(13.43)	(11.71)	(17.61)
Standard error	–	–	–	0.761*	–
				(8.32)	
Standard error squared	–	–	–	–	0.300*
					(2.14)
Adjusted R^2	–	–	–	0.049	0.01

Notes: The dependent variable in all columns is the variance-ratio minus 1, *VR1*. The number of observations is 1,560. Column (1) reports the simple (unweighted) average variance-ratio. Column (2) reports the unrestricted WLS weighted average variance-ratio minus 1, with the inverse variance as weights (Stanley and Doucouliagos, 2015). Column (3) calculates the WAAP, which is the WLS weighted average on only those estimates that have adequate power (>80%) (Ioannidis et al., 2017; Stanley et al., 2017). Column (4) displays the results from the FAT-PET model (Eq. 3), while Column (5) reports the results from the PEESE model (Eq. 4). Columns (4) and (5) are estimated using weighted least squares (WLS), with the inverse variance as weights. Parentheses report *t*-statistics, using robust standard errors.
*denotes statistical significance at least at the 5 percent level. We raise the critical value for the PET coefficient to 3.5 to allow for small-sample bias. However, the t-values here are always larger than 10, which simulations show is more than sufficient to keep Type I errors very small.

confidence interval. Simulations show that WLS dominates random effects when there is publication bias and is practically as good as random effects if there is no selective reporting (Stanley and Doucouliagos, 2015; Stanley and Doucouliagos, 2017; Stanley et al., 2017). These simulation studies also show how WLS is always as good as and often much better than fixed effect. Thus, there is little to lose and potentially much to gain by using WLS in the place of both 'fixed' and 'random effects' weighted averages and meta-regressions (Stanley and Doucouliagos, 2015; Stanley and Doucouliagos, 2017).

More recently, we show how careful attention to statistical power can reduce bias further by calculating WLS only on those estimates that can be shown to have adequate power (i.e., power ≥ 80%) – WAAP (Stanley et al., 2017). The large survey empirical economics conducted by Ioannidis et al. (2017) finds that: the typical area of economics research has nearly 90% of its estimates underpowered, low power and bias are related, and that calculating WLS on only those estimates which are sufficiently powered (WAAP) typically cuts the average size of reported effects almost exactly in half.

Returning to Table 12.4, note how WLS and WAAP are successively smaller than the simple mean, just as one would expect if there were selective reporting.

In fact, WAAP, PET and PEESE are approximately half the size of the average reported *VR1*, exactly as this recent survey discovers to be typical in economics (Ioannidis et al., 2017). Column (4) reports the FAT-PET (Eq. 3) and Column (5) presents the PEESE model results (Eq. 4). As is normally the case when there is publication selection, these weighted averages and the selection bias corrected meta-averages are significantly lower than the simple average, and here they are all of approximately the same magnitude. The *t*-statistics exceed the higher 3.5 critical value (or even a much higher critical value of 10) for all of these averages, be they simple, weighted, or publication bias corrected. All averages suggest a rejection of the EMH for Asian and Australasian stock markets and the FAT (coefficient on standard error) is statistically significant (Column (4)), suggesting some net positive publication bias in this literature. All of these findings are confirmed in the multiple MRA context where other research and market dimensions are considered – see Table 12.5.

WLS estimates of the multiple MRA model, Eq. (5), are presented in Table 12.5. We construct these models so that the baseline represents daily returns in Australia and New Zealand.[20] That is, when all explanatory (or moderator) variables are zero, the constant estimates *VR1* for daily returns in Australasia in 1992 (the sample mean). Column 1 controls for potential publication bias, average year, whether the data is monthly or weekly (with daily as the base), the holding period length used to construct the VR (*HoldingPeriodA* = *HoldingPeriod* – the Australasian mean) and market capitalization (*MarketCapA* = *MarketCap* – the Australasian mean). Column (2) adds the dummy variable *LesserIncome*. Column (3) explores further the difference between countries by including 14 country dummies; it serves as our core MRA model.[21]

Columns (4) to (8) explore the robustness of these results to various alternate models.[22] Column 4 uses Robust Regression. Columns 5 and 6 report results from unbalanced panel-data MRA models that include study level effects (see Nelson and Kennedy 2009; Stanley and Doucouliagos 2012). Column 5 reports the results from the fixed-effects panel data WLS model, while column 6 present results from the random-effects panel data WLS model. Both the random and fixed effects panel data models are weighted using inverse variance weights. Column 7 reports results using 'random effects' MRA, using modified inverse variance weights, $1/(se_{ij}^2 + \tau^2)$; where τ^2 is the between-study or heterogeneity variance.[23] While conventional practice among meta-analysts argues in favor of the random-effects model, there is growing concern about this practice, particularly in the presence of publication selection (Stanley and Doucouliagos, 2012 and 2017). Finally, there is no consensus on how clustering should be treated in the very unbalanced data used in MRA. Column 8 reports the results from a multilevel, linear hierarchical model that is one way of handling any data dependence within studies. In Table 12.5 we use market capitalization as the key external variable. We also re-estimate these models replacing market capitalization with economic freedom. For the sake of space, only the coefficient on economic freedom is reported in panel B of Table 12.5 (the full results are available from the authors).

Table 12.5 Multiple meta-regression results (dependent variable is the *VRI*)

Variables	WLS (1)	WLS (2)	WLS (3)	Robust (4)	FE Panel (5)	RE Panel (6)	Random effects (7)	Multi-level (8)
Constant	0.108*	0.054*	0.046*	0.093*	0.017	0.018	0.098*	0.016
	(8.70)	(4.27)	(4.16)	(11.38)	(1.42)	(1.54)	(4.36)	(1.41)
Standard error	1.024*	1.079*	1.106*	0.599*	1.416*	1.402*	0.342*	1.563*
	(9.21)	(9.13)	(11.65)	(9.87)	(17.12)	(7.10)	(4.54)	(4.17)
Average year	−0.003*	−0.006*	−0.007*	−0.007*	−0.007*	−0.007*	−0.012*	−0.007*
	(−3.03)	(−5.47)	(−6.39)	(−12.71)	(−6.76)	(−7.34)	(−7.66)	(−7.07)
Monthly	−0.168*	−0.172*	−0.191*	−0.163*	−0.143*	−0.152*	−0.204*	−0.146*
	(−10.86)	(−10.67)	(−12.03)	(−14.16)	(−8.46)	(−8.95)	(−10.18)	(−8.71)
Weekly	0.028	0.033*	−0.006	−0.009	0.022*	0.010	0.028	0.017
	(1.45)	(1.70)	(−0.39)	(−1.15)	(1.92)	(0.89)	(1.61)	(1.58)
HoldingPeriodA	−0.000	−0.000	−0.000	0.002*	−0.001*	−0.001*	0.001*	−0.001*
	(−0.31)	(−0.97)	(−1.30)	(10.43)	(−4.18)	(−4.33)	(5.31)	(−4.38)
MarketCapA	−0.0004*	−0.0001	−0.002*	−0.001*	−0.001*	−0.002*	−0.002*	−0.001*
	(−4.18)	(−1.11)	(−4.60)	(−6.16)	(−5.69)	(−6.28)	(−4.08)	(−5.97)
LesserIncome		0.085*						
		(5.85)						
Bangladesh			−0.062*	−0.024	−0.022	−0.037	0.087	−0.027
			(−2.61)	(−0.72)	(−0.45)	(−0.76)	(1.23)	(−0.56)
China			0.025	0.069*	−0.051*	0.004	0.119*	−0.030
			(1.00)	(5.94)	(−2.62)	(0.20)	(3.35)	(−1.58)
India			0.086*	0.088*	0.082*	0.088*	0.125*	0.085*
			(5.05)	(5.63)	(3.47)	(3.84)	(3.03)	(3.65)
Indonesia			0.110*	0.125*	0.113*	0.116*	0.274*	0.114*
			(4.01)	(7.66)	(5.21)	(5.23)	(6.63)	(5.29)
Malaysia			0.288*	0.243*	0.248*	0.268*	0.328*	0.255*
			(6.84)	(11.01)	(8.20)	(8.78)	(6.42)	(8.51)
Philippines			0.155*	0.160*	0.157*	0.161*	0.242*	0.158*
			(8.55)	(10.54)	(7.90)	(7.93)	(6.08)	(8.03)
Sri Lanka			0.275*	0.540*	0.273*	0.273*	0.576*	0.273*
			(3.87)	(22.10)	(8.47)	(8.33)	(8.58)	(8.53)

(*Continued*)

Table 12.5 (Continued)

Variables	WLS (1)	WLS (2)	WLS (3)	Robust (4)	FE Panel (5)	RE Panel (6)	Random effects (7)	Multi-level (8)
Thailand	—	—	0.116*	0.121*	0.112*	0.116*	0.183*	0.114*
			(5.09)	(7.51)	(5.30)	(5.39)	(4.76)	(5.41)
Pakistan	—	—	0.027	0.073*	−0.023	−0.016	0.151*	−0.021
			(0.99)	(4.30)	(−0.84)	(−0.61)	(3.55)	(−0.79)
Korea	—	—	−0.046	−0.003	−0.007	−0.010	−0.066*	−0.008
			(−1.31)	(−0.21)	(−0.34)	(−0.46)	(−1.86)	(−0.36)
Hongkong	—	—	0.200*	0.121*	0.176*	0.195*	0.173*	0.183*
			(3.89)	(4.49)	(4.65)	(5.16)	(2.94)	(4.90)
Japan	—	—	−0.043*	−0.060*	−0.047*	−0.043*	−0.029	−0.046*
			(−2.48)	(−4.91)	(−2.95)	(−2.67)	(−0.94)	(−2.87)
Singapore	—	—	0.242*	0.181*	0.220*	0.235*	0.198*	0.226*
			(6.88)	(9.63)	(8.51)	(9.04)	(4.59)	(8.81)
Taiwan	—	—	0.200*	0.158*	0.162*	0.170*	0.249*	0.164*
			(5.86)	(12.00)	(8.38)	(8.76)	(7.79)	(8.61)
$VR1_d$	0.108* (8.70)	0.054*	0.046*	0.093*	0.017	0.018	0.098*	0.016
		(4.27)	(4.16)	(11.38)	(1.42)	(1.54)	(4.36)	(1.41)
$VR1_w$	0.136*	0.087*	0.040*	0.084*	0.038*	0.028*	0.125*	0.034*
	(6.51)	(3.95)	(2.30)	(7.47)	(2.37)	(1.74)	(4.92)	(2.13)
$VR1_m$	−0.060*	−0.117*	−0.145*	−0.070*	−0.126*	−0.134*	−0.106*	−0.129*
	(−3.18)	(−5.75)	(−7.22)	(−4.86)	(−6.10)	(−6.41)	(−3.81)	(−6.30)
Adjusted R^2	0.139	0.178	0.359		0.371	0.354	0.510	
B: EcofreedomA	−0.025*	0.004	−0.069*	−0.092*	−0.039*	−0.066*	−0.081*	−0.053*
	(−3.90)	(0.45)	(−3.02)	(−8.25)	(−2.06)	(−3.61)	(−2.51)	(−2.86)

Notes: The dependent variable in all columns is the variance-ratio minus 1. The number of observations is 1,554. Cell entries in parentheses report *t*-statistics. All estimates use weighted least squares (WLS), with the inverse variance as weights and using robust standard errors for Columns (1)–(3). Columns (4)–(6) test the robustness of the basic WLS findings using robust regression (4), fixed-effects panel methods (5), random-effects panel methods (6), random effects weights (7), and multi-level (8) methods. $VR1_d$, $VR1_w$, and $VR1_m$ denote the estimated Variance Ratio using daily, weekly and monthly data for the base (Australasia); figures in brackets are *t*-statistics testing VR1 = 0.
*denotes statistically significant at least at the 5% level, one-tail test. R^2 in Columns (4) and (5) are for variations among the reported *t*-values in this research literature. Panel B reports the coefficient on economic freedom, replacing this with market capitalization. This model uses the same specification but for the sake of brevity the coefficients on the other variables are not reported.

Most of the results from the MRA models are essentially the same (see Table 12.5). In particular, the results for *Standard error*, *Average Year*, and *Monthly* are very robust. However, *HoldingPeriodA* is unstable, being statistically significant in some models but not in others and also changing sign in some cases. Although *Weekly* is not robustly greater than the base, daily, all columns of Table 12.5 estimate the average VR1 to be positive at the weekly frequency – see the bottom of Table 12.5.

The MRA coefficients can be used to estimate the average VR for different data frequencies. The bottom panel of Table 12.5 reports these VR1 estimates and tests of the null of the EMH for daily data ($VR1_d$), weekly data ($VR1_w$), and monthly data ($VR1_m$) for the base (Australasia) when evaluated at sample means.[24] Table 12.6 reports these tests of the EMH for each country; for each country there is some evidence of violation of the EMH. In general, for daily and weekly data there is evidence of positive autocorrelation (momentum) in Asian and Australasian stock markets. For monthly data the results suggest negative autocorrelation or mean reversion.

Recall that the VR1 is essentially an estimate of the weighted sum of all the autocorrelations up to the k holding period, with the greatest weight placed on lags 1 and 2. Hence, we can interpret it as a correlation coefficient. Our results show that the degree of stock market inefficiency is largest among several of the least developed countries, namely Indonesia, the Philippines, and Sri Lanka; with Sri Lanka being the most inefficient. However, market inefficiency is also relatively large in Taiwan. Moreover, some of the estimates suggest that the *absolute* value of the VR1 is greater with monthly data. Thus, we can conclude that market inefficiency is larger for the longer data frequency than it is for the shorter data frequency. While these estimates do not directly quantify trading profits net of transaction costs, they do suggest that the degree of predictability is potentially of economic significance, on average.

6. Discussion

Several important findings emerge from the MRA models.

Standard Error is always statistically significant with a positive coefficient, suggesting publication selection bias. This finding is the opposite of what one would expect from small-sample bias alone. In Appendix A, we show that the variance ratio increases with larger samples size, but our MRA results show that VR1 increases with the standard error. Ceteris paribus, the standard error will be inversely related to the sample size. Thus, rather than a preference to support the conventional view, EMH, there appears to be some selective reporting of variance ratios that are greater than one (VR1 > 0), relative to those that are less than one. This does not mean that all or even most researchers engage in this practice. It takes only a small minority of negative *VR1* estimates to be suppressed to be detected statistically. Selection bias can inflate the evidence against or in favor of the EMH. Hence, it is important to accommodate or correct this bias. This is what the MRA models in Table 12.5 achieve; they provide tests for the EMH after allowing for selection bias, enabling more valid inferences to be made.

The coefficient on *Average Year* is negative and is robustly statistically significant, suggesting that the VR ratio falls by about 0.07 per decade. We offer three explanations for this finding. First, it may simply reflect the so-called Proteus effect, or the decline effect, whereby it has been observed that empirical effects are declining over time (Ioannidis, 2008). Declining effects are often attributed to initial studies reporting much larger effects as a result of selection of results that favor novel findings; for example, the earlier studies might have been eager to report a rejection of the EMH. The subsequent literature then finds smaller effects as a broader range of estimates are published. Schwert (2001) speculates that this has indeed occurred in the EMH literature.

A second and arguably more plausible explanation is that this 'decline effect' may reflect structural changes that have resulted in less momentum in stock returns and thereby improved stock market efficiency over time. This is consistent with the results from the US stock market (Kim et al., 2011; Ito and Sugiyama, 2009; Gu and Finnerty, 2002). For example, technical advancements in trading systems and platforms, improved transaction flows in stock exchanges, high frequency trading, reduced bid-ask spreads, greater media coverage, increased liquidity, financial products such as exchange-traded funds and greater general awareness of stock markets, can all contribute to increased stock market efficiency. This can also be related with declining level of microstructure factors of emerging stock markets, as Lagoarde-Segot (2009) has found. A third explanation for declining effects was advanced by Schwert (2001: 939) who claims that even if the anomalies existed in the sample period in which they were first identified, the activities of practitioners who implement strategies to take advantage of anomalous behavior can cause the anomalies to disappear (as research findings cause the market to become more efficient)." In essence, Schwert (2001) is arguing that when the market is inefficient in a particular way, the inefficiency is to some degree self-correcting. Once a particular pattern of returns is highlighted and published by researchers, arbitragers can exploit them for profit, which tends to dissolve the pattern in question. Nonetheless, investor irrationality and market inefficiency may persist indefinitely (Shliefer and Summers, 1990). A final point worth noting is that the negative sign on *Average Year* indicates that stock market efficiency improves over time. This finding is consistent with Lo's (2004) adaptive markets hypothesis.

Monthly always has a negative and statistically significant coefficient in the MRA, suggesting that, on average, the use of monthly data results in VR estimates less than one – Tables 12.5 and 12.6. Monthly data reveals negative autocorrelation in stock returns for the majority of countries, i.e., mean reversion. This means that the variance in stock returns is less than proportional to the investment horizon, whereas market efficiency requires this variance to be proportional. In contrast, on average, the use of daily and weekly data results in positive autocorrelation in stock returns and VR estimates greater than one. The use of monthly observations means that the analysis focuses on patterns that repeat,

Table 12.6 Country-specific MRA tests of the EMH, daily, weekly and monthly data

Country	Daily data VR1$_d$ (1)	Weekly data VR1$_w$ (2)	Monthly data VR1$_m$ (3)
Bangladesh	0.060*	0.054*	−0.131*
	(4.49)	(2.74)	(−6.21)
China	0.104*	0.099*	−0.086*
	(5.10)	(4.28)	(−3.36)
Korea	0.002	−0.003	−0.188*
	(0.07)	(−0.09)	(−5.19)
Hong Kong	0.029*	0.023	−0.162*
	(2.30)	(1.22)	(−7.42)
India	0.152*	0.146*	−0.039*
	(10.87)	(7.88)	(−1.89)
Indonesia	0.211*	0.205*	0.020
	(9.66)	(7.36)	(0.75)
Japan	−0.053*	−0.058*	−0.243*
	(−4.86)	(−3.38)	(−11.49)
Malaysia	0.156*	0.151*	−0.035
	(7.94)	(6.60)	(−1.48)
Philippines	0.220*	0.215*	0.030
	(15.00)	(10.80)	(1.39)
Sri Lanka	0.377*	0.371*	0.186*
	(5.44)	(5.24)	(2.64)
Singapore	0.152*	0.147*	−0.038*
	(14.38)	(8.33)	(−1.97)
Taiwan	0.224*	0.219*	0.034
	(6.47)	(6.64)	(0.90)
Thailand	0.173*	0.167*	−0.018
	(7.99)	(6.47)	(−0.66)
Australasia	0.046*	0.040*	−0.145*
	(4.16)	(2.30)	(−7.22)

Notes: The cells report estimates using the MRA coefficients from Table 5, Column (3), evaluated at the mean of the samples for average year and market capitalization. Figures in brackets are *t*-statistics. VR1$_d$, VR1$_w$, and VR1$_m$ denote the estimated Variance Ratio using daily, weekly and monthly data, respectively.
*denotes statistically significant at least at the 5% level, one-tail test.

at most, every two months. We would expect that lagged prices will be less important for explaining future prices the longer is interval at which prices are observed, because serial correlation should decay as the lag length increases.

The two exogenous variables, *MarketCap* and *Ecofreedom* both have the expected negative sign in all specifications except Column (2) of Table 12.5 which adds a dummy variable for lesser income countries. *MarketCap* and *Ecofreedom* are not significant in this specification because these factors tend to have the same effect on market efficiency as economic development. It seems that *LesserIncome* captures the effect of all of these forces. Otherwise, the MRA confirms that more developed stock markets, as measured by market capitalization, are also more efficient. Similarly, the MRA confirms that countries with less regulation (more market liberalization) experience greater market efficiency. Our results broadly confirm those of Kaminsky and Schmukler (2008: 256), who find that financial cycles are dampened in the long run by "improvements in property rights, transparency, and overall contractual environment", all important components of economic freedom.[25]

The development level variable, *Lesserinc*, has a positive and statistically significant coefficient, confirming that stock markets are less efficient in the less developed nations. The coefficients on the individual country dummies provide more detailed evidence on the degree to which stock market efficiency varies across countries. In general, stock markets in the less developed countries (e.g., Sri Lanka, Indonesia, and the Philippines) are less efficient than those from higher income countries. Kim and Shamsuddin (2008) report similar findings in their investigation of the weak-form efficiency of Asian stock markets using the VR test.

7. Summary and conclusions

The efficiency of markets is one of the cornerstones of finance theory, with profound implications for the functioning of markets and the role of regulators. When markets are efficient, prices reflect fundamental values and hence they allocate scarce funds to their highest valued use. Its prominence in economics and finance notwithstanding, there continues to be considerable debate in the theoretical and empirical literature regarding the EMH. For example, Engel and Morris (1991: 21) conclude that "the evidence on mean reversion is mixed. Thus, more evidence is needed before declaring the stock market inefficient." This paper explores the EMH in Asian and Australasian markets. We apply meta-regression analysis to 1,560 estimates of the EMH that use the Variance Ratio test across 16 nations. We intentionally adopt a cross-country comparison, enabling us to analyze stock market efficiency from a relative (comparative) perspective.

Our results indicate that the weight of the evidence from Variance Ratio tests is a rejection of the EMH for Asian nations. Stock market efficiency is particularly weaker in the less developed and more regulated economies. An interesting pattern of results emerges among the different data frequencies. We find small to medium sized inefficiencies among daily and weekly returns and negative autocorrelation among monthly returns. Our results suggest that there is a degree of inefficiency in Asian stock markets and hence potentially some room for technical analysis and mutual fund managers to outperform the market.[26]

Market efficiency is often viewed as a final steady state. However, perhaps it is more appropriate to view market efficiency as a process rather than a state. Viewed this way, it is clear from the meta-analysis that stock markets in Asian are becoming more efficient. We find that efficiency has been improving over time and that market capitalization and economic freedom (market linearization) both increase stock market efficiency. These factors mean that it is dubious whether there remain opportunities to outperform the stock market, except in the least developed stock markets and the less liberal nations.

Our focus in this paper has been on Asian stock markets and the Variance Ratio test of the EMH. Meta-analysis could be profitably employed to other regions, especially other emerging economies such as those in the Middle East and Latin America. A particularly important extension would be to apply meta-regression analysis to other tests of the EMH, such as the stock market predictability literature that uses regression analysis.

Notes

1 Traders and investors are interested in exploiting any inefficiency in stock market prices by profiting from predictable patterns. Regulators seek to make stock markets efficient because when prices reflect fundamental values they help to allocate new investments to their highest valued use.

2 Although widely regarded as an important tool to improve integrity and credibility of empirical research (see, for example, Cummings, 2014; and Ioannidis and Doucouliagos, 2013), meta-analysis has not been applied extensively in the finance literature. Notable meta-analytic studies in finance include Capon et al. (1990), van Ewijk et al. (2012), and Ferdnandes et al. (2014).

3 This choice is driven by the Asian countries analyzed in the primary literature.

4 According to the bestseller, *Flash Boys*, large banks are making billions by placing their program trading computers physically closer to the New York Stock Exchange's computer (Lewis, 2014).

5 Other autocorrelation-based tests include Box-Ljung type tests (e.g., Escanciano and Lobato, 2009), spectral tests (e.g., Escanciano and Velasco, 2006), and non-parametric tests (e.g., Wright, 2000). The variance ratio test is more widely used in the empirical literature, as it possesses better small sample properties (see Charles et al., 2011).

6 Throughout the paper we measure the effect size as VR − 1, rather than VR, which we denote as VR1. VR1 measures the deviation from market efficiency, which we use it for expositional purposes. Inferences are *identical* whether we use VR or VR-1, when the interpretation is properly adjusted.

7 In the case of the EMH, re-estimation can involve taking different samples, time periods, countries, indices, etc.

8 Recall that we use VR − 1. Hence, the test of the EMH is the null of $\beta_0 = 0$. If we used VR, then the test of the EMH involves the null of $\beta_0 = 1$.

9 Ed Tufte (2006: 687) famously remarked that t-statistics that fall in the range between 1.6 and 2 lie in the "Zone of Boredom, Ambiguity, and Unpublishability".

10 It is often claimed that including unpublished studies reduces or even eliminates publication selection bias. Stanley and Doucouliagos (2012) argue that this belief is mistaken. When there is a well-known preference for statistically significant results, theses and working papers will also report, preferentially, statistically significant findings in preparation for subsequent publication. MRAs that have coded and analyzed published vs. unpublished studies, sometimes find that there are no differences and at other times that published studies show evidence of stronger selection for statistical significance. In any case, unpublished papers cannot be assumed to be free of 'publication bias' or selective reporting.

11 Some studies focus only on the statistical significance of the VR but do not report standard errors. The results from these studies are broadly in line with our own findings.

12 We also removed a single extreme value with a very large VR1 (in excess of 8) that was estimated with poor precision.

13 In unreported regressions we also included a dummy for the Asian financial crisis, assigning a value of 1 for estimates that relate purely to the post-financial crisis period. This variable was never statistically significant in any of the MRA models.

14 Of the 1,560 VR1 estimates included in our sample, 434 relate to monthly data and 526 relate to weekly data, with the remainder relating to daily data. We include in *Monthly* 13 observations for quarterly returns and 11 observations for annual returns.

15 We also calculated this length as fractions of monthly data, i.e., the length of the holding period for weekly and daily frequencies was converted into monthly. For example, $k = 20$ for daily data is converted into a one month holding period.

16 If a dummy variable for heteroskedastic VR estimates is included in the MRA, it is never statistically significant.

17 An exception to this interpretation occurs if the variance ratio tends to be less than one, as we find among monthly frequencies.

18 Market capitalization and economic freedom are highly correlated with a correlation coefficient of 0.85. Hence, we treat these variables as alternate measures rather than including both in the MRA; neither is statistically significant when both are included in the MRA.

19 Kaminsky and Schmukler (2008) construct a new database of market liberalization. However, their index does not cover many of the countries in our database. The Economic Freedom of the World index is more comprehensive and available for all the countries in our database.

20 In unreported regressions we used an alternate specification where the baseline of the MRA is high income countries, using the World Bank's classification system: Australia, New Zealand, Singapore, Taiwan, Hong Kong, Japan, and South Korea. The results are essentially the same as those reported in the text.

21 Note that we pool all estimates for China. In unreported regressions, we considered separate dummies for Shanghai and Shenzen indices but these results are not qualitative different to those presented in the text.

22 We do not report OLS results here as these are not recommended for meta-regression models; OLS treats every observation equally and ignores the fact that precision varies across estimates and studies.

23 The term 'random effects' in Column (7) refers to the weights used in the meta-analysis sense of this term; whereas in Column (6), it refers to the normal econometrics usage, as a panel data estimator.

24 In other words, these MRAs reported in Table 5 are used to make individual predictions using sample mean values of market capitalization and average year. *Standard error* is set to zero because VR1 is widely known to have small-sample bias, regardless of selective reporting or publication bias – see Appendix A. Even if *Standard error* were not a proxy for bias, it should still be set equal to zero because estimates get better and better (higher statistical power) with larger samples and smaller standard errors.

25 Kaminsky and Schmukler (2008) find that there is an increase in the short turn but in the long run, cycles are less pronounced.

26 Recall however that transaction costs and taxation considerations are *not* considered in VR tests.

Bibliography

Amihud, Y. (2002) Illiquidity and stock returns: Cross-section and time-series effects. *Journal of Financial Markets* **5**, 31–56.

Angrist, J. D. and Pischke, J. S. (2008) *Mostly Harmless Econometrics: An Empiricist's Companion*, Princeton University Press, Princeton.

Bachelier, L. 1900. *Théorie de la Speculation*, Paris.

Barber, B. M. and Odean, T. (2001) Boys will be boys: Gender, overconfidence, and common stock investment. *Quarterly Journal of Economics* **116**(1), 261–292.

Bender, J. C., Osler, C. L. and Simon, D. (2013) Noise trading and illusory correlations in US equity markets, *Review of Finance* **17**, 625–652.

Bom, P. R. D. and Ligthart, J. E. (2008) *How Productive Is Public Capital? A Meta-analysis*. CESifo Working Paper No. 2206.

Boudoukh, J., Richardson, M. P. and Whitelaw, R. F. (1994) A Tale of Three Schools: Insights on Autocorrelations of Short-horizon Stock Returns. *Review of Financial Studies* **7**, 539–573.

Cameron, A. C., Gelbach, J. B., and Miller, D. L. (2008) Bootstrap-based improvements for inference with clustered errors, *Review of Economics and Statistics* **90**(3), 414–427.

Campbell, J. Y., Lo, A. W. and MacKinlay, A. C. (1997) *The Econometrics of Financial Markets*. Princeton University Press, Princeton.

Capon, N., Farley, J. U., Hoenig, S. (1990) Determinants of financial performance: A meta-analysis, *Management Science* **36**(10), 1143–1159.

Charles, A. and Darné, O. (2009) Variance ratio tests of random walk: An overview, *Journal of Economic Surveys* **23**, 503–527.

Charles, A., Darné, O. and Kim, J. H. (2011) Small sample properties of alternative tests for martingale difference hypothesis, *Economics Letters* **110**, 151–154.

Chen, W. W. and Deo, R. S. (2006) The variance ratio statistic at large horizons, *Econometric Theory* **22**, 206–234.

Choi, I. (1999) Testing the random walk hypothesis for real exchange rates, *Journal of Applied Econometrics* **14**, 293–308.

Chow, K. V. and Denning, K. C. (1993) A simple multiple variance ratio test, *Journal of Econometrics* **58**, 385–401.

Comerton-Forde, C. and Putniņš, T. J. (2014) Stock price manipulation: Prevalence and determinants, *Review of Finance* **18**, 23–66.

Conrad, J. S. and Kaul, G. (1988) Time varying expected returns, *Journal of Business* **61**, 409–425.

Cornell, B. and Rutten, J. C. (2006) Market efficiency, crashes and securities litigation, *Tulane Law Review* **81**, 442–471.

Cumming, G. (2014) The new statistics: Why and how, *Psychological Science*, **25**(1), 7–29.

De Bondt, W. F. M. and Thaler, R. H. (1985) Does the stock market overreact? *Journal of Finance* **40**(3), 793–805.

DeFusco, R., Mishra, S. and Raghunandan, K. (2010) Changes in the information efficiency of stock prices: Additional evidence, *The Financial Review* **45**(1), 153–165.

Dominguez, M. A. and Lobato, I. N. (2003) Testing the martingale difference hypothesis, *Econometrics Review* **22**, 351–377.

Doran, J. S., Peterson, D. R. and Wright, C. (2010) Confidence, opinions of market efficiency, and investment behavior of finance professors, *Journal of Financial Markets* **13**(1), 174–195.

Doucouliagos, H. and Stanley, T. D. (2013) Theory competition and selectivity: Are all economic facts greatly exaggerated? *Journal of Economic Surveys* **27**, 316–339.

Escanciano, J. C. and Lobato, I. N. (2009) An automatic portmanteau test for serial correlation, *Journal of Econometrics* **151**, 140–149.

Escanciano, J. C. and Velasco, C. (2006) Generalized spectral tests for the martingale difference hypothesis, *Journal of Econometrics* **134**, 151–185.

Fama, E. F. (1970) Efficient capital markets: A review of theory and empirical work, *Journal of Finance* **25**(2), 383–417.

Fama, E. F. (1991). Efficient capital market II, *Journal of Finance* **46**(5), 1575–1617.

Fama, E. F. and French, K. (1988a) Permanent and temporary components of stock prices, *Journal of Political Economy* **96**, 246–273.

Fama, E. F. and French, K. (1988b) Dividend yield and expected stock returns, *Journal of Financial Economics* **22**, 3–25.

Fernandes, D., Lynch, J. G. and Netemeyer, R. G. (2014) Financial literacy, financial education, and downstream financial behaviors, *Management Science* **60**(8), 1861–1883.

Ferson, W. E., Heuson, A. and Su, T. (2005) Weak-form and semi-strong-form stock return predictability revisited. *Management Science* **51**(10), 1582–1592.

Fischel, D. R. (1989) Efficient capital markets the crash and the fraud on the market theory, *Cornell Law Review* **74**, 907–922.

Garcia, P., Hudson, M. A. and Waller, M .L. (1988) The pricing efficiency of agricultural futures markets: An analysis of research results, *Southern Journal of Agricultural Economics* 119–130.

Griffin, J. M., Kelly, P. J. and Nardari, F. (2010) Do market efficiency measures yield correct inferences? A comparison of developed and emerging markets, *Review of Financial Studies* **23**(8), 3225–3277.

Grossman, S. J. and Stiglitz, J. E. (1980) On the impossibility of informationally efficient markets, *The American Economic Review* **70**(3), 393–408.

Gu, A. Y. and Finnerty, J. (2002) The evolution of market efficiency: 103 years daily data of Dow, *Review of Quantitative Finance and Accounting* **18**(3), 219–237.

Gunther, M. and Herath, S. (2010) Efficiency of the real estate market: A meta-analysis, *17th Annual European Real Estate Society Conference*. ERES: Conference. Milan, Italy.

Harvey, C. (1995) Predictable risk and returns in emerging markets, *Review of Financial Studies* **8**, 773–816.

Havranek, T. (2015) Measuring intertemporal substitution: The importance of method choices and selective reporting, *Journal of the European Economic Association* **13**(6): 1180–1204.

Hunter, J. E. and Schmidt, F. L. (2004) *Methods of Meta-Analysis: Correcting Error and Bias in Research Findings*, Sage, New York.

Ioannidis, J. P. A. (2008) Why most true discovered associations are inflated, *Epidemiology* **19**, 640–648.

Ioannidis, J. P. A. and Doucouliagos, C. (2013) What's to know about credibility of empirical economics? *Journal of Economic Surveys* **27**(5), 997–1004.

Ioannidis, J. P. A., Stanley, T. D. and Doucouliagos, C. (2017). The power of bias in economics research, *The Economic Journal* **127**, F236–265.

Ito, M. and Sugiyama, S. (2009) Measuring the degree of time varying market inefficiency, *Economics Letters* **103**(1), 62–64.

Jegadeesh, N. and Titman, S. (1993) Returns to buying winners and selling losers: Implications for stock market efficiency, *Journal of Finance* **48**(1), 65–91.

Kaminsky, G. L. and Schmukler, S. L. (2008) Short-run pain, long-run gain: Financial liberalization and stock market cycles, *Review of Finance* **12**, 253–292.

Keef, S. P. and Roush, M. L. (2007) A meta-analysis of the international evidence of cloud cover on stock returns, *Review of Accounting and Finance* **6**(3), 324–338.

Kim, J. H. (2006) Wild bootstrapping variance ratio tests, *Economics Letters* 92, 38–43.

Kim, J. H. (2009) Automatic variance ratio test under conditional heteroskedascity, *Finance Research Letters* 6(3), 179–185.

Kim, J. H. and Shamsuddin, A. (2008) Are Asian stock markets efficient? Evidence from new multiple Variance Ratio tests, *Journal of Empirical Finance* 15(3), 518–532.

Kim, J. H., Shamsuddin, A. and Lim, K.-P. (2011) Stock return predictability and the adaptive markets hypothesis: Evidence from century-long U.S. data, *Journal of Empirical Finance* 18, 868–879.

Lagoarde-Segot, T. (2009) Financial reforms and time-varying microstructures in emerging equity markets, *Journal of Banking and Finance* 33(10), 1755–1769.

Lesmond, D. A., Ogden, J. and Trzcinka, C. (1999) A new estimate of transaction costs, *Review of Financial Studies* 12, 1113–1141.

Lewis, M. (2014) *Flash Boys*, W.W. Norton, New York.

Lim, K.-P. and Brooks, R. D. (2011) The evolution of stock market efficiency over time: A survey of the empirical literature, *Journal of Economic Surveys* 25, 69–108.

Lo, A. W. (2004) The adaptive markets hypothesis: Market efficiency from an evolutionary perspective, *Journal of Portfolio Management*, 15–29.

Lo, A. W. and MacKinlay, A. C. (1988) Stock market prices do not follow random walks: Evidence from a simple specification test, *Review of Financial Studies* 1(1), 41–66.

Lo, A. W. and MacKinlay, A. C. (1989) The size and power of the variance ratio test in finite samples: a Monte Carlo investigation, *Journal of Econometrics* 40, 203–238.

Lo, A. W. and MacKinlay, A. C. (1990). An econometric analysis of nonsynchronous trading, *Journal of Econometrics* 45, 181–212.

Malkiel, B. G. (2003). The efficient market hypothesis and its critics, *Journal of Economic Perspectives* 17(1), 59–82.

Mandelbrot, B. (1963) The variation of certain speculative prices, *Journal of Business* 36, 394–419.

Moulton, B. R. (1990) An illustration of a pitfall in estimating the effects of aggregate variables on micro unit, *The Review of Economics and Statistics* 72(2), 334–338.

Neely, C. J.,Weller, P. A. and Ulrich, J. (2009) The adaptive markets hypothesis: Evidence from the foreign exchange market. *Journal of Financial and Quantitative Analysis* 44(2), 467–488.

Park, C. H. and Irwin, S. H. (2007) What do we know about the profitability of technical analysis? *Journal of Economic Surveys* 21, 786–826.

Poterba, J. A. and Summers, L. H. (1988) Mean reversion in stock prices, *Journal of Financial Economics* 22, 27–59.

Reilly, D., Lucey, B. and Gurdgiev, C. (2011) *Real Estate and the Stock Market: A Meta-regression Analysis*. Paper presented at the 2011 Cambridge MAER-NET Colloquium, Cambridge University, September 16–18th, England.

Richardson, M. and Smith, T. (1991) Tests of financial models in the presence of overlapping observations, *Review of Financial Studies* 4, 227–254.

Roberts, C. J. and Stanley, T. D. (2005). *Issues in Meta-Regression Analysis and Publication Bias in Economics*, Blackwell, Oxon.

Samuelson, P. (1965) Proof that properly an anticipated prices fluctuate randomly, *Industrial Management Review* 6, 41–49.

Schwert, G. (2003) Anomalies and market efficiency. In G. Contantinides, G., Harris, M. and Stulz, R. M. (Eds.), *Handbook of the Economics of Finance* (pp. 937–972), Amsterdam, North Holland.

Shamsuddin, A. and Kim, J. H. (2010) Short-horizon return predictability in international equity markets, *The Financial Review* **45**(2), 469–484.

Shiller, R. J. (1984) Stock prices and social dynamics, *Brookings Papers in Economic Activity* **2**, 457–498.

Shliefer, A. and Summers, L. H. (1990) The noise trader approach to finance, *Journal of Economic Perspectives* **4**, 19–33.

Shleifer, A. and Vishny, R. W. (1997) The limits of arbitrage, *Journal of Finance* **52**, 35–55.

Stanley, T. D. (2008) Meta-regression methods for detecting and estimating empirical effects in the presence of publication selection, *Oxford Bulletin of Economics and Statistics* **70**(1), 103–127.

Stanley, T. D. and Doucouliagos, C. (2015) Neither fixed nor random: Weighted least squares meta-analysis, *Statistics in Medicine* **34**, 2116–2127.

Stanley, T. D., Doucouliagos, C. and Ioannidis, J. P. A. (2017) Finding the power to reduce publication bias, *Statistics in Medicine* **36**, 1580–1598.

Stanley, T. D. and Doucouliagos, H. (2010) Picture this: A simple graph that reveals much ado about research, *Journal of Economic Surveys* **24**(1), 170–191.

Stanley, T. D. and Doucouliagos, H. (2012) *Meta-Regression Analysis in Economics and Business*. Routledge, Oxford.

Stanley, T. D. and Doucouliagos, H. (2014) Meta-regression approximations to reduce publication selection bias, *Research Synthesis Methods* **5**, 60–78.

Stanley, T. D. and Doucouliagos, H. (2017) Neither fixed nor random: Weighted least squares meta-regression analysis, *Research Synthesis Methods* **8**, 19–42.

Stanley, T. D., Doucouliagos, H., Giles, M., Heckemeyer, J., Johnston, R. J., Laroche, P., Nelson, J. P., Paldam, M., Poot, J., Pugh, G., Rosenberger, R. and Rost, K. (2013) Meta-analysis of economics research reporting guidelines, *Journal of Economic Surveys* **27**(2), 390–394.

Tufte, E. (2006) American Political Science Review top twenty citations, *American Political Science Review* **100**(4), 667–687.

van Ewijk, C., Henri, L. F. de Groot, A. J. (Coos) Santing, (2012) A meta-analysis of the equity premium, *Journal of Empirical Finance* **19**(5), 819–830.

Wright, J. H. (2000) Alternative variance – Ratio tests using ranks and signs, *Journal of Business and Economic Statistics* **18**, 1–9.

Yen, G. and Lee, C. F. (2008) Efficient market hypothesis (EMH): Past, present and future, *Review of Pacific Basin Financial Markets and Policies* **11**(2), 305–329.

Zhang, C. Y. and Jacobsen, B. (2013) Are monthly seasonals real? A three century perspective, *Review of Finance* **17**, 1743–1785.

Appendix A

Meta-regression analysis for variance ratio tests

The purpose of this Appendix is to report simulation results from meta-regression models of variance ratio tests that accommodate possible publication selection bias. Past studies have investigated similar MRA methods when regression coefficients or transformations of regression coefficients are being summarized and modeled (e.g., Stanley, 2008; Stanley, Jarrell and Doucouliagos, 2010). Although the FAT-PET-MRA model that is developed and employed in these papers remains the foundation of the tests investigated here (Stanley and Doucouliagos, 2012), application to variance ratio testing introduces new challenges. In particular, the variance ratio is known to have small-sample bias (Lo and MacKinlay, 1988) and publication selection may 'go both ways.' Typically, publication selection is for statistical significant results (Card and Krueger, 1995; Doucouliagos and Stanley, 2013), which in this application implies a rejection of market efficiency. Some researchers may have priors that the market is inefficient and experiment with their models, data ranges, and methods to find a variance ratio that differs from 1 (either greater than 1 or less than 1). Other researchers may believe that the investors are rational and markets are efficient and dismiss some large variance ratios as faulty. That is, there may be selection across different studies in both directions, for statistical significance and for statistical insignificance.

Second, even in the absence of reporting or publication selection, small-sample bias will cause the effect size, $VR1 = VRT - 1$, to be correlated with its sample size and thereby inversely with its own standard error. The conventional FAT-PET-MRA (equation (3)) will therefore be affected by this small-sample bias, which may or may not distort the precision-effect test (PET) of the overall market efficiency (MEPET). The central purpose of these simulations is to investigate the statistical properties of MEPET for this application and thereby insure the validity of our MRA methods in assessing the research literature's evidence of market efficiency. Table A.1 reports this small-sample bias.

Past simulations have only reported the performance of these MRA models of publication bias when there are various incidences of selection for statistical significance but not when selection may be for statistical *insignificance*. This too may potentially invalidate the FAT-PET-MRA by adding a yet another correlation of the reported effect to its standard error. We do not wish to suggest that

Table A.1 Small-sample bias of the variance ratio (10,000 replications)

VR1 Sample size	Bias of the Variance Ratio
25	−0.077
50	−0.038
100	−0.019
200	−0.011
500	−0.0043
1000	−0.0020

Table A.2 Type I errors of MEPET (10,000 replications)

MRA sample size	H_0: β_0= 0 Critical Value = 1.96	H_0: β_0= 0 Critical Value = 3.50
50	0.056	0.002
100	0.075	0.002
250	0.128	0.004
500	0.206	0.010
1000	0.351	0.024

these challenges invalidate the precision-effect test. In fact, the below simulations findings support the use of PET for application to variance-ratio testing. In this Appendix, we merely wish to address these challenges directly and thereby ensure the validity of a modified precision-effect test for market-efficiency research.

These simulations are designed to be realistic and to follow the statistical properties that we observe in this particular research literature on market efficiency. First, returns are generated randomly assuming that prices follow a random walk,

$$r_t = 0.035 + \varepsilon_t, \tag{A1}$$

where ε_t is N(0, 0.035^2). This allows us to gauge the size and type I errors of MEPET.

Table A.1 reports the average small-sample bias of the variance ratio over 10,000 replications. Table A.1 merely corroborates the known small-sample bias of variance ratio testing. Although this bias is thought to be rather small (Lo and MacKinlay, 1988), it is of sufficient magnitude for our FAT-PET-MRAs to detect and be influenced by it. As a result of this small-sample bias, our precision-effect test (H_0:β_0 = 0) for equation (3) has inflated type I errors when conventional critical values are used – see Table A.2. To investigate the power of PET, returns are generated randomly assuming that they are correlated to their past values, AR(1). Next, either 100, 200, 500, 800 or 1,000 returns are used to calculate the Lo-MacKinlay variance ratio test statistics (q = 2). This process is repeated any number of times to represent the number of tests (MRA sample size) reported by a research literature.

Table A.2 reports the observed size of MEPET (i.e., the frequency that market efficiency is rejected even though it is true) for various MRA samples sizes. The

MRA sample size represents the number of tests reported in a given empirical literature. As Table A.2 shows, the inflation of the type I error increases as PET has access to a larger number of reported tests. Therefore, if we do not modify PET to accommodate these inflated type I errors, it would be unreliable for this application. Rejecting H_0: $\beta_0 = 0$ might then imply either market inefficiency or a mistaken rejection of market efficiency. Thus, it is crucial that this type I error inflation be controlled if PET is to be used.

The last column of Table A.2 reports the observed size of MEPET when the critical value is 3.5. That is, we consider H_0: $\beta_0 = 0$ to be rejected only when its t-value is 3.5 or larger. Note how all observed type I errors are less than the nominal value (0.025) for the conventional critical value = 1.96. For this reason our modified market efficiency precision-effect test (MEPET) uses a critical value of 3.5.

In practice, empirical research is likely to be more complex than what we have simulated thus far. As discussed above, some researchers might not report all of the test results that they obtain; thereby selecting what is reported. Table A.3 displays the stimulations results when proportions of statistical significant and statistically insignificant VRTs are selected. In our meta-analysis of market efficiency, 38% of the reported findings are statistically significant. Thus, these simulations assume that 40% could be selected to be statistically significant, as a worse-case scenario. Likewise, we also allow 40% to be selected to be statistically insignificant. To encompass the range of possible selection we assume that either: 40/40/20%, 60/0/40%, 0/60/40% or 0/0/100% are selected to be statistically significant, insignificant or not selected, respectively. Although all returns are generated randomly, we control for selection by forcing the above percent of the VRs in our MRA sample to be statistically significant (or insignificant). In the 'no selection' condition, the first VR1 (significant or not) obtained is added to the MRA sample. In a second set of simulations, we allow returns to be correlated ($\rho=.1$ or $\rho=.2$).

Our simulations are made further realistic by using an MRA sample size of 1,000, which is approximately the number of VRTs found in our meta-analysis (1,339). Table A.3 shows that there are acceptably small type I errors (≤ 0.024) when there is no heterogeneity or moderate heterogeneity ($I^2=56\%$) – see column 1. Furthermore, in all these cases, MEPET is able to detect even small departures from a random walk ($\rho=.1$) – see column 2 of Table A.3. When there is only moderate excess heterogeneity and 1,000 reported variance-ratio tests, MEPET is a nearly perfect test. Nonetheless, there remains one crucial research dimension that might reverse or qualify these results – large excess heterogeneity

Excess heterogeneity is found in all meta-analyses of economics research (Stanley and Doucouliagos, 2012). That is, the observed variation among reported estimates (or tests) is larger than what one could expect from the reported standard errors alone. Past simulations have found that such excess heterogeneity is the most important characteristic in a research literature (Stanley, 2008; Stanley et al., 2010). The simulations reported in Table A.3 generate

Table A.3 Publication selection, type I error and power of MEPET (MRA sample size = 1,000 with 1,000 replications)

Hetero-geneity*	Incidence of Publication Selection†	1:Random Walk Level of MEPET Critical value= 3.5	2: Correlated (ρ=.1) Power of MEPET Critical value= 3.5	3: Correlated (ρ=.2) Power of MEPET Critical value= 3.5
None	No selection	.024	1.000	1.000
	0/40/60%	.022	1.000	1.000
	40/0/60%	.000	1.000	1.000
	40/40/20%	.000	1.000	1.000
$I^2 = 56\%$	No selection	.007	1.000	1.000
	0/40/60%	.000	1.000	1.000
	40/0/60%	.004	1.000	1.000
	40/40/20%	.000	1.000	1.000
$I^2 = 95\%$	No selection	.000	.131	1.000
	0/40/60%	.000	.000	.000
	40/0/60%	.085	.883	1.000
	40/40/20%	.000	.000	.000

*Heterogeneity is measured by $I^2 = \sigma_h^2/(\sigma_h^2+\sigma_\varepsilon^2)$ (Higgins and Thompson, 2002)

†The incidence of publication selection is reported as the percent that are selected to be statistically significant/insignificant/not selected.

excess heterogeneity by adding a second random term to the equation that generates the returns – recall Appendix equation (1). To quantify this heterogeneity, we use Higgins and Thompson's (2002) $I^2=\sigma_h^2/(\sigma_h^2+\sigma_\varepsilon^2)$; where σ_h^2 is the between-study heterogeneity variance and σ_ε^2 is the within-study sampling variance. I^2 measures the proportion of the total variation due to unexplained heterogeneity. Although the exact value of I^2 varies for each random sample, Appendix Table 3 reports its average value when there is either no selection or balanced selection (40/40/20%).

Moderate excess heterogeneity ($I^2 = 56\%$) causes no problem for MEPET. In fact, the Type I errors are smaller, and the power remains perfect – 100%. However, extreme heterogeneity ($I^2 = 95\%$) offers another challenge for MEPET. When there such large heterogeneity, power can fall precipitously and the Type I errors rises (8.5%) if there is only selection for significant VRT findings – see column 1 of Table A.3. Unfortunately, our meta-analysis finds an observed I^2 of 94%. Because the Type I error can be larger than the conventional $\alpha = .05$ with such extreme heterogeneity, we believe that something further must be done to be absolutely sure that our findings imply that a rejection of market rationality.

Several remedies come to mind. First, we could increase the critical value and thereby drive all the observed type I errors to zero. Simulations show that a critical value of 10 is more than sufficient. Yet, our MEPET has a t-value much larger than 10, thereby ensuring that our evidence against market efficiency is not a type I error (recall Table 4).

The only remaining concern is the low power of MEPET for some incidences of publication selection when there is extreme heterogeneity. But low power is not an issues for this particular application because everything is statistically significant when we use 10 as the critical value (see Table 12.4). Given that large power is found for both versions of MEPET only when there is selection only for statistically significant VRTs (column 2 Table A.3), our meta-analysis of this market efficiency seems to indicate that there is publication selection for the rejection of market efficiency (confirming FAT reported in Table 12.4). However, MEPET power would be expected to increase as the correlation among returns increase. Column 3 of Table A.3 reports the power of MEPET when the first-order correlation among returns is .2. In this case, power for the no selection case increases to 100%. Thus, the exact incidence of selection is not clear from our meta-analysis. Although not reflected in these simulations, our findings are also consistent with smaller incidences of selection in both directions as long as the larger proportion is selected for statistical significance.

Appendix B

Studies included in the meta-analysis (n = number of estimates used from each study)

1 Alam, M. I., Hasan, T. and Kadapakkam, P. J. (1999) An application of variance-ratio test of five Asian stock markets, *Review of Pacific Basin Financial Markets and Policies* **2**(3), 301–315. (n = 40)

2 Ayadi, O. F. and Pyun, C. S. (1994) An application of variance ratio test to the Korean securities market, *Journal of Banking and Finance* **18**, 643–658. (n=40)

3 Chakraborty, M. (2006) Market efficiency for the Pakistan stock market: Evidence from the Karachi stock exchange, *South Asia Economic Journal* **7**, 67–81. (n=42)

4 Chang, K. P. and Ting, K-S. (2000) A variance ratio test of the random walk hypothesis for Taiwan's stock market, *Applied Financial Economics* **10**, 525–532. (n=87)

5 Chen, F. and Jarrett, J. E. (2011) Financial crisis and the market efficiency in the Chinese equity markets, *Journal of the Asia Pacific Economy* **16**(3), 456–463. (n=32)

6 Cheung, K-C. and Coutts, J. A. (2001) A note on weak form market efficiency in security prices: Evidence from the Hong Kong stock exchange, *Applied Economics Letters* **8**, 407–410. (n=14)

7 Claessens, S., Dasgupta, S. and Glen, J. (1995) Return behavior in emerging stock markets, *The World Bank Economic Review* **9**, 131–151. (n=16)

8 Cohen, B. H. (1999) Derivatives, volatility and price discovery, *International Finance* **2**(2), 167–202. (n=12)

9 Darrat, A. F. and Zhong, M. (2000) On testing the random-walk hypothesis: A model-comparison approach, *The Financial Review* **35**, 105–124. (n=20)

10 Füss, R. (2005) Financial liberalization and stock price behaviour in Asian emerging markets, *Economic Change and Restructuring* **38**, 37–62. (n=112)

11 Groenewold, N. and Ariff, M. (1998) The effects of de-regulation on share-market efficiency in the Asia-Pacific, *International Economic Journal* **12**(4), 23–47. (n=36)

12 Guidi, F. and Gupta, R. (2013) Market efficiency in the ASEAN region: Evidence from multivariate and cointegration tests, *Applied Financial Economics* **23**(4), 265–274. (n=40)

13 Hassan, M. K. and Chowdhury, S. S. H. (2008) Efficiency of Bangladesh stock market: Evidence from monthly index and individual firm data, *Applied Financial Economics* **18**, 749–758. (n= 4)

14 Hiremath, G. S. and Kamaiah, B. (2010) Some further evidence on the behaviour of stock returns in India, *International Journal of Economics and Finance* **2**(2), 157–167. (n=8)

15 Huang, B-N. (1995) Do Asian stock market prices follow random walks? Evidence from the variance ratio test, *Applied Financial Economics* **5**, 251–256. (n=105)

16 Hung, J-C. (2009) Deregulation and liberalization of the Chinese stock market and the improvement of market efficiency, *The Quarterly Review of Economics and Finance* **49**, 843–857. (n=48)

17 Islam, A. and Khaled, M. (2005) Tests of weak-form efficiency of the Dhaka stock exchange, *Journal of Business, Finance and Accounting* **32**(7), 1613–1624. (n=18)

18 Karemera, D., Ojah, K. and Cole, J. A. (1999) Random walks and market efficiency tests: Evidence from emerging equity markets. *Review of Quantitative Finance and Accounting* **13**, 171–188. (n=128)

19 Kawakatsu, H. and Morey, M. R. (1999) Financial liberalization and stock market efficiency: An empirical examination of nine emerging market countries, *Journal of Multinational Financial Management* **9**, 353–371. (n=59)

20 Lai, M-M., Balachandher, K.G. and Nor, F. M. (2002) An examination of the random walk model and technical trading rules in the Malaysian stock market, *Quarterly Journal of Business and Economics* **41**(1), 81–104. (n=56)

21 Lee, U. (1992) Do stock prices follow random walk? Some international evidence, *International Review of Economics and Finance* **1**(4), 315–327. (n=32)

22 Lee, C. F., Chen, G.-M. and Rui, O.M. (2001) Stock returns and volatility on China's stock market, *The Journal of Financial Research* **24**(4), 523–543. (n=16)

23 Lock, D.B. (2007) The Taiwan stock market does follow a random walk, *Economics Bulletin* **7**(3), 1–8. (n=16)

24 Long, M. D., Payne, J. D. and Feng, C. (1999) Information transmission in the Shanghai equity market, *The Journal of Financial Research* **22**(1), 29–45. (n=4)

25 Lu, C., Wang, K., Chen, H. and Chong, J. (2007) Integrating A- and B-share markets in China: The effects of regulatory policy changes on market efficiency, *Review of Pacific Basin Financial Markets and Policies* **10**(3), 309–328. (n=47)

26 Patro, D. K. and Wu, Y. (2004) Predictability of short-horizon returns in international equity markets, *Journal of Empirical Finance* **11**(4), 553–584. (n=360)

27 Rashid, A. (2006) Random walk tests for KSE-100 index: Evidence and implications, *Business Review* **1**(1), 80–95. (n=24)

28 Youssef, A. and Galloppo, G. (2013) The efficiency of emerging stock markets: Evidence from Asia and Africa, *Global Journal of Business Research* **7**(4), 1–7. (n=46)

29 Worthington, A. and Higgs, H. (2006). Weak-form market efficiency in Asian emerging and developed equity markets: Comparative tests of random walk behaviour, *Accounting Research Journal* **19**(1), 54–63. (n=120)

Index

Note: Italicized page numbers indicate a figure on the corresponding page. Page numbers in bold indicate a table on the corresponding page.